Index to the 1871 Census of Ontario

RENFREW AND THE NORTH

Bruce S. Elliott
General Editor

Dan Walker
Assistant

David L. Brown
EDP Coordinator

Irena Nosco
Programming

Coordinators:
Barbara Bowles, Thunder Bay District Branch
Bruce S. Elliott, Ottawa Branch
Aileen Gerrie, Nipissing District Branch
Merlene Lee, Sault Ste. Marie District Branch

Compilers:

Doris Adams
Mary Bathurst
Rose Blair
Barbara Bowles
Walter Brown
G. Cazabon
Thomas I. Coram
Robert C. Corrigan
Brenda Cross
M. Deeley-Gartner
Pat Denhart
Mary Dunnill
Joan Duquette
Helen Elford
Bruce S. Elliott
Iris Elliott

Marjorie Fennell
Aileen Gerrie
Mary P. Gleeson
Mary Heasman
Louise Hope
Alice Hughes
Iona Joy
Merlene Lee
Peggy Mackey
Jean Mather
Jean MacDougall
Roy McGilvray
Donna McLeod
Rod McLeod
Norma Morrison
Joseph A. Murphy
and family

Rolande O'Brien
Catherine O'Keefe
Shelley J. Pearen
J. Peters
R. Peters
Richard Hugh Pinnell
May Prange
Doug Redmond
Hazel Redmond
Mary Louise Roach
Kathryn Welsh Ryan
Donald Schell
Bernice Severson
Lou Shank
Christina Thiele
Dan Walker

MULTI·PRIORES·MULTAE·PATRIAE

Ontario Genealogical Society
Toronto
1992

Canadian Cataloguing in Publication Data

Main entry under title:

Index to the 1871 census of Ontario : Renfrew and the
North

ISBN 0-920036-44-9

 1. Renfrew (Ont. : County)--Census, 1871--Indexes.
2. Ontario, Northern--Census, 1871--Indexes.
3. Renfrew (Ont : County)--Genealogy--Indexes.
4. Ontario, Northern--Genealogy--Indexes. 5. Registers
of births, etc.--Ontario--Renfrew (County)--Indexes.
6. Registers of births, etc.--Ontario, Northern--
Indexes. 7. Canada--Census, 1871--Indexes.
I. Elliott, Bruce S.   II. Bowles, Barbara
III. Gerrie, Aileen   IV. Lee, Merlene   V. Ontario
Genealogical Society.

FC3095.R4I63 1992   929'.371381   C92-090116-6
F1059.R4I63 1992

Cover illustration: Arnprior Marble Works, P.T. Somerville, Arnprior, Ontario,
from H. Belden & Co., <u>Historical Atlas of Lanark & Renfrew Counties, Ont.</u>
(1880-81), p. 46.

General Introduction

The original nominal returns of the various nineteenth-century censuses are among the most commonly used and most useful of genealogical sources, providing the name, age, birthplace, religion, ethnic origin, and occupation of every resident at a point in time, in this instance 2 April 1871. It is the only source that comes close to being a comprehensive listing of the population.

The advantages of having an index to the census records of an entire province are many. The existence of an index allows a person engaged in genealogical or biographical research to locate a given individual quickly, even if the place of residence is unknown. It will therefore be of great value to genealogical beginners, who often do not know precisely where their ancestors lived. It will also be of tremendous benefit to descendants of Ontario families resident in the United States and the Canadian West, for whom the place of residence in Ontario of their pioneer ancestors remains a mystery, and the index should prove useful to genealogists in Europe who are attempting to trace elusive families who may have emigrated to Canada in the nineteenth century. Those whose ancestors left Ontario before 1871 will also find it useful for identifying regions of the province in which particular surnames were found, thus suggesting areas from which the ancestor might have come. Because the index includes every head of family and stray individual in the province (unlike land records and indexes to wills and newspapers) it will become a prime source for Ontario one-name studies. Once the comprehensive provincial listing is available it will be possible to identify all families of a given surname in the province and to move on from this starting point to determine whether or not, in the case of unusual surnames, all share a common ancestry. The usefulness of this index extends beyond the field of family history. Social scientists studying internal migration will for the first time have an easy way of tracing the later whereabouts of residents who left specific communities in the 1850s and 1860s.

Why 1871? There are a number of reasons why we selected this year. A major consideration was the fact that the 1871 returns appear to be the most complete and probably the most legible of the Canadian censuses. The returns are generally easier to read than the earlier ones, and in many parts of the province the spelling and handwriting in 1881 were far worse than they had been ten years earlier. Indexing the 1871 returns presented less threat of duplication than would have been the case had another year been selected; most of the indexing that had already been done involved the 1852 and 1861 censuses. 1871 also nicely antedated the massive movement of Ontario population to the Canadian and American West which began in earnest in the late 1870s. Finally, at the time the project was begun the 1881 returns had only recently been opened, but were still subject to some restrictions and the microfilms were not widely available; the 1891 census had not yet been released for purposes of historical research.

This index to the 1871 census of Ontario was undertaken as a project of the Ontario Genealogical Society to mark the organization's twenty-fifth anniversary in 1986. The project began in January 1982 when Bruce Elliott of Ottawa and Laurena Storey of London conceived the idea. Elliott drew up a proposal to OGS Council which was greeted with enthusiasm by the representatives of the Branches and approved by Council on February 13, 1982. Each Branch named a Coordinator to oversee work in its own area and received listings and instructions from Bruce Elliott, who served as Provincial Coordinator. The project was officially inaugurated at the Society's provincial Seminar held in Guelph that May.

Through the kind intercession of Dr. John Clarke an agreement was reached with Machine-Readable Archives of the National Archives of Canada in the autumn of 1982 for computerization of the data extracted by the Society's members from the microfilms of the original census schedules. Work began in the spring of 1983 and the first batch of completed forms was delivered to the Archives in December of that year. By the end of 1985 98.5 per cent of the initial transcription had been completed by more than 400 volunteers and 26 Branch Coordinators, and the inputting of corrections made during double-checking of preliminary printouts against the microfilms, again by Branch volunteers, commenced in February 1986.

This volume is one of thirty in a series which began publication in 1986. When the project has been completed the Society will also make available in microform a single A-Z series for the entire province, containing some 400,000 names. It will eventually be possible for scholars and members of the public to request custom-made printouts and statistical cross-tabulations from the Archives for specialized research projects: families of African origin in the province, percentages of Irish or Scottish Catholics and Protestants in a specific municipality or the province as a whole, lists of photographers in a given region, and so forth. Thus the OGS 25th Anniversary Project will result not only in the production of alphabetical indexes to the population of Ontario just after Confederation but in the creation of a computer-manipulable data base which will be of use to scholars in various disciplines.

This volume indexes the 1871 census of the County of Renfrew and the northern districts of Algoma, Manitoulin, Muskoka, Nipissing, and Parry Sound. The head of each family recorded in the personal schedules has been listed, with complete data concerning age, sex, birthplace, religion, ethnic origin, and occupation, and a coded reference to the municipality and page number. We have also indexed any individual bearing a surname different from that of the head of family, designating such a person as a "stray", and have included all names recorded in the deaths schedules, which follow the personal schedules on the microfilm.

Many university and public libraries in Canada have copies of the census films, and they may also be borrowed on Interlibrary Loan from the National Archives of Canada in Ottawa by any library possessing a microfilm reader.

Bruce S. Elliott,
Provincial Coordinator
and General Editor.

How to Find an Indexed Individual in the Census

To find an indexed individual in the 1871 census, locate the name of the municipality and the National Archives of Canada microfilm reel number using the numerical table below. The first part of the code identifies the Electoral District (frequently but not always corresponding to county or city), the second the Sub-District (corresponding to township, town, village, or city ward), the third the enumerator's division, and the final column the page number. The names and code numbers of the Districts, Sub-Districts, and Divisions, as well as the page numbers, appear at the top of each page of the original microfilmed census. Thus an individual for whom the location reference reads

081 A 2 21

was resident in McNab Township, Renfrew County (081 A), and can be located on the 21st page of the 2nd division of McNab, on reel C-10,020.

The codes for Renfrew and the North follow.

District	Sub-District	Division	National Archives Microfilm Reel No.
081. RENFREW SOUTH	A. McNab	1-2	C-10,020
	B. Arnprior village		C-10,020
	C. Bagot & Blythfield		C-10,020
	D. Brougham		C-10,020
	E. Matawatchan & Griffith		C-10,020
	F. Sebastopol		C-10,020
	G. Brudenell & Lyndock	1	C-10,020
	Radcliffe & Raglan	2	C-10,020
	H. Horton	1-2	C-10,020
	I. Renfrew village		C-10,020
	J. Admaston	1	C-10,020-21
		2	C-10,021
	K. Grattan		C-10,021
082. RENFREW NORTH	A. Ross		C-10,021
	B. Bromley		C-10,021
	C. Westmeath	1-2	C-10,021
	D. Pembroke township		C-10,021
	E. Pembroke village		C-10,021
	F. Stafford		C-10,021
	G. Wilberforce		C-10,021-22
	H. Algona		C-10,022
	I. Alice & Fraser		C-10,022
	J. Petawawa		C-10,022
	K. Rolph, Buchanan, Wylie, & McKay	1-2	C-10,022
	L. Head		C-10,022
083. NIPISSING SOUTH	A. Madawaska East	1-2	C-10,022
	B. Madawaska West	1-2	C-10,022
	C. Bonnechere		C-10,022
	D. Petawawa South		C-10,022
	E. Petawawa North		C-10,022
	F. Petawawa Centre	1-2	C-10,022

	G. Petawawa West		C-10,022
084. NIPISSING NORTH	A. Rocher Capitaine		C-10,022
	B. Deux Rivieres		C-10,022
	C. Matawan South		C-10,022
	D. Matawan West		C-10,022
	E. Matawan North		C-10,022
	F. Jocko River		C-10,022
	G. Montreal River	1-2	C-10,022
	H. Temiscaming West		C-10,022
	I. Tamagamingue	1-2	C-10,022
085. MUSKOKA	A. Morrison		C-10,022
	B. Muskoka		C-10,022
	C. Monck		C-10,022
	D. Watt & Cardwell		C-10,022-23
	E. Humphry & Medora		C-10,023
	F. Wood		C-10,023
	G. Conger		C-10,023
	H. Draper, Ryde, Oakley		C-10,023
	I. Macaulay		C-10,023
	J. Stephenson		C-10,023
	K. McLean, Ridout, Franklin, Brunel	1-2	C-10,023
	L. Lake Vernon		C-10,023
086. PARRY SOUND	A. The Sound	1-3	C-10,023
	B. Aumick Lake		C-10,023
	C. Maganetawan	1-2	C-10,023
087. MANITOULIN	A. Manitoulin East		C-10,023
	B. Manitoulin Centre	1-3	C-10,023
	C. Manitoulin West		C-10,023
088. ALGOMA EAST	A. Killarney		C-10,023
	B. Spanish River		C-10,023
	C. Mississaga		C-10,023
089. ALGOMA CENTRE	A. Bruce Mines		C-10,023
	B. Sault Ste Marie		C-10,023
090. ALGOMA WEST	A. Batchewaning		C-10,024
	B. Michipicoten		C-10,024
	C. Pic		C-10,024
	D. St Ignace (Silver Islet)		C-10,024
	E. Nipigon		C-10,024
	F. Kaministikuia		C-10,024

A page number "D" indicates an entry in the Deaths Schedules, microfilmed immediately following the personal schedules for each division. Some local libraries still have an old microfilm version of the 1871 census in which only the personal schedules are included; if this is true of your library, you will have to obtain the new films from Ottawa to consult the deaths schedules.

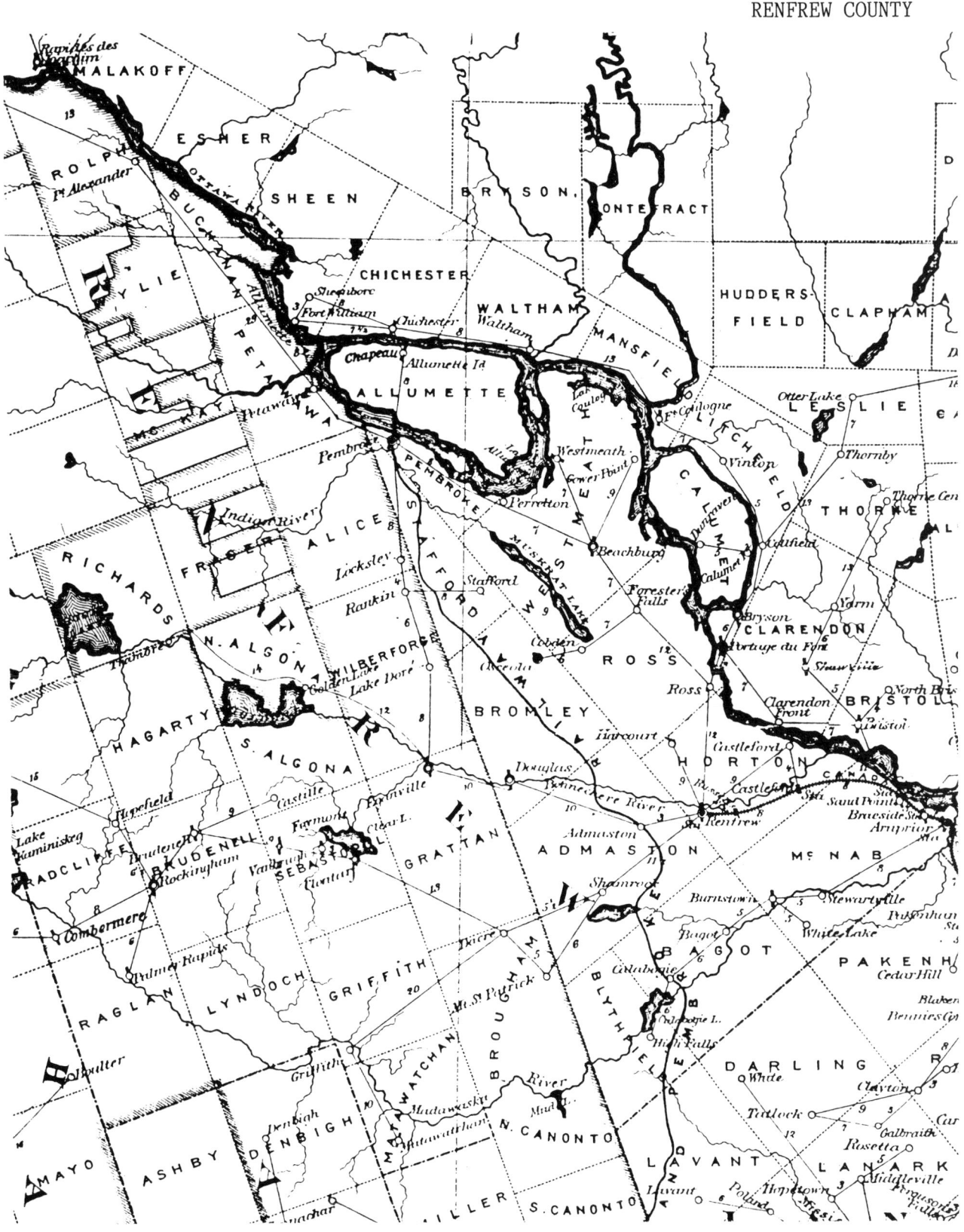

Detail from "New Railway and Postal Map of the Dominion of Canada", Sheet No. 10 in The New Standard Atlas of the Dominion of Canada (Montreal and Toronto: Walker and Miles, 1875), National Archives of Canada, National Map Collection, NMC-80253.

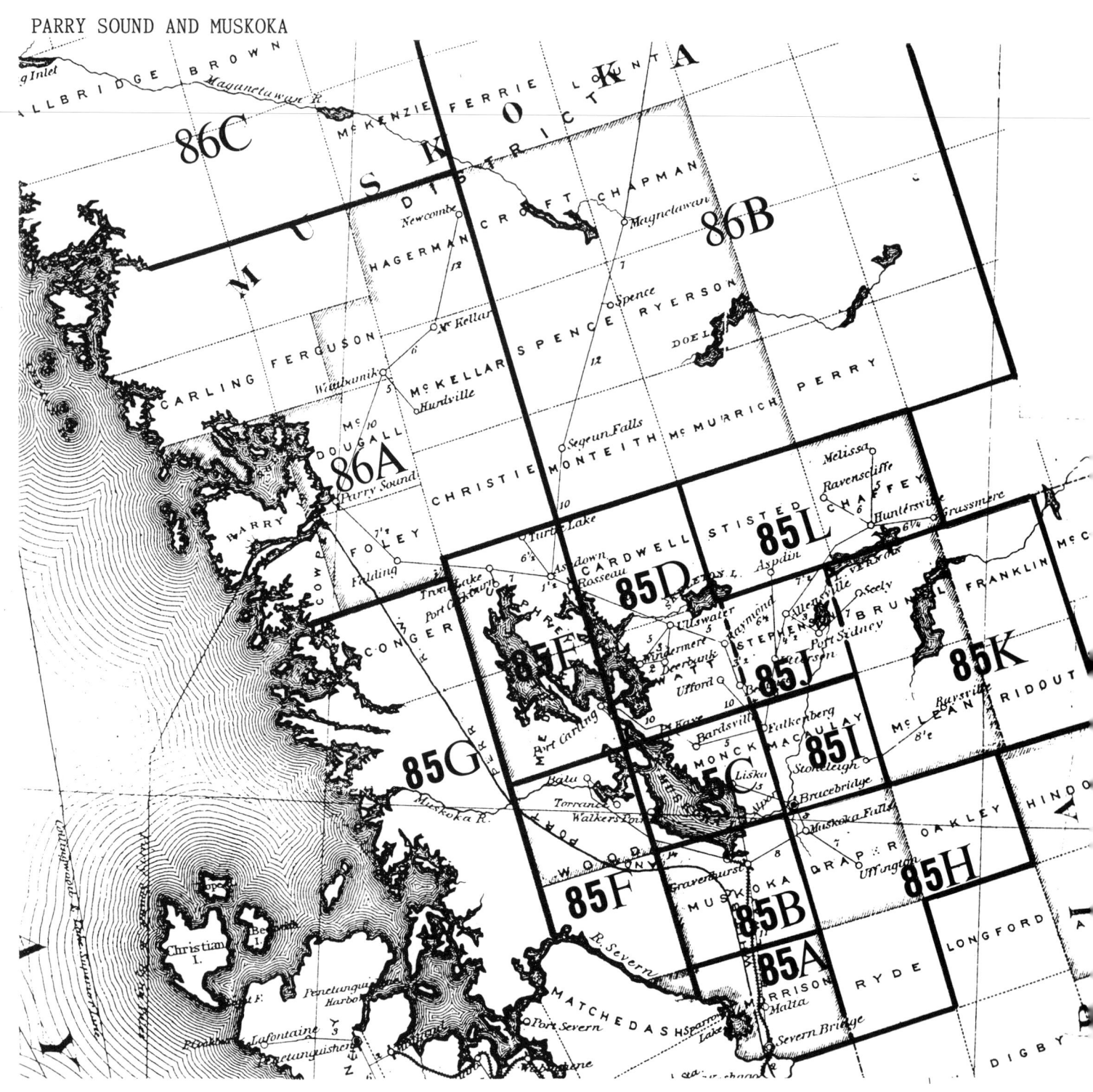

Detail from "New Railway and Postal Map of the Dominion of Canada", Sheet No. 10 in The New Standard Atlas of the Dominion of Canada (Montreal and Toronto: Walker and Miles, 1875), National Archives of Canada, National Map Collection, NMC-80253. Overlying is a grid representing the Subdivision boundaries in the Muskoka (085) and Parry Sound (086) Enumeration Districts, derived from descriptions contained in Censuses of Canada 1608 to 1876, Vol. 5 of Census of Canada 1870-71 (Ottawa: Maclean, Roger & Co., 1878), p. 406.

Descriptions of Subdistrict boundaries in Northern Ontario

No maps depicting boundaries of the 1871 enumeration subdistricts in northern Ontario appear to exist. In Renfrew County the townships served as the basic units of enumeration, as was the case in most of southern Ontario, and so we have included in this book the appropriate section of the 1875 postal map, which shows township boundaries as well as numerous post office locations, as has been our custom in previous volumes. We also print the section of the same map that covers the Parry Sound and Muskoka enumeration districts, but we have added to it an overlay grid that depicts the limits of the subdistricts as they were described verbally in the printed statistical volumes from the original 1871 enumeration. Because the subdistrict boundaries for Nipissing, Manitoulin, and Algoma were beyond the territory covered in the postal map, and were based largely upon the limits of timber licences granted for the 1866-67 season, it has not proved possible to include maps that show the subdistrict boundaries there. The reader may, however, ascertain district boundaries by examining the map that appears on the back cover. The physical descriptions of the subdistrict limits appear below, taken from <u>Censuses of Canada 1608 to 1876,</u> Vol. 5 of <u>Census of Canada 1870-71</u> (Ottawa: Maclean, Roger & Co., 1878), pp. 404-6.

Census District No. 83, SOUTH NIPISSING :

a. Madawaska East,—being so much of the said Census District as comprises the Timber Berths on the River Madawaska and its tributaries, bounded to the northward by the Census Sub-district of Bonnechère hereinafter described, and to the westward by the westerly boundary of the Timber Berths of Licenses numbers four hundred and thirty-nine and four hundred and forty of the season ending on the thirtieth day of April 1867, and by the north-easterly boundary of the Township of Clyde.

b. Madawaska West,—being so much of the said Census District as comprises the Timber Berths on the River Madawaska and its tributaries and the tract to the westward thereof, bounded to the eastward by the Census Sub-district of Madawaska East, to the northward by the northerly boundaries of the Timber Berths of Licenses numbers four hundred and sixty, three hundred and sixteen and three hundred and ninety-five of the season ending on the thirtieth day of April, 1867, and the north-westerly boundary of the last mentioned Timber Berth, and the prolongation thereof south-westerly.

c. Bonnechère,—being so much of the said Census District as comprises the Timber Berths on the River Bonnechère, bounded to the westward by the westerly boundary of the Timber Berths of Licenses numbers two hundred and fifty-four and two hundred and fifty-eight of the season ending on the thirtieth day of April, 1867.

d. Petawawa South,—being so much of the said Census District as comprises the Timber Berths on the south Branch of the River Petawawa and on the Indian River, bounded to the westward by the westerly boundary of the Timber Berths of Licenses, numbers three hundred and eight and three hundred and nine of the season ending on the thirtieth day of April, 1867.

e. Petawawa North,—being so much of the said Census District as comprises the Timber Berths on the River Petawawa and Chalk River, bounded to the westward by the westerly boundary of the Timber Berths of Licenses numbers two hundred and seventy-five and three hundred and forty-three of the season ending on the thirtieth day of April 1867.

f. Petawawa Centre,—being so much of the said Census District as comprises the Timber Berths on the River Petawawa and its tributaries, and Lake Opeongo, bounded to the eastward by the Census Sub-district of Bonnechère, Petawawa South and Petawawa North, and to the westward by the westerly boundary of the Timber Berths of License numbers three hundred and ninety-four, four hundred and sixty-seven, four hundred and sixty-eight and four hundred and sixty-nine of the season ending on the thirtieth day of April, 1867.

g. Petawawa West,—being so much of the said Census District as comprises the Timber Berths on the River Petawawa and its tributaries, and the tract to the westward thereof, bounded to the southward by the Census Sub-district of Madawaska West, and to the eastward by the Census Sub-District of Petawawa Centre and the eastern boundary of the Timber Berth of License number four hundred of the season ending on the thirtieth day of April, 1867.

Census District No. 84, NORTH NIPISSING :

a. Rocher Capitaine,—being so much of the said Census District as comprises the Timber Berths on and appertaining to the River Ottawa, bounded to the westward by the westerly boundary of the Timber Berths of Licenses numbers three hundred and sixty and three hundred and sixty-three of the season ending on the thirtieth day of April, 1867.

b. Deux Rivières,—being so much of the said Census District as comprises the Timber Berths on the River Ottawa, bounded to the eastward by the Census Sub-district of Rocher Capitaine, and to the westward by the Timber Berths of Licenses numbers two hundred and seven and five hundred and five of the season ending on the thirtieth day of April, 1867.

c. Matawan South,—being so much of the said Census District as comprises the Timber Berths on the River Matawan and its tributaries, bounded to the eastward by the Census Sub-district of Deux Rivières, to the northward by the River Matawan and the northerly boundaries of the Timber Berths of Licenses numbers three hundred and thirteen and two hundred of the season ending on the thirtieth day of April, 1867, and to the westward by the westerly boundaries of the Timber Berths of Licenses numbers two hundred, four hundred and ninety, and eighty-four of the season ending on the thirtieth day of April, 1867, and thence by the line of watershed between the streams falling into the River Amable du Fond on the one hand, and those falling into Lake Nipissing on the other.

d. Matawan West,—being so much of the said Census District as comprises the Timber Berths on the River Matawan and its tributaries, and on Lake Nipissing, and the tract to the westward thereof, bounded to the eastward by the Census Sub-district of Matawan South, to the northward by the northerly boundaries of the Timber Berths of Licenses numbers one hundred and ninety-eight and five hundred and seventeen of the season ending on the thirtieth day of April, 1867, and by Lake Nipissing and French River, and to the westward by the Indian Reserve on the north Shore of Lake Nipissing, and including the islands in Lake Nipissing and French River.

e. Matawan North,—being so much of the said Census District as comprises the Timber Berths on the River Ottawa and appertaining thereto, and the tract to the westward thereof, bounded to the southward by the Census Sub-districts of Matawan South and Matawan West, to the northward by the northerly boundaries of the Timber Berths of Licenses numbers two hundred and eighty-one and two hundred and thirty-four of the season ending on the thirtieth day of April, 1867, and the prolongation thereof to the line of watershed between the streams falling into the River Ottawa on the one hand, and those falling into Lake Nipissing on the other, and to the westward by the easterly boundary of the Indian Reserve on the north shore of Lake Nipissing and prolongation thereof to and along the line of watershed between the streams falling into the River Ottawa on the one hand, and those falling into Lake Nipissing on the other.

f. Jacko River,—being so much of the said Census District as comprises the Timber Berths on the River Ottawa and Lake Temiscamang and appertaining thereto, and the tract to the westward thereof, bounded to the southward by the Census Sub-district of Matawan North, to the northward by the southerly boundary of the Timber Berth of License number four hundred and twenty-six, and the northerly boundary of the Timber Berth of License number two hundred and forty-seven of the season ending on the thirtieth day of April, 1867, and the prolongation of the last mentioned boundary to the line of watershed between the streams falling into the River Ottawa on the one hand, and those falling into Lake Nipissing on the other, and to the westward by the said line of watershed.

g. Montreal River,—being so much of the said Census District as comprises the Timber Berths on Lake Temiscamang and the Montreal River and the tract to the northward and westward thereof, bounded to the southward by the Census Sub-district of Jacko River, to the northeastward by the Timber Berths of Licenses numbers four hundred and one, two hundred and ninety-seven and four hundred and ninety-eight of the season ending on the thirtieth day of April, 1867, and the prolongation of the southwesterly boundary of the last mentioned Timber Berth, to and along the line of watershed between the streams falling into Lake Temiscamang on the one hand and those falling into the Montreal River on the other to the boundary of the Province, and to the southwestward by the line of watershed between the streams falling into the Montreal River on the one hand, and those falling into Lake Tamagamingue on the other.

h. Temiscamang West,—being so much of the said Census District as comprises the Timber Berths on Lake Temiscamang and the tract to the northward thereof, bounded to the southward and southwestward by the Census Sub-District of Montreal River.

i, Tamagamingue,—being so much of the said Census District as is bounded to the southward by the Census Sub-District of Matawan West, and to the northeastward by the Census Sub-Districts of Matawan North, Jacko River and Montreal River.

Census District No. 85, MUSKOKA :

a. Morrison.—Municipality, Township.
b. Muskoka.—Municipality, Township.
c. Monck —Municipality, Township
d. Watt and Cardwell.—One Municipality, Two Townships.
e. Humphry and Medora.—Townships.
f. Wood —being so much of the said Census-District as is bounded to the eastward by the Census Sub-districts of Morrison, Muskoka and Monck, to the northward by the Township of Medora, and to the westward by a prolongation of the westerly boundary of the same Township
g. Conger,—being so much of the said Census-District as is bounded to the eastward by the Census Sub-District of Wood, and by the Townships of Medora and Humphry.
h. Draper, Ryde and Oakley.—One Municipality, three Townships.
i. Macaulay.—Municipality, Township.
j. Stephenson.—Municipality, Township.
k. McLean, Brunel, Ridout and Franklin.—four Townships.
l. Lake Vernon.—being so much of the said Census District as is bounded to the westward by the Township of Cardwell, and to the southward by the Townships of Stephenson, Brunel and Franklin.

Census District No. 86, PARRY SOUND :

a. The Sound,—being so much of the said Census District as is bounded to the eastward by the easterly boundary of the Townships of Christie, McKellar and Hagerman, and to the northward by the northerly boundary of the Township of Hagerman, and the prolongation thereof westerly.
b. Aumick Lake,—being so much of the said Census-District as is bounded to the westward by the eastern Boundary of the Census Sub-district of the Sound, and the prolongation thereof northerly.
c. Maganetawan,—being so much of the said Census District as is bounded to the southward and eastward by the Census Sub-Districts of the Sound and Aumick Lake.

Census District No. 87, MANITOULIN :

a. Manitoulin East,—being so much of the said Census District as has not been ceded by the Indians, bounded to the westward by Manitowaning Bay and South Bay and a line drawn due south from the southerly extremity of the former to the latter.
b. Manitoulin Centre,—being so much of the said Census-District as is bounded to the eastward by the Census Sub District of Manitoulin East, and to the westward by Julia Bay and by a line drawn from the southeasterly extremity thereof to the northeasterly extremity of Lake Wolsey, and by Lake Wolsey and a line drawn from the southeasterly extremity thereof to Portage Bay.
c. Manitoulin West,—being so much of the said District as is bounded to the eastward by the Census Sub-district of Manitoulin Centre.

Census District No. 88, EAST ALGOMA :

a. Killarney.—being so much of the said Census District as is bounded to the westward and north-westward by the line drawn due north and south from the westerly extremity of LaCloche Island to and along the watershed between the streams falling into the Spanish River on the one hand, and those falling into White Fish River on the other, to White Fish Lake, and from thence by a line drawn due north.
b. Spanish River.—being so much of the said Census-District as is bounded to the eastward and southeastward by the Census Sub-District of Killarney,—and to the westward by the westerly boundary of the Townships of Spragge and Esten and the prolongation thereof.
c. Mississaga,—being so much of the said Census District as is bounded to the eastward by the Census Sub-District of Spanish River.

Census District No. 89, CENTRE ALGOMA :

a. Bruce Mines,—being so much of the said Census District as is bounded to the north-westward and westward by the south-easterly and easterly boundaries of the Indian Reserve, on Lake George, and the prolongation of the easterly boundary thereof.
b. Sault Ste. Marie,—being so much of the said Census District as is bounded to the south-eastward and eastward by the Census Sub-district of Bruce Mines.

Census District No. 90, WEST ALGOMA :

a. Batchewaning,—being so much of the said Census District as is bounded to the northward by a line drawn due east from the southerly angle of the Mining Location at Cape Gargantua.
b. Michipicoten,—being so much of the said Census District as is bounded to the southward by the Census Sub-district of Batchewaning, and to the north-westward by a line drawn due north-east from Otter Head.
c. Pic,—being so much of the said Census District as is bounded to the south-eastward by the Census Sub-district of Michipicoten, and to the westward by a line drawn due north and south from the easterly extremity of Copper Island.
d. St. Ignace,—being so much of the said Census District as is bounded to the eastward by the Census Sub-district of Pic, and to the north-westward and northward by Thunder Bay, a line drawn

from the north-easterly extremity thereof to the north-westerly extremity of Black Bay, thence by Black Bay, the Portage and Nipigon Bay.

e. Nipigon,—being so much of the said Census District as is bounded to the eastward by the Census Sub-district of Pic, to the southward and south-eastward by the Census Sub district of St. Ignace, and to the south-westward by a line drawn due northwest from the mouth of Black Sturgeon River.

f. Kaministiquia,—being so much of the said Census District as is bounded to the north-eastward by the Census Sub distric: of Nipigon, and to the south-eastward by the Census Sub district of St. Ignace.

Explanation of columns, left to right

Surname   Surnames are entered as they appear in the census. We have attempted to provide cross-references to more difficult entries, but the degree to which this has been possible has depended upon the local knowledge of the indexers. We have assumed that the user of this index will exercise creativity in coming up with alternate spellings and have not attempted to cross-index spellings the user should be expected to come up with himself. Thus we assume that someone looking for McDonnell will also check under MacDonnell and indeed under McDonald, and that someone looking for an O'Grady will also check Grady and Johnson Johnstone. On the other hand, it is not so reasonable to expect a reader to check under Lhulin for Laughlin or King for the French-Canadian name Roy, so cross-references to these spellings have been included, if the local indexers have been aware of the proper form of the name.

In some parts of the province native people bearing no surnames were recorded in the census. These individuals have been listed under the heading "INDIAN". Native people having surnames have been indexed in the normal way.

Forenames 1 and 2   Forenames or Christian names are recorded as stated in the census. Thus William George Smith may appear as William, Willm, Wm, William G, W G, George, George W, etc. Smith may also be entered as Smyth. Do not expect the 1871 enumerator to have been as fussy about the spelling of names as you are!

Stray   We have indexed all heads of families and individuals bearing surnames different from that of the head of family. We have designated the latter "strays", and they are indicated by a "1" in this column. A "2" in this column designates an entry in the Deaths Schedules (schedule 2), microfilmed immediately following the Personal Schedules.

Sex   Women have been designated by a "1" in this column to facilitate computer retrieval.

Age   Remember that census ages are often approximate at best and may not correspond to ages recorded in other sources. Ages under one year have been left blank or indicated "0".

Birthplace   Birthplace is usually a province or country. "O" is Ontario, "Que" is Quebec.

Religion   Religious denominations were entered in so many ways in the original returns (we found about two dozen ways of entering Anglicans alone - Church of England, English Ch., C of E, Episcopalian, Episcopal, etc.) that the Archives has employed a series of two-letter codes to standardize the references for computer retrieval. The list of codes is an expanded version of that recommended by the Social Science Federation of Canada's Working Group on Historical Census Microdata Usage in "Guidelines for the Transcription of Historical Census Data for Quantitative Research" (1978). A full alphabetical explanation of these codes is appended to this Introduction.

Origin   The census enumerator was instructed to record paternal ethnic origin. Thus a person whose mother was born in Scotland and father in Ireland was recorded as Irish. This led to some strange anomalies, such as the Indian reserve in the Prairie west in which most of the mixed-blood residents were recorded as Scottish, using the census definition of ethnicity, though all were legally treaty Indians. Despite some entries to the contrary, "American" was not considered to be an acceptable reply to the question.

<u>Occupation</u>   Occupations have been entered as given in the original enumeration, with some standardization of spelling. "F" indicates a farmer, "Lab" a labourer. Some lengthy occupational designations may be cut off in mid-word if they exceed the space we have allocated for this column.

<u>Muncipality and Page Reference</u>   See the explanation of these columns above: "How to find an indexed individual in the census".

Religion Codes

Because there were so many different ways of writing one religion, the Archives has standardized religion into a two-letter code. Most of these are easy to understand. Thus "CP" is Canada Presbyterian, "CE" is Church of England, "WM" is Wesleyan Methodist, and so on. Some of the more obscure denominations have more difficult codes. The alphabetical list following does not include every long-hand version one will find in the original census schedules, but the major variations are given. We recognize that some of these variants indicate the same denomination, e.g. CE and EP, and even CI, but feeling that there was some value to retaining the original terminology where possible, these have been assigned separate designations.

AA	African Association Baptist	KB	Close Communion Baptist
AD	Adventists	LD	Latter Day Saints
AP	American Presbyterian	LU	Lutheran/Evangelical Lutheran
AT	Atheist		
BA	Baptist	MC	I. Meth. C.
BB	Bible Believer	MD	Mahometan
BC	Bible Christian	ME	Methodist
BE	British Episcopal Methodist	MI	Meth. I.
BR	Brethren	MO	Mormon
CB	Christian Brethren	MN	Mennonite
CC	Christian Conference Baptist	MS	Messiah
CD	Christadelphian	MV	Moravian
CE	Church of England, Anglican	NC	New Connexion Methodist
CI	Church of Ireland	NG	Not Given
CM	Calvinistic Methodist	NP	N. Presbyterian
CN	Christian	OB	[Other Baptist]
CO	Congregationalist	OM	[Other Methodist]
CP	Canada Presbyterian/C. Presb.	OP	[Other Presbyterian]
CS	Church of Scotland/Kirk/ Scotch Presb., etc.	PA	Pagan
		PB	Plymouth Brethren
CX	Church of Christ	PE	Est. Presb.
DE	Deist	PM	Primitive Methodist
DI	Disciple (of Christ)	PR	Protestant
EA	Evangelical Association	PS	Presbyterian
EM	Episcopal Methodist/ Methodist Episcopal	PU	Puritan
		QU	Quaker/Friends
EP	Episcopal(ian)	RB	Reformed Baptist/R. Baptist
EU	Evangelical Union	RC	(Roman) Catholic
EV	Evangelical	RM	R. Methodist
FK	Free Kirk/Free Presb., etc.	RP	Reformed Presb.
FT	Free Thinker (of England)	SD	Seventh Day Adventist
FW	Free Will Baptist/Free Christian	SP	Spiritualist
		SW	Swedenborgian/New Jerusalem
GB	Regular Baptist/see also RB	TU	Tunker
IF	Infidel	UB	United Brethren
IL	Illegible	UN	Union Baptist
IM	I. Meth. E.	UP	United Presbyterian/ U. Kirk Presbyterian
IN	Independent		
IP	Irish Presbyterian	UT	Unitarian
IR	Irvingite/Catholic Apostolic	UV	Universalist
JM	J. Meth. E.	VM	Evangelical Methodist
JU	Jew	WM	Wesleyan Methodist
		WP	W. Presbyterian
		XC	C. C. Baptist
		ZZ	[Strange References]

SURNAME	NAME1	NAME2	STRAY	SEX	AGE	BIRTHPL	RELIGION	ORIGIN	OCCUP	DIST	SUB_DIST	DIV	PAGE
	AMELIA		1	1	18	IRELAND	RC	IRISH		082	E		10
	ANGELIC		2	1	5	O	RC			088	A		D
	ANNAY		1	1	14	GERMANY	LU	GERMAN		082	J		9
	JACOB		1		18	GERMANY	LU	GERMAN	LAB	082	J		9
	MARAY		1	1	9	O	RC	FRENCH		084	I	2	1
	PETER		1	1	11	O	RC	FRENCH		084	I	2	1
	WILLIAM		1		5	O	CP	IRISH		082	C	1	63
	WILLIAM	JAMES	1			ONT	RC	FRENCH		081	C		37
ABARE	JOSEPH				32	US	RC	FRENCH	FISHERMAN	089	A		63
ABBEY	CHARLES				25	O	WM	ONTARIO	F	087	B	3	9
ABBOTT	FRANCISE				41	GERMANY	LU	GERMAN	F	082	J		16
ABBOTT	JOHN		1		30	IRELAND	CE	IRISH	FISHERMAN	081	H	2	21
ABBOTT	WILLIAM	VAN			40	ENGLAND	CE	ENGLISH		089	B		7
ABLESON	WILLIAM				62	ENGLAND	WM	ENGLISH	SHOE MAKER	089	A		44
ABLEW	ALICK				56	QUEBEC	RC	FRENCH		081	J	1	18
ABREY	GEORGE	BROCKETT			32	O	WM	ENGLISH	MERCHANT	087	B	3	1
ABREY	LOUIS				38	QUEBEC	RC	FRENCH	F	081	J	1	40
ABREY	PETER				25	ONT	RC	FRENCH	F	081	J	1	9
ACKESON	ARCHIBALD				46	IRELAND	CE	IRISH	INNKEEPER	082	C	1	1
ACKFORD	JAMES				61	SCOTLAND	CP	SCOTCH	CARPENTER	081	A	2	1
ACKLAND	JOHN		1		33	O	CE	IRISH	SHOEMAKER	081	B		6
ACTON	ARTHUR				37	ENGLAND	CE	ENGLISH	FARMER	081	G	1	28
ACTON	PHILIP		1		18	ENGLAND	CE	ENGLISH	LABOURER	081	G	1	28
ACTON	RICHARD				44	ENGLAND	CE	ENGLISH	FARMER	081	G	1	30
ACTURNOS	MICAL		1		52	QUEBEC	RC	FRENCH	LAB	083	E		2
ADAIR	JOHN				35	O	NC	IRISH	CARPENTER	085	I		2
ADAMS	ABRAHAM				30	O	CE	IRISH	F	081	E		1
ADAMS	ALPHEUS				25	US	ME	ENGLISH	F	087	B	2	6
ADAMS	ANN			1	43	ENGLAND	WM	ENGLISH	BOARDING HOUSE	088	B		5
ADAMS	EDWIN				48	ENGLAND	EM	ENGLISH	F	085	E		22
ADAMS	GIDEON				32	O	WM	ENGLISH	CLERK	082	C	1	5
ADAMS	JANE		2		86	IRELAND	CP			083	C		D
ADAMS	JOHN				30	NB	CE	IRISH	DOCTOR	085	B		9
ADAMS	JOHN				30	US	CS	ENGLISH	HUNTER	088	B		20
ADAMS	MARTHA		2	1	54	IRELAND	CE			081	G	1	D
ADAMS	ROBERT				57	IRELAND	CE	IRISH	FARMER	081	G	1	11
ADAMS	SAMUEL				32	USA	CE	ENGLISH	F	085	L		7
ADAMS	THOMAS				33	O	CE	IRISH	F	081	E		1
ADAMS	THOMAS		1		26	USA	CE	ENGLISH	F	085	L		7
ADAMS	W	H	1		35	IRELAND	CP	IRISH	SERVANT	081	B		41
ADAMS	WM	HENRY			66	ENGLAND	CE	IRISH		081	E		2
ADDISOM	MATHEW				28	O	CE	IRISH	WATCHMAKER	081	I		4
AGAWANAKWAT	(WIFE)		2	1	31	US	RC	INDIAN		087	A		D
AGER	RICHARD		1		17	IRELAND	CE	IRISH	PRINTER	081	B		56
AGNEW	JAMES				29	IRELAND	RC	IRISH	FARMER	082	B		59
AGOWISSE	ANTOINE				45	US	RC	INDIAN	F & FISHERMAN	087	A		12
AGWASE	DOMINIC				37	US	RC	INDIAN	F & FISHERMAN	087	A		22
AHARE	PATRICK				45	IRELAND	RC	IRISH	F	081	J	1	11
AHBETAHKEZHIK	DOMINIC				40	O	RC	INDIAN	F & FISHERMAN	087	C		3
AHBETAHKEZHIK	FRANCIS				23	O	RC	INDIAN	F & FISHERMAN	087	C		5
AHBETAHKEZHIK	FRANCIS	WAHBEGWOWHNAI			25	US	RC	INDIAN	F & FISHERMAN	087	C		4
AHBETAHKEZHIK	JOHN				35	US	RC	INDIAN	F & FISHERMAN	087	C		5
AHBETAHWONAHBISHKUN	JOS				28	O	RC	INDIAN	F & FISHERMAN	087	C		10
AHDAHZHAWA	JOHN				70	US	RC	INDIAN	F & FISHERMAN	087	C		9
AHIABEUS	JOSEPH				32	US	RC	INDIAN	F & FISHERMAN	087	A		40
AHWISHTOOYAH	AMABE				36	O	RC	INDIAN		087	A		44
AHWONOKEMAH	PETER				42	US	RC	INDIAN	COOPER & F	087	B	1	21
AHWONOQUET	PETER				33	US	CE	INDIAN	LABOURER	087	B	1	17
AIKLE	HENERY				35	IRELAND	CE	IRISH	FARMER	082	D		13
AIRLEY	ROBERT				56	SCOTLAND	CP	SCOTCH	F	081	H	1	14
AIRTH	DAVID				50	SCOTLAND	CP	SCOTCH	FARMER	081	I		1
AIRTH	HENRY				52	SCOTLAND	CS	SCOTCH	F	081	H	1	1
AIRTH	HENRY		2		84	SCOTLAND	CP		F	081	I		D
AIRTH	MIRION		2	1	80	SCOTLAND	CP			081	I		D
AIRTH	OPHELIA			1	31	O	BA	SCOTCH		081	I		16
AIRTH	ROBERT				49	SCOTLAND	CP	SCOTCH	MERCHANT	081	I		20
AIRTH	WILLIAM				40	O	CS	SCOTCH		081	I		3
AJAWAB'S	(DAUGHTER)			1		ONTARIO	PA	INDIAN	HUNTER & TRAPPER	090	E		20
AJAWAKAMIG	(WIDOW)			1		ONTARIO	PA	INDIAN	HUNTER & TRAPPER	090	E		19
AJAWANAKWAH	J	BTE			35	US	RC	INDIAN	F & FISHERMAN	087	A		34
AKOTCHISH	(2ND WIDOW)			1		ONTARIO	PA	INDIAN	HUNTER & TRAPPER	090	E		7
ALDERMAN	THOMAS				33	ENGLAND	CE	ENGLISH	F	085	H		15
ALEXANDER	JANET			1	60	SCOTLAND	CP	SCOTCH	F	081	C		28
ALEXANDER	MCDONALD				23	ONTARIO	RC	IRISH	FARMER	081	G	2	3
ALEXANDER	PERCIVILLE				44	IRELAND	CE	IRISH	FARMER	082	B		9
ALEXANDER	SAMUEL				33	SCOTLAND	PS	SCOTCH	F	085	D		30
ALEXANDER	WILLIAM					QUE	CS	SCOTCH		081	A	1	67
ALFRED	ISAAC				24	O	CP	IRISH	LABOURER	085	B		8
ALGIE	JOSEPH				25	ENGLAND	WM	ENGLISH	F	086	A	2	4
ALLAM	JAMES				30	O	CP	SCOTCH	SURVEYOR	081	I		11
ALLAN	GALDAN		1		61	ENGLAND	CE	ENGLISH	TANNER	081	I		13
ALLARD	WILLIAM				22	ENGLAND	CO	ENGLISH	F	086	A	1	8
ALLEN	JANE			1	25	O	CP	IRISH	FARMERESS	082	C	2	2
ALLEN	JANE		1	1	29	O	PS	IRISH	SERVANT	082	E		57
ALLEN	JOHN				60	SCOTLAND	FK	SCOTCH	F	081	J	1	82
ALLEN	MICHEAL				48	IRELAND	RC	IRISH	F	081	A	1	53
ALLEN	ROBERT				37	ONTARIO	CS	ENGLISH	F	082	A		55
ALLEN	ROBERT	C			92	SCOTLAND	CS	SCOTCH	F	082	A		5
ALLEN	SARAH	JANE	1	1	11	UNITED STATES	WM	GERMAN		085	C		8
ALLEN	WILLIAM				30	QUE	CP	IRISH	MERCHANT TAILOR	081	B		8
ALLEN	WILLIAM				22	ONT	FK	SCOTCH	F	081	J	1	83
ALLISON	ANDREW				35	O	CS	SCOTCH	BLACKSMITH	081	A	1	18
ALLUM	CARROL				32	GERMANY	WM	GERMAN	W METH MINISTER	082	G		98
ALMOND	EDWARD				42	ENGLAND	CE	ENGLISH	F	086	A	1	8
ALPORT	AGUSTUS	I			55	NS	CP	ENGLISH	F	085	B		25
ALSNAR	OTTO				35	GERMANY	LU	GERMAN	F	082	J		8
ALSTON	JOHN				50	SCOTLAND	CS	SCOTCH	HOTELKEEPER	081	A	1	12
AMADJIWE	J	BT			32	O	RC	INDIAN	HUNTER	088	A		11
AMBERY	NELSON		1		22	NORWAY	NG	NORWEGIAN	LAB	085	F		5
AMBRIDGE	AMY		1	1	22	ENGLAND	CE	ENGLISH	TAILORESS	082	E		34
AMCKEWA	JACOB				40	US	WM	INDIAN	HUNTER	086	C	2	2
AMES	CHARLES				29	GERMANY	CE	GERMAN	F	085	E		29
AMES	JOSEPH				27	UNITED STATES	EP	ENGLISH	OVERSEER	090	D		6
AMIKOS	ISABELLA			1	2	O	RC			082	H		D
AMIKOS	JOHN					O	RC			082	H		D
AMIKOS	VINCENT				28	QUE	RC	INDIAN	HUNTER AND FISHERMAN	082	H		27

SURNAME	NAME1	NAME2	STRAY	SEX	AGE	BIRTHPL	RELIGION	ORIGIN	OCCUP	DIST	SUB_DIST	DIV	PAGE
AMIOT	CHARLOTTE		1	1	7	0	RC	FRENCH		089	B		30
AMIOT	JULIE		1	1	7	0	RC	FRENCH		089	B		30
AMIOTTE	ABRAHAM				25	0	RC	FRENCH	FISHERMAN	089	A		64
AMIOTTE	ALBIRT				22	0	RC	FRENCH	FISHERMAN	089	A		63
AMIOTTE	PHILOMEN			1	21	0	RC	FRENCH		089	A		63
AMOS	HENRY	THOS			49	ENGLAND	CE	ENGLISH	BUILDER	085	I		9
AMUICK	JOHN				55	0	WM	INDIAN	HUNTER	086	A	3	7
ANDERS	WILLIAM				36	IRELAND	PR	IRISH	FARMER	081	G	2	8
ANDERSON	ANDREW				36	SCOTLAND	CP	SCOTCH	F	085	E		26
ANDERSON	ANGUS				36	0	RC	INDIAN	F & FISHERMAN	087	A		34
ANDERSON	DUNCAN				76	SCOTLAND	CP	SCOTCH	LAB	081	A	2	24
ANDERSON	EDWARD				63	IRELAND	CE	IRISH	F	085	J		11
ANDERSON	HAMILON				44	IRELAND	PB	IRISH	F	082	L		8
ANDERSON	HENRY	N			50	SCOTLAND	PS	SCOTCH	F	085	A		1
ANDERSON	JAMES				39	SCOTLAND	CS	SCOTCH	FARMER	084	D		2
ANDERSON	JAMES		1		23	0	CP	IRISH	F LABOURER	085	H		21
ANDERSON	JAMES		1		19	SCOTLAND	PS	SCOTCH	LUMBERMAN	086	B		2
ANDERSON	JOHN				44	SCOTLAND	CS	SCOTCH	F	081	A	1	32
ANDERSON	JOHN				56	SCOTLAND	CS	SCOTCH		081	C		9
ANDERSON	JOHN				24	0	CP	IRISH	F	082	C	1	27
ANDERSON	JOHN				37	IRELAND	EM	IRISH	F	082	C	1	42
ANDERSON	JOHN				34	QUE	CP	SCOTCH	F	082	C	1	47
ANDERSON	JOHN				39	SWEDEN	LU	SWEDISH	F	087	B	3	12
ANDERSON	JONAS				36	SWEDEN	PS	SWEDISH	F	087	B	3	4
ANDERSON	MALCOM		1		2	0	WM	IRISH		082	D		26
ANDERSON	PETER				42	SCOTLAND	CS	SCOTCH	F	081	A	1	63
ANDERSON	THOMAS		1		8	ONT	RP	IRISH		082	I		10
ANDERSON	THOMAS				31	IRELAND	RP	IRISH	FARMER	082	I		14
ANDERSON	WILLIAM				24	QUE	CP	SCOTCH	F	082	C	1	47
ANDERSON	WILLIAM				40	IRELAND	RP	IRISH	FARMER	082	I		14
ANDREVOUT	ELIZABETH		1	1	31	USA	RC	AMERICAN	SISTERS OF CHARITY	087	A		1
ANDREW	CROZIER				44	IRELAND	CE	IRISH	F	081	H	1	10
ANDREW	JOHN				38	ENGLAND	WM	ENGLISH	MINER	089	A		21
ANDREW	MICHAEL				38	QUE	RC	INDIAN	LAB	081	B		85
ANDREW	WILLIAM				48	IRELAND	CP	IRISH	F	086	A	2	3
ANDREWS	JAMES				57	IRELAND	PS	IRISH	F	081	K		2
ANDREWS	LOLA			1	48	0	WM	SCOTCH	SEAMSTRESS	082	C	2	9
ANDREWS	MATHEW				33	IRELAND	CP	IRISH	FARMER	082	B		52
ANDREWS	ROBERT				55	IRELAND	PS	IRISH	F	081	K		2
ANDREWS	SOPHIA		1	1	56	ENGLAND	CE	ENGLISH		081	H	2	18
ANDREWS	THOMAS				35	IRELAND	PS	IRISH	BOOT SHOEMAKER	082	B		51
ANDREWS	THOMAS				39	ENGLAND	CE	ENGLISH	ENGINEER	082	E		59
ANDREWS	WILLIAM				30	SCOTLAND	CP	SCOTCH	CARPENTER	081	A	2	24
ANDUNNOSSWAS	JOHN				30	0	RC	INDIAN	F	087	C		4
ANGER	THOMAS				31	ENGLAND	PM	FRENCH	MINISTER	085	I		8
ANGUS	JAMES				49	0	CS	SCOTCH	F	081	A	1	42
ANGUS	WILLIAM				27	QUE	PS	SCOTTISH	PAINTER	082	E		76
ANIKON	BAPTISTE				40	ONTARIO	RC	INDIAN	HUNTER	083	F	2	1
ANIMEKEWANNE	J	BTE			23	0	RC	INDIAN	COOPER & F	087	A		39
ANIMIKWAAM	PAUL				47	US	RC	INDIAN	F & FISHERMAN	087	A		27
ANSELL	ASHER				34	ENGLAND	JU	ENGLISH	TOBACCONIST	082	E		41
ANSLEY	JULIUS				74	ENGLAND	CE	ENGLISH	F	085	D		31
ANSTER	JOHN				73	IRELAND	RC	IRISH	F	081	J	1	53
ANTLER	CHARLES				45	GERMANY	LU	GERMAN	FARMER	082	I		46
ANTOINE	JOSEPH				19	QUE	RC	INDIAN	HUNTER	084	I	1	5
ANTONIE	GIRRARD				64	QUE	RC	FRENCH	F	081	H	1	8
ANTWAIN	EANASE				40	ONTARIO	RC	INDIAN	HUNTER	083	D		2
APEQUASH	GEORGE				55	0	RC	INDIAN	FISHERMAN	089	B		23
APPLEBY	JOHN				46	IRELAND	CE	IRISH	F	082	A		59
APPLER	GODSLIP				45	GERMANY	LU	GERMAN	FARMER	082	I		18
ARCHAMBEO	JOSEPH		1		42	QUEBEC	RC	FRENCH	LAB	083	E		2
ARCHAMBOU	JOSEPH				32	QUE	RC	FRENCH	LAB	082	C	1	23
ARCHAMBOU	MICHEAL				46	QUE	WM	FRENCH	LAB	082	C	1	11
ARCHER	RICHARD				50	ENGLAND	CE	ENGLISH	BAKER	081	I		19
ARCHER	WILLIAM		1		22	0	ME	ENGLISH	SERVANT	085	I		13
ARENS	HENRY				30	PRUSSIA	PR	PRUSSIAN	F	085	A		4
ARGUE	HENRY				54	IRELAND	WM	IRISH	F	082	A		42
ARLOW	JACOB				45	PRUSSIA	RC	PRUSSIAN	FARMER	083	A	1	19
ARMISTRONG	MARY GENE			1	3	QUE	RC	IRISH		084	E		2
ARMITAGE	BENGAMIN				55	IRELAND	RC	IRISH	LABOURER	082	D		16
ARMSTRONG	ALBERT				26	0	CP	IRISH	PHYSICIAN	081	B		80
ARMSTRONG	ANDREW				60	IRELAND	PS	IRISH	F	085	J		11
ARMSTRONG	FOSTER				28	QUE	RP	IRISH	F	082	K	1	18
ARMSTRONG	HONORA	MARGARET	1	1	2	0	CE	IRISH		081	K		65
ARMSTRONG	I				60	IRELAND	WM	IRISH	F	086	A	1	4
ARMSTRONG	JAMES				36	0	CE	IRISH	COOPER	082	G		51
ARMSTRONG	JAMES				31	ONTARIO	CE	IRISH	CLERK	083	C		4
ARMSTRONG	JOHN				68	IRELAND	CE	IRISH	COOPER	082	G		55
ARMSTRONG	JOHN				30	IRELAND	CE	IRISH	F	085	E		16
ARMSTRONG	JOHN				25	0	CP	SCOTCH	LUMBERMAN	085	H		21
ARMSTRONG	JOHN		1		21	IRELAND	WM	IRISH	LAB	085	I		16
ARMSTRONG	JOHN				23	0	WM	ENGLISH	F	085	L		11
ARMSTRONG	JOHN				25	IRELAND	WM	IRISH	CONTRACTOR	086	A	1	27
ARMSTRONG	JOHN				55	IRELAND	CE	IRISH	F	086	A	2	11
ARMSTRONG	MARY		1	1	20	0	CE	IRISH		081	B		6
ARMSTRONG	MATHEW				37	ENGLAND	CE	ENGLISH	F	085	J		21
ARMSTRONG	NANCY			1	32	QUE	WM	IRISH		082	D		20
ARMSTRONG	ROBERT	JR			40	IRELAND	CE	IRISH	F	085	A		17
ARMSTRONG	SAMUEL				24	IRELAND	WM	IRISH	STOREKEEPER	086	A	2	6
ARMSTRONG	SAMUEL				60	IRELAND	WM	IRISH	F	086	A	2	6
ARMSTRONG	THOMAS				38	0	CE	IRISH	F	082	G		61
ARMSTRONG	THOMAS				55	IRELAND	CP	IRISH	F	085	I		35
ARMSTRONG	THOMAS				24	0	CE	IRISH	F	086	A	2	11
ARNALD	PHILIP				55	ENGLAND	RC	ENGLISH	TURNKEY	082	D		15
ARNAUD	ELIAS	D			23	ENGLAND	CE	ENGLISH	BANKER	081	B		76
ARNOLD	JAMES		1		19	0	CS	SCOTCH	LABOURER	088	A		8
ARNOLD	LEVI				29	0	PM	ENGLISH	F	085	C		27
ARNOT	JOHN				30	0	CS	SCOTCH	F	081	A	1	62
ARNOT	WILLIAM	LAMONT			54	SCOTLAND	CS	SCOTCH	F	081	A	1	56
ARONS	ANDREW		1		40	CANADA	PR	ENGLISH	FARM SERVANT	085	A		10
ARROLL	SARAH		1	1	13	QUE	WM	IRISH		089	B		1
ARROLL	WILLIAM		1		16	QUE	WM	IRISH	FARMER	089	B		1
ARTHUR	GEORGE				40	ENGLAND	CE	ENGLISH	BRICK AND TILE MAKER	085	I		12
ARTHUR	WM				35	0	WM	IRISH	F	085	J		22
ASA	ABRAM				35	0	WM	INDIAN	HUNTER	086	A	3	1
ASANCE	SOLOMON				70	0	WM	INDIAN	F	086	A	3	4

SURNAME	NAME1	NAME2	STRAY	SEX	AGE	BIRTHPL	RELIGION	ORIGIN	OCCUP	DIST	SUB_DIST	DIV	PAGE
ASHDOWN	JAMES				46	ENGLAND	NG	ENGLISH	MERCHANT	085	E		1
ASHDOWN	WILLIAM				31	ENGLAND	CP	ENGLISH		085	H		9
ASHICK	FREDRICK				39	GERMANY	LU	GERMAN	FARMER	082	G		29
ASSANCE	DAVID				47	O	RC	INDIAN	F & FISHERMAN	087	A		42
ASSANCE	JOSEPH				47	O	RC	INDIAN	F	087	B	1	9
ASSIGINACK	BENJAMIN				41	US	RC	INDIAN	F	087	B	1	22
ASSIGINACK	LOUIS		2		4	O	RC	INDIAN		087	B	1	D
ASSIGINAK	AMABLE				82	US	RC	INDIAN	F	087	A		16
ASSIGINAK	DANIEL				40	US	RC	INDIAN	MECHANIC & F	087	A		17
ASSIGINAK	HYACINTHE		2		28	O	RC	INDIAN	F	087	A		D
ASSIGINAK	JOSEPH				42	US	RC	INDIAN	SHOEMAKER & F	087	A		17
ASSIGINAK	LOUIS				47	US	RC	INDIAN	CARPENTER & F	087	A		16
ASSIGINAK	VINCENT		2		9	O	RC	INDIAN		087	A		D
ASSINAB'S	(DAUGHTER)			1		ONTARIO	PA	INDIAN	HUNTER & TRAPPER	090	E		9
ASSINEWAY	JOHN	B			42	O	RC	INDIAN	CARPENTER	088	B		11
ASSINIIWE	JEAN	BTE			64	US	RC	INDIAN	F	087	A		5
ASSINIIWE	WILLIAM				30	O	RC	INDIAN	F & FISHERMAN	087	A		6
ASSINIWE	VINCENT				59	US	RC	INDIAN	F	087	A		15
ASSINWE	FRANCES			1	23	O	RC	INDIAN	F	087	A		16
ASTLEFORD	EMILIE		1	1	14	O	WM	ENGLISH		082	D		10
ASTLEFORD	THOS		1		17	O	WM	ENGLISH		082	D		10
ASTLEY	ROBERT				46	ENGLAND	CE	ENGLISH	PAINTER	085	D		13
ATAWISH	CECIL				60	US	RC	INDIAN	F	087	A		35
ATCHISON	GEORGE				53	IRELAND	RP	IRISH	FARMER	082	I		6
ATCHISON	JAMES				30	IRELAND	CP	IRISH	FARMER	082	I		15
ATCHISON	JAMES	ALEXANDER	2			ONT	CP			082	I		D
ATCHITCHAKOWS	JOSEPH				29	US	RC	INDIAN	F & FISHERMAN	087	A		40
ATKIN	SCOTT				42	SCOTLAND	WM	SCOTCH	F	085	D		24
ATKINSON	JOHN				37	ENGLAND	CE	ENGLISH	F	081	J	1	47
ATKINSON	JOHN				58	ENGLAND	CE	ENGLISH	F	085	D		13
ATKINSON	JOHN				34	IRELAND	EP	IRISH	F	087	B	3	1
ATKINSON	MARGARETE		1	1	57	O	WM	ENGLISH		085	B		4
ATKINSON	ROBERT				38	ENGLAND	CE	ENGLISH	F	085	D		7
ATKINSON	THOMAS		1		36	SCOTLAND	PM	SCOTCH	F	085	D		25
ATTRIDGE	CATHERINE		2			O	WM			085	K	1	D
ATTRIDGE	EDWARD				23	O	WM	IRISH	F	085	K	1	3
ATTRIDGE	JAMES				52	ENGLAND	CE	ENGLISH	FARMER	089	A		49
AULT	JOHN		1		24	O	WM	SCOTCH	F	085	H		14
AUMOND	JANET			1	53	SCOTLAND	CS	SCOTCH	F	081	C		49
AUSTIN	WILLIAM	WESLEY			35	O	CE	ENGLISH	MERCHANT	081	K		73
AUTIO	PAUL				46	QUE	RC	FRENCH	F	082	H		18
AVERELL	DAVID	M			35	IRELAND	FK	IRISH	LUMBERMAN	086	C	1	10
AVERENE	JULIUS				37	GERMANY	WM	GERMAN	F	082	C	2	48
AVRIL	JOHN				23	ONTARIO	CE	IRISH	GEN MGR	084	D		1
AWASSIGIJIK	PIERRE				50	US	RC	INDIAN	F & FISHERMAN	087	A		34
AWASSIN'S	(WIFE)			1		ONTARIO	PA	INDIAN	HUNTER & TRAPPER	090	E		21
AYLLERD	JOHN				34	ENGLAND	FW	IRISH	F	085	K	2	4
AZMER	EDWARD				21	O	CE	GERMAN	CARPENTER	081	B		39
BABEKEPESICK	SIMM				23	O	RC	INDIAN	LABOURER	090	F		12
BADERMAN	WM				25	GERMANY	LU	GERMAN	F	082	G		30
BADGER	CATHERINE		2	1	23	O				086	A	1	D
BADGER	JAMES				53	ENGLAND	WM	ENGLISH	F	086	A	1	20
BADGLEY	IRVIN				26	O	EM	ENGLISH	LAB	081	B		48
BAGLEY	JAMES	T			31	ENGLAND	UT	ENGLISH	F	085	A		13
BAGS	ELIZA		1	1	20	O	CP	IRISH		081	B		55
BAGS	JOHN		1		21	O	CP	IRISH		081	B		55
BAHDIWUAYH	PIERRE				28	US	RC	INDIAN	LABOURER	089	B		38
BAIBOMCOWMAI	BENOIT				27	O	RC	INDIAN	F	087	B	1	10
BAIBONERUNG	J	BAPTISTE			69	USA	RC	INDIAN	F	087	B	1	2
BAIBONERUNG	JEAN	BAPTISTE			38	USA	RC	INDIAN	F	087	B	1	2
BAILEY	EDWARD				28	ENGLAND	PM	ENGLISH	F	085	I		20
BAILEY	JAMES				27	ENGLAND	WM	ENGLISH	MINER	089	A		7
BAILEY	JOHN				56	SCOTLAND	CS	SCOTCH	F	081	C		57
BAILEY	JOHN				45	IRELAND	PR	IRISH	F	085	A		11
BAILEY	JOHN				29	ENGLAND	PM	ENGLISH	F	085	I		20
BAILEY	MARGARET		1	1	22	O	PS	IRISH		082	E		30
BAILEY	NATHAN		1		23	O	PS	SCOTTISH	TEAMSTER	082	E		30
BAILEY	SAMUEL				50	ONTARIO	CE	IRISH	F	082	A		35
BAILEY	THOMAS		1		21	ENGLAND	WM	ENGLISH	MINER	089	A		37
BAILLIE	WILLIAM				44	ENGLAND	CE	ENGLISH	LAB	081	H	2	38
BAILY	ALEXANDER		2		58	O	RC		F	085	F		D
BAILY	JULIE			1	43	O	RC	FRENCH		085	E		20
BAILY	MICHAEL				46	O	RC	FRENCH	F	085	E		23
BAILY	ROBERT				34	QUE	ME	ENGLISH	LUMBERMAN	086	C	1	10
BAIN	ALEX				68	SCOTLAND	FK	SCOTCH	FARMER	081	J	1	36
BAIN	ALEXANDER				46	SCOTLAND	CP	SCOTCH	F	085	B		4
BAIN	JAMES				62	SCOTLAND	FK	SCOTCH	WEAVER	081	J	1	35
BAIN	THOMAS				47	SCOTLAND	CP	SCOTCH	F	085	B		4
BAIN	WILLIAM				26	ONT	FK	SCOTCH	F	081	J	1	36
BAIN	WILLIAM		1		43	ENGLAND	CE	ENGLISH	LABOURER	085	D		19
BAIRD	DAVID				35	SCOTLAND	RP	SCOTCH	FARMER	082	I		4
BAIRD	GRACE		1	1	8	ONT	RP	SCOTCH		082	I		11
BAIRD	JOHN	D			56	QUE	CE	SCOTCH	F	082	K	1	17
BAIRD	WILLIAM				33	O	CE	IRISH	F	082	C	1	23
BAITAULD	AUGUST				45	PRUSSIA	CE	GERMAN	FARMER	082	B		53
BAKER	ADALINE		1	1	19	O	RC	IRISH	SERVANT GIRL	082	D		17
BAKER	CATHARINE				45	O	RC	IRISH		086	C	1	9
BAKER	RICHARD				50	ENGLAND	CE	ENGLISH	GUNSMITH	086	A	1	32
BAKER	SAMUEL				55	ENGLAND	WM	ENGLISH	SHOEMAKER	085	B		12
BAKER	WILLIAM				32	ENGLAND	CE	ENGLISH	BRICKMAKER	081	A	2	13
BAKER	WILLIAM		1		44	ENGLAND	WM	ENGLISH	SHOE MAKER	085	I		3
BALDWIN	ELIZABETH			1	53	QUE	CP	IRISH		081	B		73
BALDWIN	SHEARMAN				29	O	PM	ENGLISH	F	085	I		22
BALDWIN	SHERMAN		1		14	O	EM	IRISH	LAB	081	B		60
BALDWIN	WILLIAM	H	1		17	UNITED STATES	EM	IRISH	LAB	081	B		60
BALEACK	LOUIS				52	QUE	RC	ENGLISH	SAWYER	082	E		76
BALFOUR	ROBERT				23	O	EM	IRISH	LAB	081	B		22
BALGER	JOHN				40	IRELAND	RC	IRISH	CARPENTER	081	J	1	9
BALGER	PATRICK				30	IRELAND	RC	IRISH	F	081	J	1	8
BALGER	WILLIAM				40	IRELAND	RC	IRISH	F	081	J	1	5
BALGER	WILLIAM				40	IRELAND	RC	IRISH	F	081	J	1	4
BALL	GEORGE				34	O	CE	ENGLISH	MILLWRIGHT	081	B		38
BALL	GEORGE				63	ENGLAND	CE	ENGLISH	F	085	H		18
BALL	MARY	ANN		1	60	ENGLAND	CE	ENGLISH		081	B		71
BALL	PETER		1					IRISH	LUMBERMAN	086	C	1	9
BALL	THOMAS		1		42	ENGLAND	CE	ENGLISH	F	085	K	1	3

SURNAME	NAME1	NAME2	STRAY	SEX	AGE	BIRTHPL	RELIGION	ORIGIN	OCCUP	DIST	SUB_DIST	DIV	PAGE
BALL	THOMAS	REV	1		26	ENGLAND	CE	ENGLISH	CLERGYMAN	085	C		22
BALLENTINE	ROBERT				30	ENGLAND	WM	ENGLISH	F	085	L		10
BALMAN	JACOB				34	WURTEMBURG	LU	GERMAN	F	085	A		5
BAMBACK	CHARLES				42	GERMANY	LU	GERMAN	COOPER	090	D		2
BAME	CHARLES				47	GERMANY	LU	GERMAN	FARMER	082	I		55
BAMER	GOTLIP				56	GERMANY	WM	GERMAN	F	082	G		16
BAMPTON	CHARLES				40	IRELAND	RC	IRISH	BUILDER	089	B		7
BAMPTON	CHARLES		2		7	0	RC			089	B		D
BANDY	RICHARD				41	ENGLAND	EM	ENGLISH	F	081	A	1	8
BANDY	ROBERT				39	ENGLAND	CE	ENGLISH	F	081	A	1	4
BANE	DANIEL				32	SCOTLAND	PS	SCOTCH	F	085	J		5
BANERLE	WILLIAM		1		29	GERMANY	UV	GERMAN	TEACHER	090	D		1
BANGS	AGNES			1	40	QUE	CP	SCOTCH		081	B		49
BANGS	CAROLINE		1	1	60	QUE	EM	ENGLISH		081	B		12
BANGS	JAMES				35	ONTARIO	RC	IRISH	FARMER & HOTEL KEEPE	084	C		5
BANGS	JOHN				39	ONTARIO	CE	ENGLISH	MERCHANT & POSTMASTE	084	C		5
BANING	ALLICE		1	1	58	SCOTLAND	CP	SCOTCH		081	B		82
BANING	MARY	ANN	1	1	19	0	CP	IRISH		081	B		82
BANKS	JOHN		1		28	IRELAND	RC	IRISH	LUMBERMAN	088	B		5
BANNERMAN	JOHN				25	SCOTLAND	RP	SCOTCH	MERCHANT	081	I		10
BANNERMAN	WILLIAM				28	SCOTLAND	CP	SCOTCH	LUMBERER	081	A	1	42
BANNING	WILLIAM				26	0	CP	IRISH	LAB	081	B		81
BAOSE	WALTER				33	ONT	CS	SCOTCH	F	081	J	1	31
BARBEAU	ANTOINE				39	0	PS	FRENCH	MILLER	086	A	1	26
BARBER	JAMES				28	0	PS	ENGLISH	F	085	D		24
BARBER	JOHN				62	SCOTLAND	CP	SCOTCH	F	082	C	2	3
BARBER	ROBERT				27	0	CP	SCOTCH	CARRIAGEMAKER	081	B		28
BARD	CHARLES				31	ENGLAND	IN	ENGLISH	F	085	C		5
BARD	FREDRICK				27	ENGLAND	CE	ENGLISH	F	085	C		5
BARKER	WILLARD				29	0	WM	ENGLISH	F	086	A	1	24
BARKOAN	JOSEPH				46	QUE	RC	FRENCH	FARMER	081	F		4
BARNET	HANNORA		1	1	17	0	RC	IRISH	SERVANT	081	B		80
BARNET	SUSAN				49	IRELAND	CE	IRISH	LADY FARMER	081	C		12
BARNETT	ALEXANDER				31	0	CE	IRISH	LUMBER MERCHANT	081	I		16
BARNS	JOHN				40	SCOTLAND	CS	SCOTCH	F	081	H	2	19
BARR	ELIZABETH			1	65		CP	SCOTCH		081	A	1	30
BARR	HENRY				27	ONTARIO	PS	SCOTTISH	FARMER	082	B		61
BARR	JAMES				32	0	CP	SCOTCH	F	081	A	1	30
BARR	JAMES				61	SCOTLAND	CP	SCOTCH	F	082	C	1	45
BARR	JENET		1	1	42	ONT	CP	IRISH	HOUSEKEEPER	081	J	1	42
BARR	JOHN				51	IRELAND	CP	IRISH	F	082	C	1	45
BARR	MACKIE				36	ONT	CS	SCOTCH	F	081	J	1	83
BARR	MATTHEW		2		85	SCOTLAND	CP		F			1	D
BARR	WALTER		1		19	0	CS	SCOTCH	APPRENTICE	082	C	2	64
BARR	WILLIAM				34	0	CS	SCOTCH	F	081	H	1	7
BARREN	WILLIAM				30	0	CO	INDIAN	SCHOOL TEACHER	085	G		1
BARRETT	DENNIS				50	IRELAND	RC	IRISH	F	081	A	2	32
BARRETT	JAMES		1		18	US	CE	IRISH	LAB	085	F		5
BARRETT	WALTER		1		12	0	PM	ENGLISH		089	A		8
BARREY	WALTER				44	0	OP	ENGLISH	F	081	E		18
BARRIE	ROBERT				66	SCOTLAND	CP	SCOTCH	F	081	J	1	71
BARRON	ALEXANDER				59	SCOTLAND	CS	SCOTCH	F	085	I		18
BARRON	EDDARE		1		13	0	RC	FRENCH		082	C	1	50
BARRON	ELENOR		1	1	7	0	RC	FRENCH		082	C	1	50
BARRON	FRANCEWAY		1		64	QUE	RC	FRENCH	CARPENTER	082	C	1	49
BARRON	FRANCEWAY		1		9	0	RC	FRENCH		082	C	1	50
BARRON	JOSEPH		1		16	0	RC	FRENCH	FARM LAB	082	C	1	50
BARRON	JOSEPHINE		1	1	46	QUE	RC	FRENCH		082	C	1	49
BARRON	JOSEPHINE		1	1	15	0	RC	FRENCH		082	C	1	50
BARRY	ISAAC				33	0	CE	IRISH	F	086	A	1	21
BARRY	JAMES				50	IRELAND	RC	IRISH	F	081	C		52
BARRY	JOHN				36	0	CE	ENGLISH	F	081	A	1	15
BARRY	JOHN				41	IRELAND	RC	IRISH	TINSMITH	082	E		35
BARRY	MARY			1	67	IRELAND	CE	IRISH		081	A	1	15
BARTHREW	HYACUTH				50	QUEBEC	RC	FRENCH	LUMBERMAN	083	A	1	12
BARTLE	JOHN				42	ENGLAND	WM	ENGLISH	MINER	089	A		28
BARTLETT	G	W			19	ENGLAND	CE	ENGLISH	F	081	C		43
BARTLEY	ELLIN		1	1	17	0	EM	ENGLISH		085	J		14
BARTLEY	MARY		1	1	16	0	WM	SCOTCH	SERVANT	085	H		20
BARTOME	JOSEPH				28	QUE	RC	FRENCH	SHANTYMAN	082	E		50
BARTRAGE	WILLIAM				50	IRELAND	RC	IRISH	LAB	081	A	2	14
BARTRAND	HYACENTHE		1		47	QUEBEC	RC	FRENCH	SHANTYMAN	081	G	1	4
BASHAM	PETER				35	QUE	RC	FRENCH	F	081	E		12
BASHORT	PETTER				50	0	CE	GERMAN	LAB	081	H	1	19
BASSETT	EDWARD				36	IRELAND	RC	IRISH	LAB	081	B		79
BASSIE	EDWARD				56	QUEBEC	RC	FRENCH	SHOEMAKER	081	J	1	86
BATEMAN	WILLIAM				39	ENGLAND	WM	ENGLISH	MACHINIST & ENGINEER	085	I		14
BATEMATA	THOMAS				41	IRELAND	CE	IRISH	F	085	D		28
BATEN	WILLIAM				56	SCOTLAND	UP	SCOTCH	F	085	D		10
BATES	EZRA	E			33	0	CE	SCOTCH	POSTMASTER	081	B		77
BATES	MATHEW				65	IRELAND	CE	IRISH	F	082	A		12
BATRAZE	CELIA		1	1	15	0	RC	IRISH	SERVANT	081	A	2	17
BATTRAM	JOHN	V			33	ENGLAND	NG	ENGLISH	CARPENTER	085	I		10
BATZ	VALTIN				35	GERMANY	LU	GERMAN	F	082	G		19
BAUDIN	ISRAEL				29	QUE	RC	FRENCH	COOPER	088	A		13
BAUDRIE	MRS			1	60	SCOTLAND	CS	SCOTCH		081	J	1	85
BAUERMAN	JOHN				28	SCOTLAND	CP	SCOTCH	LAB	081	A	2	16
BAUNIGUANY	K				46	FRANCE	RC	FRENCH	COOK	088	A		8
BAUPRIE	BEN				45	QUE	RC	FRENCH	LABOURER	082	E		75
BAXTER	DAVID				24	IRELAND	WM	IRISH	F	085	L		1
BAXTER	HUGH				36	ONTARIO	ME	IRISH	F	083	C		18
BAXTER	JOHN				39	ENGLAND	CE	ENGLISH	F	085	D		2
BAYLEE	ALEXANDER				38	IRELAND	WM	IRISH	F	085	J		26
BAYLEE	C	O'DELL			24	IRELAND	CE	IRISH	SCHOOL TEACHER	085	C		11
BEACH	ABEL				52	0	JM	ENGLISH	CONVEYANCER	082	C	2	1
BEACH	JOHN				49	0	JM	IRISH	SHOEMAKER	082	C	2	13
BEACH	JOHN		1		21	0	CE	ENGLISH	COOK	085	E		27
BEACH	JOSEPH				37	0	JM	ENGLISH	F	082	C	2	64
BEACH	LEVI				43	0	JM	ENGLISH	MILLER	082	C	2	43
BEACH	WILLIAM		1		17	0	CE	ENGLISH	SHANTY MAN	085	E		27
BEADERMAN	AUGUSTUS		1		20	GERMANY	CE	GERMAN	SERVANT	082	E		55
BEADLEY	DAVID				40	QUE	CP	IRISH	F	082	C	2	25
BEAHAN	SARAH			1	73	IRELAND	RC			082	H		D
BEALL	WILLIAM				63	ENGLAND	CE	ENGLISH	F	082	C	2	17
BEAM	AUGUST				29	GERMANY	WM	GERMAN	F	082	G		82
BEAMAN	HARMAN				28	PRUSSIA	PS	PRUSSIAN	TENANT	081	J	1	43

SURNAME	NAME1	NAME2	STRAY	SEX	AGE	BIRTHPL	RELIGION	ORIGIN	OCCUP	DIST	SUB_DIST	DIV	PAGE
BEAMISH	WILLIAM		1		23	QUE	CE	IRISH	CABINETMAKER	082	E		60
BEARTLING	NEAL		1		19	O	CP	SCOTCH	F LABOURER	085	H		21
BEASLEY	WILLIAM				43	ENGLAND	CE	ENGLISH	FARMER	086	B		8
BEASTLY	MARTIN				31	IRELAND	RC	IRISH	F	082	K	1	8
BEASTLY	WILLIAM				60	IRELAND	RC	IRISH	F	082	K	1	8
BEATON	STEPHEN				27	ONT	CP	SCOTCH		081	J	1	35
BEATTY	EDWARD		1		27	QUE	PS	IRISH	FARMER	086	B		7
BEATTY	GEORGE				33	IRELAND	WM	IRISH	F	085	A		29
BEATTY	JOHN				32	O	WM	IRISH	CROWN LAND AGENT	086	A	1	29
BEATTY	WILLIAM				36	IRELAND	WM	IRISH	MERCHANT	086	A	1	33
BEATY	GEORGE	W	2			O	CP			082	E		D
BEATY	JOHN				40	ONTARIO	CS	IRISH	FARMER	084	D		3
BEATY	THOMAS		2			O	CE			081	B		D
BEATY	WALTER				30	O	CP	SCOTTISH	CARPENTER	082	E		66
BEATY	WILLIAM				25	IRELAND	CE	IRISH	CLERK	081	B		31
BEAUBIEN	JOHN				35	QUE	RC	INDIAN	HUNTER	081	K		28
BEAUCHAMP	MARGRET		1	1	64	SCOTLAND	CP	SCOTCH		081	I		1
BEAUDREAU	GILBERT				22	QUEBEC	RC	FRENCH	F	083	C		4
BEAUDRIE	ELY				28	QUE	RC	FRENCH	LAB	081	I		19
BEAUDRY	EUSABE				36	QUE	RC	FRENCH	FARMER	084	E		3
BEAUPRE	JOHN		1		19	O	JM	SCOTCH	F	082	C	2	13
BEAUPRE	MARTIN		1		16	O	JM	SCOTCH		082	C	2	13
BEAUPRE	SILVESTER		1		13	O	JM	SCOTCH		082	C	2	13
BEAVEN	E	W			37	ENGLAND	CE	ENGLISH	CLERGYMAN	081	B		40
BEAVEN	ELEANOR	G	2	1		O	CE			081	B		D
BEBONISE	PIERRE				45	US	RC	INDIAN	F & FISHERMAN	087	A		25
BECK	JACOB				34	GERMANY	RC	GERMAN	MINER	090	F		17
BECK	JAMES		2			US	ME			090	F		D
BECK	JOHN				39	FRANCE	RC	GERMAN	GENERAL MANAGER	090	F		18
BECKER	AUGUST				48	GERMANY	FW	GERMAN	FARMER	081	G	1	40
BECKER	CAROL				46	GERMANY	LU	GERMAN	F	082	H		14
BECKET	JAMES				50	IRELAND	CE	IRISH	F	081	K		25
BECKET	JOHN				62	ENGLAND	CE	IRISH	F	081	K		24
BECKET	WILLIAM				42	IRELAND	CE	IRISH	F	081	K		25
BECKETT	ALFRED	R			33	O	CE	ENGLISH	F	085	K	2	8
BECKETT	GEORGE				24	O	CE	IRISH	F	086	A	2	8
BEDDARD	ALVINE		1	1	19	QUE	RC	FRENCH	SERVANT	082	D		21
BEECH	JAMES				35	O	EM	GERMAN	F	085	D		8
BEEDERMAN	AUGUST				32	GERMANY	LU	GERMAN	F	082	G		89
BEELOW	HARMAN				23	GERMANY	LU	GERMAN	F	081	K		57
BEEMAN	CEPHAS		1		21	O	WM	ENGLISH	PRINTER	082	E		30
BEERS	LESSEA		1	1	16	O	CE	SCOTCH		082	K	1	11
BEERS	SARAH		1	1	14	O	CE	SCOTCH		082	K	1	11
BEG	PIERRE				45	O	RC	INDIAN	HUNTER	084	H		1
BEGONIER	MARGARET		1	1	30	O	RC	FRENCH	SEAMSTRESS	089	A		52
BEHAN	DAVID				48	IRELAND	RC	IRISH	F	081	K		36
BEHAN	JAMES				32	IRELAND	RC	IRISH	BOOKKEEPER	082	E		54
BEHM	AUGUST				32	PRUSSIA	LU	PRUSSIAN	F LABOURER	081	J	1	50
BEHM	CHARLES						NG		SEE BAME	082	I		55
BEHMISE	FREDERICK		1		21	GERMANY	FW	GERMAN		081	G	1	41
BEHMISE	JULAS		1		27	GERMANY	FW	GERMAN	FARMER	081	G	1	41
BEIDEMAN	CHAS				28	PRUSSIA	LU	PRUSSIAN	F	082	G		81
BEIDERMAN	GOTLIP				55	GERMANY	LU	GERMAN	F	082	G		27
BEIGG	BEN				39	ENGLAND	CE	ENGLISH	F	085	J		3
BELANGE	MICHAEL				37	QUE	RC	FRENCH	F	081	E		14
BELANGE	NICALO				42	QUE	RC	FRENCH	F	081	E		13
BELANGE	OCTALIE				20	QUE	RC	FRENCH	F	081	E		14
BELANGER	ANDREW				48	RED RIVER	RC	FRENCH	LAB	090	F		14
BELANGER	JOSEPH				27	ONT	RC	FRENCH	F	081	C		56
BELANGIE	MARSELLE		1		20	QUE	RC	FRENCH	FARMER	081	D		22
BELANGIE	URSONE		1	1	20	O	RC	FRENCH		081	D		22
BELESKY	ALBERT				59	PRUSSIA	RC	PRUSSIAN	FARMER	083	A	1	17
BELEY	BENJAMIN	SNOWDRI			30	ENGLAND	CN	ENGLISH	F	085	E		1
BELFORD	CHARLES				36	O	BA	IRISH	SHANTYING	081	H	2	6
BELFORD	JOHN				53	IRELAND	CE	IRISH	GARDENER	082	C	1	10
BELILE	ADOLPHUS		1		29	O	RC	FRENCH	F	081	K		34
BELILE	JULIAN				48	QUE	RC	FRENCH	LAB	081	K		34
BELILE	LOUIS		1		3	O	RC	FRENCH		081	K		34
BELILE	MARY		1	1	20	QUE	RC	FRENCH		081	K		34
BELILE	MARY		1	1	1	O	RC	FRENCH		081	K		34
BELL	ALBERT				62	IRELAND	CE	IRISH	F	086	A	1	11
BELL	ALEXANDER				25	IRELAND	CE	IRISH	F	082	A		8
BELL	DAVID				49	SCOTLAND	PS	SCOTTISH	LUMBER MERCHANT	082	E		38
BELL	DUNCAN				38	SCOTLAND	BA	SCOTCH	F	085	A		20
BELL	GEORGE				60	IRELAND	CP	IRISH	F	085	D		15
BELL	JAMES				39	UNITED STATES	CE	IRISH	GENERAL AGENT	081	B		84
BELL	JAMES				26	O	PM	ENGLISH	MINISTER P METHODIST	089	A		23
BELL	JOHN				33	O	CP	SCOTCH	GROCER	081	B		16
BELL	JOHN		1		21	O	CE	SCOTCH	CLERK	081	I		30
BELL	JOHN				51	SCOTLAND	CP	SCOTTISH	LUMBER MERCHANT	082	E		5
BELL	JOHN				60	O	CE	SCOTCH	HUNTER	089	B		28
BELL	JOSEPH				44	SCOTLAND	PS	SCOTTISH	LUMBER MERCHANT	082	D		4
BELL	JOSEPH				30	O	RC	SCOTCH	BOATMAN	089	B		28
BELL	MARGARET		1	1	15	O	CE	IRISH	SERVANT	089	B		2
BELL	MARGRET		2	1	80	SCOTLAND	PS			082	D		D
BELL	MARY		1	1	11	O	WM	IRISH	SERVANT	089	B		1
BELL	PETER				40	O	RC	SCOTCH	TRADER	089	B		27
BELL	PETER	WARREN			39	ONTARIO	PR	SCOTCH	CHIEF TRADER H B CO	090	B		1
BELL	RICHD	JAMES			39	ENGLAND	CE	ENGLISH	MERCHANT & CLERK	085	I		43
BELL	ROBERT				48	SCOTLAND	RP	SCOTCH	FARMER	082	I		9
BELL	SOPHIE		2	1	4	O	RC			089	B		D
BELL	WILLIAM				46	SCOTLAND	PS	SCOTTISH	FARMER	082	D		5
BELL	WILLIAM		2		79	SCOTLAND	PS		SHIAW MAKER	082	D		D
BELL	WILLIAM				50	IRELAND	CP	IRISH	P L SURVEYOR	082	E		16
BELLAIRE	MICHL				35	QUE	RC	FRENCH	TEAMSTER	082	E		21
BELLAMY	JOAB				40	O	WM	ENGLISH	CARPENTER	081	A	1	54
BELLAMY	JUSTICE				25	O	WM	ENG	TINSMITH	081	B		60
BELLEAU	MICHEL				48	O	RC	FRENCH	BOATMAN	089	B		26
BELLEFEUILLE	GABRIEL	JNR			34	O	RC	FRENCH	LAB	082	J		1
BELLEFEUILLE	GABRIEL	SR			61	QUE	RC	FRENCH	F	082	J		1
BELLEFEUILLE	THEOPHILE				30	O	RC	FRENCH	HOTELKEEPER	082	J		19
BELLERBY	HENERY				70	ENGLAND	CE	ENGLISH	GENTLEMAN	081	I		16
BELLILL	LOUIS				39	QUE	RC	FRENCH	CARPENTER	081	B		74
BELLINGS	FRANCIS				47	IRELAND	RC	IRISH	FARMER	082	B		2
BELLINGSLEY	JOHN				34	O	EM	ENGLISH	F	085	D		4
BELLO	PETER				50	QUE	RC	FRENCH	LAB	082	C	1	28

SURNAME	NAME1	NAME2	STRAY	SEX	AGE	BIRTHPL	RELIGION	ORIGIN	OCCUP	DIST	SUB_DIST	DIV	PAGE
BELMENT	JAMES				40	ENGLAND	CE	ENGLISH	F	085	J		5
BELVAL	FRANK				75	QUE	RC	FRENCH	FARMER	089	A		54
BELVAL	FRANK		1		24	O	RC	FRENCH	LABOURER	089	A		54
BELVAL	JOHN		1		21	O	RC	FRENCH	FISHERMAN	089	A		59
BEMANAKINANG	BERNARD				33	US	RC	INDIAN	FISHERMAN & LAB	087	A		18
BEMANAKINANG	FABIEN				40	US	RC	INDIAN	F & FISHERMAN	087	A		18
BEMANAKINANG	JOSEPH				45	US	RC	INDIAN	MASON & F	087	A		18
BEMANAKINANG	LOUIS				36	US	RC	INDIAN	F & FISHERMAN	087	A		18
BEMANAKINANG	MARGARET		1		42	US	RC	INDIAN	F	087	A		18
BEMANAKINANG	MICHEL				72	US	RC	INDIAN	MASON & F	087	A		17
BEMISSENODAWA	PIERRE				43	US	RC	INDIAN	F	087	A		35
BENAGER	ELLIOTT								SEE ELLIOTT	085	I		29
BENBOW	JOHN				21	ENGLAND	CE	ENGLISH	F	085	L		4
BENBOW	WM				21	ENGLAND	CE	ENGLISH	F	085	L		4
BENET	JOHN				24	O	RC	IRISH	F	082	L		1
BENJAMIN	ANTOINE				46	QUEBEC	WM	FRENCH	F	081	J	1	40
BENJAMIN	GEORGE				45	ENGLAND	CE	ENGLISH	BRICKLAYER	082	E		20
BENNAR	FERDINAN		1		30	QUE	RC	FRENCH	LAB	081	A	2	17
BENNET	FRANCIS				27	QUE	CP	FRENCH	F	081	H	1	6
BENNET	MOSES				29	ENGLAND	BA	ENGLISH	F	087	B	3	11
BENNET	PETER		1							085	A		19
BENNET	RICHARD		1		30	IRELAND	RC	IRISH	CARPENTER	081	K		66
BENNET	WILLIAM				48	ENGLAND	CE	ENGLISH	F	085	H		8
BENNETT	BRIDGET		1	1	26	IRELAND	RC	IRISH	SEAMSTRESS	081	K		70
BENNETT	EDMUND				32	IRELAND	RC	IRISH	F	082	H		1
BENNETT	JAMES				57	ENGLAND	CE	ENGLISH	F	082	A		12
BENNETT	JAMES				27	ENGLAND	EM	ENGLISH	F	082	A		26
BENNETT	JOHN				58	IRELAND	RC	IRISH	FARMER	081	F		17
BENNETT	LEVI				34	QUE	NG	FRENCH	F	081	C		28
BENNETT	LOUIS				26	QUE	RC	FRENCH	LAB	081	I		28
BENNETT	MARGARET		1	1	14	O	CP	SCOTCH		085	I		18
BENNETT	MARGRET		1	1	18	O	CP	SCOTCH		081	B		13
BENNETT	MATTHIAS				54	IRELAND	RC	IRISH	F	082	H		2
BENNETT	NICHOLAS				35	IRELAND	CE	IRISH	F	085	D		18
BENNETT	WILLIAM				73	IRELAND	CE	IRISH	F	081	H	2	34
BENNETTS	HURBERT		1		18	IRELAND	CE	IRISH	LABOURER	089	B		16
BENNETTS	MARY		1	1	19	IRELAND	CE	ENGLISH		089	B		9
BENNIE	ROBERT				30	O	CP	SCOTCH	F	082	C	1	51
BENNY	GEORGE				60	SCOTLAND	CP	SCOTCH	WEAVER	082	C	1	63
BENOIT	FRANCES				27	ONTARIO	RC	INDIAN	HUNTER	083	D		1
BENOITT	EDMO		1		23	QUE	RC	FRENCH	WATCHMAKER	082	E		30
BENSON	PATRICK				35	O	RC	IRISH	F	082	L		5
BENSON	THOMAS		1		60	IRELAND	CE	IRISH	FARMER	081	F		14
BENTEN	THOMAS	JR			37	IRELAND	RC	IRISH	LAB	081	B		83
BENTRUM	WILLIAM				70	SCOTLAND	CP	SCOTCH	F	085	H		20
BENZINGER	FRIDNE				34	GERMANY	LU	GERMAN	F	085	A		31
BERFORD	FRANCIS	M			56	IRELAND	CE	FRENCH	F	085	K	2	9
BERGER	AMOS				24	O	EM	ENGLISH	F	085	D		4
BERGER	GORDON				55	O	PM	GERMAN	F	085	D		23
BERGER	WILLIAM				27	GERMANY	LU	GERMAN	F	082	G		14
BERKWELL	HUGH				50	ENGLAND	CE	ENGLISH	FARMER	081	G	1	19
BERLAND	PHELIX				27	QUEBEC	RC	FRENCH	LAB	083	F	1	1
BERMAN	JOSEPH		1		40	IRELAND	CE	IRISH	FARMER	086	B		8
BERNARD	ADELINE		1	1	32	QUE	RC	FRENCH	SERVANT	082	E		40
BERNARD	BENAN				35	US	RC	INDIAN	SAILOR	088	A		2
BERNARD	JOHN				32	ENGLAND	CE	ENGLISH	F	081	J	1	11
BERNDT	DAVID				37	GERMANY	BA	GERMAN	FARMER	081	F		31
BERNESKEY	ANTHONY				60	PRUSSIA	RC	PRUSSIAN	FARMER	083	A	1	6
BERNETTS	JAMES				60	ENGLAND	CE	ENGLISH	GENERAL MANAGER	089	A		44
BERNIER	CELANIS		1	1	16	QUE	RC	FRENCH		082	D		19
BERNSON	SARAH		1	1	24	QUE	CE	ENGLISH	WAITER	082	C	1	3
BERRY	ALEXANDER		1		8	O	CP	SCOTCH		081	I		8
BERTRAND	FELIX				27	QUEBEC	RC	FRENCH	LUMBERER	083	F	2	1
BERTRAND	FRANCIS				26	O	RC	FRENCH	F	082	C	1	56
BERTRAND	FRANCIS		1		12	QUE	RC	FRENCH	FARM LAB	082	C	1	60
BERTRAND	PABERION	F			59	QUE	RC	FRENCH	F	082	C	1	56
BERTRAND	SAMUEL				45	QUEBEC	RC	FRENCH	FARMER	084	B		3
BERTRAND	THEOFILE				25	QUE	RC	FRENCH	F	082	C	1	47
BERTREND	ANTOINE		1		17	QUE	RC	FRENCH	BLACKSMITH	082	E		37
BESAU	HORACE				33	USA	RC	FRENCH	MILLER	082	B		57
BESLEY	GEORGE	BARLOW			25	ENGLAND	CE	ENGLISH	F	085	E		30
BESLEY	WILLIAM		1		28	ENGLAND	CE	ENGLISH	YEOMAN	085	B		14
BESLEY	WM	BARLOW			27	ENGLAND	CE	ENGLISH	F	085	E		30
BESOINE	AUGUSTINE				45	O	RC	FRENCH	TRADER	090	A		1
BESSAM	SOVEFEE		2	1	49	GERMANY	WM			081	I		D
BESSENT	RICHARD		1		32	ENGLAND	CE	ENGLISH	CARPENTER	085	E		25
BEST	JOSEPH		1		25	O	WM	ENGLISH	SEAMAN	089	A		3
BEST	SAMUEL	G			42	CANADA	PS	SCOTCH	MERCHANT	085	E		6
BESTIAN	LOUIS		1		50	QUEBEC	RC	FRENCH	FARMER	084	B		5
BETEMAN	WILLIAM				32	ENGLAND	CE	ENGLISH	CARPENTER	081	I		21
BETHUNE	DONALD				42	QUE	CP	SCOTCH	F	081	A	2	41
BETHUNE	PETER				40	O	CP	SCOTCH	F	081	A	2	41
BETTLES	JOHN				46	ENGLAND	WM	ENGLISH	F	082	C	2	40
BETTLES	NOAH		2			O	WM			082	C	2	D
BEVIS	HENRY	BASIL	1		29	ENGLAND	CE	ENGLISH	MINISTER	081	K		61
BEVRIDGE	ROBERT				51	SCOTLAND	PS	SCOTCH	CARPENTER	086	A	1	25
BEZWAH	J	BTE			56	US	RC	INDIAN	F	087	A		45
BEZWAH	J	BTE			30	O	RC	INDIAN	F	087	A		45
BICKMORE	HENRY				27	ENGLAND	CE	ENGLISH	F	085	C		19
BIESENTHAL	AUGUST				25	GERMANY	LU	GERMAN	F	082	H		25
BIESENTHAL	GOTTLAIB				46	GERMANY	LU	GERMAN	FARMER	082	I		60
BIESENTHAL	HERMAN		1		8	ONT	LU	GERMAN		082	I		62
BIESENTHAL	JOHN		1		17	GERMANY	LU	GERMAN		082	I		61
BIESENTHAL	LOUISA		1	1	6	ONT	LU	GERMAN		082	I		62
BIESENTHAL	MARY		1	1	10	ONT	LU	GERMAN		082	I		61
BIESENTHAL	MICHAEL				54	GERMANY	LU	GERMAN	FARMER	082	I		63
BIESENTHAL	WILLIAM		1		13	ONT	LU	GERMAN		082	I		61
BIESENTHAL	WILLIAM				26	GERMANY	LU	GERMAN	FARMER	082	I		62
BIESETHAL	FERDINAND		1		18	GERMANY	LU	GERMAN	FARM SERVANT	082	I		42
BIGGER	GEORGE				49	O	OP	SCOTCH	MERCHANT	081	I		24
BIGGER	JOHN				61	O	CP			085	E		29
BIGGINGS	EDWARD				40	ENGLAND	WM	ENGLISH	GAOLER	089	B		13
BIGGS	GEORGE				24	ONT	CP	ENGLISH	FARMER	082	I		38
BIGGS	JOSEPH				35	NB	CE	ENGLISH	FARMER	082	I		42
BIGGS	SAMUEL				58	NB	CP	ENGLISH	FARMER	082	I		37
BIGGS	WILLIAM				30	NB	CP	ENGLISH	FARMER	082	I		42

SURNAME	NAME1	NAME2	STRAY	SEX	AGE	BIRTHPL	RELIGION	ORIGIN	OCCUP	DIST	SUB_DIST	DIV	PAGE
BIGS	ARON				24	NB	CP	ENGLISH	F	082	F		20
BILADEAU	JOSEPH				40	QUEBEC	CE	FRENCH	LABOURER	082	B		49
BILDSON			2			0	WM			085	L		D
BILDSON	JOHN				30	ENGLAND	CE	ENGLISH	F	085	L		9
BILLALE	JOSEPH				46	QUEBEC	PR	FRENCH	SHOEMAKER	081	G	2	7
BILLEDO	JOSEPH				22	QUE	RC	FRENCH	LAB	081	B		74
BILODEAU									SEE BILLEDO	081	B		74
BINION	EDWARD		1		24	CALCUTTA E I	CE	ENGLISH	GROCER	085	B		13
BINKEY	AUGUST				35	GERMANY	LU	GERMAN	L	082	G		82
BINKEY	JACOB				42	GERMANY	RC	GERMAN	F	082	G		33
BIRD	ENA		1	1	26	GERMAN	EV	GERMAN		082	F		24
BIRK	HENRY		1		10	ENGLAND	CE	ENGLISH		085	I		29
BIRNIE	ALEXR		1		27	SCOTLAND	PS	SCOTTISH	BLACKSMITH	082	E		60
BIRON	ALEXANDER		1		56	0	RC	FRENCH		089	B		28
BIRON	ANGELIQUE		1	1	50	0	RC	INDIAN		089	B		28
BIRON	CECIL		2	1	4	0	RC			089	B		D
BIRON	CHARLES				38	0	RC	FRENCH	BOATMAN	089	B		17
BIRON	GABRIEL		2		20	0	RC			089	B		D
BIRON	JOACHIM				50	0	RC	FRENCH	FERRY MAN	089	B		8
BIRON	JOSEPH				40	0	RC	FRENCH	BOATMAN	089	B		30
BISAILLON	JOSEPH				41	0	RC	FRENCH	FISHERMAN	089	A		62
BISAILLON	JULIAN				45	0	RC	FRENCH	FISHERMAN	089	A		65
BISENBANK	JOHN				41	PRUSSIA	RC	PRUSSIAN	LAB	090	D		7
BISHOP	JOHN				53	IRELAND	CE	IRISH	FARMER	089	A		54
BISHOP	THOMAS				30	0	CE	IRISH	LABOURER	089	A		55
BISHOP	WM		1		35	ENGLAND	CE	ENGLISH	LABOURER	088	A		7
BISIT	FRANCIS		1		24	0	CP	SCOTCH	TEACHER	081	B		28
BISSETT	VIOLET		1	1	23	0	CS	SCOTCH		090	F		22
BLACK	AGNES		1	1	12	ONTARIO	CS	SCOTCH		082	A		21
BLACK	ANGUS				33	SCOTLAND	PS	SCOTCH	F	085	C		17
BLACK	ARCHIBALD				65	SCOTLAND	CS	SCOTCH	F	085	C		18
BLACK	CHARLET		1	1	10	ONTARIO	CS	SCOTCH		082	A		21
BLACK	GEORGE				38	SCOTLAND	CS	SCOTCH	F	082	A		14
BLACK	JAMES				63	SCOTLAND	CS	SCOTCH	F	082	A		6
BLACK	JAMES		1		7	ONTARIO	CS	SCOTCH		082	A		21
BLACK	MARGT		1	1	16	ONTARIO	CS	SCOTCH		082	A		21
BLACK	ROBERT		1		46	ONTARIO	CP	SCOTTISH	FARMER	082	B		70
BLACK	ROBERT				20	0	CP	SCOTCH	LUMBERMAN	083	C		1
BLACK	THEODORE				25	QUE	CE	SCOTCH	BOOKKEEPER	081	B		28
BLACK	WILLIAM				49	SCOTLAND	CP	SCOTCH	F	081	J	1	30
BLACK	WILLIAM		1		25	ONTARIO	CS	SCOTCH	F	082	A		15
BLACK	WILLIAM				32	0	CE	IRISH	F	082	F		32
BLACKALL	THOMAS				62	IRELAND	RC	IRISH	FARMER	081	F		6
BLACKBURN	CALL				35	0	PS	SCOTCH	C S TEACHER	082	G		75
BLACKBURN	JOHN					0	CP					1	D
BLACKBURN	JOHN		1		30	0	CP	SCOTCH	F	081	A	1	70
BLACKBURN	MARION		1	1	23	0	CP	SCOTCH		081	A	1	70
BLACKBURN	WILLIAM		1		6	0	CP	SCOTCH		081	A	1	71
BLACKBURN	WILLIAM				54	SCOTLAND	PS	SCOTCH	F	081	H	2	11
BLACKMON	CHARLES				26	ENGLAND	CE	ENGLISH	F	085	H		7
BLACKWELL	GEORGE				64	IRELAND	OM	IRISH	F	081	H	1	11
BLACKWELL	JAMES				32	IRELAND	EM	IRISH	F	082	A		74
BLACKWELL	MARY	ANN		1	4	CANADA	WM	IRISH		085	A		15
BLACKWELL	RICHARD				34	IRELAND	EM	IRISH	F	082	A		65
BLACKWELL	THOMAS				30	ONTARIO	EM	IRISH	F	082	A		65
BLACKWELL	WILLIAM				25	ONTARIO	EM	IRISH	F	082	A		74
BLACKWOOD	DONALD				25	0	CE	SCOTCH	TRADER	090	F		19
BLACKWOOD	SAMUEL				56	IRELAND	PS	IRISH	MEDICAL DOCTOR	081	K		61
BLACKWOOD	WILLIAM		1		21	0	PS	SCOTCH	CLERK	090	F		19
BLAIR	JAMES				44	IRELAND	PS	IRISH	F	085	E		8
BLAIR	JOHN				50	IRELAND	CS	IRISH	F	082	A		30
BLAIR	JOHN				74	IRELAND	CE	IRISH	SHOEMAKER	082	C	2	35
BLAIR	JOHN				50	IRELAND	CE	IRISH	SHOEMAKER	082	C	2	35
BLAIR	MRS			1	50	IRELAND	CE	IRISH		081	J	1	86
BLAIR	ROBERT				30	ONTARIO	CS	IRISH	F	082	A		19
BLAIR	ROBERT				55	SCOTLAND	PS	SCOTCH	F	086	A	1	26
BLAIR	ROBERT	F			25	0	PS	SCOTCH	F	086	A	1	23
BLAIR	WILLIAM				78	SCOTLAND	CP	SCOTCH	SHOEMAKER	081	A	1	22
BLAIR	WILLIAM				60	IRELAND	CS	IRISH	F	082	A		31
BLAIS	SESAREY		1	1	8	0	RC	FRENCH		082	J		1
BLAKLEY	MALCOLM		1		20	QUE	CP	IRISH		081	B		27
BLANE	DAVID		1		44	SCOTLAND	CP	SCOTCH		081	A	1	43
BLANE	ISABELLA		1	1	37	0	CP	SCOTCH	F	081	A	1	43
BLANE	JOHN		1			0	CP	SCOTCH		081	A	1	43
BLANE	MARION		1	1	71	SCOTLAND	CP	SCOTCH				1	78
BLASDELL	FLORANCE		1	1	1	0	CE	IRISH		081	B		28
BLASDELL	J	C			67	UNITED STATES	CE	IRISH	MECHANIC	081	B		37
BLASDELL	J	C JR			28	0	CE	IRISH		081	B		38
BLASDELL	LOIS		1	1	21	0	CE	ENGLISH		081	B		27
BLAYLOCK	ELIZABETH		1	1	26	0	PS	SCOTTISH	TAILORESS	082	E		60
BLEAKEMAN	GEORGE				30	ISLE OF MAN	CE	MANX	F	085	E		30
BLEASE	FREDERICK				33	GERMANY	LU	GERMAN	F	082	H		14
BLEASNER	FERNHAM				49	GERMANY	CE	DUTCH	LAB	081	B		47
BLESKEY	JOSEPH				55	PRUSSIA	RC	PRUSSIAN	FARMER	083	A	1	4
BLESKEY	LOUIS				30	PRUSSIA	RC	PRUSSIAN	FARMER	083	A	1	17
BLICHE	NARCISS				45	QUE	RC	FRENCH	FARMER	082	I		43
BLINCO	GEORGE		1		26	US	CE	ENGLISH	F	086	A	2	13
BLOCK	WHILIMENE			1	35	GERMANY	LU	GERMAN		082	G		15
BLOEDON	FERDINAND				28	GERMANY	FW	GERMAN	F	082	H		23
BLONDIN	GEORGE				34	QUE	RC	FRENCH	MACHINIST	081	I		32
BLONNIK	PAUL		1		33	POLAND	RC	POLISH	LAB	083	C		19
BLUGNIER	BENJIMAN				36	QUE	RC	FRENCH	MINE LABOURER	089	A		40
BLUSTER	GEORGE				30	ENGLAND	CE	ENGLISH	F	085	H		15
BOAL	JOHN	SR			70	IRELAND	CE	IRISH		082	D		23
BOAL	MARY		2	1		0	CE			082	D		D
BOARD	JOHN				42	ENGLAND	CE	ENGLISH	F	085	F		3
BOAST	JOHN				56	ENGLAND	CE	ENGLISH	LABOURER	082	E		37
BOCASH	TERRAS				28	0	RC	INDIAN	HUNTER	084	I	1	7
BOCHER	IAN	FORREST	2	1		0	CP			081	H	1	D
BOFFEY	BARRICK		1		18	ENGLAND	CE	ENGLISH	LAB	081	B		69
BOGART	JACOB				45	0	WM	GERMAN	F	085	D		21
BOHAN	MICHAEL				36	IRELAND	RC	IRISH	LAB	081	A	2	16
BOHOLTS	CHARLES				28	GERMANY	EV	GERMAN	FARMER	082	I		20
BOHOLTS	FRANCES				53	GERMANY	EV	GERMAN	FARMER	082	I		64
BOISENEAW	BAPTIST		1		20	QUE	RC	FRENCH	LAB	082	K	1	15
BOISINEAU	MAGLOISE				49	0	RC	FRENCH	CARPENTER	089	B		7

SURNAME	NAME1	NAME2	STRAY	SEX	AGE	BIRTHPL	RELIGION	ORIGIN	OCCUP	DIST	SUB_DIST	DIV	PAGE
BOISOW	CHARLES				61	GERMANY	WM	GERMAN	BRICKMAKER	081	I		32
BOISSINEAU	BASSIL		2		3	0	RC			089	B		D
BOISSINEAU	FRANCOIS				40	0	RC	FRENCH	CARPENTER	089	B		32
BOISSINEAU	FRANCOIS		2		2	0	RC			089	B		D
BOISSINEAU	JOSEPH				28	0	RC	FRENCH		089	B		2
BOISSINEAU	JOSEPH		2		4	0	RC			089	B		D
BOISSINEAU	LEON				24	0	RC	FRENCH		089	B		2
BOISSINEAU	NARCISSE				40	0	RC	FRENCH	CARPENTER	089	B		31
BOISSINEAU	THEOPHILE				39	0	RC	FRENCH	BOAT BUILDER	089	B		32
BOISSINEAU	THERESE		2	1		0	RC			089	B		D
BOIVIN	MICHEL								SEE DRINKWINE	081	E		21
BOLAN	JOHN				50	IRELAND	RC	IRISH	F	082	A		50
BOLAND	JOHN				56	IRELAND	CE	IRISH	FARMER	082	B		65
BOLAND	THOMAS				19	IRELAND	RC	IRISH	FARMER	081	F		8
BOLAND	THOMAS				39	IRELAND	CE	IRISH	STOREKEEP	082	B		56
BOLAND	WILLIAM		1		21	IRELAND	CE	IRISH	LAB	083	C		1
BOLDUC	GASTIEN		1		40	QUE	RC	FRENCH	LUMBERMAN	088	B		18
BOLE	GEORGE				26	0	CE	IRISH		081	B		56
BOLEAW	JOSEPH		1		23	FRANCE	RC	FRENCH	BUSHMAN	084	E		1
BOLGER	MARTIN				55	IRELAND	RC	IRISH	CARPENTER	081	D		1
BOLGER	NICHOLAS		1		17	0	RC	IRISH	SHOEMAKER	081	K		71
BOLT	JOHN				53	GERMANY	EV	GERMAN	FARMER	082	I		66
BOLTON	GEORGE				27	0	CE	ENGLISH	F	085	J		15
BOLTON	GEORGE	C	1		31	QUEBEC	CE	ENGLISH		082	A		49
BOLTON	JOHN				23	ONTARIO	RC	ENGLISH	F	082	A		82
BOLTON	WILLIAM				34	ONTARIO	CE	IRISH	FARMER	084	D		4
BOMIAH	PETER				55	QUE	RC	FRENCH	LAB	081	B		2
BOND	JOHN				50	SCOTLAND	CE	SCOTCH	WAVER	081	G	1	48
BOND	THOMAS		1		0	0	CE	SCOTCH		081	G	1	49
BONE	JOHN				52	GERMANY	WM	GERMAN	F	082	H		23
BONFIELD	JAMES				50	IRELAND	RC	IRISH	LUMBERMAN MILKMAN	081	K		63
BONIAQUISIC	JOSEPH				40	0	RC	INDIAN	HUNTER	089	A		58
BONIAQUISIE	JOSEPH				31	0	RC	INDIAN	HUNTER	089	A		48
BONKY	WILLIAM				39	GERMANY	LU	GERMAN	FARMER	082	I		16
BONNA	ISACK		1		30	QUE	RC	FRENCH	FARMER	084	G	1	1
BONNAN	FRANCWAY				50	QUE	RC	FRENCH	LAB	082	C	1	56
BONNESKEY	JOHN				25	PRUSSIA	RC	PRUSSIAN	FARMER	083	A	1	19
BONNETCAME	PENE		1		31	0	RC	INDIAN	HUNTER	090	F		6
BONO	CICELY			1	60	IRELAND	RC	IRISH	F	081	H	1	9
BONTZ	WILLIAM				40	GERMANY	ME	GERMAN	F	085	A		2
BOOKER	THOMAS				29	0	EM	ENGLISH	F	085	I		32
BOORN	CHRISTIAN				45	GERMANY	LU	GERMAN	FARMER	082	I		22
BOORN	EARNEST				36	GERMANY	LU	GERMAN	FARMER	082	I		22
BOOTH	WILLIAM				45	IRELAND	CE	ENGLISH	F	085	K	2	4
BORMAN	CHARLES	FREDERICK					NG		SEE POORMAN	082	I		45
BORRON	EDWARD	B			50	ENGLAND	UV	ENGLISH	MINING INSPECTOR	090	F		20
BORVOIN	GRAQUIRE		1		22	QUE	RC	FRENCH	TANNER	082	E		47
BOSEIL	GANORE				47	QUE	RC	FRENCH	F	081	E		13
BOSEWELL	ANNE		2	1	81	IRELAND	CE			082	F		D
BOSHARD	JACOB				40	PRUSSIA	WM	GERMAN	F	082	G		84
BOSTON	MARIA		1	1	18	0	CE	ENGLISH	SERVANT	082	E		6
BOSTON	SUSAN		1	1	25	0	CE	IRISH	SEAMSTRESS	082	E		3
BOSTON	THOMAS				24	0	CE	IRISH	F	082	F		13
BOSTON	THOMAS						NG		SEE BOSTON	082	F		13
BOSTWICK	JOHN				57	US	PM	ENGLISH	F	085	B		9
BOSTWICK	JOHN	P	1		50	QUE	CE	IRISH	GENTLEMAN	082	D		1
BOTTRELL	MARY		1	1	85	ENGLAND	CM	ENGLISH		085	B		24
BOTTRELL	WILLIAM				49	ENGLAND	EM	ENGLISH	F	086	A	1	6
BOUCHARD	FRANCIS					ONTARIO	RC	FRENCH	GUIDE	090	E		4
BOUCHARD	GILBERT					ONTARIO	RC	FRENCH	LABOURER	090	E		4
BOUCHARD	HUGH		1		25	0	RC	IRISH	SERVANT	081	A	2	17
BOUCHARD	JOSEPH		1		62	QUEBEC	RC	FRENCH		084	A		1
BOUCHARD	LOUIS				40	0	RC	INDIAN	LABOURER	090	C		1
BOUCHARD	LOUIS					HUDSON'S BAY	RC	FRENCH	PENSIONER	090	E		1
BOUCHARD	MRS			1		ONTARIO	RC	FRENCH	SERVANT TO H B CO	090	E		4
BOUCHARD	NICHOLAS					ONTARIO	RC	FRENCH	LABOURER	090	E		4
BOUCHER	FELIX		1		19	QUEBEC	RC	FRENCH	FARMER	084	C		2
BOUCHER	JOSEPH				60	QUE	RC	FRENCH	CARPENTER	090	F		22
BOUCHER	OLIVIER				34	QUE	RC	FRENCH	CLERGYMAN	082	D		19
BOUCHER	TOUSSAINT				70	QUEBEC	RC	FRENCH	FISHERMAN & TRAPPER	090	B		1
BOUCHER	WILLIAM				45	ONTARIO	CE	IRISH	LUMBERER	083	B	1	1
BOUDETTE	DELA		1	1	19	QUE	RC	FRENCH	SEAMSTRESS	082	E		44
BOUDRIE	MESHALL				50	0	RC	FRENCH	LUMBERMAN	086	C	1	4
BOUGHIE	PHILLIMORE				29	0	RC	FRENCH	LUMBERMAN	086	C	1	4
BOUHOLTS	FRANCIS		1		20	GERMANY	LU	GERMAN	FARM SERVANT	082	I		42
BOULTON	GEORGE				30	0	WM	SCOTCH	TINSMITH	081	B		60
BOULTON	MARGARET		2	1	60	IRELAND	RC		INNKEEPER	081	H	2	D
BOULTON	MARTHA		1	1	26	0	WM	ENGLISH		081	B		41
BOULTON	WILLIAM				25	0	RC	IRISH	INNKEEPER	081	H	2	35
BOURDRIE	BESREES				24	0	RC	FRENCH		086	C	1	5
BOURDRIE	MESHALL				26	0	RC	FRENCH	LUMBERMAN	086	C	1	5
BOURGEOS	JOSEPH				28	0	RC	FRENCH	LAB	082	K	1	16
BOURJOUS	CHARLES				33	QUE	RC	FRENCH	LUMBERMAN	088	C		11
BOURK	GEORGE				34	0	RC	IRISH	LABOURER	082	E		52
BOURK	LOUIS		1		32	GERMANY	LU	GERMAN	F	082	C	2	39
BOURKE	ADALINE		1	1	16	ONT	RC	ENGLISH		082	I		28
BOURKE	EDWD				58	IRELAND	RC	IRISH	GAOLER	082	E		7
BOUSDRIC	ALBERT	JOSEPH	2		6	0	RC			086	C	1	D
BOUSELAIS	EUGENE		1		25	QUE	RC	FRENCH	LUMBERMAN	086	C	1	7
BOUSETTE	GEORGE				34	QUE	RC	FRENCH	BILLIARD SALOON	082	E		71
BOUSH	WILLIAM				34	GERMANY	LU	GERMAN	FARMER	082	I		54
BOUVIER	JOSEPH	REVD			47	FRANCE	RC	FRENCH	CLERGYMAN	081	B		18
BOVAIR	PETER				50	QUE	WM	FRENCH	F	082	C	2	41
BOVIN	DENIS				39	QUE	RC	FRENCH	FARMER	081	D		19
BOWER	MICHAEL				63	IRELAND	CE	IRISH	F	085	A		15
BOWERMAN	THOS	M			37	0	CE	ENGLISH	SCHOOL TEACHER	085	I		7
BOWERS	WILLIAM				33	0	PS	IRISH	F	086	A	1	4
BOWES	DANIEL				33	0	RC	IRISH	F	082	K	1	3
BOWES	JAMES				39	ONTARIO	CP	SCOTTISH	FARMER	082	B		50
BOWES	JOHN				64	IRELAND	RC	IRISH	F	085	A		10
BOWIE	CHARLES				60	RED RIVER	RC	FRENCH		088	B		11
BOWIE	JOSEPH				50	RUPERT LAND	RC	FRENCH	FUR TRADER	088	C		6
BOWIE	PETER				52	RED RIVER	RC	FRENCH	FUR TRADER	088	C		7
BOWKER	JOHN				57	ENGLAND	CE	ENGLISH	OFFICER OF CUSTOMS	089	A		4
BOWLAND	JAMES		1		26	0	CE	IRISH	BARBOY	082	G		61
BOWLAND	JANE		1	1	26	0	CE	IRISH		082	G		61

SURNAME	NAME1	NAME2	STRAY	SEX	AGE	BIRTHPL	RELIGION	ORIGIN	OCCUP	DIST	SUB_DIST	DIV	PAGE
BOWLAND	THOMAS				29	O	CE	IRISH	F	081	K		55
BOWLAND	THOMAS				60	IRELAND	CE	IRISH	F	081	K		57
BOWLAND	WILLIAM				37	O	CE	IRISH	F & LUMBERMAN	081	K		74
BOX	ALEXANDER				37	ENGLAND	CE	ENGLISH	F	081	A	1	14
BOX	JOHN				38	ENGLAND	CP	ENGLISH	STOREKEEPER	081	A	1	18
BOXWEL	THOMAS				52	IRELAND	CE	IRISH	FARMER	082	F		2
BOYD	ANDREW		1		26	O	WM	IRISH	CARPENTER	085	A		28
BOYD	JAMES	F			40	ONT	ME	IRISH	F	085	A		20
BOYD	JAMES	JR			22	O	PS	IRISH	F	085	A		28
BOYD	JOHN				33	IRELAND	CE	IRISH	F	085	J		9
BOYD	W	S	1		25	CANADA	DI	ENGLISH	FISHERMAN	087	B	2	2
BOYDE	JOSEPH				47	O	CP	IRISH	F	081	A	2	53
BOYER	AMELIA		1	1	12	PRUSSIA	EV	PRUSSIAN	SERVANT	085	A		8
BOYER	BENJIMINE				23	O	RC	FRENCH	LABOURER	089	B		32
BOYER	HENRY		1		25	ENGLAND	WM	ENGLISH	BOOKKEEPER	085	I		16
BOYER	JAMES				36	ENGLAND	CE	ENGLISH	F	085	I		21
BOYER	MARY ANN		1	1	21	O	RC	INDIAN		088	B		27
BOYER	MICHEAL				68	O	RC	FRENCH	LABOURER	089	B		40
BOYER	MICHEAL				30	O	RC	FRENCH	FISHERMAN	089	B		43
BOYER	MICHEL		2		5	O	RC			089	B		D
BOYLE	HENRY				66	IRELAND	EM	IRISH	F	082	G		43
BOYLE	JOHN				55	IRELAND	RC	IRISH	MINE LABOURER	089	A		20
BOYLE	ROBERT		2		1	ONTARIO	CE			083	C		D
BOYLE	WILLIAM				40	O	CE	IRISH	F	083	C		1
BOYNE	ALEXANDER		1		28	ENGLAND	CE	ENGLISH	LAB	081	B		54
BOYS	JAMES				28	IRELAND	PS	IRISH	F	085	D		20
BOYS	JAMES				73	IRELAND	RP	IRISH	F	085	D		22
BRABOUR	WILLIAM				30	GERMANY	LU	GERMAN	F	082	H		25
BRACE	T	M			56	US	WM	ENGLISH	MILLOWNER	081	H	2	37
BRACKENBURY	ROBERT				44	ENGLAND	WM	ENGLISH	CLERK	086	A	1	29
BRADEY	TERRENCE				40	IRELAND	RC	IRISH	LAB	081	B		19
BRADLEY	GEORGE		1		39	ENGLAND	WM	ENGLISH	F	085	H		18
BRADLEY	MICHAEL				31	O	EM	ENGLISH	LAB	081	B		62
BRADLEY	PATRICK				56	IRELAND	RC	IRISH	FARMER	081	D		10
BRADLEY	THOS		1		60	QUE	RC	FRENCH	F	081	B		12
BRADON	ELIAS	HENRY	1		7	ONT	WM	IRISH		081	C		44
BRADON	WILLIAM		1		8	ONT	WM	IRISH		081	C		44
BRADSHAW	GEORGE				31	O	DI	ENGLISH	F	085	K	2	9
BRADY	BRIDGET			1	55	IRELAND	RC	IRISH	FARMER	081	D		1
BRADY	HUGH				55	IRELAND	RC	IRISH	FARMER	082	B		2
BRADY	ISABELLA			1	73	SCOTLAND	RC	SCOTCH	WEAVER	082	C	1	54
BRAMBERGER	AUGUST				26	GERMANY	LU	GERMAN	F	082	G		28
BRAMBERGER	GOTLIP				53	GERMANY	LU	GERMAN	F	082	G		23
BRAMILY	JOHN				37	ENGLAND	CE	ENGLISH	CLARK	081	I		4
BRANDO	HIRAM		1		13	O	BA	ENGLISH		087	B	3	7
BRANNAN	PATRICK				65	IRELAND	CE	IRISH	F	082	J		5
BRANSEAU	JOHN				35	QUE	RC	FRENCH	SADDLER	081	I		12
BRANSSOW	MICHIAL				60	QUE	RC	FRENCH	SADLER	081	I		16
BRANT	ALBERT		1		20	GERMANY	RC	GERMAN	SERVANT	081	A	2	32
BRANT	FREDRICK				50	GERMANY	CE	GERMAN	MASON	081	B		66
BRASCH	LOUACE						NG		SEE BRUSH	082	I		62
BRASS	CRISTAY				48	GERMANY	LU	GERMAN	F	082	F		21
BRASSEAU	JULIE			1	46	O	RC	FRENCH		089	B		25
BRASSINU	PIERRE		1		61	QUE	RC	FRENCH	LABOURER	089	B		23
BRASSO	ANTOINE				56	QUE	RC	FRENCH	LABOURER	082	E		36
BRASSO	LEON				30	QUE	RC	FRENCH	SHANTYMAN	082	E		36
BRAY	EDWARD				47	ENGLAND	WM	ENGLISH	F	085	K	2	1
BRAY	JOHN				43	ENGLAND	WM	ENGLISH	MINER	089	A		2
BRAZO	BENJAMIN				68	O	RC	FRENCH	F	082	F		15
BRAZO	BENJAMIN				34	O	RC	FRENCH	F	082	F		15
BRAZO	JOSEPH				32	O	RC	FRENCH	F	082	F		15
BREADY	ANNE		1	1	48	IRELAND	RC	IRISH		082	D		3
BREEN	ALICE		1	1	12	O	PS	IRISH		081	F		14
BREEN	GOWSA		2	1		O	CE			082	B		D
BREEN	MARGRET		1	1	22	O	RC	IRISH	SERVANT	081	A	2	19
BREEN	MARY		1	1	32	IRELAND	PS	IRISH		081	F		14
BREEN	MICHAEL		1		9	O	PS	IRISH		081	F		14
BREEN	PATRICK				34	IRELAND	RC	IRISH	FARMER	082	B		40
BREENE	JOHN				37	IRELAND	RC	IRISH	F	082	G		68
BREENE	JOHN				65	IRELAND	RC	IRISH	F	082	G		77
BREES	JOSEPH				27	O	WM	UNKNOWN	F	085	F		3
BREHAN	KATE		1	1	25	O	RC	IRISH	SERVANT	081	A	2	29
BREMNER	GEORGE		1		20	ONT	CP	SCOTCH	LABOURER	081	J	1	61
BREMNER	JOHN				59	SCOTLAND	CS	SCOTCH	F	081	J	1	61
BREMNER	MRS			1	50	SCOTLAND	CS	SCOTCH	F	081	J	1	87
BRENAN	MARK		1		17	O	RC	IRISH	AP CABINETMAKER	082	E		56
BRENAN	MICHAEL				34	IRELAND	RC	IRISH	LUMBERMAN	082	H		36
BRENNAN	ANDREW				37	O	CE	IRISH	F	082	G		95
BRENNAN	EDWARD				50	IRELAND	RC	IRISH	WEAVER	081	D		19
BRENNAN	ELIZA			1	45	IRELAND	RC	IRISH	GROCER	081	B		7
BRENNAN	ELIZABETH			1	55	IRELAND	RC	IRISH	FARMER	082	I		37
BRENNAN	JOHN				50	IRELAND	RC	IRISH	F	081	A	2	49
BRENNAN	KATE		1	1	19	QUE	RC	IRISH	SERVANT	082	E		15
BRENNAN	LAWRENCE				60	IRELAND	RC	IRISH	FARMER	081	D		18
BRENNAN	MARTIN				28	O	RC	IRISH	CARPENTER	081	B		41
BRENNAN	MICHEAL		1		14	O	RC	IRISH	SERVANT	081	A	2	19
BRENNAN	PATRICK				32	IRELAND	RC	IRISH	BLACKSMITH	081	K		71
BRENNAN	PATRICK				60	IRELAND	RC	IRISH	COOPER	083	C		7
BRENNAN	ROBERT				25	ONTARIO	RC	IRISH	F	083	C		7
BRENNAN	SAMUEL	JNR	1		16	O	RP	IRISH	F	082	J		5
BRENNAN	SAMUEL	SNR			40	IRELAND	RP	IRISH	F	082	J		5
BRENNAN	THOMAS		2			O	RC			081	D		D
BRENNAN	THOS		1		18	IRELAND	RC	IRISH	SADDLER	082	E		60
BRENNEN						O	RC			084	C		D
BRENNEN	MICHAEL				48	IRELAND	RC	IRISH	F	085	K	2	5
BRENNEN	WILLIAM				36	QUEBEC	RC	IRISH	FARMER	084	C		2
BRENNER	GEORGE				76	SCOTLAND	RP	SCOTCH	F	081	K		11
BRENNER	JOHN				44	O	EM	SCOTCH	F	081	K		13
BRENNETT	PETER				36	ONTARIO	RC	FRENCH	LUMBERER	083	A	2	4
BRESCO	ROBERT				23	O	CE	ENGLISH	F	082	F		32
BRESEL	MARY		1	1	22	O	RC	IRISH		081	I		21
BRESINGHAM	THOMAS		1		12	O	RC	IRISH		082	K	1	13
BRESNAHAM	FRANCIS				47	IRELAND	EM	IRISH	LAB	081	B		44
BRESNAHAM	JOSEPH		1		65	IRELAND	RC	IRISH	F	081	K		30
BRESSENHAM	FRANCES			1	58	IRELAND	WM	IRISH		082	G		57
BRESSENHAM	JOHN				28	O	WM	IRISH		082	G		56

SURNAME	NAME1	NAME2	STRAY	SEX	AGE	BIRTHPL	RELIGION	ORIGIN	OCCUP	DIST	SUB_DIST	DIV	PAGE
BREWER	JOHN				42	QUE	CE	SCOTCH	F	081	A	2	48
BRIDE	MARY		1	1	19	IRELAND	RC	IRISH		089	A		43
BRIDGE	JOHN				55	ENGLAND	CE	ENGLISH	LAB	081	I		28
BRIDGEMAN	JOHN				70	IRELAND	RC	IRISH	FARMER	081	D		12
BRIDGEMAN	MAURICE				40	IRELAND	RC	IRISH	FARMER	081	G	2	2
BRIDGEN	CHARLES				43	ENGLAND	CE	ENGLISH	LAB	081	I		40
BRIDGES	JOHN				53	ENGLAND	CE	ENGLISH	F	081	C		18
BRIDGES	ROBERT				30	0	CP	ENGLISH	F	081	C		11
BRIDGES	THOMAS				27	0	CE	SCOTCH	F	081	C		10
BRIDGLAND	SAMUEL		1		23	0	CE	ENGLISH	DOCTOR	085	I		6
BRIENS	HENERY				58	IRELAND	CE	IRISH	F	085	B		10
BRIESE	AUGUST				28	GERMANY	LU	GERMAN	F	085	C		5
BRIESEMEISTER	WILLIAM				46	GERMANY	LU	GERMAN	FARMER	082	I		60
BRIGGS	SOLOMON				30	0	PM	ENGLISH	F	085	B		4
BRIGGS	THOMAS		1		9	0	CE	ENGLISH		085	C		14
BRILL	AGNES		1	1	9	0	CP	IRISH		081	B		58
BRILL	BENJAMIN				38	QUE	EM	ENGLISH	CARPENTER	081	A	2	20
BRILL	HANAH		1	1	21	0	CP	ENGLISH	MILLINER	081	B		9
BRILL	WILLIAM				30	ONT	EM	ENGLISH	F	081	C		27
BRIMES	GEORGE				27	0	PS	SCOTCH	LUMBERMAN	081	I		18
BRIMSTIN	JAMES				36	IRELAND	WM	IRISH	F	085	I		42
BRINDLE	JAMES	SR			59	ENGLAND	RC	ENGLISH	F	082	J		4
BRISBOIE	PAUL		1		29	QUEBEC	RC	FRENCH	LAB	083	E		2
BRISCO	BRIAN				37	ENGLAND	CE	ENGLISH	F	081	J	1	51
BRISCO	JAMES				64	ENGLAND	CE	ENGLISH	F	081	J	1	85
BRISCO	JOHN				26	ONT	CE	ENGLISH	F	081	J	1	84
BRISCO	THOS				33	ONT	CE	ENGLISH	F	081	J	1	51
BRISCO	WILLIAM				62	ENGLAND	CE	ENGLISH	F	081	J	1	85
BRISKY	AUGUST				34	GERMANY	BA	GERMAN	FARMER	081	F		21
BRISLER	CHRISTE		1		53	GERMANY	LU	GERMAN		082	F		21
BRISO	WILLIAM				26	ONT	CE	ENGLISH	F	081	J	1	49
BRISSON	HENRY				28	QUE	RC	FRENCH	LUMBERMAN	088	B		3
BRITTAN	ALFRED				34	ENGLAND	CE	ENGLISH	FARMER	086	B		9
BROAD	JAMES		1		85	ENGLAND	RC	ENGLISH	SERVANT	082	E		29
BROADBENT	HENRY		1		20	ENGLAND	CE	ENGLISH	COMMON WORKMAN	086	A	1	32
BROADLEY	ENOS				27	ENGLAND	CE	ENGLISH	F	085	F		1
BROCK	JO					0	LU	ENGLISH	MILLHAND	085	A		31
BROCK	JOSEPH				28	0	CE	IRISH	F	085	B		8
BROCK	THOMAS				34	IRELAND	WM	IRISH	CLERGYMAN	081	B		76
BROCK	WILLIAM		1		23	0	CE	ENGLISH	SCHOOL TEACHER	082	K	1	15
BRODIE	DAVID	JOHN	1		17	CANADA	PS	SCOTCH		085	E		6
BRODIE	REBECCA		1	1	81	ENGLAND	CE	ENGLISH		085	H		16
BROHAM	ROBERT		1		7	ONTARIO	WM	IRISH		082	A		11
BROHARTS	FREDRICK				44	GERMANY	LU	GERMAN	FARMER	082	I		76
BROMFIELD	J	W	1		19	ENGLAND	CE	ENGLISH	HUNTER	085	E		25
BROMFIELD	SAMUEL		1		19	ENGLAND	CE	ENGLISH	LABOURER	085	E		30
BROMLEE	ELIZABETH			1	40	IRELAND	CE	IRISH		082	A		82
BROMLEY	EDWIN		1		17	0	WM	IRISH	CLERK	082	C	2	67
BROMLEY	EDWIN		1		20	ENGLAND	CE	ENGLISH	CABINETMAKER	082	E		34
BROMLEY	HENRY				59	IRELAND	CE	IRISH	F	082	C	1	13
BROMLEY	JAMES				63	ENGLAND	CE	ENGLISH	CONVEYANCER	081	I		23
BROMLEY	JAMES				47	IRELAND	CE	IRISH	F	082	C	1	28
BROMLEY	JAMES				52	IRELAND	WM	IRISH		082	C	1	30
BROMLEY	THOS				23	0	ME	IRISH	LABOURER	082	E		33
BRONCOMMIER	JOSEPH		1		43	QUE	RC	FRENCH	LABOURER	084	E		5
BRONDEAST	JOHN				25	0	CE	FRENCH	FUR TRADER	088	B		14
BROOKS	ARCHIBALD				38	0	PM	FRENCH	F	085	I		23
BROOKS	JAMES				46	QUE	RC	ENGLISH	F	082	C	1	63
BROOKS	JOHN	J	1		40	0	CP	SCOTCH	CARPENTER	090	D		8
BROOKS	NOT GIVEN		2	1		0	PM			085	I		D
BROOM	CHAS				52	GERMANY	LU	GERMAN	F	082	L		7
BROOM	FRANCIS				50	ENGLAND	CE	ENGLISH	F	082	A		19
BROOM	JAMES		1		20	ONTARIO	CS	ENGLISH	LAB	082	A		20
BROOM	THOMAS				53	ENGLAND	WM	ENGLISH	F	082	A		18
BROOMLY	ALFRED				22	ENGLAND	CE	ENGLISH	F	081	J	1	73
BROPHY	JOHN		1		19	0	RC	IRISH	SHANTYMAN	085	E		27
BROPHY	JOHN				22	0	RC	IRISH		086	B		1
BROSE	CHARLES				35	ONT	CS	SCOTCH	F	081	J	1	30
BROUGHAN	JENETT			1	28	IRELAND	RC	IRISH		082	G		56
BROUGHEN	PATRICK				38	IRELAND	WM	IRISH	LAB	082	C	1	66
BROUTICH	CAROLINE		1	1	21	GERMANY	WM	GERMAN	SERVANT	082	E		8
BROWEN	JAMES				28	0	CS	IRISH	F	082	F		38
BROWEN	ROBERT				50	IRELAND	CE	IRISH	F	082	F		39
BROWEN	WILLIAM				61	IRELAND	CS	IRISH	F	082	F		38
BROWN	ADAM		1		35	0	CE	SCOTCH	CARPENTER	088	A		7
BROWN	ADILAIDE		1	1	20	0	CP	SCOTTISH		082	E		64
BROWN	ALEX				42	SCOTLAND	CP	SCOTCH	F	081	J	1	68
BROWN	ALEX				45	SCOTLAND	PS	SCOTCH	F	081	J	1	69
BROWN	ALFRED				24	ENGLAND	CE	ENGLISH	F	085	K	1	1
BROWN	AUGUSTUS				24	0	CE	ENGLISH	INNKEEPER	082	C	2	27
BROWN	CATHERINE		2	1	5	0	CP			082	C	2	D
BROWN	CHARLES				35	IRELAND	CE	IRISH	F	082	C	1	37
BROWN	CHARLES		1		65	IRELAND	CE	IRISH		083	A	1	8
BROWN	DANIEL				47	IRELAND	CP	SCOTCH	WHEELWRIGHT	082	C	2	22
BROWN	DAVID				63	SCOTLAND	CP	SCOTCH	TANNER	081	A	2	2
BROWN	DAVID				31	0	CE	ENGLISH	F	082	C	2	28
BROWN	DELORMA				27	ONTARIO	EM	ENGLISH	SHOEMAKER	082	A		23
BROWN	DOUGALE				30	NS	CP	SCOTCH	HOTELKEEPER	085	B		8
BROWN	FRANCIS				22	UNITED STATES	WM	IRISH	CLERK	083	B	2	1
BROWN	FRANK				60	QUE	RC	FRENCH	F	090	F		18
BROWN	FREDRICK		1		22	GERMANY	ME	GERMAN	LABOURER	082	D		8
BROWN	GEORGE				44	ONT	CP	SCOTCH	F	081	J	1	72
BROWN	GEORGE				71	SCOTLAND	CS	SCOTCH	CARPENTER	081	J	1	72
BROWN	GEORGE				31	0	CS	IRISH	F	085	C		17
BROWN	GEORGE		1		18	ENGLAND	CE	ENGLISH	LAB	085	E		22
BROWN	HANNA			1	47	ONTARIO	EM	ENGLISH		082	A		72
BROWN	HENRY				59	0	CE	IRISH	FARMER	086	B		7
BROWN	HIRAM				25	0	EM	IRISH	LAB	081	H	2	32
BROWN	HUGH				65	IRELAND	RC	IRISH	F	081	K		47
BROWN	HYTABLE		1	1	28	0	JM	ENGLISH		082	C	2	10
BROWN	ISABELLA		1	1	17	0	WM	IRISH	MILLINER	081	B		69
BROWN	JAMES				27	SCOTLAND	CS	SCOTCH	F	081	A	1	52
BROWN	JAMES				50	N BRUNSWICK	EM	IRISH	LAB	081	B		60
BROWN	JAMES				36	SCOTLAND	PS	SCOTCH	COOPER	081	J	1	54
BROWN	JAMES				60	IRELAND	CE	IRISH	F	082	F		37
BROWN	JAMES		1		23	0	RC	IRISH	LAB	085	F		5

SURNAME	NAME1	NAME2	STRAY	SEX	AGE	BIRTHPL	RELIGION	ORIGIN	OCCUP	DIST	SUB_DIST	DIV	PAGE
BROWN	JAMES		1		23	QUE	CP	SCOTCH	LAB	090	F		25
BROWN	JENNE		1	1	36	O	CP	SCOTCH		081	A	2	44
BROWN	JOHN				32	ONT	PS	SCOTCH	F	081	J	1	72
BROWN	JOHN				30	IRELAND	CE	IRISH	F	082	A		8
BROWN	JOHN				30	O	CE	ENGLISH	F	082	C	2	27
BROWN	JOHN				50	IRELAND	CE	IRISH	F	082	C	2	52
BROWN	JOHN		1		15	GERMANY	WM	GERMAN	SERVANT	082	G		92
BROWN	JOHN				30	ONTARIO	RC	INDIAN	HUNTER	083	F	2	1
BROWN	JOHN		1		20	SCOTLAND	NG	IRISH	HATTER	085	E		22
BROWN	JOHN				22	O	CP	SCOTCH	FOREMAN OF LUMBER SH	085	E		27
BROWN	JOHN				24	IRELAND	CE	IRISH	SAWYER OR FARMER	085	I		12
BROWN	JOHN				23	O	CP	ENGLISH	CARPENTER	085	I		27
BROWN	LEWIS				35	O	JM	ENGLISH	FARM LAB	082	C	2	4
BROWN	MANUS		1		14	O	RC	IRISH		081	K		30
BROWN	MARGRET			1	38	O	CP	SCOTCH		081	A	2	45
BROWN	MARGRET		1	1	30	O	WM	IRISH	SERVANT	081	H	1	2
BROWN	MARGRET		1	1	37	O	CE	ENGLISH	WEAVER	082	C	2	6
BROWN	MARTHA		1	1	63	SCOTLAND	CP	SCOTCH		082	G		42
BROWN	MARY		1	1	18	O	RC	IRISH	SERVANT	082	E		68
BROWN	MILES				46	ONT	WM	ENGLISH	F	082	A		78
BROWN	MIRIAM		1	1	19	O	PR	IRISH	SERVANT GIRL	082	D		3
BROWN	NICHOLES				50	ONT	WM	SCOTCH	F	081	J	1	47
BROWN	PETER				54	SCOTLAND	PS	SCOTCH	HM CUSTOMS	089	B		14
BROWN	PETER	JAMES	1		14	ONT	RC	IRISH		082	I		35
BROWN	ROBERT				42	SCOTLAND	PS	SCOTCH	F	081	J	1	67
BROWN	ROBERT				38	IRELAND	CE	IRISH		082	C	2	63
BROWN	ROBERT				39	SCOTLAND	PS	SCOTCH	F	085	J		13
BROWN	SARAH			1	51	IRELAND	CE	IRISH		085	B		23
BROWN	SUSAN		1	1	21	ONTARIO	CE	IRISH		082	A		55
BROWN	SUSAN		1	1	54	IRELAND	PS	IRISH		082	E		73
BROWN	THOMAS				32	O	CS	IRISH	F	082	F		31
BROWN	THOMAS				60	ENGLAND	RP	SCOTCH	FARMER	082	I		10
BROWN	THOMAS				33	ENGLAND	CE	ENGLISH	F	085	D		32
BROWN	WALTER				51	SCOTLAND	CS	SCOTCH	F	081	A	1	54
BROWN	WILLIAM		1		25	IRELAND	RC	IRISH	LAB	081	H	2	22
BROWN	WILLIAM		1		20	ONT	WM	IRISH	LAB	082	A		27
BROWN	WILLIAM				47	ENGLAND	WM	ENGLISH	STONE MASON	085	C		10
BROWN	WILLIAM				70	SCOTLAND	CS	SCOTCH	CARPENTER	085	I		15
BROWN	WILLIAM				38	O	RC	FRENCH	FISHERMAN	089	A		58
BROWN	WILLIAM				26	ENGLAND	CE	ENGLISH	CIVIL ENGINEER	090	F		18
BROWN	WILLIAM	HENRY			36	IRELAND	CP	IRISH	FARMER	082	I		15
BROWNE	ANN			1	52	IRELAND	CE	IRISH		081	H	2	19
BROWNE	JACOB				44	O	WM	DUTCH	BLACKSMITH	082	C	2	47
BROWNELL	JACOB				43	O	BA	GERMAN	F	085	H		12
BROWNING	ANDREW	H			28	ENGLAND	CE	SCOTCH	F	085	B		24
BROWNLEE	JAMES				23	O	BA	IRISH	F	086	A	2	2
BROWNLEE	NATHANIEL		1		15	QUE	WM	IRISH	SADDLER & HARNESS MA	082	C	2	5
BROWNLEE	THOMAS				47	O	CE	IRISH	F	082	C	1	18
BROWNLIE	JAMES				38	SCOTLAND	PS	SCOTCH	F	086	A	1	3
BRUCE	COLLIN				42	SCOTLAND	CS	SCOTCH	F	082	A		2
BRUCE	GEORGE		1		30	O	CS	SCOTCH	LABOURER	088	A		7
BRUCE	JOHN				35	IRELAND	CE	IRISH	F	081	E		7
BRUCE	ROBERT				75	IRELAND	CE	IRISH	FARMER	081	D		9
BRUCE	THOMAS				40	IRELAND	WM	IRISH	F	085	I		30
BRUCE	THOMAS	JOHN	2	1	1	O	WM			085	I		D
BRUN	MAURICE				50	IRELAND	RC	IRISH	FARMER	082	B		68
BRUNDAG	ALFRED	W	1		8	O	CP	IRISH		082	C	2	25
BRUNDAG	ELIZABETH		1	1	29	O	CP	IRISH	SEAMSTRESS	082	C	2	25
BRUNEAU	JOSEPH				24	QUE	RC	FRENCH	SHANTYMAN	082	D		18
BRUNETT	MANOS				18	O	RC	FRENCH		081	B		67
BRUNILY	FREDERICK				24	ENGLAND	CE	ENGLISH	F	081	H	1	6
BRUNNETTE	EDWARD				42	QUE	RC	FRENCH	LAB	081	B		43
BRUNO	SILVESTAS				23	QUE	RC	FRENCH	LUMBERMAN	086	C	1	3
BRUSH	FRANCIS		1	1	20	GERMANY	RC	GERMAN	FARM LABOURER	081	K		52
BRUSH	LOUACE				35	GERMANY	LU	GERMAN	FARMER	082	I		62
BRUSHA	JOSEPH				32	QUE	RC	FRENCH	F	081	K		35
BRUSHA	JULIAN		2			O	RC			081	K		D
BRYANT	ROBERT		1		48	IRELAND	CE	ENGLISH	MINE LABOURER	089	A		24
BRYANT	THOMAS				25	O	CE	ENGLISH	MINE LABOURER	089	A		24
BRYARD	STEPHEN				27	QUE	RC	FRENCH	SHOEMAKER	081	C		38
BRYCE	THOMAS		1		27	O	EP	IRISH	FARMER	090	D		2
BRYERS	NELSON		1		65	IRELAND	CP	IRISH	F	085	B		3
BRYERS	ROBERT		1		21	IRELAND	CE	IRISH	F	085	B		3
BRYSON	MARGRET		1	1	22	O	CP	IRISH	SERVANT	081	B		76
BUBEY	FRACIS				40	FRANCE	RC	FRENCH	LAB	082	F		20
BUCAUSE	AUGUST		1		17	GERMANY	WM	GERMAN	SERVANT	082	E		5
BUCHAN	DAVID		1		36	ONTARIO	PR	SCOTCH	MERCHANT	081	G	2	13
BUCHAN	HUGH				45	O	CP	SCOTCH		081	B		52
BUCHAN	JOHN				40	SCOTLAND	CE	SCOTCH	WATCHMAN	086	C	1	1
BUCHAN	WILLIAM				39	O	CP	SCOTCH	JOBBER	081	B		17
BUCHANAN	AGNES		1	1	19	PRINCE RUPERTS LAND	CE	SCOTCH		089	B		9
BUCHANAN	JAMES		1		55	IRELAND	CE	IRISH	SEAMAN	089	B		24
BUCHANAN	JOHN				56	SCOTLAND	CP	SCOTCH	F	082	C	1	52
BUCHANAN	WILLIAM				25	US	CE	IRISH	SAILOR	089	B		25
BUCHANNAN	DAVID				63	SCOTLAND	CS	SCOTCH	F	082	C	1	52
BUCHANNAN	JAMES				37	O	CP	SCOTCH	F	082	C	1	64
BUCHANNAN	PETER				31	O	CP	SCOTCH	F	082	C	1	55
BUCHER	ELLEN		1	1	19	O	ME	ENGLISH		082	D		8
BUCHER	HARIAT		1	1	56	QUE	ME	ENGLISH		082	D		8
BUCK	THOMAS				50	ENGLAND	CE	ENGLISH	F	085	E		15
BUCK	WM				45	ENGLAND	WM	ENGLISH	F	085	L		12
BUCK	WM	JUNR	1		20	ENGLAND	WM	ENGLISH	F	085	L		12
BUCKERFIELD	WILLIAM	H			34	ENGLAND	CE	ENGLISH	F	085	D		23
BUCKINSHAW	EDWARD				38	ENGLAND	CE	ENGLISH	CARPENTER	085	B		10
BUCKLAND	AMELIA		1	1	21	ENGLAND	CE	ENGLISH	SERVANT	085	I		39
BUCKLAND	AMELIA		1	1	45	ENGLAND	CE	ENGLISH	HOUSE-KEEPER	085	I		39
BUCKLEY	JOHN		1		24	IRELAND	RC	IRISH	CARPENTER	088	B		3
BUCKLEY	MICHAEL				40	IRELAND	RC	IRISH	LAB	081	A	2	8
BUCKLEY	PATRICK				40	IRELAND	RC	IRISH	F	082	G		72
BUCKNER	JAMES				31	O	CE		F	086	A	2	10
BUCKSHOT	AMIGAN		1		30	ONTARIO	RC	INDIAN	HUNTER	083	C		19
BUDDEN	CHARLES	T	1		21	ENGLAND	CE	ENGLISH	F	085	I		3
BUDDER	FREDRICK				43	GERMANY	LU	GERMAN	L	082	G		13
BUDDER	JOHN				24	GERMANY	EM	GERMAN	F	082	G		89
BUDERICK	MARTIN				58	GERMANY	WM	GERMAN	FARMER	081	G	1	46
BUDREW	THOMAS				18	O	WM	IRISH		085	J		20

SURNAME	NAME1	NAME2	STRAY	SEX	AGE	BIRTHPL	RELIGION	ORIGIN	OCCUP	DIST	SUB_DIST	DIV	PAGE
BUDRIC	JOHN				22	O	RC	FRENCH	F	082	H		33
BUDRIC	LOUIS				48	QUE	RC	FRENCH	F	082	H		32
BUDRICK	MARTIN				23	PRUSSIA	PR	PRUSSIAN	FARMER	081	G	2	2
BUFFAN	M	S	1	1	70	ENGLAND	CE	ENGLISH		081	I		29
BUKER	HENRY				24	O	PM	ENGLISH	COOPER	085	I		23
BULGER	DANIEL		1		15	ONTARIO	RC	IRISH	FARMER	082	B		33
BULGER	DANIEL				58	IRELAND	RC	IRISH	F	082	G		80
BULGER	MARGARET		1	1	23	O	RC	IRISH		081	K		73
BULGER	WILLIAM		1		13	ONTARIO	RC	IRISH		082	A		51
BULHILL	CHARLETT		1	1	60	QUE	RC	FRENCH		081	I		33
BULHILL	ELLEN		1	1	20	QUE	RC	FRENCH		081	I		33
BULLERANT	HENRY				30	ENGLAND	PM	ENGLISH	F	085	H		9
BULLERANT	JOSEPHUS				31	ENGLAND	PM	ENGLISH	F	085	H		20
BULLNER	JOHN		1		19	UNITED STATES	RC	GERMAN	LAB	090	D		2
BULMER	EDWARD				37	ONTARIO	CE	ENGLISH	F	082	A		21
BULMER	ROBERT				48	ENGLAND	EM	ENGLISH	F	082	A		23
BUNION	JOHN				70	IRELAND	RC	IRISH	F	082	F		29
BUNION	MICHEL				60	IRELAND	RC	IRISH	FARMER	082	D		25
BUNN	GEORGE				37	ENGLAND	CE	ENGLISH	F	085	D		6
BUNNON	RICHARD		1		20	O	RC	IRISH	LABOURER	082	E		5
BUNUS	JOHN		1		22	IRELAND	RC	IRISH	MILLWRIGHT	081	A	2	16
BUNYAN	ELIZA		1	1	22	O	RC	IRISH	SERVANT	082	E		18
BUNYAN	ELLEN		1	1	18	O	RC	IRISH	SERVANT	082	E		42
BUNYAN	MARY		1	1	25	O	RC	IRISH	SERVANT	082	E		18
BURBAGE	WILLIAM				56	IRELAND	RC	IRISH	FARMER	081	G	1	4
BURBIDGE	JAMES				44	IRELAND	RC	IRISH	FARMER	081	G	1	49
BURDEN	WILLIAM	F			49	ENGLAND	CE	ENGLISH	HOTEL KEEPER	085	I		3
BURDENOE	NAROUS				38	QUE	RC	FRENCH	F	081	E		21
BURGES	ANN		1	1	24	O	CE	IRISH		082	G		67
BURGES	ELIZA		2	1		O	CE			082	G		D
BURGES	SAMUEL				31	O	EM	IRISH	F	082	G		76
BURGES	THOMAS				47	SCOTLAND	CP	SCOTCH	F	085	E		28
BURGES	WILLIAM		1		21	O	RC	IRISH	RAILWAYMAN	081	A	2	29
BURGES	WILLIAM				36	O	CE	IRISH	F	082	G		76
BURGESS	JEMIMA		1	1	27	O	CE	IRISH		082	F		11
BURGESS	WILLIAM				45	IRELAND	CE	IRISH	F	082	F		10
BURGESS	WILLIAM	L			65	IRELAND	CE	IRISH	FARMER	082	B		71
BURGETT	JOSEPH				50	PRUSSIA	RC	PRUSSIAN	FARMER	083	A	1	18
BURGO	ANTONIO				34	QUEBEC	RC	FRENCH	FARMER	082	B		55
BURJETT	GEORGE		1				NG	FRENCH		088	B		2
BURK	CARL				37	GERMANY	BA	GERMAN	FARMER	081	F		10
BURK	DAVID	F			40	O	WM	IRISH	FARMER	086	B		8
BURK	ELIZABETH		1	1	1	IRELAND	RC	IRISH		081	F		1
BURK	ESTER		1	1	28	O	RC	IRISH		082	C	1	20
BURK	JAMES				55	IRELAND	RC	IRISH	LAB	081	A	2	8
BURK	JAMES		1		19	O	RC	IRISH	CLERK	082	E		48
BURK	PATRICK				30	O	RC	IRISH	LABOURER	082	D		20
BURK	THOMAS				50	IRELAND	CE	IRISH	F	081	K		5
BURKE	AUGUST				38	GERMANY	LU	GERMAN	L	082	G		82
BURKE	FRANCOIS				58	QUE	RC	FRENCH	F	081	K		37
BURKE	JOHN				53	IRELAND	RC	IRISH	F	081	K		17
BURKE	MARY		2	1	30	O	RC			081	K		D
BURKE	PETER				40	IRELAND	RC	IRISH	FARMER	081	G	1	27
BURKITT	GEORGE				24	O	CE	ENGLISH	STORE CLERK	089	A		46
BURL	THOMAS				34	ONT	RC	ENGLISH	RAFTSMAN	082	I		50
BURLANKET	LOUIS				29	ONT	FK	FRENCH	LABOURER	081	J	1	73
BURLANQUET	WILLIAM		1		22	ONT	WM	FRENCH	F LABOURER	081	J	1	81
BURLENGUET	ELESEBETH		2	1	56		WM			081	I		D
BURLINGUET	JOHN				58	QUE	WM	FRENCH	CARPENTER	081	I		20
BURMASTER	FREDRIEK				37	GERMANY	LU	GERMAN	F	082	J		14
BURNEPH	JOSEPH		1		3	O	RC	IRISH		081	K		16
BURNET	JAMES		1		33	O	CE	ENGLISH	WEAVER	081	B		15
BURNET	JAMES				34	ENGLAND	EP	ENGLISH	F	087	B	3	4
BURNET	JOHN				26	O	BA	ENGLISH	F	087	B	3	6
BURNETT	JOHN				30	O	CP	IRISH	F	082	C	2	2
BURNETT	PHILIP		1				NG	FRENCH		088	B		2
BURNETT	WILLIAM		1		33	O	CP	IRISH	F	082	C	2	3
BURNS	EDWARDS		1		42	IRELAND	RC	IRISH	LABOURER	082	D		3
BURNS	ELIZABETH		1	1	6	O	OP	SCOTCH		081	E		18
BURNS	GEORGE				46	IRELAND	PB	IRISH	SHANTYMAN	082	L		8
BURNS	JAMES				25	O	WM	SCOTCH	F	086	A	1	17
BURNS	JOHN				52	SCOTLAND	RP	SCOTCH	CARPENTER	081	I		3
BURNS	JOHN				30	IRELAND	RC	IRISH	F	081	J	1	14
BURNS	JOHN				50	IRELAND	RC	IRISH	F	081	J	1	62
BURNS	JOSEPH				28	ONTARIO	WM	IRISH	BLACKSMITH	082	A		80
BURNS	JOSEPH		1		30	O	WM	IRISH	BLACKSMITH	082	E		31
BURNS	MARTIN				35	IRELAND	RC	IRISH	FARMER	081	G	2	8
BURNS	PATRICK				70	IRELAND	RC	IRISH	F	081	H	2	40
BURNS	THIMOTY				65	IRELAND	RC	IRISH	F	082	J		13
BURNS	THOMAS		2		28	IRELAND	RC		FARMER	081	H	2	D
BURNS	THOMAS				21	IRELAND	RC	IRISH	INNKEEPER	084	E		2
BURNS	THOMAS		1		22	O	CP	IRISH	LUMBERMAN	086	B		2
BURNS	WILLIAM				32	IRELAND	RC	IRISH	F	081	K		16
BURRELL	ANDREW				25	ONT	RC	ENGLISH	FARMER	082	I		40
BURRELL	ANDREW		2		77	ENGLAND	RC		FARMER	082	I		D
BURRELL	KATE		1	1	20	O	RC	ENGLISH	SERVANT	082	E		61
BURRIS	ANN		1	1	98	IRELAND	CE	IRISH		082	C	1	47
BURRIT	ALFRED				35	O	CE	ENGLISH	CAPTAIN OF TUG	086	A	1	26
BURRITT	CLEMENCE				61	O	CE	ENGLISH	CARPENTER	081	B		27
BURRITT	ELIHU				31	ONTARIO	CE	ENGLISH	CARPENTER& HOTELKEEP	084	B		3
BURRITT	JAMES	H	1		22	O	CE	FRENCH	LAW STUDENT	082	E		9
BURROWS	JOHN				50	IRELAND	CE	IRISH	F	085	K	1	2
BURT	WILLIAM		1		9	O	RC	ENGLISH		089	A		64
BURTON			2	1		O	WM			081	H	2	D
BURTON	JOHN				27	O	CE	ENGLISH	F	081		1	75
BURTON	JOHN				38	ONTARIO	RC	IRISH	FARMER	084	A		2
BURTON	WILLIAM				46	ENGLAND	PM	ENGLISH	TAILOR	085	I		36
BURTON	WILLIAM	JR			47	O	WM	ENGLISH	F	081	H	2	14
BURTON	WILLIAM	SR			74	ENGLAND	CS	ENGLISH	F	081	H	2	12
BURWASH	CHARLOT			1	39	QUE	CP	ENGLISH		081	B		1
BURWELL	JOHN				44	O	EM	ENGLISH	F	081	H	2	27
BUSH	ALVIN				57	ONT	WM	ENGLISH	MILLWRIGHT	081	C		44
BUSH	JOHN		1		24	CANADA	PS	ENGLISH	LAB	087	B	2	1
BUSH	PHILIP				28	CANADA	PS	ENGLISH	F	087	B	2	3
BUSH	WALTER		1		20	CANADA	PS	SCOTCH	LAB	087	B	2	2
BUSH	WILLIAM				31	US	CE	ENGLISH	F	086	A	1	7

SURNAME	NAME1	NAME2	STRAY	SEX	AGE	BIRTHPL	RELIGION	ORIGIN	OCCUP	DIST	SUB_DIST	DIV	PAGE
BUSSA	JOHN		1		23	O	RC	FRENCH	LABOURER	089	B		16
BUSSA	JOHN		2		2	O	RC			089	B		D
BUSTIRE	JOSEPH				30	O	RC	FRENCH	LUMBERMAN	086	C	1	8
BUSTLAR	HENERY		1		35	QUEBEC	RC	FRENCH	FARMER	083	A	2	4
BUTCHART	JAMES	C			40	SCOTLAND	WM	SCOTCH	CARPENTER	089	B		31
BUTHER	MARTIN				50	GERMANY	EM	GERMAN	F	082	G		88
BUTLER	JOHN				36	O	CE	IRISH	TINSMITH	081	B		19
BUTLER	MICHAEL				24	IRELAND	RC	IRISH	LABOURER	082	E		21
BUTLER	WILLIAM				35	IRELAND	RC	IRISH	F	082	A		29
BUTT	CHARLES				42	GERMANY	LU	GERMAN	F	082	G		81
BUTT	EDWARD		1		26	IRELAND	CE	IRISH	LUMBERMAN	088	B		5
BUTT	LUEY				36	GERMANY	LU	GERMAN	F	082	G		83
BUTT	NILLIAN		1		18	ENGLAND	CE	ENGLISH	CLERK	081	B		30
BUTTERTON	OLIVER		1		17	ENGLAND	CE	ENGLISH	F	085	E		30
BUTTLE	BENGEMAN				64	IRELAND	CE	IRISH	F	082	F		37
BUTTLE	HENERY				47	IRELAND	CE	IRISH	F	082	F		33
BUTTLER	C	F			27	ENGLAND	CE	ENGLISH	F	085	D		14
BUTTLER	HENRYETTA		1	1	18	ONT	CE	IRISH		082	I		30
BUTTLER	PIERCE				40	IRELAND	RC	IRISH	FARMER	081	G	1	7
BUTTONS	CHARLES				25	O	RC	INDIAN	F & FISHERMAN	087	B	1	6
BUTTRELL	SAMUEL				29	ENGLAND	CE	ENGLISH	F	086	A	1	5
BUTTY	ELIZABETH		1	1	23	GERMANY	LU	GERMAN	SERVANT	082	E		61
BYCE	HENRY				54	ONTARIO	UV	ENGLISH	MILLWRIGHT	082	A		16
BYERS	CHARLES				43	PRUSSIA	LU	GERMAN	F	081	C		30
BYERS	JOHN	NELSON			29	O	CE	SCOTCH	DOCTOR	085	I		11
BYERS	WM	H	1		13	O	PS	IRISH		082	E		47
BYRES	ALBERT		1		5	O	CP	IRISH		082	G		61
BYRES	JAMES				27	ONTARIO	CP	IRISH	FARMER	082	B		44
BYRES	JAMES				77	ONTARIO	CP	SCOTTISH	FARMER	082	B		50
BYRES	JANE			1	45	IRELAND	CE	IRISH		082	G		8
BYRES	NULIE		1	1	26	GERMANY	ME	GERMAN		082	D		9
BYRNE	JOHN				36	IRELAND	RC	IRISH	F	081	A	1	6
BYRNE	MICHAEL				50	IRELAND	RC	IRISH	PRIEST	081	K		72
BYRNES	PETER				50	IRELAND	RC	IRISH	FARMER	081	D		13
CABINEAU	JOSEPH				60	NORTH WEST	RC	INDIAN	F	081	H	2	31
CADA	ANTOINE				32	O	RC	INDIAN	F & FISHERMAN	087	C		3
CADA	MARY			1	42	US	RC	INDIAN	F	087	C		3
CADAT	CHARLES				28	O	RC	FRENCH	LABOURER	089	B		26
CADDEN	BRIDGET			1	56	FERN IRELAND	RC	IRISH		082	E		65
CADIEUX	LOUIS		1		26	QUE	RC	FRENCH	MINER	090	F		17
CADOT	MICHEL				40	MANITOBA	RC	FRENCH	BOATMAN	089	B		44
CAHEL	HORATIO				40	O	RC	IRISH		082	C	1	28
CAHILL	CATHERINE		1	1	87	IRELAND	RC	IRISH		081	H	2	39
CAHILL	MICHAEL				55	IRELAND	RC	IRISH	FOREMAN	081	A	2	15
CAIBAISHKUNG	ANTOINE				24	O	RC	INDIAN	F & FISHERMAN	087	A		44
CAIN	ISAC		1		60	UNITED STATES	WM	GERMAN	SERVANT	082	I		69
CAIRNS	DAVID				41	SCOTLAND	CS	SCOTCH	CARPENTER	085	H		23
CAIRNS	WILLIAM				29	O	CE	SCOTCH	FARMER	086	B		7
CAIRNY	JAMES				37	IRELAND	RC	IRISH	SHOEMAKER	081	I		21
CALBECK	ROBERT				37	IRELAND	CE	IRISH	F	082	F		34
CALDWELL	ALEXANDER				45	SCOTLAND	PS	SCOTCH	WEAVER	081	K		2
CALE	JAMES		1		32	ONT	CE	IRISH	FARM LABOUR	081	J	1	46
CALHOON	MARY		1	1	36	SCOTLAND	NG	SCOTCH	SEAMSTRESS	082	C	2	6
CALIES	CHARLES				55	PRUSSIAN	CE	PRUSSIAN	F	081	J	1	75
CALLAGHAN	BRIDGET		1	1	16	O	RC	IRISH	SERVANT	081	B		73
CALLAGHAN	PATRICK				70	IRELAND	RC	IRISH	F	081	A	2	39
CALLAGHAN	SARAH		1	1	16	O	RC	IRISH	SERVANT	081	B		76
CALLAHAN	MICHAEL				55	IRELAND	RC	IRISH	FARMER	081	D		24
CALLARD	JOHN	C			41	ENGLAND	WM	ENGLISH	F	085	K	2	5
CALLENDAR	AGNES		1	1	23	NB	PS	SCOTTISH		082	D		5
CALLIGAN	THOMAS				40	IRELAND	RC	IRISH	LAB	081	A	2	7
CALVIN	CHARLES				34	GERMANY	CE	GERMAN		081	B		64
CALVIN	JAMES		1		22	IRELAND	WM	ENGLISH	LABOURER	084	F		1
CALWAY	JOHN				37	QUEBEC	CE	ENGLISH	LUMBERMAN	086	C	1	9
CAMARAN	JOHN				52	SCOTLAND	PS	SCOTCH	F	081	J	1	77
CAMARON	SOPHIE		1	1	60	SCOTLAND	FK	SCOTCH		081	J	1	73
CAMBELL	MALCOM		1		82	SCOTLAND	CS	SCOTCH	WEAVER	082	F		9
CAMBLEY	JAMES				30	ONT	RC	IRISH	FARMER	082	B		4
CAMELEY	TERRANCE				35	IRELAND	RC	IRISH	F	082	K	1	13
CAMELL	DUNCAN				29	SCOTLAND	PS	SCOTCH	F	086	A	1	2
CAMERON	ALEXANDER		2		41	SCOTLAND	CS		F			1	D
CAMERON	ALEXANDER				34	O	CP	SCOTCH		081	A	2	52
CAMERON	ALEXANDER				40	SCOTLAND	PS	SCOTCH	F	090	F		19
CAMERON	ALEXENDER				74	SCOTLAND	CP	SCOTCH	FARMER	089	B		4
CAMERON	ALLAN				31	O	CP	SCOTCH	LAB	081	A	1	22
CAMERON	ALLEN				31	QUE	PS	SCOTTISH	MERCHANT	082	E		29
CAMERON	ANGUS				79	SCOTLAND	CP	SCOTCH	F	081	A	1	24
CAMERON	ANGUS				36	SCOTLAND	CP	SCOTCH	F	081	A	1	28
CAMERON	ANN			1	35	SCOTLAND	PS	SCOTCH		090	F		19
CAMERON	ANNIE		1	1	30	O	BA	SCOTTISH	SERVANT	082	E		28
CAMERON	ARCHIBALD				26	O	CP	SCOTCH	F	081	A	1	22
CAMERON	CATHARINE		2	1	3	O	CP					1	D
CAMERON	CHARLES		1		2	ONT	CP	SCOTCH		081	C		29
CAMERON	COLIN				52	SCOTLAND	CP	SCOTCH	LUMBERER	083	C		5
CAMERON	DONALD				40	SCOTLAND	CP	SCOTCH	F	081	A	1	24
CAMERON	DONALD				47	ONTARIO	CP	SCOTTISH	STOREKEEPER	082	B		58
CAMERON	DONALD		1		27	QUEBEC	CS	SCOTCH		084	A		1
CAMERON	DUNCAN				26	O	CP	SCOTCH	F	081	A	1	22
CAMERON	DUNCAN				35	O	CP	SCOTCH	F	082	C	2	28
CAMERON	DUNCAN				31	O	CS	SCOTCH	ENGINEER	085	I		10
CAMERON	HUGH				35	O	RP	SCOTCH	F	081	H	1	5
CAMERON	HUGH				36	SCOTLAND	CP	SCOTCH	MINISTER	082	C	2	11
CAMERON	JANE		1	1	12	O	PS	SCOTCH		089	A		30
CAMERON	JANET		1	1	30	SCOTLAND	CP	SCOTCH		081	C		29
CAMERON	JOHN				38	O	CP	SCOTCH	LAB	081	A	1	21
CAMERON	JOHN				45	SCOTLAND	CP	SCOTCH	F	081	A	1	24
CAMERON	JOHN		2		82	O	RP		F	081	H	1	D
CAMERON	JOHN				30	ONTARIO	CP	SCOTCH	LUMBERER	083	C		5
CAMERON	JOHN	S			41	SCOTLAND	CS	SCOTCH	LUMBERMAN	088	B		2
CAMERON	LOCHLIN				28	O	CP	SCOTCH		081	A	2	52
CAMERON	MARGRET		1	1	2	O	CP	SCOTCH		081	A	1	21
CAMERON	ROBERT		1		34	ONT	CP	SCOTCH	F	081	C		29
CAMERON	WILLIAM				61	SCOTLAND	CP	SCOTCH	HOTEL KEEPER	085	E		26
CAMERON	WILLIAM				55	SCOTLAND	WM	SCOTCH	F	086	A	2	11
CAMERON	WM		1		25	O	CS	SCOTCH	LABOURER	088	A		7
CAMP	GEORGE	B			54	ENGLAND	CE	ENGLISH	F	085	E		28

SURNAME	NAME1	NAME2	STRAY	SEX	AGE	BIRTHPL	RELIGION	ORIGIN	OCCUP	DIST	SUB_DIST	DIV	PAGE
CAMPAGANA	CHARLES				25	QUE	RC	FRENCH	F	082	C	1	49
CAMPBELL	ANGUS		1		4	O	OP	SCOTCH		081	E		18
CAMPBELL	ANGUS				60	SCOTLAND	EM	SCOTCH	F	081	H	2	27
CAMPBELL	ANN		1	1	84	IRELAND	WM	IRISH	W	082	A		60
CAMPBELL	ARCHIBALD				50	SCOTLAND	CP	SCOTCH	LAB	081	A	2	10
CAMPBELL	ARCHIBALD				21	QUE	CP	SCOTCH	HOTELKEEPER	081	B		53
CAMPBELL	DANIEL				51	SCOTLAND	CS	SCOTCH	F	082	A		34
CAMPBELL	DONALD				33	SCOTLAND	PS	SCOTCH	MINE LABOURER	089	A		33
CAMPBELL	DOUGAL				78	SCOTLAND	CP	SCOTCH	F	081	A	2	46
CAMPBELL	DUNCAN				84	SCOTLAND	CS	SCOTCH	F	081	A	1	48
CAMPBELL	DUNCAN				25	O	CP	SCOTCH	F	081	A	2	61
CAMPBELL	DUNCAN				32	ONT	PS	SCOTCH	F	081	J	1	69
CAMPBELL	GEORGE	C			46	PEI	WM	SCOTCH	F	082	A		8
CAMPBELL	HUGH				30	O	EM	SCOTCH	HOTEL KEEPER	085	I		3
CAMPBELL	ISABELLA		1	1	57	SCOTLAND	CP	SCOTCH		081	B		28
CAMPBELL	ISABELLA		1	1	2	O	OP	SCOTCH		081	E		18
CAMPBELL	JAMES				38	SCOTLAND	CP	SCOTCH	F	081	A	1	2
CAMPBELL	JAMES				43	O	CS	SCOTCH	F	081	A	1	64
CAMPBELL	JAMES				22	ONT	PS	SCOTCH	F	081	J	1	69
CAMPBELL	JAMES				28	O	BA	SCOTCH	SHANTYMAN	082	G		54
CAMPBELL	JAMES				32	SCOTLAND	CP	SCOTCH	CARPENTER	085	H		25
CAMPBELL	JANET			1	36	O	CS	SCOTCH		081	A	1	59
CAMPBELL	JOHN				42	SCOTLAND	CP	SCOTCH	F	081	A	1	13
CAMPBELL	JOHN				70	SCOTLAND	CP	SCOTCH	F	081	A	1	37
CAMPBELL	JOHN				53	SCOTLAND	CP	SCOTCH	F	081	A	2	46
CAMPBELL	JOHN				37	O	CP	SCOTCH	F	081	A	2	48
CAMPBELL	JOHN				64	IRELAND	WM	IRISH	F	081	A	2	58
CAMPBELL	JOHN				23	O	BA	SCOTCH	F	081	A	2	61
CAMPBELL	JOHN				30	ONT	PS	SCOTCH	F	081	J	1	68
CAMPBELL	JOHN				60	SCOTLAND	PS	SCOTCH	F	081	J	1	69
CAMPBELL	JOHN				24	ONT	PS	SCOTCH	F	081	J	1	69
CAMPBELL	JOHN				24	ONT	CS	SCOT	F	082	A		34
CAMPBELL	JOHN				32	ONTARIO	CP	SCOTTISH	FARMER	082	B		8
CAMPBELL	JOHN		1		60	SCOTLAND	PS	SCOTTISH		082	D		31
CAMPBELL	JOHN		1		35	O	CP	IRISH	F LABOURER	085	B		19
CAMPBELL	KATIE		1	1	8	O	CP	SCOTCH		081	A	2	48
CAMPBELL	LEWIS		1		25	QUE	RC	FRENCH	LUMBERMAN	088	B		2
CAMPBELL	LUCY			1	38	O	PS	SCOTCH	HOTELKEEPER	081	K		62
CAMPBELL	MALCOLM				45	O	CP	SCOTCH	F	081	A	2	45
CAMPBELL	MARGRET		1	1	10	O	CP	SCOTCH	SERVANT	081	A	2	19
CAMPBELL	MARY		1	1	22	O	WM	SCOTTISH	DOMESTIC	082	E		8
CAMPBELL	MARY	JANE	1	1	33	O	CS	SCOTCH		081	A	1	57
CAMPBELL	PETER		1		10	O	CS	SCOTCH		081	A	1	58
CAMPBELL	PETER				58	SCOTLAND	PS	SCOTCH	F	081	J	1	68
CAMPBELL	PETER				45	O	BA	SCOTCH	BLACKSMITH	082	G		54
CAMPBELL	ROBERT				40	IRELAND	ME	IRISH	F	085	B		24
CAMPBELL	SAMUEL				39	IRELAND	PS	IRISH	F	085	J		6
CAMPBELL	SARAH		2	1	14	O	ME			085	B		D
CAMPBELL	WILLIAM				45	SCOTLAND	CP	SCOTCH	F	081	J	1	56
CAMQ	AGUSTUS		1		26	IRELAND	WM	IRISH	FOREMAN	084	E		3
CANE	CHARLES		1		20	O	RC	IRISH	LAB	085	F		5
CANN	WM				52	ENGLAND	CE	ENGLISH	F	085	L		1
CANNELL	EDWARD				55	ISLE OF MAN	CE	ENGLISH	F	085	A		25
CANNIFF	PETER	L	1		24	O	EM	ENGLISH	BOOKKEEPER	086	C	1	1
CANNINE	PATRICK				38	IRELAND	RP	IRISH	FARMER	082	I		5
CANNING	JOHN				46	IRELAND	WM	IRISH	F	085	A		30
CANNON	GILBERT		1		16	O	CP	SCOTTISH		082	E		7
CANNON	JOHN				70	IRELAND	RC	IRISH	FARMER	082	B		21
CANNON	MARGRET		2	1	81	SCOTLAND	CP			082	C	2	D
CANNON	WILLIAM				54	SCOTLAND	CP	SCOTCH	NOTARY PUBLIC	082	C	2	14
CANTIN	LOUIS		1		22	QUEBEC	RC	FRENCH	LUMBERMAN	083	A	1	8
CANWAY	PATRICK		1		55	IRELAND	RC	IRISH	LABOURER	081	J	1	24
CARANAGH	BRIDGIT		1	1	50	ONTARIO	RC	IRISH		082	B		32
CARBY	HONORAH		2	1		ONT	RC			081	C		D
CARDA	NARSISE				46	QUE	RC	FRENCH	SHANTYMAN	082	G		60
CARDEN	SILV		1		22	O	RC	IRISH	LABOURER	082	E		33
CARDIFF	GEORGE				31	ONT	RC	IRISH	F	081	J	1	16
CARDIFF	GEORGE				38	ONT	FK	IRISH	F	081	J	1	84
CARDIFF	JANE		1	1	24	ONT	RC	IRISH	SERVANT MAID	081	J	1	85
CARDIFF	JOHN				29	ONT	CP	IRISH	F	081	J	1	66
CARDIFF	MARK				50	IRELAND	CE	IRISH	F	081	J	1	31
CARDIFF	RICHARD				58	IRELAND	CE	IRISH	F	081	J	1	82
CARDIFF	THOS				58	IRELAND	CE	IRISH	F	081	J	1	83
CARDIFFE	GEORGE				62	IRELAND	CE	IRISH	F	081	J	1	83
CARDIFFE	MICHAEL		1		14	ONT	RC	IRISH		081	J	1	76
CARDIN	MARY		1	1	16	O	RC	FRENCH	SERVANT	089	A		61
CARDRIAL	FORDNA		1		26	QUE	RC	FRENCH	LAB	082	J		13
CARDY	AUGUSTUS				33	QUE	RC	FRENCH	LUMBERMAN	086	C	1	8
CARL	THOMAS				37	IRELAND	RC	IRISH	F	082	K	1	16
CARLEY	MARY		1	1	16	O	RC	IRISH		081	B		13
CARMICHAEL	ELIZABETH			1	49	SCOTLAND	CS	SCOTCH	F & LUMBER	082	C	1	65
CARMICHAEL	JANE		1	1	14	O	CP	SCOTCH	SERVANT	081	B		59
CARMICHAEL	JOHN				36	O	CP	IRISH	CARPENTOR	081	A	2	21
CARMICHAEL	JOHN				48	SCOTLAND	CP	SCOTCH	F	081	A	2	49
CARMICHAEL	MARGRET			1	42	O	CP	SCOTCH		081	A	1	49
CARMICHAEL	MARIAN		1	1	17	O	CP	IRISH		081	A	2	24
CARMICHAEL	MARY		1	1	67	IRELAND	RC	IRISH		081	A	2	21
CARMICHAEL	ROBERT				40	IRELAND	PS	IRISH	LAB	081	H	2	24
CARMICHAEL	THOMAS				49	IRELAND	RP	IRISH	FARMER	082	I		7
CARMODY	JEREMIAH				60	IRELAND	RC	IRISH	F	081	J	1	23
CARNAGIE	ALEXANDER				40	IRELAND	CE	IRISH	FARMER	082	I		39
CARNAGIE	ALEXANDER	SR			83	IRELAND	CE	IRISH		082	I		39
CARNAGIE	DANIEL				37	IRELAND	CE	IRISH	F	082	C	2	48
CARNAGIE	WILLIAM				37	IRELAND	CE	IRISH	F	082	C	2	48
CARNEY	DANIEL				55	IRELAND	RC	IRISH	F	082	F		27
CARNEY	JAMES				44	IRELAND	RC	IRISH	F	082	F		30
CARNEY	JOHN				65	IRELAND	RC	IRISH	F	082	F		27
CARNEY	JOHN				39	ENGLAND	WM	ENGLISH	MERCHANT	089	B		3
CARNEY	RICHARD				69	ENGLAND	CE	ENGLISH	SHERIFF	089	B		8
CARNEY	SUSAN		1	1	16	O	RC	IRISH		081	B		5
CARNEY	WILLIAM				42	IRELAND	RC	IRISH	F	082	F		26
CARNEY	WILLIAM	H			41	ENGLAND	WM	ENGLISH	MERCHANT	089	B		5
CARR	GEORGE				15	ENGLAND	CE	ENGLISH		085	E		25
CARR	MARGARET		1	1	19	O	CP	SCOTCH		081	B		19
CARR	PATRICK				54	IRELAND	RC	IRISH	F	081	J	1	9
CARRADICE	JOHN		1		52	SCOTLAND	PS	SCOTCH	CARPENTER	087	B	2	1

SURNAME	NAME1	NAME2	STRAY	SEX	AGE	BIRTHPL	RELIGION	ORIGIN	OCCUP	DIST	SUB_DIST	DIV	PAGE
CARRCAJEAN	JOSEPH				20	ONTARIO	RC	INDIAN	LABOURER H B CO	090	E		17
CARRIER	CATHERINE		1	1	20	ONT	RC	FRENCH	MILLINER	081	C		41
CARRIER	JANE		1	1	19	ONT	RC	FRENCH		081	C		37
CARROLL	JAMES		1		16	QUE	CP	ENGLISH	LAB	081	B		85
CARSE	HENRY				28	0	WM	IRISH	F	082	C	1	44
CARSON	DAVID				34	QUE	WM	IRISH	F	082	C	1	36
CARSON	GEORGE		1		40	IRELAND	CP	IRISH	LAB	081	B		54
CARSON	JOHN				45	IRELAND	RP	IRISH	FARMER	082	I		3
CARSON	SAMUEL		1		17	0	CE	IRISH	SERVANT	087	C		7
CARSON	WILLIAM		1		30	IRELAND	PS	IRISH	BOOKKEEPER	082	E		30
CARSS	GEORGE				30	0	WM	IRISH	FORWARDER	081	B		26
CARSS	WILLIAM				30	0	WM	IRISH	MERCHANT	081	B		49
CARSWELL	ALLAN		1		40	UNKNOWN	NG	SCOTCH	LUMBERER	081	C		52
CARSWELL	ALLAN	I	2		1	0	CP			081	I		D
CARSWELL	ALLEN				51	SCOTLAND	CP	SCOTCH	F	082	C	1	48
CARSWELL	BENJAMIN				75	QUE	WM	ENGLISH	FARMER	081	D		4
CARSWELL	DAVID				38	0	CS	SCOTCH	F	081	H	2	4
CARSWELL	JAMES				34	0	CP	SCOTCH	TIMBER MERCHANT	081	I		10
CARSWELL	MARGRET		1	1	55	SCOTLAND	CS	SCOTCH		081	A	1	63
CARSWELL	ROBERT				45	SCOTLAND	CP	SCOTCH	F			1	78
CARSWELL	THOMAS				50	SCOTLAND	CS	SCOTCH	F	082	C	1	49
CARTER	JOHN		1		55	UNITED STATES	WM		MILLWRIGHT	081	I		26
CARTER	WILLIAM		1		55	US	ME	ENGLISH		081	K		15
CARTHBERT	ALEX		1		30	0	RC	SCOTCH	SHANTYMAN	085	E		27
CARTHRITE	JOSEPH		1		23	QUE	CE	IRISH	F	085	I		38
CARTIER	CHARLES		1		50	QUEBEC	RC	FRENCH	PILOT	084	D		1
CARTMAN	JOHN				49	ENGLAND	CE	ENGLISH	F	082	A		42
CARTMAN	ROBERT				51	ENGLAND	CE	ENGLISH	F	082	A		22
CARTY	FRANCUS				64	IRELAND	RC	IRISH	FARMER	081	G	1	11
CARTY	JAMES				28	IRELAND	RC	IRISH	FARMER	081	G	1	11
CARTY	JOHN				26	IRELAND	RC	IRISH	FARMER	081	G	1	18
CARTY	JOHN				40	IRELAND	RC	IRISH	FARMER	081	G	1	46
CARTY	THOMAS				40	IRELAND	RC	IRISH	F	081	C		33
CARUISE	ROBERT		1		22	SCOTLAND	FK	SCOTCH	LABOURER	081	J	1	83
CASADU	CATHERIN		1	1	18	IRELAND	WM	IRISH		082	C	1	37
CASERYE	LOUISS		1		18	0	RC	FRENCH	SERVANT	081	A	2	2
CASEY	ANN		2	1	55	IRELAND	RC			081	G	1	D
CASEY	JOHN				28	IRELAND	RC	IRISH	MERCHANT	081	K		66
CASEY	PATRICK				60	IRELAND	RC	IRISH	SHOEMAKER	081	G	1	43
CASHMORE	THOMAS				39	ENGLAND	CE	ENGLISH	BRICKMAKER	082	E		55
CASIDY	MAREY	JANE	1	1	21	0	RC	IRISH		082	J		14
CASK	JAMES		1		20	0	RC	INDIAN	LAB	090	F		8
CASKEY	JANE	MRS		1	70	IRELAND	CP	IRISH		081	A	2	28
CASS	JNO				45	ONT	ME	INDIAN	HUNTER & TRAPPER	090	B		9
CASSELMAN	WM	J			46	0	EM	GERMAN	F	085	K	2	1
CASSIDY	JAMES				29	0	CP	SCOTCH	F	082	C	2	27
CASSWELLER	JOSEPH				41	ENGLAND	BA	ENGLISH	F	085	E		7
CASWELL	DAVID				31	QUE	WM	ENGLISH	FARMER	081	D		4
CASWELL	THOMAS				26	ENGLAND	WM	ENGLISH	F	085	J		21
CASY	PATT		1		23	0	RC	IRISH	LAB	085	F		5
CATANOTH	DANIEL		1		24	0	PS	SCOTCH	COOK	086	B		2
CATCHI	BAPTISTE				60	0	RC	INDIAN	HUNTER & TRAPPER	090	A		4
CATING	JOHN				29	QUEBEC	RC	IRISH	LUMBERER	083	C		5
CATON	THOMAS				35	0	CE	IRISH	MILLWRIGHT	086	A	1	8
CATTLE	SAMUEL				44	ENGLAND	CE	ENGLISH	WEAVER	082	D		6
CAUCHRAN	JOHN				29	QUE	CS	IRISH	FARMER	082	I		77
CAUCHRAN	WILLIAM				29	ONT	RP	IRISH	FARMER	082	I		6
CAUDIOCE	ANDREW		1		24	QUE	RC	FRENCH		081	A	2	17
CAUGHLIN	MATHEW				52	IRELAND	RC	IRISH	F	081	K		53
CAUSLAY	BENJIMEN				25	0	RC	FRENCH	LUMBERMAN	088	C		9
CAUSLAY	SOLOMAN				78	US	RC	GERMAN	FARMER	088	C		6
CAVAN	MICHAEL	C			38	IRELAND	RC	IRISH	LABOURER	082	E		20
CAVANAGH	JOHN				50	IRELAND	WM	IRISH	F	085	E		12
CAVANAH	EDWD				41	IRELAND	RC	IRISH	F	081	C		12
CAVES	THOMAS				57	IRELAND	JM	IRISH	F	082	C	2	16
CAWGAGIB	JOHN				38	US	RC	INDIAN	CARPENTER	089	B		41
CAWLEY	THOMAS				51	IRELAND	RC	IRISH	F	081	K		20
CAYAN	BAPTISTE				32	QUE	RC	FRENCH	SHANTYMAN	082	E		36
CEALARD	JOSIAH				35	ENGLAND	PB	ENGLISH	F	085	E		29
CECILE	TOUSANT				55	QUE	RC	FRENCH	F	082	C	1	9
CEUR	FREDRICK				25	GERMANY	WM	GERMAN	LAB	081	I		26
CHABOT									SEE SHABBOTT	081	B		76
CHALMERS	WM				34	SCOTLAND	PS	SCOTCH	F	085	J		9
CHAMBERLAIN	D	C			32	0	WM	FRENCH	MERCHANT	082	E		2
CHAMBERLAIN	ELIZA			1	22	QUE	WM	ENGLISH	SEAMSTRESS	082	C	1	3
CHAMBERLAIN	HIRAM				22	0	WM	ENGLISH	F	082	C	1	22
CHAMBERLAIN	NATHAN				58	QUE	CP	ENGLISH	F	082	C	2	11
CHAMBERLAIN	WYMAN	A			50	0	WM	ENGLISH	TANNER & F	082	C	1	14
CHAMBERLIN	DAVID				25	0	BA	ENGLISH	F	085	C		15
CHAMBERS	ANNE		1	1	28	ENGLAND	CE	ENGLISH		085	I		3
CHAMBERS	GEORGE		1		35	IRELAND	RC	IRISH	LAB	090	D		6
CHAMBERS	JOHN				60	IRELAND	CE	IRISH	TAILOR	082	C	1	17
CHAMBERS	JOHN				61	IRELAND	PS	IRISH	F	085	J		15
CHAMPAGNE	JOE				39	QUE	RC	FRENCH	SHANTYMAN	082	E		40
CHAMPAGNE	PIERRE								SEE CHOMPANZ	082	C	1	58
CHAMPANG	XEVIER				33	QUE	RC	FRENCH	F	082	C	1	62
CHANCE	JAMES				40	ENGLAND	CE	ENGLISH	CLERGYMAN	089	B		36
CHANDERAND	MELINDA		1	1	22	0	CP	SCOTCH	SCHOOL TEACHER	082	F		21
CHANNONHOUSE	JOHN				31	0	CE	IRISH	MEDICAL DOCTOR	081	K		61
CHANT	ANNA	M	1	1	22	ENGLAND	NG	ENGLISH		089	B		19
CHAPAU	MARY		1	1	24	QUE	RC	FRENCH	SERVANT	082	E		29
CHAPMAN	ELIZ	JANE	1	1	26	ENGLAND	WM	SCOTCH	SCHOOL TEACHER	085	A		22
CHAPMAN	JAMES				36	QUEBEC	WM	ENGLISH	FARMER	084	D		4
CHAPMAN	JAMES				33	ENGLAND	CE	ENGLISH	F	086	A	1	14
CHAPMAN	RICHARD				45	ENGLAND	PM	ENGLISH	F	085	B		19
CHAPMAN	RICHARD				28	ENGLAND	PM	ENGLISH	F	085	H		23
CHAPMAN	WILLIAM		1		21	0	CE	ENGLISH	LUMBERMAN	086	B		2
CHAPMAN	WILLIAM				38	ENGLAND	WM	ENGLISH	MINER	089	A		26
CHAPMAN	WM	D			34	QUE	WM	ENGLISH	HARDWARE MERCHANT	082	E		47
CHARBONNEAU									SEE SHERBINO	081	B		16
CHARBONNEAU									SEE SHARBINO	081	B		16
CHARBONNEAULT	JOSEPH		1		35	QUE	RC	FRENCH	LAB	082	J		13
CHARBOT	MARY			1	30	0	RC	INDIAN	WASHERWOMAN	090	F		18
CHARBUT	PETER				44	QUEBEC	RC	INDIAN	HUNTER	083	B	2	1
CHARETTE	BABTIST				58	0	RC	FRENCH	F	082	F		27
CHARION	EDWARD				45	QUEBEC	RC	FRENCH	LUMBERMAN	083	A	2	1

SURNAME	NAME1	NAME2	STRAY	SEX	AGE	BIRTHPL	RELIGION	ORIGIN	OCCUP	DIST	SUB_DIST	DIV	PAGE
CHARLABOIS	PAUL		1		23	QUEBEC	RC	FRENCH	LABOURER	083	A	1	12
CHARLEBOIS	ANDRE				49	QUE	RC	FRENCH	LABOURER	082	E		74
CHARLEBOIS	JOSEPH				61	QUE	RC	FRENCH	LABOURER	082	E		52
CHARLES	JAMES				41	IRELAND	CE	IRISH	F	085	A		16
CHARLES	JOHN				47	IRELAND	CE	IRISH	FARMER	082	I		35
CHARRETT	OLEVER		1		33	QUE	RC	FRENCH	LAB	082	J		1
CHARRON									SEE SHOROW	081	B		14
CHARRON	JACQUES				21	ONTARIO	RC	IRISH	LABORER	083	G		1
CHARSLAY	CHARLES		1		47	ENGLAND	CE	ENGLISH	TAILOR	081	A	1	18
CHARTAIN	LUKE				48	0	RC	FRENCH	F	087	B	3	7
CHARTRAND	NASSAIRE		1		39	QUE	RC	FRENCH	LAB	081	K		75
CHARTRANT	FRANCISE				50	QUE	RC	FRENCH	LAB	082	J		11
CHASE	NELSON				60	QUE	CP	ENGLISH	F	081	A	1	21
CHATELLA	LOUIS				32	0	RC	INDIAN	LAB	090	F		26
CHATREAU	EUDITH		1	1	16	0	RC	CANADIAN	SERVANT	087	A		2
CHATTERTON	WM	EDWARD			41	ENGLAND	WM	ENGLISH	FARMER	081	G	1	12
CHEESEBROUGH	JOHN		1		21	ENGLAND	WM	ENGLISH	F	085	J		9
CHENEY	FRANCIS				27	0	RC	FRENCH	GROCER	085	I		6
CHERRY	MOSES				70	ENGLAND	WM	ENGLISH	S CARPENTER	085	A		26
CHERRY	WILLIAM				49	SCOTLAND	PS	SCOTCH	WEAVER	081	J	1	54
CHESSER	DONALD		1		29	QUE	RC	IRISH	PEDLAR	082	E		18
CHESTER	EMMA		1	1	17	0	WM	SCOTTISH		082	E		22
CHESTER	HOWARD		1		13	ENGLAND	CE	ENGLISH	FARMER	086	B		7
CHESTER	THOMAS		1		23	ENGLAND	CE	ENGLISH	FARMER	086	B		7
CHETTLE	WILLIAM				40	ENGLAND	CE	ENGLISH	F	085	H		4
CHEWAUESE	JAS				23	0	RC	INDIAN	HUNTER	088	B		27
CHICAN	MAXIAM				30	QUE	RC	FRENCH	F	084	D		6
CHICOSA	LOUIS		1		30	0	RC	INDIAN	LAB	090	F		25
CHILDERHOSE	HENRY				52	IRELAND	CE	IRISH	F	082	A		55
CHILDERHOSE	JOHN				63	IRELAND	CE	IRISH	F	082	F		36
CHILDERHOSE	JOHN				31	IRELAND	CE	IRISH	MANUFACTURER OF WOOL	082	G		56
CHILDERHOSE	ROBERT				75	IRELAND	CE	IRISH	POSTMASTER	082	F		12
CHILDERHOSE	STEVEN				38	IRELAND	CE	IRISH	F	082	F		9
CHILDERHOSE	THOMAS				51	IRELAND	CE	IRISH	F	082	F		12
CHILDERHOSE	WILLIAM				50	IRELAND	CE	IRISH	F	081	H	2	12
CHIPMAN	RICHARD				39	ENGLAND	WM	ENGLISH	FARMER	089	A		13
CHIPOR	JOHN				42	POLAND	RC	POLISH	F	083	C		19
CHIPPEYUR	MICHAEL				50	PRUSSIA	RC	PRUSSIAN	FARMER	083	A	1	19
CHIPYERE	MATHIAS				25	PRUSSIA	RC	PRUSSIAN	FARMER	083	A	1	16
CHIRCHILL	JOHN				48	0	WM	IRISH	COOPER	081	I		27
CHISHOLM	ANN		1	1	20	SCOTLAND	CP	SCOTCH		085	L		12
CHISHOLM	DAVID		1		13	0	RC	IRISH		081	K		69
CHISHOLM	EMELY		1	1	22	SCOTLAND	CP	SCOTCH		085	L		12
CHISHOLM	GEORGE				41	0	WM	ENGLISH	SEAMAN	089	A		6
CHISHOLM	JOHN	W			45	CANADA	CE	SCOTCH	COOPER	087	B	2	1
CHISHOLM	MARGARET		1	1	15	0	RC	IRISH		081	K		69
CHISHOLM	MARY	ANN	1	1	17	0	RC	IRISH	TEACHER	081	K		69
CHOMPANZ	PIERRE				56	QUE	RC	FRENCH	F	082	C	1	58
CHONI	JOHN	PETER	1		63	FRANCE	RC	FRENCH	PRIEST	090	F		10
CHRISTIE	JOHN				25	0	RC	FRENCH	LAB	090	F		7
CHUCK	JOSEPH				26	ENGLAND	CE	ENGLISH	PAINTER	081	I		24
CHURCH	GEORGE				37	0	OM	ENGLISH	F	081	H	1	13
CHURCH	HARIET		1	1	34	ONT	CE	ENGLISH		081	C		54
CHURCH	HORROS	J			47	QUE	WM	ENGLISH	LAWYER	082	D		21
CHURCH	JAMES				44	ONTARIO	EM	ENGLISH	F	082	A		74
CHURCH	JOSEPH				31	ONT	WM	ENG AMERICAN	F	081	C		41
CHURCH	THOMAS				38	ONT	NG	ENG AMERICAN	F	081	C		42
CHURCH	TRENSIE		2	1	36	0	OM			081	H	1	D
CHURCH	TRENSIE		2	1		0	OM			081	H	1	D
CHURCH	WILLIAM				23	ONT	NG	ENG AMERICAN	F	081	C		42
CHURCHILL	ANNE		1	1	21	ONT	WM	SCOTCH	SERVANT	081	J	1	74
CHURCHILL	ASA				70	US	CE	ENGLISH	F	086	A	1	20
CHURCHILL	JOHN		1		23	ONT	WM	SCOTCH	FARM LABOUR	081	J	1	74
CHYER	GEORGE		1		26	QUE	RC	GERMAN	LAB	090	D		1
CIRETTE	AMBROISE				30	0	RC	FRENCH	EXPLORER	090	F		9
CLADWORTHY	WILLIAM	JOHN			50	IRELAND	PS	IRISH	F	081	K		51
CLAMO	CHARLES				19	QUEBEC	RC	FRENCH	FARMER	081	G	2	2
CLAREY	THOS				33	0	RC	IRISH		082	D		11
CLARK	ANDREW				43	0	CE	IRISH	F	082	F		10
CLARK	EDWD				36	IRELAND	WM	IRISH	SADDLER	082	E		58
CLARK	GEORGE				32	IRELAND	CE	IRISH	BLACKSMITH	082	E		57
CLARK	HUGH		1		26	0	CE	IRISH	SHOEMAKER	081	B		6
CLARK	ISAAC				58	SCOTLAND	PS	SCOTCH	F	085	J		19
CLARK	JAMES				31	IRELAND	CE	IRISH	F	085	I		24
CLARK	JAMES		1		42	LEINSTER	RC	IRISH	F	087	A		1
CLARK	JOHN				52	IRELAND	PS	IRISH	BLACKSMITH	086	A	1	9
CLARK	MOSES		1		24	QUE	CE	ENGLISH	MILLER	081	I		30
CLARK	NORMAN				18	ENGLAND	CE	ENGLISH	F	085	K	2	7
CLARK	PULASTER				27		CE		STOREKEEPER	086	C	1	2
CLARK	RICHARD				28	0	PS	IRISH	F	085	J		22
CLARK	RICHARD		1		25	ENGLAND	CE	ENGLISH	BLACKSMITH	086	B		3
CLARK	SCYLER		2		4	0	CE			085	B		D
CLARK	THOMAS				47	QUE	CE	IRISH	F	081	H	2	20
CLARK	THOMAS		1		35	0	PS	SCOTTISH	LABOURER	082	D		4
CLARK	THOMAS	SEN			80	IRELAND	CE	IRISH	WEAVER	081	H	2	21
CLARK	WILLIAM		1		22	0	CP	SCOTCH	CLERK	081	A	2	28
CLARK	WILLIAM		1		30	0	CE	IRISH	F	081	H	2	19
CLARK	WILLIAM				29	NEW BRUNSWICK	CP	SCOTCH	MANAGER	084	B		2
CLARK	WILLIAM				26	0	CS	ENGLISH	LUMBERMAN	088	B		20
CLARK	WM				40	ENGLAND	CO	ENGLISH	F	085	L		6
CLARKE	ALEXANDER				53	SCOTLAND	CP	SCOTCH	SAILOR	089	B		25
CLARKE	ANN			1	56	SCOTLAND	CS	SCOTCH		087	B	2	9
CLARKE	DONALD	JR			30	SCOTLAND	CS	SCOTCH	F	087	B	2	9
CLARKE	DONALD	SEN			40	SCOTLAND	CS	SCOTCH	F	087	B	2	9
CLARKE	ELIZABETH		1	1	12	0	PS	SCOTCH		089	A		34
CLARKE	FRANK				48	US	RC	INDIAN	LABOURER	089	B		38
CLARKE	GEORGE				28	0	CE	IRISH	F	082	G		25
CLARKE	GEORGE				60	IRELAND	CE	IRISH	F	082	G		25
CLARKE	GEORGE				54	0	CE	IRISH	MERCHANT	085	B		8
CLARKE	GEORGE				37	ENGLAND	PM	ENGLISH	MINE LABOURER	089	A		23
CLARKE	JOHN				22	0	CE	IRISH	F	082	G		25
CLARKE	JOHN				40	0	CE	ENGLISH	FARMER	089	A		57
CLARKE	MILES				45	IRELAND	CE	IRISH	F	082	G		26
CLARKE	REBECCA		2	1		0	NG			082	G		D
CLARKE	THOMAS				34	0	CE	IRISH	F	082	G		24
CLARKE	THOMAS		1		9	0	RC	ENGLISH		089	A		56

SURNAME	NAME1	NAME2	STRAY	SEX	AGE	BIRTHPL	RELIGION	ORIGIN	OCCUP	DIST	SUB_DIST	DIV	PAGE
CLARKE	THOS				35	IRELAND	CE	IRISH	MERCHANT	082	E		9
CLARKE	WM				57	IRELAND	CE	IRISH	F	082	G		36
CLARKSON	WILLIAM		1		18	ENGLAND	RC	ENGLISH	LABOURER	086	A	1	31
CLEARY	JAMES		1		5	O	RC	IRISH		082	K	2	1
CLEMMO	FELIS		1		8	O	RC	FRENCH		082	C	1	56
CLEMONT	JOSEPH		1		12	O	RC	FRENCH		082	K	2	4
CLEMONT	LOVII		1	1	38	O	RC	FRENCH		082	J		1
CLEMONT	MARGERIT		1	1	10	O	RC	FRENCH		082	K	2	4
CLEMS	MERO				50	QUE	RC	FRENCH	FARMER	081	D		12
CLENDENNING	PHILIP				44	O	CS	IRISH	F	086	A	2	12
CLERIHUE	JAMES				33	QUE	WM	SCOTCH	MERCHANT	085	I		5
CLERY	CURNILUS				36	IRELAND	RC	IRISH	CARPENTER	081	I		19
CLEVE	MARGRET		2	1		O	WM			081	I		D
CLIFFORD	EDWARD		1		41	ENGLAND	CE	ENGLISH	F	085	E		5
CLIFFORD	HENRY				60	ENGLAND	CE	ENGLISH	STORE KEEPER	085	H		26
CLINE	SIMEON				25	O	WM	ENGLISH	MERCHANT	085	E		1
CLIPSHAM	MICHAEL				31	ENGLAND	WM	ENGLISH	BLACKSMITH	085	A		22
CLLIFORD	THOMAS				26	ENGLAND	CE	ENGLISH	F	086	A	2	13
CLOSE	DAVID				56	IRELAND	NG	IRISH	F	081	C		50
CLOSE	JANE	E	1	1	20	ONT	NG	IRISH		081	C		53
CLOSE	MARGARET			1	44	ONT	CE	ENG		081	C		49
CLOSE	RACHAEL		1	1	18	O	WM	SCOTCH		081	B		15
CLOSS	ANN	C	1	1	14	O	WM	IRISH	SERVANT	081	B		69
CLOUREN	RICK				23	QUE	RC	POLISH	BLACKSMITH	081	I		38
CLOUTHIER	FRANCESE				40	QUE	RC	FRENCH	INNKEEPER	082	K	2	4
CLUFF	WILLIAM		1		24	ENGLAND	CE	ENGLISH	LAB	081	B		54
CLYDESDALE	THOMAS				26	SCOTLAND	PS	SCOTCH	F	085	J		9
COAL	FRANCES				37	ONT	CP	ENGLISH	FARMER	082	I		52
COAL	JAMES				44	O	CE	IRISH	F	081	E		5
COALE	JOHN				33	O	OM	ENGLISH	F	081	H	1	16
COBB	MARGT		1	1	22	QUE	CP	SCOTTISH	DOMESTIC	082	E		7
COBOURN	ALEXANDER				60	IRELAND	RP	IRISH	FARMER	082	I		11
COBOURN	BENJAMIN				30	ENGLAND	CE	IRISH	FARMER	082	I		34
COBOURN	CHARLOT		1	1	32	O	CP	IRISH	SERVANT	081	B		38
COBOURN	GEORGE				32	ENGLAND	CE	IRISH	FARMER	082	I		34
COBOURN	JOHN		1		76	IRELAND	CE	IRISH	F	081	A	2	58
COBOURN	JOHN				45	IRELAND	CP	IRISH	FARMER	082	I		27
COBOURN	JOHN				40	IRELAND	WM	IRISH	FARMER	082	I		68
COBOURN	WILLIAM				50	IRELAND	CE	IRISH	FARMER	082	I		34
COBURN	JAMES				56	IRELAND	WM	IRISH	FARMER	082	D		26
COBURN	MARGRET	BURNS	2	1	15	O	WM			082	D		D
COBURN	ROBT				58	IRELAND	WM	IRISH	FARMER	082	D		30
COCHANCE	JACQUES				28	ONTARIO	RC	INDIAN	HUNTER	084	A		4
COCHANCE	SUSAN			1	50	QUE	RC	INDIAN	F	082	J		18
COCHLAN	JOHN		1		30	O	WM	IRISH		081	B		13
COCHRAIN	HANNAH		1	1	55	O	CE	FRENCH		081	I		13
COCHRAN	MARY			1	52	IRELAND	RP	IRISH	FARMER	082	I		6
COCHRAN	SAMUEL				32	IRELAND	NC	IRISH	F	086	A	1	11
COCHRAN	THOMAS				70	IRELAND	RC	IRISH	FARMER	081	G	1	20
COCHRAN	WILLIAM				46	IRELAND	RP	IRISH	FARMER	082	I		8
COCHRANE	ANDREW				48	O	CP	SCOTCH	F	081	A	1	7
COCHRANE	JOHN		1		16	ONT	CP	IRISH	LABOUR	081	J	1	85
COCHRANE	JOHN				59	SCOTLAND	PS	SCOTCH	F	081	K		7
COCHRANE	JOHN				31	O	NG	SCOTCH	CARPENTER	081	K		8
COCHRANE	THOMAS				28	O	PS	SCOTCH	F	081	K		8
COCHRANE	WILLIAM				37	NB	CE	IRISH	F	085	H		10
COCK	FREDERICK				56	ENGLAND	DE	ENGLISH	F	085	K	2	4
COCKBURN	DANIEL				25	O	CP	SCOTCH	STORE KEEPER	085	E		23
COCKBURN	DAVID				38	ENGLAND	CE	ENGLISH	WOODCARVER	082	E		54
COCKBURN	JOHN				38	ENGLAND	CE	ENGLISH	BOAT BUILDER	082	E		55
COCKBURN	JOHN	P			35	O	CP	SCOTCH	MERCHANT	085	B		13
COCKBURNE	GEORGE		1		22	ENGLAND	PS	SCOTCH	GENT	085	J		24
COCKEGESE	JAMES				24	O	NR	INDIAN	HUNTER	088	C		4
COCKGABIE	EDWARD				68	ONTARIO	RC	INDIAN	HUNTER	083	E		1
COCKRAM	CHARLES				22	ENGLAND	WM	ENGLISH	F	085	L		6
CODE	JAMES				60	IRELAND	CE	IRISH	FARMER	082	B		70
COFFE	JAMES				40	O	CE	ENGLISH	F	082	F		29
COFFEE	ANN		1	1	75	ENGLAND	CE	ENGLISH		082	A		42
COFFY	GEORGE				50	O	CE	ENGLISH	SPINNER	082	C	2	45
COGHLAN	JAMES				37	IRELAND	RC	IRISH	F	083	C		15
COGHLAN	PATRICK				32	IRELAND	RC	IRISH	F	083	C		15
COGHLAN	THOMAS				64	IRELAND	RC	IRISH	F	083	C		15
COIN	PATRICK				19	QUE	RC	IRISH	ACCOUNTANT	082	C	2	67
COINE	JOHN		2			SCOTLAND	CP			082	C	2	D
COINN	WILLIAM				31	ONTARIO	RC	IRISH	FARMER	081	G	1	11
COLBAY	RIELIE		1	1	22	ENGLAND	CE	ENGLISH		085	D		27
COLE	FREDRICK				33	GERMANY	PR	GERMAN	F	082	G		16
COLE	HERCULIS				31	ONTARIO	RC	IRISH	FARMER	081	G	2	4
COLE	JOHN				25	IRELAND	CE	IRISH	F	087	B	2	8
COLE	JOSEPH				58	ENGLAND	CE	ENGLISH	F	086	A	1	21
COLE	MARTIN				38	GERMANY	LU	GERMAN	F	082	G		3
COLE	THOMAS				42	O	EM	ENGLISH	F	081	H	2	29
COLE	WILLIAM		1		2	O	OP	IRISH		081	E		19
COLE	WILLIAM				30	O	WM	ENGLISH		081	H	2	30
COLE	WRIGHT				25	ENGLAND	CE	ENGLISH	FARMER	085	E		28
COLEMAN	JAMES				36	IRELAND	RC	IRISH	BUTCHER	082	E		32
COLEMAN	WILLIAM	S			34	ONTARIO	CE	ENGLISH	MERCHANT	082	A		1
COLLAN	JOSEPH				60	O	RC	FRENCH	FISHERMAN	090	A		2
COLLANS	JOSEPH				30	QUE	RC	FRENCH	LAB	081	I		34
COLLENDER	RICHARD				36	SCOTLAND	CP	SCOTCH	CARPENTER	081	B		83
COLLET	GEORGE				37	ENGLAND	CE	ENGLISH	WATCHMAKER	085	B		11
COLLETT	ARTHUR				29	ENGLAND	CE	ENGLISH	F	086	A	1	30
COLLIAN	EDWARD		1		25	O	RC	IRISH	PAINTER	081	B		13
COLLIDGE	WILLIAM				65	ENGLAND	PM	ENGLISH	F	085	I		38
COLLIN	JOHN	B			35	O	RC	INDIAN	LAB	090	F		24
COLLIN	MICHEL				74	RED RIVER	RC	FRENCH	CANOE BUILDER	090	F		9
COLLIN	SAMUEL					ONTARIO	RC	FRENCH	SERVANT H B CO	090	E		15
COLLINS	ADELAIDE		2	1	1	O	RC			081	D		D
COLLINS	CATHERINE		1	1	65	IRELAND	RC	IRISH		081	F		19
COLLINS	EDWARD				65	IRELAND	RC	IRISH	F	085	A		2
COLLINS	ELIZABETH		1	1	11	O	WM	FRENCH		081	I		21
COLLINS	GEORGE				28	IRELAND	RC	IRISH	ENGINEER	085	B		9
COLLINS	JAMES				60	IRELAND	RC	IRISH	LABOURER	081	D		8
COLLINS	JAMES		1		38	IRELAND	RC	IRISH	SCHOOL TEACHER	082	E		18
COLLINS	JOHN	E			46	IRELAND	WM	IRISH	F	082	C	2	18
COLLINS	MARGARITE		1	1	21	UNITED STATES	RC	IRISH		090	D		3

SURNAME	NAME1	NAME2	STRAY	SEX	AGE	BIRTHPL	RELIGION	ORIGIN	OCCUP	DIST	SUB_DIST	DIV	PAGE
COLLINS	PATRICK		1		45	IRELAND	RC	IRISH	SHANTYMAN	082	E		18
COLLINS	RICHARD				60	IRELAND	RC	IRISH	F	081	J	2	5
COLLINS	SUSAN		1	1	25	IRELAND	RC	IRISH		081	F		19
COLLINS	THOMAS				52	IRELAND	WM	IRISH	F	082	C	1	64
COLLINS	THOMAS				36	ENGLAND	WM	ENGLISH	MINER	089	A		42
COLLINS	WILLIAM				40	IRELAND	WM	IRISH	F	082	C	2	15
COLLINS	WM		1		21	0	CE	ENGLISH	CLERK	082	E		2
COLOSE	FREDRICK				44	GERMANY	LU	GERMAN	FARMER	082	G		29
COLSMITH	WILLIAM		2		3	0	LU			082	B		D
COLSON	CHARLES				63	ENGLAND	CO	ENGLISH	F	085	H		1
COLSON	THOMAS				32	ENGLAND	BA	ENGLISH	F	085	H		19
COLSOVA	ANN		1	1	20	GERMANY	WM	GERMAN	SERVANT	081	G	1	31
COLTER	GEORGE				59	IRELAND	UF	IRISH	F	085	D		15
COLTON	ANTOINE				30	ONTARIO	RC	ENGLISH	FARMER & HUNTER	084	B		4
COLTON	JAMES				50	IRELAND	RC	IRISH	FARMER	081	G	1	22
COLTON	MARY		2	1	40	ONTARIO	RC			081	G	1	D
COLTON	THOMAS				40	IRELAND	RC	IRISH	FARMER	081	G	1	22
COLVAN	JAMES				40	IRELAND	RC	IRISH	F	081	H	1	16
COMANDO	ALECK	C			32	0	RC	INDIAN	HUNTER	084	I	1	2
COMANDO	JOSEPH				32	0	RC	INDIAN	HUNTER	084	I	1	1
COMANDO	JOSEPH		1		70	UNITED STATES	RC	INDIAN	HUNTER	084	I	1	4
COMB	FREDRICK				40	GERMANY	LU	GERMAN		082	G		15
COMBER	RODRICK		1		49	IRELAND	RC	IRISH		082	G		50
COMBER	SAMSOM				62	ENGLAND	CE	ENGLISH	FARMER	081	I		1
COMBES	GEORGE		1		4	0	CP	SCOTCH		081	I		13
COMBES	THOMAS				28	0	CE	ENGLISH	LAB	081	I		8
COMERY	PETER				57	SCOTLAND	CP	SCOTCH	F	082	C	1	54
COMFORTER	JAMES				34	IRELAND	RC	IRISH	FARMER	081	G	2	9
COMMENDENT	LOUIS				40	ONTARIO	RC	INDIAN	HUNTER	084	C		6
COMOR	PATRICK				30	IRELAND	RC	IRISH	F	081	C		15
CONAWAY	THOMAS		1		29	0	RC	SCOTCH	SHANTYMAN	085	E		27
CONDELL	CHARLES				35	IRELAND	RC	IRISH	LAB	081	A	2	31
CONDELL	JOHN				30	IRELAND	RC	IRISH	F	081	A	2	31
CONDELL	PATRICK				30	IRELAND	RC	IRISH	LAB	081	A	2	31
CONDIE	ALEXANDER				44	0	CP	SCOTCH	F	082	C	2	3
CONDIE	JAMES				70	SCOTLAND	CP	SCOTCH	F	082	C	2	10
CONDIE	JAMES				46	0	CP	SCOTCH	F	082	C	2	21
CONDIE	JAMES		1		12	0	CP	SCOTCH		082	C	2	27
CONDIE	MALCOLM				56	0	CP	SCOTCH	F	082	C	2	13
CONDIE	THOMAS				38	0	CP	SCOTCH	F	082	C	2	9
CONDLE	PATRICK				41	IRELAND	RC	IRISH	F	081	A	2	56
CONDON	JOHN				56	IRELAND	RC	IRISH	F	081	C		9
CONDY	ELIZABETH		1	1	9	ONTARIO	CS	IRISH		082	A		13
CONE	DAVID	H			37	AMERICAN	EM	ENGLISH	LAB	081	B		48
CONE	HENRY				39	US	EM	SCOTCH	CARPENTER	081	A	2	22
CONLEY	JAMES				40	IRELAND	RC	IRISH	FARMER	082	B		36
CONLEY	OWEN				61	ONTARIO	RC	IRISH	FARMER	082	B		37
CONNALEY	MICHAEL				55	IRELAND	RC	IRISH	FARMER	081	G	1	45
CONNELL	JOHN				80	UNITED STATES	EM	SCOTCH	PENSIONER	081	B		60
CONNELL	WILLIAM		1		26	SCOTLAND	CP	SCOTCH	LAB	090	D		7
CONNELLY	THOS				34	IRELAND	RC	IRISH	COOPER FARMER	081	J	1	19
CONNERS	ANN		1	1	3	0	RC	IRISH		081	K		19
CONNERS	CATHRINE		1	1	2	ONTARIO	RC	IRISH		081	G	1	23
CONNERS	HUGH				27	IRELAND	RC	IRISH	FARMER	081	G	1	17
CONNERS	MICHAEL				49	IRELAND	RC	IRISH	SERVANT	081	A	2	3
CONNOGHAN	JOHN				28	IRELAND	RC	IRISH	F	081	K		45
CONNOGHAN	JOHN				55	IRELAND	RC	IRISH	F	081	K		45
CONNOLL	JAMES		1		24	0	CP	IRISH	LAB	081	B		85
CONNOLLY	JAMES				48	IRELAND	RC	IRISH	FARMER	081	F		3
CONNOLLY	JAMES		1		21	IRELAND	RC	IRISH	FARM LABOURER	081	K		4
CONNOLLY	PATRICK				47	IRELAND	RC	IRISH	FARMER	081	F		1
CONNOR	MICHAEL				45	IRELAND	RC	IRISH	LAB	081	A	2	10
CONNOR	THOMAS				60	IRELAND	RC	IRISH	F	081	C		34
CONNORS	JESY		2	1	24	SCOTLAND	RC			081	E		D
CONNORS	JOHN				37	IRELAND	RC	IRISH	F	081	E		11
CONNORS	JOHN				32	IRELAND	RC	IRISH	FARMER	081	F		18
CONNORS	JOHN				62	IRELAND	RC	IRISH	F	082	H		30
CONNORS	JOHN				40	IRELAND	RC	IRISH	F	082	H		12
CONNORS	MARTIN				36	IRELAND	RC	IRISH	F	082	L		4
CONNORS	PATRICK				34	IRELAND	RC	IRISH	F	081	J	1	34
CONOLEY	JAMES				45	QUE	CE	IRISH	LAB	085	I		17
CONOLY	ANNE			1	22	IRELAND	RC	IRISH	SCHOOL MISTRESS	082	H		27
CONRAD	WILHAMINA			1	42	PRUSSIA	LU	PRUSSIAN		085	A		18
CONROY	MARY	JANE	1	1	5	0	RC	IRISH		081	E		8
CONROY	PATRICK		1		16	0	RC	IRISH	SERVANT	082	E		56
CONSTAN	SIMON				40	QUE	RC	INDIAN	F	081	E		8
CONSTANT	JOSEPH				70	QUE	RC	INDIAN	HUNTER	081	D		22
CONTOIS	SORIL				46	QUE	RC	FRENCH	F	082	G		80
CONTRA	MOSES				30	QUE	RC	FRENCH	F	082	H		18
CONTRA	ORGET				29	QUE	RC	FRENCH	F	082	H		19
CONWAY	CATHRINE		1	1	5	0	RC	IRISH		082	L		3
CONWAY	ELLAN		1	1	2	0	RC	IRISH		082	L		3
CONWAY	GEORGE				60	IRELAND	RC	IRISH	FARMER	083	A	2	1
CONWAY	JOHN		1		9	0	RC	IRISH		082	L		3
CONWAY	MARY	JANE	1	1	7	0	RC	IRISH		082	L		3
CONWAY	MICHAEL				44	IRELAND	RC	IRISH	F	081	J	1	33
CONWAY	MICHAEL				49	IRELAND	RC	IRISH	F	082	L		2
CONWAY	MICHAEL				43	IRELAND	RC	IRISH	FARMER	083	A	1	9
CONWAY	MRS		1	1	60	IRELAND	RC	IRISH		081	J	1	23
CONWAY	PATRICK				50	IRELAND	RC	IRISH	F	081	J	1	25
CONWAY	RICHARD	W			32	0	WM	IRISH	CLOTHIER	081	B		21
CONWAY	THOMAS				26	QUEBEC	RC	IRISH	FARMER	083	A	2	3
CONWAY	THOS				56	IRELAND	RC	IRISH	F	081	J	1	22
COOK	AARON				61	ENGLAND	CE	ENGLISH	FARM LABOURER	089	A		15
COOK	ALANSON				24	0	CP	SCOTCH	MERCHANT	081	A	2	28
COOK	CHARLES		1		23	ENGLAND	WM	ENGLISH	MINER	089	A		37
COOK	HENRY		1		25	ENGLAND	WM	ENGLISH	MINER	089	A		37
COOK	JAMES		1		26	0	RP	IRISH	LAB	082	K	1	14
COOK	JAMES				60	SCOTLAND	PS	SCOTCH	FARMER	089	B		19
COOK	JOHN				41	0	WM	ENGLISH	F	085	J		3
COOK	JOHN				58	ENGLAND	WM	ENGLISH	MINER	089	A		34
COOK	JOSEPH		1		19	ENGLAND	CE	ENGLISH	F LAB	085	J		23
COOK	JOSIAH				31	ENGLAND	WM	ENGLISH	MINER	089	A		5
COOK	MAREY		1	1	24	IRELAND	RP	IRISH	SERVANT	082	K	1	14
COOK	RICHARD		2		1	0	OM			089	A		D
COOK	THOMAS				32	SCOTLAND	CP	SCOTCH	F	081	H	1	3

SURNAME	NAME1	NAME2	STRAY	SEX	AGE	BIRTHPL	RELIGION	ORIGIN	OCCUP	DIST	SUB_DIST	DIV	PAGE
COOK	THOMAS		1		64	ENGLAND	WM	ENGLISH	MINE LABOURER	089	A		37
COOK	WILLIAN				25	GERMANY	LU	PRUSSIAN	F	085	A		1
COOKE	EMILY	CHARLOTTE		1	25	QUE	PB	AMERICAN		084	E		4
COOKE	GEORGE				30	ENGLAND	NG	ENGLISH	BAKER	085	I		8
COOKE	MARY		2	1	53	ENGLAND	CE			085	H		D
COOKE	MICHAEL				50	IRELAND	CE	IRISH	F	085	H		5
COOKMAN	THOMAS				56	IRELAND	RC	IRISH	F	081	A	1	5
COOLAS	ALBERT				52	PRUSSIA	RC	PRUSSIAN	FARMER	083	A	1	2
COOLAS	JACOB				65	PRUSSIA	RC	PRUSSIAN	FARMER	083	A	1	7
COONAN	EDWARD				50	IRELAND	RC	IRISH	F	081	A	2	5
COONEY	MARTHA		1	1	33	US	CE	IRISH		085	B		11
COOPER	ALEXANDER				42	SCOTLAND	CP	SCOTCH	STONE CUTTER	085	I		26
COOPER	EDMON				30	ENGLAND	CE	ENGLISH	F	085	E		26
COOPER	EMANUEL				40	ENGLAND	WM	ENGLISH	HOTEL KEEPER	085	B		7
COOPER	JAMES				52	IRELAND	CE	IRISH	F	085	E		6
COOPER	JOSEPH		1		10	0	RC	INDIAN		088	A		9
COOPER	ROBERT		1		60	IRELAND	CE	IRISH	F	085	C		11
COPELAND	JAS				59	IRELAND	PS	IRISH	HOTELKEEPER	082	E		47
COPP	MICHEAL				40	IRELAND	RC	IRISH	F	082	K	1	3
COPPER	JOSEPH				31	0	WM	ENGLISH	CARPENTER	085	I		10
COPPS	DANIEL				39	IRELAND	RC	IRISH	FARMER	081	G	1	6
COPPS	JOHN				36	IRELAND	RC	IRISH	LUMBERMAN	083	A	1	14
COPPS	PATRICK				24	QUEBEC	RC	IRISH	FARMER	081	G	1	16
CORAGON	WILLIAM				28	IRELAND	RC	IRISH	FARMER	081	G	1	34
CORASA	OCTAB				36	QUE	RC	FRENCH	LAB	081	A	2	25
CORAZZI	A				39	ITALY	CE	ITALIAN	MUSICIAN	081	B		69
CORBETT	MRS		1	1	50	IRELAND	RC	IRISH		081	J	1	67
CORBIER	DANIEL				32	0	RC	INDIAN	F & FISHERMAN	087	B	1	8
CORBIER	HENRY	JR			29	0	RC	INDIAN	F	087	B	1	8
CORBIER	HENRY	SENIOR			47	0	RC	INDIAN	TRADER	087	B	1	2
CORBIER	JOSEPH				22	0	RC	INDIAN	F	087	B	1	9
CORBIER	MARGARET		1	1	20	0	RC	FRENCH		088	B		2
CORBIERE	JOHN				51	0	RC	FRENCH	TRADER	089	B		30
CORBIERE	JOHN				28	0	RC	FRENCH	BOATMAN	089	B		32
COREELE	FEPI				88	QUE	RC	FRENCH	F	082	C	1	10
CORIER	JOSEPH		1		22	QUE	RC	FRENCH	BLACKSMITH	082	E		37
CORMAC	BESSY		2	1	3	0	CP			082	E		D
CORMACK	JOHN	G			32	0	CP	SCOTTISH	DRUGGIST	082	E		9
CORMAGH	NEIL				36	IRELAND	CE	IRISH	F	082	J		18
CORMEA	HENRY		1		24	QUEBEC	RC	FRENCH	LUMBERMAN	083	A	1	12
CORMICHAEL	JAMES				89	SCOTLAND	CS	SCOTCH	F	082	A		33
CORNEY	FRANCIS		1		6	US	RC	IRISH		085	E		8
CORNEY	JOHN		1		14	US	RC	IRISH	F	085	E		8
CORNFORTH	HENRY				45	ENGLAND	CE	ENGLISH	STORE KEEPER	085	D		9
CORNWELL	JAMES				33	US	CE	ENGLISH	LUMBERMAN	085	H		22
CORO	LOUIS		1		19	QUE	RC	FRENCH	LAB	081	B		18
CORO	WILLIAM		1		15	QUE	RC	FRENCH	SERVANT	081	A	2	50
CORRIER	JAMES				47	QUE	RC	FRENCH	FARMER	082	I		50
CORRIGAN	CATHERINE			1	50	IRELAND	CE	IRISH		085	H		19
CORRIGAN	JAMES		1		41	QUE	CE	SCOTCH	FARM LAB	082	C	1	61
CORRIGAN	MARTIN				32	IRELAND	RC	IRISH	F	083	C		14
CORRIGAN	MARY		1	1	23	IRELAND	RC	IRISH		081	C		51
CORRIGAN	MICHAEL				28	IRELAND	RC	IRISH	F	082	H		3
CORRIGAN	ROBERT				24	QUE	CE	IRISH	F	085	H		18
CORTMASH	HENERY		1		42	QUEBEC	RC	FRENCH	LAB	083	E		2
CORTSWICK	MARTIN				48	GERMANY	LU	GERMAN	F	082	H		13
COSGROVE	ARCHD		1		26	0	CE	IRISH	FARM SERVANT	085	A		24
COSMACK	ALBERT				28	GERMANY	CE	GERMAN	FARMER	081	G	1	41
COSTELLO	CATHERINE		1	1	32	ONTARIO	RC	IRISH	SCHOOL TEACHER	081	C		19
COSTELLO	CATHERINE		1	1	19	0	RC	IRISH	SERVANT	081	K		72
COSTELLO	FRANCIS				37	0	RC	IRISH	F	081	H	1	2
COSTELLO	HANNAH		1	1	24	IRELAND	RC	IRISH	SEAMSTRESS	081	K		70
COSTELLO	JOHN				29	IRELAND	RC	IRISH	MERCHANT	081	I		3
COSTELLO	JOHN				60	IRELAND	RC	IRISH	FARMER	082	B		47
COSTELLO	JOHN				60	IRELAND	RC	IRISH	F	083	C		9
COSTELLO	RICHARD		1		21	IRELAND	RC	IRISH		081	B		67
COSTELLO	THOMAS				65	IRELAND	RC	IRISH	FARMER	082	B		46
COSTELLO	WILLIAM				47	0	RC	IRISH	F	081	H	1	2
COSTELO	FRANCIS				30	0	CE	IRISH	F	082	C	2	56
COSTELO	SAMUEL				50	IRELAND	CE	IRISH	F	082	F		11
COSTELO	THOMAS				32	IRELAND	CE	IRISH	F	082	C	2	58
COSTELO	WILLIAM				72	IRELAND	CE	IRISH	F	082	C	2	53
COSTELOW	MARY		1	1	20	0	RC	IRISH		081	B		18
COSTOLO	CATHRINE		1	1	15	ONTARIO	RC	IRISH		081	G	1	17
COSTOLO	RICHARD		2		1	0	CE			082	F		D
COSTOLO	WILLIAM				64	IRELAND	RC	IRISH	BLACKSMITH	081	G	1	4
COTE	ANTOINE				55	QUE	RC	FRENCH	FARMER	089	A		52
COTE	GRIGOIRE				35	QUE	RC	FRENCH	LUMBERMAN	081	K		63
COTHIER	JAMES		1		25	ENGLAND	CE	ENGLISH	COPPER SMELTER	089	A		46
COUCHE	NANCY			1	40	RED RIVER	RC	INDIAN		090	F		10
COUCHE	RICHARD				61	ENGLAND	WM	ENGLISH	MINER	089	A		21
COUGHLAN	JOHN				34	IRELAND	RC	IRISH	FARMER	081	G	1	15
COUGHLAN	JOHN				60	IRELAND	RC	IRISH	FARMER	081	G	1	48
COUGHLAN	PATRICK				30	IRELAND	RC	IRISH	FARMER	081	G	1	47
COUGHLAN	SIMON		2		65	IRELAND	RC		FARMER	081	G	1	D
COUGHLAN	THOMAS				35	IRELAND	RC	IRISH	FARMER	081	G	1	38
COUGHLIN	JOHN				21	ONTARIO	RC	IRISH	BLACKSMITH	081	G	1	17
COUGHLIN	MATTHIAS				24	ONTARIO	RC	IRISH	FARMER	081	G	1	20
COUGHLIN	THOMAS				60	IRELAND	RC	IRISH	FARMER	083	A	1	9
COULSON	JOHN				37	IRELAND	CE	IRISH	F	085	C		11
COULTER	DAVID				32	0	CE	IRISH	MINER	089	A		31
COULTER	JAMES				22	0	WM	IRISH	BLACKSMITH	086	A	1	32
COULTER	JOHN	YOUNG			27	0	CE	IRISH	CLERK	081	K		72
COULTER	JOSEPH				40	IRELAND	CP	IRISH	F	085	F		4
COULTER	MARGARET			1	39	0	PS	SCOTCH	SEAMSTRESS	081	K		62
COULTER	ROBERT				44	IRELAND	WM	IRISH	F	085	E		11
COURT	FREDRICK				51	GERMANY	LU	GERMAN	FARMER	082	I		63
COURT	FREDRICK				29	GERMANY	LU	GERMAN	FARMER	082	I		78
COUSIN	ISABELLA		1	1	3	0	WM	IRISH		081	E		20
COUSINS	JOHN				54	ENGLAND	CE	ENGLISH	CUSTOMS OFFICER	090	F		21
COUZNER	JOHN		1		18	0	CE	ENGLISH	BOOKKEEPER	082	E		30
COVERDALE	RICHARD				38	ENGLAND	CE	ENGLISH	FARMER	089	B		21
COVNER	FRANCIS				39	IRELAND	RC	IRISH	CARPENTER	082	B		12
COWAN	ALEXANDER				65	SCOTLAND	CS	SCOTCH	WEAVER	081	A	1	54
COWAN	ALEXANDER		1		40	IRELAND	PS	IRISH	F	085	C		4
COWAN	DONALD		1		8	0	EM	SCOTCH		085	I		16

SURNAME	NAME1	NAME2	STRAY	SEX	AGE	BIRTHPL	RELIGION	ORIGIN	OCCUP	DIST	SUB_DIST	DIV	PAGE
COWAN	MARGARET		1	1	15	0	CS	ENGLISH	SERVANT	085	I		15
COWAN	SARAH		1	1	10	0	EM	SCOTCH		085	I		16
COWARD	WILLIAM				39	ENGLAND	CE	ENGLISH	LAB	081	A	2	11
COWBIE	MARTON		1		30	GERMANY	LU	GERMAN	LABOURER	082	D		22
COWDREY	BETCY			1	34	ONTARIO	EM	ENGLISH		082	A		11
COWDRIE	GEORGE				45	0	WM	ENGLISH	F	082	C	2	16
COWDRY	RUTH		2	1	11	ONTARIO	EM			082	A		D
COWIE	JOHN				40	SCOTLAND	CP	SCOTCH	F	082	C	2	20
COX	HUGH				48	IRELAND	CE	IRISH	F	085	A		11
COX	JAMES				29	ENGLAND	WM	ENGLISH	CARPENTER	081	B		79
COX	JAMES				32	IRELAND	CE	IRISH	F	081	E		10
COX	MATILDA		1	1	21	QUE	WM	ENGLISH	SERVANT	082	E		58
COX	MICHAEL				31	IRELAND	CE	IRISH	F	081	K		5
COX	WILLIAM				47	IRELAND	PR	IRISH	F	085	A		14
COXFORD	JOHN				40	ENGLAND	ME	ENGLISH	FARMER	082	D		6
COYNE	JOHN				28	0	RC	IRISH	FARMER	081	F		24
COYNE	JOHN				66	ENGLAND	RC	IRISH	F	081	K		43
COYNE	PATRICK				46	IRELAND	RC	IRISH	F	083	C		3
COYNE	PHINEUS				40	IRELAND	RC	IRISH	F	081	K		49
COYOH	HYACINTH				49	QUE	RC	FRENCH	LAB	081	B		17
COZETTD	CHRISTIAN				49	GERMANY	LU	GERMAN	FARMER	082	I		68
CRAIG	DONALD				32	QUE	CE	SCOTCH	AGENT	081	B		17
CRAIG	GEORGE				45	SCOTLAND	CP	SCOTCH	BAKER	081	B		49
CRAIG	LAVINA		1	1	12	0	RC	IRISH		081	B		57
CRAIG	WILLIAM		1		30	0	CS	SCOTCH	SCHOOL TEACHER	081	A	1	60
CRAM	GEORGE		1		28	US	BA	IRISH	FISHERMAN	090	A		6
CRAM	JAMES				53	SCOTLAND	CP	SCOTCH	F	081	A	1	9
CRAM	PETTER				44	0	RP	SCOTCH	LAB	081	H	1	5
CRAM	WILLIAM				60	SCOTLAND	CP	SCOTCH	CARPENTER	081	A	1	10
CRANE	CHARLOTTE		1	1	1	0	CS	ENGLISH		081	A	1	34
CRANE	EDWARD		1		40	ENGLAND	CE	ENGLISH	F	081	A	1	33
CRANE	ELIZABETH		1	1	38	0	CS	IRISH		081	A	1	34
CRANE	ISABELLA		1	1	3	0	CS	ENGLISH		081	A	1	34
CRANE	JOHN		1		9	0	CS	ENGLISH		081	A	1	34
CRANE	MARY	ANN	1	1	5	0	CS	ENGLISH		081	A	1	34
CRANSTON	J	G			37	UNITED STATES	CP	SCOTCH	PHYSICIAN	081	B		69
CRATTON	WILLIAM		1		83	SCOTLAND	PS	SCOTCH		082	G		62
CRAWFORD	ARCHIBALD				44	IRELAND	WM	IRISH	MINE LABOURER	089	A		21
CRAWFORD	DAVID				45	SCOTLAND	PS	SCOTCH	FARMER	089	B		20
CRAWFORD	JOHN	W			52	IRELAND	CS	IRISH	F & MERCHANT	082	A		47
CRAWFORD	ROBERT				36	SCOTLAND	PS	SCOTCH	CHIEF TRADER H B CO	090	E		1
CRAWFORD	THOMAS				63	IRELAND	RC	IRISH	F	081	K		59
CRAWFORD	WILLIAM				60	IRELAND	EM	IRISH	F	085	D		28
CREBE	ALFRED				37	ENGLAND	WM	ENGLISH	MINER	089	A		5
CREBO	PHILIP		1		29	ENGLAND	CE	ENGLISH	MINER	089	A		37
CREBO	WILLIAM				44	ENGLAND	CE	ENGLISH	BLACKSMITH	089	A		42
CREELEY	JOHN				38	IRELAND	RC	IRISH	F	082	L		6
CREHAN	CARL				58	PRUSSIA	CP	GERMAN	FARMER	082	B		54
CREIGHTON	ADAM				40	ENGLAND	CE	SCOTCH	SAWYER	081	B		36
CREIGHTON	HERBERT		2		1	0	CE			081	B		D
CREOR	ANN		2	1	11	GERMAN	LU			082	G		D
CREOR	CHRISTIANA				38	GERMANY	LU	GERMAN	F	082	G		92
CRESOLL	JOHNNY				35	PRUSSIA	RC	PRUSSIAN	FARMER	083	A	1	5
CRESOR	GEORGE				40	ENGLAND	PM	ENGLISH	F	085	D		26
CRESOR	HENRY				40	ENGLAND	CE	ENGLISH	F	085	D		23
CRESOR	JOHN				34	ENGLAND	CE	ENGLISH	F	085	D		27
CRESOR	MARIA		2	1	32	ENGLAND	CE	ENGLISH		085	D		D
CRETON	JOHN				24	0	CP	SCOTCH	LAB	081	I		13
CREUR	DANIEL				65	GERMANY	LU	GERMAN	L	082	G		14
CRIAS	FRANNS		1		29	GERMANY	RC	GERMAN	LABOURER	082	D		17
CRICKLAND	WM				42	IRELAND	CE	IRISH	F	085	J		12
CRISTFIELD	CHARLES		1		26	ENGLAND	CE	ENGLISH	CLERK	085	F		5
CROBAR	THOMAS				39	ONT	WM	GERMAN	FARMER	082	I		73
CROCK	JOHN				33	GERMANY	LU	GERMAN	FARMER	082	I		53
CROMACK	M	H	1		22	0	CE	ENGLISH	SPINNER	081	B		15
CRONE	JOHN				38	GERMANY	LU	GERMAN	F	082	G		16
CROSIER	ANN		1	1	2	ONT	CP	IRISH		082	I		3
CROSIER	ARCHIBALD		1		8	ONT	CP	IRISH		082	I		3
CROSIER	JOHN				40	IRELAND	CE	IRISH	F	081	J	1	43
CROSIER	MARGRET		1	1	5	ONT	CP	IRISH		082	I		3
CROSIER	MARTHA		1	1	14	QUE	RP	IRISH		082	I		2
CROSIER	MARY	JANE	1	1	12	ONT	CP	IRISH		082	I		3
CROSIER	SARIAH		1	1	10	ONT	CP	IRISH		082	I		3
CROSKERY	JAMES				42	0	CP	IRISH	F	082	C	2	28
CROTTE	JOSEPH				33	QUE	RC	FRENCH	RAFTSMAN	082	E		12
CROW	LIGGETT			1	50	0	RC	INDIAN		090	F		6
CROW	WILLIAM				45	RED RIVER	RC	INDIAN	HUNTER	090	F		11
CROWN	ROBERT	STEVEN	2			0		CP		082	C	2	D
CROZIER	ANDREW				44	IRELAND	CE	IRISH	F	081	H	1	10
CROZIER	CHRISTOPHER				37	IRELAND	EM	IRISH	F	082	A		64
CROZIER	CHRISTOPHER				75	IRELAND	CE	IRISH	F	082	A		71
CROZIER	MARGT		1	1	40	IRELAND	CP	IRISH	SERVANT	082	E		28
CROZIER	OCTAVE				50	IRELAND	CP	IRISH	F	082	C	2	26
CROZIER	ROLAND				30	IRELAND	CE	IRISH	F	082	A		71
CRUER	FRANCIS		1		17	GERMANY	LU	GERMAN	F	082	G		61
CRUER	JOHN				41	GERMANY	WM	GERMAN	FARMER	082	G		13
CRUER	MARY		1	1	13	GERMANY	LU	GERMAN		082	G		61
CRUER	WILLIAM				56	GERMANY	PR	GERMAN	L	082	G		16
CRUGER	JOHN				50	PRUSSIA	CE	GERMAN	FARMER	082	B		56
CUDDY	MARGRET			1	50	IRELAND	RC	IRISH		081	G	1	1
CUDDY	MICHAEL				24	IRELAND	RC	IRISH	FARMER	081	G	1	44
CUESLA	STEPHEN				36	RED RIVER	RC	FRENCH	LUMBERMAN	088	C		9
CUISSON	EXAVIA				45	QUE	RC	FRENCH	FARMER	084	E		2
CULAS	ANTHONY				60	PRUSSIA	RC	PRUSSIAN	F	081	J	1	12
CULBERTSON	BOLTON				36	ONT	PS	IRISH	F	081	J	1	23
CULBERTSON	THOMAS				38	IRELAND	CE	IRISH	HOTELKEEPER	082	B		58
CULHANE	DAN'L				60	IRELAND	RC	IRISH	F	081	C		9
CULHANE	DANIEL				28	IRELAND	RC	IRISH	F	081	C		3
CULHANE	DANIEL				50	IRELAND	RC	IRISH	F	081	C		17
CULHANE	DANIEL	SENR			60	IRELAND	RC	IRISH	F	081	C		3
CULHANE	JOHN				60	IRELAND	RC	IRISH	FARMER	081	G	2	11
CULL	JOHN				68	IRELAND	RC	IRISH	FARMER	081	G	1	7
CULL	JOHN				35	IRELAND	RC	IRISH	FARMER	081	G	1	26
CULL	MICHAEL				33	IRELAND	RC	IRISH	F	083	C		11
CULL	THOMAS				27	IRELAND	RC	IRISH	FARMER	081	G	1	13
CULL	WILLIAM				32	IRELAND	RC	IRISH	FARMER	081	G	1	13

SURNAME	NAME1	NAME2	STRAY	SEX	AGE	BIRTHPL	RELIGION	ORIGIN	OCCUP	DIST	SUB_DIST	DIV	PAGE
CULLEN	ELIZA			1	16	0	PS	SCOTCH		086	C	1	2
CULLIGAN	MICHAEL		2		17	IRELAND	RC		F	082	B		D
CULLIGAN	PATRICK				40	IRELAND	RC	IRISH	FARMER	082	B		65
CULLIS	RICHARD				48	ENGLAND	WM	ENGLISH	BUTCHER	089	A		8
CULLY	THOMAS				41	ONT	RC	IRISH	FARMER	082	I		33
CUMBER	JOHN		1		39	ENGLAND	CE	ENGLISH	LAB	081	B		54
CUMING	MICHEAL		1		22	0	RC	IRISH	LAB	082	K	1	12
CUMMING	ALEXR				48	SCOTLAND	PS	SCOTCH	F	085	J		23
CUMMING	JAMES				28	ONTARIO	CS	SCOTCH	F	082	A		57
CUMMINGS	JAMES				28	0	CE	SCOTCH	FUR TRADER	088	B		14
CUNNIGHAM	ELIZABETH		1	1	20	0	EM	IRISH	SERVANT	081	A	1	19
CUNNINGHAM	ANN		1	1	60	IRELAND	CE	IRISH		081	A	1	28
CUNNINGHAM	ANNIE		2	1		ONT	RC			081	J	1	D
CUNNINGHAM	ANNIE	ISABELLA	1	1	7	0	CE	IRISH		081	A	1	28
CUNNINGHAM	JOHN				28	IRELAND	CE	IRISH	F	081	A	1	28
CUNNINGHAM	JOHN				39	IRELAND	RC	IRISH	MERCHANT	082	E		4
CUNNINGHAM	MICHAEL				40	IRELAND	RC	LIRISH	F	081	J	1	27
CUNNINGHAM	MICHAEL		1		30	IRELAND	RC	IRISH	SHANTYMAN	084	B		3
CUNNINGHAM	PATRICK				55	IRELAND	RC	IRISH		081	B		65
CUNNINGHAM	THOS				34	IRELAND	RC	IRISH	F	081	J	1	57
CUNNINGHAM	TIMOTHY				34	IRELAND	RC	IRISH	F	081	J	1	91
CUNNINGHAM	WILLIAM				60	IRELAND	RC	IRISH	FARMER	081	D		24
CUOR	MARTIN				44	GERMANY	LU	GERMAN	F	082	G		85
CURLEY	HUE				50	IRELAND	RC	IRISH	F	082	F		35
CURLEY	LAWRENCE				63	IRELAND	RC	IRISH	F	081	K		27
CURNANE	JOHN				60	IRELAND	RC	IRISH	FARMER	081	D		12
CURRIE	THOMAS				18	0	CP	SCOTCH	SERVANT	085	E		28
CURRIER	FRANCIS		1		28	IRELAND	RC	IRISH	HOTEL KEEPER	083	C		6
CURRY	ABRAHAM				30	ONT	WM	IRISH	FARMER	082	I		27
CURRY	ERASTUS				36	0	WM	IRISH	CLERGYMAN	089	B		4
CURRY	FRANCES				40	IRELAND	RC	IRISH	F	081	J	1	62
CURRY	GEORGE				74	0	WM	IRISH	FRAMER	082	D		29
CURRY	GEORGE	JR			37	0	WM	IRISH	FARMER	082	D		29
CURRY	JAMES				67	IRELAND	RC	IRISH	F	081	J	1	64
CURRY	JOHN				45	IRELAND	RC	IRISH	F	081	J	1	64
CURRY	JOHN				46	0	WM	IRISH	F	082	C	1	16
CURRY	THOMAS				70	IRELAND	RC	IRISH	F	081	K		21
CURRY	WILLIAM				28	0	WM	SCOTCH	F	082	C	2	45
CURTAIN	MORRIS		1		40	IRELAND	RC	IRISH	LAB	081	J	2	4
CURTIN	PATRICK				60	IRELAND	RC	IRISH	F	081	J	1	4
CURTIS	JAMES				46	IRELAND	CP	IRISH	F	081	J	1	42
CUSAC	ANDREW		1		20	0	RC	IRISH		086	B		1
CUSAS	JOHN		1		23	0	RC	IRISH		086	B		1
CUSH	CHARLES				31	GERMANY	RC	GERMAN	FARMER	082	I		46
CUSHING	ARTHUR	M	1		28	QUE	CE	ENGLISH	SHANTY CLERK	082	E		20
CUSHING	E	J			44	QUE	CE	ENGLISH	HOTEL KEEPER	082	E		19
CUSINA	LOUIS				22	0	RC	FRENCH	LAB	081	I		34
CUTCHUCK	PETER				41	GERMANY	RC	GERMAN	F	082	G		81
CUTHBERT	JAMES				58	SCOT	RP	SCOTCH	SHOEMAKER	085	A		28
CUTHBERT	JAMES	EVANS			46	IRELAND	CS	IRISH	STOREKEEPER	081	A	1	11
CUTHBERT	WILLIAM		2		2	0	CS					1	D
CUYLER	STEPHEN				51	0	WM	DUTCH	MILLWRIGHT	085	B		22
CUZINO	LOUIS				60	QUE	RC	FRENCH	RAFTSMAN	082	E		12
CWISI	JOHN				50	GERMANY	CE	GERMAN	F	081	C		32
DABUCK	INCAH				46	POLAND	RC	POLISH	LAB	081	I		36
DACEY	DUNCAN		1		29	0	CP	SCOTCH	SEWING MACHINE AGENT	081	A	1	20
DACLT	INSCHINIE		1	1		0	RC	IRISH		081	I		43
DAGENAIS									SEE DASHENA	081	B		14
DAGENAS	JOSEPH				60	0	RC	FRENCH	F	082	K	1	16
DAGG	THOMAS				40	0	CE	IRISH	F	081	H	2	34
DAILEY	ELLEN			1	40	IRELAND	RC	IRISH		082	A		80
DAILEY	PETER		1		25	IRELAND	RC	IRISH	LABOURER	088	A		7
DAILEY	ROBERT				26	IRELAND	CP	IRISH	F	085	I		44
DAILY	PATRICK		1		22	QUEBEC	RC	IRISH	CLERK	084	C		4
DAIN	JOHN				47	IRELAND	CE	IRISH	F	081	H	1	11
DAISEY	DANIEL				30	IRELAND	RC	IRISH	F	081	J	1	5
DALE	ESTER		1	1	25	IRELAND	CE	IRISH		082	E		33
DALE	JOHN		1			0	CE	IRISH		082	E		33
DALE	SAMUEL		1		26	IRELAND	CE	IRISH	LABOURER	082	E		33
DALEY	JOHN				35	IRELAND	RC	IRISH	BLACKSMITH	089	A		42
DALEY	MICHAEL				36	IRELAND	RC	IRISH	FARMER	081	G	1	17
DALGLESH	AMY		2	1	14	ONT	CP			081	J	1	D
DALGLISH	PETER				50	SCOTLAND	CP	SCOTCH	F	081	J	1	39
DALY	JAMES				25	ONTARIO	RC	IRISH	FARMER	082	B		19
DALY	JAMES				40	IRELAND	RC	IRISH	F	083	C		14
DALY	JOSEPH				45	IRELAND	RC	IRISH	FARMER	082	B		11
DALY	MICHAEL				46	IRELAND	RC	IRISH	F	081	K		38
DALY	PATRICK				30	ONTARIO	RC	IRISH	FARMER	082	B		17
DALY	STEVEN				60	IRELAND	RC	IRISH	FARMER	082	B		17
DALY	THOMAS				60	IRELAND	RC	IRISH	FARMER	082	B		27
DALY	THOMAS				25	IRELAND	RC	IRISH	F	083	C		9
DANE	PAUL				60	IRELAND	CE	IRISH	F	085	C		27
DANIAL	PETER		1		36	SWEDEN	LU	SWEDISH	LABOURER	084	G	1	1
DANIELS	RICHARD				29	ENGLAND	CE	ENGLISH	TINSMITH	085	I		5
DARCEY	JOSEPH		1		38	IRELAND	RC	IRISH		082	E		17
DARGAS	JOSEPH				35	PRUSSIA	RC	PRUSSIAN	FARMER	083	A	1	3
DARIL	BENJAMIN		1		24	QUE	RC	FRENCH	RAFTSMAN	084	D		8
DARINK	HENRYETTA		1	1	65	GERMANY	LU	GERMAN		082	I		18
DARLING	JAMES				21	SCOTLAND	CS	SCOTCH	F	085	L		12
DARLING	JOHN				45	SCOTLAND	CS	SCOTCH	F	085	L		11
DARLING	MARGARET		1	1	19	0	CS	SCOTCH	F	085	L		11
DARMADY	JAMES				55	IRELAND	RC	IRISH	F	083	C		9
DART	JOHN		1		17	0	PM	ENGLISH	LUMBERMAN	086	B		2
DARWIN	CHARLES	A			34	UNITED STATES	CE	GERMAN	WATCHMAKER	081	B		72
DASANSEAU	AMABLE		1		22	QUE	RC	FRENCH	LUMBERMAN	088	B		18
DASHENA	DUNCAN				30	QUE	RC	FRENCH	COOPER	081	B		14
DASHNEAU	GEORGE				46	QUEBEC	RC	FRENCH	COOPER	082	B		34
DASHNEY	FRANCIS				32	QUE	RC	FRENCH	F	081	E		21
DAUPHINE	MARIE		1	1	60	0	RC	FRENCH	WORK WOMAN	089	B		16
DAUSSA	PAUL				59	0	RC	FRENCH	FISHERMAN	089	A		61
DAVEAU	HYACINTH				66	QUE	RC	FRENCH	BOAT MAN	089	B		26
DAVEAU	HYACINTHE				38	0	RC	FRENCH	BOATMAN	089	B		13
DAVEAU	JOSEPH				40	0	RC	FRENCH	BOATMAN	089	B		13
DAVID	AUGUST				53	PRUSSIA	PR	PRUSSIAN	F	085	A		8
DAVID	DENNIS		1		35	QUEBEC	RC	FRENCH	LAB	083	E		2
DAVIDSON	GEORGE		1		45	IRELAND	RC	IRISH	LAB	082	A		45

SURNAME	NAME1	NAME2	STRAY	SEX	AGE	BIRTHPL	RELIGION	ORIGIN	OCCUP	DIST	SUB_DIST	DIV	PAGE
DAVIDSON	JAMES				60	IRELAND	RC	IRISH	FARMER	082	D		18
DAVIDSON	JOHN				55	SCOTLAND	PS	SCOTCH	INDIAN AGENT	089	B		10
DAVIDSON	JOSEPH		1		17	0	RC	SCOTCH		084	D		8
DAVIDSON	WILLIAM				41	IRELAND	CS	IRISH	F	081	K		22
DAVIS	ANN		1	1	22	0	CE	ENGLISH		082	C	2	17
DAVIS	DAVID				76	ENGLAND	CE	ENGLISH	F	085	C		25
DAVIS	EDWARD				77	IRELAND	CE	IRISH	F	082	G		27
DAVIS	HENERY				41	IRELAND	CE	IRISH	F	082	F		40
DAVIS	JAMES		1		34	IRELAND	CE	IRISH	CARPENTER	081	G	1	20
DAVIS	JAMES				46	0	CE	IRISH	F	085	B		16
DAVIS	JOHN		1		15	0	CE	IRISH	LAB	081	K		14
DAVIS	RICHARD				40	IRELAND	CE	IRISH	FARMER	082	I		41
DAVIS	RICHD		1		57	ENGLAND	CE	ENGLISH	LABOURER	082	E		14
DAVIS	ROSAN		1	1	19	0	RC	IRISH	SERVANT	081	A	2	17
DAVIS	RUTH		1	1	46	ENGLAND	CE	ENGLISH		082	C	2	17
DAVIS	THOMAS				45	ENGLAND	CE	ENGLISH	F	085	C		23
DAVIS	WILLIAM				58	IRELAND	CE	ENGLISH	F	082	G		27
DAVIS	WILLIAM	HENRY			44	0	RC	IRISH	TAILOR	081	K		73
DAVISON	ALBERTI		1	1	3	0	EM	SCOTCH		085	I		31
DAVISON	JAMES				45	IRELAND	CP	IRISH	F	082	C	2	22
DAVISON	MARY	ANNE	1	1	57	IRELAND	PS	IRISH		082	D		23
DAVISON	MARY	ANNE	1	1	17	QUE	PS	IRISH		082	D		23
DAVISON	ROBERT				50	IRELAND	WM	IRISH	F	082	C	2	35
DAVISON	WILLIAM				36	ENGLAND	CE	ENGLISH	F	085	D		15
DAWSAY	PETER				42	QUE	RC	FRENCH	CARPENTER	081	B		37
DAWSON	ABRAM				53	IRELAND	EM	IRISH	CLERGYMAN	082	G		20
DAWSON	JAMES				61	ENGLAND	PM	ENGLISH	F	085	D		21
DAWSON	THOMAS	J	1		22	WALES	CE	ENGLISH	SERVANT	085	E		1
DAWSON	WILLIAM				40	ENGLAND	CE	ENGLISH	F	085	D		25
DAY	JOHN				44	ENGLAND	WM	ENGLISH	FARMER	089	A		49
DAY	THOMAS				42	ENGLAND	WM	ENGLISH	SHOEMAKER	085	I		9
DE BELENHARD	JOHN				37	SCOTLAND	CE	SCOTCH	F	085	J		24
DE LA RONDE	CATHARINE			1	32	ONTARIO	RC	FRENCH		090	E		22
DE LA RONDE	CHARLES	F			64	HUDSON'S BAY	RC	FRENCH	POST MASTER	090	E		1
DE LA RONDE	HENRY				35	ONTARIO	RC	FRENCH	CLERK	090	E		1
DEACON	JOHN				48	0	WM	IRISH	COUNTY JUDGE	082	E		18
DEACON	THOMAS				38	0	WM	IRISH	BARRISTER	082	E		10
DEALY	JOSEPH				40	IRELAND	RC	IRISH	FARMER	081	G	2	5
DEALY	MARTIN				40	IRELAND	RC	IRISH	FARMER	081	G	2	11
DEAN	ELIZA		1	1	18	ENGLAND	CE	ENGLISH	SERVANT	085	I		4
DEAN	THOS				46	IRELAND	PS	IRISH	BLACKSMITH	082	E		27
DEAR	WILLIAM				48	ENGLAND	CE	ENGLISH	F	086	A	1	13
DECHAMP	ALPHONSE		2		18	0	RC		VOYAGEUR	090	F		D
DECHAMP	JOSEPH				35	0	RC	FRENCH	LAB	090	F		7
DECHAMP	LOUISA		2	1	35	0	RC			090	F		D
DECHAMP	MICHAEL				33	0	RC	FRENCH	LAB	090	F		6
DECOTTS	ALEXANDER		1		28	QUE	RC	FRENCH	LAB	090	F		19
DEFERGNE	PERE		1		79	QUE	RC	FRENCH		082	E		73
DEGERDO	MOSES				50	0	RC	FRENCH	F	082	F		18
DEHAITE	CIRILLE		1		23	QUE	RC	FRENCH	LUMBERMAN	088	B		18
DEHIE	PAUL		1		30	QUEBEC	RC	FRENCH	SHANTYMAN	084	C		3
DEJARDIN	JOHN				60	QUEBEC	RC	FRENCH	LUMBERER	081	C		36
DEKANATTER	CHRISTOPHER				53	PRUSSIA	LU	PRUSSIAN	CARPENTER	090	D		2
DELAHAY	ROBT				43	IRELAND	WM	IRISH	MERCHANT	082	E		8
DELANEY	DANIEL				46	IRELAND	RC	IRISH	F	083	C		10
DELANEY	THOMAS				34	IRELAND	RC	IRISH		081	A	2	4
DELANY	JOHN		1		25	0	RC	IRISH	FARM LABOURER	081	K		64
DELANY	JULIA			1	54	IRELAND	RC	IRISH		081	F		24
DELARE	SEVARE				36	QUE	RC	FRENCH	F	081	K		36
DELARGE	BENJAMIN				48	QUE	ME	FRENCH	F	081	C		29
DELARGE	MARY		2	1		ONT	WM			081	C		D
DELBECK	BATICE		1		96	ONT	RC	FRENCH	F	082	C	2	39
DELBECK	OLISEW				37	QUE	RC	IRISH	LAB	082	C	2	39
DELEBOUGH	JOSEPH				33	ONT	EM	FRENCH	F	082	A		80
DELEHAY	JOHN				21	IRELAND	WM	IRISH	MERCHANT	082	A		49
DELIBOUGH	JACOB		1		28	ONT	EM	FRENCH	F	082	A		79
DELIBOUGH	MARY	ANN		1	62	ONT	EM			082	A		79
DELIGA	EMILY		1	1	18	QUEBEC	RC	FRENCH		081	G	1	45
DELONIE	JOSEPH				35	0	RC	FRENCH	FARMER	081	D		22
DELORIA			2			0	RC			081	D		D
DELORME	BAPTIST				49	QUE	RC	FRENCH	HEWER	082	G		56
DELORYIA	OLIVER				60	QUE	RC	FRENCH	F	081	C		29
DELOUGHERY	MICHAEL				62	IRELAND	RC	IRISH	F	081	K		44
DELOUGHRY	JOSEPH				27	IRELAND	RC	IRISH	F	082	G		63
DELOUGHRY	THOS				60	IRELAND	RC	IRISH	F	082	G		71
DEMENSKY	MICHAEL				40	PRUSSIA	RC	PRUSSIAN	FARMER	083	A	1	16
DEMERRAH	GUSTAVAS				41	0	RC	FRENCH	F	086	A	1	32
DEMISON	OLIVER		1		49	QUEBEC	RC	FRENCH	SHOEMAKER	081	C		51
DEMPSEY	THOS				50	IRELAND	RC	IRISH	F	081	C		53
DEMPSEY	WILLIAM				35	SCOTLAND	EP	IRISH	FISHERMAN	087	B	3	4
DENCIN	CHRISTY				56	GERMANY	WM	GERMAN	F	082	G		30
DENEHAN	WILLIAM				28	IRELAND	RC	IRISH	F	081	J	1	14
DENIHAN	BRIDGET		2	1		ONT	RC			081	J	1	D
DENIHAN	JAMES				55	IRELAND	RC	IRISH	F	081	J	1	62
DENIO	JOHN				45	UNITED STATES	MO	ENGLISH	COOPER	089	A		59
DENISON	FRANCIS				21	PRUSSIA	PR	PRUSSIAN	FARMER	081	G	2	2
DENISON	HENERY				27	ONTARIO	PR	ENGLISH	FARMER	081	G	2	6
DENISON	JOHN				36	QUEBEC	PR	ENGLISH	FARMER	081	G	2	6
DENISON	JOHN				70	ENGLAND	RP	ENGLISH	PRINTER	083	A	1	15
DENISON	ROBERT				30	0	WM	IRISH	BAKER	082	E		39
DENISON	WILLIAM				27	0	CE	IRISH	SHOEMAKER	082	E		38
DENISON	WM				28	0	CP	IRISH	F	082	G		67
DENLEY	WILLIAM				58	ENGLAND	CE	ENGLISH	JOINER	089	B		16
DENNIS	JAMES								SEE DUNNE	081	J	1	44
DENNIS	WILLIAM	C			24	ENGLAND	CE	ENGLISH	CARPENTER	085	H		22
DENNISON	JOHN				56	0	CP	IRISH	F	082	G		35
DENOMIE	JEAN	BAPTISTE			69	QUE	RC	FRENCH	LABOURER	089	B		6
DEPOTTE	JOSEPH		1		30	QUEBEC	RC	FRENCH	FARMER	084	C		2
DEREL	WILLIAM				32	0	CP	SCOTCH	F	082	F		14
DERENZEY	EDWARD				37	0	WM	IRISH	MERCHANT	082	A	2	25
DERGETTE	HARRIETTE		1	1	17	QUE	RC	FRENCH		082	C		57
DEROCHE	CLEOPHES				22	UNITED STATES	RC	FRENCH	BOOTS AND SHOEMAKER	081	I		22
DEROCHE	JOSEPH				45	QUE	RC	FRENCH	CARPENTER	081	I		23
DEROCHER	JOSEPH		1		20	QUEBEC	RC	FRENCH	RAFTSMAN	084	D		1
DEROSIA	THEOPPILE				41	0	RC	FRENCH	LAB	082	C	1	31
DEROSIE	EDWARD				37	0	RC	FRENCH	F	082	H		6

SURNAME	NAME1	NAME2	STRAY	SEX	AGE	BIRTHPL	RELIGION	ORIGIN	OCCUP	DIST	SUB_DIST	DIV	PAGE
DEROSIE	LOOIE				38	QUE	RC	FRENCH	FARMER	082	D		18
DERRING	CHAS				26	GERMANY	EV	GERMAN	F	082	G		93
DERRING	WILLIAM				40	GERMANY	EV	GERMAN	F	082	G		86
DESCHAMPS	PIERRE				42	ONTARIO	RC	FRENCH	INDIAN TRADER	090	E		22
DESERMONT	FRANCIS				42	QUEBEC	RC	FRENCH	FARMER	084	B		4
DESJARDIN	ABARE						NG		SEE DEGERDO	082	F		16
DESJARDIN	MOISE						NG		SEE DEGERDO	082	F		18
DESJARDINE	GEDEON				22	QUE	RC	FRENCH	BLACKSMITH	082	E		37
DESJARDINS	ABARE				41	0	RC	FRENCH	F	082	F		16
DESLOGES	J	A	1		24	QUE	RC	FRENCH	MEDICAL DOCTOR	082	E		48
DESMOULINS	ISADOR				50	QUE	RC	FRENCH	LABOURER	090	C		3
DESONNIA	FRANCIS				40	QUE	RC	FRENCH	LAB	081	B		29
DESORMIA	JOSEPH				62	QUE	RC	FRENCH	CASTER	081	B		30
DESORMIA	JOSEPH				37	QUE	RC	FRENCH	LABORER	081	B		30
DETWILLER	JOHN				26	0	WM	SCOTCH	BLACKSMITH	086	C	1	2
DEUKIS	MICHAEL				45	0	RC	INDIAN	TRADER	084	I	1	7
DEUNOR	FREDERICK				47	GERMANY	CE	GERMAN	LAB	081	B		60
DEVERS	ROBERT		1		24	ENGLAND	RC	ENGLISH	CLERK	088	B		3
DEVIN	HUGH				40	0	RC	IRISH	LABOURER	082	D		28
DEVINE	ANDREW				54	IRELAND	RC	IRISH	F	081	H	1	21
DEVINE	FELIX				49	IRELAND	RC	IRISH	MERCHANT	081	I		8
DEVINE	JAMES				35	ONTARIO	RC	IRISH	FARMER	082	B		29
DEVINE	JOHN				40	IRELAND	RC	IRISH	F	081	H	1	20
DEVINE	MATTHEW				56	IRELAND	RC	IRISH	CORDONIER	081	C		51
DEVINE	MICHAEL				44	ONTARIO	RC	IRISH	FARMER	082	B		32
DEVINE	PHILIP				43	ONTARIO	RC	IRISH	F	083	C		18
DEVINE	ROBERT				45	IRELAND	RC	IRISH	FARMER	081	G	1	9
DEVINE	SOLOMON	SNR			46	QUE	CE	IRISH	F	082	J		1
DEVINE	THOMAS		2		1	0	CE			082	J		D
DEVINE	WILLIAM				58	ENGLAND	RC	IRISH	FARMER	081	G	1	35
DEVLIN	CHARLES				41	0	CE	IRISH	BLACKSMITH	082	E		44
DEVLIN	HARIETT		1	1	21	0	RC	IRISH	FURRIER	082	E		41
DEVLIN	JAMES				36	ONTARIO	WM	IRISH	F	082	A		23
DEVLIN	THOS		1		28	0	BA	IRISH	AXEMAKER	082	E		73
DEWAR	DANIEL				40	QUEBEC	CP	SCOTTISH	BLACKSMITH	082	B		57
DEWAR	DONALD				42	SCOTLAND	CP	SCOTCH		081	A	2	52
DEWAR	DUNCAN						NG		SEE DURE	081	A	2	53
DEWAR	EVERS				15	ONTARIO	RC	SCOTCH	CLERK FOR DANIALE MC	081	G	1	40
DEWAR	JOHN				42	0	CP	SCOTTISH	TANNER SHOEMAKER	082	E		46
DICK	ANDREW				39	SCOTLAND	PS	SCOTCH	TRADER	090	C		2
DICK	DAVID				43	SCOTLAND	FK	SCOTCH	F	081	K		8
DICKER	JOHN	L			24	ENGLAND	PR	ENGLISH	F	085	A		9
DICKIE	ROBERT				50	SCOTLAND	CS	SCOTCH	F	081	J	1	34
DICKINSON	GEORGE		1		25	ONTARIO	CE	ENGLISH	PHYSICIAN	084	C		5
DICKINSON	THOMAS				39	ENGLAND	CE	ENGLISH	F	086	A	1	18
DICKS	MARTHA		1	1	78	ENGLAND	CE	ENGLISH		085	I		36
DICKSON	ADAM				28	SCOTLAND	CP	SCOTCH	F	082	C	1	57
DICKSON	EMMA		1	1	12	0	CE	SCOTCH		089	B		5
DICKSON	GEORGE				57	ENGLAND	RC	ENGLISH	COOPER	082	E		50
DICKSON	JAMES				63	SCOTLAND	CP	SCOTCH	F	081	A	1	51
DICKSON	JAMES				51	SCOTLAND	CP	SCOTCH	F	082	C	1	61
DICKSON	JAMES	B			36	0	PS	IRISH	LUMBERMAN	082	D		2
DICKSON	JOHN				30	SCOTLAND	CP	SCOTCH	F	081	A	1	52
DICKSON	ROBERT				61	SCOTLAND	CS	SCOTCH	WEAVER	081	A	1	53
DICKSON	SYLVESTER		1		20	0	CP	IRISH	DRUGGIST APPRENTICE	082	E		9
DICKSON	THOMAS				37	SCOTLAND	CP	SCOTCH	F	082	C	1	61
DICKSON	THOMAS				50	ENGLAND	PS	ENGLISH	F	085	E		12
DICKSON	WILLIAM				23	0	CP	SCOTCH	MERCHANT	081	I		31
DICKSON	WM	W			30	0	CP	IRISH	SURGEON	082	E		26
DIDLO	HENRY				28	GERMANY	PR	GERMAN	F	085	A		9
DIERKS	CHARLES				35	GERMANY	LU	GERMAN	F	085	A		7
DIERKS	HENRY				36	PRUSSIA	LU	PRUSSIAN	F	085	A		7
DILIAM	HENRY				25	GERMANY	EV	GERMAN	EVANGELICAL CLERGYM	082	I		58
DILL	CHARLES	HENRY			45	USA	BA	ENGLISH	GENERAL MANAGER	086	C	1	11
DILL	GEORGE				24	ONTARIO	LU	HESSIAN	FARMER	084	C		4
DILL	JACOB	W			30	0	CE	GERMAN	MERCHANT	085	I		5
DILLABOUGH	J		2			0	EM			081	B		D
DILLABOUGH	WILLIAM				40	0	EM	GERMAN	LAB	081	B		24
DILLAN	JAMES				30	IRELAND	RC	IRISH	F			1	77
DILLANE	JOHANNA		1	1	13	0	RC	IRISH		081	F		10
DILLANE	MARY		1	1	15	0	RC	IRISH		081	F		15
DILLON	DENNIS				43	IRELAND	RC	IRISH	MERCHANT	081	C		38
DILLON	EDWARD				35	IRELAND	RC	IRISH	F	081	A	2	50
DILLON	JOHN				60	IRELAND	RC	IRISH	F	081	C		35
DILLON	T	H			50	IRELAND	RC	IRISH	YEOMAN	081	C		57
DILNO	ROBERT				89	0	WM	DUTCH		089	B		21
DILWORTH	ROBT				24	ENGLAND	RC	ENGLISH	F	085	A		24
DIMMA	ADAM				40	QUE	CP	SCOTCH	F	085	F		3
DINEE	ANTWINE				27	QUE	RC	FRENCH	LAB	081	I		34
DINNER	WILLIAM				47	ENGLAND	CE	ENGLISH	F	085	C		15
DINNING	WEBSTER		1		21	0	RC	UNKNOWN	LAB	085	F		5
DITCHBURN	JOHN				32	ENGLAND	CE	ENGLISH	F	085	E		9
DIVAR	WILLIAM				26	ENGLAND	WM	IRISH	F	085	I		37
DIVINE	JAMES				39	0	RC	IRISH	F	082	C	2	34
DIVINE	LYTTLE				45	0	RC	IRISH	F	082	C	2	34
DIXON	DAVID				42	SCOTLAND	CP	SCOTCH	F	085	I		25
DIXON	JAMES				33	IRELAND	BA	IRISH	TRADER	090	F		15
DIXON	JOHN				26	ONTARIO	RC	SCOTTISH	FARMER	082	B		38
DIXSON	AUGUSTUS		1		28	ENGLAND	CE	ENGLISH	YEOMAN	085	B		14
DIXSON	JAMES				54	IRELAND	CE	IRISH	F	082	L		1
DOBBIE	ROBERT				28	ONT	CS	IRISH	F	081	C		50
DOBBIN	JOHN				33	SCOTLAND	WM	SCOTCH	F	085	I		10
DOBIE	WILLIAM				32	ENGLAND	PS	SCOTCH	STORE CLERK	089	A		38
DOBRING	MARTIN		1		16	GERMANY	LU	GERMAN	WAGONMAKER AP	082	E		68
DOBRING	MARTIN						NG		SEE DUBRING	082	I		62
DOBSON	JAMES				46	ENGLAND	CE	ENGLISH	F	082	F		5
DOBSON	WILLIAM				72	ENGLAND	CE	ENGLISH	F	082	F		38
DOBSON	WILLIAM				36	0	CE	ENGLISH	F	082	F		39
DOCHARTY	GEORGE				33	0	CE	IRISH	DOOR SASH & BL MAK	081	B		15
DOCHERTY	EVEN	JAMES	1		11	0	CE	ENGLISH		082	C	2	18
DOCHERTY	OSMOND	G	1		9	0	CE	ENGLISH		082	C	2	18
DOCHERTY	SARAH	JANE	1	1	34	SCOTLAND	CE	ENGLISH		082	C	2	18
DODD	THOMAS		1		31	SCOTLAND	CP	SCOTCH	BUSHRANGER	090	D		1
DODGE	EDWARD				39	0	RC	ENGLISH	F	081	E		13
DODGE	JERRY				30	0	RC	FRENCH	FARMER	081	D		20
DODGE	JOHN				34	0	RC	FRENCH	FARMER	081	D		22

SURNAME	NAME1	NAME2	STRAY	SEX	AGE	BIRTHPL	RELIGION	ORIGIN	OCCUP	DIST	SUB_DIST	DIV	PAGE
DODGE	JOSEPH				34	O	RC	FRENCH	FARMER	081	D		23
DODGE	PETER				36	ONTARIO	RC	FRENCH	F	081	C		2
DOELY	WILLIAM				26	O	CP	SCOTCH	F	085	I		31
DOERING	HENRYGTIA						NG		SEE DARINK	082	I		18
DOHERTY	JOHN				28	IRELAND	CO	IRISH	F	085	D		14
DOHERTY	JOHN				27	IRELAND	WM	IRISH	F	085	H		2
DOHERTY	WILLIAM				49	IRELAND	CO	IRISH	F	085	D		17
DOIL	JOHN				55	IRELAND	RC	IRISH	CARPENTER	081	I		14
DOISON	PETER		1		22	O	RC	INDIAN		087	C		10
DOLAN	HONORA		2	1	6	IRELAND	RC			081	K		D
DOLAN	MICHAEL		1		21	O	RC	IRISH	SHOEMAKER	081	B		6
DOLAN	MICHAEL				60	IRELAND	RC	IRISH	WEAVER	081	G	1	32
DOLAN	PATRICK				35	IRELAND	RC	IRISH	F	081	K		18
DOLAN	PHILL		1		22	O	RC	IRISH	SHANTYMAN	082	E		18
DOLLAR	JOSEPH				40	O	RC	FRENCH	FISHERMAN	089	A		43
DOLLAR	ROBERT				45	SCOTLAND	CS	SCOTCH	IRON MOULDER	085	I		24
DOLOYON	DIMERS				51	QUEBEC	RC	FRENCH	LUMBERMAN	083	E		2
DOMBRUSKY	ADDAM				49	PRUSSIA	RC	PRUSSIAN	FARMER	083	A	1	1
DOMBRUSKY	CHRISTIE				47	PRUSSIA	RC	PRUSSIAN	FARMER	083	A	1	1
DONAHOE	THOMAS				60	IRELAND	RC	IRISH	FARMER	081	F		20
DONAHUE	ROBERT				28	IRELAND	CE	IRISH	FARMER	081	G	1	38
DONAHUY	WILLIAM		1		40	IRELAND	CE	IRISH		083	A	1	14
DONALLY	ROBERT				52	IRELAND	WM	IRISH	F	085	C		1
DONAN	MARTIN				37	GERMANY	EV	GERMAN	F	082	G		86
DONAN	MARTIN				38	GERMANY	LU	GERMAN	F	082	G		87
DONEGAN	JOSEPH				60	IRELAND	RC	IRISH	FARMER	082	B		13
DONELLY	FANNY		2	1	53	IRELAND	CE			085	C		D
DONELLY	WILLIAM				44	IRELAND	RC	IRISH	F	082	L		1
DONELLY	WILLIAM				62	IRELAND	CE	IRISH	F	085	C		4
DONEY	JOSEPH				44	ENGLAND	CE	ENGLISH	MINER	089	A		12
DONIGHA	LYDIA		1		22	O	WM	ENGLISH		086	C	1	1
DONILSON	ARCHIBALD		1		21	ONTARIO	CE	IRISH	LUMBERMAN	083	A	1	10
DONILSON	JAMES				27	ONTARIO	WM	IRISH	FARMER	083	A	1	11
DONNELLY	JOHN				65	IRELAND	RC	IRISH	F	081	H	1	2
DONNILY	HANNORA		1	1	20	IRELAND	RC	IRISH	SERVANT	081	I		27
DONOHOE	JANE		1	1	54	IRELAND	WM	IRISH		082	C	1	11
DONOHOE	JERRY				27	NEWFOUNDLAND	RC	IRISH	LUMBERER	083	C		5
DONOHOE	THOMAS				33	IRELAND	RC	IRISH	F	081	E		10
DONOHUE	TIMOTHY				45	IRELAND	RC	IRISH	F	082	H		35
DONOVAN	DANIEL				30	IRELAND	RC	IRISH	F	081	E		8
DONOVAN	JOHN				40	IRELAND	RC	IRISH	F	081	E		7
DONOVAN	PATRICK				45	IRELAND	RC	IRISH	F	081	E		7
DONOVAN	THOMAS				30	IRELAND	RC	IRISH	SHOEMAKER	081	K		62
DONOVAN	TIMOTHY				66	IRELAND	RC	IRISH	F	081	C		36
DONOVAN	WILLIAM		1		49	IRELAND	RC	IRISH	F	090	F		10
DONVO	HANORA		1	1	9	ONTARIO	RC	IRISH		082	B		26
DOOCOONAIS	(4TH CHILD)		2			O	IF			090	C		D
DOOL	JOHN				57	IRELAND	PS	SCOTCH	F	081	E		2
DOOLAN	TIMOTHY				38	IRELAND	RC	IRISH	F	081	J	2	7
DOOLY	JEREMIAH				45	IRELAND	RC	IRISH	F	081	C		33
DOOLY	PATRICK				26	IRELAND	RC	IRISH	FARMER	081	G	1	14
DOOLY	WILLIAM				70	IRELAND	RC	IRISH	F	081	C		34
DOONER	BERNARD				52	IRELAND	RC	IRISH	FARMER	081	G	1	19
DOONER	FRANCIS				65	IRELAND	RC	IRISH	MECHANIC	082	B		15
DOONER	JAMES				64	IRELAND	RC	IRISH	FARMER	081	G	1	9
DOONER	JOHN				56	IRELAND	RC	IRISH	FARMER	081	G	1	10
DOPSON	RICHARD				40	O	CE	IRISH	CARPENTER	082	E		66
DORAN	EDWARD				39	O	WM	IRISH	LABOURER	082	D		26
DORAN	JOHN				45	O	RC	IRISH	STIPENDIARY MAGISTRA	082	D		15
DORAN	WILLIAM				31	UNITED STATES	PS	IRISH	BOATSMAN	082	D		2
DORE	MACHAEL				59	IRELAND	RC	IRISH		081	A	2	4
DORIE	J		1		22	QUE	RC	FRENCH	LABOURER	088	A		7
DORION	DONALD				28	ONTARIO	RC	FRENCH	FARMER	084	B		5
DORION	JULIA		1	1	19	ONTARIO	RC	FRENCH	SERVANT	084	C		6
DORION	NARCIS				68	QUE	RC	FRENCH	LABOURER	084	E		5
DORION	NARCISSE				36	QUEBEC	RC	FRENCH	FARMER	084	B		4
DORION	STEPHEN		1		40	QUE	RC	FRENCH	LAB	081	B		74
DORION	WILLIAM		1		28	QUEBEC	RC	FRENCH	RAFTSMAN	084	D		1
DORNBUSH	ALBERT		1		31	GERMANY	RC	GERMAN	LAB	090	D		7
DOTA	ALBERT				25	POLAND	RC	POLISH	F	083	C		18
DOTY	HATTIE		1	1		US	NG			085	H		26
DOTY	JASPER		1			US	NG			085	H		26
DOTY	LEWEY		1	1	11	US	CP	SCOTCH		085	H		26
DOUBLEDEE	ELIZA		1	1	58	ENGLAND	CE	ENGLISH		089	A		57
DOUCETTE	ELMIERE			1	12	O	RC	FRENCH		084	E		1
DOUCETTE	EUGENE		1		16	O	RC	FRENCH		084	E		1
DOUCETTE	FILIMINE			1	14	O	RC	FRENCH		084	E		1
DOUGAL	PETER				35	SCOTLAND	CP	SCOTCH	WAGGONMAKER	081	I		22
DOUGHERTY	DOMINIE				48	IRELAND	RC	IRISH	TAILOR	082	G		60
DOUGHERTY	MARY		1	1	25	O	RC	IRISH	SCHOOL TEACHER	082	D		19
DOUGHERTY	SARAH		1	1	38	IRELAND	CE	IRISH		082	C	1	46
DOUGHTERY	FRANCIS				60	IRELAND	RC	IRISH	LAB	081	I		26
DOUGLAS	ADAM		1		18	O	CP	SCOTCH	LAB	081	B		84
DOUGLAS	ALEYR		1		36	SCOTLAND	CE	SCOTCH	BLACKSMITH	081	A	2	16
DOUGLAS	GEORGE				25	IRELAND	CE	IRISH	SHANTYMAN	084	B		2
DOUGLAS	JAMES				48	ENGLAND	CE	IRISH	STORE KEEPER			1	81
DOUGLAS	JAMES				60	SCOTLAND	CP	SCOTCH	F	085	B		15
DOUGLAS	JOHN				53	SCOTLAND	EM	SCOTCH	F	081	A	1	56
DOUGLAS	JOHN						NG		SEE DUGLAS	082	F		3
DOUGLAS	JOHN				68	IRELAND	PS	IRISH	FARMER	089	B		22
DOUGLAS	MARIA		1	1	16	O	EM	SCOTCH		081	B		70
DOUGLASS	JOHN				72	SCOTLAND	OP	SCOTCH	F	081	E		20
DOUGLESS	JAMES				46	IRELAND	CE	IRISH	F	082	C	2	56
DOUSETTE	CYRLLE				36	QUE	RC	FRENCH	LUMBERMAN	086	C	1	2
DOVRIER	JOHN				67	IRELAND	RC	IRISH	FARMER	082	B		1
DOW	JOHN		1		21	O	CP	SCOTCH		086	B		1
DOWELL	FRANCIS				38	ENGLAND	CE	ENGLISH	BAKER	086	A	1	31
DOWIS	WILLIAM		1		30	ENGLAND	CE	ENGLISH	CARPENTER	085	I		16
DOWLAR	EZABELLA		1	1	44	IRELAND	PR	IRISH		082	D		9
DOWLER	JOHN				41	IRELAND	CE	IRISH	F	082	K	1	19
DOWN	ROBERT				40	ENGLAND	EP	ENGLISH	MINER	090	D		1
DOWNEY	JAMES		1		49	IRELAND	RC	IRISH	ENGINEER	090	D		7
DOWNEY	JOHN		1		22	UNITED STATES	RC	IRISH	ENGINEER	090	D		9
DOWNEY	SAMUEL				30	IRELAND	CE	IRISH	F	085	B		23
DOWNEY	THOMAS				62	IRELAND	CE	IRISH	F	085	B		23
DOWSLEY	MARTIN				58	IRELAND	RC	IRISH	BRICKLAYER & CONTRAC	082	E		53

SURNAME	NAME1	NAME2	STRAY	SEX	AGE	BIRTHPL	RELIGION	ORIGIN	OCCUP	DIST	SUB_DIST	DIV	PAGE
DOWSLEY	SAMUEL				30	IRELAND	RC	IRISH	PLASTERER	082	E		54
DOWSON	ELLEN	C	1	1	58	ENGLAND	CP	ENGLISH		081	B		66
DOWSWELL	A	H			61	ENGLAND	CP	ENGLISH	SADDLER	081	B		80
DOXSTEDER	ARCHIBALD				40	QUE	CP	ENGLISH	F	085	B		22
DOYLE	ALEXANDER				30	ONTARIO	RC	IRISH	TAVERN KEEPER	084	A		4
DOYLE	CATHERINE		1	1	23	O	RC	IRISH	SERVANT	082	G		27
DOYLE	DENIS		1		70	IRELAND	RC	IRISH	F	082	H		29
DOYLE	DENIS		1		40	IRELAND	RC	IRISH	F	082	H		29
DOYLE	JAMES		1		65	IRELAND	RC	IRISH	SCHOOL TEACHER	081	F		15
DOYLE	JOHN				59	IRELAND	RC	IRISH	F	081	J	1	76
DOYLE	JOHN		1		24	CANADA	PS	SCOTCH	LAB	087	B	2	1
DOYLE	JOSEPH				30	IRELAND	RC	IRISH	FARMER	081	G	1	20
DOYLE	MARY			1	26	O	RC	IRISH	SERVANT	084	E		2
DOYLE	MORACE		1		50	IRELAND	RC	IRISH	BRICKLAYER	082	E		18
DOYLE	MRS		2	1	55	IRELAND	RC			081	J	1	D
DOYLE	ROBERT		1		1	O	RC	IRISH		082	G		27
DRAGOR	AUGUST		1		28	GERMANY	WM	GERMAN		082	I		58
DRAGOR	AUGUST		1		28	GERMANY	WM	GERMAN		082	I		58
DRAGOR	FREDRICA		1	1	67	GERMANY	WM	GERMAN	FARMER	082	I		58
DRAKE	MATILDA	EM	1	1	16	QUE	WM	ENGLISH	ADOPTED CHILD	085	I		15
DRAPER	ASAHEL				48	O	ME	IRISH	F	085	A		27
DRAPER	CHARLES				24	O	ME	ENGLISH	FARMER	085	A		26
DREYCOTT	THOMAS				45	ENGLAND	CE	ENGLISH	F	085	E		3
DRINKWINE	MICHAEL				25	QUE	RC	FRENCH	F	081	E		21
DRINNAN	JAMES				34	IRELAND	CE	IRISH	F	082	C	1	42
DRISCOLL	J	C			35	O	RC	IRISH	GROCER	081	B		5
DRISDELL	J	S			25	O	CP	SCOTCH	BLACKSMITH	081	B		70
DRIVER	WILLIAM				30	O	CE	SCOTCH	CARPENTER	089	B		41
DRIZIER	SHEVERY		1		20	QUE	RC	FRENCH	LAB	081	B		82
DROCHE	MARY		2	1		O	RC			081	I		D
DROHAN	ROBERT				24	IRELAND	RC	IRISH	FARMER	081	G	1	16
DRUVE	WILLIAM				38	GERMANY	LU	GERMAN	F	082	G		88
DRYADELE	ROBERT				48	O	CP	SCOTCH	CABINETMAKER	081	I		8
DRYSDEL	JAMES				32	SCOTLAND	CP	SCOTCH	F	082	C	2	12
DRYSDELL	GEORGE		1		16	O	CP	SCOTCH		081	A	2	25
DUBEE	GERMAIN				31	QUEBEC	RC	FRENCH	LABORER	083	G		1
DUBERVILLE	THOMAS		1		22	US	CE	ENGLISH	LAB	081	K		61
DUBERVILLE	WILLIAM				27	O	RC	FRENCH	F	081	K		39
DUBOIS	FRANCIS				89	QUE	RC	FRENCH	F	082	C	1	53
DUBOIS	JOHN				24	O	RC	INDIAN	LABOURER	090	C		2
DUBOIS	JOSEPH				29	O	RC	FRENCH	CARTER	089	B		7
DUBOIS	JOSEPH				67	O	RC	FRENCH	CLERK	090	A		4
DUBOIS	JOSEPH				68	ONT	RC	INDIAN	TRADER	090	B		7
DUBOIS	LOUIS				39	QUE	RC	FRENCH	LAB	081	I		34
DUBOIS	NANCY		2	1	8	O	RC			090	A		D
DUBOIS	NOT GIVEN		2			O	RC			090	A		D
DUBRING	MARTIN				50	GERMANY	LU	GERMAN	FARMER	082	I		62
DUBRY	EDWARD				48	QUE	RC	FRENCH	LUMBERER	081	D		21
DUCEAT	LOUIS		1		23	QUE	RC	FRENCH	LUMBERMAN	088	B		18
DUCEAT	THEODORE		1		21	QUE	RC	FRENCH	LUMBERMAN	088	B		18
DUCHARME	MARY			1	35	O	RC	INDIAN		090	F		12
DUCHARME	OLIVIER				50	QUE	RC	FRENCH	F	081	K		32
DUCHENES	MARGARET		1	1	3	O	RC	CANADIAN	STUDENT	087	A		1
DUCHENS	ANGELINE		1	1	12	O	RC	CANADIAN	STUDENT	087	A		1
DUCHNES	WILLIAM				37	QUE	RC	FRENCH	TRADER & HUNTER	084	D		5
DUCK	JOSEPH				40	ENGLAND	CE	ENGLISH	SHOEMAKER	085	I		13
DUCK	MARTIN		1		22	GERMANY	LU	GERMAN	WAGONMAKER	082	E		68
DUDGEON	ANN		1	1	70	IRELAND	CE	IRISH		081	B		74
DUDLEY	JOSUA				50	IRELAND	CE	IRISH	LABOURER	082	E		68
DUDLEY	THOMAS				28	ENGLAND	PM	ENGLISH	SHOE MAKER	085	I		3
DUFF	ALEXANDER				29	O	CP	SCOTCH	STOREKEEPER	081	A	1	60
DUFF	IZETT				67	SCOTLAND	CP	SCOTCH	F	081	A	1	33
DUFF	JOHN				43	ENGLAND	CE	ENGLISH	F	085	L		10
DUFF	PETER				30	SCOTLAND	CP	SCOTCH	F	081	A	1	3
DUFFEY	JAMES		1		20	IRELAND	RC	IRISH		086	B		1
DUFFY	DANIEL	H			40	IRELAND	RC	IRISH	LABOURER	082	E		68
DUFFY	JOHN				64	IRELAND	RC	IRISH	FARMER	081	F		1
DUFONTS	AMABLE				70	QUEBEC	RC	INDIAN	HUNTER	084	C		1
DUFONTS	IGNACE				25	QUEBEC	RC	INDIAN	HUNTER	084	C		1
DUGAN	GEORGE				27	ENGLAND	CE	ENGLISH	CARPENTER	082	G		22
DUGEN	ROSEANN			1	45	IRELAND	RC	IRISH	F	082	F		22
DUGGAN	DANIEL				57	IRELAND	RC	IRISH	FARMER	081	D		1
DUGGAN	PATRICK				34	IRELAND	RC	IRISH	STEAMER CAPTAIN	082	D		32
DUGGAN	PHILL		1		35	IRELAND	RC	IRISH	SHANTYMAN	082	E		18
DUGLAS	JOHN				39	IRELAND	CE	IRISH	FARMER	082	F		3
DUILT	VICTOR				31	QUE	RC	FRENCH	SADDLER	081	I		43
DUIRE	PATRICK		1		25	ONTARIO	RC	IRISH	LABOURER	081	G	1	40
DUKE	EDWARD				40	O	CE	IRISH	F	082	J		17
DUKE	JOHN		1		35	IRELAND	CE	IRISH	FARM LAB	082	C	1	8
DULAC	AMAND		1		23	QUE	RC	FRENCH	LAB	086	C	1	2
DULET	MAYLLENES				34	QUE	RC	FRENCH	LAB	081	I		42
DUMA	JOSEPH		1		11	O	RC	FRENCH		081	A	2	31
DUMBRESKY	THOMAS				26	PRUSSIA	RC	PRUSSIAN	FARMER	083	A	1	18
DUMOIT	ANTOINE				87	O	RC	FRENCH	FARMER	089	A		50
DUMONT	ANTONIE		1		60	QUE	RC	FRENCH	LUMBERMAN	088	C		10
DUMONTE	WILLIAM		1		45	QUE	RC	FRENCH	BUSHMAN	084	E		3
DUMOT	JOSEPH		1		11	QUE	RC	FRENCH		081	B		30
DUNBAR	JAMES				55	IRELAND	RC	IRISH	F	082	A		83
DUNBAR	MARGRET		1	1	22	O	CP	SCOTCH		081	B		77
DUNCAN	JAMES				19	SCOTLAND	QU	SCOTCH		086	B		1
DUNCAN	THOMAS				45	IRELAND	CE	IRISH	F	085	A		24
DUNCAN	WILLIAM		1		25	IRELAND	CE	IRISH	F	085	E		18
DUNCAN	WILLIAM		1		18	SCOTLAND	CP	SCOTCH	F	085	I		24
DUNCEN	JAMES		1		8	O	CP	SCOTCH		081	H	1	3
DUNFIELD	GEORGE				40	IRELAND	PS	IRISH	F	081	J	1	31
DUNFIELD	JAMES				50	IRELAND	WM	IRISH	F	081	J	1	36
DUNFIELD	WILLIAM		1		60	IRELAND	CP	IRISH	FARM LABOURER	081	J	1	31
DUNIGAN	JAMES				40	IRELAND	RC	IRISH	F	082	A		63
DUNIGAN	PATRICK				36	IRELAND	RC	IRISH	F	082	H		35
DUNIGAN	PATRICK				50	IRELAND	RC	IRISH	F	082	H		35
DUNK	FRANCIS	E	1	1	7	O	PS	SCOTCH		085	J		25
DUNK	JOHN		1		31	ENGLAND	CE	ENGLISH	F	085	J		25
DUNK	MARTHA		1	1	4	O	PS	SCOTCH		085	J		25
DUNK	MARY	JANE	1	1	29	IRELAND	PS	IRISH		085	J		25
DUNK	SOPHIA		1	1	66	ENGLAND	CE	ENGLISH		085	J		25
DUNLAP	ELIZABETH			1	40	QUE	WM	IRISH	HOUSEKEEPER	082	D		8

SURNAME	NAME1	NAME2	STRAY	SEX	AGE	BIRTHPL	RELIGION	ORIGIN	OCCUP	DIST	SUB_DIST	DIV	PAGE
DUNLAP	JOHN				55	QUE	ME	SCOTTISH	FARMER	082	D		7
DUNLAP	MAGERIT		1	1	16	0	RC	IRISH	SERVANT	082	K	1	1
DUNLOP	GABE				60	0	RC			081	H	1	17
DUNLOP	JAMES				53	IRELAND	RC	IRISH	F	081	J	1	65
DUNLOP	JAMES		1		23	0	RC	IRISH	LABOURER	082	E		47
DUNLOP	JAMES				30	SCOTLAND	PS	SCOTCH	F	082	L		2
DUNLOP	JOHN				57	IRELAND	EP	IRISH	F	081	J	1	75
DUNLOP	JOHN				29	0	EP	SCOTCH	F	087	B	3	4
DUNLOP	ROBERT				44	0	RC	IRISH	F	081	H	1	16
DUNLOP	THOMAS		2		7	0	RC			081	H	1	D
DUNLOP	WILLIAM				45	0	RC	IRISH	F	081	H	1	20
DUNN	JAMES				65	IRELAND	EM	IRISH	F	082	C	1	37
DUNN	JOHN		1		21	QUEBEC	CP	IRISH	LABORER	084	C		3
DUNN	RICHARD				37	ENGLAND	PM	ENGLISH	MINER	089	A		46
DUNN	THOMAS				28	ONTARIO	RC	IRISH	FARMER	082	B		47
DUNN	WILLIAM				67	ENGLAND	CE	ENGLISH	FARMER	083	A	1	8
DUNN	WILLIAM				40	ENGLAND	CE	ENGLISH	FARMER	083	A	1	9
DUNN	WILLIAM				36	ONTARIO	CE	ENGLISH	FARMER	083	A	2	3
DUNN	WILLIAM				21		CP	SCOTCH	FARMER	085	E		32
DUNN	WILLIAM	JOSEPH			38	QUEBEC	CE	ENGLAND	FARMER	083	A	1	8
DUNNE	CHARLES				67	QUE	RC	IRISH	F	081	A	2	60
DUNNE	JAMES				58	IRELAND	RC	IRISH	F	081	J	1	44
DUNNELLY	JOSEPH				32	IRELAND	RC	IRISH	CLERK	083	A	1	14
DUPEE	FRANCIS				48	QUE	RC	FRENCH	CARPENTER	081	I		34
DUPIE	RAMAGE				38	QUE	RC	FRENCH	MILLWRIGHT	081	B		43
DUPIES	EDMOND		2		39	QUE	RC	FRENCH	FARMER	084	E		D
DUPIES	EUSTINE				38	0	RC	FRENCH		084	E		1
DUPIEUE	MOSES				59	QUE	RC	FRENCH		082	C	1	36
DUPLISES	ALEXIS		1		23	QUE	RC	FRENCH	CARRIAGEMAKER	081	K		72
DUPONT	GIDEON				21	QUE	RC	FRENCH	SHANTYMAN	082	E		45
DUPRINE	JOSEPH				29	QUE	RC	FRENCH		082	C	1	34
DUPUIS	HENRY		1		22	ENGLAND	CE	ENGLISH	LAB	090	F		25
DUPUIS	MAXIME				36	QUE	RC	FRENCH	F	082	C	1	47
DUPUIS	PIERE				40	ONTARIO	RC	FRENCH	FARMER	083	A	1	13
DUPUIS	VANSANT				34	ONTARIO	RC	FRENCH	FARMER	083	A	1	11
DURANQUIT	DOMNICK				58	FRANCE	RC	FRENCH	PRIEST	090	F		10
DURBROW	ANN		1	1	16	0	CP	ENGLISH		081	A	1	69
DURBROW	THOMAS				60	ENGLAND	CP	ENGLISH	F	081	A	1	71
DURE	DUNCAN				55	SCOTLAND	CP	SCOTCH	F	081	A	2	53
DURICK	DANIEL				46	IRELAND	RC	IRISH	F	082	F		7
DURRELL	JAMES				33	0	PS	IRISH	FARMER	082	D		8
DURRICK	PATRICK		1		33	IRELAND	RC	IRISH	TAILOR	082	E		16
DUSETT	CAROLINE		1	1	18	QUE	RC	FRENCH	TAILORESS	082	E		42
DUTCOTO	LEWIS				23	QUE	RC	FRENCH	LUMBERMAN	088	B		6
DUVAL	ADOLPHE		1		24	QUE	RC	FRENCH	F	090	F		16
DUVAL	ALFRED				40	QUE	RC	FRENCH	FARMER	081	F		8
DUVALLE	PIERE		1		28	QUEBEC	RC	FRENCH	FARMER	083	A	2	3
DWIRE	THOMAS				49	IRELAND	RC	IRISH	F	082	G		69
DWYER	CONNOR				56	IRELAND	RC	IRISH	F	081	K		59
DWYER	JOHN				68	IRELAND	RC	IRISH		081	J	1	87
DWYRE	JOHN				52	IRELAND	RC	IRISH	F	082	H		30
DWYRE	STEPHEN				30	0	RC	IRISH	F	082	H		30
DYER	JAMES		1		19	0	CP	AFRICAN	LAB	085	H		26
DYER	LAURENCE				26	CANADA	WM	ENGLISH	F	085	A		8
DYKE	JOHN				27	ENGLAND	CE	ENGLISH	FUR TRADER	088	C		4
EADE	JAMES				33	ENGLAND	WM	ENGLISH	MINER	089	A		22
EADY	GEORGE				30	0	WM	ENGLISH	MERCHANT	081	I		5
EADY	GEORGE	SEN			57	GIBRALTER	WM	ENGLISH	F	081	H	2	17
EADY	JAMES				37	0	EM	ENGLISH	LAB	081	H	2	13
EADY	ROBERT				28	0	WM	ENGLISH	F	081	H	2	17
EADY	ROBERT	SEN			54	0	WM	ENGLISH	F	081	H	2	15
EADY	WILLIAM				28	0	EM	ENGLISH	F	081	H	2	16
EAMS	WILLIAM				38	UNITED STATES	WM	ENGLISH	LABOURER	081	B		32
EANEAS	MOCOSE	LIEUS			31	ONTARIO	RC	INDIAN	HUNTER	083	D		1
EANS	LOUIS				34	QUE	RC	FRENCH	F	082	H		31
EARL	ALVAN	MENSEL			40	ONTARIO	WM	IRISH	PHYSICIAN	084	C		4
EARL	THOS				55	IRELAND	RC	IRISH	F	081	J	1	66
EASTROP	HARRY		1		23	ENGLAND	BA	ENGLISH	CARPENTER	082	E		75
EBEL	FREDERICK				46	GERMANY	BA	GERMAN	FARMER	081	F		23
EBITANY	PAUL				47	US	RC	INDIAN		087	A		34
ECKFORD	CHRISTINA		2	1		0	WM			082	C	2	D
ECKFORD	GEORGE				29	SCOTLAND	CS	SCOTCH	F	082	C	2	59
ECKFORD	JAMES				30	0	CS	SCOTCH	F	082	C	2	59
ECKFORD	JOHN				34	0	PM	SCOTCH	F	085	D		26
ECKFORD	WILLIAM				36	0	WM	SCOTCH	F	082	C	2	19
ECKFORD	WILLIAM				64	SCOTLAND	CS	SCOTCH	F	082	C	2	58
ECKLAND	THOS				42	ONTARIO	CE	IRISH	F	082	A		44
EDDY	JOHN				24	SCOTLAND	WM	ENGLISH	FARMER	082	B		60
EDDY	JOSEPH				68	SCOTLAND	CP	SCOTCH	F	085	H		9
EDEY	CHARLES				35	0	EM	ENGLISH	F	081	A	2	35
EDEY	EDMOND				62	QUE	EM	ENGLISH	HOTELKEEPER	081	B		12
EDEY	HENRY				37	QUE	EM	ENGLISH	WHEELWRIGHT	081	B		47
EDMONDS	GILBERT				47	ONTARIO	EM	SCOTCH	F	082	A		73
EDMONDS	JOHN				30	ONTARIO	EM	SCOTCH	F	082	A		74
EDMONDS	LORENZO	DOW			22	ONTARIO	EM	SCOTCH	F	082	A		70
EDMONDS	OBEDIAH				36	0	EM	GERMAN	F	081	H	2	16
EDMUNDS	WILLIAM		1		26	0	WM		MERCHANT	081	I		44
EDOWWISHKOSH	JOHN				36	US	CO	INDIAN	F & FISHERMAN	087	C		1
EDOWWISHKOSH	JOSEPH	WIDOW OF		1	32	US	RC	INDIAN	F & FISHERMAN	087	C		1
EDOWWISHKOSH	SAMSON				60	US	RC	INDIAN	F & FISHERMAN	087	C		1
EDWARDS	ABRAHAM				35	ONT	CE	IRISH	FARMER	082	I		30
EDWARDS	ALEXR				31	0	EM	IRISH	F	081	H	2	33
EDWARDS	ELIZABETH		1	1	21	ONT	CE	ENGLISH	SEAMSTRESS	082	I		43
EDWARDS	EVAN				42	0	WM	IRISH	F	082	G		23
EDWARDS	FRANCIS		1		38	ONT	CE	IRISH	FARMER	082	I		12
EDWARDS	FRANCIS		2		38	ONT	CE		FARMER	082	I		D
EDWARDS	ISAC				26	ONT	CE	IRISH	FARMER	082	I		52
EDWARDS	JOHN				21	IRELAND	CE	IRISH	F	082	G		65
EDWARDS	JOHN	WILLIAM	2			ONT	CE			082	I		D
EDWARDS	JOSEPH		1		22	US	WM	IRISH	SERVANT	081	A	2	29
EDWARDS	LOVAN				22	ENGLAND	CE	ENGLISH	F	085	D		22
EDWARDS	MARGARET				58	IRELAND	EM	IRISH		082	H	2	15
EDWARDS	MARY	ANN	1	1	20	ONTARIO	CE	ENGLISH	SCHOOL TEACHER	081	G	1	35
EDWARDS	MARY	JANE	1	1	26	ONT	RP	IRISH		082	I		12
EDWARDS	REBECCA			1	67	IRELAND	WM	IRISH		082	G		24
EDWARDS	REBECCA	MOON	1	1		ONT	RP	IRISH		082	I		12

SURNAME	NAME1	NAME2	STRAY	SEX	AGE	BIRTHPL	RELIGION	ORIGIN	OCCUP	DIST	SUB_DIST	DIV	PAGE
EDWARDS	RICHARD				26	ONT	CE	IRISH	FARMER	082	I		57
EDWARDS	SERAH		1	1	27	O	WM	IRISH	SEAMSTRESS	082	E		63
EDWARDS	THOMAS				33	O	EM	IRISH	F	081	H	2	27
EDWARDS	THOS				40	US	WM	IRISH	F	082	G		23
EDWARDS	THOS				39	O	WM	IRISH	TANNER	082	G		95
EDWARDS	WAKEMAN	JC			30	FRANCE	CE	ENGLISH	F	085	D		5
EDWARDS	WESLEY				23	O	WM	IRISH	F	082	G		24
EDWARDS	WILLIAM				33	ONTARIO	WM	ENGLISH	FARMER	082	B		32
EDWARDS	WILLIAM				29	ONTARIO	PM	IRISH	FARMER	082	B		61
EDWARDS	WILLIAM				45	O	WM	IRISH	F	082	G		24
EDWARDS	WILLIAM				62	IRELAND	CE	IRISH	F	082	G		30
EDY	EDWARD				29	QUE	PR	ENGLISH	FARMER & HOTELKEEPER	082	G		53
EECHE	CHISTIAN				37	GERMANY	CE	GERMAN	LAB	081	B		58
EGAN	EDWARD				50	IRELAND	RC	IRISH	F	082	J		6
EGAN	JOHN		2		77	IRELAND	RC		F	082	C	2	D
EGAN	JOHN		1		48	IRELAND	RC	IRISH	BOOKKEEPER	082	E		28
EGAN	JOHN				28	ENGLAND	RC	IRISH	LIGHT HOUSE KEEPER	088	A		12
EGAN	JOSEPHINE		2	1	4	O	RC	IRISH		088	A		D
EGAN	MARY		1	1	28	O	RC	IRISH	SERVANT	082	E		25
EGAN	MARY		2	1	3	O	RC	IRISH		088	A		D
EGAN	MICHAEL		1		70	IRELAND	RC	IRISH	FARMER	081	J	1	63
EGAN	TIMOTHY				62	IRELAND	RC	IRISH	FARMER	082	B		24
EGAN	WILLIAM				30	IRELAND	RC	IRISH	SHOEMAKER	082	B		6
EGAN	WILLIAM				30	IRELAND	RC	IRISH	FARMER	082	B		24
EGAN	WINIFRED		1	1	20	O	RC	IRISH	SERVANT	082	E		25
EGART	GEORGE				40	QUE	WM	DUTCH	BOOKKEEPER	081	B		31
EGGLEFIELD	THOMAS				44	QUE	EM	ENGLISH	CARPENTER	085	I		44
EGGLESTON	NEWTON				46	UNITED STATES	CP	ENGLISH	BAILIFF	082	C	2	14
EGNOSS	CATHERINE			1		O	RC			082	H		D
EGNOSS	JAMES				2	O	RC			082	H		D
EIERK	EDWARD				44	GERMANY	CE	GERMAN	F	081	A	2	43
EKUBEK	ANTWAN				48	POLAND	RC	POLISH	LAB	081	I		38
ELDER	JANE		1	1	75	SCOTLAND	FK	SCOTCH		081	K		9
ELDER	WILLIAM				27	SCOTLAND	CP	SCOTCH	F	085	B		21
ELGAR	CHARLES				29	ENGLAND	CE	ENGLISH	F	085	H		18
ELLDIN	WILLIAM				38	ENGLAND	CE	ENGLISH	F	086	A	1	6
ELLIOT	JOHN				45	SCOTLAND	PS	SCOTCH	FARMER	086	B		8
ELLIOT	ROBERT				21	IRELAND	PM	IRISH	F	086	B		4
ELLIOTT	ABNER				50	O	WM	INDIAN	MISSIONARY	086	A	3	1
ELLIOTT	BENAGER				38	O	WM	ENGLISH	BLACKSMITH	085	I		29
ELLIOTT	DAWSON				41	IRELAND	EM	IRISH	F	082	A		67
ELLIOTT	GEORGE				43	IRELAND	WM	IRISH	F	085	D		32
ELLIOTT	HENRY				42	IRELAND	WM	IRISH	F	082	A		52
ELLIOTT	THOMAS				43	IRELAND	WM	IRISH	F	082	A		7
ELLIOTT	WILLIAM				31	ONTARIO	CE	IRISH	CARPENTER	083	C		14
ELLIOTT	WILLIAM		1		30	IRELAND	CE	IRISH	CARPENTER	085	E		18
ELLIS	ISABELLA		1	1	20	QUE	CP	SCOTCH		081	A	2	53
ELLIS	JAMES				47	SCOTLAND	PS	SCOTCH		086	A	1	12
ELLIS	JOHN				50	IRELAND	CE	IRISH	F	081	K		23
ELLIS	ROBERT	B			23	O	WM	ENGLISH	CLERK	088	B		2
ELLIS	SAMUEL				55	IRELAND	WM	IRISH	F	086	A	1	16
ELLISS	THOMAS				51	QUE	WM	ENGLISH	FARMER	082	D		9
EMBELA	LUCK				48	QUE	RC	FRENCH	MOULDER	081	I		32
EMBRES	SYLVESTER								SEE SYLVESTER	085	F		5
EMERSON	JOHN				71	ENGLAND	ME	ENGLISH	F	085	D		5
EMERSON	MATTHEW				29	ENGLAND	PM	ENGLISH	F	085	D		10
EMERSON	MELCHIZEDEL				27	ENGLAND	PM	ENGLISH	F	085	D		27
ENDGLES	ANNY			1	46	ENGLAND	CE	ENGLAND		081	I		42
ENDIGOOSE	LOUIS				36	ONT	ME	INDIAN	HUNTER & TRAPPER	090	B		9
ENGLAND	BEN				58	IRELAND	CE	IRISH	F	081	J	1	14
ENGLAND	EDWARD				40	NB	CE	SCOTCH	F	082	C	2	33
ENGLES	ANTWINE				73	POLAND	RC	POLISH	LAB	081	I		36
ENGLISH	JOHN				53	IRELAND	RC	IRISH	F	081	J	1	7
ENGLISH	RICHARD		1		37	CANADA	PS	SCOTCH	LUMBER MANUFACT	087	B	2	3
ENNIS	HENRY				26	O	EM	GERMAN	F	085	K	2	8
ENNIS	JOHN				70	ENGLAND	CE	IRISH	F	085	I		29
ENNIS	ROBERT				37	IRELAND	CE	IRISH	F	085	B		5
ENNIS	WILLIAM				46	IRELAND	CE	IRISH	MASON	085	B		6
ENRIGHT	DENNIS				30	IRELAND	RC	IRISH	F	081	J	1	91
ENRIGHT	DONALD				47	IRELAND	RC	IRISH	F	081	J	1	91
ENRIGHT	JAMES				55	IRELAND	RC	IRISH	F	081	C		16
ENRIGHT	JOHN				30	IRELAND	RC	IRISH	F	081	J	1	26
ENRIGHT	JOHN		1		26	IRELAND	RC	IRISH	LABOURER	081	J	1	78
ENRIGHT	JOHN				24	IRELAND	RC	IRISH	F	081	J	1	80
ENRIGHT	JOHN				65	IRELAND	RC	IRISH	F	081	J	1	91
ENRIGHT	OWEN				32	IRELAND	RC	IRISH	F	081	J	1	91
ENRIGHT	PATRICK				34	IRELAND	RC	IRISH	F	081	J	1	5
ENRIGHT	PATRICK				47	IRELAND	RC	IRISH	F	081	J	1	92
ENRIGHT	STEPHEN				29	IRELAND	RC	IRISH	FARMER	081	C		16
ENRIGHT	THOS				60	IRELAND	RC	IRISH	F	081	J	1	26
ENRIGHT	THOS				53	IRELAND	RC	IRISH	F	081	J	1	88
ENRIGHT	TIMATHY				60	IRELAND	RC	IRISH	F	081	J	1	24
ENSKA	MICHEAL				56	PRUSSIA	RC	POLISH	F	082	J		15
ENTY	EDWARD				46	USA	WM	AFRICAN	F	085	K	2	7
EMWAOSL	DANIEL				62	US	RC	INDIAN	F & FISHERMAN	087	A		25
ERBARE	JOSEPH		1		21	QUE	RC	FRENCH	FARM LAB	082	C	1	27
ERITCHIK	ALBERT		1		10	PRUSSIA	RC	PRUSSIAN		083	A	1	3
ERITCHIK	ANNIE		1	1	8	ONTARIO	RC	PRUSSIAN		083	A	1	3
ERITCHIK	CATHARINE		1	1	17	PRUSSIA	RC	PRUSSIAN		083	A	1	3
ERWIN	JAMES				38	IRELAND	PS	IRISH	F	081	K		50
ESSEX	JOHN				25	ENGLAND	CE	ENGLISH	COOPER	081	A	2	14
ETSON	ALFRED		1		22	ENGLAND	CE	ENGLISH	SCHOOL TEACHER	082	A		77
EURCHEKE	ROBERT		1		14	GERMANY	RC	GERMAN	SERVANT	081	B		54
EUSELE	MALONSON				49	QUE	RC	FRENCH		082	C	1	35
EUSTACH	GRATTAN				41	QUE	RC	FRENCH		082	C	1	23
EVANS	JAMES		1		30	O	WM	GERMAN	LAB	082	K	1	7
EVANS	JOHN		1		34	IRELAND	CE	IRISH	CLERK	082	E		9
EVANS	OLEIVE		1	1	26	O	WM	GERMAN		082	K	1	7
EVANS	OLEIVE		1	1	6	O	WM	GERMAN		082	K	1	7
EVANS	PHILLOMENA		1	1	38	QUE	WM	GERMAN	F	082	K	1	13
EVANS	ROSE	ANN	1	1	7	ONTARIO	CS	IRISH		082	A		16
EVANS	S	T A			37	QUE	CE	IRISH	LAND SURVEYOR	082	E		8
EVANS	SAMUEL				52	ENGLAND	WM	ENGLISH	MINER	089	A		23
EVANS	THOMAS				79	ENGLAND	CE	ENGLISH	MOULDER	082	J		18
EVANS	WILLIAM		2		17	O	WM		F	081	H	1	D
EVERETT	JOSEPH	H			28	O	CE	ENGLISH	CARPENTER	085	I		4

SURNAME	NAME1	NAME2	STRAY	SEX	AGE	BIRTHPL	RELIGION	ORIGIN	OCCUP	DIST	SUB_DIST	DIV	PAGE
EVERINGHAM	ANDREW				64	0	WM	DUTCH	F	086	A	1	21
EVERY	JEFFERSON				38	0	BA	ENGLISH	HUNTER TRAPPER	085	K	1	1
EVINS	JOHN		1		16	0	CS	IRISH	CLARK	081	I		30
EVIT	MARGARET			1	52	IRELAND	PS	IRISH		085	C		19
EVOY	DANIEL				26	QUE	RC	FRENCH	LUMBERMAN	088	C		11
EWERBECK	JOHN				39	PRUSSIA	LU	PRUSSIAN	F	085	A		19
EWIIWE	MARIE		1	1	43	US	RC	INDIAN		087	A		35
EWING	GORDON	M			45	SCOTLAND	BA	SCOTCH	F	085	C		16
EZNOSS	CRISTIANN		1	1		0	RC	INDIAN		082	H		27
EZNOSS	LAMEL				27	0	RC	INDIAN	HUNTER AND FISHERMAN	082	H		27
EZNOSS	MARY		1	1	60	QUE	RC	INDIAN		082	H		28
EZNOSS	NORSEACE		1		9	0	RC	INDIAN		082	H		27
EZNOSS	PHILEMAN		1	1	28	QUE	RC	INDIAN		082	H		27
EZNOSS	SIMON		1		35	0	RC	INDIAN	HUNTER AND FISHERMAN	082	H		27
FABWAY	CHRISTIAN				39	GERMANY	LU	GERMAN	SHOEMAKER	082	G		4
FAHEY	MERIA				29	0	RC	IRISH		082	L		3
FAHEY	NICHOLAS				64	IRELAND	RC	IRISH	F	081	K		20
FAIJENT	CHARLOTTE			1	50	0	RC	INDIAN		090	F		13
FAILL	JOSEPH				26	0	RC	INDIAN	HUNTER	088	B		23
FAILL	MARYANN			1	60	0	RC	INDIAN		088	B		23
FAIRER	JOSEPH				33	ENGLAND	WM	ENGLISH	F	085	D		34
FALIN	OLLIVER		1		10	QUE	RC	FRENCH		082	E		43
FALLANE	RICHARD				50	IRELAND	RC	IRISH	LABOURER	082	D		11
FALLON	JAMES		1		36	IRELAND	RC	IRISH	SCHOOL TEACHER	081	F		15
FALLON	JOHN				48	IRELAND	RC	IRISH	F	082	K	1	19
FANANHONE	CARL				47	GERMANY	LU	GERMAN	F	081	K		53
FARGUSON	WILLIAM				30	SCOTLAND	RP	SCOTCH	TEACHER	081	I		20
FARLINE	JAMES				42	0	RC	ENGLISH	BOAT BUILDER	089	A		53
FARMER	GEORGE				19	0	RB	WELSH	SHOEMAKER	081	B		6
FARMER	WILLIAM				23	WALES	RB	WELSH	SHOEMAKER	081	B		5
FARMER	WILLIAM		1		21	0	CE	ENGLISH	TANNER	082	D		17
FARNSWORTH	WILLM				37	USA	FW	ENGLISH	F	085	K	2	8
FARQUAHARSON	DAVID				49	SCOTLAND	CS	SCOTCH	F	081	J	1	85
FARQUHARSON	MARGRET		1	1	32	SCOTLAND	CP	SCOTCH		081	H	1	
FARR	ARTHUR		2		18	ENGLAND	CE		F	085	K	2	D
FARR	CHRISTOPHER				55	ENGLAND	CE	ENGLISH	F	085	K	2	6
FARR	JOHN	C			27	ENGLAND	CE	ENGLISH	F	085	J		15
FARREL	POARTLZ				36	IRELAND	RC	IRISH	F	082	H		21
FARRELL	EDWARD				63	IRELAND	CE	IRISH	F	081	H	2	37
FARRELL	WILLIAM				31	QUE	CP	IRISH	LUMBER AGENT	085	B		24
FARREST	JOHN				66	SCOTLAND	CP	SCOTCH	F	081	J	1	80
FAUGHNAU	JAMES				30	IRELAND	RC	FARMER		082	B		28
FAUGHT	LAWERENCE				50	IRELAND	WM	IRISH	SHOEMAKER	082	G		7
FAULKNER	JOHN		1		40	QUE	PS	IRISH	F	085	J		11
FAWCETT	THOMAS				22	ENGLAND	WM	ENGLISH	F	085	H		13
FEELY	THOMAS				40	IRELAND	RC	IRISH	F	081	K		45
FELIX	MARIEA			1	27	QUE	RC	FRENCH	SERVANT	084	F		1
FELLETER	MARY		1	1	26	0	RC	IRISH		081	C		12
FELLETER	WILLIAM				67	IRELAND	RC	IRISH	F	081	C		12
FELTZ	HARMAN				21	GERMANY	LU	GERMAN	F	081	K		58
FENCHNY	WILLIAM				48	0	CP	SCOTCH	LUMBER MERCHANT	081	I		17
FENERTY	PETER				56	IRELAND	RC	F		081	A	2	32
FENTON	DAVID		1		35	QUEBEC	RC	SCOTCH	CARPENTER	084	C		5
FENTON	DAVID		1		4	ONTARIO	RC	HALFBREED		084	C		6
FENWICK	JOHN				28	ENGLAND	WM	ENGLISH	MINER	089	A		42
FERARD	MARTIN		1		54	TOUR	RC	FRENCH	PRIEST	087	A		1
FERER	DAVID				35	IRELAND	IM	IRISH	FARMER	082	B		31
FERGERSON	ANGUS				51	SCOTLAND	PS	SCOTCH	MINE LABOURER	089	A		28
FERGURSON	ALXANDER				29	0	WM	SCOTCH	CARPENTER	081	I		23
FERGUS	JOHN				61	IRELAND	RC	IRISH	F	081	C		8
FERGUS	PATRICK				22	IRELAND	RC	IRISH	F	081	C		58
FERGUSON	CATHERINE			1	48	ONTARIO	CS	SCOTCH		082	A		32
FERGUSON	DANIEL				50	0	CP	SCOTCH	MANAGER	082	C	1	59
FERGUSON	DAVID				39	0	CE	SCOTCH	F	085	K	2	6
FERGUSON	DONALD				48	0	CS	SCOTCH	F	081	A	1	23
FERGUSON	DRUMMOND		1		29	0	CP	SCOTCH	BLACKSMITH	084	E		4
FERGUSON	DUNCAN				51	SCOTLAND	CP	SCOTCH	F	081	J	1	19
FERGUSON	DUNCAN		1		52	SCOTLAND	CP	SCOTTISH	CLERK	082	B		58
FERGUSON	JAMES				33	SCOTLAND	CP	SCOTCH	F	081	J	1	61
FERGUSON	JAMES				44	ONTARIO	CS	SCOTCH	F	082	A		82
FERGUSON	JOHN				31	SCOTLAND	CP	SCOTCH	F	081	J	1	61
FERGUSON	JOHN				26	ONTARIO	CS	SCOTCH	F	082	A		60
FERGUSON	MARGARET		1	1	19	0	WM	SCOTCH		081	B		7
FERGUSON	PETER				46	SCOTLAND	CS	SCOTCH	F	081	C		46
FERGUSON	PETER				35	ONTARIO	CS	SCOTCH	LAB	082	A		49
FERGUSON	PETER				39	ONTARIO	CS	SCOTCH	F	082	A		69
FERGUSON	ROBERT				40	IRELAND	WM	IRISH	TAILOR	085	I		27
FERGUSON	ROBT				51	SCOTLAND	CS	SCOTCH	F	081	C		55
FERGUSSON	DONALD				47	0	CS	SCOTCH	F	081	H	2	23
FERGUSSON	ROBERT				34	0	CS	SCOTCH	F	081	H	2	23
FERLAND	SEVERN				49	QUE	RC	FRENCH	MERCHANT	082	E		40
FERNET	ROBERT		1		18	QUE	RC	FRENCH	SERVANT	081	D		9
FESSKEY	CHARLES				27	0	RC	FRENCH	LAB	081	B		16
FETCHEY	JAMES				34	ONTARIO	CP	SCOTTISH	BLACKSMITH	082	B		57
FETHERSTON	T	C			30	ENGLAND	CE	ENGLISH	PAINTER	081	A	2	39
FETHERSTON	THOMAS				28	0	WM	ENGLISH	F	085	B		4
FETTERLY	HIRAM	L			21	0	WM	GERMAN	F	085	K	2	1
FETTERLY	IRA				50	0	WM	UNKNOWN	F	085	L		2
FETTERLY	JOHN	P			62	0	WM	GERMAN	F	085	K	2	3
FETTERLY	PETER				38	0	WM	ENGLISH	F	085	L		8
FICK	WILLIAM				52	PRUSSIA	LU	GERMAN	F	082	G		19
FIDLER	WILLIAM				42	0	PS	ENGLISH	LIVERY KEEPER	082	E		36
FIELD	GEORGE				66	ENGLAND	CE	ENGLISH	F	082	K	1	1
FIELD	WILLIAM		1		25	ENGLAND	CE	ENGLISH	ENGINEER	082	K	2	2
FIFE	CHARLES				32	SCOTLAND	CS	SCOTCH	F	082	A		40
FIFE	DAVID				42	0	PM	SCOTCH	F	085	D		25
FILHABER	FRANCIS				42	GERMANY	BA	GERMAN	MASON	081	F		10
FILLOROS	HANNAH		2	1	3	0	NG			085	A		D
FILLY	JAMES				60	ENGLAND	RC	ENGLISH	F	081	K		27
FIMRINS	JOHN				40	0	RC	ENGLISH	F	083	C		2
FINAN	JOHN				60	IRELAND	CE	IRISH	F	081	H	2	41
FINCH	JACOB				33	0	WM	ENGLISH	F	085	J		14
FINCHERY	W	JAMES	2		7	0	CP			081	I		D
FINDLAY	ALEXANDER				52	SCOTLAND	CE	SCOTCH	FARMER	089	B		39
FINDLAY	JAMES				37	QUE	CP	SCOTCH	LUMBER MERCHANT	082	C	2	1
FINDLAY	WALTER				48	SCOTLAND	RP	SCOTCH	LUMBER & F	082	C	1	5

SURNAME	NAME1	NAME2	STRAY	SEX	AGE	BIRTHPL	RELIGION	ORIGIN	OCCUP	DIST	SUB_DIST	DIV	PAGE
FINDLY	JAMES				45	SCOTLAND	RP	SCOTCH	LUMBERMAN	082	K	1	20
FINERTY	JOHN				26	IRELAND	RC	IRISH	FARMER	081	G	1	8
FINLAYSON	J	MCNAIR			52	SCOTLAND	PS	SCOTCH	F	086	A	1	23
FINLAYSON	JNO				48	0	RC	INDIAN	CLERK H B CO	090	C		1
FINN	ISAAC		1			ONT	CS	IRISH		081	C		49
FINN	JANET	ISSAB	1	1	3	ONT	CS	IRISH		081	C		49
FINN	JOHN		1		37	ONT	CS	IRISH	FARMER	081	C		49
FINN	JUDITH		1	1	27	ONT	CS	IRISH		081	C		49
FINN	MARGARET		1	1	5	ONT	CS	IRISH		081	C		49
FINNCANE	PATRICK				50	IRELAND	RC	IRISH	F	082	H		4
FINNEL	JOHN				34	ENGLAND	CE	ENGLISH	F	085	D		2
FINNELL	SAMUEL		1		69	ENGLAND	CE	ENGLISH	F	085	D		3
FINNERS	JOSEPH		1		24	0	RC	IRISH	SHOEMAKER	081	K		65
FINNEY	ISRAEL	JOHN	1		23	USA	ME		LUMBERMAN	086	C	1	11
FINUCANE	JOHN				60	IRELAND	RC	IRISH	F	081	J	1	3
FIRTH	JOHN		1		29	ENGLAND	CP	ENGLISH	CARPENTER	085	E		23
FISHER	ALBERT				24	PRUSSIA	EP	PRUSSIAN	LAB	090	D		7
FISHER	ALEXANDER				27	SCOTLAND	PS	SCOTCH	MINER	089	A		34
FISHER	CATHARINE		1	1	82	SCOTLAND	CP	SCOTCH		081	A	1	17
FISHER	CATHERINE		1	1	50	IRELAND	RC	IRISH	SERVANT	082	E		25
FISHER	ELIZA		1	1	24	QUE	CE	IRISH	SERVANT	082	E		20
FISHER	GEORGE		1		35	UNITED STATES	WM	ENGLISH	COPPER SMELTER	089	A		35
FISHER	JOHN				54	QUE	CS	SCOTCH	F	081	A	1	32
FISHER	JOHN				26	0	CE	IRISH	F	086	A	2	11
FISHER	JOHN				33	SCOTLAND	PS	SCOTCH	MINER	089	A		37
FISHER	REBEKA		2	1	77	ENGLAND	WM	ENGLISH		085	B		D
FISHER	RICHARD				69	SCOTLAND	PS	SCOTCH	FARMER	089	A		54
FISHER	THOMAS				40	SCOTLAND	PS	SCOTCH	MINER	089	A		30
FISHER	WILLIAM				40	GERMANY	LU	GERMAN	F	082	J		16
FITZGERALD	BRIDGET		1	1	17	ONTARIO	RC	IRISH		082	B		11
FITZGERALD	DAVID		1		12	IRELAND	RC	IRISH		082	B		1
FITZGERALD	HANNAH		1	1	18	ONT	RC	IRISH	SERVANT	081	J	1	20
FITZGERALD	HANORA		1	1	8	ONTARIO	RC	IRISH		082	B		33
FITZGERALD	HONORA		1	1	12	0	RP	IRISH		081	K		10
FITZGERALD	JOHN				56	IRELAND	RC	IRISH	FARMER	081	D		1
FITZGERALD	JOHN		1		14	ONTARIO	RC	IRISH	F	082	B		3
FITZGERALD	PATRICK				54	IRELAND	RC	IRISH	F	081	J	2	6
FITZGERALD	PATRICK		1		7	ONTARIO	RC	IRISH		082	B		17
FITZMARICE	JOHN		1		70	IRELAND	RC	IRISH		081	I		41
FITZMARICE	MICHAEL				37	IRELAND	RC	IRISH	BLACKSMITH	081	I		40
FITZMORRIS	EDWARD				33	IRELAND	RC	IRISH	F	085	C		17
FITZMORRIS	THOMAS				31	IRELAND	RC	IRISH	F	085	C		18
FITZMORRIS	THOMAS				67	IRELAND	RC	IRISH	F	085	C		21
FITZMURCE	HONNORD		2	1		0	RC			081	I		D
FITZMURICE	JAMES				28	IRELAND	RC	IRISH	BLACKSMITH	081	I		19
FITZNER	ADAM		1		25	GERMANY	LU	GERMAN	BUTCHER	082	G		29
FITZNER	BERNARD		1		17	GERMANY	LU	GERMAN	TAILOR	082	G		29
FITZNER	FREDRICK		1		21	GERMANY	LU	GERMAN	SERVANT	082	G		29
FITZNER	HARMEN		1		24	GERMANY	LU	GERMAN	GARDNER	082	G		29
FITZNER	JULIUS		1		19	GERMANY	LU	GERMAN	TAILOR	082	G		29
FITZNER	ROBERT		2			0	WM			082	G		D
FITZNER	WILLIAM				30	GERMANY	WM	GERMAN	F	082	G		93
FITZPATRICK	HENRY				60	IRELAND	RC	IRISH	FARMER	082	B		18
FITZPATRICK	JAMES				52	IRELAND	RC	IRISH	ENGINEER	082	A		49
FITZPATRICK	JOHN		1		30	0	RC	IRISH	SHANTYMAN	082	E		18
FITZPATRICK	MARGARET		1	1	50	IRELAND	RC	IRISH		081	F		10
FITZPATRICK	MICHAEL				31	ONTARIO	RC	IRISH	FARMER	082	B		19
FITZSIMONS	KATE		1	1	18	0	RC	IRISH	SERVANT	081	A	2	29
FITZWILLIAM	BRIDGET		1	1	35	IRELAND	RC	IRISH	SISTERS OF CHARITY	087	A		1
FLAHERTY	JAMES				39	IRELAND	CE	IRISH	INNKEEPER	090	F		18
FLAMOND	J	BTE			47	0	RC	INDIAN	F & FISHERMAN	087	A		7
FLANGEN	THOMAS		1		60	IRELAND	RC	IRISH	COOPER	081	I		28
FLANIGAN	JOHN				41	0	CE	IRISH	ENGINEER	086	C	1	10
FLANIGHAN	MICHAEL		1		35	QUE	RC	IRISH	LAB	090	F		15
FLANNAHAN	PATRICK								SEE HANNAHAN	081	J	2	5
FLANNERY	CATHERINE			1	35	ENGLAND	RC	ENGLISH		082	E		7
FLAVIN	PATRICK				31	IRELAND	RC	IRISH	MINER	090	D		3
FLEECE	ALBERT				80	PRUSSIA	RC	PRUSSIAN	FARMER	083	A	1	18
FLEECE	JOHN				38	PRUSSIA	RC	PRUSSIAN	FARMER	083	A	1	3
FLEMING	DAN		1		20	SCOTLAND	PS	SCOTTISH	PRINTER	082	E		30
FLEMING	JAMES				27	IRELAND	RC	IRISH	F	082	H		17
FLEMING	JOHN		1		23	SCOTLAND	PS	SCOTTISH	GARDENER	082	E		28
FLEMING	JOHN				65	IRELAND	RC	IRISH	F	082	H		17
FLESHMAN	WILLIAM				38	GERMANY	CE	GERMAN	BLACKSMITH	081	K		55
FLETCHER	CHARLES		2		50	ENGLAND	CE			081	I		D
FLETCHER	FRANCIS		1		20	0	WM	ENGLISH	F	085	L		6
FLETCHER	GEORGE				21	0	WM	ENGLISH	F	085	L		6
FLETCHER	JOHN				48	SCOTLAND	PS	SCOTCH	FARMER	089	B		19
FLETCHER	MICHIAL				49	ENGLAND	CE	ENGLISH	F	081	H	1	13
FLETCHER	ROBERT				40	ENGLAND	CE	ENGLISH	PAINTER	081	B		36
FLETCHER	SARAH		1	1	31	0	WM	IRISH	TAILORESS	082	E		30
FLETCHER	WM	T	1		24	ENGLAND	CE	ENGLISH	CARPENTER	085	E		25
FLEUREY	ANDREW		1		25	FRANCE	RC	FRENCH	LAB	084	I	2	1
FLINBIDY	TIMOTHY				40	IRELAND	RC	IRISH	FARMER	082	B		27
FLINT	R	S			28	QUE	WM	ENGLISH	COOPER	081	A	2	23
FLINT	WILLIAM	R	2			0	CE			081	A	2	D
FLOOD	FRANCIS				30	0	CE	IRISH	F	082	C	1	3
FLOOD	JOHN				34	ONTARIO	EM	IRISH	F	082	A		9
FLOOD	WILLIAM				79	IRELAND	CE	IRISH	F	082	A		11
FLORENCE	JAMES				29	ENGLAND	CE	ENGLISH	FARMER	089	B		12
FLORIEN	FERMA		1		30	QUE	RC	FRENCH	BUSHMAN	084	E		3
FLOYD	EDWARD				36	ONTARIO	CE	IRISH	FARMER	084	D		3
FLUCHER	JOHN				22	IRELAND	ME	IRISH	F	086	B		4
FLUKER	GEORGE				40	ENGLAND	CE	ENGLISH	FARMER	082	I		70
FOLEY	JOHN				37	IRELAND	RC	IRISH	CARPENTER	081	K		65
FOLEY	JOHN				40	IRELAND	RC	IRISH	F	082	G		76
FOLEY	MARTIN				45	IRELAND	RC	IRISH	F	081	J	2	5
FOLEY	MICHAEL				28	IRELAND	RC	IRISH	FARMER	082	B		38
FOLEY	MICHAEL				57	IRELAND	RC	IRISH	FARMER	082	B		42
FOLGARINGLE	GODTLIP				40	GERMANY	LU	GERMAN	FARMER	082	I		56
FOLKS	JOHN				59	WALES	PM	WELSH	F	085	D		15
FOOTT	HELEN		1	1	2	US	CE	IRISH		089	B		26
FOOTT	HELENA	LOUISA	2	1		0	CE			089	B		D
FOOTT	WADE	GEORGE			43	IRELAND	CE	IRISH	MERCHANT	089	B		24
FORAN	EDWARD				25	0	RC	IRISH	FARMER	081	F		4
FORAN	JAMES				33	0	RC	IRISH	FARMER	081	F		2

SURNAME	NAME1	NAME2	STRAY	SEX	AGE	BIRTHPL	RELIGION	ORIGIN	OCCUP	DIST	SUB_DIST	DIV	PAGE
FORAN	JOHN				55	IRELAND	RC	IRISH	FARMER	082	B		45
FORAN	JOHN		1		3	O	RC	IRISH		082	K	1	10
FORAN	MICHAEL				40	O	RC	IRISH	FARMER	081	F		17
FORAN	MICHAEL	JR			33	IRELAND	RC	IRISH	FARMER	081	F		3
FORAN	MICHAEL	SR			64	IRELAND	RC	IRISH	FARMER	081	F		2
FORAN	PATRICK				32	IRELAND	RC	IRISH	FARMER	081	F		15
FORAN	PATRICK				62	IRELAND	RC	IRISH	F	082	K	1	5
FORAN	ROSE	ANN	1	1	15	O	RC	IRISH		081	F		17
FORAN	WILLIAM				28	O	RC	IRISH	FARMER	081	F		5
FORBES	ANDREW				26	O	CP	SCOTTISH	MERCHANT	082	E		26
FORBIS	JOHN				41	SCOTLAND	CP	SCOTCH	F	085	E		29
FORBS	GEORGE				27	O	CE	IRISH	MD	082	C	2	5
FORD	BENJAMIN				32	ONTARIO	CP	SCOTTISH	BLACKSMITH	082	B		6
FORD	GEORGE				23	O	WM	ENGLISH	TELEGRAPH OP	082	E		27
FORD	THOMAS				39	ENGLAND	BA	ENGLISH	LABOURER	082	E		21
FORECYTHE	FRANCES				35	ENGLAND	WM	ENGLISH	F	085	L		3
FOREMAN	WILLIAM				47	ENGLAND	CE	ENGLISH	F	085	E		20
FOREST	CHARLES		1		19	IRELAND	CP	IRISH	LAB	085	H		25
FOREST	JOHN				84	SCOTLAND	CP	SCOTCH	F	081	A	1	43
FOREST	JOHN				29	ONTARIO	CP	SCOTTISH	FARMER	082	B		62
FORESTER	OLIVER				42	ONTARIO	CE	ENGLISH	POSTMASTER	082	A		1
FORGE	FRANK				33	ENGLAND	PM	ENGLISH	F	085	D		25
FORGIE	CLARK	BRICE	1		3	O	WM	IRISH		082	D		26
FORREST	ANDREW				55	SCOTLAND	CP	SCOTCH	F	081	H	1	3
FORREST	ELIZABETH		2	1	20	ONT	CP			081	J	1	D
FORRESTER	THOMAS				31	SCOTLAND	WM	SCOTCH	F	085	H		17
FORSTER	WILLIAM	T			42	UNITED STATES	EP	ENGLISH	MACHINIST	090	D		5
FORSYTH	DONALD				50	SCOTLAND	PS	SCOTCH	BLACKSMITH	086	A	1	13
FORSYTH	EDW		2		1	O	WM			086	A	1	D
FORSYTH	EDWARD				38	O	WM	ENGLISH	SCHOOL TEACHER	086	A	1	8
FORSYTH	JOHN				64	SCOTLAND	CP	SCOTCH	F	085	I		41
FORSYTH	JOHN				34	SCOTLAND	CP	SCOTCH	F	085	I		42
FORSYTHE	FRANCIS		1		31	ENGLAND	WM	ENGLISH	CARPENTER	085	I		16
FORTIER	ALFRED				25	QUE	RC	FRENCH	STORE CLERK	082	E		50
FORTIER	CYRILLE				37	QUE	RC	FRENCH	FARMER	082	I		41
FORTIER	FIERDINAND				27	QUE	RC	FRENCH	LUMBERMAN	088	C		11
FORTIER	JOSEPH				24	QUE	RC	FRENCH	LUMBERMAN	088	C		11
FORTIER	NURE				30	QUE	RC	FRENCH	LUMBERMAN	088	C		11
FORTIN	ANTOINE				35	QUE	RC	FRENCH	CARPENTER	089	B		16
FORTUNE	PETER		1		49	NB	RC	IRISH	LUMBERER	082	L		6
FOSHA	PIERRE				49	QUE	RC	FRENCH	LUMBERMAN	081	K		13
FOSS	FRED				71	GERMANY	LU	GERMAN	F	081	H	1	10
FOSSET	ISACK				38	O	PM	ENGLISH	F	085	J		15
FOSTER	ARCHIBALD				33	O	WM	ENGLISH	TANNER	082	D		17
FOSTER	BENJAMIN				30	O	WM	ENGLISH	WHEELWRIGHT	085	B		11
FOSTER	GEORGE				53	ENGLAND	WM	ENGLISH	F	085	H		22
FOSTER	IRA		1		21	O	WM	IRISH	TINSMITH	082	E		59
FOSTER	JOHN				49	ENGLAND	XC	ENGLISH	F	085	D		8
FOSTER	JOHN				25	ENGLAND	WM	ENGLISH	F	085	H		8
FOSTER	JOHN				63	IRELAND	CE	IRISH	F	085	I		37
FOSTER	JOHN	WILLIAM			30	ENGLAND	CE	ENGLISH	F	085	E		30
FOSTER	THOMAS				35	QUE	RC	FRENCH	F	081	C		6
FOSTER	THOMAS				42	IRELAND	CE	IRISH	F	085	C		25
FOSTER	WILLIAM				43	IRELAND	CE	IRISH	F	081	K		3
FOSTER	WILLIAM				28	O	CE	IRISH	WAGONMAKER	082	E		67
FOSTER	WILLIAM				24	O	WM	ENGLISH	F	085	B		9
FOTIEN	JOSEPH				56	QUE	RC	FRENCH	FARMER	082	I		43
FOUBERT	ALEXES		1		27	QUE	RC	FRENCH	LUMBERMAN	088	B		18
FOUBERT	CHARLES		1		30	QUE	RC	FRENCH	LUMBERMAN	088	B		18
FOUBERT	FREDERICK		1		22	QUE	RC	FRENCH	LUMBERMAN	088	B		18
FOUBERT	OLIVER		1		24	QUE	RC	FRENCH	LUMBERMAN	088	B		18
FOUNTAIN	MICHAEL				34	QUE	RC	FRENCH	LAB	081	B		61
FOUNTAIN	PETER				33	QUE	WM	FRENCH	F	082	K	1	17
FOURNIER	ANTONIE		1		19	US	RC	FRENCH	LUMBERMAN	088	B		17
FOURNIER	JOHN		1		40	US	RC	FRENCH	LUMBERMAN	088	B		17
FOURNIER	LEVIS		1		26	US	RC	FRENCH	LUMBERMAN	088	B		17
FOURNIER	LEWIS		1		23	US	RC	FRENCH	LUMBERMAN	088	B		17
FOWD	MARGRET			1	34	O	FW	IRISH	DRESSMAKER	081	I		23
FOWLER	JOHN				34	ENGLAND	CE	ENGLISH	F	082	J		6
FOWLER	JOSEPH				44	QUE	RC	US	FOREMAN	084	E		1
FOX	J	WILLIAM			26		NG			085	E		30
FOX	JOHANNA		1	1	60	IRELAND	CE	IRISH		081	A	1	61
FOX	JOHN				27	IRELAND	RC	IRISH	SHOEMAKER	081	H	2	26
FOX	JOHN	W	1		26	ENGLAND	CE	ENGLISH	LAB	085	E		30
FOX	RICHARD				26	ENGLAND	PM	ENGLISH	ENGINEER	089	A		28
FOX	THOMAS				41	ENGLAND	WM	ENGLISH	MINER	089	A		31
FOY	FRANCIS				50	QUE	CE	IRISH	F	082	G		52
FOY	JOHN				45	IRELAND	RC	IRISH	FARMER	081	F		1
FOY	MICHAEL		1		12	O	RC	IRISH		081	A	2	19
FOY	MICHAEL				55	IRELAND	RC	IRISH	FARMER	081	D		7
FOY	NICHOLAS				28	IRELAND	RC	IRISH	F	081	K		50
FOY	PATRICK				60	IRELAND	RC	IRISH	FARMER	081	G	1	24
FOY	PETER				45	QUEBEC	CE	IRISH	F	083	C		5
FRAMPTON	JOSEPH				29	ENGLAND	CE	ENGLISH	CARPENTER	085	B		5
FRANCES	ELISAH				42	ONT	WM	SCOTCH	F	081	J	1	41
FRANCES	SAMUAL				56	I	WM	IRISH	WOOLEN MANUFACTURER	081	I		41
FRANCIS	EDWARD				25	ONT	WM	IRISH	F	081	J	1	39
FRANCIS	FREDRICK				26	O	WM	IRISH	F	086	A	1	21
FRANCIS	HU		1		62	IRELAND	PS	IRISH	PAINTER	082	E		33
FRANCIS	JOSEPH				30	QUEBEC	RC	INDIAN	HUNTER	083	B	2	1
FRANCIS	POUPORE		2		71	QUE	RC		F	082	C	1	D
FRANCIS	W	B			23	ENGLAND	CP	ENGLISH	WATCHMAKER	081	B		85
FRANCOUR	LOUIS				50	QUE	RC	FRENCH	F	082	K	1	8
FRANKE	FREDRICK				30	GERMANY	LU	GERMAN	MINISTER	082	I		61
FRAPIER	FABIEN				27	QUE	RC	FRENCH	SHANTYMAN	082	E		63
FRASER	ABRAHAM				45	SCOTLAND	PS	SCOTCH	F	081	J	1	53
FRASER	ALEXANDER		1		22	O	CP	SCOTCH	BLACKSMITH	081	A	1	43
FRASER	ALEXANDER				76	SCOTLAND	CP	SCOTCH	F	081	C		24
FRASER	ALEXANDER		1		17	ONT	CP	SCOTCH	FARM LABOURER	081	J	1	80
FRASER	ALEXANDER				50	SCOTLAND	CS	SCOTCH	F	082	A		26
FRASER	ALEXANDER				40	O	CP	SCOTCH	MERCHANT	082	C	1	65
FRASER	ALEXANDER		1		23	ENGLAND	EP	SCOTCH	CLERK	084	G	1	1
FRASER	ALEXANDER				34	SCOTLAND	PS	SCOTCH	F	085	D		20
FRASER	ANNIE	S	2	1	1	O	CP			082	E		D
FRASER	CHARLES				67	SCOTLAND	CP	SCOTCH	F	081	A	1	20
FRASER	CHARLES				33	SCOTLAND	PS	SCOTTISH	BOOKKEEPER	082	E		60

SURNAME	NAME1	NAME2	STRAY	SEX	AGE	BIRTHPL	RELIGION	ORIGIN	OCCUP	DIST	SUB_DIST	DIV	PAGE
FRASER	CHARLES		1		33	SCOTLAND	CP	SCOTCH	CLERK	084	C		5
FRASER	CHARLES	E	1		14	O	WM	SCOTCH		082	C	1	4
FRASER	CHRISTINA	LOUISA	1	1	4	O	CP	SCOTCH		081	A	1	23
FRASER	GEORGE				41	SCOTLAND	CP	SCOTCH	BOOK STATIONER	081	B		5
FRASER	GEORGE	A	1		16	O	WM	SCOTCH	HARNESSMAKING	082	C	1	4
FRASER	HECTOR				34	O	CS	SCOTTISH	BANK AGENT	082	E		39
FRASER	HUGH				29	O	PS	SCOTTISH	WAGON CARRIAGEMAKER	082	E		58
FRASER	HUGH				63	SCOTLAND	PS	SCOTCH	F	087	B	3	9
FRASER	JAMES				36	SCOTLAND	CP	SCOTCH	LAB	081	B		35
FRASER	JAMES		2		1	ONT	PS			081	J	1	D
FRASER	JAMES	A			36	IRELAND	CE	IRISH	WHARFINGER	081	H	2	21
FRASER	JESSY		1	1	10	O	WM	FRENCH		082	E		2
FRASER	JOHN		1		2	O	CS	SCOTCH		081	A	1	32
FRASER	JOHN		1		20	O	CP	SCOTCH	F	081	A	1	43
FRASER	JOHN				28	O	PS	SCOTTISH	CARPENTER	082	E		72
FRASER	JOHN		1		50	O	WM	SCOTCH	SCHOOL TEACHER	085	J		17
FRASER	MARION		2	1	31	O	CP					1	D
FRASER	MARION		2	1		O	CP					1	D
FRASER	ROBERT	N	1		11	O	WM	SCOTCH		082	C	1	4
FRASER	THOMAS				41	SCOTLAND	CP	SCOTCH	F	081	A	1	43
FRASER	THOMAS		1		18	O	WM	SCOTCH	LAB	082	C	1	4
FRASER	THOMAS		1		30	O	CE	IRISH		082	C	1	19
FRASER	THOMAS				38	O	CP	SCOTCH	AGENT	082	C	2	38
FRASER	WILLIAM				50	SCOTLAND	CP	SCOTCH	F	081	C		30
FRASER	WILLIAM		1		20	O	WM	SCOTCH	BLACKSMITH	082	C	1	3
FRASER	WILLIAM				34	SCOTLAND	PS	SCOTCH	PLASTERER	085	A		21
FRASIER	JOHN				55	SCOTLAND	CP	SCOTCH	F	085	L		10
FRAZIER	ASA	FOSTER	1		7	O	WM	ENGLISH		082	D		13
FRAZIER	DANIAL				68	IRELAND	CE	IRISH	FARMER	082	D		13
FRAZIER	JAMES	S	1		9	O	WM	ENGLISH		082	D		13
FRAZIER	JOHN	KABERT	1		5	O	WM	ENGLISH		082	D		13
FRAZIER	RICHARD				46	O	WM	SCOTTISH	FARMER	082	D		22
FRAZIER	ROBERT				25	O	WM	SCOTTISH	FARMER	082	D		19
FRAZIER	ROBERT				49	O	WM	SCOTTISH	FARMER	082	D		31
FRAZIOR	SIMOND				40	IRELAND	WM	IRISH	LABOURER	082	D		14
FREDRICK	AMELIA			1	40	GERMANY	WM	GERMAN	FARMER	082	G		12
FREDRICK	CHARLES				28	ONT	LU	GERMAN	FARMER	082	I		67
FREDRICK	CHAS				35	GERMANY	WM	GERMAN	F	082	G		21
FREDRICK	JOHN				30	GERMANY	WM	GERMAN	F	082	G		92
FREE	CATHERINE	A	1	1	11	O	CE	IRISH		082	E		49
FREE	MARTHA	ANNA	1	1	13	O	CE	IRISH		082	E		49
FREE	WILLIAM		1		15	O	CE	IRISH		082	E		49
FREELAND	GEORGE				65	IRELAND	CE	IRISH	F	082	A		7
FREELAND	JAMES				28	ONTARIO	WM	IRISH	F	082	A		41
FREEMAN	WILLIAM				30	ENGLAND	CE	ENGLISH	STONEMASON	085	F		3
FREMAH	ANTOINE				23	ONT	RC	FRENCH	F	081	J	1	17
FREMAH	LOUIS				45	QUEBEC	RC	FRENCH	F	081	J	1	17
FRENCH	CAMPBELL				27	QUE	WM	SCOTCH	LUMBERMAN	082	I		40
FRENCH	EDWIN				32	QUE	WM	ENGLISH	F	082	C	2	37
FRENCH	FRANCES				63	IRELAND	RC	IRISH	TAILOR	081	I		44
FRENCH	FRANCIS				31	IRELAND	RC	IRISH	TAILOR	081	I		18
FRENCH	JAMES				55	IRELAND	RC	IRISH	F	082	L		1
FRENCH	MICHEAL				30	IRELAND	RC	IRISH	F	081	H	1	8
FRESHETTE	LOUIS				47	O	RC	FRENCH	FISHERMAN	089	A		61
FRESHETTE	STEPHEN				24	O	RC	FRENCH	COOPER	089	A		61
FREVET	GUSTAVE				31	ENGLAND	PR	FRENCH	F	085	A		17
FRIDAY	HENRY				42	GERMANY	RC	FRENCH	MINE LABOURER	089	A		39
FRIDAY	MARY		1	1	66	GERMANY	RC	FRENCH		089	A		40
FRIEL	MARY			1	57	IRELAND	RC	IRISH		081	I		21
FRIER	SARAH			1	34	SCOTLAND	CS	SCOTCH		081	I		10
FRISSE	MCGUIRE				45	QUEBEC	RC	FRENCH	FARMER	081	G	1	39
FRIVOLT	AUGUST				45	GERMANY	EV	GERMAN	FARMER	082	I		66
FROLY	JOHN				24	PRUSSIA	PR	PRUSSIAN	FARMER	081	G	2	2
FROMSTONE	WILLIAM		1		46	ENGLAND	CE	ENGLISH		089	A		25
FROOD	ANDREW				36	ONT	FK	SCOTCH	SHOEMAKER	081	J	1	73
FROOD	ANDREW				39	ONT	CP	SCOTCH	CARPENTER	081	J	1	77
FROOD	ANNIE		1	1	19	O	CP	SCOTCH		081	A	1	50
FROOD	DANIEL				31	O	CS	SCOTCH	F	081	H	1	5
FROOD	HUGH		1		51	SCOTLAND	CE	SCOTCH	F	081	J	1	73
FROOD	JANE	DEANS	1	1	21	O	CP	SCOTCH		081	A	1	50
FROOD	JOHN				28	O	RP	SCOTCH	F	081	H	1	6
FROOD	JOHN				28	ONT	PS	SCOTCH	F	081	J	1	52
FROOD	SAMUEL				23	O	CS	SCOTCH	SERVANT	081	H	1	4
FROOD	THOMAS				55	SCOTLAND	CP	SCOTCH	F	081	A	1	49
FROOD	WILLIAM				33	ONT	CP	SCOTCH	F	081	C		30
FRUE	WILLIAM	B			42	IRELAND	BA	SCOTCH	MINER	090	D		5
FRUTEN	WILLIAM				44	IRELAND	PM	IRISH	F	085	D		17
FRY	WILLIAM		1		34	IRELAND	CE	IRISH	F	085	E		17
FRYER	WILLIAM				42	ENGLISH	CE	ENGLISH	F	085	F		2
FULFORD	FLORENCE		1	1	16	O	CP	SCOTCH		081	B		11
FULLAN	JOHN				26	O	RC	IRISH	LABOURER	082	E		74
FULLER	BENJAMIN				54	ENGLAND	CE	ENGLISH	HOTEL KEEPER	085	B		14
FULLIAN	BAPTIST		1		19	QUEBEC	RC	FRENCH	LUMBERMAN	083	A	1	8
FULLIAN	FELIX		1		20	QUEBEC	RC	FRENCH	LUMBERMAN	083	A	1	8
FULTON	JAMES		1		19	ONTARIO	CS	SCOTCH	FARM SERVANT	082	A		6
FULTON	WILLIAM				48	SCOTLAND	CP	SCOTCH	F	081	J	1	57
FURGUSON	JOHN		1		35	SCOTLAND	CP	SCOTCH	LAB	090	D		7
FURLONG	MICHAEL				45	O	RC	IRISH	HOTELKEEPER	081	K		68
FYFE	DANIEL				31	SCOTLAND	CP	SCOTCH	F			1	79
FYNN	MICHEAL				60	IRELAND	RC	IRISH		082	C	1	37
GABAW	JOSEPH				62	O	RC	INDIAN	F & FISHERMAN	087	A		8
GABAW	JOSEPH	JUN			27	O	RC	INDIAN	F & FISHERMAN	087	A		8
GABLE	GOTTLOB				59	SILESIA GERMANY	LU	GERMAN	GUNSMITH	082	E		4
GACKO	FRANCESS				45	QUE	RC	INDIAN	HUNTER	082	K	1	13
GAFFENAY	JAMES				47	IRELAND	RC	IRISH	F	082	J		12
GAFFNEY	JAMES				50	IRELAND	RC	IRISH	F	085	D		12
GAGAGOGIN	JAMES				25	O	WM	INDIAN	TRADER	090	A		1
GAGAN	JAMES				35	IRELAND	RC	IRISH	LAB	081	H	2	38
GAGISHIANGAI			2		2	O	NG			088	A		D
GAGNE	SIMON		1		30	QUE	RC	FRENCH	LAB	090	F		25
GAGNON	JOSEPH						NG		SEE GONYON	082	I		50
GALLAGHER	BERNARD				47	IRELAND	RC	IRISH	FARMER	081	F		19
GALLAGHER	FARIGAL				50	IRELAND	RC	IRISH	F	081	K		44
GALLAGHER	HUGH				34	IRELAND	RC	IRISH	FARMER	081	F		18
GALLAGHER	HUGH				33	IRELAND	RC	IRISH	CARRIAGEMAKER	081	K		72
GALLAGHER	JAMES		1		30	O	RC	IRISH	SERVANT	081	A	2	30

SURNAME	NAME1	NAME2	STRAY	SEX	AGE	BIRTHPL	RELIGION	ORIGIN	OCCUP	DIST	SUB_DIST	DIV	PAGE
GALLAGHER	JOHANNA		1		33	O	RC	IRISH		081	K		49
GALLAGHER	JOHN				46	IRELAND	RC	IRISH	FARMER	081	F		16
GALLAGHER	MICHAEL				35	IRELAND	RC	IRISH	FARMER	081	F		17
GALLAGHER	THOMAS				55	IRELAND	RC	IRISH	FARMER	082	B		52
GALLAGHER	WILLIAM				50	IRELAND	RC	IRISH	FARMER	081	F		2
GALLAHER	JOHN				46	IRELAND	RC	IRISH	FARMER	081	G	1	33
GALLAHER	PATRICK		2		6	ONTARIO	RC			081	G	1	D
GALLANDERS	JOHN		1		26	QUE	RP	IRISH	F	085	L		5
GALLIGER	RICHARD		1		24	IRELAND	PS	IRISH	LUMBERMAN	086	C	1	9
GALLOWAY	DAVID				38	ENGLAND	PM	ENGLISH	SHOEMAKER	085	I		37
GALLOWAY	MATHEW				38	O	PM	IRISH	F	085	D		5
GANAWEBI	BENOIT				26	O	RC	INDIAN	F & FISHERMAN	087	A		30
GANAWEBI	MOSES				20	O	RC	INDIAN	F & FISHERMAN	087	A		30
GANEY	WILLIAM				26	O	RC	IRISH	F	081	E		4
GANION	MERCEL				53	QUE	RC	FRENCH	LABOURER	081	B		30
GANIS	ELIZABETH		2	1	15	O	RC	INDIAN		084	I	1	D
GANNEAU	NOLBEAR				36	QUE	RC	FRENCH	BLACKSMITH	081	E		3
GANNON	EDWARD				40	IRELAND	RC	IRISH	FARMER	082	B		25
GANNON	JOHN		1		19	O	RC	IRISH	APPRENTICE WAGONMAK	082	E		59
GANNON	MICHAEL		1		80	IRELAND	RC	IRISH	WEAVER	082	C	2	49
GANNON	MICHAEL				52	IRELAND	RC	IRISH	F	082	G		77
GANNON	PATRICK				46	IRELAND	RC	IRISH	FARMER	082	B		37
GANT	HARMEN				30	GERMAN	WM	GERMAN	F	082	G		95
GARBET	JOHN				46	ENGLAND	EP	ENGLISH	F	087	B	3	8
GARDINER	CHARLES				39	IRELAND	CE	IRISH	SADDLER	082	C	2	5
GARDNER	CAROLINE		1	1	41	ENGLAND	CE	ENGLISH		085	I		8
GARDNER	WILLIAM				43	ONT	CP	SCOTCH	F	081	J	1	34
GARLAND	MARY		1	1	44	ENGLAND	WM	ENGLISH		085	J		8
GARMAN	DANIEL				35	IRELAND	RC	IRISH	F	081	J	1	16
GARNOCH	ARCHIBD				50	SCOTLAND	CP	SCOTCH	BOOKKEEPER	081	B		28
GARRELEAU	CATHERINE		1	1	8	QUE	RC	IRISH		082	C	1	8
GARSON	JOHN				39	SCOTLAND	CS	SCOTCH	FARMER	089	B		18
GARVAN	JOHN				62	IRELAND	PS	IRISH	FARMER	081	F		20
GARVEY	GEORGE		1		30	ENGLAND	CE	ENGLISH	LAB	081	B		54
GARVEY	JOHN		1		32	ENGLAND	CE	ENGLISH	LAB	081	B		54
GARVEY	WILLIAM		1		35	ENGLAND	CE	ENGLISH	LAB	081	B		54
GARVIE	HUGH				35	IRELAND	CE	IRISH	F	085	B		13
GARVIN	ARCHIBALD		1		27	O	CP	IRISH	LAB	081	A	1	38
GARVIN	JOHN				36	QUE	RP	IRISH	FARMER	082	I		14
GARVIN	PATRICK				32	IRELAND	RC	IRISH	LUMBERER	083	C		6
GASKELL	JAMES				32	ENGLAND	RC	ENGLISH	JOINER	085	D		7
GASTLE	WILLIAM				30	ENGLAND	CS	ENGLISH	SAWYER	088	B		20
GATKEY	MATHEW				48	GERMANY	LU	GERMAN	F	082	G		88
GAUDETT	JOSEPH				31	O	RC	FRENCH	JOBER	081	B		32
GAUDETTE	DENNIS				60	QUEBEC	RC	FRENCH	F	081	C		37
GAUKIE	ANTOINE		1		82	QUEBEC	RC	FRENCH		081	J	1	15
GAUKIE	ARSON				32	QUEBEC	RC	FRENCH	F	081	J	1	17
GAUKIE	LUCY		1	1	80	QUE	RC	FRENCH		081	J	1	15
GAUNTLETT	WILLIAM				30	O	WM	ENGLISH	LUMBERMAN	088	B		5
GAUTHIER	GREGORE				40	O	RC	FRENCH	F	082	K	1	9
GAUTHIER	LEMIAL				63	O	RC	FRENCH	F	082	F		14
GAUTHIER	LEMIAL						NG		SEE GOKEY	082	F		14
GAUTHIER	MICHEL						NG		SEE GOKEY	082	F		30
GAY	ELIZABETH			1	30	ENGLAND	PM	ENGLISH	SEAMSTRESS	089	A		5
GEBLER	FREDRICK				33	GERMANY	LU	GERMAN	LABOURER	082	I		57
GEETON	HENREY				60	IRELAND	CE	IRISH	F	085	J		5
GEJEGAD	JOSEPH				45	O	RC	INDIAN	F & FISHERMAN	087	A		28
GELBEAW	HENERY				35	QUE	RC	FRENCH	F	082	K	1	11
GELL	GEORGE		1		22	ENGLAND	CE	ENGLISH	F	085	I		8
GELLEON	WILLIAM				40	GERMANY	CE	GERMAN		081	B		64
GELLY	JOHN		1		22	O	PS	IRISH	F	085	I		12
GEMCEX	MARGARET		1	1	22	O	RC	FRENCH	SERVANT	082	K	1	5
GEMMEL	GOTLIP				61	GERMANY	LU	GERMAN	FARMER	081	F		14
GEMMELL	ARCH				26	ONTARIO	CS	SCOTTISH	FARMER	082	B		40
GEMMELL	DUNCAN				27	O	CP	SCOTCH	F	081	A	1	14
GEMMELL	WILLIAM				56	SCOTLAND	CP	SCOTCH	WEAVER	081	A	1	13
GEMMELL	WILLIAM		1		22	SCOTLAND	CP	SCOTCH	CARPENTER	081	A	2	16
GEMMIL	WILLIAM				35	SCOTLAND	CP	SCOTCH	F	081	A	1	31
GEMMILE	WILLIAM				30	ONTARIO	CP	SCOTTISH	FARMER	082	B		18
GEMMILL	JOHN		1		9	O	CS	SCOTCH		081	I		15
GENES	ELIZABETH								SEE GANIS	084	I	1	D
GENES	PAUL				50	O	RC	INDIAN	HUNTER	084	I	1	5
GENES	PINASEY				43	O	RC	INDIAN	HUNTER	084	I	1	5
GENGEST	JOSEPH	REV			76	FRANCE	RC	FRENCH	PRIEST	082	C	1	57
GENISHON	JOSEPH				48	ONTARIO	RC	INDIAN	HUNTER	083	D		1
GEOFFRY	PATRICK				33	IRELAND	CP	IRISH		082	C	1	25
GEONISSE	LOUIS				80	ONTARIO	RC	INDIAN	HUNTER	084	D		4
GEORGE	ANDREW				38	O	RC	IRISH	F	082	H		2
GEORGE	HENRY				46	QUE	CE	IRISH	MERCHANT	081	K		65
GEORGE	JAMES				30	SCOTLAND	PS	SCOTCH	MINER	089	A		36
GEORGE	THOMAS				32	ENGLAND	CE	ENGLISH	LABOURER	082	E		74
GEORGE	THOMAS				41	ENGLAND	FK	ENGLISH	STORE KEEPER	085	C		9
GERARD	JOSEPH				35	QUE	RC	FRENCH	SAWYER	081	B		23
GERDA	ABNER				37	O	RC	FRENCH	F	082	F		15
GERDA	ALFORD				34	O	RC	FRENCH	F	082	F		16
GERDA	GRIGWA				38	O	RC	FRENCH	F	082	F		16
GERDA	JOSEPH				28	O	RC	FRENCH	F	082	F		16
GERDA	TEFFEL				26	O	RC	FRENCH	F	082	F		16
GERMAIN	EUGENE				22	QUE	RC	FRENCH	F	084	D		7
GERMAIN	EUSTACHE				60	QUEBEC	RC	FRENCH	FARMER	082	B		28
GERMAIN	FRANCOIS		1		20	ONTARIO	RC	FRENCH	SERVANT	084	B		2
GERMAIN	MARG		1	1	18	ONTARIO	RC	IRISH		082	B		20
GEROUX	BARTHOLUME				65	QUE	RC	FRENCH	HOTELKEEPER	082	E		49
GEROUX	CHARLES				38	QUE	RC	FRENCH	FARMER	082	I		71
GEROUX	EMILLY		2	1	22	O	RC			082	E		D
GEROUX	LUKE				53	QUE	RC	FRENCH	CARPENTER	082	E		68
GEROUX	NARCIES				33	QUE	RC	FRENCH	FARMER	082	I		72
GERSIE	JOSEPH				75	QUE	RC	FRENCH	LAB	081	B		76
GERUE	EXAVIER		1		5	O	RC	FRENCH	PAINTER	081	B		54
GERUE	PROSPER				38	QUE	RC	FRENCH	LAB	081	B		62
GERUE	TILDA		1	1	35	QUE	RC	FRENCH	HOUSEKEEPER	081	B		54
GERVAH	AMBROIS				31	O	RC	FRENCH	F	082	C	1	58
GERVAH	BATTIST				72	QUE	RC	FRENCH	F	082	C	1	10
GERVAH	DERNAS				38	QUE	RC	FRENCH	F	082	C	1	55
GERVAH	GILBARE				31	O	RC	FRENCH	F	082	C	1	57
GERVAH	PHILLIP				71	QUE	RC	FRENCH	F	082	C	1	56

SURNAME	NAME1	NAME2	STRAY	SEX	AGE	BIRTHPL	RELIGION	ORIGIN	OCCUP	DIST	SUB_DIST	DIV	PAGE
GERVAH	THEOFFILLE				29	O	RC	FRENCH	F	082	C	1	58
GERVAH	VERONIQUE			1	60	QUE	RC	FRENCH	F	082	C	1	58
GERVAIS	LOUIS				28	QUE	RC	FRENCH	F	081	K		22
GERVAIS	MOSES				59	QUE	RC	FRENCH	F	081	K		33
GESTEBUSH	MARY			1	35	O	WM	INDIAN		086	A	3	6
GETTY	WILLIAM				56	IRELAND	PS	IRISH	F	085	C		23
GIANDRON	JOHN		1		22	QUE	RC	FRENCH	FARMER	084	E		3
GIBBINS	EDWD		1		30	QUE	RC	IRISH	SHANTYMAN	082	E		18
GIBBINS	WILLIAM		1		16	ENGLAND	WM	ENGLISH	CLERK	082	E		30
GIBBONS	ALEX				39	ONT	CP	ENGLISH	F	081	J	1	46
GIBBONS	ALEX				31	ONT	CE	ENGLISH	F	081	J	1	50
GIBBONS	GEORGE				55	ENGLAND	CE	ENGLISH	F	081	H	2	3
GIBBONS	JOHN				34	ONT	CE	ENGLISH	F	081	J	1	50
GIBBONS	JOHN	B			44	UNITED STATES	CS	ENGLISH	F	081	H	2	1
GIBBONS	WILLIAM				23	O	CS	ENGLISH	F	081	H	1	2
GIBBONS	WILLIAM				63	ENGLAND	WM	ENGLISH	F	081	J	1	44
GIBBONS	WM	JOSEPH			38	ENGLAND	WM	ENGLISH	F	082	K	1	1
GIBBS	ROBERT		1		23	ENGLAND	CE	ENGLISH	CARPENTER	085	E		18
GIBIDWEGIJY	MICHEL				58	US	RC	INDIAN	F & FISHERMAN	087	A		30
GIBSON	ALEX		1		38	IRELAND	RC	IRISH	MINER	090	F		17
GIBSON	CHARLETTE		1	1	14	O	CE	IRISH		082	E		16
GIBSON	EDWARD				38	ONTARIO	CS	ENGLISH	F	082	A		58
GIBSON	GEORGE				29	QUE	RC	FRENCH	LUMBERMAN	088	C		11
GIBSON	ISAAC				37	ONTARIO	CE	ENGLISH	F	082	A		58
GIBSON	JAMES				36	O	CS	ENGLISH	F	085	I		15
GIBSON	JOHN				30	ONTARIO	CE	ENGLISH	F	082	A		56
GIBSON	JOSEPH				48	QUE	RC	SCOTCH	LAB	081	B		21
GIBSON	JULIA				56	QUEBEC	CE	IRISH		082	A		58
GIBSON	MARGRET		1	1	39	QUE	CE	IRISH	HOTELKEEPER	082	E		15
GIBSON	NEIL		1		35	NEW BRUNSWICK	CS	SCOTCH	FARMER	084	A		1
GIBSON	RICHARD		1		17	O	CE	IRISH		082	E		16
GIBSON	ROBERT				37	ONTARIO	CE	ENGLISH	LABOURER	082	A		72
GIBSON	ROBERT		2		12	O	CS			085	I		D
GIBSON	ROBT	EDWD	1		9	O	CE	IRISH		082	E		16
GIBSON	THOMAS				36	ONTARIO	CE	IRISH	F	082	A		57
GIBSON	THOMAS				70	IRELAND	CE	IRISH	FARMER	084	A		1
GIBSON	WILLIAM		1		68	IRELAND	CE	IRISH	F	081	K		55
GIBSON	WILLIAM				31	O	WM	ENGLISH	F	082	C	2	16
GIBSON	WILLIAM				33	O	WM	ENGLISH	F	085	C		24
GIBSON	WILLIAM	H	1		19	O	CE	IRISH	STOREKEEPER	082	E		15
GIDLEY	SAMUEL				55	ENGLAND	WM	ENGLISH	MINER	089	A		10
GIERKE	MARTIN				60	PRUSSIA	LU	PRUSSIAN	F	085	A		5
GIGUIRE	ANDRE				28	O	RC	FRENCH	F	082	L		7
GILBERT	GEORGE				29	GERMANY	ZZ	GERMAN	F	085	H		12
GILBERT	HENRY				67	GERMANY	ZZ	GERMAN	F	085	H		11
GILBERT	HENRY	JR			33	GERMANY	ZZ	GERMAN	F	085	H		12
GILBERT	ROBERT				30	IRELAND	CE	IRISH	F	085	E		20
GILBERT	ROSA		1	1	11	MICHIGAN	RC	INDIAN	STUDENT	087	A		1
GILBONS	JOHN				32	IRELAND	RC	IRISH	FARMER	082	B		19
GILBONS	PATRICK				55	IRELAND	RC	IRISH	FARMER	082	B		21
GILBREATH	THOMAS				33	SCOTLAND	CP	SCOTCH	F	085	H		1
GILCHRIST	ANNIE		1	1	30	Q	CP	SCOTCH	SERVANT	081	B		1
GILCHRIST	EDMUND				36	SCOTLAND	PS	SCOTCH	F	086	A	1	7
GILCHRIST	ELIZA		1	1	25	QUE	CP	SCOTCH	SERVANT	081	B		1
GILCHRIST	JAMES				74	SCOTLAND	CS	SCOTCH		081	A	1	41
GILCHRIST	PETTER				40	SCOTLAND	CS	SCOTCH	MILLER	081	I		16
GILCHRIST	SUSAN		1	1	15	QUE	CE	ENGLISH	SERVANT	081	A	2	29
GILCHRIST	WILLIAM				68	ONTARIO	CS	SCOTCH	F	082	A		30
GILE	THOMAS		1		55	ENGLAND	CE	ENGLISH	MINE LABOURER	089	A		20
GILES	CHARLES				24	O	BC	SCOTCH	F	086	A	1	12
GILES	HENERY				68	IRELAND	RC	IRISH	F	081	H	1	8
GILES	JOHN				32	O	RC	IRISH	F	081	K		27
GILES	JOHN				27	QUE	PM	IRISH	F	085	D		17
GILES	MARTHA			1	55	IRELAND	EM	IRISH	F	085	D		21
GILES	ROBERT				30	O	CE	IRISH	F	085	E		25
GILES	THOMAS	H			25	O	WM	IRISH	F	085	D		27
GILICHAR	BATES				50	QUE	RC	FRENCH	LUMBERER	084	G	1	1
GILL	HENRY					ENGLAND	NG	ENGLISH		085	D		18
GILL	HENRY		1		20	ENGLAND	CE	ENGLISH	STORE CLERK	085	I		39
GILL	HUGH		1		9	CANADA	PR	SCOTCH	SERVANT	085	A		4
GILL	JOHN		1		35	ENGLAND	CE	ENGLISH	MINE LABOURER	089	A		38
GILLAN	JOHN				54	IRELAND	WM	IRISH	CARPENTER	081	J	1	70
GILLESPIE	ANNIE		1	1	40	SCOTLAND	CP	SCOTCH		081	A	1	22
GILLESPIE	GEORGE		1		20	QUE	CS	SCOTCH	F	081	A	1	63
GILLIAN	GREGIOR		1		23	QUE	RC	FRENCH	LUMBERMAN	088	C		10
GILLIAN	JOHN	ARTHUR			36	IRELAND	CE	IRISH	LAB	081	A	2	1
GILLIES	JOHN				52	SCOTLAND	PS	SCOTCH	MINE LABOURER	089	A		33
GILLIES	NIEL				47	SCOTLAND	PS	SCOTCH	MINER	089	A		27
GILLIN	BERNIERD				55	IRELAND	RC	IRISH	F	081	H	1	21
GILLIN	JAMES				42	IRELAND	CE	IRISH	F	081	H	2	6
GILLION	ELLEN		1	1	9	O	RC	IRISH	SERVANT	081	A	2	29
GILLIS	PATRICK				26	IRELAND	RC	IRISH	SHOEMAKER	081	I		7
GILLIS	SARAH		1	1	11	ONTARIO	EM	ENGLISH		082	A		72
GILLON	JOHN				24	O	CP	SCOTCH	LAB	081	B		9
GILMER	ROBERT				63	SCOTLAND	CP	SCOTCH	WEAVER	082	G		65
GILMOUR	DAVID				26	SCOTLAND	PS	SCOTCH	BLACKSMITH	086	C	1	10
GILMOUR	HUGH				35	IRELAND	CE	IRISH	F	081	H	2	39
GILMOUR	HUGH				43	ONTARIO	CS	SCOTCH	F	082	A		4
GIMLEL	CHARLES		1		23	DRUSSIA	LU	GERMAN	SHANTY CLERK	082	C	1	3
GINNIS	JOSEPH				25	ENGLAND	WM	ENGLISH	CHEMIST	089	A		11
GINNIS	PATRICK		1		24	IRELAND	RC	IRISH	LUMBERMAN	086	C	1	10
GINOSHAMY	J	BTE			50	US	RC	INDIAN	F & FISHERMAN	087	A		36
GINOSHAMY	J	BTE			26	O	RC	INDIAN	F & FISHERMAN	087	A		37
GINOSHAMY	THOMAS				45	US	RC	INDIAN	F	087	A		3
GINOSHAMY	WILLIAM				32	US	RC	INDIAN	F	087	A		4
GINOSHEMY	MICHEL				41	US	RC	INDIAN	F & BLACKSMITH	087	A		4
GIROUX	EMILIE		1	1	48	QUE	RC	FRENCH		088	A		13
GISHNEBUS	JACOB				40	O	WM	INDIAN	F	086	A	3	4
GLADEITOER	NOT GIVEN		2	1		O	WM			085	I		D
GLADEITOER	OCELIO				39	US	WM	INDIAN	MASON	085	I		9
GLAGIEN	CYTHIEN		1	1	27	QUE	CE	ENGLISH		082	E		48
GLAGIEN	JOHN	ARTHUR	1		1	O	CE	ENGLISH		082	E		48
GLAGIEN	MARY	E	1	1	3	QUE	CE	ENGLISH		082	E		48
GLAGIEN	STEPHEN	W	1		33	NB	CE	ENGLISH	LUMBER AGENT	082	E		48
GLANVILLE	JAMES				62	ENGLAND	WM	ENGLISH	MINER	089	A		47
GLANVILLE	JOHN				25	ENGLAND	WM	ENGLISH	MINER	089	A		13

SURNAME	NAME1	NAME2	STRAY	SEX	AGE	BIRTHPL	RELIGION	ORIGIN	OCCUP	DIST	SUB_DIST	DIV	PAGE
GLAP	JAMES				42	SCOTLAND	PS	SCOTCH	F	085	C		3
GLASGOW	JANE		1	1	18	IRELAND	PS	IRISH		085	C		24
GLASS	JOHN		1		35	QUE	CP	ENGLISH	F	090	F		19
GLEESON	FRANK				37	GERMANY	LU	GERMAN	OVERSEER	090	D		5
GLEESON	MARGRET		1	1	33	IRELAND	RC	IRISH	SERVANT	081	G	1	6
GLEN	ROSA				18	O	RC	IRISH	SERVANT	081	B		72
GLIEN	JOSEPH				34	O	CP	IRISH	GROCER	081	B		8
GLINDAY	ELIZABETH		1	1	35	UNITED STATES	CP	IRISH		082	C	1	13
GOBLE						O	CP			085	E		29
GODARD	NAPOLEON		1		22	QUE	RC	FRENCH	HOTEL MANAGER	082	E		43
GODDARD	EDMOND				46	ENGLAND	CP	ENGLISH	BLACKSMITH CARRIAGE	082	C	1	2
GODDIN	GILBERT				37	QUE	RC	FRENCH	F	081	E		3
GODDIN	ISIDORE				68	QUE	RC	FRENCH	F	081	E		3
GODETTE	MICHL		1		38	QUE	RC	FRENCH	LABOURER	082	E		27
GODETTE	SELINA		1	1	28	QUE	RC	FRENCH		082	E		27
GODIN	ABNER						NG		SEE GORDA	082	F		15
GODIN	ALFRED						NG		SEE GERDA	082	F		16
GODIN	CASIMERE				32	QUE	RC	FRENCH	F	081	E		11
GODIN	GREGOIRE						NG		SEE GORDO	082	F		16
GODIN	JOSEPH						NG		SEE GORDO	082	F		16
GODIN	THEOPHILE						NG		SEE GORDO	082	F		16
GODKINS	SAML				39	IRELAND	WM	IRISH	COOPER	082	E		31
GODMERE	MINEZISS				26	QUE	RC	FRENCH	SHANTY CLERK	082	E		43
GOGGIN	WILLIAM				50	IRELAND	CE	IRISH	F	085	I		38
GOGGINGS	WILLIAM		1		12	ENGLAND	RC	IRISH	SERVANT	083	C		4
GOHALIA	THOMAS		1		60	IRELAND	CE	IRISH		082	F		12
GOKEY	FELIX				42	QUE	RC	FRENCH	F	081	K		31
GOKEY	JOSEPH				54	QUE	RC	FRENCH	F	081	K		40
GOKEY	MICHEL				60	O	RC	FRENCH	F	082	F		30
GOLL	AMELIA		1	1	16	GERMANY	LU	GERMAN		081	K		56
GOLL	FREDERICA		1	1	60	GERMANY	LU	GERMAN		081	K		56
GOLL	JOHN		1		58	GERMANY	LU	GERMAN		081	K		56
GOLLINETT	ESTHER		1	1	60	QUE	RC	FRENCH		082	C	1	57
GOLTON	BROOKE		1		18	SCOTLAND	CS	SCOTCH	CLERK	084	E		5
GOMIS	ABRM				63	USA	BA	ENGLISH	F	085	L		3
GONAROOT	VALANTINE				31	PRUSSIA	RC	PRUSSIAN	FARMER	083	A	1	2
GONIE	ANTOINE		1		12	O	RC	FRENCH		081	E		17
GONNE	FRANCES		1		24	QUE	RC	FRENCH	LAB	081	B		20
GONNE	MARY	JANE	1	1	19	O	RC	FRENCH		081	B		20
GONYON	JOSEPH				45	QUE	RC	FRENCH	FARMER	082	I		50
GOOD	THOMAS		1		54	ENGLAND	CE	ENGLISH	CARPENTER	085	I		20
GOODER	WILLIAM				24	ENGLAND	EP	ENGLISH	SHOEMAKER	087	B	3	1
GOODFELLOW	JOHN				47	SCOTLAND	PS	SCOTCH	F	085	J		6
GOODFELLOW	WILLIAM				48	O	CE	IRISH	F	081	A	1	7
GOODMAN	WILLIAM				47	ENGLAND	CE	ENGLISH	COOPER	089	A		25
GOODMAS	ALBERTENIA		1	1	64	GERMANY	LU	GERMAN	SERVANT	082	J		9
GOODMAS	WILLIAM				38	POMMER	LU	GERMAN	F	082	J		8
GOODOMAN	CHARLES		1		21	GERMANY	LU	GERMAN	LAB	082	J		13
GOODS	LOUIS				28	GERMANY	LU	GERMAN	F	082	H		13
GOODS	WILLIAM				58	GERMANY	LU			082	H		D
GOODSMAN	LOUIS				48	GERMANY	CE	DUTCH	LAB	081	B		47
GOODWIN	ALEXANDER				33	O	CP	SCOTCH	LAB	081	B		59
GOODWIN	DAVID				48	O	CP	SCOTCH	F	081	A	2	2
GOODWIN	ROBERT				37	O	PS	SCOTCH	F	085	J		16
GOODWIN	WILLIAM				60	IRELAND	RC	IRISH	F	081	J	2	1
GOOLDT	FERDINAND				38	GERMANY	LU	GERMAN	FARMER	082	I		38
GOOLDT	JOHN				37	GERMANY	LU	GERMAN	FARMER	082	I		39
GOOLDTSMIDT	AUGUST				55	GERMANY	LU	GERMAN	FARMER	082	I		20
GOOLEK	MARTIN				36	GERMANY	LU	GERMAN	FARMER	082	I		80
GOORR	FREDRICK		1		3	ONT	CP	GERMAN		082	I		37
GORAN	MEDE				27	QUE	RC	FRENCH	LABOURER	081	B		31
GORBY	THOMAS				26	O	CE	IRISH	F	081	H	2	9
GORBY	THOMAS		1		68	O	RC	IRISH		081	H	2	40
GORBY	WILLIAM				58	IRELAND	CE	IRISH	F	081	H	2	20
GORDON	DONALD				41	SCOTLAND	RC	SCOTCH	F	086	B		4
GORDON	GEORGE				73	SCOTLAND	CP	SCOTCH		081	I		25
GORDON	HUGH				23	IRELAND	CE	IRISH	F	082	A		78
GORDON	HUGH	G			31	QUEBEC	RP	SCOTTISH	FARMER	082	B		55
GORDON	ROBERT				34	O	CP	SCOTCH	BLACKSMITH	081	I		25
GORDON	ROBERT				31	IRELAND	CS	IRISH	F	082	A		34
GORE	JAMES	HENRY			45	ENGLAND	CE	ENGLISH	TEACHER & FARMER	089	B		21
GORLEY	THOMAS				65	IRELAND	PS	IRISH	F	087	B	2	7
GORMAN	BENJAMIN		1		2	O	WM	IRISH		084	D		6
GORMAN	CONSTANT		1		21	ENGLAND	CE	ENGLISH	SCHOOL TEACHER	082	F		37
GORMAN	DANIEL				54	IRELAND	RC	IRISH	FARMER	081	J	1	1
GORMAN	DANIEL				53	IRELAND	RC	IRISH	FARMER	082	B		37
GORMAN	DENIS		1		13	IRELAND	RC	IRISH		082	A		83
GORMAN	FRED	A	1		18	ENGLAND	CE	ENGLISH	CLERK	082	E		26
GORMAN	HANNA		1	1	24	IRELAND	RC	IRISH	SERVANT	082	E		20
GORMAN	JOHN				50	IRELAND	RC	IRISH	FARMER	081	J	1	1
GORMAN	JOHN				36	ONT	RC	IRISH	F	081	J	1	21
GORMAN	JOHN				47	IRELAND	RC	IRISH	F	081	K		17
GORMAN	JOHN		1		16	ONTARIO	RC	IRISH	FARMER	082	B		40
GORMAN	JOHN		1		16	O	RC	IRISH	CLERK	082	E		30
GORMAN	MARTIN				37	IRELAND	RC	IRISH	SHOEMAKER	081	I		13
GORMAN	MARTIN				60	ONTARIO	RC	IRISH	F	082	A		81
GORMAN	MICH	L			47	IRELAND	RC	IRISH	TAILOR	082	E		16
GORMAN	MICHAEL		1		14	O	RC	IRISH	CLERK	081	K		64
GORMAN	MICHAEL		1		19	O	RC	IRISH	SHOEMAKER	081	K		71
GORMAN	MICHAEL				50	IRELAND	RC	IRISH	F	082	A		81
GORMAN	MICHAEL		1		14	ONTARIO	RC	IRISH		082	B		40
GORMAN	MICHL				37	O	RC	IRISH	CARPENTER	082	E		13
GORMAN	PATRICK				58	IRELAND	RC	IRISH	FARMER POSTMASTER	081	J	1	10
GORMAN	PATRICK				65	IRELAND	RC	IRISH	F	081	J	1	21
GORMAN	PETER		1		9	ONTARIO	RC	IRISH		082	B		41
GORMAN	PETER				40	IRELAND	RC	IRISH	FARMER	082	B		41
GORMAN	SAMUEL		1		11	ONTARIO	RC	IRISH		082	B		41
GORMAN	SIMON				45	IRELAND	RC	IRISH	FARMER HOTELKEEPER	081	J	1	10
GORMAN	THOMAS		1		13	ONTARIO	RC	IRISH		082	B		41
GORMAN	THOMAS				53	IRELAND	RC	IRISH	F	082	G		64
GORMAN	THOS				40	IRELAND	RC	IRISH	FARMER	081	J	1	21
GORMAN	TIMOTHY				37	IRELAND	RC	IRISH	FARMER	082	B		39
GORMAN	TIMOTHY				6	ONTARIO	RC	IRISH		082	B		41
GORMAN	WILLIAM				31	O	RC	IRISH	BLACKSMITH	081	K		1
GORMAN	WILLIAM		1		70	IRELAND	RC	IRISH	LABOURER	082	A		81
GORR	FRDRICK				52	GERMANY	LU	GERMAN	FARMER	082	I		23

SURNAME	NAME1	NAME2	STRAY	SEX	AGE	BIRTHPL	RELIGION	ORIGIN	OCCUP	DIST	SUB_DIST	DIV	PAGE
GORR	FREDERICK						NG		SEE GOORR	082	I		37
GORR	LOUISE		1	1	18	GERMANY	LU	GERMAN	SERVANT	082	E		57
GORR	WILLIAM				28	GERMANY	LU	GERMAN	FARMER	082	I		24
GORSOSKI	HENRIETTA		1	1	17	GERMANY	RC	GERMAN	SERVANT	082	E		1
GOSALIN	SAM		1		27	QUEBEC	RC	FRENCH	LUMBERMAN	083	A	1	8
GOSLIN	LOUIS				49	QUE	RC	FRENCH	FARMER	082	I		10
GOSLIN	THOMAS		1		40	IRELAND	CE	IRISH	FARM LABOURER	081	K		48
GOTH	BRYCE				35	O	CE	ENGLISH	F	081	H	2	29
GOTH	JOHN				84	ENGLAND	CE	ENGLISH		081	H	2	29
GOTHIER	JOSEPH		1		21	QUE	RC	FRENCH	CLERK	082	E		29
GOTT	JAMES				34	IRELAND	WM	IRISH	F	085	D		29
GOUCE	JOHN				50	PRUSSIA	CE	GERMAN	FARMER	082	B		11
GOUDETT	JOSEPH				29	ONTARIO	RC	FRENCH	LUMBERER	083	A	1	15
GOUGON	ARSEN				40	QUE	RC	FRENCH	F	082	K	1	9
GOULD	ARTHUR				31	ONT	CE	IRISH	F	082	A		84
GOULD	JAMES				24	ONT	EM	IRISH	F	082	A		34
GOULD	JOHN				60	IRELAND	EM	IRISH	F	082	A		84
GOULD	ROBERT				38	IRELAND	CE	IRISH	F	082	A		84
GOULD	WILLIAM				40	IRELAND	CE	IRISH	F	082	A		84
GOULEY	CHARLES				50	O	RC	FRENCH	HUNTER	084	I	1	2
GOURLEY	GEORGE		1		18	O	PS	IRISH	SADDLER	082	E		58
GOURLEY	GEORGE				50	SCOTLAND	FK	SCOTCH	TANNER	082	G		59
GOURLEY	JOHN				45	IRELAND	WM	IRISH	F	082	C	1	21
GOW	GEORGE	F			35	ENGLAND	CE	SCOTCH		085	I		1
GOW	ROBERT		1		20	O	CE	SCOTCH	LUMBERMAN	086	C	1	7
GRAB	HENRY				30	GERMANY	ZZ	GERMAN	F	085	H		12
GRAB	MICHAEL				31	GERMANY	ZZ	GERMAN	F	085	H		11
GRABER	WILLIAM				34	GERMANY	LU	GERMAN	F	082	G		17
GRACE	BENJERMAN				35	IRELAND	RC	IRISH	FARMER	081	G	1	25
GRACE	JAMES				50	IRELAND	RC	IRISH	INNKEEPER	081	G	1	6
GRACE	JAMES	J	1		17	O	RC	IRISH	SADDLER	082	E		41
GRACE	JOHN		1		18	IRELAND	RC	IRISH	SERVANT	081	I		5
GRACE	MARY	ANN	1	1	18	O	RC	IRISH	SERVANT	082	E		16
GRACE	MICHAEL				54	IRELAND	RC	IRISH	F	082	C	2	49
GRACE	MICHL		1		16	O	RC	IRISH	SHOEMAKER	082	E		47
GRACIE	JOSEPH				24	O	CS	SCOTCH	BLACKSMITH	082	C	2	65
GRACIS	MARGRET		1	1	14	O	RC	IRISH		082	D		25
GRAFF	JOHN				67	IRELAND	NR	IRISH	F TAILOR	082	A		69
GRAFFE	WILLIAM				28	ONTARIO	IM	ENGLISH	FARMER	082	B		30
GRAHAM	ALEXANDER				52	SCOTLAND	CP	SCOTCH	F	081	A	1	26
GRAHAM	CHARLES				42	IRELAND	CP	IRISH	LAB	081	B		27
GRAHAM	DAVID				43	SCOTLAND	CP	SCOTCH	F	081	J	1	70
GRAHAM	ELIZEBE		2	1	1	O	CE			082	F		D
GRAHAM	ELLEN		2	1	31	O	CE			082	G		D
GRAHAM	ISABELLA		1	1	20	ONTARIO	CE	IRISH	SERVANT	084	C		5
GRAHAM	JACOB		1		25	IRELAND	PS	IRISH	F	085	C		4
GRAHAM	JAMES				58	ONTARIO	CE	ENGLISH	FARMER	081	G	1	42
GRAHAM	JAMES				61	SCOTLAND	CP	SCOTCH	F	081	J	1	71
GRAHAM	JAMES				35	O	CE	IRISH	F	082	G		24
GRAHAM	JANE		1	1	48	IRELAND	CE	IRISH	SERVANT	086	C	1	11
GRAHAM	JOHN				29	O	CP	SCOTCH	F	081	A	1	26
GRAHAM	JOHN				27	QUE	EM	IRISH	F	082	C	1	38
GRAHAM	JOHN				25	SCOTLAND	RC	SCOTTISH	STAGE DRIVER	082	E		44
GRAHAM	JOHN		1		30	IRELAND	RC	IRISH	CARPENTER	084	G	1	1
GRAHAM	JOHN				40	ENGLAND	CE	ENGLISH	BLACKSMITH	085	A		12
GRAHAM	MARY		1	1	25	IRELAND	RC	IRISH	SERVANT	082	E		26
GRAHAM	MARY		1	1	22	QUE	RC	IRISH	SERVANT	082	E		48
GRAHAM	NANCY		1	1	22	ONTARIO	CE	IRISH	SERVANT	084	C		5
GRAHAM	R	F			27	O	PB	SCOTCH	WAGGONMAKER	081	A	2	27
GRAHAM	RICHARD				40	O	WM	IRISH	F	082	C	2	57
GRAHAM	RICHARD				37	IRELAND	CE	IRISH	F	082	H		14
GRAHAM	RICHARD		1		9	ONT	RC	IRISH		082	I		35
GRAHAM	ROBERT				71	IRELAND	CE	IRISH	F	082	C	2	50
GRAHAM	ROBERT		1		25	IRELAND	RC	IRISH	CLERK	082	E		42
GRAHAM	ROBERT		1		15	ONT	CE	IRISH		082	I		39
GRAHAM	ROBERT				36	ONT	WM	IRISH	FARMER	082	I		65
GRAHAM	ROBERT				61	IRELAND	CE	IRISH	F	090	F		17
GRAHAM	SUSAN			1	67	IRELAND	CE			082	H		D
GRAHAM	THOMAS				46	IRELAND	CE	IRISH	F	082	F		8
GRAHAM	THOS		1		32	IRELAND	RC	IRISH	DOMESTIC SERVANT	082	E		19
GRAHAM	WILLIAM				39	IRELAND	EM	IRISH	MINISTER	081	H	2	28
GRAHAM	WILLIAM				49	ENGLAND	CE	ENGLISH	MECHANIC	082	B		29
GRAHAM	WILLIAM		1		13	ONT	CE	IRISH		082	I		39
GRAHAM	WILLIAM				3	O	PS	IRISH	F	085	D		5
GRAINGER	WILLIAM				29	O	CE	ENGLISH	F	085	I		32
GRANT			1		36	QUE	PS	SCOTTISH	WAGONMAKER	082	E		63
GRANT	ALLEN	D	1		33	O	CE	SCOTTISH	WAGONMAKER	082	E		59
GRANT	CHARLES				30	O	RC	FRENCH	FISHERMAN	089	A		64
GRANT	CHARLES				50	O	RC	SCOTCH	LABOURER	089	B		29
GRANT	DONALD				35	SCOTLAND	PS	SCOTCH	F	085	C		16
GRANT	FRANCOIS		2		2	O	RC			089	B		D
GRANT	HENRY		1		22	PRUSSIA	PS	PRUSSIAN	F LABOURER	081	J	1	33
GRANT	ISABELLA		1	1	11	O	PS	SCOTCH		085	D		26
GRANT	JAMES				37	SCOTLAND	WM	SCOTCH	F	082	A		16
GRANT	JAMES				62	SCOTLAND	CS	SCOTCH	F	082	A		16
GRANT	JOHN				31	SCOTLAND	CS	SCOTCH	F	082	A		16
GRANT	JOHN		1		45	IRELAND	RC	IRISH		086	B		1
GRANT	MANI		2			O	RC			089	B		D
GRANT	ROBERT				28	QUE	CP	SCOTCH	CARPENTER	081	B		70
GRANT	W		1		20	O	CS	SCOTCH	LABOURER	088	A		8
GRAVES	AVERAL				34	IRELAND	CE	IRISH	F	085	A		18
GRAVES	GEORGE				33	O	CE	AFRICAN	F	085	B		15
GRAWBERG	MARY		1	1	62	IRELAND	ME	GERMAN		082	G		94
GRAY	JAMES				28	ONTARIO	WM	IRISH	LAB	082	A		46
GRAY	JAMES				71	SCOTLAND	CP	SCOTCH	F	085	F		4
GRAY	JOHN				40	ENGLAND	CE	ENGLISH	CARPENTER & F	082	F		2
GRAY	JOHN		2			O	RC			082	K	1	D
GRAY	ROBERT				29	O	RP	SCOTCH	SHOEMAKER	081	I		13
GRAY	ROBERT				56	SCOTLAND	CP	SCOTTISH	BOOKKEEPER	082	E		65
GRAY	SAMUEL				27	O	RC	SCOTCH	INNKEEPER	082	K	1	1
GRAY	SIMON	P	1		20	O	RC	IRISH	CLERK	082	E		42
GRAYDON	SAMUEL				43	IRELAND	CE	IRISH	F	085	J		12
GRAZ	MINNE		1	1	15	GERMANY	WM	GERMAN		082	H		11
GREATREX	BROWN		1		27	ENGLAND	CE	ENGLISH	BRICK MAKER	089	A		38
GREELY	KATE		1	1	21	O	RC	IRISH	SEAMSTRESS	081	B		11
GREELY	MARGRET		1	1	20	O	RC	IRISH	SEAMSTRESS	081	B		11

SURNAME	NAME1	NAME2	STRAY	SEX	AGE	BIRTHPL	RELIGION	ORIGIN	OCCUP	DIST	SUB_DIST	DIV	PAGE
GREEN	BUSTED				19	O	CE	IRISH	F	081	E		5
GREEN	FRANCIS				32	IRELAND	RC	IRISH	FARMER	083	A	1	15
GREEN	GEORGE				25	O	RC	IRISH	F	082	H		10
GREEN	JAMES				40	O	NG	IRISH	FARMER	081	D		4
GREEN	JOHN				22	QUE	RC	INDIAN	HUNTER	081	D		21
GREEN	JOHN				44	O	RC	IRISH	F	082	H		8
GREEN	PHILIP				36	O	RC	IRISH	F	082	H		10
GREEN	PHILIP	SR			68	IRELAND	RC	IRISH	F	082	H		9
GREEN	WILLIAM				60	IRELAND	CP	IRISH	F	082	C	2	14
GREENE	SAMUEL				46	IRELAND	CE	IRISH	F	085	K	1	1
GREENEY	ESTER		1	1	34	O	RC	IRISH	TAILORESS	082	E		39
GREENMAN	LOT		1		30	ENGLAND	BA	ENGLISH	F	085	I		18
GREEOR	JAMES		1		60	IRELAND	EM	IRISH		082	G		98
GREER	EDWARD				50	IRELAND	EM	IRISH	F	082	G		39
GREERSON	JOHN				38	ONTARIO	CS	SCOTCH	FARMER	083	A	2	3
GREEVES	JANE			1	35	IRELAND	CE	IRISH		081	K		48
GREEVES	NATHANIEL				40	SCOTLAND	CP	SCOTCH	SAWYER	081	B		36
GREGAR	AUGUST				32	PRUSSIA	WM	PRUSIA	F	081	J	1	76
GREGG	GEORGE				31	ENGLAND	CE	ENGLISH	F	085	I		24
GREGG	WILLIAM				34	ENGLAND	CE	ENGLISH	CARPENTER.	085	D		35
GREGOR	JOHN				29	PRUSSIA	ZZ	PRUSSIAN	F	085	H		11
GREGSON	JAMES				63	ENGLAND	CE	ENGLISH	FARMER	089	A		49
GREHAM	DAVID				42	SCOTLAND	WM	SCOTCH	LUMBERER	083	B	1	1
GREIG	JOHN	M			34	SCOTLAND	CP	SCOTCH	SAILOR	089	B		25
GRELIE	EDWARD				33	QUE	RC	FRENCH	LUMBERMAN	088	B		6
GRENFELL	EDWIN				30	ENGLAND	PM	ENGLISH	MINER	089	A		11
GRENFELL	JOHN				46	ENGLAND	WM	ENGLISH	ENGINEER	089	A		17
GRENIER	ISAAC				37	O	RC	FRENCH	TEACHER	081	K		73
GRESIE	FREDERICK				47	PRUSSIA	LU	PRUSSIAN	F	081	J	1	46
GRESOR	FREDERICK				32	GERMANY	RC	GERMAN	FARMER	089	B		44
GREVELL	JOSEPH				36	QUE	RC	FRENCH	HOTELKEEPER	081	I		39
GREY	JOHN				48	IRELAND	CE	IRISH	CARPENTER	088	B		3
GREY	SUSAN			1	46	QUE	CE	IRISH		088	B		3
GREY	WILLIAM				21	QUEBEC	CE	IRISH	LUMBERMAN	088	B		3
GRIEF	CHARLES						NG		SEE GRIFE	082	I		64
GRIER	PATRICK				46	IRELAND	RC	IRISH	F	082	H		11
GRIER	SAMUEL				27	IRELAND	WM	IRISH	MERCHANT	085	E		6
GRIERSON	WILLIAM				35	SCOTLAND	PS	SCOTCH	MINER	090	B		1
GRIFE	CHARLES				44	GERMANY	LU	GERMAN	FARMER	082	I		64
GRIFFIN	EDWIN				50	ENGLAND	WM	ENGLISH	F	086	A	1	18
GRIFFIN	JAMES		1		26	QUE	RC	IRISH	SHANTYMAN	082	E		15
GRIFFIN	JOHN		1		19	O	CE	ENGLISH	TINSMITH	082	E		59
GRIFFITH	ASA		1		24	US	CP	WELSH	ASSAYIST	090	F		19
GRIFFITH	GEORGE				30	IRELAND	CE	IRISH	BLACKSMITH	082	G		48
GRIFFITH	JACOB				20	O	CE	IRISH	F	082	G		39
GRIFFITH	JOHN		1		36	IRELAND	CE	IRISH	F	090	F		23
GRIFFITH	SAMUEL				28	IRELAND	CE	IRISH	SHANTYMAN	082	G		51
GRIFFITH	THOMAS				57	IRELAND	CE	IRISH	F	082	G		38
GRIFFITH	WILLIAM				31	O	CE	IRISH	CARPENTER	081	B		10
GRIFFITH	WILLIAM	C	2		2	O	CE			081	B		D
GRIFFITHS	WILLIAM				52	ENGLAND	EP	ENGLISH	F	087	B	3	1
GRIGER	MARY		1	1	16	GERMANY	LU	GERMAN	SERVANT	082	F		21
GRIMES	AUSTIN		1		12	O	RC	IRISH		081	D		13
GRIMES	AUSTIN				54	IRELAND	RC	IRISH	FARMER	081	D		13
GRIMES	CATHARINE			1	60	IRELAND	RC	IRISH		081	D		13
GRIMES	JAMES		1		14	O	RC	IRISH		081	D		13
GRIMES	JOHN		1		20	O	RC	IRISH	FARMER	081	D		13
GRIMES	JOHN				49	US	PS	ENGLISH	F	085	J		18
GRIMES	PATRICK		1		22	O	RC	IRISH	FARMER	081	D		13
GRIMES	THOMAS		2		65	IRELAND	RC	IRISH		081	D		D
GRISMOUND	MARY			1	30	QUE	RC	FRENCH		081	I		35
GRIVES	JAMES				37	SCOTLAND	PS	SCOTTISH	CARPENTER	082	D		22
GROBARGER	PETER				32	O	CP	GERMAN	F	082	C	2	23
GROBERGER	ANDREW				36	O	CE	GERMAN	F	082	J		11
GROBERGER	SARAH	ANN	1		25	O	CE	GERMAN	SERVANT	082	J		11
GROGAN	ANN		1	1	26	O	RC	IRISH	SERVANT	081	K		62
GROGAN	ANTHONY				55	IRELAND	RC	IRISH	FARMER	081	G	1	16
GROGAN	LUKE		1		14	O	RC	IRISH		081	K		21
GROGAN	MARY		1	1	18	O	RC	IRISH	SERVANT	081	D		13
GROGAN	PATRICK				51	IRELAND	RC	IRISH	F	081	J	1	24
GROGAN	PATRICK		1		18	ONT	RC	IRISH	LABOURER	081	J	1	71
GROIX	JOSEPH		1		23	QUEBEC	RC	FRENCH	RAFTSMAN	084	D		1
GROOME	JOSEPHINE		1	1	29	O	CE	ENGLISH	SCHOOL MISTRESS	089	A		4
GROSE	JOHN				27	WALES	RC	WELSH	FARMER	089	B		20
GROSE	MATTHEW				31	ENGLAND	WM	ENGLISH	MINER	089	A		38
GROSEW	HENRY				62	IRELAND	CE	IRISH	TRADER	081	I		14
GROSSELAS	CARLES				44	GERMANY	LU	GERMAN	F	082	G		92
GROTOSKEY	ALBERT				35	PRUSSIA	RC	PRUSSIAN	FARMER	083	A	1	15
GROUDNOSKI	MICHAEL				40	PRUSSIA	RC	PRUSSIAN	FARMER	083	A	1	7
GROULX	ADELINE		1		24	QUE	RC	FRENCH	SERVANT	082	D		21
GROULX	JOSEPH		1		55	QUE	RC	FRENCH	LUMBERMAN	088	B		17
GROVES	JENETT		1	1	19	ONTARIO	CE	FRENCH	SERVANT	081	G	1	29
GROVES	WILLIAM				49	IRELAND	CE	IRISH	HOTELKEEPER	082	B		49
GRUNLA	RICHARD	C			26	QUE	BA	ENGLISH	SHOEMAKER	082	D		13
GRUNT	JOHN				58	GERMANY	CE	GERMAN	F	081	C		32
GUDRUE	ROBT		1		25	QUE	RC	SCOTCH	LABOURER	088	A		7
GUEGUIN	JOHN		1		31	FRANCE	RC	FRENCH	PRIEST	084	I	2	1
GUENIE	WILLIAM				35	ONT	RC	FRENCH	F	081	J	1	54
GUERTIN	GEORGE				30	QUEBEC	RC	FRENCH	CLERK	084	B		3
GUEST	ELIZA		1	1	60	IRELAND	EM	IRISH		082	A		64
GUEST	FRANCIS				34	IRELAND	EM	IRISH	F	082	A		64
GUEST	GEORGE				32	IRELAND	EM	IRISH	F	082	A		71
GUEST	JAMES				44	IRELAND	CE	IRISH	F	082	A		77
GUEST	THOMAS				36	IRELAND	EM	IRISH	F	082	A		64
GUFFY	EDWD		1		20	O	RC	IRISH	BOOKKEEPER	082	E		26
GUGNIS	LEVIE				30	ONT	RC	FRENCH	F	081	J	1	29
GUIDI	JOSEPH		1		28	LOMBARDY	RC	ITALIAN	MILLWRIGHT	086	C	1	1
GUILMETTE	THEODORE				60	GERMANY	RC	GERMAN	COOPER	089	B		19
GUIME	LEVIE				80	QUEBEC	RC	FRENCH	F	081	J	1	26
GUINEY	CORNELIUS				31	IRELAND	RC	IRISH	F	081	E		5
GUINEY	DANIEL				35	IRELAND	RC	IRISH	FARMER	081	D		17
GUINEY	ELLEN			1	68	IRELAND	RC	IRISH		081	D		13
GUINIE	GEORGE				31	ONT	RC	FRENCH	F	081	J	1	29
GUINIE	JAMES				36	ONT	CE	FRENCH	F	081	J	1	29
GUINIE	JOHN				36	ONT	RC	FRENCH	F	081	J	1	13
GUINIE	ROBERT				29	ONT	RC	FRENCH	F	081	J	1	30

SURNAME	NAME1	NAME2	STRAY	SEX	AGE	BIRTHPL	RELIGION	ORIGIN	OCCUP	DIST	SUB_DIST	DIV	PAGE
GULLET	HENRY				38	QUE	RC	FRENCH	COOPER	081	I		39
GULLIKSON	JACKIMA		1		41	NORWAY	PS	NORWEGIAN	ENGINEER	086	C	1	1
GUNAU	SAMUEL		1		23	Q	RC	FRENCH		086	B		1
GUNK	THOMAS				60	IRELAND	PS	IRISH	F	086	A	2	1
GUNN	ALLAN				50	O	RC	SCOTCH	MILL OWNER	088	C		9
GUNTER	GUSTAV				48	GERMANY	LU	GERMAN	FARMER	082	I		19
GUNTER	JOHN				53	GERMANY	LU	GERMAN	FARMER	082	I		19
GUPPY	HENERY				44	ENGLAND	WM	ENGLISH	CARPENTER	082	D		15
GURMAN	ALFRED		1		28	Q	RC	FRENCH		086	B		1
GURT	FREDERICK				40	GERMANY	EV	GERMAN	F	082	H		21
GURT	GODFORTZ				48	GERMANY	EV	GERMAN	F	082	H		25
GURTZ	LOUIS				42	GERMANY	CE	GERMAN	F	083	C		16
GUSTA	ROSE								SEE ROSE G	081	B		30
GUTCHER	GEORGE		1		7	O	RC	FRENCH		082	K	1	9
GUTCHER	JAMES		1		19	ONTARIO	RC	FRENCH	FARM LAB	084	C		3
GUTCHER	MARY		1	1	25	O	RC	FRENCH	SERVANT	082	K	1	9
GUTCHER	WILLIAM		1		12	O	RC	FRENCH		082	K	1	8
GUTSMAN	FREDERICK				38	GERMANY	BA	GERMAN	FARMER	081	F		21
GUTZEIT	BERTHA		1	1	10	GERMANY	LU	GERMAN		081	K		58
GUTZEIT	ERNEST		1		45	GERMANY	LU	GERMAN		081	K		58
GUTZEIT	FREDERICA		1	1	46	GERMANY	LU	GERMAN		081	K		58
GUTZEIT	IDA		1	1	7	GERMANY	LU	GERMAN		081	K		58
GUTZEIT	JOHANNA		1	1	13	GERMANY	LU	GERMAN		081	K		58
GUTZEIT	PAUL		1		1	GERMANY	LU	GERMAN		081	K		58
HADDOW	AGNUS		1	1	13	O	PS	SCOTCH		089	A		41
HADDOW	JOHN		1		15	O	PS	SCOTCH	BLACKSMITH	089	A		41
HADDOW	MARGARET		1	1	18	ENGLAND	WM	SCOTCH	SERVANT	089	A		11
HADDOW	WILLIAM		1		10	O	PS	SCOTCH		089	A		41
HAENTSHAL	CHARLES				36	GERMANY	LU	GERMAN	FARMER	082	I		41
HAGAN	MICHEAL	A			34	O	RC	IRISH	INNKEEPER	082	C	1	38
HAGELSTEIN	ALEXANDER				44	GERMANY	LU	GERMAN	FARMER	081	F		29
HAGERTY	TIMOTHY				40	IRELAND	RC	IRISH	FARMER	081	G	1	19
HAGERTY	WILLIAM				48	IRELAND	RC	IRISH	F	081	K		54
HAGGARTY	BRIDGET			1	48	IRELAND	RC	IRISH	F	081	A	1	75
HAGLE	JANE		1	1	35	ENGLAND	CE	ENGLISH		085	B		21
HAIG	MARY			1	30	SCOTLAND	FK	SCOTCH	TEACHER	089	B		3
HAIGHT	J		1		20	O	CS	SCOTCH	LABOURER	088	A		8
HAIGHT	W		1		27	O	CS	SCOTCH	LABOURER	088	A		8
HAILEY	WILLIAM		1		63	ENGLAND	PR	ENGLISH	FARM SERVANT	085	A		23
HAILY	JAMES				64	IRELAND	RC	IRISH	F	082	H		20
HAIN	ROBERT				34	GERMANY	BA	GERMAN	FARMER	081	F		31
HAINES	HOMER				26	IRELAND	CE	IRISH	F	086	A	1	29
HAINPEAUX	JOSEPH		1		66	CHAMPAGNE	RC	FRENCH	PRIEST	087	A		1
HALE	JOHN				38	ENGLAND	WM	ENGLISH	BAKER	089	A		19
HALE	WILLIAM				30	O	PS	SCOTTISH	FARMER	082	D		3
HALEY	CORNELIUS				30	IRELAND	RC	IRISH	F	081	E		4
HALEY	GEORGE				50	ONTARIO	CE	ENGLISH	F	082	A		72
HALEY	HIRAM	W			33	O	WM	IRISH	F	085	I		24
HALL	GEORGE		1		10	US	RC	ENGLISH		089	B		18
HALL	JOHN				53	NB	CE	ENGLISH	F	085	H		14
HALL	RICHARD				31	IRELAND	RC	IRISH	F	081	E		5
HALL	RICHARD		1		13	O	RC	ENGLISH		089	B		17
HALL	WILARD				51	NEW BRUNSWICK	UV		F	087	B	3	10
HALLADAY	ISABELLA		1	1	21	O	CP	SCOTCH	TEACHER	081	B		85
HALLEY	MARGARET		1	1	38	ONTARIO	RC	IRISH		082	A		5
HALLIDAY	JOHN				28	O	CS	SCOTCH	LUMBERER	081	A	1	37
HALLIDAY	JOHN				67	SCOTLAND	CP	SCOTCH	F	081	C		18
HALLIDAY	JOHN				35	ONTARIO	CP	SCOTCH	F	081	C		19
HALLIDAY	TIMOTHY				56	O	CE	ENGLISH	F	082	H		14
HALLIDY	JAMES				35	SCOTLAND	CS	SCOTCH	F	081	H	2	13
HALLIDY	JOHN		1		11	O	WM	SCOTCH		081	H	1	2
HALLON	CHARLES				55	IRELAND	RC	IRISH		081	I		17
HALLY	JOHANE		1	1	40	IRELAND	RC	IRISH		081	I		43
HALLY	JOHN				24	IRELAND	RC	IRISH	F	081	J	1	90
HALPENNY	ALICE			1	43	O	WM	IRISH	HOTELKEEPER	082	E		31
HALPENNY	WILLIAM				35	O	PR	SCOTCH	MERCHANT	081	I		17
HALPENNY	WILLIAM		2		45	O	CE		HOTELKEEPER	082	E		D
HALSTAD	JESSIE		1	1		O	NG	SCOTCH		081	I		11
HALSTEAD	ROBERT		1		14	ONT	CP	SCOTCH		081	J	1	46
HALTZ	CAROLINE		1	1	22	GERMANY	NR	GERMAN	SERVANT MAID	082	D		1
HAMBLIN	JAMES				53	O	ME	SCOTTISH	FARMER	082	D		5
HAMEL	JOSUE		1		28	QUE	RC	FRENCH		082	D		19
HAMILTON	ANDREW				50	SCOTLAND	CP	SCOTCH	F	081	A	1	62
HAMILTON	ANDREW				43	ONT	WM	SCOTTISH	FARMER	082	I		73
HAMILTON	ANDREW	SR			68	SCOTLAND	WM	SCOTTISH	FARMER	082	I		74
HAMILTON	BERTHA		1	1	15	O	CP	SCOTCH		081	A	2	52
HAMILTON	DAVID				39	SCOTLAND	CP	SCOTTISH	FARMER	082	B		43
HAMILTON	DAVID				32	O	PS	SCOTCH	PHYSICIAN	089	A		9
HAMILTON	EDWARD				26	ENGLAND	CE	ENGLISH	F	085	D		8
HAMILTON	ELIZEBE		2	1	67	IRELAND	CP			082	F		D
HAMILTON	HUGH				53	IRELAND	CE	IRISH	F	081	A	1	2
HAMILTON	JAMES				33	O	CP	IRISH	F	082	F		18
HAMILTON	JAMES				65	IRELAND	CP	IRISH	F	082	F		18
HAMILTON	JAMES				41	ONT	WM	SCOTTISH	FARMER	082	I		72
HAMILTON	JERARD		2			ONT	WM			082	I		D
HAMILTON	JOHN				25	O	CP	SCOTCH	F	081	A	1	63
HAMILTON	JOHN				37	ONT	CP	IRISH	FARMER	082	I		30
HAMILTON	JOHN				40	O	CE	SCOTCH	BARRISTER	089	B		5
HAMILTON	JOHN	SR			63	IRELAND	WM	IRISH	FARMER	082	I		31
HAMILTON	MARGARET	A	1	1	84	IRELAND	WM	IRISH		082	C	1	9
HAMILTON	MARY		1	1	24	IRELAND	RC	IRISH	DOMESTIC	082	E		42
HAMILTON	ROBERT	DAY			65	SCOTLAND	CS	SCOTCH	F	081	A	1	43
HAMILTON	SAMUEL				37	ONT	CP	IRISH	FARMER	082	I		30
HAMILTON	SAMUEL		1		24	IRELAND	CE	IRISH	SERVANT	084	E		1
HAMILTON	THOMAS				30	IRELAND	CP	IRISH	LUMBERMAN	083	D		1
HAMILTON	WILLIAM				42	SCOTLAND	WM	SCOTCH	F			1	76
HAMILTON	WILLIAM				45	ENGLAND	WM	ENGLISH	ENGINEER	081	A	2	31
HAMILTON	WILLIAM				36	ONT	WM	SCOTTISH	FARMER	082	I		76
HAMILTON	WILLIAM		1	1	45	IRELAND	CE	IRISH	SERVANT	084	E		1
HAMLIN	EMILLY			1	20	O	WM	ENGLISH	SERVANT	082	E		31
HAMLIN	WILLIAM				49	O	WM	ENGLISH	F	082	C	2	66
HAMMELL	JOHN				37	IRELAND	CE	IRISH	F	085	D		22
HAMMLE	FREDRICK				37	GERMANY	LU	GERMAN	FARMER	082	I		44
HAMMOND	ALBERT		1		18	QUE	RC	FRENCH	CLERK	086	C	1	2
HAMMOND	B		1		21	SCOTLAND	CP	SCOTCH	LAB	081	A	2	16
HAMNY	ARTEMESE		1		7	O	RC	FRENCH		082	C	1	35

SURNAME	NAME1	NAME2	STRAY	SEX	AGE	BIRTHPL	RELIGION	ORIGIN	OCCUP	DIST	SUB_DIST	DIV	PAGE
HAMPEL	OSWALL				38	GERMANY	LU	GERMAN	F	082	J		9
HANA	HANA		2	1	4	0	RC			084	G	1	D
HANABURY	MARGT		1	1	22	QUE	RC	IRISH	SERVANT	082	E		47
HANCOCK	JOHN				46	ENGLAND	WM	ENGLISH	POST MASTER	089	A		18
HANCOCK	SAMUEL				52	ENGLAND	WM	ENGLISH	MINER	089	A		3
HANDLEY	GEORGE		1		37	ENGLAND	CE	ENGLISH	PAINTER	081	B		54
HANDS	HERBERT		1		19	ENGLAND	CE	ENGLISH	CLARK	082	A		1
HANES	ALEXANDER		2		4	0	CP			085	L		D
HANES	ALLEN	I			29	0	WM	ENGLISH	F	085	L		9
HANES	ERASTUS				32	0	WM	ENGLISH	F	085	J		8
HANES	FREDERICK		1		23	0	WM	ENGLISH	F	085	L		9
HANES	JAMES	F			55	0	WM	ENGLISH	F	085	L		7
HANES	JEREMIAH				59	0	WM	ENGLISH	F	085	J		10
HANES	WILLIAM	I			21	0	WM	ENGLISH	F	085	L		10
HANES	WM	F			36	0	CP	ENGLISH	F	085	L		1
HANEY	WILLIAM				32	0	RC	IRISH	MILLWRIGHT	081	B		81
HANIER	WILLIAM				35	CANADA	CE	SCOTCH	F	087	B	2	6
HANLEY	WILLIAM				47	NS	WM	ENGLISH	F	085	D		31
HANLIN	JAMES				29	IRELAND	RC	IRISH	LAB	090	D		6
HANNA	ANDREW				50	IRELAND	PS	IRISH	FARMER	089	B		21
HANNA	ANDREW		2		3	0	CP			089	B		D
HANNA	CRISTIANA			1	45	0	PM	IRISH		085	H		24
HANNA	JAMES		2		20	0	PM		LAB	085	H		D
HANNA	WILLIAM				23	0	PM	ENGLISH	STORE CLERK	085	I		2
HANNAGAN	RICHARD				57	0	WM	IRISH	F	086	A	1	23
HANNAH	EDWARD		1		20	CANADA	CE	IRISH	F	087	B	2	8
HANNAH	FRANCIS				49	IRELAND	CE	IRISH	F	087	B	2	7
HANNAH	GEORGE		1		25	0	RC	SCOTCH	LUMBERMAN	088	C		10
HANNAH	JOHN				40	IRELAND	CP	IRISH		082	C	1	17
HANNAH	ROBERT		1		18	CANADA	ME	IRISH	LAB	087	B	2	6
HANNAH	SARAH		1	1	22	CANADA	ME	IRISH		087	B	2	6
HANNAHAN	JOHN		2		2	0	RC			081	J	2	D
HANNAHAN	PATRICK				34	IRELAND	RC	IRISH	F	081	J	2	5
HANNAHAN	TIMOTHY				30	IRELAND	RC	IRISH	F	081	J	2	8
HANNAMAN	CHRISTIAN				49	PRUSSIA	LU	PRUSSIAN	F	081	J	1	74
HANRAHAN	BRIDGET			1	70	IRELAND	RC	IRISH		081	C		2
HANRAHAN	JOHN				50	IRELAND	RC	IRISH	F	081	J	1	67
HANRAHAN	PATRICK				49	IRELAND	RC	IRISH	F	081	C		1
HANSON	JOHN		1		27	ENGLAND	EP	ENGLISH	LAB	090	D		7
HANSON	WILLIAM				55	SCOTLAND	CP	SCOTCH	F	081	A	1	29
HANWELL	HENRY	T			49	ENGLAND	CE	ENGLISH	WATCHMAKER	082	E		3
HAPPETH	MARTIN				30	GERMANY	LU	GERMAN	F	082	G		84
HARA	THOMAS				42	ONTARIO	RC	IRISH	F	082	A		37
HARD	WILLIAM				54	ENGLAND	XC	ENGLISH	SHOEMAKER	085	C		8
HARDIE	ALEXANDER				28	SCOTLAND	CP	SCOTCH	F	086	A	2	11
HARDIE	ROBERT		1		23	0	CE	SCOTCH	LUMBERMAN	086	B		2
HARDING	MARTHA			1	50	ENGLAND	CE	ENGLISH	NURSE	082	E		21
HARDING	WM		1		13	ENGLAND	CE	ENGLISH	SERVANT	082	E		26
HARDY	GEORGE				58	NOVA SCOTIA	PS	ENGLISH	F	087	B	2	4
HARDY	SARAH		2	1	50	PEI	UP			087	B	2	D
HARE	RICHARD				28	ONT	WM	IRISH	FARMER	082	I		77
HARENIN	BRIDGET			1	43	IRELAND	RC	IRISH		081	B		59
HARES	HENREY				29	ENGLAND	CE	ENGLISH	F	085	J		18
HARKIMER	WILLIAM				27	0	WM	INDIAN	HUNTER	086	C	2	3
HARMELD	MARY		1	1	13	GERMANY	LU	GERMAN	SERVANT	082	G		22
HARMMONI	C	T			62	US	CE	ENGLISH	FISHERMAN	088	A		6
HARPER	HENRY				48	IRELAND	CE	IRISH	F	082	C	2	18
HARPER	ROBERT				33	0	WM	ENGLISH	F	085	C		7
HARRINGTON	ARMOIN		1		35	QUE	CP	ENGLISH	CLERK	081	B		41
HARRINGTON	CORNEILOUS				35	IRELAND	RC	IRISH	F	082	H		17
HARRINGTON	E	K			50	QUE	CP	ENG	MERCHANT	081	B		53
HARRINGTON	ERIC		1		47	QUEBEC	CE	ENGLISH	MERCHANT	081	B		30
HARRINGTON	JOHN				27	IRELAND	RC	IRISH	LAB	090	D		6
HARRINGTON	THOMAS				28	0	RC	IRISH	LAB	081	B		44
HARRIS	ABRAM				42	IRELAND	CE	IRISH	F	086	A	1	4
HARRIS	DEBERA			1	42	QUE	CE	ENGLISH	WASHWOMAN	082	E		22
HARRIS	JAMES				23	ENGLAND	CE	ENGLISH	F	086	A	1	13
HARRIS	JOHN				50	ENGLAND	WM	ENGLISH	MINE LABOURER	089	A		24
HARRIS	JOHN				21	0	WM	ENGLISH	MINER	089	A		24
HARRIS	JULIA		1	1	28	ENGLAND	CE	ENGLISH		085	I		12
HARRIS	MICHAEL		1		33	0	CE	IRISH	CIVIL ENGINEER	090	F		18
HARRIS	ROBERT	JAMES	1		23	ENGLAND	CE	ENGLISH	F	085	D		31
HARRIS	SUSAN		1	1	13	0	WM	ENGLISH		089	A		47
HARRIS	WILLIAM				28	ONTARIO	CE	IRISH	FARMER	084	C		4
HARRIS	WILLIAM				35	ENGLAND	PM	ENGLISH	MINER	089	A		4
HARRIS	WILLIAM				30	ENGLAND	PM	ENGLISH	CARPENTER	089	A		12
HARRIS	WILLIAM				45	ENGLAND	WM	ENGLISH	CARPENTER	089	A		16
HARRISON	GEORGE				32	ENGLAND	CE	ENGLISH	F	085	J		19
HARRISON	GILBERT		1		39	IRELAND	EP	IRISH	LAB	090	D		9
HARRISON	JOSEPH				42	ENGLAND	WM	ENGLISH	F	085	D		15
HARRISON	MARIA		1	1	32	0	CE	ENGLISH		085	H		26
HART	ALEXANDER				31	SCOTLAND	ME	SCOTCH	F	086	A	2	3
HART	ARCHIBALD				64	SCOTLAND	CS	SCOTCH	F	081	A	1	44
HART	ARCHIBALD				26	SCOTLAND	CS	SCOTCH	F	081	A	1	46
HART	JOHN				34	SCOTLAND	CS	SCOTCH	BLACKSMITH	081	A	1	47
HART	PATRICK				30	ONTARIO	RC	IRISH	STOREKEEPER	082	B		5
HART	SAMUEL		1		24	IRELAND	CP	IRISH		086	B		1
HARTING	JOHN		2		85	IRELAND	RC		F	081	C		D
HARTLEY	HENREY								SEE HENREY	085	B		1
HARTLY	ROBERT		1		48	ENGLAND	CE	ENGLISH	TURNKEY	089	B		13
HARTLY	WILLIAM		1		35	ENGLAND	CE	ENGLISH	MINER	090	F		17
HARTNELL	JOHN				35	IRELAND	RC	IRISH	BLACKSMITH	081	J	1	5
HARTNEY	JAMES				45	IRELAND	RC	IRISH	PRODUCE DEALER	081	B		14
HARTNY	BRIDGET			1	60	IRELAND	RC	IRISH		081	C		11
HARTNY	JAMES				85	IRELAND	RC	IRISH	F	081	C		7
HARTNY	JOHN				49	IRELAND	RC	IRISH	F	081	C		7
HARTNY	JOHN				30	ONTARIO	RC	IRISH	FARMER	081	G	1	23
HARTY	MICHAEL				45	IRELAND	RC	IRISH	F	081	J	1	67
HARTY	PATRICK				33	IRELAND	RC	IRISH	F	081	K		50
HARVEY	BERNARD				48	IRELAND	RC	IRISH	FARMER	084	A		1
HARVEY	JANE		2	1	33	IRELAND	CE			086	A	1	D
HARVEY	JEMIMA			1	44	SCOTLAND	PS	SCOTCH		089	A		3
HARVEY	JOHN				40	IRELAND	RC	IRISH	CONTRACTOR	081	B		67
HARVEY	W	S			30	ENGLAND	CE	ENGLISH	LUMBERER	082	E		4
HARVEY	WILLIAM				34	0	CE	ENGLISH	SAWYER-LOGGER	086	A	1	15
HARVIE	JAMES		1		21	0	WM	ENGLISH	F LABOURER	085	B		18

SURNAME	NAME1	NAME2	STRAY	SEX	AGE	BIRTHPL	RELIGION	ORIGIN	OCCUP	DIST	SUB_DIST	DIV	PAGE
HARYETT	WILLIAM				40	ENGLAND	CE	ENGLISH	STOREKEEPER & CONTRA	081	G	1	32
HASDLICK	MATHISS				51	PRUSSIA	RC	PRUSSIAN	F	081	J	1	11
HASEL	WILLIAM				28	PRUSSIA	LU	PRUSSIAN	F	081	J	1	79
HASELIP	JAMIMA		1	1	28	0	PS	SCOTTISH	SERVANT	082	E		33
HASELY	LUCY		1	1	36	USA	RC	AMERICAN	SISTERS OF CHARITY	087	A		1
HASKINS	CHARLES		1		39	USA	ME		TEAMSTER	086	B		7
HASKINS	RACHEL		1		65	US	EM	ENGLISH		082	A		73
HASS	AUGUST				38	GERMANY	LU	GERMAN	FARMER	082	I		53
HASS	CHARLES				42	GERMANY	LU	GERMAN	FARMER	082	I		54
HATCH	ROBERT				35	ENGLAND	CE	ENGLISH	F	086	A	1	20
HATELEY	ROBERT				50	IRELAND	CP	IRISH	F	082	C	1	51
HAUGHNAU	JAMES								SEE FAUGHNAU	082	B		28
HAUGHTON	GEORGE				37	ONT	CE	IRISH	FARMER	081	J	1	14
HAUKINS	WILLIAM				35	IRELAND	CE	IRISH	FARMER	082	B		24
HAUN	ELIZABETH		2	1		0	RC			081	B		D
HAUN	JOSEPH				41	GERMANY	RC	GERMAN	LAB	081	B		63
HAUSA	CHRIST				46	GERMANY	EV	GERMAN	F	082	G		93
HAVREY	ROBERT		1		17	0	CE	IRISH	F LAB	085	B		24
HAVRN	NATHANL				26	CANADA	PS	ENGLISH	F	087	B	2	4
HAW	JOHN				27	0	WM	IRISH	BLACKSMITH	085	I		12
HAWIKJY	MARGARET		1	1	31	MICHIGAN	RC	INDIAN	STUDENT	087	A		1
HAWKINS	HEDWARD				40	0	CE	IRISH	F	082	F		8
HAWKINS	HENERY				32	0	CE	IRISH	F	082	F		34
HAWKINS	HENRY				34	0	CE	IRISH	HOTELKEEPER	082	E		32
HAWKINS	JAMES				40	ENGLAND	WM	ENGLISH	F	082	C	2	43
HAWKINS	JAMES		1		1	0	CE	IRISH		082	F		2
HAWKINS	JOSEPH				56	ENGLAND	CE	ENGLISH	FARMER	081	G	1	42
HAWKINS	JOSEPH				38	0	CE	IRISH	F	082	F		11
HAWKINS	JOSEPH				25	0	CE	IRISH	F	082	F		11
HAWKINS	JOSEPH				29	0	CE	IRISH	F	082	F		33
HAWKINS	JOSHUA				36	0	CE	IRISH	COOPER	082	F		1
HAWKINS	THOMAS				30	0	CE	IRISH	F	082	C	2	58
HAWKINS	THOMAS				43	0	CE	IRISH	FARMER	082	F		9
HAWKINS	W	H	1		23	ENGLAND	CE	ENGLISH	CULLER	081	A	2	16
HAWKINS	WILLIAM				44	0	CE	IRISH	FARMER	082	F		2
HAWLAY	JAMES				55	IRELAND	RC	IRISH	F	082	K	1	4
HAWLEY	JOHN				38	IRELAND	RC	IRISH	FARMER	082	I		1
HAWORTH	RICHD				29	ENGLAND	CE	ENGLISH	MILL HAND	082	E		18
HAWTHORN	ROBT				52	IRELAND	CS	IRISH	F	082	A		10
HAY	ALFRED		1		24	0	WM	ENGLISH	CABINET MAKER	085	C		9
HAY	ELIZABETH		1	1	23	US	WM	IRISH	SERVANT	085	E		6
HAY	JOSEPH				28	0	PS	SCOTCH	LUMBERMAN	086	B		3
HAY	WILLIAM				32	0	CE	ENGLISH	F	085	D		19
HAY	WILLIAM				58	ENGLAND	CE	ENGLISH	F	085	I		38
HAYS	HENERY				39	0	CE	IRISH	F	082	F		4
HAYS	JAMES				66	IRELAND	RC	IRISH	FARMER	082	I		35
HAYS	MARTIN		1		30	0	WM	GERMAN	LUMBERMAN	086	B		2
HAYS	PETER				52	IRELAND	RC	IRISH	FARMER	082	I		35
HAYS	RICHARD		2		1	0	CE			082	F		D
HAYS	RICHARD				35	0	CE	IRISH	F	082	G		72
HAYTER	JOHN	R	1		16	QUE	CE	IRISH	DRUGGIST APPRENTICE	082	E		10
HAZELTON	JOHN				58	ONTARIO	CE	IRISH	CHAIRMAKER	082	B		51
HAZELTON	WILLIAM				28	0	WM	IRISH	SHOEMAKER	081	I		18
HAZLETON	JOHN		1		24	0	CE	IRISH	TINSMITH	081	I		6
HAZLETON	JOSHUA				28	0	RC	IRISH	CARPENTER	081	K		66
HAZLEWOOD	GEORGE	C			36	ENGLAND	WM	ENGLISH	COMMISSION AGENT	085	E		31
HEADMAN	IDA		1	1	5	ONT	LU	GERMAN		082	I		54
HEADRICK	DUGAL				20	SCOTLAND	CP	SCOTCH	F	085	E		29
HEADRICK	JAMES				61	SCOTLAND	CP	SCOTCH	F	081	A	1	4
HEADRICK	JOHN				51	SCOTLAND	CP	SCOTCH	F	081	A	1	15
HEADRICK	WILLIAM				56	SCOTLAND	CP	SCOTCH	F	081	A	1	13
HEALEY	THOMAS				38	IRELAND	CE	IRISH	F	086	A	1	16
HEALY	BRIDGET			1	50	IRELAND	RC	IRISH		081	C		3
HEALY	PATRICK		1		35	IRELAND	RC	IRISH	SERVANT	082	L		1
HEANEY	JAMES				24	0	RC	IRISH	STAGE PROPRIETOR	081	A	2	29
HEANEY	MARGRET			1	29	0	RC	IRISH	F	081	A	2	34
HEANY	THOMAS				43	IRELAND	RC	IRISH	F	082	L		3
HEARD	GRACE		1	1	24	CANADA	WM	SCOTCH	SERVANT	085	E		6
HEARSY	GERRVIS		1		32	IRELAND	RC	IRISH	LAB	084	D		5
HEART	SAMUEL				21	0	WM	ENGLISH	F	085	E		14
HEART	WILLIAM				48	IRELAND	PS	IRISH	CARPENTER	085	E		11
HEART	WILLIAM				48	IRELAND	PS	IRISH	CARPENTER	085	E		14
HEATH	JOSEPH				51	ENGLAND	RC	ENGLISH	TAILOR	081	B		80
HEAVEY	JAMES				62	IRELAND	RC	IRISH	FARMER	081	B		33
HEAVY	THOMAS				35	0	RC	IRISH		081	A	2	33
HEBERT	JOSEPH								SEE ERBARE	082	C	1	27
HECKING	JAMES				60	ENGLAND	FW	ENGLISH	F	085	K	2	8
HEDICAN	EDWARD				40	IRELAND	RC	IRISH	F	081	J	1	90
HEENAN	JAMES				39	IRELAND	RC	IRISH	MERCHANT	082	E		42
HEENAN	MICHAEL		2		6	ONT	RC			082	I		D
HEENAN	THOMAS				42	IRELAND	RC	IRISH	FARMER	082	I		28
HEICKS	EDWARD				24	W INDIES	WM	ENGLISH	F	085	E		12
HEIN	ERNEST	HENRY			37	ENGLAND	CE	ENGLISH	F	082	K	2	3
HEINSE	EMIL				34	GERMANY	LU	GERMAN	F	082	J		8
HELFERTY	DENNIS				51	IRELAND	RC	IRISH	F	081	K		55
HELFERTY	JOHN				35	IRELAND	RC	IRISH	F	081	K		54
HELFERTY	PATRICK				36	IRELAND	RC	IRISH	F	081	K		54
HELFORTY	BERNARD				27	ONTARIO	RC	IRISH	FARMER	082	B		64
HELFORTY	HUGH				63	IRELAND	RC	IRISH	FARMER	082	B		59
HELKINS	FANNEY		1	1	10	ONTARIO	CE	ENGLISH		081	G	1	31
HELY	AUGUSTUS				36	0	CE	IRISH		085	D		9
HEMPINSTALL	W	J			24	ENGLAND	CE	ENGLISH	F	081	A	2	7
HENDERSON	ARCHIBALD				58	SCOTLAND	CS	SCOTCH	F	081	A	1	67
HENDERSON	CHRISTINA		1	1	60	SCOTLAND	CS	SCOTCH		081	A	1	59
HENDERSON	HUGH				50	QUE	RC	IRISH	F	081	K		11
HENDERSON	JAMES		2			0	RC			082	E		D
HENDERSON	JAMES				36	SCOTLAND	CS	SCOTCH	FARMER	083	A	2	3
HENDERSON	JOSEPH				33	IRELAND	RC	IRISH	CABINETMAKER	082	E		65
HENDERSON	MARSHAL				64	IRELAND	RC	IRISH	LAB	081	A	2	13
HENDERSON	THOMAS				37	SCOTLAND	PS	SCOTCH	MINE LABOURER	089	A		29
HENERSY	MARTIN				34	0	WM	IRISH	F	082	C	1	6
HENNAN	WIBESCH		1		22	GERMANY	LU	GERMAN	SERVANT	081	A	2	2
HENNEASY	MARGARET			1		IRELAND	RC			082	H		D
HENNEASY	PATRICK				35	IRELAND	RC	IRISH	F	082	H		29
HENNESSY	THOS				50	IRELAND	RC	IRISH	F	081	J	1	87
HENNY	WILLIAM				50	IRELAND	CE	IRISH	F	085	E		7

SURNAME	NAME1	NAME2	STRAY	SEX	AGE	BIRTHPL	RELIGION	ORIGIN	OCCUP	DIST	SUB_DIST	DIV	PAGE
HENREY	HARTLEY				36	ENGLAND	CC	ENGLISH	BLACKSMITH	085	B		1
HENRY	BERNARD		1		15	O	RC	IRISH		085	K	2	6
HENRY	DAVID		1		20	O	RC	IRISH	F	085	K	2	5
HENRY	JAMES		1		22	O	RC	IRISH	F	085	K	2	5
HENRY	JOHN		1		19	O	RC	IRISH	F	085	K	2	6
HENRY	MARY		1	1	17	O	RC	IRISH		085	K	2	6
HENRY	SARAH		1	1	24	O	RC	IRISH		085	K	2	5
HENRY	WILLIAM		1		15	O	PS	SCOTTISH		082	E		61
HENSHAW	THOMAS				28	O	NC	ENGLISH	F	085	E		21
HENWOOD	ELLA		1	1	14	US	CE	ENGLISH		089	A		44
HERINGTON	MARY		1	1	70	IRELAND	CE	IRISH	F	085	B		23
HERLON	JACOB				40	POLAND	RC	POLISH		083	C		19
HERNOTTE	JULIA		1	1	13	O	RC	FRENCH		089	A		16
HERON	FRANCIS				20	ONTARIO	CE	ENGLISH	STEWARD H B CO	090	E		1
HERON	PATRICK				40	ONT	RC	IRISH	F	081	C		5
HERRICK	GERSHOM				33	IRELAND	CE	IRISH	COMM MERCHANT	082	E		26
HERRICK	MICHAEL				40	IRELAND	RC	IRISH	BLACKSMITH	081	B		61
HERRICK	THOMAS	W			44	IRELAND	CE	IRISH	PROVINCIAL LAND SURV	089	B		11
HERRING	GEORGE				30	NB	RC	IRISH	LUMBERER	083	A	2	4
HERRINGTON	WILLIAM				35	O	CP	IRISH	F	085	B		20
HERRON	JAMES				55	IRELAND	RC	IRISH	F	082	A		24
HESKETH	HENRY				37	ENGLAND	CE	ENGLISH	F	086	A	1	7
HESTER	WILLIAM				40	IRELAND	CE	IRISH	F	085	E		21
HETHERINGTON	JOHN		1		35	O	CE	SCOTCH		081	B		72
HETHERINGTON	MARIA			1	61	ENGLAND	WM	ENGLISH		089	B		1
HEULEY	JOHN		1		30	ENGLAND	CE	ENGLISH	GENTLEMAN	086	A	2	11
HEUSTIN	CATHERINE		1	1	15	O	RC	ENGLISH	SERVANT	082	G		78
HEUSTON	GEORGE		1		35	IRELAND	PS	IRISH	LAB	087	B	2	3
HEW	JACOB				26	ONT	EP	ENGLISH	F	081	J	1	52
HEWET	WILLIAM				38	SCOTLAND	CP	SCOTCH	F	082	C	2	37
HEWETT	ROBERT		1		82	SCOTLAND	PS	SCOTCH	WEAVER	082	A		6
HEWETT	THOS				50	IRELAND	CE	IRISH	F	082	G		65
HEWITT	EDWARD				51	IRELAND	CE	IRISH	F	085	B		9
HEWITT	JAMES				29	IRELAND	CE	IRISH	F	085	B		11
HEWITT	JOSEPH				50	IRELAND	CE	IRISH	F	085	C		11
HEWSTON	WILLIAM				33	O	CE	IRISH	LAB	081	B		38
HEY	GEORGE				22	ENGLAND	CE	ENGLISH	CARPENTER	085	I		8
HEY	SAMUEL				38	ENGLAND	CE	ENGLISH	F	085	I		22
HEYNES	PATRICK				56	IRELAND	RC	IRISH	FARMER	082	I		31
HIAL	ELIZABETH		1	1	18	O	CE	ENGLISH	SERVANT	089	B		36
HICKEY	ALEX R				31	QUE	RC	FRENCH	SHOEMAKER	082	E		37
HICKEY	JOHN				38	IRELAND	RC	IRISH	GENTLEMAN	082	B		67
HICKEY	JOSEPH				40	QUE	RC	IRISH	F	082	C	2	38
HICKEY	KATE		1	1	21	QUE	ME	IRISH	SERVANT	082	E		70
HICKEY	MICHAEL		1		55	MUNSTER	RC	IRISH	SCHOOL TEACHER	087	A		1
HICKEY	WILLIAM				45	IRELAND	RC	IRISH	F	081	H	1	8
HICKS	WILLIAM				58	IRELAND	CE	IRISH	F	082	C	2	20
HICKSEAY	THOMAS				69	IRELAND	RC	IRISH	LABOURER	089	B		22
HIDERMAN	FREDERICK				35	GERMANY	EM	GERMAN	F	082	J		16
HIDERMAN	MENIA		2	1	39	GERMANY	EM			082	J		D
HIEDMAN	HENRY				46	HANOVER	LU	GERMAN	F	085	A		6
HIGGINS	JAMES		1		23	O	RC	IRISH	HARNESSMAKER	081	K		69
HIGGINS	PATRICK				55	IRELAND	RC	IRISH	F	082	J		18
HIGGISON	JOHN				51	IRELAND	CE	IRISH	FARMER	082	G		1
HIGGS	JAMES				54	ENGLAND	WM	ENGLISH	PLASTERER	089	B		15
HIGHLAND	MARY		1	1	17	O	WM	IRISH		081	B		60
HIGHLAND	THOMAS				26	O	PS	IRISH	LAB	081	H	2	21
HILDITCH	WM	N	1		27	ENGLAND	CE	ENGLISH	F	085	L		9
HILL	EDWARD				22	O	CE	ENGLISH	MINE LABOURER	089	A		23
HILL	GEORGE				25	QUE	RC	ENGLISH	LAB	081	B		39
HILL	HENRY				46	IRELAND	CE	IRISH	F	082	A		52
HILL	JAMES				30	ONTARIO	CS	IRISH	F	082	A		62
HILL	JOHN				56	IRELAND	PS	IRISH	F	081	J	1	29
HILL	JOHN				26	IRELAND	CE	IRISH	LAB	082	A		50
HILL	JOHN				47	IRELAND	CE	IRISH	F	082	A		54
HILL	JOHN	SENR			66	IRELAND	CE	IRISH	F	082	A		52
HILL	JULIA			1	60	QUE	RC	FRENCH	DRESSMAKER	081	I		10
HILL	ORPHA				24	ONTARIO	CE	ENGLISH	F	083	E		1
HILL	ORPHEY		1	1	25	O	CE	SCOTCH		082	K	2	4
HILL	ROBERT				24	ONTARIO	CE	SCOTCH	LUMBERER	083	B	2	1
HILL	ROBERT	B			28	SCOTLAND	ME	SCOTCH	CARPENTER	085	E		10
HILL	ROBERT	N			44	O	NC	IRISH	MINISTER	085	K	2	9
HILL	ROWLAND				33	O	EP	ENGLISH	CLERGYMAN	087	B	3	4
HILL	THOMAS				24	ONTARIO	CE	IRISH	LAB	082	A		46
HILL	THOMAS				57	IRELAND	CE	IRISH	TAVERNKEEPER	082	A		49
HILL	THOMAS				36	IRELAND	CE	IRISH	F	082	A		53
HILL	THOMAS				55	ENGLAND	PM	ENGLISH	F	085	J		4
HILL	WILLIAM				58	SCOTLAND	CP	SCOTCH	WEAVER	081	A	1	27
HILL	WILLIAM		1		19	O	RC	FRENCH	SADDLER	081	I		42
HILL	WILLIAM		1		2	O	CE	ENGLISH		082	K	2	4
HILL	WILLIAM				45	ENGLAND	CE	ENGLISH	MINER	089	A		37
HILLIARD	THOMAS				36	IRELAND	RC	IRISH	LABOURER	082	E		36
HILSON	JAMES				29	CANADA	PS	SCOTCH	LUMBERER	087	B	2	3
HIMER	LOUIS				24	ENGLAND	WM	ENGLISH	F	085	I		39
HINDINARCH	MICHAEL		1		35	ENGLAND	CO	ENGLISH	F	085	E		7
HINT	ELIZABETH		1	1	13	O	PS	FRENCH		082	G		70
HINT	JOSEPH		1		23	O	PS	FRENCH	CARDER	082	G		70
HINT	MOSES		1		27	O	PS	FRENCH	SHANTYMAN	082	G		70
HINTON	LOUIS	E	1		19	ENGLAND	WM	ENGLISH	CLERK	085	J		7
HINTON	SAMUEL				21	ENGLAND	CE	ENGLISH	FARMER	083	A	2	1
HIRSCH	CHARLES			1	35	ENGLAND	CE	ENGLISH	CLERK	084	D		7
HOARE	GEORGE		1		25	ENGLAND	CE	ENGLISH	LAB	081	A	2	16
HOBBS	SARAH		1	1	82	SCOTLAND	CP	SCOTCH	F	086	A	2	13
HOBEN	JOHN				27	QUE	CE	IRISH	LAB	081	B		58
HODGES	CHARLES				39	ENGLAND	CE	ENGLISH	ENGINEER	086	A	1	30
HODGINS	EMILY		2	1	2	ONT	WM			081	J	1	D
HODGINS	JOHN	W			36	IRELAND	IM	IRISH	FARMER	082	B		31
HODGINS	MATHEW				74	IRELAND	EM	IRISH		082	A		65
HODGINS	WILLIAM				40	IRELAND	WM	IRISH	F	081	J	1	36
HODGSON	DAVID		1		40	UNITED STATES	EP	ENGLISH	MINER	090	D		1
HODGSON	J	C			43	UNITED STATES	WM	ENGLISH	MINER	090	D		5
HODGSON	JOSEPH		1		30	QUE	EP	ENGLISH	LAB	090	D		7
HOGABOAM			2		11	O	WM		CHILD OF C HOGABOAM	085	K	2	D
HOGABOAM	CHARLES			1	26	O	WM	GERMAN	F	085	K	2	1
HOGABOAM	DAVID				52	O	WM	SCOTCH	F	085	J		16
HOGAN	JAMES				60	IRELAND	RC	IRISH	F	081	K		47

SURNAME	NAME1	NAME2	STRAY	SEX	AGE	BIRTHPL	RELIGION	ORIGIN	OCCUP	DIST	SUB_DIST	DIV	PAGE
HOGAN	JAMES		1		40	WALES	RC	WELSH	LABOURER	082	E		38
HOGAN	JAMES				45	IRELAND	RC	IRISH	F	082	H		1
HOGAN	MARY		1	1	40	IRELAND	RC	IRISH		082	E		38
HOGAN	MATTHIAS				25	IRELAND	RC	IRISH	F	082	H		3
HOGARTH	CATHERINE			1	44	QUE	WM	IRISH	DRESSMAKER	082	E		19
HOGG	HUGH				31	SCOTLAND	PS	SCOTCH	F	085	J		11
HOGG	WILLIAM				29	0	CP	IRISH	MILLWRIGHT	081	A	2	23
HOLDCROFT	THOMAS				60	ENGLAND	CE	ENGLISH	FARMER	089	B		39
HOLDEN	ELIAS				62	ONTARIO	WM	AMERICAN	F	081	C		44
HOLDEN	HENRY				40	ONT	WM	ENGLISH	JOINER	081	C		47
HOLDEN	JOHN		1		32	ENGLAND	CE	ENGLISH	LAB	087	B	2	1
HOLDEN	SERASTIN				40	ONT	WM	ENGLISH	F	081	C		42
HOLDEN	SOLOMON				34	ONT	WM	ENG AMERICAN	F	081	C		42
HOLDEN	WILLIAM				40	IRELAND	CE	IRISH	F	085	C		27
HOLDENBECK	RALPH		1		29	US	WM	GERMAN	LUMBERMAN	088	B		5
HOLDITCH	SAMUEL				72	ENGLAND	CE	ENGLISH	F	085	C		6
HOLDITCH	WILLIAM				34	0	ME	ENGLISH	FARMER	085	I		8
HOLIDAY	THOMAS				35	ENGLAND	PM	ENGLISH	CARPENTER	085	I		31
HOLINSHED	WILLIAM				28	ENGLAND	CE	ENGLISH	F	085	K	2	2
HOLLAND	CHARLES				35	ENGLAND	WM	ENGLISH	F	085	D		34
HOLLAND	JEREMIAH		1		30	IRELAND	RC	IRISH	LUMBERMAN	082	H		8
HOLLAND	JOHN				30	IRELAND	WM	IRISH	FARMER	085	E		30
HOLLAND	WILLIAM		1		37	IRELAND	CP	IRISH	LAB	081	B		54
HOLLER	HERRIET		1	1	40	0	RC	FRENCH		088	C		9
HOLLEY	JAMES				30	0	RC	IRISH	F	081	H	2	26
HOLLEY	JOHN				32	0	RC	IRISH	F	081	H	2	26
HOLLIDAY	WILLIAM				66	SCOTLAND	CP	SCOTCH	F	081	C		41
HOLLINGER	JOHN		1		45	0	RC	IRISH	CLERK	081	I		3
HOLLINGWORTH	JOHN				41	ENGLAND	CE	ENGLISH	F	085	D		12
HOLLY	(WIDOW)			1	70	IRELAND	RC	IRISH		083	C		14
HOLLY	PATRICK				35	IRELAND	RC	IRISH	F	083	C		13
HOLLY	TIMOTHY				28	IRELAND	RC	IRISH	FARMER	081	G	1	40
HOLLY	WILLIAM				41	SCOTLAND	PS	SCOTCH	LUMBERER	081	D		21
HOLMES	BARBARA			1	50	IRELAND	PS	IRISH		081	D		5
HOLMES	GEORGE				37	IRELAND	CP	IRISH	F	085	H		23
HOLMES	HENRY				41	ENGLAND	CE	ENGLISH	MINE LABOURER	089	A		40
HOLMES	JAMES				60	IRELAND	OP	IRISH	FARMER	081	D		12
HOLMES	JOHN				65	IRELAND	CP	IRISH	FARMER	081	D		15
HOLMES	JOSEPH				30	IRELAND	OP	IRISH	FARMER	081	D		12
HOLMES	MARY		2	1	67	IRELAND	PS			081	D		D
HOLMES	ROBERT				36	IRELAND	WM	IRISH	F	090	F		18
HOLMES	WILLIAM				48	ENGLAND	CE	ENGLISH	FARMER	086	B		7
HOLODAY	ANDREW				42	IRELAND	CE	IRISH	WEAVER	082	F		12
HOLT	DANIEL				38	QUE	EM	GERMAN	CARPENTER	082	C	1	39
HOLT	SIMEON		2		2	0	EM			082	C	1	D
HOLTEN	RICHARD				26	ENGLAND	CE	ENGLISH	F	085	E		2
HOMES	MAEMORA		1	1	22	0	BA	ENGLISH	SERVANT	086	C	1	1
HOMEWTH	FREDERICK				41	GERMANY	BA	GERMAN	FARMER	081	F		32
HONRET	ANTWINE				44	QUEBEC	RC	FRENCH	CARPENTER	082	A		48
HONSBERGER	ARTHUR	E			24	0	CP	GERMAN	F	085	I		26
HOOEY	EDWARD				26	IRELAND	RP	IRISH	F	085	L		10
HOOEY	WM				26	IRELAND	CP	IRISH	F	085	L		10
HOOFMAN	WILLIAM				33	GERMANY	WM	GERMAN	F	082	G		89
HOOLIHAN	PATRICK						NG		SEE HULIHAN	082	I		39
HOOPER	DAVID				47	ENGLAND	BC	ENGLISH	MINER	089	A		8
HOOVER	SARIAH		1	1	25	ONT	WM	GERMAN	SERVANT	082	I		74
HOPES	SAMUEL				36	ENGLAND	WM	ENGLISH	CARPENTER	081	B		68
HOPKINS	MATILDA		1	1	21	0	CE	IRISH	SERVANT	082	E		16
HOPKINS	ROBERT		1		45	IRELAND	CE	IRISH	CARPENTER	082	C	2	43
HORAN	THOMAS		1		46	0	PR	IRISH	FARM SERVANT	085	A		9
HORE	ROBERT		1		88	ENGLAND	WM	ENGLISH	LABOURER	089	A		15
HORN	STEPHEN				52	ENGLAND	PM	ENGLISH	F	086	A	2	9
HORNER	ELIZA		1	1	24	0	CE	ENGLISH		082	D		21
HORNER	JOHN		1		35	0	CE	ENGLISH	LABOURER	082	D		21
HORTY	RADGER				34	ENGLAND	RC	IRISH	F	081	H	1	1
HOSKING	JOSEPH				39	ENGLAND	CE	ENGLISH	CARPENTER	089	A		29
HOSKING	WILLIAM				33	ENGLAND	CE	ENGLISH	MINER	089	A		3
HOTTIRMAN	FERDINAND				42	GERMANY	LU	GERMAN	MERCHANT	081	F		6
HOTTON	ELENNEITT		1	1	54	0	OM	ENGLISH		081	H	1	13
HOUGH	ANDREW		1		19	0	CS	GERMAN	F	081	A	1	51
HOUGH	JOHN				22	QUE	CP	GERMAN	SHOEMAKER	081	A	1	18
HOUGH	WILLIAM				53	QUE	RC	FRENCH	PILOT	081	B		56
HOUGHTEN	WM				30	ONT	ME	AMERICAN	RAFTSMAN	081	C		54
HOUGHTON	FRANK		1		26	ENGLAND	CP	ENGLISH	SADDLER	090	F		19
HOUL	EDWARD		1		5	0	RC	FRENCH		082	J		11
HOUL	LAMAY				33	QUE	RC	FRENCH	F	082	J		10
HOULD			1		24	QUE	RC	FRENCH	LUMBERMAN	088	C		10
HOULD	JOSEPH		1		28	QUE	RC	FRENCH	LUMBERMAN	088	C		10
HOULD	LEVIN		1		30	QUE	RC	FRENCH	LUMBERMAN	088	C		10
HOULD	LOUIS		1		21	QUE	RC	FRENCH	LUMBERMAN	088	C		10
HOULHAN	MARY		1	1	22	IRELAND	RC	IRISH	SERVANT	081	G	1	4
HOUSE	WILLIAM				26	0	ME	ENGLISH	F	086	B		5
HOUSTON	GEORGE				32	IRELAND	CE	IRISH	CLERK	088	B		18
HOUSTON	JOHN		1		5	0	PS	SCOTTISH		082	D		31
HOUSTON	MARGRET		1	1	40	SCOTLAND	PS	SCOTTISH		082	D		31
HOUSTON	WILLIAM		1		9	0	PS	SCOTTISH		082	D		31
HOUT	LOUIS				48	QUE	RC	FRENCH	HOTELKEEPER	082	J		1
HOWARD	DAN				38	GERMANY	LU	GERMAN	F	082	J		8
HOWARD	ELIZA			1	59	IRELAND	CE	IRISH		082	C	2	57
HOWARD	FRANCIS				31	US	WM	ENGLISH	F	086	A	1	8
HOWARD	HENRY				36	0	CE	IRISH	F	082	C	2	55
HOWARD	JAMES				45	QUE	RC	IRISH	F	081	K		51
HOWARD	JOHN		1		59	0	WM	IRISH		081	I		30
HOWARD	JOHN				27	0	CE	IRISH		082	C	1	23
HOWARD	JOHN				50	IRELAND	CE	IRISH	MINE LABOURER	089	A		21
HOWARD	JOHN	MC			30	ONTARIO	EM	IRISH	F	082	A		43
HOWARD	JOSEPH				52	IRELAND	CE	IRISH	BLACKSMITH	082	C	1	4
HOWARD	KATE		1	1	24	IRELAND	RC	IRISH		082	E		10
HOWARD	LEVI				41	QUEBEC	WM	ENGLISH	LABOURER	082	A		11
HOWARD	MARY	A	1	1	19	QUE	RC	IRISH	SERVANT	082	E		4
HOWARD	MARY	JANE	1	1	6	ONTARIO	CS	SCOTCH		082	A		26
HOWARD	PATRICK				43	IRELAND	RC	IRISH	SHOEMAKER	082	D		7
HOWARD	PATRICK				29	QUE	RC	IRISH	FARMER	082	I		35
HOWARD	PHILANDER				63	US	EM	ENGLISH	F	082	A		12
HOWARD	ROBERT				28	ENGLAND	CE	ENGLISH	HOTEL KEEPER	085	I		39
HOWARD	SIMON		1		26	IRELAND	RC	IRISH	CLERK	081	K		64

SURNAME	NAME1	NAME2	STRAY	SEX	AGE	BIRTHPL	RELIGION	ORIGIN	OCCUP	DIST	SUB_DIST	DIV	PAGE
HOWARTH	THOMAS				67	ENGLAND	CE	ENGLISH	CARDER	082	E		59
HOWDON	DEBORA		1	1	60	IRELAND	CE	IRISH		082	A		66
HOWE	JOSEPH				39	NOVA SCOTIA	PS	ENGLISH	LIGHTHOUSE KEEPER	087	B	2	1
HOWE	MICHAEL				28	IRELAND	RC	IRISH	CLERK	082	E		68
HOWELL	WILLIAM				35	O	WM	ENGLISH	SHOEMAKER	085	C		20
HOWEY	ALONZO	B	1		19	O	CP	ENGLISH	CARPENTER	081	B		85
HOWIE	JOHN				42	SCOTLAND	CS	SCOTCH	FARMER	082	A		1
HOWIE	JOHN				66	SCOTLAND	CS	SCOTCH	F	082	A		1
HUBBARD	TADIUS				32	ENGLAND	CE	ENGLISH	CABINETMAKER	081	B		70
HUBBLE	GEORGE		1		46	O	CE	ENGLISH		081	B		73
HUBNER	FREDRICK				34	GERMANY	LU	GERMAN	FARMER	082	I		45
HUCKABONE	EDWARD				47	ONTARIO	WM	IRISH	F	082	A		61
HUCKABONE	MARY			1	70	IRELAND	WM	IRISH		082	A		48
HUDON	MASSES				28	UNITED STATES	RC	FRENCH	SADELER	081	I		24
HUDSON	CHARLES				27	ONT	RC	ENGLISH	HOTELKEEPER	081	J	1	10
HUDSON	GEORGE				55	QUE	CE	ENGLISH	CARPENTER	082	E		61
HUDSON	ISABELLA			1	52	SCOTLAND	OP	SCOTCH	F	081	E		19
HUDSON	ROBERT				55	O	CE	SCOTCH	F	082	K	1	20
HUDSON	SHARLOT	J	1	1		O	WM			082	C	2	33
HUDSON	THOMAS				51	ENGLAND	PM	ENGLISH	F	086	A	2	5
HUDSON	WILLIAM				37	ONTARIO	CS	ENGLISH	F	082	A		58
HUESTON	JOHN				57	IRELAND	CE	IRISH	F	085	A		21
HUFF	WALTER				28	O	WM	GERMAN	PAINTER	086	A	1	26
HUGGARD	RICHARD				53	IRELAND	CE	IRISH	F	085	D		28
HUGHES	DANIEL				37	IRELAND	CE	IRISH	F	085	D		19
HUGHES	FRANCIS	JONES			40	WALES	CE	WELSH		089	B		15
HUGHES	GEORGE				51	O	CE	ENGLISH	F	085	A		9
HUGHES	ISSIAC				54	IRELAND	CE	IRISH	F	085	H		8
HUGHES	JOHN		1		27	QUE	RC	IRISH	SERVANT	081	B		1
HUGHES	JOHN				55	O	CE	IRISH	F	081	K		12
HUGHES	JOSEPH		1		20	O	CP	ENGLISH	LABOURER	085	B		15
HUGHES	MICHL				29	IRELAND	RC	IRISH	CABINETMAKER	082	E		56
HUGHES	PATRICK				57	IRELAND	RC	IRISH	LUMBERMAN	083	C		1
HUGHES	PETER				26	ENGLAND	CE	ENGLISH	CARPENTER	085	C		20
HUGHES	ROBERT				41	CANADA	ME	ENGLISH	F	085	A		10
HUGHEY	JOHN				31	IRELAND	CE	IRISH	F	085	H		9
HUGHEY	SUSANAH		2	1	22	IRELAND	CE			085	H		D
HUGHS	HENERY		1		5	O	FW	IRISH		081	I		23
HUGHS	PATRICK				54	IRELAND	RC	IRISH	F	081	J	1	10
HUGHS	WILLIAM				44	O	WM	IRISH		082	C	1	29
HUGHSON	ABRAM				27	O	WM	ENGLISH	F	087	B	3	12
HUGHSON	GEORGE		1		46	US	CC	ENGLISH	BOOKKEEPER	085	B		24
HUGHTON	AND		1		18	O	CP	SCOTCH	CLERK	081	B		67
HULIHAN	PATRICK				45	IRELAND	RC	IRISH	RAFTSMAN	082	I		39
HUME	GEORGE	ROBERT	1		30	QUE	WM	IRISH	CABINET MAKER	085	I		33
HUMPHREY	JOHN				38	IRELAND	CE	IRISH	F	082	A		33
HUMPHREYS	FRANCIS				56	IRELAND	WM	IRISH	F	081	H	2	30
HUMPHREYS	GEO				31	O	EM	IRISH	F	081	H	2	30
HUMPHRIES	JOHN								SEE UMPHRIES	081	J	1	48
HUMPHRIES	RICHARD				27	ONTARIO	EM	IRISH	F	082	A		70
HUNGARY	JOSEPH				22	O	RC	INDIAN	LAB	090	D		9
HUNT	ALFRED		1		28	ENGLAND	ME	ENGLISH	MERCHANT	085	I		13
HUNT	CHARLES				33	ENGLAND	CE	ENGLISH	FARMER	089	A		29
HUNT	CORNELIUS				60	IRELAND	RC	IRISH	FARMER	081	D		17
HUNT	DANIEL				60	IRELAND	RC	IRISH	FARMER	081	D		16
HUNT	GEORGE				41	CORFU IONIAN ISLAND	WM	IRISH	STORE KEEPER F	085	L		1
HUNT	JOHN				50	IRELAND	RC	IRISH	FARMER	081	C		1
HUNT	JOHN				32	O	CE	IRISH	F	082	G		48
HUNT	JOSEPH				46	ENGLAND	WM	ENGLISH	F	086	A	1	20
HUNT	ROBERT				36	ENGLAND	CE	ENGLISH	F	085	D		6
HUNT	THOMAS				40	IRELAND	RC	IRISH	SHOEMAKER	081	J	2	1
HUNT	WILLIAM		1		35	O	RC	IRISH	RAILWAYMAN	081	A	2	29
HUNT	WILLIAM				37	IRELAND	EM	IRISH	F	082	G		47
HUNTER	DAVID				38	O	EM	ENG	LAB	081	B		63
HUNTER	DAVID				53	ONTARIO	WM	IRISH	F	081	C		44
HUNTER	DAVID	JOHN	1		28	O	CP	SCOTCH	TEACHER	081	B		27
HUNTER	GEORGE				45	SCOTLAND	CS	SCOTCH	CLERK	084	E		5
HUNTER	GUY				56	O	CE	IRISH	FARMER	081	D		11
HUNTER	HENLAW				40	O	EM	ENGLISH	F	081	E		15
HUNTER	JAMES				23	SCOTLAND	PS	SCOTCH	F	085	J		26
HUNTER	JOSEPH				27	SCOTLAND	ME	SCOTCH	F	085	A		15
HUNTER	MOORE				32	ENGLAND	EM	ENGLISH	CARPENTER	088	A		9
HUNTER	S	S M			39	QUE	CP	IRISH	MERCHANT	082	E		10
HUNTER	THOMAS				29	SCOTLAND	PS	SCOTCH	F	085	A		19
HUNTER	WILLIAM				48	O	ME	ENGLISH	LUMBERMAN	081	K		14
HUNTER	WM	A			36	QUE	CE	IRISH	MERCHANT	082	E		10
HUNTINGTON	ERASTUS				55	US	WM	ENGLISH	F & INNKEEPER	082	A		27
HUNTINGTON	S	A			58	UNITED STATES	WM	ENGLISH	MILLER F & ?	082	C	1	1
HUNTLY	EDGERTON				36	ONT	ME	ENGISH	F	085	A		18
HUOT	JAMES				78	SCOTLAND	RP	SCOTCH	WEAVER	081	K		10
HURAHAN	MARY		1	1	22	O	RC	IRISH		081	B		23
HURD	ISAAC				61	O	PM	ENGLISH	F	086	A	2	9
HURD	WILLIAM				32	O	EM		F	086	A	2	10
HURLY	BRIDGET		1	1	14	O	RC	IRISH		081	K		47
HURLY	MARGARET		1	1	13	O	RC	IRISH		081	K		48
HURST	GEORGE	WILLIAM			26	O	WM	ENGLISH	SCHOOL TEACHER	082	D		32
HURST	MARY	ANN	1	1	73	IRELAND	CE	IRISH		085	I		24
HURST	ROBERT				26	IRELAND	CE	IRISH	F	085	I		36
HUSBAND	A		1		27	SCOTLAND	CS	SCOTCH	LABOURER	088	A		8
HUSBAND	JAMES		1		30	O	CE	ENGLISH	LUMBERMAN	088	C		10
HUSON	JOHN				40	IRELAND	RC	IRISH	F	082	H		1
HUSSAY	WILLIAM				41	ENGLAND	CE	ENGLISH	F	085	K	1	2
HUSTON	JAMES				40	SCOTLAND	PS	SCOTTISH	FARMER	082	D		29
HUTCHEN	ELIZABETH		1	1	66	ONTARIO	CP	SCOTCH		081	B		3
HUTCHEROFF	A		1		19	O	WM	SCOTCH	LABOURER	088	A		8
HUTCHINS	EBONEZER				39	USA	WM	ENGLISH	F	085	L		3
HUTCHINS	GEORGE				25	USA	WM	ENGLISH	F	085	L		3
HUTCHINSON	ANN			1	44	SCOTLAND	PS	SCOTCH		087	B	2	4
HUTCHINSON	RICHARD				38	ENGLAND	CE	ENGLISH	F	086	A	1	6
HUTCHINSON	SARAH		1	1	40	IRELAND	CS	IRISH	SERVANT	089	B		5
HUTSON	ANDREW				42	SCOTLAND	CS	SCOTCH	F	081	A	1	53
HUTSON	GEORGE	STODDART			25	SCOTLAND	CS	SCOTCH	F	081	A	1	64
HUTSON	JAMES				43	SCOTLAND	CS	SCOTCH	F	081	A	1	65
HUTSON	JOHN				32	SCOTLAND	CP	SCOTCH	MILLWRIGHT	081	A	1	50
HUTSON	JOHN				38	ONTARIO	RC	ENGLISH	FARMER	081	G	2	8
HUTT	SIMON		1		19	O	WM	SCOTCH		085	J		17

SURNAME	NAME1	NAME2	STRAY	SEX	AGE	BIRTHPL	RELIGION	ORIGIN	OCCUP	DIST	SUB_DIST	DIV	PAGE
HUTTON	ANDREW		1		73	SCOTLAND	PS	SCOTTISH		082	D		9
HUTTON	ARTHUR				35	IRELAND	CE	IRISH	F	085	D		30
HUTTON	BRIAN		1		11	ONT	CE	IRISH		081	J	1	86
HUTTON	CATHARINE		1	1	40	QUEBEC	CE	IRISH	HOUSEKEEPER	081	J	1	86
HUTTON	GEORGE		1		23	O	WM	IRISH	SERVANT	081	A	2	29
HUTTON	HENRY				29	ONT	WM	SCOTCH	F	081	J	1	40
HUTTON	JOHN		1		19	O	CP	SCOTCH	SERVANT	081	B		55
HUTTON	JOHN				39	ONT	WM	SCOTCH	F	081	J	1	40
HUTTON	JOHN				45	IRELAND	CS	IRISH	F	082	F		32
HUTTON	MARY		1	1	13	ONT	CE	IRISH		081	J	1	86
HYETT	GEORGE		1		20	O	CP	ENGLISH	TINSMITH	081	I		26
HYMAN	DANIEL				35	O	RC	IRISH	LAB	081	A	2	28
HYNE	CHARLES				38	GERMANY	LU	GERMAN	F	082	G		15
HYNE	WILLIAM				28	GERMANY	LU	GERMAN	F	082	G		20
HYNES	ANDREW				48	IRELAND	RC	IRISH	CONSTABLE	089	B		15
HYNES	THOMAS				26	O	WM	IRISH	CABINETMAKER	081	I		25
IGNACE	MARYANNE		1	1	50	QUEBEC	RC	INDIAN		084	B		3
ILLINOIS	MARY			1	45	RED RIVER	RC	INDIAN		090	F		13
INCH	WILLIAM				35	ENGLAND	WM	ENGLISH	F	085	I		40
INCH	WILLIAM				38	ENGLAND	CE	ENGLISH	LABOURER	089	A		36
INDIAN	(WIDOW)			1		ONTARIO	PA	INDIAN	HUNTER & TRAPPER	090	E		7
INDIAN	ABENCE				62	O	RC	INDIAN	F	087	B	1	1
INDIAN	ACHEPIBAINSE				22	ONT	RC	INDIAN	HUNTER & TRAPPER	090	B		8
INDIAN	AGUAHO				60	O	RC	INDIAN	HUNTER	090	A		3
INDIAN	AHBETAHKEZHIKCH		2		80	US	RC	INDIAN	F	087	C		D
INDIAN	AHBITAHKESHICO				36	ONT	RC	INDIAN	HUNTER & TRAPPER	090	B		8
INDIAN	AHNUTWAIAHBUNOQ		1	1	14	O	PA	INDIAN		087	C		9
INDIAN	AHTIC		1	1	70	O	CE	INDIAN		087	B	1	16
INDIAN	AHWANSE				49	O	PA	INDIAN	HUNTER	088	B		27
INDIAN	AHWONEBAHGOOQUA			1	70	US	RC	INDIAN	F	087	B	1	8
INDIAN	AIVASAMUI		2		4	ONT	RC	INDIAN		090	B		D
INDIAN	AJAWAB					ONTARIO	PA	INDIAN	HUNTER & TRAPPER	090	E		15
INDIAN	AJIMAGUA		2	1	7	O	PA	INDIAN		086	A	3	D
INDIAN	AMADJIWEGIJIK				48	O	RC	INDIAN	HUNTER	088	A		11
INDIAN	AMAGEWAYKEGICH				31	O	PA	INDIAN	HUNTER	088	B		27
INDIAN	AMIN				22	O	PA	INDIAN	HUNTER	090	F		4
INDIAN	AMUCHJEAN					O	PA	INDIAN	HUNTER & TRAPPER	090	C		17
INDIAN	ANAWEIGONCE				50	O	NR	INDIAN	CHIEF	088	A		9
INDIAN	ANGELIC		1	1	52	RED RIVER	RC	INDIAN		090	F		11
INDIAN	ANGIL			1	55	O	RC	INDIAN		084	G	2	5
INDIAN	ANIMIKI					ONTARIO	PA	INDIAN	HUNTER & TRAPPER	090	E		16
INDIAN	ANNINNECE				39	US	RC	INDIAN	F	087	A		45
INDIAN	ANTOUAKAJUAE				28	O	RC	INDIAN	FISHERMAN	088	B		17
INDIAN	ARKMAQUA		2		2		NG	INDIAN		088	C		D
INDIAN	ASABIEWIS				36	O	RC	INDIAN	HUNTER	084	G	2	2
INDIAN	ASHKAKOGAN		2		78	O	RC	INDIAN	F	087	A		D
INDIAN	ASHONAQUET				62	ONTARIO	PA	INDIAN	HUNTER	090	B		2
INDIAN	ASICTAQUIN		1	1	75	O	PA	INDIAN		090	F		3
INDIAN	ASSAMWEIVITAM					ONTARIO	PA	INDIAN	HUNTER & TRAPPER	090	E		12
INDIAN	ASSINAB					ONTARIO	PA	INDIAN	HUNTER & TRAPPER	090	E		8
INDIAN	ATCHICK					ONTARIO	PA	INDIAN	HUNTER & TRAPPER	090	E		9
INDIAN	ATIBOYANCE				46	O	NR	INDIAN	HUNTER	088	C		4
INDIAN	ATOSHIMAN				25	O	PA	INDIAN	HUNTER	090	F		3
INDIAN	AWAISIGEKOMEZOS				19	O	NR	INDIAN	HUNTER	088	C		2
INDIAN	AWUSSAMANUI			1	42	ONT	RC	INDIAN		090	B		5
INDIAN	AYENOGEYHIG				54	O	NR	INDIAN	HUNTER	088	C		2
INDIAN	BABAMASH				15	O	RC	INDIAN	HUNTER	088	B		5
INDIAN	BABOSMANOGUA		2	1	15	O	PA	INDIAN		088	B		D
INDIAN	BAJAMDSER				40	O	PA	INDIAN	HUNTER	088	C		8
INDIAN	BAMOOYAGEYHIG				23	O	NR	INDIAN	HUNTER	088	C		2
INDIAN	BAPTISTE				45	O	RC	INDIAN	HUNTER	084	G	2	4
INDIAN	BASHENEBA				50	O	PA	INDIAN	HUNTER	088	B		18
INDIAN	BEAULY				45	O	PA	INDIAN	HUNTER	090	F		1
INDIAN	BOMWAIWAIKEZKIK		1	1	30	O	PA	INDIAN		087	A		46
INDIAN	BONOKAYOSH				45	O	NR	INDIAN	HUNTER	088	C		7
INDIAN	CABEOAC				40	O	PA	INDIAN	HUNTER	088	B		16
INDIAN	CABINGH				35	O	PA	INDIAN	HUNTER	088	B		8
INDIAN	CABOOK		1		18	O	PA	INDIAN	HUNTER	090	F		4
INDIAN	CACABASLIM				24	O	RC	INDIAN	HUNTER & TRAPPER	090	A		5
INDIAN	CAHCOCOSH				35	O	NG	INDIAN		090	A		3
INDIAN	CAHKEZHESOAI				45	O	PA	INDIAN	F & FISHERMAN	087	C		7
INDIAN	CAIN				23	O	RC	INDIAN	F	087	C		3
INDIAN	CAITAHKEGOBE				45	O	PA	INDIAN	BOAT BUILDER & FISHE	087	C		11
INDIAN	CAITAHKEGOBE		2	1	3	O	PA	INDIAN		087	C		D
INDIAN	CANACOMEE		1		20	O	PA	INDIAN	HUNTER	090	F		4
INDIAN	CANDISSAI				35	ONT	RC	INDIAN	HUNTER & TRAPPER	090	B		7
INDIAN	CAPEMWAYTAK				65	O	RC	INDIAN	HUNTER	084	G	2	1
INDIAN	CARIBOO					O	PA	INDIAN	HUNTER	089	A		50
INDIAN	CARIBOO					O	PA	INDIAN	HUNTER	089	A		50
INDIAN	CASKEGANCE				36	O	NR	INDIAN	HUNTER	088	C		1
INDIAN	CHABATIKS				57	ONT	RC	INDIAN		090	B		8
INDIAN	CHEEPO				30	O	PA	INDIAN	HUNTER & TRAPPER	090	C		12
INDIAN	CHEMAUGA				40	O	PA	INDIAN	HUNTER	088	B		14
INDIAN	CHESSOMINIE				28	O	RC	INDIAN	HUNTER	090	B		3
INDIAN	CHICKOJUA				80	O	PA	INDIAN		088	B		9
INDIAN	CHIOIMO				60	O	PA	INDIAN	HUNTER	086	A	3	8
INDIAN	CHYOSEBESO		2		20	O	PA	INDIAN		088	B		D
INDIAN	CLIMCHOWES				41	O	PA	INDIAN	HUNTER	088	B		22
INDIAN	COLUMBUS			1	67	US	CE	INDIAN	F	087	B	1	10
INDIAN	COLUMBUS		2		62	US	CE	INDIAN	F	087	B	1	D
INDIAN	COMSQUABONUQUE				35	O	PA	INDIAN	HUNTER	088	B		8
INDIAN	COSCAJEE				30	O	PA	INDIAN	HUNTER	088	B		19
INDIAN	COTABOSHER				50	O	PA	INDIAN	HUNTER	088	B		7
INDIAN	COTADAMSEAUT				40	O	PA	INDIAN	HUNTER	088	C		5
INDIAN	DAKOSE				60	O	RC	INDIAN		090	A		6
INDIAN	DEWECENCE				25	O	PA	INDIAN	HUNTER	090	F		2
INDIAN	DOOCOOCHESE				40	O	PA	INDIAN	HUNTER & TRAPPER	090	C		8
INDIAN	DOOCOONACI				26	O	PA	INDIAN	HUNTER & TRAPPER	090	C		9
INDIAN	EDAWEGON		2		4	O	PA	INDIAN		086	C	2	D
INDIAN	ENCE				67	USA	RC	INDIAN	F	087	B	1	5
INDIAN	ENCESEBUN				28	O	RC	INDIAN	F	087	B	1	7
INDIAN	ENDOTOGONEW				80	O	PA	INDIAN		088	B		9
INDIAN	ENEWAYANCE				26	O	NR	INDIAN	HUNTER	088	C		3
INDIAN	ESANCE		1	1	18	O	RC	INDIAN		090	F		15
INDIAN	ESCHGUAGABA				45	O	PA	INDIAN	HUNTER	088	B		16
INDIAN	ESQUAJEESIC				55	O	PA	INDIAN	HUNTER	088	B		20

SURNAME	NAME1	NAME2	STRAY	SEX	AGE	BIRTHPL	RELIGION	ORIGIN	OCCUP	DIST	SUB_DIST	DIV	PAGE
INDIAN	FAUTAQUE				70	O	RC	INDIAN		084	H		1
INDIAN	FRANCOIS				70	O	RC	INDIAN		090	A		5
INDIAN	FRANCOS				28	O	RC	INDIAN	HUNTER	084	G	2	2
INDIAN	FRANCOS TOINE				40	O	RC	INDIAN	HUNTER	084	G	2	4
INDIAN	GABAWIDI				45	O	RC	INDIAN	HUNTER	088	B		11
INDIAN	GAGISHIANGAI				55	O	PA	INDIAN	HUNTER	088	A		14
INDIAN	GAHBINGER			1	34	ONT	RC	INDIAN		090	B		9
INDIAN	GAHGAHKEWAI				52	US	CE	INDIAN	F & COOPER	087	B	1	12
INDIAN	GAIHEZHEGONGGAI		2		3	O	CE	INDIAN		087	B	1	D
INDIAN	GAIKEZHEQONGGAI				55	O	CE	INDIAN	F & HUNTER	087	B	1	14
INDIAN	GARWAOSH				35	O	WM	INDIAN	HUNTER	090	A		1
INDIAN	GAUGAUGINCE				50	O	NR	INDIAN	HUNTER	088	A		10
INDIAN	GEORGE				18	O	PA	INDIAN	F	087	A		47
INDIAN	GESEQUT				25	O	PA	INDIAN	HUNTER	088	C		8
INDIAN	GIJIGOBINAISS				28	O	WM	INDIAN	HUNTER	088	A		10
INDIAN	GODAS			1	40	O	PA	INDIAN		086	A	3	2
INDIAN	GOTABASHEU				54	O	PA	INDIAN	HUNTER	088	B		16
INDIAN	GUAGAZANCE				60	O	RC	INDIAN		090	A		7
INDIAN	GUARONCE				100	O	PA	INDIAN		086	A	3	3
INDIAN	ICHIBAKWENININI					ONTARIO	PA	INDIAN	HUNTER & TRAPPER	090	E		20
INDIAN	ICHIETANG					ONTARIO	PA	INDIAN	HUNTER & TRAPPER	090	E		1
INDIAN	IQUBEBDUEP				36	O	NR	INDIAN	HUNTER	088	C		3
INDIAN	IQUOB				32	O	PA	INDIAN		088	B		10
INDIAN	ISHKEMAH				50	US	CE	INDIAN	F & LABOURER	087	B	1	11
INDIAN	J	BT			26	O	RC	INDIAN	HUNTER	088	A		11
INDIAN	JABUTZ				35	O	PA	INDIAN	HUNTER	088	C		8
INDIAN	JACK ON A GAN				66	O	RC	INDIAN	HUNTER	084	G	2	3
INDIAN	JACKNUOT				48	O	PA	INDIAN	HUNTER & TRAPPER	090	C		9
INDIAN	JEAN	BAPTISTE			62	O	RC	INDIAN	HUNTER	084	H		1
INDIAN	JOCKO				54	US	RC	INDIAN	F	087	A		45
INDIAN	JOHNOKON				38	O	PA	INDIAN		088	B		15
INDIAN	JOJO				60	O	PA	INDIAN	HUNTER	090	F		2
INDIAN	JOSEPH				33	O	RC	INDIAN	HUNTER	084	G	2	1
INDIAN	JOSEPH		2		21	O	RC		HUNTER	084	H		D
INDIAN	JOSET		1	1	3	O	PA	INDIAN		087	A		46
INDIAN	JOSET		1	1	20	O	PA	INDIAN		090	F		4
INDIAN	KAHBUTANAI					O	PA	INDIAN	HUNTER & TRAPPER	090	C		19
INDIAN	KAHMAHYAHWEJABO				47	O	PA	INDIAN	HUNTER	088	B		26
INDIAN	KAHTAHBAHSOSH		1		22	O	RC	INDIAN	F & FISHERMAN	087	C		9
INDIAN	KAHTAHBAHSOSH		2	1		O	RC	INDIAN		087	C		D
INDIAN	KAKAKEGE				58	O	PA	INDIAN	HUNTER	088	B		26
INDIAN	KAKAKONCE				49	O	WM	INDIAN	HUNTER	088	A		10
INDIAN	KAKIGE				72	US	PA	INDIAN	F & FISHERMAN	087	A		42
INDIAN	KAMATIG				50	O	RC	INDIAN	HUNTER	084	G	2	1
INDIAN	KAMEENOKANISE				30	ONTARIO	PA	INDIAN	HUNTER & TRAPPER	090	B		2
INDIAN	KAMSHION					ONTARIO	PA	INDIAN	HUNTER & TRAPPER	090	E		12
INDIAN	KANAGESINA					ONTARIO	RC	INDIAN	HUNTER & TRAPPER	090	E		5
INDIAN	KANDJIININI					ONTARIO	PA	INDIAN	HUNTER & TRAPPER	090	E		12
INDIAN	KANEPACHORS			1	49	ONT	RC	INDIAN		090	B		10
INDIAN	KAPEMEQUNE				55	O	RC	INDIAN	HUNTER	084	G	2	1
INDIAN	KAWASENECK				72	O	RC	INDIAN	HUNTER	090	B		4
INDIAN	KAYOSH			1	58	O	PA	INDIAN	HUNTER	088	B		27
INDIAN	KCWODINEGNA		2	1	10	O	PA	INDIAN		086	C	2	D
INDIAN	KEBRCOMAINSE				37	ONT	RC	INDIAN	HUNTER & TRAPPER	090	B		8
INDIAN	KEEMEESHIO				26	ONT	RC	INDIAN	HUNTER & TRAPPER	090	B		7
INDIAN	KEENES				67	O	RC	INDIAN	HUNTER	084	G	2	4
INDIAN	KELCHIMANITO		1	1	50	O	PA	INDIAN		090	F		1
INDIAN	KENECE		1		95	O	PA	INDIAN	F	087	C		7
INDIAN	KENECE		2		95	O	PA	INDIAN	F & FISHERMAN	087	C		D
INDIAN	KENOOSHANCE		2	1	50	O	WM	INDIAN		090	A		D
INDIAN	KEOOSHEI				80	O	WM	INDIAN		090	A		3
INDIAN	KEPUCK				25	O	PA	INDIAN	HUNTER	090	F		2
INDIAN	KEWAIGAHBOSSEQU		1	1	52	US	PA	INDIAN		087	A		46
INDIAN	KEWAIQUOUM		1		20	O	PA	INDIAN	F & FISHERMAN	087	C		8
INDIAN	KEWAITIUOQUAI		1	1	22	O	PA	INDIAN		087	A		46
INDIAN	KEWAITIVOQUAI		1	1	92	O	RC	INDIAN		087	C		10
INDIAN	KEWETAHBENESSEQ		1	1	18	O	PA	INDIAN		087	C		8
INDIAN	KEZHIKGOOBENESS				60	O	CE	INDIAN	F	087	B	1	17
INDIAN	KIBETANCE				48	O	PA	INDIAN	HUNTER & TRAPPER	090	C		12
INDIAN	KINEWAHBAI				42	USA	RC	INDIAN	F	087	B	1	3
INDIAN	KITCHCHEMOKOMON					O	PA	INDIAN	HUNTER & TRAPPER	090	C		15
INDIAN	KITCHIKITCHIGA		1	1		ONTARIO	PA	INDIAN	HUNTER & TRAPPER	090	E		20
INDIAN	KOKOMAI		1	1	82	O	PA	INDIAN		087	C		10
INDIAN	KYBINCE			1	80	O	CE	INDIAN		089	B		39
INDIAN	LAGUARDE			1		O	RC	INDIAN		090	C		14
INDIAN	LEUCWAKEGICK				27	O	PA	INDIAN	HUNTER	088	B		24
INDIAN	MACKNOOT				25	MILL LAC	PA	INDIAN	HUNTER	090	F		5
INDIAN	MAHCAHDAIWAIOSH				54	O	PA	INDIAN	F & FISHERMAN	087	C		7
INDIAN	MAHSQUEBEW		2		25	O	PA	INDIAN		087	C		D
INDIAN	MAIATCHIABANDAN					ONTARIO	PA	INDIAN	HUNTER & TRAPPER	090	E		13
INDIAN	MAINDOWOSSUNG				30	O	CE	INDIAN	F & HUNTER	087	B	1	19
INDIAN	MAINDOWOSSUNG		2		4	O	CE	INDIAN		087	B	1	D
INDIAN	MAINOKEZHIKGUK				56	O	PA	INDIAN	F & FISHERMAN	087	C		8
INDIAN	MAISHUKQUETOQUA		1	1	16	O	PA	INDIAN		087	A		47
INDIAN	MAISHUKQUETOQUA		1	1	2	O	PA	INDIAN		087	C		9
INDIAN	MAISQUOUNUN				52	O	CE	INDIAN	F & HUNTER	087	B	1	15
INDIAN	MAISQUOUNUN		2	1	3	O	CE	INDIAN		087	B	1	D
INDIAN	MAITWAIGWAH				30	O	RC	INDIAN	F & FISHERMAN	087	C		11
INDIAN	MAITWAIGWAH				30	O	RC	INDIAN	F & FISHERMAN	087	C		11
INDIAN	MAITWAIQWAB			1	50	US	RC	INDIAN		087	C		9
INDIAN	MAKONCE				40	O	RC	INDIAN		090	A		7
INDIAN	MALCHETOMBYSIE			1	48	ONT	RC	INDIAN		090	B		11
INDIAN	MALICULIBAIWESE		1		32	O	RC	INDIAN	WIDOW	087	B	1	3
INDIAN	MAMWAWAISKAWAH				38	O	NR	INDIAN	HUNTER	088	C		2
INDIAN	MANAQUDAB				35	O	PA	INDIAN	HUNTER	088	B		19
INDIAN	MANITOPINAISIE			1	38	ONT	RC	INDIAN		090	B		11
INDIAN	MANITOPINENS					ONTARIO	PA	INDIAN	HUNTER & TRAPPER	090	E		15
INDIAN	MANITOSHENS					ONTARIO	PA	INDIAN	HUNTER & TRAPPER	090	E		1
INDIAN	MANIVKEGICUD				34	O	PA	INDIAN	HUNTER	088	B		26
INDIAN	MANJISID					ONTARIO	RC	INDIAN	HUNTER & TRAPPER	090	E		17
INDIAN	MANOWABENESE				90	O	PA	INDIAN		088	B		9
INDIAN	MARGRETTE		1	1	50	RED RIVER	RC	INDIAN		090	F		11
INDIAN	MAUGOWNI				60	O	PA	INDIAN	HUNTER	088	B		25
INDIAN	MAUIVAFEISDE		2	1	3	O	PA	INDIAN		086	A	3	D
INDIAN	MAYAHNAKAHBO					O	PA	INDIAN	HUNTER & TRAPPER	090	C		16
INDIAN	MAYMAGUESS		2		48	ONT	RC		HUNTER & TRAPPER	090	B		D

SURNAME	NAME1	NAME2	STRAY	SEX	AGE	BIRTHPL	RELIGION	ORIGIN	OCCUP	DIST	SUB_DIST	DIV	PAGE
INDIAN	MEBWAYKAHBO				36	O	WM	INDIAN	HUNTER & TRAPPER	090	C		6
INDIAN	MEBWAYONEONUB					O	PA	INDIAN	HUNTER & TRAPPER	090	C		17
INDIAN	MEEKEESIPINAISH				46	ONT	RC	INDIAN	HUNTER & TRAPPER	090	B		10
INDIAN	MEENOOKESHICKA			1	54	ONT	RC	INDIAN		090	B		10
INDIAN	MEMEUSE				55	O	PA	INDIAN	HUNTER	088	B		10
INDIAN	MENEWANIKWUASH		1			ONTARIO	PA	INDIAN		090	E		15
INDIAN	MENOWALSHWK				70	O	PA	INDIAN	HUNTER	088	B		10
INDIAN	MESAKEWIN				25	O	RC	INDIAN	HUNTER	084	G	2	4
INDIAN	METWANUM				62	O	PA	INDIAN	HUNTER	088	B		12
INDIAN	MEXINNENE				62	O	RC	INDIAN	F & FISHERMAN	087	B	1	6
INDIAN	MEYHOQUANOBAW				34	O	NR	INDIAN	HUNTER	088	C		2
INDIAN	MIAHKOQUIN				60	O	PA	INDIAN	HUNTER	088	B		25
INDIAN	MICDEL					ONTARIO	PA	INDIAN	HUNTER & TRAPPER	090	E		1
INDIAN	MICHELL				57	O	PA	INDIAN	HUNTER & TRAPPER	090	C		13
INDIAN	MICHELLPPON					O	PA	INDIAN	HUNTER & TRAPPER	090	C		16
INDIAN	MICKEVACOSE			1	43	O	PA	INDIAN		088	B		24
INDIAN	MIGIZEE					O	RC	INDIAN	HUNTER & TRAPPER	090	C		11
INDIAN	MINJAKAGABAW					ONTARIO	WM	INDIAN	HUNTER & TRAPPER	090	E		13
INDIAN	MINNAWAHPENOR					O	WM	INDIAN	HUNTER & TRAPPER	090	C		3
INDIAN	MINWANIMAN					ONTARIO	PA	INDIAN	HUNTER & TRAPPER	090	E		3
INDIAN	MIOSEWAJA				40	O	PA	INDIAN	HUNTER	088	B		7
INDIAN	MIPABIC				41	O	NR	INDIAN	HUNTER	088	C		1
INDIAN	MISABY				42	O	RC	INDIAN	HUNTER	084	G	2	2
INDIAN	MISAGOSH					ONTARIO	PA	INDIAN	HUNTER & TRAPPER	090	E		10
INDIAN	MISCOBENENCE				24	O	PA	INDIAN	HUNTER	088	B		13
INDIAN	MISCOBENENCE				30	O	PA	INDIAN		088	B		13
INDIAN	MISHINNOR				34	O	WM	INDIAN	HUNTER & TRAPPER	090	C		5
INDIAN	MISHKISGO				27	O	WM	INDIAN	HUNTER & TRAPPER	090	C		6
INDIAN	MISHKOOSHKISH					O	PA	INDIAN	HUNTER & TRAPPER	090	C		14
INDIAN	MISHQUANEQUIDQU			1	60	O	NR	INDIAN	HUNTRESS	088	C		1
INDIAN	MISICJOOK		1	1	15	O	PA	INDIAN		090	F		4
INDIAN	MISOEWANIQUEB		1	1	45	O	PA	INDIAN		090	F		2
INDIAN	MISQUAHKEZHIK		1		5	US	PA	INDIAN		087	A		47
INDIAN	MISSABISMOTHUOQ			1	71	O	NR	INDIAN	HUNTRESS	088	C		2
INDIAN	MISSISQUANCE		2		5	ONTARIO	NR	INDIAN		088	C		D
INDIAN	MISTOKEWAJIS				41	O	PA	INDIAN	HUNTER	088	B		26
INDIAN	MIZIH				72	O	ZZ	INDIAN	HUNTER	089	B		39
INDIAN	MOCOHAIKIOSHK				22	O	RC	INDIAN	F	087	B	1	2
INDIAN	MOCOSITANCE				38	US	CE	INDIAN	F	087	B	1	16
INDIAN	MOCOTABIN				52	US	CE	INDIAN	F	087	B	1	13
INDIAN	MONIIAWINIWIS					ONTARIO	RC	INDIAN	HUNTER & TRAPPER	090	E		5
INDIAN	MONOMERE				70	O	PA	INDIAN	TRAPPER	086	A	3	3
INDIAN	MOODIEQUA			1	52	O	NR	INDIAN	HUNTRESS	088	C		3
INDIAN	MOOPOMIN				42	O	WM	INDIAN	HUNTER & TRAPPER	090	C		4
INDIAN	MOOSEOQUAI		1	1	32	O	PA	INDIAN		087	A		46
INDIAN	MOQUETANG		1			ONTARIO	RC	INDIAN	LABOURER	090	E		18
INDIAN	MOSES				23	O	CE	INDIAN	HUNTER	088	A		13
INDIAN	MOSES				43	O	RC	INDIAN	HUNTER & TRAPPER	090	C		6
INDIAN	MOSQUONAQUOEL				32	O	PA	INDIAN	HUNTER	088	B		17
INDIAN	MOTHER BOB			1	59	ONT	RC	INDIAN		090	B		9
INDIAN	MOUZENEKEWAZIE					O	PA	INDIAN	HUNTER & TRAPPER	090	C		18
INDIAN	MUCKEZEWAY					O	PA	INDIAN		090	C		13
INDIAN	MUCKWABIES			1	53	ONT	RC	INDIAN		090	B		10
INDIAN	MUDCHEMEGOOSH					O	PA	INDIAN	HUNTER & TRAPPER	090	C		11
INDIAN	MUHEKOSINNCK			1	58	ONT	RC	INDIAN		090	B		7
INDIAN	MUNISIUNOE				31	O	NR	INDIAN	HUNTER	088	C		2
INDIAN	MUOHQUETESS				30	O	PA	INDIAN	F & FISHERMAN	087	C		8
INDIAN	MUSEOGUOD		2		34	O	PA	INDIAN	HUNTER	088	B		D
INDIAN	MUSKAWIN			1	38	ONT	RC	INDIAN		090	B		9
INDIAN	MUSKENSE			1	47	ONT	RC	INDIAN		090	B		11
INDIAN	NABAKAINU				62	FORT FRANCES	PA	INDIAN	HUNTER	090	F		3
INDIAN	NAH BEGUN				31	O	WM	INDIAN	HUNTER & TRAPPER	090	C		4
INDIAN	NAHGOACH			1	75	O	WM	INDIAN		090	A		2
INDIAN	NAHNAHKEZHIKGOO		1	1	26	O	PA	INDIAN		087	A		47
INDIAN	NAHWAICHCHEKABB		1			O	PA	INDIAN		090	C		15
INDIAN	NAIBENAISHKUNNO		1	1	42	O	RC	INDIAN		087	C		10
INDIAN	NAIBESI				75	O	PA	INDIAN	HUNTER	088	B		25
INDIAN	NAINBWAIGOOHABE		1		7	O	PA	INDIAN		087	A		47
INDIAN	NAINEWAISHKUNG				59	O	CE	INDIAN	F	087	B	1	16
INDIAN	NAINEWAISHKUNG				60	O	PA	INDIAN	F & FISHERMAN	087	C		8
INDIAN	NAIWAIBEZOQUAI		1	1	4	O	PA	INDIAN		087	C		9
INDIAN	NAKAPIAN					ONTARIO	PA	INDIAN	HUNTER & TRAPPER	090	E		11
INDIAN	NAMAGUISH		1	1	8	O	PA	INDIAN		090	F		1
INDIAN	NAMEN					ONTARIO	RC	INDIAN	HUNTER & TRAPPER	090	E		6
INDIAN	NANAYWASH				25	O	PA	INDIAN	HUNTER	090	F		1
INDIAN	NANDAUEWIU				31	O	PA	INDIAN	HUNTER	088	B		21
INDIAN	NANISHI					ONTARIO	RC	INDIAN	HUNTER & TRAPPER	090	E		11
INDIAN	NASHDABIQUA				95	O	RC	INDIAN		090	A		8
INDIAN	NATCHEWEN			1	79	O	PA	INDIAN		088	B		27
INDIAN	NAWABANAI		2	1	11	ONT	RC			090	B		D
INDIAN	NAWANANAPUI		2		33	ONT	RC		HUNTER & TRAPPER	090	B		D
INDIAN	NAWKAMIGABOW				45	O	RC	INDIAN	COOPER	088	A		12
INDIAN	NEAGEKIAEGNUS				26	O	PA	INDIAN	HUNTER	088	B		22
INDIAN	NEBABINESSE		1		12	O	PA	INDIAN		090	F		2
INDIAN	NEBOAKEGISK				21	O	PA	INDIAN	HUNTER	088	B		24
INDIAN	NEBUMSQUA		2		16		NG	INDIAN		088	B		D
INDIAN	NEENOVWASSUN				45	ONT	RC	INDIAN	HUNTER & TRAPPER	090	B		10
INDIAN	NEGGIGOASE				52	O	NR	INDIAN	HUNTER	088	C		2
INDIAN	NEGONONQUET				67	O	RC	INDIAN	F	087	B	1	6
INDIAN	NEGONOQUOUM		1		12	US	PA	INDIAN		087	A		47
INDIAN	NEKIH WACHPEN				65	O	WM	INDIAN	HUNTER & TRAPPER	090	C		4
INDIAN	NEMAAKIWENSI		1			ONTARIO	RC	INDIAN	LABOURER	090	E		18
INDIAN	NEMAJEISIC				35	O	PA	INDIAN	HUNTER	088	C		5
INDIAN	NESETUI					O	RC	INDIAN	HUNTER & TRAPPER	090	C		10
INDIAN	NETAWASANG					ONTARIO	RC	INDIAN	HUNTER & TRAPPER	090	E		10
INDIAN	NIBEQUAH				43	O	RC	INDIAN		090	A		5
INDIAN	NINDOQUESOQUC		2	1			NG	INDIAN		088	C		D
INDIAN	NOCHEDOU				30	O	PA	INDIAN	HUNTER	088	B		22
INDIAN	NODAWANAR				40	O	PA	INDIAN	HUNTER	086	A	3	6
INDIAN	NODGTA			1	30	O	PA	INDIAN	HUNTER	088	B		14
INDIAN	NOGEGEESEGWAPE				35	O	RC	INDIAN	HUNTER	088	B		15
INDIAN	NOIAWANGEANG					ONTARIO	PA	INDIAN	HUNTER & TRAPPER	090	E		11
INDIAN	NOJWOJOBO				50	O	PA	INDIAN	HUNTER	088	B		19
INDIAN	NOQUAY				27	O	RC	INDIAN		090	A		8
INDIAN	NOWESETNOKE			1	55	O	PA	INDIAN		088	C		4
INDIAN	NOWQUAOSAJEA				80	O	PA	INDIAN	HUNTER	088	C		8

SURNAME	NAME1	NAME2	STRAY	SEX	AGE	BIRTHPL	RELIGION	ORIGIN	OCCUP	DIST	SUB_DIST	DIV	PAGE
INDIAN	NOWQUOWN		1		8	0	NG	INDIAN		087	A		
INDIAN	NOWWAHGWONOQUAI		1	1	12	0	PA	INDIAN		087	A		46
INDIAN	NOWWETAIKEZHIK				25	0	CE	INDIAN	LABOURER & F	087	B	1	20
INDIAN	ODARUMAGEWAI			1	60	0	PA	INDIAN		086	A	3	6
INDIAN	OGAWAUCE				49	0	PA	INDIAN	HUNTER	088	B		24
INDIAN	OGITCHITAPINONS					ONTARIO	PA	INDIAN	HUNTER & TRAPPER	090	E		13
INDIAN	OGUSH				58	0	RC	INDIAN	HUNTER	084	H		1
INDIAN	OHGAHSAHNOOSE				38	0	RC	INDIAN	HUNTER	090	B		4
INDIAN	OJAMANCE				30	FORT FRANCES	PA	INDIAN	HUNTER	090	F		1
INDIAN	OJESWA		2		30	0	PA	INDIAN		086	A	3	D
INDIAN	OKEEFRABINAISE				24	0	PA	INDIAN	HUNTER & TRAPPER	090	B		3
INDIAN	OKEMAH				49	0	CE	INDIAN	F	087	B	1	14
INDIAN	OKEMAHKITCHE				50	0	PA	INDIAN	F & FISHERMAN & BOAT	087	C		10
INDIAN	OKEWAH			1	30	US	RC	INDIAN	F	087	B	1	6
INDIAN	OKEWENAH				36	0	PA	INDIAN		088	B		28
INDIAN	OKEZHIKGOOK				54	0	CE	INDIAN	F	087	B	1	17
INDIAN	OKONDASHKWAI					ONTARIO	PA	INDIAN	HUNTER & TRAPPER	090	E		2
INDIAN	OMAMOIE				54	0	RC	INDIAN	HUNTER & TRAPPER	090	C		9
INDIAN	OMBINNINNIE				50	0	RC	INDIAN	HUNTER & TRAPPER	090	C		10
INDIAN	OMEE			1	45	0	PA	INDIAN		090	F		1
INDIAN	OMINASANOORS			1	56	ONT	RC	INDIAN		090	B		11
INDIAN	ONIBANSE				56	0	PA	INDIAN	HUNTER & TRAPPER	090	B		3
INDIAN	ONISIAN				34	0	RC	INDIAN	HUNTER & TRAPPER	090	C		5
INDIAN	ONISTEGUAUISH				40	0	RA	INDIAN	HUNTER & TRAPPER	090	C		8
INDIAN	ONIZENAHSQUTCIW				62	US	PA	INDIAN	F	087	A		46
INDIAN	OOGEMAHOPAI			1		0	RC	INDIAN		090	C		11
INDIAN	OOGEMCIS					0	PA	INDIAN	HUNTER & TRAPPER	090	C		19
INDIAN	OPAWMAHGONAO					0	PA	INDIAN	HUNTER & TRAPPER	090	C		14
INDIAN	OQUEWIS				52	0	RC	INDIAN	F & FISHERMAN	087	B	1	4
INDIAN	OSAJAMOCK			1	60	0	PA	INDIAN		090	F		2
INDIAN	OSAWANIMIKI				42	US	PA	INDIAN	F & FISHERMAN	087	A		41
INDIAN	OSHEBAHKOSHIKGO		1	1	70	0	RC	INDIAN		087	B	1	2
INDIAN	OSHEKUGMIG				22	0	NR	INDIAN	HUNTER	088	C		1
INDIAN	OSHIGAU				40	0	PA	INDIAN	HUNTER	086	A	3	7
INDIAN	OSHKAKIPITE					ONTARIO	PA	INDIAN	HUNTER & TRAPPER	090	E		2
INDIAN	OSHKANAGOWE					ONTARIO	PA	INDIAN	HUNTER & TRAPPER	090	E		3
INDIAN	OSORQUOUMOQUAI		1	1	18	0	PA	INDIAN		087	A		47
INDIAN	OSORROWOHQUOQWO				62	0	CE	INDIAN	F & FISHERMAN	087	B	1	16
INDIAN	OSOWQUONN				67	US	RC	INDIAN	F	087	A		44
INDIAN	OTCHONOMEQUOUN				36	0	PA	INDIAN	F & FISHERMAN	087	C		8
INDIAN	OUABUTAH				40	0	PA	INDIAN	HUNTER & TRAPPER	090	C		10
INDIAN	PA QUES QUET		1		65	0	RC	INDIAN	HUNTER	084	G		1
INDIAN	PABGUMUMEQUOUM		1		16	0	PA	INDIAN	F & FISHERMAN	087	C		8
INDIAN	PAHENCE		1		18	0	PA	INDIAN	F	087	A		46
INDIAN	PAHENCE				60	0	CE	INDIAN	HUNTER & F	087	B	1	15
INDIAN	PAHPAHGWIS				34	0	NR	INDIAN	HUNTER	088	C		1
INDIAN	PAHTAHDOGAISHIN		1		100	0	PA	INDIAN	F & FISHERMAN	087	C		8
INDIAN	PAIBOMSAI				60	0	CE	INDIAN	F	087	B	1	20
INDIAN	PAIGONAIAHSUNG		1		26	0	PA	INDIAN	LAB	087	A		46
INDIAN	PAISHAHBUNOQUAI		1	1	30	US	RC	INDIAN		087	C		5
INDIAN	PAISHSKEZHIKGOO		1	1	7	0	PA	INDIAN		087	A		47
INDIAN	PAMEGESAGONQUN				40	0	PA	INDIAN	HUNTER	086	C	2	1
INDIAN	PANABE					ONTARIO	PA	INDIAN	HUNTER & TRAPPER	090	E		5
INDIAN	PAPASHKINS					ONTARIO	PA	INDIAN	HUNTER & TRAPPER	090	E		18
INDIAN	PAPEQUISEQUA			1	62	0	NR	INDIAN	HUNTRESS	088	C		3
INDIAN	PAPTEQUATUM					0	PA	INDIAN	HUNTER & TRAPPER	090	C		14
INDIAN	PASAUQUA			1	22	0	NR	INDIAN	HUNTRESS	088	C		1
INDIAN	PASHKINAASH			1		ONTARIO	PA	INDIAN	HUNTER & TRAPPER	090	E		20
INDIAN	PASKEWAY		1	1	58	ONT	RC	INDIAN		084	G	2	5
INDIAN	PATAHWONOQUETOQ		1	1	20	US	PA	INDIAN	F	087	A		47
INDIAN	PATAMAKEJICKMAB					0	PA	INDIAN	HUNTER & TRAPPER	090	C		13
INDIAN	PAUL				27	0	RC	INDIAN	HUNTER	084	G	2	3
INDIAN	PAUL				42	0	RC	INDIAN	HUNTER & TRAPPER	090	C		15
INDIAN	PAUNOQUOUAISHKU	JB			70	0	RC	INDIAN	F	087	B	1	1
INDIAN	PEGUAGESK				55	0	RC	INDIAN	HUNTER	084	G	2	2
INDIAN	PEMIJIWONOGUA			1	110	0	PA	INDIAN		086	A	3	3
INDIAN	PENAISIECA		2		5	ONT	RC			090	B		D
INDIAN	PENATOSE				38	0	PA	INDIAN	HUNTER	088	B		19
INDIAN	PENESSAWONOQUET		1		14	0	PA	INDIAN	HUNTER	087	A		47
INDIAN	PENESSEWEKEZHIK			1	55	US	CE	INDIAN	F	087	B	1	17
INDIAN	PENESY				28	0	PR	INDIAN	HUNTER	084	G	2	3
INDIAN	PEPATCH					ONTARIO	PA	INDIAN	HUNTER & TRAPPER	090	E		16
INDIAN	PESHEKEWEKEZHIK				42	0	RC	INDIAN	F & COOPER	087	B	1	3
INDIAN	PESHKONSIWAB					ONTARIO	PA	INDIAN	HUNTER & TRAPPER	090	E		18
INDIAN	PETAHWONOQUET		1		22	0	PA	INDIAN	LAB	087	A		47
INDIAN	PETATOGONSIEGNA				47	0	PA	INDIAN	HUNTER	088	B		23
INDIAN	PETEBIE			1	60	0	RC	INDIAN	HUNTER	084	G	2	4
INDIAN	PETOJANEF		1	1	20	0	PA	INDIAN	HUNTER	088	B		4
INDIAN	PEWASH					0	PA	INDIAN	HUNTER & TRAPPER	090	C		16
INDIAN	PIAHBEWASH			1	42	0	CE	INDIAN	F	087	B	1	15
INDIAN	PINDUNWAN				52	US	RC	INDIAN	F	087	A		44
INDIAN	PUNEBEKEZHIK		1		30	0	PA	INDIAN	F & FISHERMAN	087	C		8
INDIAN	QUADESEASE				28	0	PA	INDIAN		088	B		14
INDIAN	QUAHAHEJICK				38	ONT	RC	INDIAN	HUNTER & TRAPPER	090	B		12
INDIAN	QUAUABGIE				60	0	PA	INDIAN	HUNTER	088	B		23
INDIAN	QUEINGEGUN				80	0	PA	INDIAN	HUNTER	088	B		15
INDIAN	QUESES				30	0	RC	INDIAN	HUNTER	084	G	2	4
INDIAN	QUINGWISBEDNAU				44	0	RC	INDIAN	HUNTER	088	B		22
INDIAN	QUOWEZENCE				60	0	PA	INDIAN	HUNTER	088	B		12
INDIAN	RIJIGOWININI					ONTARIO	PA	INDIAN	HUNTER & TRAPPER	090	E		16
INDIAN	RIVINGIVAAGE					ONTARIO	RC	INDIAN	HUNTER & TRAPPER	090	E		17
INDIAN	ROUND EYES				30	0	RC	INDIAN	HUNTER	084	G	2	4
INDIAN	SACKCUMEGUA			1	81	0	PA	INDIAN		088	B		28
INDIAN	SACKECHWISHKNIG				56	0	PA	INDIAN	HUNTER	088	B		27
INDIAN	SAHGAH				32	0	RC	INDIAN	F	087	B	1	8
INDIAN	SAHGUTCHEWAIOSA				28	0	RC	INDIAN		087	A		47
INDIAN	SAHKEWENAIBE				67	US	PA	INDIAN	F	087	B	1	20
INDIAN	SAHQUAIBENESS				42	0	CE	INDIAN	F & LABOURER	087	B	1	11
INDIAN	SAISAIGUNOQUAI		1	1	14	0	PA	INDIAN		087	A		47
INDIAN	SAJAKEE				35	0	RC	INDIAN	LAB	090	F		12
INDIAN	SAMON					ONTARIO	PA	INDIAN	HUNTER & TRAPPER	090	E		14
INDIAN	SAMUEL				35	0	RC	INDIAN	HUNTER	084	G	2	3
INDIAN	SARRIBAK				30	0	PA	INDIAN	TRAPPER	086	A	3	3
INDIAN	SEGINAWWISHKANG					ONTARIO	PA	INDIAN	HUNTER & TRAPPER	090	E		11
INDIAN	SHABOKAEGICKEQU				60	0	PA	INDIAN		088	B		22
INDIAN	SHABWAKUGABAW					ONTARIO	PA	INDIAN	HUNTER & TRAPPER	090	E		19

SURNAME	NAME1	NAME2	STRAY	SEX	AGE	BIRTHPL	RELIGION	ORIGIN	OCCUP	DIST	SUB_DIST	DIV	PAGE
INDIAN	SHABWASING				58	0	PA	INDIAN	HUNTER	088	B		23
INDIAN	SHAHWONNO	QUAHDOQUA		1	70	0	CE	INDIAN		089	B		38
INDIAN	SHAWBOKEJICK					0	PA	INDIAN	HUNTER & TRAPPER	090	C		16
INDIAN	SHAWBOW				57	0	WM	INDIAN		086	A	3	2
INDIAN	SHAWBWAITMINEGO		1	1	30	0	CE	INDIAN	F	087	B	1	19
INDIAN	SHEMORGAN					0	PA	INDIAN	HUNTER	089	A		49
INDIAN	SHESHEEP		2			0	PA	INDIAN		090	F		D
INDIAN	SHESHONER				50	0	PA	INDIAN	HUNTER	088	B		8
INDIAN	SHESLAWIN				40	0	PA	INDIAN	HUNTER	088	B		12
INDIAN	SHEWPNBOIRUI				56	ONT	RC	INDIAN		090	B		6
INDIAN	SHIBAGIJIK				35	0	RC	INDIAN	HUNTER	088	A		11
INDIAN	SHIGAGOTCHISH					ONTARIO	PA	INDIAN	HUNTER & TRAPPER	090	E		14
INDIAN	SHIGOSOPI					ONTARIO	PA	INDIAN	HUNTER & TRAPPER	090	E		10
INDIAN	SHONGGWAISH				95	0	RC	INDIAN	F	087	C		9
INDIAN	SHORROONNAHBUNO		1	1	12	0	PA	INDIAN		087	A		47
INDIAN	SHOSQUEGEESIC				40	0	PA	INDIAN	HUNTER	088	B		9
INDIAN	SHOWGODAKIE				20	0	NR	INDIAN	HUNTER	088	C		3
INDIAN	SHOWUS				48	0	PA	INDIAN		088	C		4
INDIAN	SHOWWANOGWEN				28	0	NR	INDIAN	HUNTER	088	C		2
INDIAN	SHOWWONDAI				60	US	PA	INDIAN	F & FISHERMAN	087	A		46
INDIAN	SHOWWOWEBENESS		1		16	0	PA	INDIAN		087	A		46
INDIAN	SKUEIBIC			1	80	0	RC	INDIAN		090	A		7
INDIAN	SOCAWGJUSI				35	0	PA	INDIAN	HUNTER	088	C		5
INDIAN	SUCKDUFF				50	0	PA	INDIAN	TRAPPER	086	A	3	2
INDIAN	SUGGUTEHEWAISHK		1		52	0	CE	INDIAN	HUNTER	087	B	1	20
INDIAN	SWASWAYKEJICK				55	0	PA	INDIAN	HUNTER & TRAPPER	090	C		13
INDIAN	SWBUNCE				50	0	PA	INDIAN	HUNTER	088	B		12
INDIAN	TAHBABUNDUNG				40	0	WM	INDIAN	HUNTER	090	A		2
INDIAN	TAICUM				60	0	PA	INDIAN	HUNTER & TRAPPER	090	C		12
INDIAN	TAQUASHEGA		2		37	ONT	RC	INDIAN	HUNTER & TRAPPER	090	B		D
INDIAN	TAQUJESICK				26	0	PA	INDIAN	HUNTER	090	F		2
INDIAN	TAWANIENUI		2		3	ONT	RC			090	B		D
INDIAN	TAWINAFA		2	1	3	ONT	RC			090	B		D
INDIAN	TENANCE				40	0	PA	INDIAN	HUNTER & TRAPPER	090	C		9
INDIAN	TENASA			1	55	RED RIVER	RC	INDIAN		090	F		11
INDIAN	TEPENEGEK				28	0	RC	INDIAN	HUNTER	084	G	2	3
INDIAN	TOMGAB				63	0	PA	INDIAN	HUNTER	090	F		2
INDIAN	TOMLAID					ONTARIO	PA	INDIAN	HUNTER & TRAPPER	090	E		2
INDIAN	TONADES				42	0	PA	INDIAN	HUNTER	088	B		22
INDIAN	TOOTCHISH				30	0	ME	INDIAN	HUNTER & TRAPPER	090	B		4
INDIAN	TOOTMNINAIL				58	0	ME	INDIAN	HUNTER	090	B		4
INDIAN	WABAKEGIK				55	0	RC	INDIAN	HUNTER	084	G	2	2
INDIAN	WABANWICK				40	0	PA	INDIAN	HUNTER	088	B		21
INDIAN	WABIGOUNNAQU			1	70	0	PA	INDIAN		086	A	3	2
INDIAN	WABINIKYIKWASHK					ONTARIO	PA	INDIAN	HUNTER & TRAPPER	090	E		9
INDIAN	WABIWAKI					ONTARIO	RC	INDIAN	HUNTER & TRAPPER	090	E		19
INDIAN	WABOOSE		2	1	22	0	PA	INDIAN		090	F		D
INDIAN	WABOSAQUA		1	1	40	US	PA	INDIAN		088	B		4
INDIAN	WADOHMIYONA				60	0	PA	INDIAN	HUNTER	086	A	3	3
INDIAN	WAHBEKENECE				35	0	RC	INDIAN	FISHERMAN	087	C		10
INDIAN	WAHBEMIN		2		40	0	IF		HUNTER & TRAPPER	090	C		D
INDIAN	WAHBOWNAI				27	0	RC	INDIAN	F	087	B	1	9
INDIAN	WAHGOOSH				44	0	RC	INDIAN	F & FISHERMAN	087	C		9
INDIAN	WAHKAHZEYHIZEQU			1	21	0	NR	INDIAN	HUNTRESS	088	C		3
INDIAN	WAHSAHG			1	52	US	PA	INDIAN	F	087	A		47
INDIAN	WAHSAHKESKIKENS				30	ONT	ME	INDIAN		090	B		6
INDIAN	WAHSQUONAIKEZHI				35	US	RC	INDIAN	F & COOPER	087	A		47
INDIAN	WAIMBWEIGWON				30	0	CE	INDIAN	HUNTER & F	087	B	1	20
INDIAN	WAIMEGWANCE				62	US	RC	INDIAN	F	087	A		43
INDIAN	WAINDAHBUNOQUAI		1	1	20	0	PA	INDIAN		087	A		47
INDIAN	WAINDUBENCE				50	0	CE	INDIAN	F	087	B	1	15
INDIAN	WAINGSHCOWWAHSI		1		14	0	PA	INDIAN		087	A		46
INDIAN	WAINTEGOOSHE		1		6	0	RC	INDIAN		087	C		10
INDIAN	WAINTEGOOSHE		2		6	0	RC	INDIAN		087	C		D
INDIAN	WAISAIUN				40	0	PA	INDIAN	F & FISHERMAN	087	C		11
INDIAN	WAISAIUN		2		40	0	PA	INDIAN	F & FISHERMAN	087	C		D
INDIAN	WAIUDEGOOQUAI		1	1	57	US	PA	INDIAN		087	A		46
INDIAN	WAJATEUCE				41	0	PA	INDIAN	HUNTER	090	F		3
INDIAN	WAKWE				60	0	PA	INDIAN		088	C		4
INDIAN	WANDABAN				51	0	RC	INDIAN	HUNTER	084	G	2	2
INDIAN	WANDUBBENCE		2	1	25	0	CE	INDIAN		087	B	1	D
INDIAN	WAOGUIBONA				30	0	RC	INDIAN	HUNTER	088	B		4
INDIAN	WAPOS					ONTARIO	RC	INDIAN	HUNTER & TRAPPER	090	E		5
INDIAN	WARJOSEJEESIC				20	0	PA	INDIAN		088	B		10
INDIAN	WASAHKEJICK		2		29	ONT	RC		HUNTER & TRAPPER	090	B		D
INDIAN	WASEGIJIG'S		2	1	30	0	RC	INDIAN		087	A		D
INDIAN	WASHEGEUSHIE				70	0	RC	INDIAN		090	A		7
INDIAN	WASHESKINNIE				30	MILL LAC	PA	INDIAN	HUNTER	090	F		4
INDIAN	WASSEKIJIG					ONTARIO	RC	INDIAN	HUNTER & TRAPPER	090	E		20
INDIAN	WASSIKWENSI		2			ONTARIO	RC		HUNTER & TRAPPER	090	E		D
INDIAN	WATCHKUZAH				24	0	RC	INDIAN	HUNTER	090	A		5
INDIAN	WATTAPPE				50	FORT FRANCES	PA	INDIAN	HUNTER	090	F		3
INDIAN	WAWBAZEMISKING				19	0	NR	INDIAN	HUNTER	088	C		4
INDIAN	WAWDAHBUNOQUAI		1	1	30	US	PA	INDIAN		087	A		47
INDIAN	WAYGUAKEGICKONC	PETER			60	0	CE	INDIAN	HUNTER	088	B		22
INDIAN	WEEKABAN				50	ONTARIO	PA	INDIAN	HUNTER & TRAPPER	090	B		2
INDIAN	WEMIGWENEQUA			1	60	0	NR	INDIAN	HUNTRESS	088	C		3
INDIAN	WENEBETUNG				32	0	PA	INDIAN	HUNTER	090	F		4
INDIAN	WENIEQWANEY	LOUIS			35	0	RC	INDIAN	HUNTER	088	B		22
INDIAN	WEZEBWINGWEDQUA			1	27	0	NR	INDIAN	HUNTRESS	088	C		3
INDIAN	WHEAHWHEAH				33	0	PA	INDIAN	HUNTER & TRAPPER	090	C		12
INDIAN	WHITE				32		RC	INDIAN		084	H		1
INDIAN	WINDIGO		2			ONTARIO	RC		HUNTER & TRAPPER	090	E		D
INDIAN	WINDININEREW		1			ONTARIO	PA	INDIAN	LABORER H B CO	090	E		7
INDIAN	WINDJAB					ONTARIO	PA	INDIAN	HUNTER & TRAPPER	090	E		8
INDIAN	WOUBESCONAW				29	0	PA	INDIAN	HUNTER	088	B		13
INDIAN	WSNBABYSS			1	62	ONT	RC	INDIAN		090	B		5
INDIAN	WYABGECON				75	0	RC	INDIAN	HUNTER	088	B		15
INDIAN	WYEKOJEWANA				60	0	RC	INDIAN	HUNTER	088	C		7
INDIAN	YPEIVEGONEB					ONTARIO	PA	INDIAN	HUNTER & TRAPPER	090	E		2
INDIAN	ZEKWAGBO				55	0	PA	INDIAN	HUNTER	088	B		8
INDIAN	ZHOUSCOBASE				50	0	PA	INDIAN	HUNTER	088	B		13
INDIAN	ZHOUSGOUN				60	0	PA	INDIAN	HUNTER	088	B		13
INDIAN	ZIBISCOOGLIC				35	0	PA	INDIAN	HUNTER	088	B		8
INEDA	ANTWIN		1		68	QUE	RC	FRENCH	LAB	081	I		42
INGLES	ADAM		1		21	0	CP	SCOTCH	CLERK	081	B		80

SURNAME	NAME1	NAME2	STRAY	SEX	AGE	BIRTHPL	RELIGION	ORIGIN	OCCUP	DIST	SUB_DIST	DIV	PAGE
INGLESS	GEORGY				22	ENGLAND	CE	ENGLISH	LAB	081	I		11
INGLIS	JOHN				42	SCOTLAND	CP	SCOTCH	WEAVER	081	A	1	25
INGLIS	WILLIAM				77	SCOTLAND	CP	SCOTCH	WEAVER	081	A	1	27
INGRAM	W	H			41	ENGLAND	PB	ENGLISH	CARPENTER	085	E		31
INIS	JAMES				22	ONTARIO	CS	SCOTCH	F	082	A		56
INNIS	HENRY		1		10	0	CP			085	H		9
INNIS	JOHN				60	SCOTLAND	UP	SCOTCH	F	085	D		11
INNIS	MALCOM		1		48	0	PS	SCOTCH	LUMBERMAN	086	B		2
INVERDUS	FRANCIS				36	QUE	RC	FRENCH	JOBBER LUMBERMAN	082	C	1	31
IRBIS	SIDNEY		1		36	ENGLAND	CE	ENGLISH	F	085	D		33
IRESS	ISAAC				49	ENGLAND	BA	ENGLISH	F	085	D		16
IRONSIDE	ANNE			1	60	0	PS	SCOTCH		089	B		14
IRONSIDE	J	S			36	0	PS	SCOTCH	CLERK H B CO	090	C		1
IRONSIDES	MCGREGOR				33	CANADA	CS	ENGLISH	CLERK	087	B	2	10
IRVINE	ELIZABETH		2	1	9	ONT	RC			082	I		D
IRVINE	WILLIAM				62	IRELAND	RC	IRISH	FARMER	082	I		32
IRVING	ANDREW				50	NB	CP	SCOTTISH	CO REGISTRAR	082	E		6
IRWIN	ARCHIBALD		1		46	IRELAND	PS	IRISH	LABOURER	089	B		19
IRWIN	JAMES				34	IRELAND	CE	IRISH	SURGEON	082	E		12
IRWIN	RICHARD				32	IRELAND	CE	IRISH	HOTEL KEEPER	085	E		17
IRWIN	THOMAS				49	IRELAND	WM	IRISH	F	086	A	2	4
IRWIN	WILLIAM				29	IRELAND	CE	IRISH	F	086	B		5
IRWINE	ARTHUR				60	IRELAND	BA	IRISH	F	085	B		1
ISAAC	ELIZA		2	1	25	0	WM			086	C	2	D
ISAAC	JOHN				30	0	WM	INDIAN	HUNTER	086	C	2	1
ISHDAN	JAMES				29	ENGLAND	CE	ENGLISH	CARPENTER	081	I		1
ISHKEMAH	JANE		1	1	13	0	CE	INDIAN		087	C		9
ISHKEMAH	MOSES		1		25	0	CE	INDIAN	F	087	B	1	20
IVERY	WILLIAM		1		35	ENGLISH	CE	ENGLISH	LUMBERMAN	083	A	1	12
IVEY	ROBERT				45	ENGLAND	WM	ENGLISH	MINER	089	A		24
JACK	JAMES				48	SCOTLAND	CS	SCOTCH	F	082	A		3
JACK	JOHN	W			60	SCOTLAND	BA	SCOTCH	F	085	C		8
JACK	WILLIAM				35	0	CP	SCOTCH	F	085	C		8
JACKLIN	ROBINSON				52	ENGLAND	CE	ENGLISH	F	086	A	1	12
JACKO	ALEXANDRE				37	0	RC	INDIAN	F & FISHERMAN	087	A		24
JACKSON	CHARLES				40	ENGLAND	CP	ENGLISH	FARMER	083	A	1	14
JACKSON	DAVID				35	ENGLAND	CE	ENGLISH	BUTCHER	089	A		43
JACKSON	EDWARD				26	0	PM	IRISH	MINER	089	A		1
JACKSON	ELIZA		1	1	22	0	CE	IRISH	DOMESTIC SERVANT	082	E		8
JACKSON	HARRISON				29	0	WM	IRISH	F	082	C	1	13
JACKSON	HENREY				26	ENGLAND	CE	ENGLISH	F	085	L		11
JACKSON	HENRY				28	ENGLAND	CE	ENGLISH	F	085	L		6
JACKSON	HUGH				30	ENGLAND	CE	ENGLISH	LABOURER	089	A		41
JACKSON	JAMES		1		26	SCOTLAND	CS	SCOTCH	SHANTY CLERK	081	A	1	59
JACKSON	JANE			1	34	IRELAND	CE	IRISH		082	G		31
JACKSON	JAS	H			55	ENGLAND	EP	ENGLISH	MERCHANT	085	A		12
JACKSON	JOHN				37	IRELAND	CE	IRISH	F	082	G		32
JACKSON	JOHN				44	IRELAND	EM	IRISH	F	082	G		36
JACKSON	JOHN				36	ENGLAND	PM	ENGLISH	BLACKSMITH	085	C		7
JACKSON	JOSEPH				36	QUE	WM	IRISH	F	082	C	1	12
JACKSON	JOSEPH		2		2	0	WM			082	C	1	D
JACKSON	MARGARET		1	1	48	SCOTLAND	PS	SCOTCH		085	C		3
JACKSON	NOAH	W			33	0	WM	IRISH	F	082	C	1	11
JACKSON	ROBERT				49	IRELAND	CE	IRISH	F	081	A	2	33
JACKSON	ROBERT				37	ENGLAND	CE	ENGLISH	HOTEL KEEPER	089	A		45
JACKSON	THOS				42	IRELAND	CE	IRISH	F	082	G		31
JACKSON	WILLIAM				40	ENGLAND	CE	ENGLISH	LABOURER	089	A		45
JACOB			2			0	RC			081	D		D
JACOB	FRANCIS				50	0	RC	INDIAN	HUNTER	081	D		21
JACQUES	MAGGY		1	1		ONTARIO	RC	INDIAN		084	A		4
JAKO	JOSEPH				51	0	RC	INDIAN	F	087	A		24
JAMES	CHAS				35	CANADA	ME	IRISH	F & CORONER	087	B	2	8
JAMES	CHRISTOPHER				35	QUEBEC	CE	IRISH	FARMER	084	C		3
JAMES	ELIZA			1	65	IRELAND	WM	IRISH		081	G	1	12
JAMES	GEORGE				44	0	WM	IRISH	F	082	G		42
JAMES	HENRY				40	ENGLAND	CE	ENGLISH	MINER	089	A		40
JAMES	HUGH				73	IRELAND	CE	IRISH	F	085	E		19
JAMES	JANE		1	1	26	0	CE	IRISH	SERVANT	081	K		74
JAMES	NATHANIEL				73	IRELAND	CE	IRISH	F	081	K		12
JAMES	RICHARD		2		66	IRELAND	WM		SCHOOL TEACHER	081	G	1	D
JAMES	SOLOMON				46	0	WM	INDIAN	TRADER	086	A	3	5
JAMES	THOMAS				45	IRELAND	CE	IRISH	F	081	K		4
JAMESOM	WILLIAM				27	SCOTLAND	CS	SCOTCH	MERCHANT	081	I		3
JAMESON	ALLAMD				48	SCOTLAND	CP	SCOTCH	TAILOR MERCHANT	081	I		11
JAMESON	JOHN				26	ONT	WM	SCOTCH	F	081	J	1	43
JAMIA	OLIVYA				32	ONTARIO	RC	FRENCH	FARMER	083	A	2	2
JAMIESON	AGNES		1	1	18	ONT	WM	SCOTCH		081	C		50
JAMIESON	ANN			1	45	QUE	CE	IRISH		081	K		56
JAMIESON	ARCHY				24	ONTARIO	NR	SCOTCH	BLACKSMITH	082	A		24
JAMIESON	HENRY				27	0	CS	SCOTCH	F	081	H	1	16
JAMIESON	JAMES				29	ONTARIO	CS	SCOTCH	F	082	A		19
JAMIESON	JOHN				57	SCOTLAND	CS	SCOTCH	F	081	H	2	17
JAMIESON	WILLIAM				54	SCOTLAND	CS	SCOTCH	F	081	H	1	17
JAMIESON	WILLIAM				24	ONTARIO	CS	SCOTCH	F	082	A		20
JAMVILLE	PETER				46	QUE	RC	FRENCH	FARMER	089	A		51
JANKE	FREDRICK						NG		SEE YONKAY	082	I		54
JANSEK	EZRIE				47	QUE	RC	FRENCH	F	085	E		27
JARVIS	FRANCIS		1		9	ONTARIO	RC	IRISH		082	B		9
JAWAN	JEAN	BTE			39	US	RC	INDIAN	F & FISHERMAN	087	A		28
JAWAN	JOSEPH				28	0	RC	INDIAN	F & FISHERMAN	087	A		28
JAWAN	PIERRE				40	US	RC	INDIAN	F & COOPER	087	A		27
JAWAN	THERESE			1	66	US	RC	INDIAN	F	087	A		27
JAWANANAKWAD	ISAAC				28	0	RC	INDIAN	SHOEMAKER & F	087	A		20
JAWANANAKWAT	JACQUES				62	US	RC	INDIAN	F & FISHERMAN	087	A		19
JAWANANAKWAT	PIERRE				35	US	RC	INDIAN	F & FISHERMAN	087	A		19
JAWANEBIN	LOUIS				57	US	RC	INDIAN	F & FISHERMAN	087	A		30
JAY	EDGAR				36	UNITED STATES	CP	ENGLISH	MACHINIST	090	D		1
JAYOTT	LYRANNIER		1	1	20	QUE	RC	FRENCH		082	I		43
JEAY	GEORGE		2			0	CE			086	B		D
JEAY	GEORGE		2			0	CE			086	B		D
JEAY	JOHN				45	ENGLAND	CE	ENGLISH	F	086	B		3
JEFFERSON	MOORE				46	ONT	RC	ENGLISH	LABOURER	081	J	1	56
JEFFERY	RICHARD				42	ENGLAND	CE	ENGLISH	MINER	089	A		42
JEFFREY	JOSEPH				23	IRELAND	FK	IRISH	F	082	A		73
JEFFREY	SAMUEL				26	IRELAND	EM	IRISH	F	082	A		72
JEFFREY	SAMUEL				48	IRELAND	CS	IRISH	F	082	A		73

SURNAME	NAME1	NAME2	STRAY	SEX	AGE	BIRTHPL	RELIGION	ORIGIN	OCCUP	DIST	SUB_DIST	DIV	PAGE
JEFFRIES	HENREY				23	ENGLAND	CE	ENGLISH	F	085	J		1
JEFFRY	JAMES		1		10	O	EP	ENGLISH	STUDENT	087	B	3	11
JEFFRY	JEFFREY				27	IRELAND	CS	IRISH	F	082	A		62
JEFFRY	JOHN		1		6	O	EP	ENGLISH	STUDENT	087	B	3	11
JEFFRY	WILLIAM		1		8	O	EP	ENGLISH	STUDENT	087	B	3	11
JENEST	JOSEPH		1		27	QUE	RC	FRENCH	LUMBERMAN	088	C		11
JENKIN	ANDREW				40	O	WM	IRISH	LAB	081	A	1	34
JENKINS	CHARLES				35	IRELAND	CP	IRISH	F	085	B		20
JENKINS	ELIZA			1	70	IRELAND	CE	IRISH		081	C		44
JENKINS	GEORGE				23	ONT	CE	IRISH	RAFTSMAN	081	C		45
JENKINS	JOHN				29	ONT	CE	IRISH	F	081	C		54
JENKYNS	E	H			31	ENGLAND	CE	ENGLISH	MINISTER	082	E		11
JENNER	JAMES				25	ENGLAND	CE	ENGLISH	F	085	J		24
JENNESSEAUX	JOSEPH		1		61	CHAMPAGNE	RC	FRENCH	SCHOOL TEACHER	087	A		1
JENNINGS	MARY			1	42	ENGLAND	WM	ENGLISH		089	A		10
JENOW	JOHN				33	GERMANY	CE	GERMAN	F	083	C		17
JERO	FRANK				27	O	RC	FRENCH	LABOURER	089	A		58
JEROME	LOUIS		1		31	QUE	RC	FRENCH	SERVANT	090	F		10
JERRAH	CHARLES				27	O	RC	FRENCH	F	081	K		18
JERUE	FRANCIS		1		76	QUE	RC	FRENCH	F	081	H	2	25
JERVA	FRANCIS				45	QUEBEC	RC	FRENCH	F	082	A		62
JERVAH	CHARLES				58	QUE	RC	FRENCH	FARMER	081	D		6
JERVATUSAW	CADILTE			1	30	US	RC	INDIAN		089	B		41
JESSIE	CHRISTIANA		1	1	7	O	CE	ENGLISH		089	B		21
JESSIE	GEORGE		1		8	O	CE	ENGLISH		089	B		4
JESSIE	JOHN	THOMAS	1		12	O	CP	ENGLISH		089	B		22
JESSIE	OWEN	P	1		11	O	CE	ENGLISH		089	B		21
JESSIE	SAYAH		2	1		O	ME			081	B		D
JESSOP	JAMES				40	O	WM	ENGLISH	F	082	G		62
JESSOP	JAMES	J			27	O	CE	ENGLISH	F	085	L		5
JESSOP	JAMES	S			50	ENGLAND	CE	ENGLISH	F	085	L		5
JESSOP	ROBERT		1		19	O	CE	ENGLISH	F	085	L		10
JESSUP	EDWARD				26	O	CE	SCOTCH	LUMBERMAN	083	C		1
JESSUP	JOHN				43	O	PS	ENGLISH	F	081	K		61
JESSUP	WILLIAM				37	O	CE	ENGLISH	F	081	K		29
JESSUP	WILSON		1		21	O	CE	ENGLISH	BLACKSMITH	081	K		71
JESTIN	GEORGE				55	IRELAND	CM	IRISH	F	085	F		3
JETSEAW	CHARLES		1		27	QUE	RC	FRENCH	ENGINEER	088	B		6
JETTY	BENJAMIN				48	QUE	RC	FRENCH CANADIAN	F	082	C	2	62
JIGARE	JOHN				42	QUE	RC	FRENCH	LABOURER	089	A		50
JILBERT	JEREMIAH				53	ENGLAND	EP	ENGLISH	MINER	090	D		4
JINKINS	EDWARD				30	IRELAND	CE	IRISH	F	086	B		5
JISHIBEKWATO	FRANCOIS				87	US	RC	INDIAN	F	087	A		28
JISHIBEKWATO	PIERRE				42	US	RC	INDIAN	F & FISHERMAN	087	A		29
JOBINVILLE	JOSEPH				71	QUE	RC	FRENCH	FARMER	089	B		23
JOCKO	NARCISSE		2		20	O	RC	INDIAN		087	A		D
JOCKO	PETER				47	O	RC	INDIAN	HUNTER	084	I	1	6
JOE	MARY		1	1	50	QUE	RC	INDIAN		084	E		2
JOHES	JOHN				34	GERMANY	LU	GERMAN	F	082	G		87
JOHN	JAMES				44	O	RC	INDIAN	HUNTER	084	I	1	1
JOHN	JOSEPH				30	O	RC	INDIAN	HUNTER	086	C	2	1
JOHNES	HUGH		1		24	IRELAND	CE	IRISH	LABOURER	081	B		30
JOHNS	ROBT	KIMBER			36	ENGLAND	CE	ENGLISH	SCHOOL TEACHER	085	C		19
JOHNSON	ABRAHAM				45	O	CE	ENGLISH	FARM LABOURER	089	A		15
JOHNSON	BENJAMIN	H			53	IRELAND	CE	IRISH	F	085	D		29
JOHNSON	CHARLES				40	IRELAND	CE	IRISH	LAB	082	C	2	60
JOHNSON	DANIEL				32	ONTARIO	ME	ENGLISH	STOREKEEPER	081	G	2	7
JOHNSON	HENERY				48	IRELAND	CE	IRISH	F	082	F		17
JOHNSON	HENRY				32	SWEDEN	CE	SWEDISH	F	085	J		4
JOHNSON	JAMES				40	ENGLAND	CE	ENGLISH	BRICKMAKER	082	F		13
JOHNSON	JANNET		1	1	60	SCOTLAND	CP	SCOTTISH	SERVANT	082	E		5
JOHNSON	JOHN				60	SCOTLAND	CP	SCOTCH	F	082	C	2	13
JOHNSON	MARY		1	1	16	O	WM	IRISH	SERVANT	085	B		13
JOHNSON	MARY		1	1	5	O	RC	INDIAN		085	G		1
JOHNSON	MARY	J	1	1	16	O	CE	ENGLISH	SERVANT	082	E		29
JOHNSON	PATRICK		1		22	O	RC	IRISH		086	B		1
JOHNSON	ROBERT				27	O	EP	IRISH	F	087	B	3	11
JOHNSON	SOPHIA		1	1	24	O	RC	FRENCH	SERVANT	089	A		58
JOHNSON	THOMAS				30	IRELAND	CE	ENGLISH	F	085	E		10
JOHNSON	WILLIAM		1		36	ENGLAND	CE	ENGLISH	CLERK	085	B		8
JOHNSON	WILLIAM				50	IRELAND	CS	IRISH	F	085	C		18
JOHNSTON	ADAM				45	IRELAND	WM	IRISH	F	085	A		30
JOHNSTON	AGNESS			1	60	SCOTLAND	PS	SCOTTISH		082	D		9
JOHNSTON	ALBERT		2			O	CE			081	B		D
JOHNSTON	ALEXANDER				31	QUE	WM	IRISH	F	081	H	2	22
JOHNSTON	ANDREW				55	IRELAND	CE	IRISH	INNKEEPER	082	C	2	1
JOHNSTON	ARTHUR				30	IRELAND	CE	IRISH	F	083	F	2	1
JOHNSTON	ELISABETH		1	1	38	IRELAND	CP	IRISH		081	B		56
JOHNSTON	ELLIOTT				60	IRELAND	CE	IRISH	F	081	H	2	20
JOHNSTON	GEORGE				29	QUE	WM	IRISH	F	081	H	2	22
JOHNSTON	HENERY				28	QUE	CE	IRISH	FARMER	082	D		26
JOHNSTON	HENRY		1		39	O	EP	DUTCH	F	087	B	3	3
JOHNSTON	HENRY		1		40	ENGLAND	CE	IRISH	LABOURER	089	A		47
JOHNSTON	HUGH				56	IRELAND	PS	SCOTCH	L	082	G		70
JOHNSTON	JAMES		1		36	SCOTLAND	CP	SCOTCH	BAKER	081	B		55
JOHNSTON	JAMES				64	IRELAND	EM	IRISH	F	081	H	2	28
JOHNSTON	JAMES				43	IRELAND	CS	IRISH	F	082	A		25
JOHNSTON	JAMES				47	SCOTLAND	WM	SCOTTISH	FARMER	082	I		71
JOHNSTON	JAMES				60	SCOTLAND	CP	SCOTCH	CARPENTER	085	E		28
JOHNSTON	JAMES				45	IRELAND	CE	IRISH	CARPENTER	085	H		3
JOHNSTON	JAMES				30	IRELAND	CE	IRISH	F	085	H		20
JOHNSTON	JAMES	WM			49	ENGLAND	CE	ENGLISH	BLACKSMITH	082	C	2	3
JOHNSTON	JOHN				29	IRELAND	EM	IRISH	F	081	H	2	28
JOHNSTON	JOHN				52	IRELAND	CS	IRISH	F	082	A		27
JOHNSTON	JOHN				30	SCOTLAND	CS	SCOTCH	F	082	A		57
JOHNSTON	JOHN				68	IRELAND	EM	IRISH	F	082	A		73
JOHNSTON	KATE		1	1	24	QUE	RC	IRISH		081	A	2	15
JOHNSTON	LANE				47	IRELAND	RP	IRISH	F	085	K	2	4
JOHNSTON	NANCY		2	1	2	ONTARIO	CS			082	A		D
JOHNSTON	R	H			19	O	CE	IRISH	FARMER	085	E		31
JOHNSTON	ROBERT				34	ONTARIO	CS	IRISH	F	082	A		26
JOHNSTON	SAML				42	IRELAND	CP	IRISH	F	082	C	2	68
JOHNSTON	SAMUEL				42	O	CE	IRISH	BUTCHER	081	B		22
JOHNSTON	SAMUEL				29	IRELAND	CS	IRISH	F	082	A		20
JOHNSTON	SUSAN			1	50	IRELAND	CE	IRISH		081	K		24
JOHNSTON	THOMAS				30	IRELAND	CE	IRISH	FARMER	081	F		13

SURNAME	NAME1	NAME2	STRAY	SEX	AGE	BIRTHPL	RELIGION	ORIGIN	OCCUP	DIST	SUB_DIST	DIV	PAGE
JOHNSTON	THOMAS				20	IRELAND	WM	IRISH	F	085	A		30
JOHNSTON	THOS		1		21	0	WM	SCOTCH	SURVEYOR	081	B		30
JOHNSTON	WILLIAM				38	0	CE	IRISH		081	K		25
JOHNSTON	WILLIAM		1		75		CP	ENGLISH		082	D		1
JOHNSTONE	W	R			23	CANADA	PS	DUTCH	LAB	087	B	2	2
JOICE	JOSEPH				29	QUE	RC	FRENCH	LAB	081	B		36
JOICE	ROBERT		2			0	CE			081	E		D
JOICE	THOMAS				33	0	CE	ENGLISH	F	081	E		2
JOICE	THOMAS		1		21	0	CE	IRISH	PAINTER	082	E		33
JOICHIM	OCTAVIE		1	1	20	QUE	RC	FRENCH	GOVERNESS	082	E		29
JOINT	THOMAS				65	IRELAND	CE	IRISH	F	083	C		5
JOLECHAR	NANCY		1	1	16	0	RC	FRENCH		084	I	2	1
JOLICOEUR	NANCIE			1		0	RC	FRENCH		084	I	2	1
JOLLI	ETHIENNE		1		85	QUE	RC	FRENCH	SERVANT	082	E		48
JOME	ALLEN				45	AMERICA	RC	IRISH	FOREMAN	083	A	1	14
JONES	ALBERT		1		3	0	RC	ENGLISH		082	K	1	15
JONES	CHARLES				54	IRELAND	CE	IRISH	F	085	B		11
JONES	CHARLES				55	IRELAND	CE	IRISH	F	085	F		2
JONES	CHARLES				50	IRELAND	CS	IRISH	F	085	I		42
JONES	EDWARD				47	IRELAND	CE	IRISH	CARPENTER & JOINER	090	A		3
JONES	ELIZA			1	54	ENGLAND	WM	ENGLISH	F	086	A	1	3
JONES	ELIZABETH		1	1	12	0	PB	IRISH		085	D		30
JONES	EMILLY			1	37	QUE	RC	FRENCH	WASHINGWOMAN	082	E		75
JONES	HARRY				75	US	WM	GERMAN	BLACKSMITH	082	C	1	17
JONES	HENRY				30	0	CE	ENGLISH	F	081	A	1	9
JONES	HUGH				42	QUE	PS	SCOTCH	CARPENTER	089	A		39
JONES	JAMES		1		7	0	PS	SCOTTISH		082	D		30
JONES	JAMES				35	QUEBEC	RC	IRISH	LUMBERER	083	B	2	1
JONES	JOHN		1		3	0	PS	SCOTTISH		082	D		30
JONES	JOHN		1		5	0	RC	ENGLISH		082	K	1	15
JONES	JOHN				80	IRELAND	WM	IRISH	CORDWAINER	089	A		26
JONES	JOSEPH				21	ENGLAND	CE	ENGLISH	F	086	A	1	3
JONES	JULIA		1	1	11	ONTARIO	RC	IRISH		082	A		15
JONES	MARY		1	1	5	0	PS	SCOTTISH		082	D		30
JONES	OLIVER				41	0	CC	ENGLISH	FARMER	085	I		6
JONES	PETER		1		32	0	CO	INDIAN	COOPER	085	G		1
JONES	PETER				35	0	CE	INDIAN	LABOURER	089	B		37
JONES	SAMUEL				40	0	EP	IRISH		087	B	3	2
JONES	THOMAS				35	ENGLAND	CE	ENGLISH	F	085	B		17
JONES	THOMAS				83	IRELAND	CE	IRISH	FARMER	089	A		55
JONES	WM	HENRY			30	WALES	CE	WELSH	F	085	F		1
JONMENY	MADOR				29	QUE	RC	FRENCH	FARMER	088	C		9
JONNS	SOLOMON				46	QUE	PS	SCOTTISH	FARMER	082	D		28
JORDAIN	JEAN BAPTISTE				29	0	RC	FRENCH		090	A		7
JORDAIN	MARCIPO				27	0	RC	FRENCH		090	A		7
JORDAIN	NOT GIVEN		2			0	RC			090	A		D
JORDAN	EDWARD		1		17	QUE	RC	IRISH		082	D		13
JORDAN	ELIZABETH		1	1	12	QUE	RC	IRISH		082	D		13
JORDAN	GODFRED				43	GERMANY	LU	GERMAN	FARMER	082	I		5
JORDAN	JAMES				65	SCOTLAND	PS	SCOTTISH	FARMER	082	D		24
JORDAN	MICHAEL		1		12	QUE	RC	IRISH		082	D		13
JORDAN	PATRICK				40	IRELAND	RC	IRISH	SHANTYMAN	082	G		5
JORDAN	SAMUEL		1		62	GERMANY	LU	GERMAN	SHOEMAKER	081	F		21
JORDAN	WILLIAM		1		10	QUE	RC	IRISH		082	D		13
JORDON	HUGH	G							SEE GORDON	082	B		55
JORDON	JANE		1	1	23	ONTARIO	CS	ENGLISH		082	A		4
JORDON	JOHN		1		21	ONTARIO	CS	ENGLISH	F	082	A		4
JOSEPH	PETER				28	0	RC	INDIAN	HUNTER	086	C	2	4
JOSEPH	PHILIP				44	QUEBEC	RC	FRENCH	BLACKSMITH	081	J	1	81
JOURDIN	MELLIEN				46	QUE	RC	FRENCH	LAB	081	H	1	5
JOURDON	EDWARD				40	IRELAND	RC	IRISH	MASON	082	D		12
JOYOTT	STEAPHEN				36	QUE	RC	FRENCH	FARMER	082	I		44
JUBE	PEIRRE				75	QUE	RC	FRENCH	FUR TRADER	088	C		5
JUBY	WILLIAM				22	ENGLAND	CE	ENGLISH	LABORER	083	G		1
JUDD	FREDRICK				27	ENGLAND	CE	ENGLISH	BAKER	085	C		5
JUNELLE	ANTOINE				52	QUE	RC	FRENCH	LUMBERMAN	089	A		52
JUNKENS	JOHN				41	0	WM	IRISH	CARPENTER	081	B		26
JUNOP	MARTIN		1			0	EV			082	H		D
JUNOP	MARTIN				25	GERMANY	EV	GERMAN	F	082	H		26
KABBAWSA	GEORGE				19	US	CE	INDIAN	LABOURER	089	B		35
KADDATZ	AUGUSTUS				54	GERMANY	LU	GERMAN	FARMER	081	F		30
KALIES	ALBERT				38	POLAND	RC	POLISH	LAB	081	I		36
KAMABINAKEG	SIMON				35	QUEBEC	RC	INDIAN	HUNTER	083	C		6
KANABINAJEG	CATHERINE		2	1	1	ONTARIO	RC			083	C		D
KANABINAJEG	JACQUES		2	1	2	ONTARIO	RC			083	C		D
KANE	JOHN				40	IRELAND	RC	IRISH	F	081	J	2	4
KANE	JOHN		1		16	0	CE	ENGLISH		088	C		10
KANE	PATRICK				50	IRELAND	RC	IRISH	F	081	J	2	4
KANNAH	ELIZABETH		1	1	65	0	RC	IRISH		081	B		18
KANOSH	JOLLINEAU				60	US	RC	FRENCH	CLERK	089	B		11
KANT	CHARLES				28	GERMANY	LU	GERMAN	F	082	G		3
KANT	FERDINAND				31	GERMANY	LU	GERMAN	F	082	H		9
KANT	JOHN				32	GERMANY	LU	GERMAN	F	082	G		3
KAOGOME	JOSEPH				52	US	RC	INDIAN	F & FISHERMAN	087	A		26
KATTILE	JOHN				46	SCOTLAND	PS	SCOTCH	FARMER	089	A		49
KATTYLE	THOMAS				38	SCOTLAND	PS	SCOTCH	MINE LABOURER	089	A		19
KAVANAGH	MARGT		1	1	20	IRELAND	RC	IRISH	SERVANT	082	E		26
KAVIJIGOKIVE	MARY		1	1	70	QUEBEC	RC	INDIAN		083	C		6
KAY	JAMES				56	SCOTLAND	PS	SCOTCH	F	085	J		24
KAYASHKI	(1ST WIDOW)			1		ONTARIO	PA	INDIAN	HUNTER & TRAPPER	090	E		6
KAYASHKI	(2ND WIDOW)			1		ONTARIO	RC	INDIAN	HUNTER & TRAPPER	090	E		7
KAYE	CHARLES				45	ENGLAND	PM	ENGLISH	F	085	C		2
KAYE	JAMES				28	IRELAND	CE	ENGLISH	F	085	C		26
KAYS	RICHARD				42	IRELAND	CE	IRISH	F	082	F		31
KEALL	THOMAS				60	IRELAND	PM	ENGLISH	F	085	I		35
KEALY	THOMAS		2		23	ONT	RC	IRISH	F	081	C		D
KEANEN	JOHN				36	0	CP	IRISH	SHANTY FOREMAN	082	G		54
KEARNEY	BRIDGET		1	1	26	IRELAND	RC	IRISH	SERVANT	082	E		14
KEARNS	ANN			1	47	IRELAND	RC	IRISH		081	K		15
KEARNS	WILLIAM				20	0	CP	SCOTCH	F	085	E		29
KEARNY	MICHAEL	JAMES			41	IRELAND	RC	IRISH	SHOEMAKER	081	K		68
KEATING	JAMES		1		39	QUE	CE	IRISH	LAB	084	D		5
KEATING	PETER		1		20	0	WM	SCOTCH	LABOURER	088	A		7
KEBASSIN	DAVID				35	RED RIVER	RC	INDIAN	LAB	090	F		6
KEBESHKANY	LOUIS				54	US	RC	INDIAN	F	087	A		32
KECHEBENA	CHARLES				36	0	WM	INDIAN	TRAPPER	086	A	3	4

SURNAME	NAME1	NAME2	STRAY	SEX	AGE	BIRTHPL	RELIGION	ORIGIN	OCCUP	DIST	SUB_DIST	DIV	PAGE
KECHEBENA	JOSEPH				80	0	WM	INDIAN		086	A	3	4
KECHINE	J	W			30	SCOTLAND	CS	SCOTCH	LABOURER	088	A		8
KEDDIE	ALEXANDER				60	SCOTLAND	CP	SCOTCH	MACHINIST	081	B		48
KEEFER	JACOB				40	0	CP	ENGLISH	F	090	F		19
KEEFFE	JOHN				35	IRELAND	RC	IRISH	F	082	H		18
KEELY	MARY	ANN	1	1	45	IRELAND	EM	IRISH	SERVANT	082	G		98
KEGIKWAGIWE	JOSEPH				72	US	RC	INDIAN	F & FISHERMAN	087	A		39
KEGIKWAGIWE	JOSEPH	JR			42	US	RC	INDIAN	F & FISHERMAN	087	A		39
KEHL	GOTLIP				42	GERMANY	FW	GERMAN	F	082	H		23
KEHO	JOHN		1		36	IRELAND	RC	IRISH	SHOEMAKER	082	E		33
KEHOE	ELIZABETH		1	1	27	0	CS	IRISH	SERVANT	081	A	1	32
KEILY	PATRICK				28	ONTARIO	RC	IRISH	FARMER	081	G	2	1
KEIRNEY	JOHN				42	0	RC	IRISH	BLACKSMITH	081	B		52
KEKLES	ALFORD		1		21	0	ME	ENGLISH	BOATSMAN	082	D		7
KEKLES	MARGARET		1	1	18	0	ME	ENGLISH		082	D		7
KEKLES	WILLIAM		1		23	0	ME	ENGLISH	BLACKSMITH	082	D		7
KELBY	WILLIAM				35	IRELAND	CE	IRISH	RAFTSMAN	082	E		24
KELLETT	MARY	JANE		1	26	QUE	RC	FRENCH	SEAMSTRESS	082	E		69
KELLEY	EDWARD				50	IRELAND	RC	IRISH	F	081	E		6
KELLO	GEORGE				67	GERMANY	EV	GERMAN		082	G		97
KELLO	JOHN				40	GERMANY	EV	GERMAN	F	082	G		96
KELLY	AGNES		1	1	1	0	RC	IRISH		081	I		34
KELLY	ALICE			1	50	IRELAND	RC	IRISH	WIDOW	082	B		23
KELLY	BARNEY				60	IRELAND	RC	IRISH	F	083	C		12
KELLY	BENJIMAN				55	QUEBEC	PR	IRISH	FARMER	081	G	2	4
KELLY	BRIDGET		1	1	22	IRELAND	RC	IRISH	SERVANT	082	E		18
KELLY	CATHERINE		1	1	22	QUE	RC	IRISH	DOMESTIC	082	E		10
KELLY	CHRISTOPHER				50	IRELAND	RC	IRISH	FARMER	082	D		2
KELLY	CORNELIUS				27	ONTARIO	PR	IRISH	BLACKSMITH	081	G	2	9
KELLY	DANIEL				37	IRELAND	RC	IRISH	LABOURER	082	E		34
KELLY	FRANCIS		1		20	QUEBEC	RC	IRISH	F	082	A		24
KELLY	HUGH		1		43	0	RC	IRISH	F	082	L		5
KELLY	JAMES				69	QUEBEC	RC	IRISH	SHOEMAKER	081	J	1	20
KELLY	JAMES				40	QUEBEC	RC	IRISH	FARMER	081	J	1	21
KELLY	JAMES				26	IRELAND	RC	IRISH	F	081	K		45
KELLY	JAMES		1		64	IRELAND	PS	IRISH	F	085	E		8
KELLY	JOHN				63	IRELAND	RC	IRISH	F	081	J	1	20
KELLY	JOHN				56	IRELAND	RC	IRISH	F	081	K		45
KELLY	JOHN				62	IRELAND	RC	IRISH	FARMER	084	B		2
KELLY	JOHN				40	IRELAND	PS	IRISH	F	085	C		11
KELLY	JOHN				38	IRELAND	RC	IRISH	F	085	E		22
KELLY	JOHN		1		35	IRELAND	RC	IRISH	DOCTOR	089	B		15
KELLY	JOHN	JR			36	IRELAND	RC	IRISH	FARMER	081	F		6
KELLY	MARGARET		1	1	21	QUE	RC	IRISH		081	C		4
KELLY	MARY		1	1	56	0	RC	IRISH		082	L		5
KELLY	MARY	ANN	1	1	24	ONTARIO	RC	IRISH		082	A		24
KELLY	MICHAEL				35	IRELAND	RC	IRISH	F	081	J	1	4
KELLY	MICHAEL				30	IRELAND	RC	IRISH	LABOURER	082	E		51
KELLY	MOSES				60	IRELAND	RC	IRISH	FARMER	081	F		20
KELLY	PATRICK				45	IRELAND	RC	IRISH	FARMER	081	F		6
KELLY	PATRICK		1			IRELAND	RC	IRISH		081	I		26
KELLY	PATRICK				58	IRELAND	RC	IRISH	F	081	J	1	8
KELLY	SIMON				36	IRELAND	RC	IRISH	FARMER	081	F		4
KELLY	THOMAS		1		23	0	RC	IRISH	TINSMITH	081	I		6
KELLY	WILLIAM		1		70	IRELAND	RC	IRISH		081	H	2	23
KELORAN	MARIAH		1	1	20	0	RC	IRISH	SERVANT	081	B		71
KELOW	WILLIAM		1		9	GERMANY	EM	GERMAN		082	G		89
KELSON	CHARLES		1		60	ENGLAND	CE	ENGLISH	JOINER	084	A		1
KEMP	ELIAS				44	0	WM	SCOTCH	F	086	A	1	24
KEMP	HENRY		1		18		CE	ENGLISH	LAB	081	B		25
KENDELL	GEORGE				26	UNITED STATES	LU	GERMAN	CARPENTER	090	D		4
KENEDA	ADAM				44	SCOTLAND	CP	SCOTCH	GAOLER	082	F		21
KENEDA	WILLIAM				82	SCOTLAND	CP	SCOTCH	F	082	F		17
KENEDAY	KATE		1	1	16	0	RC	IRISH		082	D		8
KENEDY	ELIZABETH		1	1	23	0	PS	SCOTTISH		082	D		5
KENEDY	JOHN		1		32	SCOTLAND	PS	SCOTTISH	SHANTY FOREMAN	082	D		5
KENEDY	KATHICE		1	1	6	ONT	WM	SCOTCH		081	C		50
KENNADA	CHRISTOPHER		2		5	0	RC			081	B		D
KENNADA	THOMAS				55	IRELAND	RC	IRISH	LAB	081	B		28
KENNADY	ANDREW		1		14	ONT	CE	IRISH		082	I		68
KENNADY	JAMES				25	ONT	CP	IRISH	FARMER	082	I		30
KENNADY	JOHN				33	ONT	RP	IRISH	FARMER	082	I		1
KENNADY	JOHN				25	ONT	RC	IRISH	FARMER	082	I		28
KENNADY	JOSEPH				51	IRELAND	RC	IRISH	FARMER	082	I		25
KENNADY	MARY		1	1	16	ONT	CE	IRISH		082	I		68
KENNADY	WILLIAM		1		14	0	CP	IRISH		081	B		71
KENNEDAY	R		1		21	SCOTLAND	CP	SCOTCH	MILLWRIGHT	081	A	2	16
KENNEDAY	ROBERT				45	0	CP	SCOTCH	LAB	081	B		44
KENNEDY	ALEXANDER		1			0	CS	SCOTCH	LUMBERMAN	088	C		10
KENNEDY	CATHERINE			1	46	IRELAND	RC	IRISH		081	K		52
KENNEDY	DANALD				30	ONT	CE	IRISH	F	081	J	1	45
KENNEDY	ELLEN		1	1	18	0	RC	IRISH	SERVANT	082	E		44
KENNEDY	HANORA		1	1	11	0	RC	IRISH		082	E		44
KENNEDY	JOHN		1		54	IRELAND	RC	IRISH	LABOURER	082	E		42
KENNEDY	MICHAEL				35	IRELAND	RC	IRISH	F	081	K		46
KENNEDY	PATRICK				40	IRELAND	RC	IRISH	MERCHANT	081	C		41
KENNEDY	WILLIAM				37	SCOTLAND	CP	SCOTTISH	LUMBER AGENT	082	E		71
KENNEDY	WILLIAM				29	IRELAND	WM	IRISH	SHOEMAKER	085	I		5
KENNELLY	EDWARD				40	IRELAND	RC	IRISH	F	081	K		59
KENNELLY	MARTIN				50	IRELAND	RC	IRISH	F	081	J	1	65
KENNELLY	MARTIN				40	IRELAND	RC	IRISH	F	081	J	1	89
KENNEY	ANNE		1	1	50	IRELAND	RC	IRISH	SERVANT	082	E		25
KENNPEK	CHARLES				30	POLAND	RC	POLISH	LAB	081	I		37
KENNY	ELIZABETH		1	1	27	0	CP	GERMAN		082	C	1	63
KENNY	JOHN				31	0	WM	IRISH	F	082	C	2	30
KENNY	JOHN				40	0	CE	IRISH	F	082	C	2	51
KENNY	JOSEPH				22	ONTARIO	RC	IRISH		083	A	1	14
KENNY	MARGRET			1	59	IRELAND	WM	IRISH		082	C	2	30
KENNY	MARGT		1	1	23	0	WM	IRISH	DRESSMAKER	082	E		11
KENSLEY	PAUL				49	ENGLAND	CE	ENGLISH	CARENTER	088	A		9
KENT	DARWIN				45	0	CS	ENGLISH	HOTEL KEEPER	085	I		15
KENWARD	WILLIAM				25	ENGLAND	CE	ENGLISH	LAB	081	B		61
KEOPSEL	WILLIAM		1		24	GERMANY	LU	GERMAN	SERVANT	082	E		47
KEOTASSIN	JOHN	B			45	0	RC	INDIAN	LAB	090	F		21
KEOWN	MATHEW		1		19	QUE	RC	IRISH	SADDLER	082	E		58
KERAVIN	BARTHOLOMEW				40	IRELAND	RC	IRISH	FARMER	081	G	1	31

SURNAME	NAME1	NAME2	STRAY	SEX	AGE	BIRTHPL	RELIGION	ORIGIN	OCCUP	DIST	SUB_DIST	DIV	PAGE
KERAVIN	JAMES		2		65	IRELAND	RC		FARMER	081	G	1	D
KERAVIN	MICHAEL				26	ONTARIO	RC	IRISH	FARMER	081	G	1	6
KERAVIN	THOMAS				30	IRELAND	RC	IRISH	FARMER	081	G	1	21
KERBRON	JOSEPH		1		18	QUE	RC	FRENCH	LAB	090	F		14
KERMER	ELISBEATH		1	1	22	PRUSSIA	CE	PRUSSIAN	SERVANT	082	J		3
KERNIGH	GEORGE				30	0	CE	IRISH	CARPENTER	082	G		54
KERR	ANDREW		1		37	IRELAND	CE	IRISH	FARMER	086	B		9
KERR	ANDREW	A			62	SCOTLAND	CS	SCOTCH	F	081	H	2	6
KERR	DUNCAN		1		24	0	CP	SCOTCH	FIREMAN	090	D		2
KERR	ELIZABETH		2	1	58	SCOTLAND	CS			082	A		D
KERR	FRANCIS				38	SCOTLAND	CP	SCOTCH	LAB	081	B		2
KERR	HUGH				41	IRELAND	RC	IRISH	BLACKSMITH	090	F		25
KERR	JAMES				32	ONTARIO	CS	SCOTCH	F	082	A		39
KERR	JOHN				57	SCOTLAND	CS	SCOTCH	F	082	A		22
KERR	JOHN	F			63	SCOTLAND	CP	SCOTCH	F	081	C		50
KERR	ROBERT				21	QUE	PS	IRISH	FARMER	086	B		7
KERRIGAN	ANN			1	35	IRELAND	RC	IRISH		081	C		8
KESEL	LOUIS		1		24	QUEBEC	RC	FRENCH	LUMBERMAN	083	E		2
KESICK	MASHAN				40	0	RC	INDIAN	HUNTER	084	I	1	3
KESO	FRAMSWAY				50	0	RC	INDIAN	HUNTER	084	I	1	7
KEWABINAISIE	MICHEL				55	ONT	RC	INDIAN	HUNTER & TRAPPER	090	B		5
KEWATEGIJY	PAUL				29	0	RC	INDIAN	F & FISHERMAN	087	A		39
KEWODIN	PETER				30	0	WM	INDIAN	HUNTER	086	A	3	5
KEYS	JOSEPH				51	IRELAND	CP	IRISH	F	082	C	1	44
KEYS	SUSAN		1	1	12	US	CE	ENGLISH		089	B		1
KEYS	THOS				50	IRELAND	RC	IRISH	F	081	J	1	28
KEYS?	WILLIAM		1		18	0	CS	IRISH	APRENTICE	082	C	2	64
KEZHICK	PETER				33	US	WM	INDIAN	SCHOOL TEACHER	087	C		6
KEZHIK	EDOWE				58	0	CE	INDIAN	F & HUNTER	087	B	1	16
KICKBUSH	WILLIAM				35	GERMANY	LU	GERMAN	F	082	G		81
KICKOSA	CONSTA	JOHN			81	ONT	RC	ALGONQUIN INDIAN	INDIAN HUNTER	081	C		51
KID	GEORGE				45	US	NR	ENGLISH	F	081	A	2	48
KIDD	RICHARD				35	ONT	WM	IRISH	HUNTER & FARMER	082	I		78
KIDD	THOMAS				44	ONT	CE	IRISH	FARMER & HUNTER	082	I		78
KIDDER	JOSEPH				37	QUEBEC	CE	ENGLISH	FARMER	084	A		3
KIEL	SOPHIA		2	1	70	GERMANY	CE			081	F		D
KIELY	FRANCIS				65	IRELAND	RC	IRISH	LAB	081	J	2	3
KIELY	JOHN				80	IRELAND	RC	IRISH	F	081	J	2	4
KIELY	JOHN				40	IRELAND	RC	IRISH	F	081	J	2	4
KIELY	PATRICK				28	IRELAND	RC	IRISH	F	081	J	2	8
KIEMASHOO	JANE		2	1		ONT	RC			090	B		D
KILBY	JAMES				28	0	CE	ENGLISH	F	082	H		25
KILBY	SAMUEL				22	0	RP	ENGLISH	F	082	H		20
KILBY	THOMAS				62	HOLLAND	RC	ENGLISH	FARMER	081	F		27
KILFOIL	FRANCIS				21	ONT	RP	IRISH	FARMER	082	I		15
KILFOY	ELLEN			1	30	IRELAND	RC			082	H		D
KILFOY	JAMES				40	IRELAND	RC	IRISH	F	082	H		8
KILGORE	WILLIAM				42	IRELAND	RC	IRISH	F	081	J	1	79
KILGOUR	JAMES				32	0	CE	IRISH	F	082	C	1	21
KILLANN	DANIEL				24	IRELAND	CE	IRISH		082	G		55
KILLEEN	DENNIS				38	0	RC	IRISH	LAB	081	A	2	24
KILLEORAN	MICHAEL				38	IRELAND	RC	IRISH	F	081	C		38
KILLORAN	DOMINICK				76	IRELAND	RC	IRISH	F	081	C		38
KILLORAN	MARY			1	56	IRELAND	RC	IRISH	F	081	C		47
KILLORNE	CATHERINE		1	1	1	0	RC	IRISH		081	K		18
KILLORNE	JAMES		1		27	IRELAND	RC	IRISH	LAB	081	K		18
KILLORNE	MARGARET		1	1	26	IRELAND	RC	IRISH		081	K		18
KILORAN	JAMES		1		20	ONT	RC	IRISH		082	A		28
KILORAN	JOHN				32	ONT	RC	IRISH	F	082	A		27
KILORAN	MICHAEL				29	ONTARIO	RC	IRISH	F	082	A		5
KILORAN	OWEN				27	ONTARIO	RC	IRISH	F	082	A		28
KILSON	JOHN		1		20	0	RC	IRISH	LAB	081	K		74
KIM	MARY		1	1	30	GERMANY	RC	GERMAN	NUN	090	F		11
KIMBERLY	ELISHA				33	0	CP	ENGLISH	CARPENTER	081	A	1	56
KIMBERLY	SAMUEL				36	0	BA	ENGLISH	F	081	A	2	38
KIMBERLY	WILLIAM				38	0	BA	ENGLISH	F	081	A	2	38
KIMBLE	WILLIAM				24	QUEBEC	CE		LUMBERMAN	086	C	1	6
KIMMER	JAMES				23	ENGLAND	CE	ENGLISH	F	085	E		17
KIMPTON	JOHN		1		37	ENGLAND	CP	ENGLISH	TEAMSTER	090	F		19
KINCH	EDWARD				32	ONTARIO	CE	IRISH	F	082	A		38
KINCH	WM				21	IRELAND	WM	IRISH	F	085	J		26
KINCHLEY	MARY		1	1	28	QUE	RC	IRISH	SERVANT	082	C	1	26
KINDER	JOSEPH				39	ENGLAND	CE	ENGLISH	FARMER CLERK AT B CN	081	G	1	29
KING	ABRAHAM				26	0	RC	FRENCH	FISHERMAN	089	A		59
KING	ANN	WEST		1	27	0	NG	INDIAN		085	E		21
KING	CATHERINE		1	1	28	0	PS	SCOTTISH	TAILORESS	082	E		39
KING	CHARLES	G	1		25	ENGLAND	CE	ENGLISH	F	085	J		21
KING	DAVID				45	UNITED STATES	NG	INDIAN	F	085	G		1
KING	EDWARD				35	USA	NC	AFRICAN	F	085	K	2	2
KING	ELIZABETH		1	1	62	SCOTLAND	CP	SCOTCH		082	F		6
KING	HUGH				31	SCOTLAND	CP	SCOTCH	F	086	A	2	5
KING	JAMES		1		92	SCOTLAND	CS	SCOTCH		081	A	1	35
KING	JAMES				24	0	EM	SCOTCH	F	082	G		36
KING	JOHN				25	0	CP	SCOTCH	AXEMAKER	082	G		62
KING	JOHN				33	0	NG	INDIAN	HEAD CHIEF	085	G		1
KING	JOHN				43	ENGLAND	CE	ENGLISH	F	085	K	2	6
KING	JOHN				25	0	RC	FRENCH	FISHERMAN	089	A		65
KING	JOSEPH		1		55	QUE	RC	FRENCH	LUMBERMAN	089	A		52
KING	JOSEPH				47	0	RC	FRENCH	COOPER	089	A		60
KING	JOSEPH				73	QUE	RC	FRENCH	FISHERMAN	089	A		65
KING	JULIE			1	24	0	NG	INDIAN		085	E		19
KING	LEWIS				38	0	RC	INDIAN	F	085	G		1
KING	LOUIS				40	QUE	RC	FRENCH	LAB	081	B		43
KING	MARGARET		2	1	20	0	NG			085	F		D
KING	MARY		2	1	1	0	RC			089	A		D
KING	PETER	SNR			50	SCOTLAND	RP	SCOTCH	F	082	K	1	2
KING	RICHARD				39	ENGLAND	WM	ENGLISH	MINER	089	A		7
KING	ROBERT				58	SCOTLAND	EM	SCOTCH	F	082	G		35
KING	WILLIAM				44	0	NG	ENGLISH	HUNTER	085	E		22
KING	WILLIAM	K	2		100	0	NG		HUNTER	085	F		D
KINGHINE	ANN		2	1	34	IRELAND	CE			082	G		D
KINGHINE	SUSAN		2	1		0	CE			082	G		D
KINGSHOTT	JAMES				59	ENGLAND	CE	ENGLISH	F	085	D		10
KINGSHOTT	WILLIAM				24	0	PS	ENGLISH	F	085	D		6
KINGSTON	THOMAS				32	ENGLISH	CE	ENGLISH	CLERK	083	A	1	12
KINNELLY	DANIEL				63	IRELAND	RC	IRISH	FARMER	081	D		23

SURNAME	NAME1	NAME2	STRAY	SEX	AGE	BIRTHPL	RELIGION	ORIGIN	OCCUP	DIST	SUB_DIST	DIV	PAGE
KINNELLY	JOHN				35	IRELAND	RC	IRISH	FARMER	081	D		23
KINNELLY	MARTIN				68	IRELAND	RC	IRISH	FARMER	081	D		15
KINNELLY	MICHAEL				30	IRELAND	RC	IRISH	FARMER	081	D		26
KINNELLY	MORTIMER		1		25	O	RC	IRISH	FARMER	081	D		16
KINNELLY	PATRICK				34	IRELAND	RC	IRISH	FARMER	081	D		18
KINNEY	TERRY				34	IRELAND	RC	IRISH	ENGINEER	082	D		2
KINSELLA	ANNIE		1	1	17	IRELAND	RC	IRISH		090	D		1
KINSLEY	KATE		2	1	16	ENGLAND	CE			088	A		D
KINTZING	WILLIAM	D	1		24	USA	CE	GERMAN	CLERK	086	C	1	11
KIOSHK	BENOIT				39	US	RC	INDIAN	F & COOPER	087	A		23
KIOSHK	PIERRE				32	US	RC	INDIAN	F & FISHERMAN	087	A		23
KIPLING	ANN		1	1	60	IRELAND	CE	IRISH		086	B		8
KIPPEAN	HANNA		1	1	30	GERMANY	ME	GERMAN	SERVANT	082	E		68
KIPPEN	ANDREW				58	SCOTLAND	CS	SCOTCH	SAWYER	081	C		19
KIPPEN	DUNCAN				28	ONT	CS	SCOTCH	F	081	C		21
KIRBY	DORITHEA		1		29	O	RC	IRISH	SCHOOL TEACHER	082	D		19
KIRBY	GEORGE				34	ENGLAND	PM	ENGLISH	F	085	J		6
KIRBY	NATHANIEL				49	ENGLAND	WM	ENGLISH	F	085	C		9
KIRBYSON	NICHOLAS				68	ENGLAND	CE	ENGLISH	F	085	J		8
KIRK	ELESEBATH		1	1	70	O	RP	SCOTCH		082	K		14
KIRK	JAMES				38	O	CP	IRISH	F	081	A	1	6
KIRK	JOHN				50	ENGLAND	PM	ENGLISH	F	085	I		28
KIRK	WALTER		1		63	SCOTLAND	RP	SCOTCH	LAB	082	K	1	14
KIRK	WILLIAM				25	ENGLAND	CE	ENGLISH	F	085	I		1
KIRKLING	THOMAS				42	IRELAND	CE	IRISH	F	085	E		5
KIRKMAN	ROBERT	FRANCIS			44	ENGLAND	WM	ENGLISH	SMITH	085	E		3
KIRKNESS	THOMAS				30	SCOTLAND	CP	SCOTCH	LAB	090	F		20
KIRKPATRICK	JAMES	T	1		22	O	CP	SCOTCH	MERCHANT	085	B		13
KIRKPATRICK	WILLIAM				31	IRELAND	CE	IRISH	F	085	H		7
KITCHEKAKAKE	AMABLE				35	O	RC	INDIAN	F & FISHERMAN	087	A		42
KITCHEKAKAKE	CECIL				52	US	RC	INDIAN	F	087	A		42
KITCHEN	JOHN				26	ENGLAND	WM	ENGLISH	F	085	L		7
KITCHIBATISS	CHARLES				75	US	RC	INDIAN	F	087	A		33
KITCHIBATISS	J	BTE			41	US	RC	INDIAN	F & COOPER	087	A		33
KITCHIKEKEKE	FRANCIS				30	O	RC	INDIAN	F & FISHERMAN	087	A		33
KITCHIKIWIVISIN	(WIDOW)			1		ONTARIO	PA	INDIAN	HUNTER & TRAPPER	090	E		12
KITCHING	RITCHARD				45	SCOTLAND	CS	SCOTCH	F	085	H		22
KITT	CHARLES				23	ONTARIO	RC	IRISH	FARMER	083	A	1	14
KITT	JAMES				32	ONTARIO	RC	IRISH	FARMER	081	G	1	5
KITT	MICHAEL				62	QUEBEC	RC	IRISH	FARMER	081	G	1	2
KITT	SAMUEL				32	ENGLAND	RC	ENGLISH	TAILOR	082	D		11
KITT	WILLIAM				50	ONTARIO	RC	IRISH	FARMER	081	G	1	2
KNAUT	LAURA		1	1	12	UNITED STATES	EP	GERMAN		090	D		6
KNEWSHAW	WM				44	ENGLAND	CE	SCOTCH	F	085	J		25
KNIGHT	GABRIEL				47	ENGLAND	WM	ENGLISH	MINER	089	A		16
KNIGHT	JAMES				29	ENGLAND	WM	ENGLISH	MINER	089	A		9
KNIGHT	JOHN				48	ENGLAND	WM	ENGLISH	MINER	089	A		26
KNIGHT	JOHN				25	ENGLAND	WM	ENGLISH	MINER	089	A		29
KNIGHT	JOSEPH				29	O	CP	ENGLISH	F	081	H	1	4
KNIGHT	JOSEPH	SEN			52	O	EM	ENGLISH	F	081	H	2	31
KNIGHT	THOMAS				24	O	CS	SCOTCH	BLACKSMITH	081	I		23
KNIGHT	THOMAS				81	ENGLAND	CE	ENGLISH	BRICKMAKER	082	A		2
KNIGHT	THOMAS				29	ENGLAND	CE	ENGLISH	F	085	E		17
KNOT	JAMES		1		16	O	CE	ENGLISH	BLACKSMITH	082	D		17
KNOTT	JAMES				39	O	CP	ENGLISH	SAWYER	082	E		67
KNOTT	JAMES				28	ENGLAND	CE	ENGLISH	F	085	J		8
KNOTT	JANE		1	1	9	ONT	CE	IRISH		082	I		69
KNOTT	JOHN				52	QUE	WM	ENGLISH	CARPENTER	082	D		18
KNOTT	ROBERT				55	IRELAND	CE	IRISH	F	085	B		10
KNOTT	WILLIAM				26	ENGLAND	CE	ENGLISH	F	085	L		3
KNOWLES	ELIZABETH		1	1	21	ENGLAND	WM	ENGLISH		081	B		26
KNOWLES	WILLIAM		1		23	O	CE	ENGLISH	LUMBERMAN	086	C	1	7
KNOX	CAROLINE			1	54	ENGLAND	CE	ENGLISH	SCHOOL MISTRESS	081	D		9
KOCH	AUGUST		1		4	PRUSSIA	LU	PRUSSIAN		085	A		8
KOCH	ERNEST		1		2	O	LU	PRUSSIAN		085	A		8
KOCH	HENRY		1		9	PRUSSIA	LU	PRUSSIAN	SERVANT	085	A		8
KOCH	JOHN				41	PRUSSIA	LU	PRUSSIAN	F	085	A		6
KOCH	WILLIAM		1		6	O	LU	PRUSSIAN		085	A		8
KOGCOSH	JOHN				63	O	RC	INDIAN	FISHERMAN	089	B		23
KOGCOSH	PETER				40	O	RC	INDIAN	BOAT MAN	089	B		24
KOHLER	AUGUSTIN		1		50	ALSACE	RC	FRENCH	PRIEST	087	A		1
KOHN	FREDERICK				45	GERMANY	CE	GERMAN	F	085	J		5
KOLSMIDT	CARL				45	PRUSSIA	LU	GERMAN	FARMER	082	B		13
KONINI	BENOIT				40	QUEBEC	RC	INDIAN	HUNTER	083	C		4
KOPKA	WILLIAM				43	GERMANY	LU	GERMAN	F	082	C	2	39
KOPLIN	GOTLIP		1		50	GERMANY	FW	GERMAN	F	082	H		23
KOPLIN	HENRETIA		1	1	50	GERMANY	FW	GERMAN		082	H		23
KOSMACK	FERDINAND				38	GERMANY	LU	GERMAN	FARMER	081	F		28
KOTTMANN	CHRISTOPHER				52	GERMANY	RC	GERMAN	CATHOLIC PRIEST	089	B		32
KRANZ	CATHERINE		1		40	GERMANY	LU			082	H		D
KRANZ	NICHOLOS				37	GERMANY	LU	GERMAN	F	082	H		22
KREEGER	FREDERIC		1		26	PRUSSIA	RP	GERMAN	FARMER	081	G	1	24
KREUGER	MARY						NG		SEE GRIGER	082	F		21
KRIER	FREDERICK				38	GERMANY	BA	GERMAN	FARMER	081	F		31
KRIER	JOHANNA			1	56	GERMANY	LU	GERMAN		081	F		7
KROP	DORATHE		1	1	70	GERMANY	BA	GERMAN		081	F		32
KRUER	FREDRICK		1		66	GERMANY	WM	GERMAN		082	G		12
KRUER	FREDRICKA		1	1	66	GERMANY	WM	GERMAN		082	G		12
KRUER	JOHN				64	GERMANY	LU	GERMAN	L	082	G		18
KRUNSKY	ANDREW				67	PRUSSIA	RC	PRUSSIAN	FARMER	081	G	2	1
KRUTZ	MINIE		1	1	15	PRUSSIA	LU	GERMAN	SERVANT	082	E		6
KUDDY	JOHN				30	ONTARIO	RC	IRISH	F	083	C		12
KUETZINY	ALEXANDER	EMIL	1		15	GERMANY	RC	GERMAN		081	K		22
KULUS	BACHER			1	55	POLAND	RC	POLISH		081	I		36
KURKEY	ANTOINE				45	GERMANY	RC	GERMAN	F	082	G		34
KURTH	CARL		2		85	GERMANY	LU			081	F		D
KWIWIS	(WIDOW)				72	US	RC	INDIAN	F	087	A		6
KYLE	WILLIAM				46	O	CP	IRISH	CARTER	081	B		77
LA DUKE	FRANCIS		1		22	O	RC	FRENCH	LUMBERMAN	088	B		2
LA PLANJT	LUZA				30	QUE	RC	FRENCH		088	B		4
LA TAW	FRANCIS		1		40	QUEBEC	RC	FRENCH	LUMBERER	083	A	2	4
LA TOUR	JOSEPH				40	O	RC	FRENCH	F	082	L		6
LAABS	HENRY				32	GERMANY	LU	GERMAN	FARMER	082	I		5
LABARGE	CHARLES				33	QUE	RC	FRENCH	FARMER	082	I		50
LABARGE	DENIS				34	QUE	RC	FRENCH	LAB	081	A	2	17
LABARGE	EUSTACHE		1		22	QUEBEC	RC	FRENCH	LUMBERER	083	C		7

SURNAME	NAME1	NAME2	STRAY	SEX	AGE	BIRTHPL	RELIGION	ORIGIN	OCCUP	DIST	SUB_DIST	DIV	PAGE
LABARGE	JOSEPH		1		24	QUE	RC	IRISH	SERVANT	081	F		21
LABARGE	NARCICS				33	QUE	RC	FRENCH	FARMER AND RAFTSMAN	082	I		48
LABEAU	ALPHONSE		1	1	22	QUE	RC	FRENCH	SERVANT	082	E		54
LABEAU	OLIVER				48	QUE	RC	FRENCH	F	082	C	1	62
LABELLE	JOSEPH		1		21	QUEBEC	RC	FRENCH	LAB	083	C		14
LABELLE	LOUIS				39	QUE	RC	FRENCH	BLACKSMITH	082	E		72
LABLANE	BAPTISTE				40	ONTARIO	RC	FRENCH	FARMER	083	A	2	3
LABLEAU	THEOFFILE				39	QUE	RC	FRENCH	F	082	C	1	50
LABO	MARTIN				39	O	CE	FRENCH	F	082	C	2	20
LABONDE	DENIS		2		1	O	RC			082	B		D
LABONTE	JULIAN		2	1	20	O	RC			081	K		D
LABONTE	MARY		1	1	3	O	RC	FRENCH		081	K		34
LABONTE	OLIVE		1	1	1	O	RC	FRENCH		081	K		34
LABOU	JERIME		1		16	QUE	RC	FRENCH	FARM SERVANT	082	I		44
LABOW	JENY				23	QUE	RC	FRENCH	F	090	F		16
LABROSSE	BENJAMIN				26	QUE	RC	FRENCH	LAB	082	C	1	21
LABROSSE	LOUIS		1		29	O	RC	FRENCH	LAB	082	C	1	59
LABROSSE	OCTAVE				20	O	RC	FRENCH	SERVANT	082	C	1	19
LABUN	JOSEPH	JN			27	O	RC	FRENCH		082	C	1	29
LABUN	JOSEPH	SNR?			53	QUE	RC	FRENCH	F	082	C	1	27
LABWART	LOUACE		1		37	QUE	RC	FRENCH	JOURNEYMAN CARPENTER	082	I		72
LACARRE	JOHN		1		40	QUEBEC	RC	FRENCH	FARMER	081	G	1	4
LACHANCE	FRANCIS				52	INDIA	RC	FRENCH	F	082	C	1	50
LACHENE	ZOTIQUE		1		21	QUE	RC	FRENCH	LABOURER	084	E		4
LACHNANE	ELLON			1	40	IRELAND	RC	IRISH	F	081	J	1	63
LACLAIRE	DAVID				54	QUE	RC	FRENCH	LABOURER	089	A		45
LACLARE	PETER				29	QUE	RC	FRENCH		082	C	1	30
LACY	JOHN				35	ENGLAND	WM	ENGLISH	F	082	C	1	15
LADELL	CAROLINE		2	1	18	ENGLAND	CE			085	J		D
LADELL	G	H			48	ENGLAND	CE	ENGLISH	F	085	J		15
LADENITE	JOHN		1		13	O	RC	FRENCH	LAB	081	B		29
LADERONT	ALEXANDER				25	QUE	RC	FRENCH	LAB	082	C	1	32
LADEROUT	LEAS		1	1	16	O	RC	FRENCH	SERVANT	082	J		13
LADEROUT	LEON	SNR			45	QUE	RC	FRENCH	F	082	J		7
LADEROUT	PIERE				36	QUE	RC	FRENCH	F	082	C	1	57
LADERUTE	MICHEL				20	QUE	RC	FRENCH	LAB	081	A	2	14
LADICERE	JOSEPH				28	QUE	RC	FRENCH	CARPENTER	082	E		45
LADUCUR	WILLIAM				50	QUEBEC	RC	FRENCH	FARMER	083	A	1	13
LADUROUTY	CHARLES				34	QUE	RC	FRENCH	F	081	E		14
LAFAVE	ALEXANDER				31	QUE	RC	FRENCH	FARMER	082	I		44
LAFAVE	ANTOIN				39	QUE	RC	FRENCH	FARMER	082	I		43
LAFAVE	JOSEPH				24	QUE	RC	FRENCH	LABOURER	082	E		46
LAFAVE	LOUACE				40	QUE	CE	FRENCH	FARMER	082	I		51
LAFAVE	MARGRET		2	1	37	QUE	RC			082	I		D
LAFAVE	OLIVER				35	QUE	RC	FRENCH	FARMER	082	I		47
LAFES	EMES				45	O	RC	INDIAN	BASKETMAKER	082	F		28
LAFLAIR	JOSEPH				50	QUE	RC	FRENCH	F	082	C	2	28
LAFLEUR	ALEXCA		1		17	QUE	RC	FRENCH	LAB	082	K	1	1
LAFLEUR	ALEXIS		1		72	QUE	RC	FRENCH	LAB	082	J		2
LAFLEUR	CHARLES				50	QUEBEC	RC	FRENCH	F	083	C		3
LAFLEUR	CHARLES				28	QUEBEC	RC	FRENCH	FARMER	084	A		1
LAFLEUR	MAREY		1	1	18	QUE	RC	FRENCH		082	J		1
LAFLEUR	MOSES		1		15	QUE	RC	FRENCH		082	J		2
LAFLURE	BEN	N	1		45	QUE	PS	FRENCH	LABOURER	082	E		16
LAFLURE	NARCIESE		1		18	O	RC	FRENCH	LAB	081	B		86
LAFORD	JOSEPH				88	QUE	RC	FRENCH		089	B		22
LAFRAMBOISE	POLION				24	QUEBEC	RC	FRENCH	FARMER	084	B		4
LAFRANCE	DOMINIC		1		21	QUE	RC	FRENCH	LAB	083	C		1
LAGAM	WILLIAM				47	SCOTLAND	CP	SCOTCH	CORDER & B C	081	I		29
LAGARDE	MELISIA		1	1	9	O	RC	FRENCH		090	F		9
LAGNAH	LOUIS				36	O	RC	FRENCH	FARM LAB	082	C	1	49
LAGREE	ALFRED				29	ONT	RC	FRENCH	HOTELKEEPER	081	C		57
LAGREE	EDWARD				23	ONT	RC	FRENCH	F	081	C		40
LAGREE	J	CESAR			60	QUEBEC	RC	FRENCH	F	081	C		37
LAGREE	JOSEPH				58	QUEBEC	RC	FRENCH	F	081	C		36
LAGREE	SAMUEL				32	ONT	RC	FRENCH	HOTELKEEPER	081	C		39
LAGUARDE	LALOUISE			1	43	ONT	RC	INDIAN		090	B		7
LAGUARDE	SANSON				43	ONT	RC	INDIAN	HUNTER & TRAPPER	090	B		6
LAGUARDE	THOMAS	J	2			ONT	RC			090	B		D
LAGUARDE	TOMMIE				26	ONT	RC	INDIAN	HUNTER & TRAPPER	090	B		7
LAGUEN	ALFRED				36	QUE	RC	FRENCH	LAB	082	C	1	48
LAHAYE	OCTAVE				50	QUE	RC	CANADIAN	TRADER	087	A		2
LAJEUNESSE									SEE LASHENISE	081	B		15
LAJOIR	JAMES		1		28	QUE	RC	FRENCH	LUMBERMAN	088	C		11
LALAS	EDWARD				60	IRELAND	RC	IRISH	F	081	A	1	6
LALOND	JOHN				46	QUE	RC	FRENCH	LUMBERMAN	086	C	1	3
LALONDE	EPHREM				19	QUEBEC	RC	FRENCH	RAFTSMAN	084	D		1
LALONDE	JOSEPH				56	QUE	RC	FRENCH	MINE LABOURER	089	A		31
LAMARCH	TENNIERE				60	QUE	RC	FRENCH	F	082	C	1	55
LAMARS	JOHN				27	O	RC	FRENCH	F	082	C	1	21
LAMARSH	WILLIAM				27	QUE	RC	FRENCH	TEAMSTER	081	B		37
LAMB	ELI				25	O	WM	ENGLISH	F	085	B		18
LAMB	JOB				35	ENGLAND	CE	ENGLISH	F	085	C		20
LAMBERT	EDWARD				36	FRANCE	RC	FRENCH	CARPENTER	089	A		57
LAMBERT	FRANCIS		1		19	ONT	RC	IRISH	F LABOURER	081	J	1	42
LAMBERT	JOHN				39	SCOTLAND	PS	SCOTCH	F	085	C		14
LAMBERT	MICHAEL				45	QUE	RC	FRENCH	LAB	090	F		7
LAMBERT	PETER				54	QUEBEC	RC	FRENCH	F	081	J	1	28
LAMBERT	W		1		27	QUE	RC	FRENCH	LABOURER	088	A		7
LAMING	JOHN				36	ENGLAND	WM	ENGLISH	FARMER	089	B		19
LAMOLE	NAPOLEON		1		12	O	RC	FRENCH		082	E		65
LAMONT	DONALD				32	SCOTLAND	CP	SCOTCH	F	085	H		12
LAMONT	GEORGE				27	SCOTLAND	CP	SCOTCH	F	085	H		11
LAMONT	HUGH				59	SCOTLAND	PS	SCOTCH	F	085	H		2
LAMORANDIER	ALIXIS				64	MICHIGAN	RC	FRENCH CAN	FARMER	088	A		5
LAMORANDIERE	ALEX				28	O	RC	FRENCH CAN	FISHERMAN	088	A		4
LAMORANDIERE	CHS				53	US	RC	FRENCH	TRADER	088	A		3
LAMOT	ALEXANDRE				53	QUE	RC	FRENCH	F	082	J		10
LAMOTT	FRANCESE				26	QUE	RC	FRENCH	F	082	J		11
LAMPHIRE	THOMAS				81	ENGLAND	EP	ENGLISH	KEEPER OF LIGHTHOUSE	090	D		9
LAMPKEY	JOHN				56	GERMANY	RC	GERMAN	F	082	G		93
LAMPKEY	LUEY				40	GERMANY	LU	GERMAN		082	G		92
LAMURANDIERE	P	R			26	O	RC	FRENCH	TRADER	088	A		3
LAMURE	JOSEPH				49	QUE	RC	ALGONQUIAN INDIAN	HUNTER	082	J		17
LANCASTER	EDWARD	L			40	ENGLAND	CE	ENGLISH	F	085	H		22
LANCE	CHARLES				50	GERMANY	CS	GERMAN	F	081	H	2	32

SURNAME	NAME1	NAME2	STRAY	SEX	AGE	BIRTHPL	RELIGION	ORIGIN	OCCUP	DIST	SUB_DIST	DIV	PAGE
LANCE	MICHAEL		1		13	O	RC	FRENCH		082	E		5
LANCE	MICHEAL				77	QUE	RC	GERMAN	LAB	082	J		2
LANCE	RICHARD				37	ENGLAND	CE	ENGLISH	F	085	D		2
LANCHESTER	ROBERT				39	ENGLAND	CE	ENGLISH	F	085	H		16
LAND	JOHN				47	O	WM	ENGLISH	F	086	A	1	5
LANDERS	JOHN				40	ENGLAND	CE	ENGLISH	GARDENER	082	E		61
LANDIN	WILLIAM		1		15	QUE	RC	ENGLISH	FARM LAB	082	C	1	21
LANDRIGEN	ELIZABETH			1	28	QUE	RC	SCOTCH		081	B		79
LANDRIO	LENO		1	1	22	O	RC	FRENCH		081	K		38
LANDRIO	MICHEL		1		32	O	RC	FRENCH	LUMBERMAN	081	K		38
LANE	ANN		2	1	44	IRELAND	RC		F	082	B		D
LANE	BENJAMIN				48	O	WM	DUTCH	F	087	B	3	12
LANE	JEREMIAH				49	IRELAND	RC	IRISH	LAB	081	A	2	9
LANE	JOHN		1		29	IRELAND	RC	IRISH	SHOEMAKER	081	B		6
LANE	JOHN				50	IRELAND	RC	IRISH	FARMER	081	D		1
LANE	JOHN		1		54	QUE	CE	ENGLISH	CLERK	084	D		8
LANE	JOHN	E	1		9	O	CE	ENGLISH		082	E		2
LANE	THOMAS				58	IRELAND	RC	IRISH	FARMER	082	B		46
LANE	WILLIAM				46	IRELAND	RC	IRISH	F	081	C		35
LANG	AUGUST				49	GERMANY	WM	GERMAN	F	082	G		98
LANG	H	W			46	QUE	CE	SCOTCH	GUNSMITH	081	B		11
LANG	MICHAEL				46	IRELAND	RC	IRISH	LAB	081	B		59
LANG	NANCY		1	1	20	O	WM	SCOTTISH		082	E		1
LANGAN	MATHEW				26	IRELAND	RC	IRISH	LAB	081	B		56
LANGDON	EMILY	JANE	1		28	ENGLAND	WM	ENGLISH	SERVANT	085	I		11
LANGEVIN	STANIS				24	ONTARIO	RC	FRENCH	SHANTYMAN	084	C		7
LANGFORD	ISAAC				50	IRELAND	WM	IRISH	CARPENTER & FRAMER	085	I		31
LANGFORD	THOMAS				50	IRELAND	WM	IRISH	F	085	K	1	3
LANGLOIS	CERELE				21	QUE	RC	FRENCH	LAB	081	B		86
LANGTON	ALFRED				32	ENGLAND	CE	ENGLISH	F	085	D		1
LANGTON	WENMAN				39	ENGLAND	CE	ENGLISH	F	085	D		5
LANGTREE	JAS		1		28	ENGLAND	RC	ENGLISH	LUMBERMAN	088	B		3
LANIGAN	WILLIAM		1		10	O	RC	IRISH		089	A		57
LANNON	JOHN				40	IRELAND	RC	IRISH	LABOURER	082	E		13
LANSE	MICHEL				40	O	RC	FRENCH	F	082	F		30
LAPAGE	JOSEPH				34	O	RC	FRENCH	FARM LAB	082	C	1	29
LAPINIER	JOSEPH				28	O	RC	FRENCH	F	082	C	1	7
LAPLANE	FRANCIS				61	QUE	RC	FRENCH		082	C	1	31
LAPLANT	ANTOIN				70	QUE	RC	FRENCH	FARMER	082	I		48
LAPLANT	JEREMIAH				36	QUE	RC	FRENCH	FARMER AND RAFTSMAN	082	I		48
LAPLANT	PARRE				26	QUE	RC	FRENCH	FARMER AND RAFTSMAN	082	I		48
LAPLANT	XAVIER				24	QUE	RC	FRENCH	FARMER	082	I		26
LAPLANTE	ADILIEDE		1	1		O	RC	FRENCH		081	E		17
LAPLANTE	MARY		1	1	36	QUE	RC	FRENCH		082	I		49
LAPLONTE	JOSEPH				70	QUE	RC	FRENCH	LUMBERMAN	089	A		16
LAPLONTE	LOUIS				65	QUE	RC	FRENCH	CARPENTER	089	A		16
LAPOINT	CHARLEY				36	QUE	RC	FRENCH	F	081	E		18
LAPOINTE	CHARLEY				33	QUE	RC	FRENCH	F	081	E		11
LAPOLICE	GEORGE				41	QUE	RC	FRENCH	MILLER	081	K		67
LAPOPE	FRANCIS				25	O	RC	FRENCH	MASON	082	E		61
LAPORTE	JOSEPH				69	QUE	RC	FRENCH	LAB	081	B		29
LAPOUSIER	JOSEPH				35	ONTARIO	RC	FRENCH		084	B		1
LAPRARIE	M		1		27	QUE	RC	FRENCH	LABOURER	088	A		7
LAPRINIERE	CHARLES				61	QUE	RC	FRENCH		082	C	1	34
LAQUAH	DAVID				34	QUE	RC	FRENCH	LAB	082	C	1	59
LARAGUE	MATILDA		1	1	9	O	RC	FRENCH		082	J		2
LARIVE	ANNE	F	2	1		O	PS		F	081	A	2	D
LARIVES	GEORGE				24	O	CP	FRENCH	SHOEMAKER	081	A	2	21
LARMONDEU	FELIX				41	QUE	RC	FRENCH	F	082	J		13
LARMONDEU	FELIX	JNR	2		16	O	RC			082	J		D
LARMOUTH	ELIZA		1	1	13	O	CP	SCOTCH		081	B		6
LAROCHELLE	DELOEDE			1	42	QUE	RC	FRENCH	F	082	K	1	16
LAROCHELLE	THOMAS				38	QUE	RC	FRENCH	F	082	H		19
LAROCQUE	PETER		1		22	QUEBEC	RC	FRENCH	LAB	083	E		2
LARON	MARYAN			1	50	O	RC	FRENCH		084	I	1	2
LARONDE	DENNIS				46	QUEBEC	RC	FRENCH	FARMER	082	B		21
LARONDE	PAUL				33	QUEBEC	RC	HALFBREED	HUNTER	084	D		4
LARONE	ALEX				50	QUEBEC	RC	FRENCH	F	081	C		14
LARONE	ALEXANDER				66	QUE	RC	INDIAN	F	082	C	2	33
LARONE	BARNAR				67	O	RC	INDIAN	HUNTER	084	I	1	3
LARONE	JOSET			1	30	O	RC	FRENCH		084	I	1	6
LAROSE	FRANK		1		61	US	RC	FRENCH	BOATMAN	089	B		12
LAROSE	JENOSE				49	O	RC	FRENCH	LABOURER	089	B		36
LAROSE	MARIE		1	1	50	O	RC	FRENCH	TAILORESS	089	B		12
LAROSE	NARCICE			1	42	QUE	RC	FRENCH	HOTELKEEPER	082	E		43
LAROSE	OLIVIER				32	QUEBEC	RC	FRENCH		084	A		4
LAROUE	GASANT				50	O	RC	FRENCH	LAB	082	C	2	40
LAROUE	SUSUNNAH		1	1	98	O	RC	FRENCH		082	C	2	40
LAROUGH	JOSEPH		1		22	QUE	RC	FRENCH		086	C	1	4
LAROUX	EUSTACH				39	QUE	RC	INDIAN	LAB	082	C	1	64
LARRETT	FANNY			1	38	IRELAND	CP	IRISH		082	C	2	21
LARVY	AKEN				53	QUE	EM	FRENCH	LAB	081	A	2	22
LARWILL	ONESIPORUS				45	QUEBEC	WM	ENGLISH	FARMER	081	G	1	28
LASAGE	JOSEPH				22	O	RC	FRENCH	LABOURER	089	B		38
LASAGE	MADILINE			1	80	US	RC	FRENCH	BARK WORK	089	B		34
LASHENISE	JOHN				26	QUE	RC	FRENCH	LAB	081	B		15
LASSAM	WILLIAM		1		32	GERMANY	LU	GERMAN	JOURNEYMAN CARPENTER	082	I		55
LAST	HARRY				56	ENGLAND	CE	ENGLISH	F	085	J		18
LATER	DAVID		1		21	QUE	CE	IRISH	F	085	L		5
LATER	JAMES				29	QUE	CE	IRISH	F	085	L		4
LATOUR	MALINDA		2	1	40	QUE	RC			082	G		D
LATOUR	MARY		2	1	15	QUE	RC			082	G		D
LATOUR	PETER				45	QUE	RC	FRENCH	RAFTSMAN	082	G		74
LAUDENBERGER	FRED		1		31	GERMANY	LU	GERMAN	CLERK	090	F		17
LAUGHERN	CHARLES				22	ONTARIO	RC	IRISH	LUMBERMAN	083	D		1
LAUGHRAN	JOHN		1		19	O	RC	IRISH	SHANTY CLERK	082	E		49
LAUGHRAN	LARRY		1		24	O	RC	IRISH	SHANTY CLERK	082	E		49
LAUGHRAN	PATRICK		1		17	O	RC	IRISH	CLERK	082	E		49
LAUGHRIN	JOHN				50	IRELAND	RC	IRISH	LUMBERMAN	081	K		69
LAUHN	BETSE				59	QUE	RC	FRENCH	LAB	081	I		35
LAUNDRIE	JOSEPH				38	QUE	RC	FRENCH	F	082	H		33
LAURENCE	LOUIS				34	GERMANY	RC	GERMAN	MINER	090	F		17
LAURIE	DUNCAN				40	SCOTLAND	CP	SCOTCH	MINER	090	D		1
LAVALEE	OCTAVE		1		24	QUE	RC	FRENCH	TEAMSTER	090	F		14
LAVALLEY	PROSPER				51	QUE	RC	IRISH	LAB	081	B		57
LAVAYLETTE	NODARE				29	QUE	RC	FRENCH	F	081	E		6

SURNAME	NAME1	NAME2	STRAY	SEX	AGE	BIRTHPL	RELIGION	ORIGIN	OCCUP	DIST	SUB_DIST	DIV	PAGE
LAVEC	FRANCIS				45	QUEBEC	RC	FRENCH	FARMER	083	A	2	2
LAVELLE	AUSTIN				45	IRELAND	RC	IRISH	F	083	C		13
LAVELLE	PATRICK				30	IRELAND	RC	IRISH	F	083	C		12
LAVELLEE	CELESTA				44	QUE	CS	FRENCH	F			1	79
LAVELLETTE	GREGORIE				57	QUE	RC	FRENCH	HARNESSMAKER	081	B		54
LAVENDER	ROBERT				29	0	JM	IRISH	WHEELWRIGHT	082	C	2	4
LAVENDURE	LOUIS				60	QUE	RC	FRENCH	F	081	A	2	56
LAVENE	EXAVER		1		20	QUE	RC	FRENCH	LAB	082	K	1	14
LAVENTURE	DUNCAN				31	0	BA	IRISH	SHANTYING	081	H	2	10
LAVENTURE	DUNCAN		2			0	BA			081	H	2	D
LAVERDARE	FRANCIS				72	QUE	RC	FRENCH	F	082	C	1	24
LAVERLOCHER	JOHN	NICKER			57	FRANCE	RC	FRENCH	PRIEST	084	I	2	1
LAVEVE	PETER				26	QUEBEC	RC	FRENCH	LUMBERER	083	B	1	1
LAVILLE	JAMES				40	QUE	RC	IRISH	F	082	C	2	49
LAVINE	CATHERINE			1	47	IRELAND	RC	IRISH	TRADER	081	C		39
LAVINE	JOSEPH				53	QUEBEC	RC	FRENCH	F	081	C		21
LAVIOLETTE	CHARLES				29	QUE	RC	FRENCH	SADELER	081	I		24
LAVOIE	ANDREW				21	QUEBEC	RC	FRENCH	F	083	C		7
LAVOIE	CHARLES		1		30	QUE	RC	CANADIAN	COOK	087	A		1
LAW	JOHN				40	QUE	CE	ENGLISH	F	085	J		11
LAW	MRS			1	59	IRELAND	RC	IRISH		081	J	1	23
LAW	ROBERT				55	IRELAND	PB	IRISH	LUMBERMAN	082	K	1	6
LAW	WILLIAM		1		13	0	RC	IRISH		081	K		72
LAW	WM				50	IRELAND	CE	IRISH	F	085	L		5
LAWCONLAV	ANTOINE				40	PRUSSIA	RC	PRUSSIAN	FARMER	083	A	1	17
LAWLESS	PATRICK				61	IRELAND	RC	IRISH	F	082	C	1	12
LAWORAUDIEUX	NANCY		1	1	13	0	RC	INDIAN	STUDENT	087	A		1
LAWRENCE	WM	M			50	ENGLAND	CE	ENGLISH	F	085	K	2	5
LAWRIE	AGNES			1	72	SCOTLAND	CP	SCOTCH		081	A	1	37
LAWSIN	RANKIN				26	SCOTLAND	PS	DUTCH	F	085	E		13
LAWSON	ALEXANDER				48	SCOTLAND	PS	SCOTCH	F	085	D		31
LAWSON	CYRUS				28	0	WM	SCOTCH	F	085	E		13
LAYCOCK	AGNES		1	1	15	0	CP	SCOTCH		081	A	2	26
LAYCOCK	ANNA		1	1	17	0	EM	ENGLISH	SERVANT	081	B		66
LAYCOCK	GEORGE				48	0	CE	IRISH	LAB	081	A	2	12
LAYCOCK	JOHN				40	0	EM	IRISH	BLACKSMITH	081	A	2	20
LAYMAN	CHRISTY				33	GERMANY	LU	GERMAN	F	082	G		5
LAYMAN	MARTIN				33	GERMANY	LU	GERMAN	FARMER	082	I		77
LAYMAN	MATTHE				44	PRUSSIA	LU	GERMAN	F	082	G		73
LEA	THOMAS				50	ENGLAND	CE	ENGLISH	F	085	K	1	1
LEACH	GEORGE				29	IRELAND	WM	IRISH	WHEELWRIGHT	082	C	1	12
LEACH	HENERY				52	0	CE	IRISH	F	082	F		8
LEACH	JAMES				40	0	CE	IRISH	HOTELKEEPER	082	E		32
LEACY	MARY		1	1	24	IRELAND	RC	IRISH		081	H	2	36
LEADER	JONATHAN				27	0	PM	ENGLISH	COOPER	085	I		19
LEADER	ROBERT				22	0	CE	ENGLISH	CARPENTER	085	I		18
LEANY	EDWD				35	IRELAND	RC	IRISH	SADDLER	082	E		59
LEARY	DENNIS		1		25	IRELAND	RC	IRISH	LAB	090	D		6
LEARY	PATRICK				37	IRELAND	RC	IRISH	LAB	081	A	2	1
LEASHMAN	ROBERT				23	0	WM	SCOTCH	STOREKEEPER	081	B		25
LEBARGE	JOSEPH		1		45	QUE	RC	FRENCH	LAB	082	L		5
LEBARGE	JOSEPH		1		9	0	RC	FRENCH		082	L		5
LEBARGE	RUBEN		1		7	0	RC	FRENCH		082	L		7
LEBARON	AMOS				38	US	JM	FRENCH	F	082	C	2	63
LEBARRON	NELSON				62	US	WM	FRENCH	F	082	C	2	9
LEBART	PETER		1		14	QUE	RC	FRENCH	SERVANT	082	J		19
LEBATT	MARGERITE			1	68	0	RC	FRENCH	WORK WOMAN	089	B		23
LEBEAU	JEROME						NG		SEE LABOU	082	I		44
LEBEAW	JOHN	L	1			0	RC	FRENCH		082	J		18
LEBEAW	LESIME		1		27	QUE	RC	FRENCH	LAB	082	J		18
LEBEAW	MAREY		1	1	23	0	RC	FRENCH	SERVANT	082	J		18
LEBEAW	MARRIOW				40	QUE	RC	FRENCH	F	082	J		18
LEBECK	MARTIN				50	GERMANY	LU	GERMAN	F	082	G		87
LEBELLE	GIDEON				45	QUE	RC	FRENCH	SHOEMAKER	082	E		62
LEBIRA	ROSSANA		1	1	85	PRUSSIA	RC	PRUSSIAN	WEAVER	083	A	1	1
LEBLAIS	BAPTISTE				36	QUE	RC	FRENCH	SHANTYMAN	082	E		53
LEBLAIS	MOSSES				20	QUE	RC	FRENCH	SHANTYMAN	082	E		49
LEBLANC	ISIDORE				48	QUE	RC	FRENCH	F	081	K		31
LEBLANNCE	OLIVER		1		16	QUE	RC	FRENCH	BUTCHER	082	E		32
LEBLAUS	LOUISE			1	42	US	RC	SCOTCH		082	E		73
LEBORACK	EDWARD				21	QUE	RC	FRENCH	LUMBERMAN	083	C		1
LEBORE	FREDRIC		1		25	GERMANY	LU	GERMAN	SERVANT	082	F		21
LECKIE	ALEXANDER				39	0	CS	SCOTCH	F	081	A	1	36
LECKIE	DAVID				28	0	CP	SCOTCH	BLACKSMITH			1	81
LECKIE	WILLIAM				41	0	CS	SCOTCH	BLACKSMITH	081	A	1	35
LECKIE	WILLIAM				49	SCOTLAND	CS	SCOTCH	F	081	A	1	41
LECLARE	ANTOINE				37	0	RC	FRENCH	F	081	E		16
LECLARE	BAPTISTE				62	QUE	RC	FRENCH	F	081	E		16
LECLARE	MARY		2	1	9	0	RC			081	E		D
LECLARE	THOMAS				26	0	RC	FRENCH	F	081	E		16
LEDDARD	CHARLES	W			53	ENGLAND	WM	ENGLISH	F	085	I		33
LEDGERWOOD	C			1	38	0	CP	SCOTCH		081	B		70
LEDGERWOOD	HANCE				30	IRELAND	CE	IRISH	F	081	A	1	6
LEDGERWOOD	JAMES				49	ONT	CP	SCOTCH	FARMER	082	I		56
LEDGERWOOD	MRS			1	37	0	CP	SCOTCH	F	082	C	1	40
LEDUC	AMELIA		1	1	32	QUEBEC	RC	ENGLISH	SERVANT	084	C		5
LEDUC	FRANCIS				50	FRANCE	RC	FRENCH	FARMER	089	A		50
LEDUKE	ABRAHAM				62	QUEBEC	RC	FRENCH	F	081	J	1	77
LEDUKE	PETER		2		24	ONT	RC			081	J	1	D
LEDUSA	JOSEPHINE		1	1	21	QUE	RC	FRENCH	SERVANT GIRL	082	D		3
LEE	FLORA		1	1	36	0	CP	IRISH	TAILORESS	082	E		16
LEE	GEORGE				35	0	CE	IRISH	F	082	C	2	52
LEE	JOHN		1		25	0	CP	IRISH	LAB	081	A	1	17
LEE	JOHN		1		2	0	CP	IRISH		081	A	1	17
LEE	JOHN				56	0	CE	IRISH	LAB	081	B		45
LEE	JOHN				44	ONTARIO	CE	IRISH	F	082	A		61
LEE	JOHN				47	IRELAND	RC	IRISH	F	082	F		24
LEE	LORETTA		1	1	31	0	EM	GERMAN		085	H		13
LEE	ROBERT				40	ONTARIO	CE	IRISH	F	082	A		44
LEE	SARAH		1	1	27	0	CP	SCOTCH		081	A	1	17
LEE	THOMAS				60	IRELAND	RC	IRISH	CARPENTER	082	D		1
LEE	WILLIAM				35	ENGLAND	CE	ENGLISH	BLACKSMITH	082	E		62
LEECH	JAMES				52	IRELAND	RP	IRISH	FARMER	082	I		7
LEECH	PETER				58	SCOTLAND	CS	SCOTCH	F	086	A	2	11
LEEHAFFER	FREDRIC				46	PRUSSIA	LU	PRUSSIAN	F	085	A		3
LEEHIGH	JOHN				29	QUE	CE	ENGLISH	CARPENTER	085	B		12

SURNAME	NAME1	NAME2	STRAY	SEX	AGE	BIRTHPL	RELIGION	ORIGIN	OCCUP	DIST	SUB_DIST	DIV	PAGE
LEFEBURG	ANTOINE						NG		SEE LAFAVE	082	I		43
LEFEBVRE	JOACHIM				31	QUEBEC	RC	FRENCH	FARMER	084	C		2
LEFEVE	FRANCIS	A	1		15	O	WM	FRENCH	SERVANT	082	G		24
LEFEVRE	VICTOR				57	FRANCE	RC	FRENCH	FARMER	089	A		52
LEFLEUR	EUSTACHE				55	QUE	RC	FRENCH	INNKEEPER	081	H	2	25
LEFLEUR	FRANCQUIS				68	RED RIVER	RC	FRENCH	FARMER	089	B		23
LEFLEUR	WILLIAM				25	QUE	RC	FRENCH	SHOEMAKER	081	D		7
LEFRANCE	PROSPERE				22	O	RC	FRENCH	LABOURER	082	D		20
LEFRY	BAPTIST		1		65	O	RC	FRENCH	FISHERMAN	089	A		64
LEGARATTE	JOSEPH				34	FRANCE	RC	FRENCH	COOK	084	A		1
LEGERWOOD	DANIEL				41	O	CP	SCOTCH	TEACHER	082	C	2	7
LEGG	CATHERINE		2	1		O	RC			082	C	2	D
LEGG	CHARLES				70	IRELAND	RC	IRISH	F	082	F		18
LEGG	JOHN				40	IRELAND	RC	IRISH	LABOURER	082	E		24
LEGG	RODEY				40	IRELAND	RC	IRISH	LABOURER	082	D		16
LEGG	THOMAS				28	IRELAND	RC	IRISH	MERCHANT	082	C	2	5
LEGGETT	HENERY				27	O	CE	IRISH	WAGONMAKER	081	I		4
LEGREE	CHARLES				27	ONT	RC	FRENCH	F	081	J	1	16
LEHMANN	ALBERT				35	GERMANY	LU	GERMAN	F	085	A		3
LEHMANN	GUSTAVE				39	PRUSSIA	EV	PRUSSIAN	F	085	A		8
LEICH	DAVID				36	O	PS	SCOTTISH	SHOEMAKER	082	E		43
LEIGHTON	WILLIAM				27	SCOTLAND	PS	SCOTCH	F	086	B		3
LEIR	PARICK				45	IRELAND	RC	IRISH	F	081	A	1	9
LEITCH	EDWARD				38	O	CE	IRISH	F	082	G		67
LEITCH	JAMES				30	SCOTLAND	CS	SCOTCH	F	081	H	1	13
LEITCH	JAMES	JR			40	ONT	RP	SCOTCH	FARMER	082	I		12
LEITCH	JAMES	SR			68	SCOTLAND	RP	SCOTCH	FARMER	082	I		12
LEITCH	MARY	ANN	1	1	22	IRELAND	CE	IRISH	SEAMSTRESS	082	G		22
LEITCH	PETER				39	ONT	RP	SCOTCH	FARMER	082	I		12
LEITCH	ROBERT				38	SCOTLAND	CS	SCOTCH	F	081	H	1	17
LEITCH	WILLIAM				43	O	CE	IRISH	F	082	G		34
LEITH	CHARLOTTE		1	1	2	O	EM	SCOTCH		085	D		8
LEITH	DAVID				59	SCOTLAND	BA	SCOTCH	F	086	A	1	9
LELARGE	SARRAH			1	11	ONTARIO	CE	ENGLISH		083	E		1
LEMARCHE	FLERICE			1	57	QUE	RC	FRENCH		081	K		25
LEMARCHE	THOFIELE				27	O	RC	FRENCH	F	081	K		25
LEMAY	JEAN	BAPTIST			59	O	RC	FRENCH		089	B		28
LEMERAND	EMLY		2	1		O	RC			084	B		D
LEMERAND	XAVIER				48	IRELAND	PS	IRISH	PILOT AND HEWER	084	B		2
LEMKA	WILLIAM				38	GERMANY	LU	GERMAN	F	082	J		15
LEMURRIE	CHARLES				30	O	RC	FRENCH	FARMER	089	A		53
LEMURRIE	JOHN				23	O	RC	FRENCH	FARMER	089	A		53
LENCEY	SARAH		1	1	1	O	RC	IRISH		081	I		21
LENNOX	THOS				54	SCOTLAND	PS	SCOTCH	PLASTERER	087	B	2	8
LENON	WILLIAM				34	ONTARIO	PR	IRISH	FARMER	081	G	2	4
LENORSH	PETER				37	QUEBEC	RC	FRENCH	FARMER	084	D		3
LEOCHEPELLE	FRANCIS		1		24	QUE	RC	FRENCH	FOREMAN	084	D		8
LEON	ANTWIN				42	QUE	RC	INDIAN	HUNTER	081	A	2	59
LEONARD	ISRIAL				29	O	NR	ENGLISH	SERVANT	081	A	2	39
LEONARD	JOHN				22	IRELAND	RC	IRISH	FARMER	081	F		20
LEPEIRE	LOUIS		1		14	QUE	RC	FRENCH	SERVANT	082	E		26
LEPELL	GEORGE				33	UNITED STATES	WM		MILLER	081	I		30
LEPOINTE	JOSEPH				30	O	RC	INDIAN	HUNTER & TRAPPER	090	A		4
LEPORT	CHARLES				28	QUEBEC	RC	FRENCH	F	082	J		18
LEPTKA	WILLIAM				37	GERMANY	RC	GERMAN	F	082	J		14
LERMEN	WILLIAM				22	O	RC	IRISH	F	081	K		13
LERO	GEORGE		1		21	UNITED STATES	RC	FRENCH	LAB	081	B		18
LERO	PETER		1		23	UNITED STATES	RC	FRENCH	LAB	081	B		18
LEROCK	ALFORIS		1		21	QUE	RC	FRENCH	LABOURER	082	D		8
LEROQ	SAMUEL				39	QUE	CE	DUTCH	F	084	D		6
LEROY	DAVID				28	QUE	RC	FRENCH	F	082	K	1	5
LEROY	ROBERT				37	QUE	RC	GERMAN	F	082	K	1	18
LEROY	SARAH		2	1	4	O	RC			082	K	1	D
LESAGE	JOSEPH				43	O	RC	FRENCH	FARMER	089	B		36
LESAGE	MANI		2	1		O	RC			089	B		D
LESAGE	PETER				52	O	RC	FRENCH	FARMER	089	B		37
LESAUGE	JOHN				26	O	RC	FRENCH	FISHERMAN	089	A		64
LESAUGE	LOUIS		1		19	US	RC	FRENCH	FISHERMAN	089	A		63
LESAUGE	MOSES				53	O	RC	FRENCH	FISHERMAN	089	A		64
LESHEL	LOUIS		1		48	QUEBEC	RC	FRENCH	LUMBERMAN	083	E		2
LESORT	MICHAEL				40	QUE	RC	FRENCH	LAB	082	C	1	59
LESTER	SARAH		1	1	26	QUE	CE	IRISH		081	B		22
LETOUR	FRANCES	ANN	1	1	6	O	RC	FRENCH		081	K		44
LETOUR	MARGARET		1	1	14	O	RC	FRENCH	SERVANT	081	K		69
LETOUR	PETER				40	QUE	RC	FRENCH	LUMBERMAN	081	K		74
LETT	RALPH				46	IRELAND	EM	IRISH	F	082	G		97
LETT	RALPH	W			50	IRELAND	CE	IRISH	F	082	G		7
LETT	THOMAS				36	IRELAND	EP	IRISH	F	082	G		43
LETT	THOS	BEN			41	IRELAND	PR	IRISH	F	082	G		8
LEUIPING	ANTVINE				49	QUE	RC		LAB	081	I		43
LEULOFF	FERDINAND				26	GERMANY	LU	GERMAN	F	082	G		20
LEULOFF	FREDRICK				31	GERMANY	LU	GERMAN	F	082	G		14
LEULOFF	WILLIAM				45	GERMANY	WM	GERMAN	F	082	G		12
LEVALLY	MATILDA		1	1	20	QUE	RC	FRENCH	SERVANT	082	E		51
LEVECK	VICTOR				22	QUEBEC	RC	FRENCH	SHANTY LABOURER	083	B	1	1
LEVEITH	LECE		1	1	21	O	RC	FRENCH	TEACHER	082	D		21
LEVEQUE	SAVARIN				33	QUEBEC	RC	FRENCH	CARPENTER	084	C		4
LEVERE	ANTOINE				27	QUEBEC	RC	FRENCH	F	083	C		11
LEVERE	ANTOINE				77	QUEBEC	RC	FRENCH	F	083	C		15
LEVERE	SERAPHIN				33	QUEBEC	RC	FRENCH	F	083	C		17
LEVEY	JOHN				33	QUE	RC	FRENCH	F	081	E		11
LEVINE	AMELIA		2	1	30	GERMANY	LU			081	F		D
LEVINE	JOHN				46	GERMANY	LU	GERMAN	FARMER	081	F		22
LEVINGSTON	ELIZABETH			1	55	IRELAND	CE	IRISH		082	A		77
LEVINGSTON	JAMES				67	IRELAND	WM	IRISH	F	082	A		60
LEVINS	THOMAS		1		16	ONT	CS	SCOTCH		082	A		34
LEVINS	WILLIAM				34	IRELAND	CE	IRISH	F	082	A		34
LEVINS	WILLIAM		1		25	O	CE	ENGLISH	LUMBERMAN	088	C		10
LEWIS	DAVID				28	O	EP	IRISH	F	087	B	3	8
LEWIS	DAVID				26	O	EM	IRISH	F	087	B	3	9
LEWIS	EDWARD				45	ENGLAND	BA	ENGLISH	SHIPWRIGHT	082	E		23
LEWIS	GEORGE				50	ONT	CE	IRISH	FARMER	082	I		52
LEWIS	ROBERT				35	SCOTLAND	PS	SCOTCH	LAB	087	B	2	4
LEWIS	SPANIARD				27	O	RC	INDIAN	HUNTER & TRADER	088	B		12
LEWIS	THOMAS				36	ENGLAND	CE	ENGLISH	F	085	J		26
LEWIS	W	C			46	O	WM	IRISH	HOTELKEEPER	081	A	2	29

SURNAME	NAME1	NAME2	STRAY	SEX	AGE	BIRTHPL	RELIGION	ORIGIN	OCCUP	DIST	SUB_DIST	DIV	PAGE
LEWIS	WILLIAM				47	0	CE	IRISH	F	081	H	2	31
LHINNER	JOSEPH	M			44	CANADA	ME	ENGLISH	F	085	A		2
LIBBE	PHILIP				36	IRELAND	CE	ENGLISH	F	082	F		4
LIBBY	JOHN				35	IRELAND	CE	ENGLISH	F	082	F		3
LIBBY	MATTHEW				40	IRELAND	CE	ENGLISH	F	082	G		22
LIBERA	FRANCIS		1		17	GERMANY	RC	GERMAN	SHOEMAKER	081	K		65
LIDTKY	WILLIAM				39	GERMANY	EV	GERMAN	FARMER	082	I		59
LIEDKE	WILLIAM						NG		SEE LIDTKY	082	I		59
LIESK	MATTHEW				33	GERMANY	LU	GERMAN	FARMER	082	I		49
LIFFERY	PETER	SR			58	QUE	RC	FRENCH	F	082	H		21
LIFSK	MARTIN				35	GERMANY	LU	GERMAN	FARMER	082	I		49
LIMINGTON	JAMES		1		80	IRELAND	CE	IRISH	F LABOURER	085	A		29
LIMINGTON	MARY		2	1	31	CANADA	ME			085	A		D
LIMMONS	ARTHUR				23	ENGLAND	PR	ENGLISH	F	085	A		10
LINDERMAN	WILLIAM				49	GERMANY	LU	GERMAN	FARMER	082	I		16
LINDLEY	ANNE		1	1	27	ENGLAND	WM	ENGLISH		085	D		12
LINDSAY	JAMES				46	SCOTLAND	PS	SCOTCH	F	081	H	2	9
LINDSAY	JOHN				54	SCOTLAND	CP	SCOTCH	F	081	A	1	65
LINDSAY	JOHN				35	IRELAND	CE	IRISH	F	085	C		1
LINDSAY	THOMAS				42	SCOTLAND	PS	SCOTCH	F	081	H	2	8
LINDSAY	WILLIAM				50	SCOTLAND	CP	SCOTCH	MILLOWNER	081	A	1	20
LINDSAY	WILLIAM				34	SCOTLAND	PS	SCOTCH	F	081	H	2	10
LINEY	THOMAS		1		25	0	CE	ENGLISH	FARM LAB	082	C	1	41
LINK	ELIZABETH		1	1	21	GERMANY	LU	GERMAN		082	G		29
LINK	FREDRICK		1		19	GERMANY	LU	GERMAN	FARMER	082	G		29
LINKLATER	THOMAS				40	SCOTLAND	CS	SCOTCH	FUR TRADER	088	B		14
LINN	RICHARD				40	IRELAND	CS	IRISH	F	085	C		18
LIPKEY	JOHN				33	GERMANY	PR	GERMAN	F	082	G		16
LIPSET	JOHN		1		64	IRELAND	CE	IRISH	FARMER	081	D		4
LIPSET	ROBERT				70	IRELAND	CE	IRISH	FARMER	081	D		5
LIPSET	ROBERT				28	0	CE	IRISH	FARMER	081	D		5
LIPSEY	JOHN				25	0	CE	IRISH	SERVANT	081	D		7
LISHE	BARBARA			1	48	SCOTLAND	PS	SCOTCH		087	B	2	5
LITLE	BARBERA		1	1	29	IRELAND	CP	IRISH		081	B		63
LITLE	ELENOR		1	1	38	IRELAND	RC	IRISH		082	C	1	38
LITLE	JOHN				46	IRELAND	CP	IRISH	F	082	C	1	38
LITLE	MARGRET			1	64	IRELAND	CE	IRISH		082	E		15
LITLE	WILLIAM				22	0	CP	IRISH		082	C	1	41
LITTLE	ANN		1	1	10	0	WM	IRISH		082	F		19
LITTLE	ANN	JANE	1	1	35	IRELAND	CE	IRISH		082	E		11
LITTLE	BENJAMIN				41	IRELAND	WM	IRISH	BUTCHER	082	E		29
LITTLE	JAMES				42	IRELAND	CE	IRISH	F	082	A		53
LITTLE	JOSUA		1		21	0	WM	IRISH	LABOURER	082	E		30
LITTLE	LUCINDA		1	1	6	0	CE	IRISH		082	E		11
LITTLE	PETER		2		20	0	PA		HUNTER	090	F		D
LITTLE	ROBERT				62	IRELAND	RP	IRISH	F	081	K		9
LITTLE	SAMUEL				35	ONT	WM	IRISH	FARMER	082	I		58
LITTLE	STEWART		1		40	IRELAND	CE	IRISH	BOOKKEEPER	082	E		11
LITTLE	SUSAN	R	1	1	1	0	CE	IRISH		082	E		11
LITTLE	THOMAS				36	0	WM	ENGLISH	FARMER	082	D		18
LITTLE	THOMAS				23	ONT	WM	IRISH	FARMER	082	I		58
LIVINGSTON	JOHN				45	SCOTLAND	CS	SCOTCH	ACCOUNTANT	089	B		6
LIVINGSTON	NEIL				50	SCOTLAND	CP	SCOTCH	JOINER	085	B		19
LIVINGSTON	SUSAN		1		45	IRELAND	CE	IRISH		081	C		53
LIVINGSTON	SUSANA		1	1	13	ONT	NG	IRISH		081	C		53
LIVINGSTONE	HUGH				54	SCOTLAND	RP	SCOTCH	F	081	K		11
LIVINGSTONE	NEIL				46	0	RP	SCOTCH	F	081	K		10
LIVINGSTONE	WILLIAM				71	SCOTLAND	RP	SCOTCH	F	081	K		10
LLOYD	ANNIE			1	53	ENGLAND	CE	ENGLISH		085	A		13
LLOYD	HENRY	R			20	QUE	WM	SCOTTISH	CLERK	082	E		11
LLOYD	JOHN				40	ENGLAND	CE	ENGLISH	BOOKKEEPER	082	E		4
LLOYD	JOHN		1		62	SCOTLAND	WM	SCOTTISH	MERCHANT	082	E		10
LLOYD	SERAH		1	1	61	IRELAND	WM	IRISH		082	E		10
LLOYD	WILLIAM				28	QUE	WM	SCOTTISH	DRUGGIST	082	E		11
LLOYD	WILLIAM				27	ENGLAND	CE	ENGLISH	BOARD H KEEPER	086	B		3
LOBB	SAMUEL				45	ENGLAND	CE	ENGLISH	MINE LABOURER	089	A		11
LOCKHEED	THOMAS		1		28	IRELAND	CE	IRISH	STAVE MAKER	088	B		21
LOFTIS	ANNIE		1	1	17	0	RC	IRISH	SERVANT	081	B		84
LOGAN	JAMES				27	ONTARIO	CS	IRISH	LAB	082	A		50
LOGAN	JAMES		1		25	0	WM	SCOTCH	F LAB	085	J		16
LOGAN	SOPHA			1	45	ONTARIO	CS	IRISH	F	082	A		44
LONEY	MARGARET		1	1	10	ONTARIO	EM	IRISH		082	A		65
LONG	BENJAMIN				52	ENGLAND	WM	ENGLISH	F	085	J		17
LONG	JAMES				43	ENGLAND	WM	ENGLISH	AUCTIONEER	085	I		11
LONG	WILLIAM				49	GERMANY	FW	GERMAN	F	082	H		11
LONGBO	J	B				QUE	RC	FRENCH	LAB	081	I		26
LONGHURST	FREDERICK				27	0	WM	ENGLISH	F	085	J		26
LONGISE	PETER				22	0	RC	FRENCH	LUMBERMAN	086	C	1	10
LONGLOW	MARY			1	36	QUE	RC	FRENCH	WASHWOMAN	082	E		24
LONZO	ANNIE		1	1	16	0	RC	FRENCH		081	K		37
LONZO	EDWARD		1		23	QUE	RC	FRENCH		081	K		37
LORMER	WILLIAM				31	SCOTLAND	PS	SCOTCH	F	085	E		5
LOROCHE	JOSEPH				45	QUE	RC	FRENCH	F	082	K	1	1
LORTIE	FRANCIS		1		26	QUE	RC	FRENCH	LUMBERMAN	088	B		2
LOTHIAN	E		1		24	QUE	CP	SCOTCH	LAB	090	D		1
LOTT	DAVID		1		30	QUE	RC	FRENCH	LUMBERMAN	088	C		11
LOUACE	JAMES				49	ONT	CE	IRISH	FARMER	082	I		51
LOUBITZ	CHRISTIAN				41	GERMANY	LU	GERMAN	FARMER	082	I		22
LOUCKS	HENRY	H			33	0	CE	FRENCH	BARRISTER	082	E		9
LOUDEN	JOHN		1		22	SCOTLAND	CP	SCOTCH	F	085	L		10
LOUDITT	GEORGE		1		16	0	RC	ENGLISH	HUNTER	090	F		6
LOUDITT	SAMUEL				31	JAMES BAY	CP	SCOTCH	LAB	090	F		20
LOUDITT	SARAH		2	1		0	CP			090	F		D
LOUGH	ALEXANDER		1		14	0	CP	SCOTCH		081	A	1	1
LOUGH	ROBERT		1		16	0	CP	SCOTCH	STORE CLERK	081	A	1	1
LOUGH	WILLIAM		1		18	0	CP	SCOTCH		081	A	1	1
LOUGHEAD	THOMAS				37	IRELAND	PR	IRISH	F	085	A		17
LOUGHEAD	WILLIAM				24	ONT	PR	IRISH	F	085	A		16
LOUGHEED	ROBERT				28	IRELAND	CE	IRISH	F	085	I		39
LOUGHEED	SAMUEL				38	IRELAND	CP	IRISH	F	085	I		42
LOUIS	CHARLES				23	0	RC	FRENCH	LAB	090	F		9
LOUIS	SIMON				32	0	RC	FRENCH	LAB	090	F		21
LOUIS	SOLOMON		2		10	0	RC			088	A		D
LOUKEY	LAGERUNED				33	QUE	RC	UNKNOWN	LAB	082	C	2	38
LOUNT	CHARLES	W			45	0	WM	ENGLISH	BARRISTER	085	C		21
LOUSAW	ELIER				41	QUE	RC	FRENCH	SHOEMAKER	081	B		37

SURNAME	NAME1	NAME2	STRAY	SEX	AGE	BIRTHPL	RELIGION	ORIGIN	OCCUP	DIST	SUB_DIST	DIV	PAGE
LOUSON	PETER				52	QUE	RC	FRENCH	F	082	C	1	32
LOUTHIER	JOSEPH				65	QUE	RC	FRENCH	LAB	082	C	1	63
LOVE	JAMES		1		19	CANADA	PS	SCOTCH	LAB	087	B	2	3
LOVE	ROBERT		1		23	CANADA	PS	SCOTCH	LAB	087	B	2	3
LOVE	THOMAS								SEE LANE	082	B		46
LOVE	THOMAS		1		21	CANADA	PS	SCOTCH	LAB	087	B	2	3
LOVELY	PATRICK				52	IRELAND	RC	IRISH	F	085	D		19
LOWE	DAVID				44	SCOTLAND	PS	SCOTCH	BAKER	085	C		10
LOWE	JOHN				51	IRELAND	CE	IRISH	FARMER	082	I		74
LOWE	JOHN				22	ENGLAND	WM	ENGLISH	FISHERMAN	088	A		6
LOWE	MARY		2	1	58	IRELAND	CP					1	D
LOWE	THOMAS				30	IRELAND	WM	IRISH	FARMER	082	I		74
LOWE	WILLIAM				55	IRELAND	CP	IRISH	F	081	A	1	69
LOWE	WILLIAM		1		19	INDIA	CE	ENGLISH	F	085	K	2	7
LOWERY	WILLIAM		1		50	IRELAND	CE	IRISH	LABOURER	082	E		25
LOWIN	SAMUEL				56	ENGLAND	BA	ENGLISH	CARPENTER	081	D		10
LUCAS	JAMES				47	ENGLAND	PS	ENGLISH	F	085	C		15
LUCE	BENJIMAN		1		11	UNITED STATES	RC	ENGLISH		089	A		56
LUDGATE	ANTONY				44	IRELAND	CE	IRISH	LAB	081	A	1	13
LUDGATE	JOHN				45	IRELAND	RC	IRISH	F	081	K		40
LUDGATE	MICHAEL				32	IRELAND	RC	IRISH	F	081	K		48
LUGOW	FRANCES		1	1	16	AUSTRIA	RC	AUSTRIAN	SERVANT	082	E		71
LUKE	BENJAMEN				67	IRELAND	CE	IRISH	MINE LABOURER	089	A		14
LUKE	JOHN				23	GERMANY	RC	GERMAN	F	082	G		87
LULOFF	JOHN				43	GERMANY	LU	GERMAN	F	082	H		21
LUMMIX	SAMUEL				31	0	CE	IRISH	BLACKSMITH	081	B		8
LUMMIX	SAMUEL		2			0	CE			081	B		D
LUMSDEN	ANN		1	1	14	0	CS	IRISH		081	A	1	61
LUMSDEN	JAMES				54	SCOTLAND	PS	SCOTCH	F	086	A	1	9
LUMSDON	EDWARD				33	0	CE	ENGLISH	LABOURER	082	D		21
LUNNE	RICHARD				50	ENGLAND	CE	ENGLISH	F	081	J	1	55
LUNNEY	ELIZA		1	1	20	0	RC	IRISH		082	E		13
LURLEY	JOSEPH				46	NOVA SCOTIA	PS	DANISH	MILL WRIGHT	087	B	2	1
LUTES	CHARLES				45	GERMANY	PS	DUTCH	F	086	A	1	28
LYLE	JAMES				34	IRELAND	OP	IRISH	F	082	G		62
LYN	DANIEL				46	IRELAND	RC	IRISH	F	081	A	2	60
LYN	HUGH				41	IRELAND	RC	IRISH	F	081	A	2	60
LYN	MICHAEL				35	0	RC	IRISH		081	A	2	61
LYNCH	CATHERINE			1	50	IRELAND	RC	IRISH		081	J	2	2
LYNCH	DENNIS				62	IRELAND	RC	IRISH	F	081	J	1	23
LYNCH	JAMES				60	IRELAND	CE	IRISH	F	081	H	2	33
LYNCH	JERAMIAH				55	IRELAND	RC	IRISH	F	081	J	1	25
LYNCH	JOHN				56	IRELAND	RC	IRISH	SHOEMAKER	081	G	2	3
LYNCH	JOHN		2			0	RC			081	J	2	D
LYNCH	THOMAS		2		14	0	RC			081	J	2	D
LYNCH	TIMOTHY				38	IRELAND	RC	IRISH	F	081	J	2	3
LYNN	JAMES				33	0	RC	ENGLISH	DOCTOR OF MEDICINE	081	I		9
LYNN	SAMUEL	GOODENOUGH			55	ENGLAND	RC	ENGLISH	CROWN LAND AGENT	081	K		61
LYON	JOHN				41	SCOTLAND	CP	SCOTCH	BAILIFF	081	B		50
LYON	MARY	ANN	2	1	19	0	CP			081	B		D
LYON	RICHARD								SEE RICHARD L	081	B		85
LYON	ROBINSON				60	SCOTLAND	CP	SCOTCH	HOTELKEEPER	081	B		29
LYON	WILLIAM				73	SCOTLAND	CP	SCOTCH	SHOEMAKER	081	B		48
LYONS	ALEXANDER				48	QUE	CE	ENGLISH	FARMER	082	D		27
LYONS	ANN	P J	1	1	7	IRELAND	CE	IRISH		082	G		65
LYONS	FRANCES		1	1	4	IRELAND	CE	IRISH		082	G		66
LYONS	GEORGE		1		56	SCOTLAND	PS	SCOTCH	SERVANT	089	A		15
LYONS	HENRY				35	IRELAND	CE	IRISH	FARMER	082	B		30
LYONS	JOHN				36	IRELAND	RC	IRISH	F	082	K	2	1
LYONS	ROBERT	A			41	SCOTLAND	PS	SCOTCH	LUMBER MERCHANT & GE	087	B	2	2
LYONS	SUSAN		1	1	33	IRELAND	CE	IRISH		082	G		65
LYONS	SUSAN		1	1	5	IRELAND	CE	IRISH		082	G		65
LYONS	THOS				60	IRELAND	RC	IRISH	F	081	J	1	71
LYONS	WILLIAM		1		24	ENGLAND	CE	ENGLISH	SERVANT	085	B		8
LYSK	CHRISTOPHER				24	GERMANY	LU	GERMAN	F	082	G		72
LYSK	JOHN				29	PRUSSIA	LU	PRUSSIAN	F	082	G		72
LYSNAN	MARTIN				37	GERMANY	LU	GERMAN	F	082	G		3
LYTLE	JOHN				27	0	CP	IRISH		082	C	1	41
LYTTON	LORENZO	NIXON			49	IRELAND	CE	IRISH	F	085	I		21
MAAP	CHRISTIAN				43	GERMANY	LU	GERMAN	FARMER	082	I		22
MAAP	GUSTAV				47	GERMANY	LU	GERMAN	FARMER	082	I		21
MAAS	CHARLES		1		57	GERMANY	NC	GERMAN	FARMER	082	I		5
MAAS	HANNAH		1	1	62	GERMANY	NC	IRISH		082	I		5
MACARTHY	MAURICE		1		25	IRELAND	CE	IRISH	F	085	C		27
MACDONALD	JOHN	A			36	0	CP	SCOTCH	FARMER	084	E		4
MACDONALD	MICHEL				31	MANITOBA	RC	SCOTCH	HUNTER & FARMER	081	C		41
MACFIE	JAMES		1		44	SCOTLAND	CP	SCOTCH	F	086	A	2	6
MACHOR	MATTHEW				40	GERMANY	LU	GERMAN	F	082	G		85
MACKAY	BRYAN				30	0	RC	IRISH	HOTEL KEEPER	087	B	3	1
MACKAY	WILLIAM		2		3	0	RC			087	B	3	D
MACKENZIE	RODERICK	DOUGLAS			24	SCOTLAND	CE	SCOTCH	CLERK	084	C		2
MACKEY	ALEXANDER				30	0	RC	SCOTCH	LAB	081	B		21
MACKEY	CILIA		1	1	13	SCOTLAND	CS	SCOTCH		081	B		25
MACKEY	MATILDA			1	32	0	CE	ENGLISH		081	B		73
MACKIE	DANIEL				25	0	RC	IRISH	LABOURER	089	B		44
MACKIE	DAVID				66	SCOTLAND	CP	SCOTCH	CARPENTER			1	79
MACKLAM	GEORGE				41	SCOTLAND	PS	SCOTCH	CARPENTER	081	H	2	7
MACKWASON	JOHN				40	0	CE	INDIAN	LUMBERMAN	089	B		33
MACKY	CATHARINE		1	1	61	IRELAND	RC	IRISH		082	L		2
MACKY	JOHN				51	IRELAND	RC	IRISH	FARMER	081	G	1	14
MACKY	LAURANCE		1		57	IRELAND	RC	IRISH	F	082	L		1
MACLEAN	DONALD	J			33	NS	CP	SCOTCH	CLERGYMAN	081	B		33
MACWABBA	CATHERINE			1	80	QUEBEC	RC	INDIAN		084	D		4
MADDEN	PATRICK		1		20	0	RC	IRISH	LAB	081	B		55
MADDEN	THOS		1		18	0	RC	IRISH	LAB	081	B		55
MADDON	CHRIS	H			41	IRELAND	ME	IRISH	F	085	A		14
MADELLE	JOHN				58	IRELAND	WM	IRISH	F	085	J		20
MADEN	THOMAS		1		47	IRELAND	RC	IRISH		081	A	1	36
MADIGAN	DANIEL				24	ONTARIO	RC	IRISH	FARMER	081	G	2	1
MADIGAN	DENNIS				56	IRELAND	RC	IRISH	F	082	G		11
MADIGAN	MARY		1	1	34	IRELAND	RC	IRISH	SERVANT	081	K		69
MADIGAN	THOMAS				59	IRELAND	RC	IRISH	F	081	J	2	7
MADISON	JOSEPH				51	QUE	RC	FRENCH	F	082	K	1	5
MADORE	CATHARIN		1	1		0	RC	FRENCH		082	C	1	8
MAGAMONKA	JAMES				25	0	WM	INDIAN	HUNTER	086	C	2	4
MAGAMONKA	JOHN				40	0	WM	INDIAN	HUNTER	086	C	2	4

SURNAME	NAME1	NAME2	STRAY	SEX	AGE	BIRTHPL	RELIGION	ORIGIN	OCCUP	DIST	SUB_DIST	DIV	PAGE
MAGEE	HANAH		1	1	10	O	RC	SWEDE		082	H		22
MAGGOBU	FRANCIS				60	O	RC	INDIAN	HUNTER	090	F		8
MAGHUE	EDWARD				58	QUEBEC	RC	FRENCH	F	081	J	1	18
MAGHUE	PETER				32	ONT	RC	FRENCH	F	081	J	1	18
MAGILLIVERY	WILLIAM		1		18	O	RC	SCOTCH		086	B		1
MAGINLY	RICHARD				30	O	RC	IRISH	F	082	L		3
MAGLENCY	MICHAEL				30	PRUSSIA	RC	PRUSSIAN	FARMER	083	A	1	18
MAGOR	WILLIAM				58	ENGLAND	CE	ENGLISH	F	085	E		2
MAGRATH	BRIDGET		1			O	RC			082	H		D
MAGRATH	DANIEL				40	IRELAND	RC	IRISH	F	082	H		16
MAGRATH	WILLIAM				32	IRELAND	RC	IRISH	F	082	H		16
MAGU	MATHEW				35	O	CE	ENGLISH	F	082	C	2	20
MAGUIRE	JOHN				42	IRELAND	CE	IRISH	F	085	A		16
MAGUTNAK	JACOB				62	O	RC	INDIAN	INDIAN CHIEF	090	F		10
MAHAIN	ROGER				28	IRELAND	CE	IRISH	F	085	E		19
MAHAN	JAMES				55	IRELAND	RC	IRISH	FARMER	081	G	1	35
MAHAN	JOHN				51	IRELAND	RC	IRISH	LAB	081	B		45
MAHAN	MARGRET		1	1	25	IRELAND	RC	IRISH		081	B		41
MAHAN	WILLIAM				67	IRELAND	RC	IRISH	FARMER	081	F		9
MAHAR	MARY			1	60	IRELAND	RC	IRISH		081	F		27
MAHAR	MATHEW				26	O	RC	IRISH	FARMER	081	F		27
MAHER	BRIDGET		1	1	20	O	RC	IRISH	SERVANT	081	K		71
MAHER	JAMES		1		48	IRELAND	RC	IRISH	F	082	L		4
MAHEW	FRANCIS				45	QUE	RC	FRENCH	FARMER	082	I		24
MAHEW	NARCISS				40	QUE	RC	FRENCH	FARMER	082	I		47
MAHIEU	ANTONINE				62	QUE	RC	FRENCH	F	082	C	1	60
MAHINEY	WM				37	IRELAND	CE	IRISH	F	085	L		9
MAHON	BRIDGET		1	1	17	ONTARIO	RC	IRISH		082	A		33
MAHON	LUCY	ANNE	1	1	22	ONTARIO	RC	IRISH		082	B		5
MAHON	MARIA		1	1	14	ONTARIO	RC	IRISH		082	B		5
MAHON	THOMAS		1		19	ONTARIO	RC	IRISH		082	B		5
MAHONEY	JAMES				55	IRELAND	RC	IRISH	F	081	C		15
MAHONEY	MICHAEL				26	IRELAND	RC	IRISH	SHOEMAKER	081	G	1	47
MAHONY	JOHN		1		20	IRELAND	RC	IRISH	SHOEMAKER	081	K		71
MAHY	JAMES				41	QUE	CE	ENGLISH	PAINTER	082	E		34
MAIANGOWI	LOUIS				52	US	RC	INDIAN	F	087	A		26
MAINEY	MARGARET		2	1		O	RC			082	G		D
MAINGAIN	PAUL				110	QUEBEC	RC	INDIAN	HUNTER	083	E		1
MAINPRISE	JOHN		1		25	O	CE	SCOTCH	MILLER	085	A		14
MAIONGOWE	BENJAMIN				28	O	RC	INDIAN	F & FISHERMAN	087	A		30
MAISHEQUONGGAI	ALBERT				21	O	CE	INDIAN	LABOURER	087	B	1	14
MAISHEQUONGGAI	JOHN				65	O	CE	INDIAN	F & CHIEF	087	B	1	14
MAITAHBAI	PETER				40	O	CE	INDIAN	F	087	B	1	12
MAKATEOTAWA	ALEXANDRE				29	O	RC	INDIAN	F & COOPER	087	A		38
MAKATEOTAWA	LOUIS				32	US	RC	INDIAN		087	A		37
MAKATEOTAWA	PIERRE				61	US	RC	INDIAN	F & FISHERMAN	087	A		37
MAKATEOTAWA	PIERRE	JR			34	US	RC	INDIAN	F & FISHERMAN	087	A		37
MALBEF	JOSEPH				28	QUE	RC	FRENCH	F	082	L		3
MALETT	ALEXR				46	QUE	RC	FRENCH	PILOT ON RAFT	082	E		63
MALETTE	GILBERT				51	QUE	RC	FRENCH	FARMER	082	I		49
MALEY	JAMES				60	IRELAND	RC	IRISH	FARMER	081	G	1	18
MALKAHHARRAH	GUY		2		30	O	ME		HUNTER & TRAPPER	090	C		D
MALLAN	ARTHUR		1		30	O	RC	IRISH	COOK	085	F		5
MALLARD	DAVID				58	ENGLAND	WM	ENGLISH	F	087	B	3	3
MALLARD	MARGRET		1	1	97	IRELAND	CE	IRISH		081	A	1	15
MALLARD	THOMAS				30	O	ME	ENGLISH	CARPENTER	086	C	1	4
MALLET	ANTION		1		45	QUE	RC	FRENCH	LAB	084	D		5
MALONE	BERNARD		1		20	US	WM	IRISH		081	A	2	29
MALONE	BERNARD				26	IRELAND	RC	IRISH	FARMER	081	G	1	1
MALONE	EDWARD				35	IRELAND	RC	IRISH	FARMER	081	G	1	5
MALONE	GEORGE				36	IRELAND	RC	IRISH	FARMER	081	G	1	1
MALONE	JAMES				36	IRELAND	RC	IRISH	SHOEMAKER	081	G	1	6
MALONE	PATRICK				25	IRELAND	RC	IRISH	FARMER	081	G	1	6
MALONE	PHILLIP				30	IRELAND	RC	IRISH	FARMER	081	G	1	2
MALONEY	MICK		1		20	QUE	RC	IRISH	SHANTYMAN	082	E		18
MALONEY	PATRICK				45	IRELAND	RC	IRISH	F	082	G		79
MALORY	ANN		2	1	39	O	EM			085	D		D
MALOY	PATRICK				45	IRELAND	RC	IRISH		082	C	1	35
MALPAS	EDWARD	W			25	ENGLAND	CE	ENGLISH	MERCHANT	085	I		6
MANDAMIS	AMABLE				25	ONTARIO	RC	INDIAN	HUNTER	083	C		6
MANDERS	JAMES		1		45	HUDSON BAY	EP	ENGLISH	BUSHRANGER	090	D		9
MANDERS	MARY		1	1	23	IRELAND	RC	IRISH	SERVANT	082	E		20
MANEY	PAT				55	IRELAND	RC	IRISH	SHOEMAKER	082	G		78
MANGAN	CHARLES		1		4	IRELAND	RC	IRISH		081	K		19
MANGAN	MARGRET		2	1		O	RC			081	A	2	D
MANGAN	MARTIN		1		32	IRELAND	RC	IRISH	PLASTERER	081	K		19
MANGAN	MARY		1	1	28	IRELAND	RC	IRISH		081	K		19
MANGAN	MATHEW		1	1	2	IRELAND	RC	IRISH		081	K		19
MANGAN	MATHEW				28	IRELAND	RC	IRISH	F	081	K		20
MANGAN	PATRICK				45	IRELAND	RC	IRISH	F	081	J	1	55
MANGAN	PATRICK				42	IRELAND	RC	IRISH	F	085	I		14
MANGANE	JOHN				31	IRELAND	RC	IRISH	F	081	J	1	59
MANGEN	JOHN				37	IRELAND	CE	IRISH	INNKEEPER	082	D		29
MANGHIR	AUGUST		1		13	GERMANY	CE	GERMAN		081	G	1	34
MANGHIR	HENRY		1		8	GERMANY	CE	GERMAN		081	G	1	34
MANINGTON	EDMOND		1		36	ENGLAND	CE	ENGLISH	HUNTER	085	E		17
MANION	MARTIN	SR			67	IRELAND	RC	IRISH	F	082	H		3
MANION	PATRICK		1		24	O	RC	IRISH	LUMBERMAN	082	H		8
MANITOWABI	LOUIS				60	US	RC	INDIAN	F & FISHERMAN	087	A		13
MANITOWABI	PIERRE				30	US	RC	INDIAN	F & FISHERMAN	087	A		13
MANITOWABI	SIMON				24	US	RC	INDIAN	F & FISHERMAN	087	A		14
MANLY	DAVID				48	IRELAND	RC	IRISH	F	081	J	2	2
MANN	JAMES		1		25	O	CS	SCOTCH	DOCTOR MEDICINE	081	I		10
MANNING	BRIDGET			1	55	IRELAND	RC	IRISH	F	083	C		17
MANNING	JAMES		1		24	O	RC	IRISH	SHANTY MAN	085	E		27
MANSON	JOHN				30	IRELAND	CE	IRISH	CARPENTER	081	D		9
MANSOR	WILLIAM				27	O	CP	ENGLISH	F	085	E		30
MANTIFLE	CHAS				60	GERMANY	LU	GERMAN	F	082	G		4
MANY	JOHN		1		24	O	RC	IRISH	F	082	G		79
MANY	LAURENCE				42	IRELAND	RC	IRISH	FARMER	081	F		24
MAQUASH	BATISE		1		18	O	RC	INDIAN	LABOURER	089	A		48
MAQUASH	LOUIS		1		20	O	RC	INDIAN	LABOURER	089	A		48
MAQUASH	MISHELL		1		13	O	RC	INDIAN		089	A		48
MAQUILLEN	JOHN		1		27	IRELAND	RC	IRISH		086	B		1
MARCELLA	EDWARD		1		13	MOOSE FACTORY	CP	INDIAN		090	F		20
MARCELLA	GEORGE		1		30	MOOSE FACTORY	CP	FRENCH	LAB	090	F		20

SURNAME	NAME1	NAME2	STRAY	SEX	AGE	BIRTHPL	RELIGION	ORIGIN	OCCUP	DIST	SUB_DIST	DIV	PAGE
MARCELLA	JAMES				35	HUDSON'S BAY	RC	FRENCH	LABOURER	090	E		1
MARCH	JANE		1	1	72	SCOTLAND	CS	SCOTCH		089	B		9
MARCILA	PETER				50	QUE	RC	FRENCH	F	081	E		21
MARCOTT	HENRY		1		23	QUE	WM	FRENCH	FARM LAB	082	C	1	27
MARCOTTE	ADOLPHUS		1		21	QUE	RC	FRENCH	LAB	090	D	1	1
MARCOTTE	ELI				52	QUE	RC	FRENCH	F	082	C	1	7
MARCUS	MARTIN				38	GERMANY	EV	GERMAN	F	082	H		24
MARIA	MERION		1		8	ONTARIO	RC	FRENCH		084	D		1
MARION	PETER				53	QUE	RC	FRENCH	GENTLEMAN	082	E		69
MARK	DANIEL		1		27	O	CE	IRISH	BLACKSMITH	082	E		33
MARKEE	LOUIS				22	QUE	RC	FRENCH	LAB	086	B		5
MARKEL	JEREMIAH		1		17	O	WM	SCOTCH		085	J		17
MARKEL	MATHEW				57	O	WM	SCOTCH	F	085	J		17
MARKHAM	SARAH		1	1	20	O	BA	ENGLISH		086	C	1	1
MARKS	ELIZABETH		1	1	34	QUE	CE	ENGLISH	SEAMSTRESS	081	B		11
MARKS	GEORGE				41	IRELAND	CE	IRISH	STORE KEEPER	089	A		22
MARKS	JOHN				45	IRELAND	CE	IRISH	MERCHANT	089	A		55
MARKS	MARTIN				57	POLAND	RC	POLISH	F	081	C		32
MARKS	SAMUEL				27	IRELAND	CE	IRISH	FISH MERCHANT	089	A		65
MARKS	THOMAS				36	IRELAND	CE	IRISH	STORE KEEPER	089	A		44
MARKSONQUAW	JAMES				30	O	CE	INDIAN	LUMBERMAN	089	B		34
MARLOW	PETER				25	QUE	RC	FRENCH	FARMER	082	I		71
MARRAH	ALEX		1		21	SCOTLAND	PS	SCOTCH	F	085	J		16
MARRAW	WILLIAM				43	IRELAND	EM	IRISH	F	081	J	1	51
MARRON	JOHN				29	IRELAND	CE	IRISH	FARMER	082	I		76
MARSELLAS	CHARLES				61	UNITED STATES	CP	NOT GIVEN	SHOEMAKER	081	B		68
MARSHALL	GEORGE				36	ONTARIO	CS	ENGLISH	F	082	A		53
MARSHALL	GEORGE				26	QUE	CE	ENGLISH	FARMER	089	B		20
MARSHALL	HENRY		1		30	GERMANY	RC	GERMAN	LAB	090	D		7
MARSHALL	JAMES				35	ONTARIO	WM	ENGLISH	F	082	A		59
MARSHALL	JOHN				41	ONTARIO	CE	ENGLISH	BLACKSMITH	082	A		45
MARSHALL	ROBERT				52	ENGLAND	CE	ENGLISH	FARMER	089	B		20
MARSHALL	THOMAS	GEORGE			49	IRELAND	CE	IRISH	F	084	D		5
MARSHALL	WM				25	SCOTLAND	CP	SCOTCH	F	085	L		1
MARSTON	ALEXANDER				48	ONTARIO	CE	ENGLISH	F	083	C		3
MARTELL	ABRAHAM		1		24	UNITED STATES	RC	FRENCH	FISHERMAN	089	A		63
MARTELL	N		1		25	QUE	RC	FRENCH		081	I		39
MARTIN	BRIDGET			1	56	IRELAND	RC	IRISH		082	E		43
MARTIN	CHARLES				35	ENGLAND	CE	ENGLISH	SHOE MAKER	085	E		4
MARTIN	CHRISTEIN				64	GERMANY	LU	GERMAN	F	082	J		9
MARTIN	CHRISTOPHER				24	IRELAND	PR	IRISH	F	082	G		50
MARTIN	CHRISTOPHER				70	IRELAND	CE	IRISH	F	085	D		21
MARTIN	EDWARD				25	CANADA	WM	ENGLISH	LAB	087	B	2	2
MARTIN	FELIX				74	QUE	RC	FRENCH	PILOT	081	B		37
MARTIN	FRANK		1		23	QUE	RC	FRENCH	LUMBERMAN	086	C	1	7
MARTIN	GEORGE				25	QUEBEC	RC	FRENCH	LABORER	083	F	2	1
MARTIN	GEORGE				50	ENGLAND	CE	ENGLISH	CORDWAINER	085	E		3
MARTIN	GILBERT		1		16	Q	RC	FRENCH		086	B		1
MARTIN	HILLYARD				40	QUE	RC	FRENCH	WAGGONMAKER	081	B		8
MARTIN	ISABELLA			1	48	SCOTLAND	CE	SCOTCH		081	H	2	2
MARTIN	JAMES				25	IRELAND	RC	IRISH	LAB	081	A	2	35
MARTIN	JAMES		2		18	IRELAND	CE	IRISH		085	D		D
MARTIN	JAMES				37	ENGLAND	WM	ENGLISH	MINER	089	A		1
MARTIN	JAMES		1		34	SCOTLAND	RC	SCOTCH	LAB	090	F		16
MARTIN	JANE			1	40	O	PS	IRISH	F	082	G		46
MARTIN	JENNET			1	50	SCOTLAND	CS	SCOTCH	F	081	H	1	1
MARTIN	JOHN				36	QUE	RC	IRISH	STATION AGENT	081	B		32
MARTIN	JOHN				49	O	WM	IRISH	MASON	081	B		74
MARTIN	JOHN				60	SCOTLAND	CS	SCOTCH	F	081	H	1	1
MARTIN	JOHN				31	O	CE	IRISH	F	082	C	2	26
MARTIN	JOHN				35	IRELAND	CE	IRISH	F	082	G		37
MARTIN	JOHN				48	ENGLAND	CE	ENGLISH	F	085	J		23
MARTIN	MARY		1	1	11	O	RC	IRISH		082	E		62
MARTIN	MATHEW				30	GERMANY	LU	GERMAN	F	082	G		89
MARTIN	MAXIME		1		25	QUE	RC	FRENCH	LAB	090	F		25
MARTIN	ROBERT				46	IRELAND	RP	IRISH	FARMER	082	I		9
MARTIN	SISTER			1	45	FRANCE	RC	FRENCH	NUN SUPERIOR	090	F		11
MARTIN	THOMAS				65	ENGLAND	CE	ENGLISH	FARMER	081	G	1	31
MARTIN	THOMAS				40	ONTARIO	CE	IRISH	FARMER	082	B		49
MARTIN	WILLIAM				30	ENGLAND	CE	ENGLISH	MERCHANT CLERK	081	G	1	34
MARTIN	WM				35	ENGLAND	WM	ENGLISH	F	085	L		10
MARTINEAU	NARCISSE				45	QUE	RC	FRENCH	F	090	F		16
MARTINS	FERDINAND		1		24	GERMANY	LU	GERMAN	NAVY OFFICER	081	F		30
MARTYN	THOMAS				41	IRELAND	FW	ENGLISH	F	081	A	1	72
MASENHUNMET	ADAM				45	GERMANY	CE	GERMAN	CARPENTER	085	E		15
MASEQUANQUE	MARY		1	1	25	O	RC	INDIAN		090	F		24
MASHECK	PAUL				25	O	RC	INDIAN	HUNTER	084	I	1	6
MASKIMMING	JOHN				27	IRELAND	CP	IRISH	FARMER	082	I		27
MASKIMMING	THOMAS				54	IRELAND	CP	IRISH	FARMER	082	I		28
MASON	BENJAMIN				28	O	CP	ENGLISH	F	082	C	1	28
MASON	F	W	1		22	O	CE	ENGLISH	CLOTH FINISHER	081	B		15
MASON	JOHN				33	IRELAND	RC	IRISH	MILLWRIGHT	081	B		81
MASON	PETER		1		30	NG		GREEK	LAB	081	A	2	17
MASON	SAMUEL				39	IRELAND	EM	IRISH	F	081	H	2	43
MASON	SAMUEL		1		61	IRELAND	EM	IRISH	CARPENTER	082	A		74
MASON	WILLIAM				65	UNITED STATES	OB	AFRICAN	F	085	C		16
MASSEY	GEORGE				37	IRELAND	CE	IRISH	F	085	E		24
MASSON	BRIDGET		1	1	26	IRELAND	RC	IRISH		081	C		16
MASSON	HONORAH		1	1	11	ONT	RC	IRISH		081	C		16
MASSON	JAMES		1		1	QUEBEC	RC	FRENCH		081	C		16
MASSON	JOHANNA		1	1	14	ONT	RC	IRISH		081	C		16
MASSON	JOHN		1		19	ONT	RC	IRISH	FARMER	081	C		16
MASSON	LOUIS		1		28	QUEBEC	RC	FRENCH	FARMER	081	C		16
MASSON	MARY		1	1	16	ONT	RC	IRISH		081	C		16
MASSON	MICHAEL		1		22	ONT	RC	IRISH	RAFTSMAN	081	C		16
MASTAR	ALEXANDER		2			O	RC			089	B		D
MASTAR	ANGELIQUE		2	1	22	O	RC			089	B		D
MASTAT	JOHN	BAPTIST			37	O	RC	FRENCH	BOATMAN	089	B		16
MASTAT	RAYMOND		1		86	QUE	RC	FRENCH		089	B		12
MATCHE	JIMIE				45	ONT	ME	INDIAN	HUNTER & TRAPPER	090	B		6
MATCHET	ISAAC				37	IRELAND	PS	IRISH	F	085	J		21
MATCHIIWITA	ONESIME				52	US	RC	INDIAN	F & FISHERMAN	087	A		26
MATHESON	K		1		28	SCOTLAND	CS	SCOTCH	BAKER	088	A		8
MATHESON	WILLIAM				28	SCOTLAND	PS	SCOTCH	CLERK	084	I	1	3
MATHEW	WILLIAM				44	GERMANY	CE	GERMAN	FARMER	086	B		6
MATHEWS	HUGH				45	IRELAND	CE	IRISH	F	085	H		24

SURNAME	NAME1	NAME2	STRAY	SEX	AGE	BIRTHPL	RELIGION	ORIGIN	OCCUP	DIST	SUB_DIST	DIV	PAGE
MATHEWS	JOHN		1		30	0	CP	IRISH	LAB	084	D		5
MATHEWS	LEONARD				33	0	BA	DUTCH	F	086	A	1	7
MATHEWS	NEHEMIAH				41	ENGLAND	PM	ENGLISH	F	085	H		5
MATHEWSON	LAUGHLEN				40	0	CS	SCOTCH	F	082	C	2	54
MATHEWSON	ROBERT				26	SCOTLAND	PS	SCOTCH	F	081	J	1	44
MATHEWSON	THOMAS				38	0	CP	SCOTCH	F	082	C	2	31
MATHEWSON	WILLIAM				28	SCOTLAND	PS	SCOTCH	F	086	A	1	13
MATHIASE	WILLIAM				47	0	WM	GERMAN	F	085	H		13
MATHISON	ROBT		1		19	0	PS	SCOTTISH	AP CABINETMAKER	082	E		56
MATHISON	WILLIAM				28	0	PS	IRISH	FARMER	082	D		30
MATHISON	WILLIAM		2		71	SCOTLAND	PS			082	D		D
MATTHEWS	EDWARD				27	ENGLAND	CE	ENGLISH	CARPENTER	085	I		33
MATTHEWS	JOHN				49	IRELAND	CP	IRISH	FARMER	082	I		36
MATTICE	HANS				50	GERMANY	RC	GERMAN	LAB	081	B		61
MAU	MICHAEL				50	GERMANY	LU	GERMAN	FARMER	082	I		60
MAUDE	FRANCIS	C			42	ENGLAND	CE	ENGLISH	F	085	H		22
MAUGIER	THOMAS				40	IRELAND	RC	IRISH	LAB	081	A	2	6
MAVES	AUGUST				32	GERMANY	LU	GERMAN	FARMER	082	I		17
MAVES	FREDRICK				52	GERMANY	WM	GERMAN	FARMER	082	I		17
MAVIS	THOMAS		1		23	0	CE	SCOTCH	CARPENTER	090	F		19
MAWGOSE	ANTONIE				60	0	PA	INDIAN	HUNTER	088	B		25
MAWHANEY	JOHN				50	IRELAND	CE	IRISH	F	085	H		24
MAWHINEY	MARIANIE		2	1	39	NB	CE			085	H		D
MAXVIL	ROBERT		1		8	0	CE	ENGLISH		082	F		1
MAXWELL	ALEXR				65	SCOTLAND	CP	SCOTCH	F	081	C		53
MAXWELL	SARAH		1	1	13	ONT	CE	ENGLISH		082	I		74
MAY	ALBERT				19	0	WM	ENGLISH	F	085	E		20
MAY	ANNE		1	1	65	IRELAND	CE	IRISH		082	H		14
MAY	ELLEN		1	1	32	0	CE	SCOTCH		081	A	2	25
MAY	FREDERICK				35	0	WM	ENGLISH	F	085	K	2	3
MAY	GEORGE				41	ENGLAND	PM	ENGLISH	F	085	K	2	2
MAY	HENRY		1		24	ENGLAND	CE	ENGLISH	COACHMAN	085	I		5
MAY	HUMPHREY				27	0	EP	0	COOPER	087	B	3	3
MAY	JAMES				25	0	EP	0	COOPER	087	B	3	2
MAY	JANE		1	1	21	0	CE	IRISH		088	A		13
MAY	PHILIP				50	0	CE	IRISH	COOPER	088	A		13
MAY	RICHARD				33	0	WM	ENGLISH	F	085	K	2	2
MAY	SARAH		1	1	29	0	CP	SCOTCH	SERVANT	081	A	2	2
MAY	THOMAS				62	ENGLAND	WM	ENGLISH	F	085	E		21
MAY	WILLIAM		1		35	ENGLAND	CG	ENGLISH	SHANTYMAN	082	E		18
MAYAU	PAUL				30	QUE	RC	FRENCH	SHANTYMAN	082	E		74
MAYHEW										081	J	1	18
MAYHEW	ELKANAH				34	0	WM	FRENCH	AXEMAKER	081	I		41
MAYHEW	JOSEPH				72	UNITED STATES	WM	FRENCH	F	081	H	1	2
MAYHUE	FREE				43	ONT	WM	FRENCH	F	081	J	1	80
MAYHUE	JOSEPH				43	ONT	WM	FRENCH	F	081	J	1	38
MAYHUE	JOSEPH				27	ONT	CP	FRENCH	F	081	J	1	86
MAYHUE	PETER				29	ONT	CE	ENGLISH	F	081	J	1	53
MAYLEH	CATHARINE		1	1	60	IRELAND	RC	IRISH		081	J	1	4
MAYNARD	JAS	E			38	ENGLAND	BA	ENGLISH	MERCHANT TAILOR	081	B		10
MAYNARD	JOHN				62	ENGLAND	WM	ENGLISH	GARDENER	085	I		21
MAYO	PETER				46	ONTARIO	RC	FRENCH	FARMER	081	G	2	6
MAZ	SAMUEL				30	IRELAND	CE	IRISH	F	082	H		15
MCABE	MARY		1	1	60	IRELAND	EM	IRISH		082	G		62
MCABE	ROBERT				40	0	EM	IRISH	F	082	G		61
MCADAM	DANIEL				36	NS	RC	SCOTCH	LAB	081	A	2	60
MCADAM	DUNCAN		1			0	CP	SCOTCH				1	81
MCADAM	JAMES				35	0	CP	IRISH	STATION AGENT	081	A	2	28
MCADAM	JOHN				48	IRELAND	CE	IRISH	SCHOOL TEACHER	081	I		4
MCADAM	WILLIAM				32	0	CP	IRISH	FOREMAN	081	A	1	57
MCADAM	WILLIAM				74	IRELAND	CP	IRISH	FARMER	082	D		1
MCADAMS	MRS			1	60	IRELAND	RC	IRISH	FARMER	081	J	1	2
MCAFFARY	DUNCAN				24	0	PS	SCOTCH	HOTEL KEEPER	085	J		8
MCAFIKE	ROSE			1	45	IRELAND	RC	IRISH	F	082	F		23
MCALESTER	JOHN				32	ONTARIO	CE	IRISH	FARMER	082	B		49
MCALISTER	JAMES				37	IRELAND	CP	IRISH	F	085	B		16
MCALISTER	WILLIAM				33	SCOTLAND	CP	SCOTCH	MINER	090	D		1
MCALLISTER	DUNCAN				50	SCOTLAND	CS	SCOTCH	WEAVER	081	A	1	55
MCALLISTER	JAMES				27	ONTARIO	CS	SCOTCH	F	082	A		39
MCALLISTER	JANE		2	1	73	SCOTLAND	CS					1	D
MCALLISTER	MRS	F	1	1	40	0	RC	SCOTCH		088	C		9
MCALPIN	JOHN				30	SCOTLAND	PS	SCOTCH	MILL OWNER	085	J		26
MCANDREW	JOHN				48	SCOTLAND	CS	SCOTCH	MERCHANT	081	I		30
MCARTHUR	ARCH				20	QUE	CE	ENGLISH	LAB	081	A	2	16
MCARTHUR	JAMES				45	SCOTLAND	CS	SCOTCH	F	081	H	2	5
MCAULY	JOHN				48	IRELAND	CE	IRISH	FARMER	082	I		69
MCBAIN	SARAH		1	1	6	QUE	CP	SCOTCH		081	A	2	17
MCBANE	FLORA		1	1	19	CANADA	PS	SCOTCH		087	B	2	8
MCBANE	JOHN				48	SCOTLAND	PS	SCOTCH	FARMER	089	A		51
MCBLANE	ALECK		1		26	SCOTLAND	PS	SCOTCH	F	085	D		34
MCBOWEN	JAMES				50	IRELAND	WM	IRISH	F	086	A	2	2
MCBRIDE	ARCHIBALD				33	SCOTLAND	CP	SCOTCH	LAB	081	B		75
MCBRIDE	JAMES				30	IRELAND	CP	IRISH	F	085	H		25
MCBRIDE	PHOENIX				25	0	CP	IRISH	F	085	B		17
MCBRIDE	THOMAS				35	IRELAND	WM	IRISH		082	C	1	25
MCBRIDE	WILLIAM				32	IRELAND	CP	IRISH	F	085	H		1
MCCABE	EDWARD				47	IRELAND	RC	IRISH	F	081	E		11
MCCABE	JAMES				55	IRELAND	CE	IRISH	F	085	B		14
MCCABE	JOHN				50	IRELAND	CE	IRISH	SHOEMAKER	081	B		64
MCCABE	THOMAS				66	IRELAND	CP	IRISH	F	082	H		11
MCCACHRAN	WILLIAM				40	IRELAND	CE	IRISH	FARMER	082	I		32
MCCAGHERTY	CATHARINE		1	1	26	0	CE	IRISH		082	C	1	13
MCCAGHERTY	CATHERIN		1	1	20	0	CE	IRISH		082	C	1	19
MCCAGHERTY	ELIZA		2	1	56	IRELAND	CP			082	C	1	D
MCCAGHERTY	ELIZABETH		1	1	5	0	CE	IRISH		082	C	1	13
MCCAGHERTY	PATRICK				60	IRELAND	CP	IRISH	WEAVER	082	C	1	26
MCCAGHERTY	THOMAS	JAMES	1		4	0	CE	IRISH		082	C	1	19
MCCALE	JOHN				21	IRELAND	RC	IRISH	F	081	J	1	91
MCCALLAM	JOHN				42	IRELAND	EM	IRISH	F	081	H	2	16
MCCALLAM	SARAH		2	1	41	0	EM			081	H	2	D
MCCALLUM	A	C			35	SCOTLAND	CP	SCOTCH	BOOKKEEPER	081	A	2	27
MCCALLUM	DUNCAN				75	SCOTLAND	CS	SCOTCH	F	081	A	1	47
MCCALLUM	DUNCAN		2		4	ONT	CP			081	C		D
MCCALLUM	DUNCAN				40	0	CO	SCOTCH	F	085	D		14
MCCALLUM	ELIZABETH		1	1	26	SCOTLAND	CP	SCOTCH	MILLINER	081	B		69
MCCALLUM	GEORGE				40	QUE	CP	SCOTCH	LAB	081	A	2	26

SURNAME	NAME1	NAME2	STRAY	SEX	AGE	BIRTHPL	RELIGION	ORIGIN	OCCUP	DIST	SUB_DIST	DIV	PAGE
MCCALLUM	JOHN				40	O	CS	SCOTCH	SHOEMAKER	081	A	1	36
MCCALLUM	JOHN				28	ONT	CP	SCOTCH	F	081	C		28
MCCALLUM	WILLIAM		2		2	ONT	CP			081	C		D
MCCAMBRAGE	THOMAS		1		36	IRELAND	CE	IRISH	FARM SERVANT	084	E		2
MCCANN	EDWARD				31	IRELAND	RC	IRISH	FARMER	082	B		15
MCCANS	HUGH				43	IRELAND	PS	IRISH	BLACKSMITH	085	E		9
MCCARTER	DAVID				34	SCOTLAND	CP	SCOTCH	LAB	081	B		24
MCCARTHEY	FELIX				60	IRELAND	RC	IRISH	F	082	K	1	7
MCCARTHY	FLORENCE				61	IRELAND	RC	IRISH	MASON	082	C	2	33
MCCARTHY	JOHN				24	O	RC	IRISH	F	081	J	2	1
MCCARTHY	JOHN				50	IRELAND	RC	IRISH	F	083	C		7
MCCARTHY	PATRICK				57	IRELAND	RC	IRISH	F	081	J	2	1
MCCARTY	ALICE			1	59	IRELAND	RC	IRISH		082	E		20
MCCARTY	ANNIE		2	1	73	IRELAND	RC			081	J	1	D
MCCARTY	EUGANIE				27	IRELAND	RC	IRISH	F	081	E		8
MCCARTY	FELIX				30	IRELAND	RC	IRISH	F	082	K	2	1
MCCARTY	FLORANCE				22	US	RC	IRISH	F	082	K	2	2
MCCARTY	FRANCES				32	ONT	RC	IRISH	F	081	J	1	60
MCCARTY	JAMES				44	ONT	RC	IRISH	F	081	J	1	60
MCCARTY	JEREMIAH				32	IRELAND	RC	IRISH	F	082	K	2	1
MCCARTY	JOHN				37	ONT	RC	IRISH	F	081	J	1	59
MCCARTY	JOHN				45	IRELAND	RC	IRISH	F	082	C	2	12
MCCASKEL	FINLAY				61	SCOTLAND	CS	SCOTCH	F	085	D		24
MCCASKILL	DONALD				59	ONTARIO	CS	SCOTCH		082	A		38
MCCASKILL	GEORGE				31	ONTARIO	CS	SCOTCH	F	082	A		41
MCCASKILL	KENNETH				90	SCOTLAND	CS	SCOTCH		082	A		39
MCCASKILL	SAMUEL		1		23	O	PS	SCOTCH	LUMBERMAN	086	B		2
MCCAULEY	JOHN				26	IRELAND	CE	IRISH	F	082	G		31
MCCAUTION	DONALD				39	ONT	RP	SCOTCH	FARMER	082	I		14
MCCAUTION	JOHN	ARCHIBALD	1		2	ONT	WM	SCOTCH	FARMER	082	I		27
MCCAWLEY	JOHANNA		2	1		O	RC			081	F		D
MCCAWLEY	JOHN				39	IRELAND	PS	IRISH	F	085	E		9
MCCAWLEY	PATRICK				45	IRELAND	RC	IRISH	FARMER	081	F		15
MCCHESNEY	GERINIA				40	QUE	CP	SCOTCH	LAB	081	B		84
MCCHESNEY	JOHN		1		20	QUE	CE	IRISH	FARM LAB	082	C	1	38
MCCHESNIE	WESLEY	S	1		22	QUE	CE	IRISH	FARM LAB	082	C	1	39
MCCLAREN	ISABELLA			1	60	SCOTLAND	WM	SCOTCH		086	A	1	17
MCCLAREN	WILLIAM				26	O	WM	SCOTCH		086	A	1	17
MCCLELLAN	DAN		1		21	O	RC	SCOTCH	SHANTYMAN	085	E		27
MCCLELLAN	ROBT				52	IRELAND	CP	IRISH	F	082	C	2	27
MCCLELLAND	DAVID				41	IRELAND	RC	IRISH	F	082	J		14
MCCLELLAND	DAVID				36	O	ME	IRISH	F	085	A		28
MCCLELLAND	HUGH				73	IRELAND	RP	IRISH	FARMER	082	I		8
MCCLELLAND	JOHN				25	IRELAND	WM	IRISH	POST MASTER	086	A	1	25
MCCLELLAND	MOSES				38	IRELAND	ME	IRISH	F	085	A		23
MCCLENNAN	JOHN				68	IRELAND	CE	IRISH	F	082	G		9
MCCLENNAN	WM				43	IRELAND	CE	IRISH	F	082	G		9
MCCLOUD	JOHN		1		21	O	PS	SCOTCH	LUMBERMAN	086	C	1	11
MCCOLLUM	ARCHABLE				46	SCOTLAND	CP	SCOTCH	F	085	E		26
MCCOMB	GEORGE				29	QUE	CE	IRISH	MERCHANT	081	B		2
MCCONEGHY	JAMES				55	IRELAND	WM	IRISH	F	081	H	2	21
MCCONEGHY	JANE		1	1	15	O	CE	IRISH	SERVANT	081	A	1	73
MCCONEGHY	JOHN				31	O	PS	IRISH	F	081	H	2	22
MCCONEGHY	ROBERT				26	O	WM	IRISH	F	081	H	2	22
MCCONEGHY	ROBERT				26	O	WM	IRISH	F	081	H	2	22
MCCONNEL	GEORGE				65	SCOTLAND	PS	SCOTTISH	FARMER	082	D		27
MCCONNELL			1	1	36	IRELAND	CE	IRISH	SERVANT	082	E		12
MCCONNELL	ALEXANDER				25	O	CE	IRISH	F	086	B		5
MCCONNELL	BEN				50	QUE	WM	ENGLISH	GENTLEMAN	082	E		70
MCCONNELL	CECELIA	L	1	1	42	QUEBEC	WM	SCOTCH		084	C		2
MCCONNELL	GEORGE				27	QUE	CP	SCOTCH	F	082	C	2	34
MCCONNELL	HUGH				31	IRELAND	CE	IRISH	F	086	A	1	31
MCCONNELL	JOHN				35	IRELAND	CP	IRISH	F	085	C		1
MCCONNELL	MARIA		1	1	9	QUE	WM	FRENCH		082	E		7
MCCONNELL	RINALDO		1		19	QUEBEC	WM	SCOTCH	CLERK	084	C		2
MCCONNELL	ROBERT				61	QUE	WM	SCOTCH	F	084	D		6
MCCONNELL	WILLIAM				57	SCOTLAND	RP	SCOTCH	F	082	K	1	10
MCCOOL	ELIZA		1	1	18	O	CP	IRISH	SERVANT	082	E		26
MCCOOL	FRANCESE				52	IRELAND	RC	IRISH	F	082	J		19
MCCORMAC	JAMES				27	IRELAND	RC	IRISH	PRIEST	081	G	1	6
MCCORMAC	JOHN				36	IRELAND	RC	IRISH	F	081	K		42
MCCORMAC	M		1	1	24	QUE	CP	IRISH	SERVANT	082	E		11
MCCORMAC	PATRICK				70	IRELAND	RC	IRISH	F	081	K		28
MCCORMAC	THOS				45	IRELAND	RC	IRISH	LABOURER	082	E		62
MCCORMACK	JOHN				29	IRELAND	RC	IRISH	PRIEST	081	D		26
MCCORMIC	WILLIAM				33	O	CE	IRISH	F	082	F		32
MCCORMICK	DONALD				28	SCOTLAND	RC	SCOTCH	F	085	A		4
MCCORMICK	JAMES				46	SCOTLAND	RC	SCOTCH	F	081	A	2	45
MCCORMICK	JOHN				55	QUE	CP	SCOTCH	LAB	081	A	2	11
MCCORMICK	JOHN				55	IRELAND	RP	IRISH	F	082	K	1	9
MCCORMICK	WILLIAM				54	SCOTLAND	CP	SCOTCH	F	081	J	1	84
MCCOSHEN	DONALD						NG		SEE MCCAUTION	082	I		14
MCCOURT	JAMES				55	IRELAND	RC	IRISH	F	082	G		78
MCCOURT	THOMAS				50	IRELAND	RC	IRISH	FARMER	082	B		48
MCCOWAN	GEORGE				54	IRELAND	CE	IRISH	CARPENTER	081	C		26
MCCOWEN	THOMAS				56	IRELAND	CP	IRISH	SAILOR	083	D		1
MCCOWRIE	ANN	ELIZABETH	1	1	10	IRELAND	JM	IRISH		082	C	2	58
MCCOWRIE	THOMAS		1		5	IRELAND	JM	IRISH		082	C	2	58
MCCOY	DANIEL				50	ONT	CS	SCOTCH	F & BLACKSMITH	082	A		29
MCCOY	HENERY	T			26	O	CP	SCOTCH	F	081	E		6
MCCOY	HENRY				63	U STATES	WM	SCOTCH	F	081	J	1	27
MCCOY	JANE		1	1	26	O	RC	IRISH		081	B		17
MCCOY	JOHN				31	QUEBEC	CE	SCOTCH	F	081	J	1	5
MCCOY	OWEN				70	IRELAND	RC	IRISH	F	082	A		15
MCCRACKEN	JANE			1	24	O	CP	IRISH	DRESSMAKER	082	E		11
MCCRACKIN	ELIZABETH				43	IRELAND	CE	IRISH	INNKEEPER	082	C	2	42
MCCRACKIN	MARY			1	48	IRELAND	WM	IRISH	F	082	C	2	36
MCCRAE	JOHN				44	SCOTLAND	CP	SCOTCH	CARPENTER	081	A	1	31
MCCRAE	MARY			1	49	QUE	RC	SCOTCH		081	B		13
MCCRAIG	HARRY		1		26	O	CP	SCOTCH	F LABOURER	085	H		22
MCCRAIGHT	J		1		35	IRELAND	CE	IRISH	SAWYER	088	A		7
MCCRAY	BETRISET		2	1	2	O	CP			085	I		D
MCCRAY	JOHN				36	QUE	CP	SCOTCH	BLACKSMITH FARMER	085	I		24
MCCREA	COLIN		1		29	O	PS	SCOTTISH	LABOURER	082	E		33
MCCREA	EDWARD				47	IRELAND	RC	IRISH	MERCHANT	081	C		51
MCCREA	JAMES	L			26	ONT	NG	IRISH	LUMBERER	081	C		51

SURNAME	NAME1	NAME2	STRAY	SEX	AGE	BIRTHPL	RELIGION	ORIGIN	OCCUP	DIST	SUB_DIST	DIV	PAGE
MCCUE	ANDREW				38	IRELAND	RC	IRISH	F	081	J	1	59
MCCULLOCH	JOHN				54	SCOTLAND	CS	SCOTCH	F	082	A		45
MCCULLOCH	JOHN				45	IRELAND	CP	IRISH	F	085	H		14
MCCULLOCH	THOMAS				50	ENGLAND	CE	ENGLISH	FARMER	089	B		18
MCCULLOCH	THOMAS	JOHN	2		2	0	CP			085	H		D
MCCULLOCH	WILLIAM				43	ONTARIO	CS	SCOTCH	F	082	A		43
MCCULLOUGH	JOSEPHINE		1	1	16	0	RC	IRISH	SERVANT	087	A		2
MCCURDIE	WILLIAM				54	IRELAND	PS	IRISH	F	085	C		24
MCDADE	JOHN		1		17	0	RC	IRISH		081	B		18
MCDANIEL	LEWIS				33	SCOTLAND	CS	SCOTCH	F	081	H	1	4
MCDANIEL	ROBERT				34	IRELAND	CE	IRISH	FARMER	082	I		31
MCDANIELS	JAMES				30	IRELAND	CE	IRISH	LAB	090	F		25
MCDAVIT	MARY		1	1	9	0	RC	IRISH				1	77
MCDEIRMED	JAMES				50	SCOTLAND	CP	SCOTCH	CARPENTER	081	B		53
MCDERMAID	ROBERT				34	0	CS	SCOTCH	F	081	A	1	46
MCDERMENT	MARY		1		27	0	CS	SCOTCH	SERVANT	081	I		42
MCDERMID	J	A	2			0	CP			081	B		D
MCDERMID	JOHN				34	SCOTLAND	RP	SCOTCH	CLARK	081	I		9
MCDERMID	PETER				38	ON SEA	CS	SCOTCH	F	081	H	2	42
MCDERMINT	CHRISTINA			1	42	0	PS		SERVANT	084	F		1
MCDERMOT	HENRY				66	IRELAND	RC	IRISH	FARMER	082	B		12
MCDERMOT	JOHN				30	ONTARIO	CP	SCOTTISH	FARMER	082	B		18
MCDERMOT	MALCOLM				25	ONTARIO	CP	SCOTTISH	FARMER	082	B		18
MCDERMOTT	JAMES				31	IRELAND	RC	IRISH	TINSMITH	081	K		67
MCDERMOTT	MARY		1		44	IRELAND	RC	IRISH		082	A		35
MCDEVIT	CHARLES				20	0	RC	IRISH		081	B		86
MCDEVIT	EDWARD		1		3	0	CP	SCOTCH		081	A	2	54
MCDIARMID	JOHN		2		80	SCOTLAND	FW		F			1	D
MCDIARMID	JOHN				33	0	FW	SCOTCH	F	081	A	1	48
MCDOLE			1		30	QUE	CE	IRISH	CARPENTER	081	B		51
MCDONAL	JAMES				36	0	WM	IRISH	F	085	J		20
MCDONAL	JAMES				37	SCOTLAND	CE	SCOTCH	F	085	J		25
MCDONALD	ALEXANDER				51	SCOTLAND	RC	SCOTCH	F	081	A	1	51
MCDONALD	ALEXANDER						NG		SEE ALEXANDER MCD	081	G	2	3
MCDONALD	ALEXANDER				60	0	RC	SCOTCH	TEACHER	081	K		19
MCDONALD	ALEXANDER		1		53	0	RC	SCOTCH	LAB	082	K	1	1
MCDONALD	ALEXANDER				50	SCOTLAND	PR	SCOTCH	F	085	A		4
MCDONALD	ALEXANDER		1		32	SCOTLAND	PS	SCOTCH	TAILOR	089	A		25
MCDONALD	ALEXD				76	SCOTLAND	RC	SCOTCH	LUMBERMAN	081	A	2	30
MCDONALD	ALXD		1		25	SCOTLAND	RC	SCOTCH	LAB	081	A	2	17
MCDONALD	ANGUS				60	SCOTLAND	RC	SCOTCH	F	081	E		10
MCDONALD	ANGUS				41	0	RC	SCOTCH	FARMER	081	F		12
MCDONALD	ANGUS				36	SCOTLAND	RC	SCOTCH	FARMER	081	G	1	48
MCDONALD	ANGUS		1		19	0	RC	SCOTCH	LUMBERMAN	086	B		2
MCDONALD	ANN		1	1	15	0	PR	SCOTCH	SERVANT	082	G		43
MCDONALD	ARCHIBALD				52	SCOTLAND	CP	SCOTCH	F	081	E		14
MCDONALD	ARCHY				38	SCOTLAND	CS	SCOTCH	BLACKSMITH	082	A		32
MCDONALD	ARCHY				55	SCOTLAND	PS	SCOTCH	F	082	G		97
MCDONALD	CATHERINE		2	1	17	0	PS		SEAMSTRESS	085	A		D
MCDONALD	CATHINE		1	1	13	0	RC	SCOTCH		081	B		13
MCDONALD	CHARLES		1		9	0	PR	SCOTCH		082	G		43
MCDONALD	DAVID				29	QUE	CP	SCOTCH	LAB	081	B		82
MCDONALD	DONALD				38	QUE	RC	SCOTCH	LAB	081	A	2	24
MCDONALD	DONALD		1		33	ONTARIO	RC	SCOTCH	COOK	081	G	1	33
MCDONALD	DONALD				52	ENGLAND	CE	SCOTCH	F	082	G		21
MCDONALD	DONALD				77	0	RC	SCOTCH	F	082	H		30
MCDONALD	DONALD				26	SCOTLAND	PS	SCOTCH	F	086	A	1	11
MCDONALD	DONALD	R			40	ONTARIO	RP	SCOTTISH	BLACKSMITH	082	B		6
MCDONALD	DONKIN				40	0	RC	SCOTCH	F	082	F		34
MCDONALD	DUNCAN				30	QUE	CS	SCOTCH	SAILOR	088	A		7
MCDONALD	DUNCAN				38	0	CS	SCOTCH	LUMBERMAN	088	C		10
MCDONALD	EDWARD				42	SCOTLAND	CP	SCOTCH	F	082	C	1	11
MCDONALD	ELIHU				45	ONTARIO	RC	SCOTCH	FARMER	081	G	1	27
MCDONALD	ELIZABETH		1	1	17	0	CE	SCOTCH	SERVANT	082	H		32
MCDONALD	FINDLY				47	0	RC	SCOTCH	SHANTYMAN	082	G		7
MCDONALD	FLORA		1	1	12	0	RC	IRISH		081	B		11
MCDONALD	GEORGE				71	ENGLAND	CP	SCOTCH	LAB	081	A	1	17
MCDONALD	GRAHAM	J	1		40	ONT	CS	IRISH		081	C		38
MCDONALD	H	JAMES			31	0	EM	SCOTCH	MERCHANT	085	I		1
MCDONALD	HANNAH		1	1	18	0	CS	SCOTCH		081	A	1	44
MCDONALD	HARRIETT	A		1	41	QUE	WM	IRISH		082	C	1	10
MCDONALD	HIRAM				58	0	EM	SCOTCH	CARPENTER	085	I		8
MCDONALD	ISABELLA		1	1	36	0	RC	SCOTCH		081	A	2	25
MCDONALD	ISOBELLA		1	1	26	0	CP	SCOTTISH	DOMESTIC	082	E		10
MCDONALD	JANE		1	1	52	SCOTLAND	PS	SCOTTISH		082	D		4
MCDONALD	JOHN				45	SCOTLAND	RC	SCOTCH	LUMBERMAN	081	A	2	19
MCDONALD	JOHN				35	0	RC	SCOTCH	FOREMAN	081	A	2	27
MCDONALD	JOHN				36	SCOTLAND	RC	SCOTCH	F	081	A	2	40
MCDONALD	JOHN				37	IRELAND	RC	IRISH	LAB	081	B		45
MCDONALD	JOHN				49	SCOTLAND	CP	SCOTCH	LAB	081	B		64
MCDONALD	JOHN				65	SCOTLAND	FK	SCOTCH	SCHOOL TEACHER	081	C		17
MCDONALD	JOHN		2			0	CP			081	E		D
MCDONALD	JOHN				37	0	RC	SCOTCH	FARMER	081	F		12
MCDONALD	JOHN				36	0	RC	SCOTCH	BARRISTER AT LAW	081	I		25
MCDONALD	JOHN				39	IRELAND	PS	IRISH	F	081	J	1	32
MCDONALD	JOHN				46	ONTARIO	CS	SCOTCH	CARPENTER	082	A		46
MCDONALD	JOHN		2		3	0	RP			082	B		D
MCDONALD	JOHN				28	0	CP	SCOTTISH	CARPENTER	082	E		12
MCDONALD	JOHN				44	0	RC	SCOTCH	F	082	F		31
MCDONALD	JOHN				47	SCOTLAND	CP	SCOTCH	F	082	G		38
MCDONALD	JOHN				30	QUEBEC	RC	HALFBREED	HUNTER	084	C		1
MCDONALD	JOHN		1		29	0	RC	SCOTCH	PHYSICIAN	090	F		19
MCDONALD	JOHN	A			40	QUE	RC	SCOTCH	LAB	081	B		78
MCDONALD	JOHN	A	1		23	0	RC	SCOTCH	LAB	081	B		86
MCDONALD	JOHN	R			49	0	RC	SCOTCH	FARMER	081	F		14
MCDONALD	JONATHON				61	SCOTLAND	CP	SCOTCH	F	082	G		38
MCDONALD	MARGARET			1	60	IRELAND	RC	IRISH	F	082	G		47
MCDONALD	MARGRET			1	58	SCOTLAND	RC	SCOTCH		081	A	2	40
MCDONALD	MARTIN				37	IRELAND	RC	IRISH	INNKEEPER	081	H	2	26
MCDONALD	MARY		1	1	23	0	CP	SCOTCH	SERVANT	081	A	2	28
MCDONALD	MARY		1	1	19	0	RC	SCOTCH		081	B		29
MCDONALD	MARY		1	1	21	0	CP	SCOTCH		082	F		6
MCDONALD	MILES		1		24	0	RC	SCOTCH	LUMBERMAN	088	B		18
MCDONALD	MURDOCK				65	SCOTLAND	CS	SCOTCH	F	081	A	1	46
MCDONALD	PAT				33	IRELAND	RC	IRISH		082	G		57
MCDONALD	PETER				33	ONT	PS	SCOTCH	F	081	J	1	33

SURNAME	NAME1	NAME2	STRAY	SEX	AGE	BIRTHPL	RELIGION	ORIGIN	OCCUP	DIST	SUB_DIST	DIV	PAGE
MCDONALD	PETER				50	SCOTLAND	CP	SCOTCH	F	082	G		37
MCDONALD	RANALD		1		53	SCOTLAND	RC	SCOTCH	LUMBERER	083	C		5
MCDONALD	RODERICK				32	0	RC	SCOTCH	HEWER	081	F		11
MCDONALD	RONALD				54	SCOTLAND	RC	SCOTCH	BLACKSMITH	081	A	2	27
MCDONALD	SARAH		1	1	22	0	CE	ENGLISH		082	F		8
MCDONALD	T	A	1		21	0	CP	IRISH	TINSMITH	081	B		55
MCDONALD	W	J			36	0	CP	SCOTCH	SURVEYOR	081	B		67
MCDONALD	WILLIAM				48	SCOTLAND	CP	SCOTCH	F	081	E		15
MCDONALD	WILLIAM				49	SCOTLAND	RC	SCOTCH	F	083	C		2
MCDONALD	WILLIAM				36	SCOTLAND	CP	SCOTCH	F	085	B		22
MCDONALL	A	JOHN			19	ONTARIO	RC	SCOTCH	CLERK	083	B	1	1
MCDONELL	ALEXANDER				46	0	CP	SCOTCH	F	082	C	2	49
MCDONELL	DONALD	A	1		30	0	RC	SCOTCH	LUMBERMAN	088	C		10
MCDONELL	DONELL				38	0	CP	SCOTCH	F	082	C	2	52
MCDONELL	ELEZA		1	1	57	IRELAND	CE	IRISH		082	C	2	51
MCDONELL	GEORGE				28	0	WM	SCOTCH	F	082	C	2	51
MCDONELL	HENRY				65	IRELAND	RC	IRISH	F	082	A		36
MCDONELL	MICHAEL		2		65	IRELAND	RC		SERVANT	081	C		D
MCDONELL	MICHAEL				40	IRELAND	RC	IRISH	F	081	K		21
MCDONELL	RODRIC				67	0	CP	SCOTCH		082	C	2	53
MCDONELL	THOMAS				36	0	CP	SCOTCH	F	082	C	2	51
MCDONELL	WILLIAM		1		73	0	CS	SCOTCH		082	C	2	52
MCDONNELL	DONALD				61	ONTARIO	RC	SCOTCH	FARMER	081	G	2	12
MCDONNELL	JOHN		1		87	0	CS	SCOTCH		082	C	2	49
MCDONOGH	PATRICK				62	IRELAND	RC	IRISH	F	081	K		19
MCDONONELD	DONALD		2		92	SCOTLAND	RC		GENTLEMAN	081	I		D
MCDONOUGLE	MICHAEL				60	IRELAND	RC	IRISH	F	082	C	2	36
MCDOUGAL	ALEX				44	SCOTLAND	CP	SCOTTISH	LUMBERER	082	E		3
MCDOUGAL	CATHERIN		1	1	14	0	RC	SCOTCH		081	B		21
MCDOUGAL	DONALD				58	QUE	RC	SCOTCH	LAB	081	B		58
MCDOUGAL	EDITH	A	2	1		0	CE			081	B		D
MCDOUGAL	JOSEPH				27	QUE	CE	SCOTCH	BLACKSMITH	081	B		50
MCDOUGAL	JOSEPH				76	UNITED STATES	RC	SCOTCH	FARM LABOURER	089	A		3
MCDOUGAL	SUSAN		1	1	32	0	CS	SCOTCH		081	A	1	
MCDOUGALL	ALEX				26	ONT	CP	IRISH	F	081	J	1	60
MCDOUGALL	ALEX				25	ONT	CS	SCOTCH	FARMER	081	J	1	80
MCDOUGALL	ALEXANDER		1		33	0	PS	SCOTCH	WATCHMAN	086	C	1	11
MCDOUGALL	ARCHIBALD		1		25	0	RC	SCOTCH	LUMBERMAN	088	C		10
MCDOUGALL	CATHERINE			1	33	0	RC	SCOTCH		081	F		9
MCDOUGALL	CATHINE			1	58	QUE	CS	SCOTCH		081	I		33
MCDOUGALL	J	L			32	0	CS	SCOTCH	F LUMBER MERCHANT	081	I		29
MCDOUGALL	JOHN				60	SCOTLAND	CS	SCOTCH	SHOEMAKER	081	I		16
MCDOUGALL	JOHN				35	ONT	CP	IRISH	F	081	J	1	60
MCDOUGALL	MALCOLM				56	SCOTLAND	PS	SCOTCH	F	087	B	2	5
MCDOUGALL	MARY		2	1	28	ONT	CP			081	J	1	D
MCDOUGALL	MRS			1	49	IRELAND	CP	IRISH	HOTELKEEPER	081	J	1	58
MCDOUSAGH	MICHAEL				28	0	WM	IRISH	F	082	C	2	48
MCDOWELL	CHARLES		1		50	IRELAND	CE	IRISH	LABOURER	089	B		22
MCDOWELL	EMILEY			1	50	SCOTLAND	RC	SCOTCH		081	A	2	18
MCDUGALD	MALCOLM				50	SCOTLAND	WM	SCOTCH	F	086	A	1	16
MCEACHEN	SIMON				50	ONTARIO	RC	SCOTTISH	FARMER	082	B		69
MCEACHEORN	DOT				37	SCOTLAND	FK	SCOTCH	F	087	B	2	9
MCEACHEORN	MARY		2	1		0	NG			087	B	2	D
MCELIGATE	JAMES				40	IRELAND	RC	IRISH	F	081	J	1	19
MCEOWN	ROBERT				45	0	CE	SCOTCH	F	085	I		22
MCEWAN	JOHN				40	SCOTLAND	CP	SCOTCH	MOULDER	081	B		4
MCEWAN	JOSEPH		1		25	0	RC	SCOTCH	LAB	081	B		82
MCEWEN	GEORGE				47	IRELAND	CE	IRISH	F	081	C		15
MCEWEN	JAMES				50	IRELAND	CE	IRISH	F	081	K		51
MCEWEN	JOHN				44	SCOTLAND	CP	SCOTTISH	PRESB MINISTER	082	E		63
MCEWEN	MARGRET	JANE	1	1	18	0	CE	IRISH	SERVANT	081	A	1	28
MCEWEN	MARGT		1	1	35	0	RC	IRISH	SERVANT	082	E		1
MCEWEN	WILLIAM				50	SCOTLAND	CS	SCOTCH	F	082	A		62
MCFADDEN	MARGARET			1	59	SCOTLAND	CS	SCOTCH	F	081	C		23
MCFADEN	LACHLIN				29	0	BA	SCOTCH	BLACKSMITH	085	B		12
MCFADYEN	CHRISTINA		1	1	48	SCOTLAND	CP	SCOTCH		081	A	1	38
MCFARLAND	DAVID				44	IRELAND	PS	IRISH	F	086	A	1	22
MCFARLANE	DUNCAN				63	SCOTLAND	CS	SCOTCH	LAB	081	C		39
MCFARLANE	DUNCAN				40	SCOTLAND	CS	SCOTCH	F	085	I		14
MCFARLANE	JAMES				32	QUE	CS	SCOTCH	WHARFINGER	081	H	2	36
MCFARLANE	JOHN		1		32	SCOTLAND	CP	SCOTCH	MINER	090	D		5
MCFARLANE	JOHN	DUNCAN	1		15	0	CS	SCOTCH		081	A	1	58
MCFARLANE	MICHAEL				48	0	WM	SCOTCH	FARMER	081	K		6
MCFARLANE	ROBERT				36	ONTARIO	CS	SCOTCH	CLERK	082	A		48
MCFARLANE	WALTER				54	SCOTLAND	CP	SCOTCH	F	081	C		48
MCFARLIN	HENRY				27	IRELAND	CE	IRISH	BUTCHER	085	I		3
MCFARLING	ANN		1	1	28	0	CS	SCOTCH	SERVANT	082	F		39
MCFARLING	WILLIAM		1		14	0	CP	IRISH		082	F		24
MCFAYDEN	ALEXANDER				31	0	CP	SCOTCH	HOTELKEEPER	081	A	1	35
MCFAYDEN	ANN		1	1	20	0	CP	SCOTCH		081	B		28
MCFAYDEN	HUGH				73	SCOTLAND	CP	SCOTCH	STONEMASON	081	C		22
MCFAYDON	ANGUS				37	QUE	CP	SCOTCH	TRADER	081	C		25
MCFIE	ARCHIBALD				35	SCOTLAND	CE	SCOTCH	FARMER & TWP CLERK	085	J		24
MCGAHERN	JAMES				70	IRELAND	RC	IRISH	FARMER	082	B		41
MCGAHERR	ROBERT				50	IRELAND	RC	IRISH	FARMER	082	B		42
MCGAINTY	MAURICE				35	IRELAND	RC	IRISH	FARMER	082	B		31
MCGARRY	JOHN				35	IRELAND	RC	IRISH	F	081	A	1	5
MCGEE	ELLEN		1	1	20	0	CP	IRISH	SERVANT	085	B		13
MCGEE	JAMES				62	IRELAND	RC	IRISH	F	081	J	1	86
MCGEE	THOMAS				63	IRELAND	RC	IRISH	F	082	A		60
MCGEE	WILLIAM				40	IRELAND	CE	IRISH	F	085	B		3
MCGERY	ALEXANDER				52	SCOTLAND	PS	SCOTCH	F	085	E		8
MCGIBBON	THOMAS				46	IRELAND	RC	IRISH	LAB	081	B		26
MCGILL	AGNES		1	1	56	SCOTLAND	CS	SCOTCH		081	I		41
MCGILL	ANDREW				30	SCOTLAND	CS	SCOTCH	F	082	F		23
MCGILL	DAVID				30	SCOTLAND	CS	SCOTCH	TAILOR	081	I		41
MCGILL	JAMES		1		25	IRELAND	CP	IRISH	SHOEMAKER	081	B		6
MCGILL	THOMAS				35	0	CE	SCOTCH	F	085	E		30
MCGILLICUDDY	JOHN		1		65	IRELAND	RC	IRISH	SCHOOL TEACHER	081	K		36
MCGILLIS	ALEXANDER				24	QUE	CP	SCOTCH	LAB	081	A	2	19
MCGILLIS	AMELIA		1	1	20	UNITED STATES	CE	ENGLISH		081	B		25
MCGILLIS	ANGUS				27	QUE	CE	SCOTCH	LAB	081	A	2	22
MCGILLIS	JAMES				58	0	RC	SCOTTISH	LABOURER	082	E		23
MCGILLISH	ALEX		1		24	QUE	CE	ENGLISH	LAB	081	A	2	16
MCGILLIVARY	JOHN				60	SCOTLAND	CP	SCOTCH	F	085	E		25
MCGILLVERY	DAVID		1		42	0	CS	SCOTCH		088	B		17

SURNAME	NAME1	NAME2	STRAY	SEX	AGE	BIRTHPL	RELIGION	ORIGIN	OCCUP	DIST	SUB_DIST	DIV	PAGE
MCGILLVERY	WILLIAM		1		35	QUE	CP	SCOTCH	CULLER	084	E		4
MCGILLVRAY	JOHN				30	QUE	CP	SCOTCH	LUMBERMAN	090	F		23
MCGILVERY	DANIEL				27	SCOTLAND	PS	SCOTCH	LUMBERMAN	086	C	1	11
MCGILVREY	DONALD		1		28	0	PS	SCOTCH	LUMBERMAN	086	C	1	7
MCGINES	JAMES		1		13	0	RC	IRISH		082	C	2	49
MCGINN	JAMES				63	ONTARIO	RC	IRISH	F	082	A		51
MCGINN	MARGT		1	1	19	0	CE	IRISH	DOMESTIC	082	E		7
MCGINNIS	HUGH		1		21	0	WM	SCOTCH	LUMBERMAN	086	B		2
MCGINNIS	JOHN				24	ONTARIO	RC	IRISH	HOTEL KEEPER	083	C		4
MCGINNIS	WILLIAM		1		20	0	CE	IRISH	DRUGGIST	081	B		13
MCGINTY	CHARLES				32	IRELAND	RC	IRISH	F	082	A		81
MCGLADE	JAMES				23	0	RC	IRISH		081	B		56
MCGLAUGHLAN	DANIEL				50	IRELAND	RC	IRISH	FARMER	082	D		20
MCGLAUGHLAN	JOSEPH				18	QUE	RC	IRISH	LABOURER	082	D		23
MCGLAUGHLIN	CHARLES				35	IRELAND	CS	IRISH	F	082	A		37
MCGLAUGHLIN	JAMES				73	IRELAND	CE	IRISH	F	082	A		29
MCGLAUGHLIN	JAMES				30	IRELAND	CE	IRISH	F	082	A		77
MCGLAUGHLIN	WILLIAM				32	IRELAND	CE	IRISH	F	082	A		29
MCGOMERY	ALEXANDER				67	QUEBEC	CE	SCOTCH	HOTELKEEPER	083	E		1
MCGOMERY	CHARLES				39	QUEBEC	CE	ENGLISH	HOTELKEEPER	083	E		2
MCGONEGAL	ANDREW				45	IRELAND	CE	IRISH	F	082	C	2	11
MCGONNIGAL	PATRICK				26	0	RC	IRISH	CARPENTER	081	B		9
MCGONNIGLE	PETER				34	0	RC	IRISH	SAWYER	081	B		78
MCGONNIGLE	WILLIAM				40	0	RC	IRISH	F	081	A	2	41
MCGOULRICK	CATHE		1	1	18	QUE	RC	IRISH	SERVANT	082	E		5
MCGOVREN	JAMES		1		19	0	RC	IRISH	SADDLER	082	E		41
MCGOWAN	THOMAS				42	SCOTLAND	CO	SCOTCH	F	086	A	1	19
MCGOWAN	WILLIAM				25	0	PS	SCOTCH	LIGHTHOUSE KEEPER	086	A	1	33
MCGRAH	MCGRAH				40	0	CE	INDIAN	F & LABOURER	087	B	1	13
MCGRATH	EDWARD				34	IRELAND	RC	IRISH	F	083	C		13
MCGRATH	JOHN				33	IRELAND	RC	IRISH	F	081	K		48
MCGRATH	MICHAEL				60	IRELAND	RC	IRISH	F	081	J	1	37
MCGRATH	PETER				53	IRELAND	RC	IRISH	F	081	J	1	9
MCGRATH	THOMAS				65	IRELAND	RC	IRISH	F	081	K		47
MCGREERY	JAMES				54	IRELAND	WM	IRISH	F	081	A	2	35
MCGREGOR	ALEX				50	SCOTLAND	CS	SCOTCH	F	081	C		10
MCGREGOR	ALEXD		1		19	0	RC	IRISH	RAILWAYMAN	081	A	2	29
MCGREGOR	CATHERIN		1	1	17	0	CP	SCOTCH		081	A	2	3
MCGREGOR	COLIN				54	SCOTLAND	CS	SCOTCH	F	081	A	1	39
MCGREGOR	DANIEL				44	SCOTLAND	CP	SCOTTISH	BRICKMAKER	082	E		66
MCGREGOR	DUNCAN		1			0	CS	SCOTCH		081	A	1	46
MCGREGOR	DUNCAN				44	0	CS	SCOTCH	F	081	H	2	3
MCGREGOR	DUNCAN				49	SCOTLAND	PS	SCOTCH	CARDER & FULLER	082	G		70
MCGREGOR	DUNCAN		1		30	0	RC	INDIAN	F & SAILOR	087	B	1	20
MCGREGOR	FLORA		1	1	24	QUE	CP	SCOTCH		081	B		60
MCGREGOR	GEORGE				30	SCOTLAND	CP	SCOTTISH	LABOURER	082	E		68
MCGREGOR	JAMES				37	0	CS	SCOTCH	F	081	H	2	12
MCGREGOR	JAMES				61	SCOTLAND	RC	SCOTCH	F	082	J		17
MCGREGOR	JANE			1	30	0	RC	SCOTCH		088	B		3
MCGREGOR	JANET			1	48	SCOTLAND	CP	SCOTTISH	SCHOOL MISTRESS	082	B		60
MCGREGOR	JOHN		2		57	SCOTLAND	CS		F			1	D
MCGREGOR	JOHN				25	0	CS	SCOTCH	SHOEMAKER	081	A	1	36
MCGREGOR	JOHN				21	0	CS	SCOTCH	F	081	A	1	38
MCGREGOR	JOHN				60	0	OP	SCOTCH	SHOEMAKER	081	E		19
MCGREGOR	JOHN				70	SCOTLAND	CS	SCOTCH	F	081	H	2	4
MCGREGOR	JOHN				50	ONTARIO	CP	SCOTTISH	FARMER	082	B		66
MCGREGOR	JOHN				39	ONT	RC	SCOTCH	FARMER	082	I		8
MCGREGOR	MARGRET		1	1	6	0	CP	SCOTCH		081	A	1	39
MCGREGOR	PETER		1		7	0	CP	SCOTCH		081	A	1	39
MCGREGOR	RICHARD				41	QUE	RC	SCOTCH	LAB	081	K		32
MCGREGOR	ROBERT				38	0	CS	SCOTCH	F	081	A	1	70
MCGREGOR	THOMAS				48	IRELAND	CE	IRISH	F	081	E		4
MCGREGOR	WILLIAM		1			0	CS	SCOTCH		081	A	1	46
MCGUCHAN	CATHERINE		1	1	68	IRELAND	RC	IRISH		082	A		36
MCGUCHAN	JOHN		1		70	IRELAND	RC	IRISH	F	082	A		36
MCGUIRE	CHARLES				56	IRELAND	RC	IRISH	FARMER	084	B		2
MCGUIRE	ELLEN			1	43	IRELAND	RC	IRISH		081	A	2	6
MCGUIRE	HUGH		1		83	IRELAND	RC	IRISH		081	C		52
MCGUIRE	JAMES				62	IRELAND	RC	IRISH	FARMER	081	G	1	5
MCGUIRE	JAMES				38	IRELAND	RC	IRISH	FARMER	081	G	1	36
MCGUIRE	JANE		1	1	70	IRELAND	RC	IRISH		081	C		52
MCGUIRE	JOHN		1		13	ONT	RC	IRISH		081	H	1	20
MCGUIRE	LAWRANCE		1		18	0	RC	IRISH	LAB	081	B		86
MCGUIRE	MICHAEL				46	IRELAND	RC	IRISH	FARMER	081	D		2
MCGUIRE	RICHARD				34	0	CE	IRISH	F	086	A	1	29
MCGUIRE	WILLIAM				50	QUE	RC	IRISH	F	081	K		7
MCHUGH	JAMES				36	IRELAND	RC	IRISH	F	081	C		4
MCHUGH	JOHN				50	IRELAND	RC	IRISH	F	081	C		3
MCHUGH	JOHN				58	IRELAND	RC	IRISH	F	081	J	1	20
MCHUGH	MARY	ANN	1	1	22	0	RC	IRISH	SERVANT	085	I		6
MCHUGH	MICHAEL				45	IRELAND	RC	IRISH	F	081	C		4
MCHUGH	PATRICK				35	IRELAND	RC	IRISH	BLACKSMITH	081	K		69
MCIBBON	HEINRY		2		55	IRELAND	CP		F	082	G		D
MCIBBON	JAMES				43	IRELAND	EM	IRISH	F	082	G		50
MCIBBON	JOSEPH				39	IRELAND	CP	IRISH	F	082	G		52
MCIBBON	JOSEPH				49	IRELAND	CP	IRISH	F	082	G		52
MCIBBON	SARAH			1	55	IRELAND	CP	IRISH	F	082	G		52
MCILROY	WILLIAM				25	SCOTLAND	CE	SCOTCH	F	086	A	1	32
MCINESNY	DENNIS				50	IRELAND	RC	IRISH	F	081	K		39
MCINIRY	JAMES				50	IRELAND	RC	IRISH	F	081	K		36
MCINNERNY	THOMAS				68	IRELAND	RC	IRISH	FARMER	081	F		23
MCINNES	ANGUS				62	SCOTLAND	CS	SCOTCH	F	081	A	1	47
MCINNES	ANGUS				44	SCOTLAND	CS	SCOTCH	F	081	A	1	48
MCINNES	ARCHIBALD				42	0	CS	SCOTCH	SHOEMAKER	081	A	1	59
MCINNES	JOHN				37	0	CS	SCOTCH	F	081	A	1	66
MCINNES	JOHN				35	0	CS	SCOTCH	F	081	A	1	68
MCINNES	JOHN				79	SCOTLAND	CS	SCOTCH	FARMER	081	I		15
MCINNES	JOHN	D			44	0	RC	IRISH		085	D		33
MCINNIS	HENRY				33	0	CS	SCOTCH	F	081	H	2	6
MCINTERE	JANE		1	1	90	IRELAND	WM	IRISH		082	C	2	58
MCINTIRE	JOHN		1		25	SCOTLAND	CP	SCOTCH	CLERK	085	E		24
MCINTOMELY	JOHN				34	ONTARIO	RC	IRISH	FARMER	081	G	1	21
MCINTOMELY	JULA		2	1	33	ONTARIO	RC			081	G	1	D
MCINTOMELY	MARTHA		1	1	22	0	RC	IRISH	SERVANT	082	J		19
MCINTOMMY	PATK				33	0	RC	IRISH	LABOURER	082	E		66
MCINTOMNEY	LUKE				60	IRELAND	RC	IRISH	LABOURER	082	E		4

SURNAME	NAME1	NAME2	STRAY	SEX	AGE	BIRTHPL	RELIGION	ORIGIN	OCCUP	DIST	SUB_DIST	DIV	PAGE
MCINTOMNEY	MARGT		1	1	20	0	RC	IRISH	SERVANT	082	E		5
MCINTOSH	ALEXANDER		1		21	0	CP	SCOTCH	F LABOURER	085	H		21
MCINTOSH	ISAAC				20	0	CP	SCOTTISH	BARBER HAIRDRESSER	082	E		41
MCINTOSH	JAMES		1		1	0	RC	IRISH				1	75
MCINTOSH	JOHN				57	0	PS	SCOTCH	F	085	C		3
MCINTOSH	JOHN		1		18	0	CP	SCOTCH	SHANTY MAN	085	E		27
MCINTOSH	MARGRET		1	1	23	0	CP	SCOTCH				1	80
MCINTOSH	MARSHAL		1			0	CP	SCOTCH				1	80
MCINTOSH	PETER				65	SCOTLAND	CP	SCOTCH	F			1	76
MCINTOSH	THOMAS		1		45	SCOTLAND	PS	SCOTCH	F	085	C		16
MCINTOSH	WILLIAM				48	SCOTLAND	CP	SCOTCH	F	082	C	2	27
MCINTYRE	A	J			31	0	CP	SCOTCH	CONTRACTOR	081	B		51
MCINTYRE	ARTHUR				51	IRELAND	CE	IRISH	F	082	G		74
MCINTYRE	DANIEL		1		64	SCOTLAND	CS	SCOTCH	GARDENER	081	A	1	58
MCINTYRE	DANIEL				66	SCOTLAND	CS	SCOTCH	F	081	A	1	59
MCINTYRE	DANIEL				43	ONT	CS	SCOTCH	F	081	C		39
MCINTYRE	DONALD				35	SCOTLAND	CP	SCOTTISH	FARMER	082	B		5
MCINTYRE	DUNCAN				57	SCOTLAND	CS	SCOTCH	F	081	H	2	3
MCINTYRE	DUNCAN				37	0	CP	SCOTCH	CARPENTER	081	I		26
MCINTYRE	F	J			31	ONTARIO	CP	SCOTCH	CONTRACTOR	083	A	1	15
MCINTYRE	FINLEY				30	ONT	PS	SCOTCH	F	081	J	1	49
MCINTYRE	GEORGE		2			0	CE			082	B		D
MCINTYRE	GREGOR				62	SCOTLAND	CS	SCOTCH	F	081	H	2	12
MCINTYRE	JAMES				28	SCOTLAND	CP	SCOTCH	F	081	A	1	28
MCINTYRE	JAMES				38	QUE	CS	SCOTCH	F	081	A	1	58
MCINTYRE	JAMES				48	SCOTLAND	CP	SCOTCH	F	081	J	1	58
MCINTYRE	JAMES				28	IRELAND	CE	IRISH	FARMER	082	B		45
MCINTYRE	JAMES				61	IRELAND	CE	SCOTCH	F	082	G		71
MCINTYRE	JOHN				71	SCOTLAND	CS	SCOTCH	F	081	A	1	57
MCINTYRE	JOHN				29	0	CP	SCOTCH	F	081	A	2	36
MCINTYRE	JOHN				54	SCOTLAND	CS	SCOTCH	F	081	C		40
MCINTYRE	JOHN				42	SCOTLAND	PS	SCOTCH	F	081	J	1	49
MCINTYRE	JOHN				30	SCOTLAND	CP	SCOTTISH	FARMER	082	B		34
MCINTYRE	JOHN				67	IRELAND	CE	IRISH	FARMER	082	B		67
MCINTYRE	JOHN				53	SCOTLAND	CS	SCOTCH	HUDSON BAY COMPANY O	090	F		21
MCINTYRE	MACOLM		2		66	SCOTLAND	CP		F	082	B		D
MCINTYRE	MALCOM				28	0	CS	SCOTCH	MERCHANT	081	I		10
MCINTYRE	MALCOM				49	S	CS	SCOTCH	MERCHANT	081	I		42
MCINTYRE	MARGARET		1	1	21	QUE	RC	IRISH		081	A	2	33
MCINTYRE	MARY		1	1	38	ONTARIO	CE	IRISH		082	B		44
MCINTYRE	MICHAEL		1		30	IRELAND	CE	IRISH	SHANTYMAN	082	B		44
MCINTYRE	PATRICK		1		19	QUE	RC	IRISH	CLERK	081	B		76
MCINTYRE	ROBERT				46	SCOTLAND	CS	SCOTCH	FARMER	081	C		39
MCINTYRE	ROBERT				51	IRELAND	CE	IRISH	F	082	G		79
MCINTYRE	ROBT		1		15	0	CE	IRISH	APPRENTICE	082	E		57
MCINTYRE	RONALD				28	SCOTLAND	PS	SCOTCH	LAB	087	B	2	2
MCINTYRE	SAMUEL		1		55	IRELAND	CE	IRISH	FARMER	082	B		44
MCINTYRE	WILLIAM				28	ONTARIO	CE	IRISH	FARMER	082	B		48
MCINTYRE	WILLIAM				57	IRELAND	RP	IRISH	F	082	J		4
MCINTYRE	WILLIAM	JOHN	1		3	0	CP	SCOTCH		081	A	1	27
MCINTYRE	WM	HENRY			53	0	RP	SCOTCH	LUMBERMAN & F	082	L		4
MCIVER	BERNARD				56	IRELAND	RC	IRISH	WAITER	082	D		11
MCIVER	ROBERT		2		45	SCOTLAND	CP		LAB	082	C	1	D
MCIVOY	JAMES		1		26	0	RC	IRISH	LUMBERMAN	086	B		2
MCJASNEY	JOSEPH				55	IRELAND	WM	IRISH	LABOURER	085	B		8
MCKAIN	GEORGE	I			38	ENGLAND	CE	ENGLISH	GENERAL MANAGER	081	E		3
MCKAIS	GEORGE	S	1		38	ENGLAND	CE	ENGLISH	G MANAGER	081	G	1	43
MCKAMUS	JAMES				25	0	CE	IRISH	F	085	J		12
MCKAY	ABRAHAM		1		2	0	RC	SCOTCH		089	B		26
MCKAY	ALEXANDER				50	SCOTLAND	CP	SCOTCH	LAB	081	B		75
MCKAY	ALEXANDER				40	SCOTLAND	CP	SCOTCH	F	085	H		8
MCKAY	ALEXANDER				46	0	CE	SCOTCH	FISHERMAN	086	C	1	5
MCKAY	ALEXANDER		1		16	US	RC	SCOTCH		089	B		26
MCKAY	ALEXANDER	W			67	US	CP	SCOTCH	HUNTER	089	B		15
MCKAY	ANDREW	C			34	SCOTLAND	CP	SCOTCH	FARMER	089	B		22
MCKAY	ANGELIQUE		1	1	35	0	RC	FRENCH		089	B		26
MCKAY	ANGUS				29	0	RC	SCOTCH	F	082	C	1	21
MCKAY	BAPTISTE				48	0	RC	SCOTCH	CARPENTER	089	B		33
MCKAY	DANIEL				39	0	RC	SCOTCH	FISHERMAN	089	B		44
MCKAY	DUNCAN				43	0	RC	SCOTCH	F	082	C	1	53
MCKAY	ELIZA	SARAH		1	40	SCOTLAND	WM	SCOTCH		085	E		26
MCKAY	HUGH				66	SCOTLAND	PS	SCOTCH	F	085	D		3
MCKAY	I	MRS	1	1	37	SCOTLAND	CE	SCOTCH	SERVANT	083	C		4
MCKAY	ISABELLA		1	1	4	0	RC	SCOTCH		089	B		26
MCKAY	JAMES				63	SCOTLAND	CP	SCOTCH	F	081	A	1	22
MCKAY	JAMES				55	IRELAND	RC	IRISH	FARMER	082	I		36
MCKAY	JAMES				57	SCOTLAND	CP	SCOTCH	F	085	B		2
MCKAY	JANE		1	1	2	0	RC	SCOTCH		089	B		16
MCKAY	JOHN		1		8	0	RC	SCOTCH		089	B		26
MCKAY	JOSEPH				32	SCOTLAND	PS	SCOTCH	F	085	C		11
MCKAY	MARYANN		1	1	6	0	RC	SCOTCH		089	B		26
MCKAY	NANCY		2	1	3	0	RC			089	B		D
MCKAY	NEIL				34	0	CP	SCOTCH	F	081	A	1	27
MCKAY	NIEL		1		36	0	RC	SCOTCH		089	B		26
MCKAY	NORMAN				25	SCOTLAND	CP	SCOTCH	LABOURER	089	B		2
MCKAY	PHILOMEN		1	1	15	0	RC	ENGLISH		084	I	2	1
MCKAY	RICHD				48	IRELAND	RC	IRISH	HOTELKEEPER	082	E		17
MCKAY	ROBERT				60	IRELAND	CE	IRISH	FARMER	082	I		26
MCKEACHAN	CATHERINE		1	1	93	IRELAND	CE	IRISH		082	I		69
MCKEAN	AUGUSTUS		1		26	IRELAND	RC	IRISH	SERVANT	089	A		46
MCKECHNIE	ALXD		1		26	QUE	CP	SCOTCH	LAB	081	A	2	17
MCKECHNIE	WM		1		21	QUE	CP	SCOTCH	LAB	081	A	2	17
MCKEE	HENRY	S	1		40	0	PB	ENGLISH	LAB	081	A	2	16
MCKEE	WILLIAM				52	IRELAND	CE	IRISH	F	084	D		5
MCKELLAR	DUNCAN				62	SCOTLAND	CP	SCOTCH		090	F		23
MCKELLOP	ARCHABALD				52	SCOTLAND	CS	SCOTCH	F	082	C	2	65
MCKELLUP	EUPHEMIA		1	1	79	SCOTLAND	CS	SCOTCH	F	081	J	1	71
MCKENLEY	ELISABATH		2	1		0	RP			082	K	1	D
MCKENLY	JOHN				33	SCOTLAND	CP	IRISH	FARMER	085	E		31
MCKENSIE	ANDREW				60	SCOTLAND	CP	SCOTCH	F	081	J	1	58
MCKENY	JAMES				56	IRELAND	RC	IRISH	F	082	L		2
MCKENZIE	ALEXANDER				49	SCOTLAND	PS	SCOTCH	MINE LABOURER	089	A		4
MCKENZIE	CHARLES				31	CANADA	PR	ENGLISH	TAVERN KEEPER	085	A		12
MCKENZIE	CHARLES				58	SCOTLAND	CP	SCOTCH	F	085	B		22
MCKENZIE	DONALD				45	NEW BRUNSWICK	PS	SCOTCH	LIGHTHOUSE KEEPER	087	B	3	11
MCKENZIE	EDWD				38	0	CP	SCOTTISH	PHYSICIAN	082	E		65

SURNAME	NAME1	NAME2	STRAY	SEX	AGE	BIRTHPL	RELIGION	ORIGIN	OCCUP	DIST	SUB_DIST	DIV	PAGE
MCKENZIE	ELIZABETH		1	1	32	0	PS	SCOTTISH		082	E		33
MCKENZIE	JAMES				33	0	PS	SCOTCH	BOARDING HOUSE KEEPE	086	C	1	7
MCKENZIE	JAS		1		32	QUE	PS	SCOTTISH	RAFTSMAN	082	E		33
MCKENZIE	JOHN		1		46	SCOTLAND	CP	SCOTCH	SERVANT	081	A	2	7
MCKENZIE	JOHN				54	SCOTLAND	CS	SCOTCH	F	081	C		14
MCKENZIE	JOHN		1		24	0	CE	SCOTCH	LAB	085	F		5
MCKENZIE	JOHN		1		28	0	CE	SCOTCH	LUMBERMAN	086	C	1	7
MCKENZIE	JOHN		1		22	UNITED STATES	CP	SCOTCH	LAB	090	D		2
MCKENZIE	JULIA		1	1	18	GERMANY	RC	GERMAN	SERVANT	081	A	2	7
MCKENZIE	PETER				74	SCOTLAND	CP	SCOTTISH	FARMER	082	I		66
MCKENZIE	RODERICK				50	SCOTLAND	CS	SCOTCH	CHIEFTRADER	088	B		10
MCKENZIE	RODERICK		2		15	BNA	CS			088	B		D
MCKENZIE	WILLIAM		1		75	SCOTLAND	CP	SCOTCH	GARDENER	081	A	2	19
MCKENZIE	WILLIAM				21	0	PS	SCOTCH	F	087	B	3	11
MCKEOWN	DONALD		1		31	SCOTLAND	FK	SCOTCH	LUMBERMAN	086	B		3
MCKEOWN	WILLIAM		1		35	IRELAND	CE	IRISH	STAVE MAKER	088	B		3
MCKEOWN	WILLIAM		1		35	IRELAND	CE	IRISH	STAVE MAKER	088	B		21
MCKERKER	JOHN				20	0	WM	SCOTCH	HOTELKEEPER	081	B		71
MCKETRICK	ROBT				46	IRELAND	CE	IRISH	F	085	I		34
MCKEY	SUTHERLAND				53	SCOTLAND	PS	SCOTCH	SEA CAPTAIN FARMER	085	J		7
MCKEY	WILLIAM				50	SCOTLAND	CP	SCOTCH	MERCHANT	081	I		9
MCKIE	CHARLOTTE			1	25	QUE	RC	FRENCH		088	B		1
MCKIE	JOSEPH				53	QUE	RC	SCOTCH	LUMBERMAN	088	B		1
MCKIE	JOSEPH		2		26	QUEBEC	RC		LUMBERMAN	088	B		D
MCKIE	WILLIAM				31	0	PS	SCOTCH	FARMER	089	B		20
MCKIERNAN	CHARLES				40	IRELAND	RC	IRISH	F	081	K		46
MCKIERNAN	JAMES				51	IRELAND	RC	IRISH	F	081	K		43
MCKIERNAN	JOHN				46	IRELAND	RC	IRISH	F	081	K		42
MCKILLOP	ALEXANDER		1		21	SCOTLAND	CP	SCOTCH	SCHOOL TEACHER	082	C	1	37
MCKINLEY	ARCHIBALD				45	SCOTLAND	CS	SCOTCH	F	085	J		2
MCKINLEY	JAMES				31	0	RC	IRISH	F	082	L		3
MCKINLEY	JOHN				35	IRELAND	RP	IRISH	BLACKSMITH	082	K	1	11
MCKINLEY	MARGRET		1	1	45	IRELAND	NG	IRISH		082	C	2	34
MCKINLEY	PETER				36	SCOTLAND	CP	IRISH	FARMER	082	B		12
MCKINNON	ALEX		1		36	PEI	PB	ENGLISH	LAB	081	A	2	16
MCKINNON	ALEXANDER		1		18	QUE	RC	SCOTCH	SERVANT	081	A	2	61
MCKINNON	DONALD		1		35	SCOTLAND	CP	SCOTCH	F LABOURER	085	H		21
MCKINSIE	ANDREW				27	ONT	CS	SCOTCH	F	081	J	1	43
MCKINZIE	DANIEL				29	0	OP	SCOTCH	HOUSE CARPENTER	082	C	1	11
MCKINZIE	PETER				60	SCOTLAND	CP	SCOTCH	F	081	A	1	26
MCKIVER	JOHN		1		48	SCOTLAND	CP	SCOTCH	WEAVER	082	C	1	15
MCKONE	JOHN				40	0	RC	IRISH	FARMER	082	D		31
MCKOUSKEY	JOHN				40	AUSTRIA	RC	AUSTRIAN	FARMER	082	I		15
MCLACHLAN	JAMES				55	SCOTLAND	CS	SCOTCH	F	081	H	2	1
MCLACHLAN	REBECA		1	1	19	0	CP	IRISH	SERVANT	081	B		53
MCLACHLIN	DANIEL				63	QUE	CP	SCOTCH	F	081	B		1
MCLACHLIN	HUGH				40	0	CP	SCOTCH	F	081	A	2	38
MCLACHLIN	JOHN	JR			26	0	CP	SCOTCH	LUMBERMAN	081	B		41
MCLAIN	JOHN				30	SCOTLAND	PS	SCOTCH	F	086	A	1	2
MCLANE	JOHN				24	0	CP	SCOTCH	F	082	C	1	38
MCLAREN	ALESS				61	SCOTLAND	CP	SCOTTISH	FARMER	082	B		7
MCLAREN	ANN			1	84	SCOTLAND	CP	SCOTCH		081	A	1	68
MCLAREN	DONALD				39	0	CP	SCOTCH	F	081	A	2	55
MCLAREN	DUNCAN				34	ONT	PS	SCOTCH	F	081	J	1	38
MCLAREN	FORBES				23	0	WM	SCOTCH	F	086	A	1	18
MCLAREN	JAMES				59	SCOTLAND	CS	SCOTCH	POSTMASTER	082	A		32
MCLAREN	JAMES				28	0	CP	IRISH	F	082	C	2	21
MCLAREN	JAMES				56	0	CP	IRISH	F	082	C	2	54
MCLAREN	JOHN				62	SCOTLAND	CS	SCOTCH	F	081	H	2	5
MCLAREN	JOHN				63	SCOTLAND	CS	SCOTCH	F	082	A		31
MCLAREN	JOHN				32	ONTARIO	CP	SCOTTISH	STOREKEEPER	082	B		7
MCLAREN	LOUGHIN		1		18	0	PS	SCOTCH	MASON	086	C	1	7
MCLAREN	MALCOLM				65	SCOTLAND	CS	SCOTCH	F	081	A	1	44
MCLAREN	MALCOLM				30	ONT	PS	SCOTCH	F	081	J	1	48
MCLAREN	MARGARET		1	1	22	0	CS	SCOTCH		081	H	2	6
MCLAREN	MATHEW				36	0	CP	IRISH		082	C	2	7
MCLAREN	PETER				50	SCOTLAND	CP	SCOTCH	F	081	A	2	17
MCLAREN	PETER				36	0	CP	SCOTCH	SHOEMAKER	082	C	2	2
MCLAREN	ROBERT				40	SCOTLAND	CP	SCOTT	FARMER	082	B		68
MCLAREN	ROBERT				31	0	CS	SCOTCH	F	082	C	2	59
MCLAREN	ROBERT	JOHN ROBERTSON			44	SCOTLAND	CP	SCOTCH	F	081	A	1	68
MCLAREN	WILLIAM				58	SCOTLAND	CS	SCOTCH	F	082	C	2	60
MCLAREN	WILLIAM	R			56	SCOTLAND	CS	SCOTCH	F	082	A		30
MCLARNE	MARY		1	1	50	SCOTLAND	CP	SCOTCH		081	I		31
MCLARREN	M		1	1	19	0	CP	SCOTTISH	SERVANT	082	E		3
MCLARREN	THOS				42	QUE	CP	SCOTTISH	TAILOR	082	E		22
MCLARTY	JOHN				28	IRELAND	RC	IRISH	FARMER	082	B		47
MCLAUCHLAN	D	JAMES			39	SCOTLAND	CE	SCOTCH	F	081	H	2	2
MCLAUCHLAN	DONALD				37	0	CP	SCOTCH	F	081	A	1	16
MCLAUCHLAN	DUNCAN				64	SCOTLAND	CS	SCOTCH	F	081	A	1	16
MCLAUCHLAN	JAMES				58	SCOTLAND	CP	SCOTCH	F	081	A	1	16
MCLAUCHLAN	JOHN				63	SCOTLAND	CP	SCOTCH	F	081	A	1	23
MCLAUCHLAN	JOHN				34	0	CS	SCOTCH	F	081	A	1	33
MCLAUCHLAN	THOMAS				65	SCOTLAND	CP	SCOTCH	F	081	A	1	29
MCLAUD	ALEX		1		24	PEI	CP	SCOTCH	MILLER	082	E		25
MCLAUD	DONALD				40	0	CP	SCOTTISH	BLACKSMITH	082	E		13
MCLAUGHLAN	ALEXANDER				40	SCOTLAND	CP	SCOTCH	F	081	A	1	32
MCLAUGHLEN	ROBERT				51	IRELAND	CE	IRISH	F	082	C	2	46
MCLAUGHLIN	JOHN				55	IRELAND	CE	IRISH	F	081	C		22
MCLAUGHLIN	JOHN				47	IRELAND	RC	IRISH	SHOEMAKER	081	G	1	36
MCLAURIN	JOHN				38	0	BA	SCOTCH	TRADER	090	F		14
MCLAY	ALEX				28	SCOTLAND	PS	SCOTCH	F	087	B	2	7
MCLAY	ALEXANDER				30	SCOTLAND	PS	SCOTCH	F	087	B	3	12
MCLAY	MARY		1	1	24	IRELAND	RC	IRISH		082	C	1	38
MCLAY	WILLIAM		1		24	US	RC	ENGLISH	BRICKLAYER	082	C	1	38
MCLEAN	ANGUS				27	SCOTLAND	PS	SCOTCH	F	085	A		13
MCLEAN	ARCHABLE				38	SCOTLAND	BA	SCOTCH	F	085	F		4
MCLEAN	ARCHIBALD		1		50	0	PS	SCOTCH		089	B		18
MCLEAN	ARCHY		1		33	CANADA	BA	SCOTCH	LAB	087	B	2	3
MCLEAN	DONALD				63	SCOTLAND	CS	SCOTCH	F	082	C	1	43
MCLEAN	DONALD				56	SCOTLAND	PS	SCOTCH	F	085	A		5
MCLEAN	DUNCAN				63	SCOTLAND	PS	SCOTCH	F	085	H		2
MCLEAN	ELIJAH		1		24	0	CP	SCOTCH	LAB	083	C		1
MCLEAN	ELIZEBATH		1	1	10	QUE	RC	ENGLISH		084	I	2	1
MCLEAN	GEORGE				39	SCOTLAND	CS	SCOTCH	HOTELKEEPER	081	A	1	60
MCLEAN	HENRY				32	QUE	WM	SCOTCH	F	085	C		3

SURNAME	NAME1	NAME2	STRAY	SEX	AGE	BIRTHPL	RELIGION	ORIGIN	OCCUP	DIST	SUB_DIST	DIV	PAGE
MCLEAN	J	L	1		38	IRELAND	RC	IRISH	CARPENTER	090	D		2
MCLEAN	JAMES				50	0	CE	SCOTCH	LAB	081	K		14
MCLEAN	JOHN				51	SCOTLAND	EM	SCOTCH	F	081	C		48
MCLEAN	JOHN				35	0	CP	SCOTCH	F	082	C	2	6
MCLEAN	JOHN				82	SCOTLAND	CP	SCOTCH	F	082	C	2	12
MCLEAN	JOHN				34	0	WM	SCOTCH	F	082	C	2	25
MCLEAN	JOHN				45	SCOTLAND	PS	SCOTCH	F	087	B	2	5
MCLEAN	LACHLAN				53	SCOTLAND	PS	SCOTCH	F	085	A		5
MCLEAN	MALCOM		1		42	SCOTLAND	PS	SCOTCH	LABOURER	084	G	1	1
MCLEAN	MARY		1	1	4	0	RP	SCOTCH		081	E		20
MCLEAN	MARY		2	1	7	0	BA			087	B	2	D
MCLEAN	MARY	JANE	1	1	9	ONTARIO	CP	SCOTTISH		082	B		7
MCLEAN	NEIL		1		28	0	PS	SCOTCH	F	085	D		34
MCLEAN	NIEL				42	SCOTLAND	BA	SCOTCH	LAB	087	B	2	6
MCLEAN	PETER				40	SCOTLAND	CP	SCOTCH	F	081	A	2	54
MCLEAN	ROBERT		1		75	SCOTLAND	RP	SCOTCH	CARPENTER	082	K	1	7
MCLEAN	SAMUEL				51	IRELAND	PS	IRISH	F	087	B	3	6
MCLEAN	SARAH		1	1	25	0	CS	SCOTCH	DRESS MAKER	089	B		9
MCLEAN	THOMAS				25	0	BA	SCOTCH	MANAGER	084	F		1
MCLEAN	WILLIAM				40	SCOTLAND	CS	SCOTCH	F	081	A	1	73
MCLEARN	LILLA		2	1		0	WM			085	C		D
MCLEECE	WILLIAM				50	IRELAND	CS	IRISH	F	082	A		31
MCLEESE	DANIEL				37	IRELAND	FK	IRISH		082	C	1	27
MCLELAHAN	CHARLES		1		38	0	CP	SCOTCH	LAB	081	A	2	17
MCLELAN	ADAM				27	SCOTLAND	WM	SCOTCH	FARMER PLASTERER	081	J	1	73
MCLELLAN	ARCHD				29	ONT	CP	SCOTCH	F	081	C		27
MCLELLAN	ARCHIBALD				52	SCOTLAND	CP	SCOTCH	F	081	C		26
MCLELLAN	DOUGALL				44	SCOTLAND	CP	SCOTCH	F	081	E		12
MCLELLAN	GEORGE				53	SCOTLAND	OP	SCOTCH	F	081	E		18
MCLELLAN	JOHN				60	SCOTLAND	CP	SCOTCH	F	081	C		26
MCLELLAN	JOHN				32	SCOTLAND	CS	SCOTCH	F	082	A		9
MCLELLAN	JOHN				67	SCOTLAND	CS	SCOTCH	COOPER & F	082	A		9
MCLELLAN	SARAH		1	1	20	SCOTLAND	CP	SCOTCH		081	B		14
MCLENNAN	F		1		27	SCOTLAND	CS	SCOTCH	LABOURER	088	A		8
MCLENNON	JOHN				50	SCOTLAND	PS	SCOTCH	CARPENTER	082	G		59
MCLEOD	ALEXANDER				42	ONT	CP	SCOTCH	FARMER	082	I		15
MCLEOD	ALEXANDER				47	SCOTLAND	CP	SCOTCH	F	085	B		25
MCLEOD	DONALD				61	ONTARIO	CP	SCOTTISH	FARMER	082	B		54
MCLEOD	DONALD				50	ONTARIO	CP	SCOTT	FARMER	082	B		62
MCLEOD	DONALD				50	SCOTLAND	PS	SCOTCH	MINE LABOURER	089	A		43
MCLEOD	JAMES		1		45	SCOTLAND	CP	SCOTCH	SERVANT	081	A	2	30
MCLEOD	JOHN				33	SCOTLAND	RC	SCOTCH	LAB	090	F		20
MCLEOD	MALCOLM				45	SCOTLAND	PS	SCOTCH	FARMER	089	A		52
MCLEOD	NORMAN				28	ONTARIO	CP	SCOTTISH	FARMER	082	B		70
MCLEOD	NORMAN		1		33	ONTARIO	CP	SCOTCH	LAB	083	C		6
MCLEOD	NORMAN				42	SCOTLAND	PS	SCOTCH	MANAGER	084	I	1	4
MCLEOD	RODERICK				51	ONTARIO	CS	SCOTTISH	FARMER	082	B		35
MCLEOD	RODERICK				25	SCOTLAND	PS	SCOTCH	MINER	089	A		30
MCLERN	ROBERT				44	0	CS	SCOTCH	F	081	H	1	7
MCLINDEN	DANIEL				54	IRELAND	RC	IRISH	MASON	081	A	1	18
MCLOTHIAN	RONALD				28	ONTARIO	RP	SCOTCH	FOREMAN	083	A	1	14
MCLOUD	AGNES		2	1	9	0	CP			082	E		D
MCLOUD	MALCOM		1		25	0	PS	SCOTTISH	LABOURER	082	E		33
MCLOUD	RODERICK				29	P E ISLAND	CP	SCOTCH	TANNER & CURRIER	081	I		28
MCLOUGHLAN	GEO		1		21	QUE	SW	IRISH	PHOTOGRAPHER	082	E		48
MCLOUGHLIN	HUGH				28	ONTARIO	PR	SCOTCH	LUMBERMAN	081	G	2	12
MCLOY	EDWARD				50	RED RIVER	PS	SCOTCH	F	086	A	1	32
MCMAHAN	JOHN				52	IRELAND	RC	IRISH	F	081	J	1	27
MCMAHAN	JOHN				45	IRELAND	RC	IRISH	F	081	J	1	78
MCMAHAN	JOHN				48	IRELAND	RC	IRISH	F	081	J	1	80
MCMAHAN	MAURICE				46	IRELAND	RC	IRISH	F	081	J	1	63
MCMAHON	JAMES				58	IRELAND	RC	IRISH	F	081	J	1	65
MCMAHON	MICHAEL				58	IRELAND	RC	IRISH	F	081	J	1	78
MCMAHON	MICHAEL				50	IRELAND	RC	IRISH	FARMER	084	A		1
MCMAHON	MICHAEL				55	IRELAND	RC	IRISH	F	085	C		21
MCMAHON	PETER				33	IRELAND	RC	IRISH	FARMER	082	B		19
MCMAHON	TIMOTHY				74	IRELAND	RC	IRISH	F	081	J	1	33
MCMANAS	ANN		1	1	40	IRELAND	RC	IRISH	SERVANT	081	I		20
MCMANAS	JAMES				31	ONTARIO	RC	IRISH	FARMER	082	B		53
MCMANAS	JOHN				40	IRELAND	RC	IRISH	FARMER	082	B		39
MCMANAS	MARY		1	1	20	IRELAND	RC	IRISH	SERVANT	081	I		10
MCMANAS	MICHAEL		2		2	0	RC			082	B		D
MCMANAS	PATRICK				24	IRELAND	RC	IRISH		081	I		27
MCMANUS	DENIS				39	0	RC	IRISH	BLACKSMITH	081	A	1	12
MCMANUS	HANNAH		1	1	30	0	RC	IRISH	SERVANT	081	B		1
MCMANUS	JOHN				60	IRELAND	RC	IRISH	LAB	081	B		73
MCMANUS	JOHN				72	IRELAND	RC	IRISH		081	I		5
MCMANUS	PATRICK				45	0	RC	IRISH	F	081	A	1	3
MCMANUS	TERRANCE				71	IRELAND	RC	IRISH	F	081	A	1	3
MCMANUS	TIMOTHY		1		46	IRELAND	RC	IRISH	LAB	081	A	1	29
MCMARTIN	CHRISTINA		1	1	23	0	PS	SCOTTISH	TAILORESS	082	E		61
MCMARTIN	DAVID		1		26	0	CE	SCOTCH	LUMBERMAN	088	B		3
MCMARTIN	DUNCAN		1		14	ONTARIO	CS	SCOTCH		082	A		4
MCMARTIN	EDWARD		1		11	ONTARIO	CS	SCOTCH		082	A		4
MCMARTIN	ESTHER		1	1	16	ONTARIO	CS	SCOTCH		082	A		4
MCMARTIN	JAMES		1		22	0	CE	SCOTCH	LUMBERMAN	088	B		3
MCMARTIN	JOHN				55	SCOTLAND	CS	SCOTCH	F	082	A		5
MCMARTIN	PETER		1		18	ONTARIO	CS	SCOTCH	F	082	A		4
MCMASTER	HUGH				29	ONTARIO	RC	SCOTCH	TAVERNKEEPER	081	G	2	7
MCMASTER	THOMAS				50	IRELAND	RP	IRISH	F	081	K		9
MCMICHAIL	ALEXR				34	SCOTLAND	CS	SCOTCH	F	085	L		12
MCMICKEN	JOHN				28	IRELAND	RC	IRISH	CLERK	084	B		1
MCMILAN	ARCHEY		1		12	QUEBEC	WM	SCOTCH		081	G	1	28
MCMILLAN	ARCHIBALD				33	0	CS	SCOTCH	F	081	A	1	66
MCMILLAN	CATHARINE		1	1	20	0	CS	SCOTCH		081	A	1	48
MCMILLAN	DAVID				32	IRELAND	IM	IRISH	F	081	E		1
MCMILLAN	DONALD				49	SCOTLAND	CP	SCOTCH	F	081	C		24
MCMILLAN	DOUGALD		2		22	0	CP		SERVANT	085	B		D
MCMILLAN	DUNCAN				50	SCOTLAND	CS	SCOTCH	F	081	A	1	49
MCMILLAN	HELLEN		2	1		0	CS					1	D
MCMILLAN	JOHN				48	SCOTLAND	CP	SCOTCH	F	081	A	1	68
MCMILLAN	PETER		2		73	SCOTLAND	CS		F			1	D
MCMILLAN	PETER				40	P	CS	SCOTCH	F	081	A	1	66
MCMILLEN	ALEXR		1		20	0	WM	IRISH	F	085	J		22
MCMILLEN	EWEN				45	0	CP	SCOTCH	LAB	081	A	2	13
MCMILLEN	JOHN		1		23	0	WM	IRISH	F	085	J		22

SURNAME	NAME1	NAME2	STRAY	SEX	AGE	BIRTHPL	RELIGION	ORIGIN	OCCUP	DIST	SUB_DIST	DIV	PAGE
MCMILLEN	MARGRET		1	1	36	0	CP	SCOTCH		081	B		29
MCMILLIAN	ANGUS				45	0	CP	SCOTCH	F	086	A	2	12
MCMULLAN	MARY		1	1	3	ONTARIO	CE	SCOTCH		081	G	1	48
MCMULLAN	RICHARD		1		11	ONTARIO	CE	SCOTCH		081	G	1	48
MCMULLEN	ALEXANDER				61	IRELAND	RC	IRISH	FARMER	082	D		3
MCMULLEN	ALEXANDER		2		24	0	CE		F	082	G		D
MCMULLEN	JOHN				52	QUE	CE	IRISH	L	082	G		51
MCMULLEN	WILLIAM				50	IRELAND	CE	IRISH	FARMER	086	A	1	1
MCMULLIN	JOHN				35	0	CP	SCOTCH	F	082	G		2
MCMULLIN	ROLAND				40	ONTARIO	CS	SCOTCH	F	082	A		57
MCMULLIN	SARAH		1	1	56	ONTARIO	RC	IRISH		082	B		36
MCMULLIN	WILLIAM				50	IRELAND	EM	IRISH	F	082	A		67
MCMUNN	RICHARD		1		15	ONT	CE	IRISH	FARM LABOUR	081	J	1	38
MCMURRAY	THOMAS				40	SCOTLAND	WM	SCOTCH	EDITOR	085	I		11
MCMURRY	ROBERT				36	SCOTLAND	CP	IRISH	F	085	H		5
MCNAB	ALEXANDER				58	SCOTLAND	CP	SCOTCH	F	081	A	1	60
MCNAB	ALEXANDER				30	QUE	CP	SCOTCH	CARPENTER	081	A	2	7
MCNAB	ALEXANDER				41	0	CP	SCOTCH	F	081	A	2	40
MCNAB	ALLAN				51	SCOTLAND	CS	SCOTCH	F	081	H	2	2
MCNAB	ARCHIBALD		1		20	0	CP	SCOTCH	BLACKSMITH			1	81
MCNAB	ARCHIBALD				55	SCOTLAND	CS	SCOTCH	F	081	A	1	41
MCNAB	CATHARINE			1	42	SCOTLAND	CP	SCOTCH		081	A	1	31
MCNAB	COLLAN				40	SCOTLAND	CS	SCOTCH		081	H	1	15
MCNAB	DOUGALD	CAMPBELL			49	SCOTLAND	CS	SCOTCH	TEACHER	081	A	1	11
MCNAB	DUNCAN				82	SCOTLAND	CP	SCOTCH	F	081	A	1	30
MCNAB	DUNCAN				41	SCOTLAND	CS	SCOTCH	F	081	A	1	40
MCNAB	FRANCIS		1		15	0	CS	SCOTCH		081	A	1	12
MCNAB	ISABELLA			1	28	0	CP	SCOTCH	F	081	A	1	62
MCNAB	ISABELLA			1	78	SCOTLAND	CP	SCOTCH		081	B		85
MCNAB	JOHN				50	SCOTLAND	CS	SCOTCH	F	081	A	1	40
MCNAB	JOHN				51	SCOTLAND	CS	SCOTCH	F	081	A	1	51
MCNAB	JOHN				73	SCOTLAND	CS	SCOTCH	F	081	H	2	2
MCNAB	JOHN	DUNCAN			49	MALTA	CP	SCOTCH	MILLER	081	A	1	61
MCNABB	ALEX		1		45	SCOTLAND	CP	SCOTCH	PROV LAND SURVEYOR	090	F		19
MCNABB	ALLEN				45	SCOTCH	CP	SCOTCH	BAST? LAB	082	C	2	17
MCNABB	RICHARD				25	0	CE	ENGLISH	MINE LABOURER	089	A		20
MCNABB	ROBERT		1		20	0	CE	IRISH	LABOURER	085	B		19
MCNABB	ROBERT		2		2	0	CE			085	B		D
MCNABB	SAMUEL				44	SCOTLAND	BA	SCOTCH	BLACKSMITH	090	F		22
MCNABB	THOMAS				26	0	CE	IRISH	F	085	B		19
MCNABB	WILLIAM				36	SCOTLAND	PS	SCOTCH	F	085	C		17
MCNAIRNAY	HUGH	CHAS			50	IRELAND	PS	SCOTCH	WEAVER	085	C		12
MCNAMARA	DENIS				50	IRELAND	RC	IRISH	HOTELKEEPER	081	B		68
MCNAMARA	JOHN				29	IRELAND	RC	IRISH	SHOEMAKER	081	K		71
MCNAMARA	MARTIN				60	IRELAND	RC	IRISH	FARMER	082	B		40
MCNAMARA	PATRICK				29	IRELAND	RC	IRISH	SHOEMAKER	081	G	1	47
MCNAMARA	PATRICK				34	IRELAND	RC	IRISH	LAB	081	K		66
MCNAMARA	THOMAS				35	IRELAND	RC	IRISH	F	081	K		41
MCNAMEE	CHARLES				35	IRELAND	PS	IRISH	F	086	A	2	2
MCNAUGHT	JOHN		1		23	0	CP	SCOTCH	LAB	090	F		19
MCNAUGHTON	ALEXANDER				72	ONTARIO	CS	SCOTCH	F	082	A		73
MCNAUGHTON	DONALD				77	SCOTLAND	CS	SCOTCH	F	081	A	1	33
MCNAUGHTON	ELIZABETH				17	ONTARIO	CS	SCOTCH		082	A		74
MCNAUGHTON	JOHN		1		55	SCOTLAND	CS	SCOTCH	LAB	081	A	1	39
MCNAUGHTON	JOHN				29	SCOTLAND	CP	SCOTCH	LAB	090	F		25
MCNAUGHTON	MARY			1	24	SCOTLAND	CS	SCOTCH	SERVANT GIRL	082	A		9
MCNEAL	ARCHY				45	IRELAND	PS	IRISH		082	G		57
MCNEE	ANNIE		1	1	23	0	CP	SCOTCH	SERVANT	081	A	2	2
MCNEE	DUNCAN				65	SCOTLAND	CP	SCOTCH	F	081	A	2	40
MCNEE	DUNCAN		1		16	0	CP	SCOTCH		081	B		33
MCNEE	JAMES				59	SCOTLAND	CP	SCOTCH	F	081	A	2	44
MCNEE	JAMES				38	SCOTLAND	CP	SCOTCH	F	085	I		41
MCNEE	ROBERT		1		16	0	CP	SCOTCH	LAB	081	A	2	16
MCNEE	ROBERT				62	0	CP	SCOTCH	F	081	A	2	42
MCNEIL	DAN		1		26	0	RC	IRISH	SHANTY MAN	085	E		27
MCNEIL	DONALD				36	SCOTLAND	PS	IRISH		086	A	1	2
MCNEIL	JAMES				32	IRELAND	RP	IRISH	FARMER	082	I		10
MCNEIL	JOHN				30	IRELAND	CP	IRISH	FARMER	084	A		2
MCNEIL	NEIL				24	SCOTLAND	NG	IRISH	F	085	I		33
MCNEIL	WILLIAM	JOHN			40	IRELAND	WM	IRISH	F	082	A		57
MCNELLY	JOHN				50	IRELAND	RC	IRISH	FARMER	081	D		19
MCNEVEN	ALEX		1		20	0	CP	SCOTCH	SHOEMAKER	081	B		6
MCNEVEN	ALEX				60	SCOTLAND	CP	SCOTCH	F	081	C		26
MCNICHOL	DUNCAN				38	ONT	CP	SCOTCH	F	081	J	1	57
MCNICHOL	JAMES	SR			73	SCOTLAND	PS	SCOTCH		085	J		19
MCNIE	ALEX				55	SCOTLAND	CS	SCOTCH	F	081	C		21
MCNIE	DUNCAN				22	ONTARIO	CS	SCOTCH	F	081	C		20
MCNIE	MARGRET		1	1	33	0	CP	SCOTCH	SERVANT	081	A	1	21
MCNIEL	ROBERT				65	IRELAND	WM	IRISH	FARMER	082	I		11
MCNIREE	THOMAS		1		25	0	CE	IRISH	CLERK	081	K		74
MCNIRNEY	NANCY		1	1	29	0	WM	ENGLISH		085	J		10
MCNIVEN	ALEXANDER		2		84	SCOTLAND	CP		F			1	D
MCNIVEN	ALEXANDER				56	SCOTLAND	CP	SCOTCH	F	081	A	1	38
MCNIVEN	ALEXANDER				32	0	CP	SCOTCH	F	081	A	1	39
MCNULTY	CHARLES				28	QUEBEC	RC	IRISH	F	081	C		4
MCNULTY	DOMNICK				80	IRELAND	RC	IRISH	FARMER	081	D		13
MCNULTY	JAMES				27	QUEBEC	RC	IRISH	F	081	C		7
MCNULTY	JOHN				40	IRELAND	RC	IRISH	F	081	C		5
MCNULTY	JOHN				36	IRELAND	RC	IRISH	FARMER	081	D		13
MCNULTY	MARTIN				30	IRELAND	RC	IRISH	FARMER	081	D		11
MCNULTY	MICHAEL				20	IRELAND	RC	IRISH	FARMER	081	D		25
MCNULTY	PATRICK				40	IRELAND	RC	IRISH	F	081	J	1	88
MCNULTY	PATRICK				65	IRELAND	RC	IRISH	F	081	J	2	6
MCPEACH	HENRY				49	IRELAND	RC	IRISH	FARMER	082	B		1
MCPEACH	JOHN				45	IRELAND	RC	IRISH	FARMER	082	B		15
MCPEACH	PATRICK				60	IRELAND	RC	IRISH	FARMER	082	B		4
MCPEAK	CATHERINE			1	29	0	RC	ENGLISH	INNKEEPER	081	H	2	24
MCPHEE	DANIEL				21	QUE	CP	SCOTCH	LAB	090	F		24
MCPHEE	JAMES				21	0	CE	SCOTCH	SADDLER & HARNESS	081	B		73
MCPHEE	JANE		1	1	24	0	CP	IRISH		081	B		56
MCPHEE	JANE	ANN	1	1	1	0	CP	IRISH		081	B		56
MCPHEE	JOHN		1		14	0	CE	SCOTCH		081	B		67
MCPHEE	JOHN				54	CANADA	ME	ENGLISH	F	085	A		3
MCPHEE	MARY			1	50	QUE	CP	SCOTCH		081	B		20
MCPHERSON	ADAM				30	0	CE	SCOTCH	CARPENTER	081	B		42
MCPHERSON	ALEXANDER				27	SCOTLAND	PS	SCOTCH	F	085	J		7

SURNAME	NAME1	NAME2	STRAY	SEX	AGE	BIRTHPL	RELIGION	ORIGIN	OCCUP	DIST	SUB_DIST	DIV	PAGE
MCPHERSON	ALEXANDER				39	SCOTLAND	CP	SCOTCH	MINER	090	D		8
MCPHERSON	ANGUS				34	O	PS	SCOTCH	F	081	E		17
MCPHERSON	ANN		2	1	3	O	CP			090	D		D
MCPHERSON	COLIN		1		61	SCOTLAND	PS	SCOTCH	F	081	K		49
MCPHERSON	COLLIN				23	O	OP	SCOTCH	F	081	E		17
MCPHERSON	DONALD				30	SCOTLAND	PS	SCOTCH	F	081	E		17
MCPHERSON	ELIZABETH		1	1	63	SCOTLAND	PS	SCOTCH		081	K		49
MCPHERSON	JAMES		1		20	O	CP	SCOTCH	SHANTY MAN	085	E		27
MCPHERSON	MALCOM				48	SCOTLAND	PS	SCOTTISH	TAILOR	082	E		38
MCPHERSON	MARY		2	1		O	CP			090	D		D
MCPHERSON	WILLIAM				44	SCOTLAND	PS	SCOTTISH	COOPER	082	B		51
MCPHILEMY	WILLIAM				45	IRELAND	EP	IRISH	F	086	A	1	17
MCPONTONY	LOUIS				31	IRELAND	RC	IRISH	FARMER	082	B		1
MCQUACKIMIE	LOUIS				69	O	RC	INDIAN	HUNTER	089	A		48
MCQUACKIMIE	LOUIS				30	O	RC	INDIAN	LABOURER	089	A		48
MCQUADE	EDWARD				50	ONTARIO	RC	IRISH	F	082	A		80
MCQUADE	JAMES				35	ONTARIO	RC	IRISH	F	082	A		36
MCQUADE	MARIA			1	80	IRELAND	RC	IRISH		082	A		36
MCQUESTEIN	JAMES				66	IRELAND	RP	IRISH	F	082	K	1	6
MCQUIRTER	THOMAS		1		21	O	WM	IRISH	FARMER	086	B		7
MCQUITTY	DAVID				59	IRELAND	EM	IRISH	F	081	H	2	30
MCQUITTY	JOSEPH				62	IRELAND	CP	IRISH	FARMER	082	B		48
MCQUITTY	PHEBE		2	1	58	IRELAND	EM			081	H	2	D
MCQUITTY	WILLIAM				31	O	OM	IRISH	F	081	H	1	16
MCRAE	JOHN				65	SCOTLAND	CP	SCOTCH	MILLER	081	I		40
MCRAY	DUNCAN		1		30	SCOTLAND	PS	SCOTCH	LUMBERMAN	086	B		2
MCRAY	JAMES				28	ONTARIO	RC	SCOTCH	LABOURER	090	E		22
MCREA	DONALD				35	SCOTLAND	CP	SCOTCH	STOREKEEPER	081	A	1	35
MCREA	JAMES				45	IRELAND	RC	IRISH	F	081	C		22
MCREA	MARGRET		1	1	30	SCOTLAND	RC	SCOTCH	SERVANT	081	H	1	14
MCREA	RICHARD				50	IRELAND	CE	IRISH	F	081	C		25
MCREADIE	WILLIAM				37	SCOTLAND	CS	SCOTCH	F	081	H	1	9
MCSOURLEY	THOS				60	IRELAND	RC	IRISH	F	082	L		6
MCSOURLEY	WM				60	IRELAND	RC	IRISH	F	082	L		6
MCSOURLY	JOHN				54	IRELAND	RC	IRISH	F	082	L		5
MCTAVISH	ADAM				40	O	CP	SCOTCH	BLACKSMITH	081	I		2
MCTAVISH	ALEXANDER				45	O	CS	SCOTCH	F	081	H	2	42
MCTAVISH	HUGH				37	O	CS	SCOTCH	F	081	H	2	36
MCVANE	ARCHD		1		28	O	PS	SCOTTISH	WAGONMAKER	082	E		59
MCVANE	MARY		1	1	26	O	PS	SCOTTISH		082	E		59
MCVEETERS	SAMUEL				35	IRELAND	CE	IRISH	F	082	A		75
MCVEETERS	SAMUEL				63	IRELAND	CE	IRISH	F	082	A		79
MCVEETERS	WILLIAM		1		40	IRELAND	CE	IRISH	F	082	A		79
MCVICAR	CHRISTINA			1	61	SCOTLAND	CP	SCOTCH		090	F		25
MCWADE	ELIAS				40	ONTARIO	CS	IRISH	F	082	A		40
MCWHIRTER	WILLIAM				45	SCOTLAND	WM	SCOTCH	F	081	A	2	57
MCWILLIAMS	JAMES				32	QUE	RC	IRISH	HOTELKEEPER	081	D		9
MCWILLIAMS	MARK				38	QUEBEC	RC	IRISH	PLASTERER	081	J	1	5
MCWILLIAMS	MAUDE		2	1	1	O	CE			081	D		D
MCWILLIAMS	THOMAS				33	QUE	RC	IRISH	STOREKEEPER	081	D		7
MDIGAN	SIMON				50	IRELAND	RC	IRISH	F	082	G		11
ME-SQAWAC-GEN	JOCKO				80	ONTARIO	RC	INDIAN	HUNTER	084	D		1
MEARS	RICHARD				50	ENGLAND	CE	ENGLISH	F	085	C		18
MECHEKEBINAISIE	ISAIAH				28	ONT	RC	INDIAN	FISHERMAN & LABOURER	090	B		12
MEE	JOHN		1		20	QUE	CE	IRISH	SERVANT	084	E		1
MEEHAN	ANDREW				31	O	RC	IRISH	HOTELKEEPER	082	E		15
MEEHEN	LAWRENCE				37	ONTARIO	RC	IRISH	FARMER	082	B		9
MEEKEN	MICHAEL				60	IRELAND	RC	IRISH	HOTELKEEPER	082	B		5
MEENEY	ELLEN		1	1	19	O	RC	IRISH	SERVANT	082	E		42
MEGANISH	PAUL				60	QUEBEC	RC	INDIAN	HUNTER	083	B	2	1
MEGGISON	WILLIAM	D			37	ENGLAND	PM	ENGLISH	F	085	I		41
MEGUIRE	JOSEPH				30	QUE	RC	FRENCH	F	082	K	1	16
MEGWANABI	JOSEPH				28	O	RC	INDIAN	F & FISHERMAN	087	A		32
MEGWAS	JOSEPH				26	O	RC	INDIAN	F & FISHERMAN	087	B	1	9
MEGWONNUBBE	ANDREW				40	US	RC	INDIAN	F & FISHERMAN	087	A		43
MEIKLE	AGNES			1	41	SCOTLAND	SCOTCH	SCOTLAND		081	B		2
MEJAKE	ETIENNE				34	US	RC	INDIAN	F	087	A		35
MELLAN	BERNARD		1		66	IRELAND	RC	IRISH	LAB	081	K		61
MELLEY	JOHN				54	IRELAND	CE	IRISH	F	081	H	2	19
MELLON	ELLEN		1	1	25	QUE	RC	IRISH	SERVANT	082	E		2
MELON	BRIDGET		1	1	35	QUE	RC	IRISH	SERVANT	082	E		29
MELON	MARY		1	1	24	QUE	RC	IRISH	SERVANT	082	E		29
MELVILLE	ANDREW				56	SCOTLAND	CS	SCOTCH	F	081	C		46
MELVILLE	FRANCES		1	1	50	IRELAND	ME	IRISH		082	E		70
MELVILLE	JOHN		1		70	SCOTLAND	PS	SCOTTISH		082	E		70
MENADICE	JOHN				20	O	PA	INDIAN	HUNTER	090	F		24
MENADICE	WILLIAM		2		60	O	PA		HUNTER	090	F		D
MENDASKANG	CHARLES				28	O	RC	INDIAN	F & FISHERMAN	087	A		29
MENTROY	JOHN				40	QUE	RC	FRENCH	LUMBERMAN	086	C	1	1
MENZIES	GEORGE	H			34	SCOTLAND	CP	SCOTCH	F	081	A	2	3
MENZIES	JANE			1	38	SCOTLAND	PS	SCOTCH		089	A		36
MENZIES	ROBERT				50	SCOTLAND	CE	SCOTCH	CARPENTER	082	C	1	41
MERCER	JOHN				25	QUE	RC	FRENCH	LAB	090	F		14
MERCHANT	CHARLES		1		23	QUE	RC	FRENCH	LAB	081	A	2	16
MERCHANT	JOSEPH				30	QUEBEC	RC	FRENCH	F	082	A		81
MERCHANT	WILLIAM		1		14	QUE	RC	FRENCH	LAB	081	A	2	16
MERCIER	ANDREW				55	QUE	RC	FRENCH	BUSHMAN	084	E		2
MERCIER	BAPTISTE				53	QUEBEC	RC	FRENCH	F	083	C		4
MERCIER	JAMES				62	ENGLAND	CE	ENGLISH		082	F		14
MERCILE	BATTIEST				44	QUE	RC	FRENCH	F	082	C	1	7
MERCILLE	HANNAH		2	1	2	O	RC			082	C	1	D
MERET	CHARLES				50	JERSEY	CE	ENGLISH	LAB	082	F		20
MERIGAN	CATHERINE		1	1	30	IRELAND	RC	IRISH	SERVANT	081	B		67
MERIGAN	JAMES		2		56	IRELAND	RC		LABOURER	082	E		D
MERION	MARIA								SEE MARIA	084	D		1
MERON	JOSEPH		1		25	QUE	RC	FRENCH	LAB	082	K	1	10
MERRIANT	NERCIESE				40	QUE	RC	FRENCH	LAB	082	C	1	60
MERRICK	CHARLES		2		76	O	CE		MILLER	081	K		D
MERRICK	CHARLES	HENRY			22	O	CE	WELSH	LUMBERMAN	081	K		63
MERRICK	CHARLOTTE		2	1	36	O	CE			081	K		D
MERRIMAN	MICHAEL		1		25	IRELAND	RC	IRISH	BLACKSMITH	081	A	1	1
MERRION	ALICE		2	1	52	QUE	RC			082	C	1	D
MERRION	SILBARE				60	QUE	RC	FRENCH	LAB	082	C	1	60
MERRIOUNT	CERIAC				55	QUE	RC	FRENCH	F	082	C	1	19
MERVON	GUY				60	QUEBEC	EM	FRENCH	F	082	A		19
MESHEMAHKENAHGE	(WIDOW)			1	60	US	RC	INDIAN	F	087	C		3

SURNAME	NAME1	NAME2	STRAY	SEX	AGE	BIRTHPL	RELIGION	ORIGIN	OCCUP	DIST	SUB_DIST	DIV	PAGE
MESHEMINONAQUAH	JEAN	BAPTISTE			62	USA	RC	INDIAN	FARMER	087	B	1	3
MESHININI	PIERRE				74	US	RC	INDIAN	F	087	A		31
MESKILL	GEORGE				28	IRELAND	RC	IRISH	FARMER	082	B		20
METCALFE	HENRY				34	0	CE	ENGLISH	BLACKSMITH	082	C	1	3
METICOMAP	PETER				30	0	PA	INDIAN	HUNTER & TRAPPER	090	C		8
METOSSAGE	FRANCOIS				55	US	RC	INDIAN	MECHANIC & F	087	A		16
METWEIASHI	(WIDOW)			1	58	US	RC	INDIAN	F	087	A		22
METWEIASHI	LEON				29	0	RC	INDIAN	F	087	A		23
METWEIASHI	WILLIAM				34	US	RC	INDIAN	COOPER & F	087	A		23
MEZIES	GEORGE		1		34	SCOTLAND	CP	SCOTCH	LAB	081	B		73
MEZIES	GEORGE				25	SCOTLAND	RP	SCOTCH	F	085	K	2	6
MICHAELIES	FERD				35	GERMANY	LU	GERMAN	FARMER	082	I		55
MICHAELIS	AUGUST				26	GERMANY	WM	GERMAN	F	082	H		16
MICHAELIS	EARNEST				30	GERMANY	WM	GERMAN	F	082	H		13
MICHAELIS	EDWARD				28	GERMANY	LU	GERMAN	F	082	H		16
MICHAELIS	FREDERICK				36	GERMANY	WM	GERMAN	F	082	H		13
MICHAELIS	WILLIAM				0		WM			082	H		D
MICHAELS	CHARLES				22	GERMANY	EV	GERMAN	FARMER	082	I		66
MICHIEL	GUSTAVE				36	GERMANY	LU	GERMAN	F	082	J		9
MICHIKEBENESE	JOSIT		2	1	30	MANITOBA	RC			090	F		D
MICHIKELINESE	DAVID				50	RED RIVER	RC	INDIAN	LAB	090	F		12
MICHIKILINSE	ANTOINE				24	0	RC	INDIAN	LAB	090	F		12
MICHIMAKWA	(WIDOW)			1		ONTARIO	PA	INDIAN	HUNTER & TRAPPER	090	E		21
MICK	DANIEL				45	IRELAND	CE	IRISH	F	082	F		4
MICK	GEORGE				56	IRELAND	EM	IRISH	F	082	F		6
MICK	JOHN				54	IRELAND	CE	IRISH	F	082	F		6
MICK	MOUNTEFER				35	IRELAND	CE	IRISH	F	082	F		9
MICK	PETER				45	IRELAND	CE	IRISH	F	082	G		32
MICKLESON	AUGUST				28	GERMANY	LU	GERMAN	F	082	G		14
MIEKLES	HERMOND				25	GERMANY	CE	GERMAN	TAILOR	081	B		63
MIETT	OLLIVER				37	QUE	RC	FRENCH	LAB	081	B		20
MIGAKWAT	LOUIS				38	US	RC	INDIAN	F & FISHERMAN	087	A		12
MILES	ALEXANDER				59	SCOTLAND	RP	SCOTCH	FARMER	082	I		12
MILIE	SISTER		1	1	22	US	RC	GERMAN	NUN	090	F		11
MILLAR	CATHERINE		1	1	36	IRELAND	WM	IRISH	SERVANT	082	E		30
MILLAR	CHRISTENE		1	1	29	0	CP	SCOTTISH		082	E		8
MILLAR	JAMES				58	SCOTLAND	PS	SCOTTISH	BUTCHER	082	E		57
MILLAR	JANE	H	1	1	11	0	ME	ENGLISH		085	A		27
MILLAR	JOHN	P			33	SCOTLAND	PS	SCOTTISH	MERCHANT	082	E		57
MILLAR	RACHAEL		1	1	25	IRELAND	CE	IRISH	SERVANT	082	E		33
MILLE	ANN		1	1	2	0	EM	GERMAN		082	G		88
MILLE	MARTIN		1		11	GERMANY	EM	GERMAN		082	G		88
MILLER	ABRAHAM		1		21	GERMANY	NG	GERMAN	SHOEMAKER	081	K		63
MILLER	ADAM				70	IRELAND	WM	IRISH	F	082	G		22
MILLER	ALEXANDER				51	SCOTLAND	PS	SCOTCH	F	081	H	2	7
MILLER	ARCHIBALD				47	SCOTLAND	CS	SCOTCH	F	081	J	1	41
MILLER	DAVID				24	0	PS	IRISH	CLERK	087	B	3	5
MILLER	DAVID				44	IRELAND	PS	IRISH	MERCHANT	087	B	3	5
MILLER	DAVID				95	IRELAND	PS	IRISH	TRADER	087	B	3	6
MILLER	EDWARD		1		32	GERMANY	LU	GERMAN	MINER	090	F		17
MILLER	HEINRICH				60	GERMANY	LU	GERMAN	L	082	G		14
MILLER	HUGH	H	1		20	0	WM	ENGLISH	F	086	B		5
MILLER	JAMES				43	SCOTLAND	CS	SCOTCH	F	081	A	1	66
MILLER	JAMES				43	QUE	CE	SCOTCH	F	082	G		6
MILLER	JAMES				33	0	WM	IRISH	F	086	B		4
MILLER	JAMES		1		18	0	CE	IRISH	LABOURER	089	A		47
MILLER	JANETT		1	1	10	0	CS	SCOTCH		081	H	2	6
MILLER	JOHN				52	SCOTLAND	CS	SCOTCH	F	081	H	2	4
MILLER	JOHN				20	0	PS	IRISH	CLERK	087	B	3	6
MILLER	ROBERT				26	US	PM	IRISH	F	085	I		40
MILLER	WILLIAM				29	0	EM	SCOTCH	F	081	A	1	54
MILLER	WILLIAM				38	0	CP	SCOTCH	COOPER	081	B		48
MILLER	WILLIAM				47	IRELAND	CP	IRISH	FARMER	082	I		66
MILLER	WILLIAN	HENRY			26	0	CE	IRISH	DOCTOR	086	C	1	11
MILLIN	ARTHUR				33	0	WM	IRISH	F	086	A	2	5
MILLS	GEORGE				45	ENGLAND	CE	ENGLISH	GARDENER	085	I		29
MILLS	ISAAC				44	IRELAND	CE	ENGLISH	F	085	I		34
MILLS	JAMES				38	0	CE	IRISH	HOTELKEEPER	081	D		8
MILLS	JANE			1	46	0	PR	ENGLISH		082	G		45
MILLS	JOHN				47	0	CS	ENGLISH	BUTCHER	081	I		14
MILLS	JOHN	G			23	0	CE	IRISH	AXEMAKER	082	E		48
MILLS	MARY	JANE	1	1	16	ONTARIO	RC	IRISH		082	B		5
MILLS	RICHARD				24	IRELAND	CE	IRISH	F	085	I		34
MILLS	ROBERT				47	0	CE	IRISH	LUMBER MERCHANT	081	I		25
MILLS	WILLIAM				31	0	CE	IRISH	CABINETMAKER	081	I		1
MILLSON	ROBERT		1		31	ENGLAND	BA	ENGLISH	LUMBERMAN	088	B		5
MILNE	ANDREW				63	SCOTLAND	CP	SCOTCH	F	085	I		18
MILNE	GEORGE				39	SCOTLAND	CP	SCOTCH	CLERK	081	B		3
MILNE	GEORGE				33	SCOTLAND	PS	SCOTCH	F	086	A	1	28
MINAKWAT	PAUL				56	US	RC	INDIAN	F	087	A		32
MINAKWAT	VINCENT				28	0	RC	INDIAN	LAB & F	087	A		32
MINARD	FRANCIS				28	0	RC	FRENCH	F	081	K		30
MINARD	JOSEPH				17	ONTARIO	RC	FRENCH	LAB	083	C		4
MINER	ELECTA			1	58	US	WM			084	D		6
MINERS	JAMES				35	ENGLAND	PM	ENGLISH	MINER	089	A		27
MINETT	CHARLES	JAMES			29	ENGLAND	CE	ENGLISH	CARPENTER	085	E		31
MINETT	ED	CHARLES	2			0	NG			085	F		D
MINISINAW	GEORGE				30	0	CE	INDIAN	LABOURER	089	B		43
MINKING	CHARLES				45	GERMANY	CE	GERMAN	LAB	081	B		62
MINOR	BASIL				48	QUEBEC	RC	FRENCH	FARMER	084	C		7
MINOR	MAXIME				47	QUEBEC	RC	FRENCH	FARMER	084	C		7
MINORE	ALFRED				32	QUE	RC	FRENCH	TINSMITH	082	E		14
MINORE	JOHANNA			1	25	0	RC	ENGLISH		082	E		50
MINORE	JOSEPH				64	QUE	RC	FRENCH	TINSMITH	082	E		26
MINORE	LIZEY		1	1	11	0	RC	FRENCH		082	E		50
MIRON	JOSEPH				27	0	RC	FRENCH	LABOURER	089	B		12
MIRON	LOUIS				30	0	RC	FRENCH	BOAT MAN	089	B		8
MIRON	RAYMOND				23	0	RC	FRENCH	BOATMAN	089	B		12
MIRON	SARAH		2	1	2	0	RC			089	B		D
MISCOPEACE	MDM		1		0	RC	INDIAN		090	C		9
MISGUADES	HARRY				35	0	WM	INDIAN	HUNTER	086	A	3	6
MISHAW	ANGUS		1		24	0	RC	SCOTCH	SHANTYMAN	085	E		27
MISHAWAS	THOMAS				53	US	RC	INDIAN	F & FISHERMAN	087	A		29
MISHEWEWO'S	(WIDOW)		1	1		ONTARIO	PA	INDIAN	HUNTER & TRAPPER	090	E		21
MISHIBINIGUNA	DANIEL				54	US	RC	INDIAN	F & FISHERMAN	087	A		21
MISHIBINIGUNA	FRANCOIS				22	0	RC	INDIAN	F	087	A		21

SURNAME	NAME1	NAME2	STRAY	SEX	AGE	BIRTHPL	RELIGION	ORIGIN	OCCUP	DIST	SUB_DIST	DIV	PAGE
MISHIBINIGUNA	MOYSE				64	US	RC	INDIAN	F	087	A		21
MISHIMUE	(WIDOW)			1		ONTARIO	PA	INDIAN	HUNTER & TRAPPER	090	E		17
MISHO	JOHN				38	O	RC	FRENCH	FISHERMAN	086	A	1	33
MISKE	MICHAEL		1		24	POLAND	RC	POLAN	LAB	081	I		42
MISKELLEY	JAMES				34	IRELAND	WM	IRISH	TINSMITH	081	B		54
MISKOMANITONS	MARY		1	1	11	O	RC	INDIAN	STUDENT	087	A		1
MISSISANGWE	MICHEL				39	US	RC	INDIAN	COOPER & F	087	A		22
MISSISSANCE	MICHELLE				65	US	PA	INDIAN	F & FISHERMAN	087	C		5
MITCHEL	BRIDGET		1	1	50	IRELAND	RC	IRISH	SPINSTER	082	C	1	37
MITCHEL	GEORGE				35	QUE	ME	ENGLISH	BLACKSMITH	082	D		7
MITCHEL	JAMES		2		1	O	CP			081	B		D
MITCHEL	JOHN				60	IRELAND	CE	IRISH	F & MILLWRIGHT	082	C	1	43
MITCHEL	W	C			36	SCOTLAND	CP	SCOTCH	WATCHMAKER	081	B		52
MITCHELL	ABRAHAM				44	ENGLAND	WM	ENGLISH	MINER	089	A		17
MITCHELL	DONALD				40	SCOTLAND	PS	SCOTCH	F	085	D		3
MITCHELL	DUNCAN				27	CANADA	PS	SCOTCH	LAB	087	B	2	2
MITCHELL	JAMES		1		41	ONTARIO	CS	SCOTCH	F	082	A		27
MITCHELL	JAMES				45	ENGLAND	PM	ENGLISH	MINER	089	A		32
MITCHELL	JOHN				55	O	CE	INDIAN	F&LABOURER&TINSMITH	087	B	1	18
MITCHELL	JOHN	L	2			O	WM			082	E		D
MITCHELL	ROBERT				22	O	PS	IRISH	F	085	D		3
MITCHELL	S	E			34	ENGLAND	WM	ENGLISH	STATIONER	082	E		27
MITCHELL	WILLIAM				31	O	CP	IRISH	FARMER	081	D		3
MIXINNENNE	LOUIS		2		1	O	RC	INDIAN		087	B	1	D
MIZEONOQUICH	JEAN	BAPTISTE			52	O	RC	INDIAN	F & HUNTER	087	B	1	4
MIZIAH	JOHN		1		61	O	RC	INDIAN	FISHERMAN	089	B		23
MIZIGON	ANTOINE				50	US	RC	INDIAN	LABOURER	089	B		41
MIZIGON	JOSELLE		1	1	20	US	RC	INDIAN		089	B		41
MIZIGON	MICHEAL				50	US	CE	INDIAN	LABOURER	089	B		42
MIZIGON	SUSAN		1	1	3	US	RC	INDIAN		089	B		41
MIZIH	GEORGE		2		2	O	RC			089	B		D
MOCOSIK	JOSEPH				55	US	RC	INDIAN	F	087	A		46
MOCOTABIN	BOB				35	US	CE	INDIAN	F	087	B	1	13
MOCOTAIKWOSHK	LOUIS				38	US	RC	INDIAN	F & FISHERMAN	087	C		2
MOFFAT	ALEXANDER				69	SCOTLAND	FK	SCOTTISH	MILLER	082	E		61
MOFFAT	ALEXR	JR			41	SCOTLAND	CP	SCOTTISH	POSTMASTER	082	E		60
MOFFAT	HENRY				48	IRELAND	CE	IRISH	F	086	A	2	8
MOFFAT	JAMES		1		10	O	PS	SCOTTISH		082	D		4
MOFFAT	JAS	P			43	SCOTLAND	PS	SCOTTISH	CROWN LAND AGENT	082	E		32
MOFFAT	JOHN		1		6	O	PS	SCOTTISH		082	D		4
MOFFAT	WILLIAM				45	SCOTLAND	CP	SCOTTISH	FARMER	082	D		1
MOFFAT	WILLIAM				26	O	WM	IRISH		086	A	2	9
MOHNS	AGUSTUS				39	GERMANY	RP	GERMAN	F	082	J		16
MOIRARTY	JAMES				28	IRELAND	RC	IRISH	FARMER	081	G	1	42
MOIRARTY	PATRICK				55	IRELAND	RC	IRISH	FARMER	081	G	1	37
MOIZON	JOHN	BATHURST			43	QUE	RC	FRENCH	M-MAKER	082	D		16
MOLES	R	J			26	O	WM	IRISH	PHOTOGRAPHER	081	B		66
MOLLOY	SUSAN			1	53	IRELAND	RC	IRISH		081	K		52
MOLONEY	JOHN				55	IRELAND	RC	IRISH	FARMER	081	D		14
MOLONEY	MICHAEL				60	IRELAND	RC	IRISH	FARMER	081	D		15
MOLONEY	PATRICK				55	IRELAND	RC	IRISH	FARMER	081	D		14
MONAGHAN	HUGH				48	IRELAND	PR	IRISH	F	085	A		16
MONAGHAN	JOHN				38	IRELAND	RC	IRISH	SAWYER	081	B		23
MONE	FRANCIS				54	IRELAND	RC	IRISH	TAILOR	082	E		11
MONE	HUGH				30	IRELAND	RC	IRISH	CARPENTER	082	E		15
MONET	JOSEPH		1		21	QUE	RC	FRENCH		081	C		54
MONETOWOB	CATHRAN			1	60	O	WM	INDIAN	TRAPPER	086	A	3	3
MONGER	I	P	1		27	UNITED STATES	UV	GERMAN	TEAMSTER	090	D		2
MONHOUSE	GEORGE		1		31	ENGLAND	ME	ENGLISH	MILLER	085	E		10
MONKMAN	WILLIAM				78	ENGLAND	CE	ENGLISH	F	086	A	1	3
MONRO	REED	PERCIVAL	1		23	SCOTLAND	CP	SCOTCH	F	085	E		23
MONSON	(WIDOW)			1		ONTARIO	PA	INDIAN	HUNTER & TRAPPER	090	E		21
MONSON	GEORGE				70	IRELAND	CE	IRISH	WEAVER	081	F		11
MONSON	LOUIS		1		19	QUE	RC	FRENCH	LAB	082	C	1	56
MONSON	PALLINE		1	1	62	QUE	RC	FRENCH		082	C	1	56
MONSON'S	(2ND SON)		2			ONTARIO	PA	INDIAN		090	E		D
MONTGOMERY	ALEXANDER				58	SCOTLAND	CE	SCOTCH	F	082	K	2	3
MONTGOMERY	DAVID				61	SCOTLAND	CS	SCOTCH	F	082	A		33
MONTGOMERY	JOHN				46	IRELAND	CP	IRISH	FARMER	082	I		70
MONTGOMERY	JOHN				24	O	EM	IRISH	F	085	D		28
MONTGOMERY	JOHN				48	IRELAND	PS	IRISH	F	086	A	1	5
MONTGOMERY	MARY			1	62	IRELAND	PS	IRISH		082	E		76
MONTGOMERY	ROBERT				70	SCOTLAND	PS	SCOTCH	MINISTER	081	K		2
MONTGOMERY	SUE		1	1	23	QUE	CP	ENGLISH	SERVANT	082	E		70
MONTGOMERY	WILLIAM				51	IRELAND	OM	IRISH	F	081	H	1	18
MONTGOMERY	WILLIAM		1		22	O	WM	SCOTCH	LABOURER	088	A		7
MONTGOMERY	WM				32	IRELAND	CE	IRISH	F	085	J		9
MONTGOMORY	WILLIAM		1		80	SCOTLAND	CP	SCOTCH		081	A	1	60
MONTIE	ALBERTINE		1	1	21	GERMANY	RC	GERMAN	SERVANT	082	E		37
MONTRE	CHAROLETTE		1	1	11	O	RC	FRENCH		082	E		35
MONTRE	JOSEPH		1		76	QUE	RC	FRENCH	HUNTER	082	E		35
MONTRE	MARIA		1	1	14	O	RC	FRENCH		082	E		35
MONTRE	MARY		1	1	32	O	RC	INDIAN		082	E		35
MONTRIAVER	JENNIE		1	1	17	O	WM	FRENCH		081	B		73
MONTROY	LEWIS				40	QUE	RC	FRENCH	FARMER	084	E		4
MOON	ARCHER				45	IRELAND	PS	IRISH	F	085	E		14
MOON	JOSEPH		1		80	ENGLAND	WM	ENGLISH		085	L		8
MOONEY	PATRICK				58	IRELAND	RC	IRISH	F	081	A	2	46
MOOR	ANDREW		1		24	O	NR	IRISH	F	086	A	2	1
MOOR	ANNE		1	1	24	IRELAND	RC	IRISH	SERVANT	081	I		41
MOOR	DAVID				31	ONT	WM	IRISH	BLACKSMITH	081	C		40
MOOR	DAVID				64	IRELAND	CP	IRISH	FARMER	082	I		65
MOOR	ELIAS				66	QUEBEC	CE	ENGLISH	MILLER	082	B		55
MOOR	JOHN	JNR			24	O	RC	ENGLISH	LAB	082	K	1	15
MOOR	MAREY		1	1	13	O	EP	SCOTCH		084	G	1	1
MOOR	MARTHA		1	1	36	IRELAND	CP	IRISH	COOK	085	B		7
MOOR	MATTHIAS				45	ENGLAND	CE	ENGLISH	RETIRED COM OFFICER	085	I		38
MOOR	STEPHEN				50	IRELAND	WM	IRISH	F	082	A		39
MOOR	STEPHEN		1		95	IRELAND	WM	IRISH		082	A		39
MOORE	ANDREW				24	O	CP	SCOTCH	DOCTOR MEDICINE	081	I		44
MOORE	BEN		1		14	O	CE	IRISH		082	L		6
MOORE	BENJAMIN				46	QUE	CE	ENGLISH	F	082	K	1	11
MOORE	BENJAMIN		1		23	O	WM	IRISH		084	D		6
MOORE	CHARLES				35	QUEBEC	CE	IRISH	F	081	J	1	32
MOORE	CHARLES				26	ENGLAND	CE	ENGLISH	F	085	D		14
MOORE	CHOROLETTE	A	1	1	9	O	CE	IRISH		082	L		6

SURNAME	NAME1	NAME2	STRAY	SEX	AGE	BIRTHPL	RELIGION	ORIGIN	OCCUP	DIST	SUB_DIST	DIV	PAGE
MOORE	DUDLY				31	ONT	CE	IRISH	F	081	J	1	26
MOORE	DYRE				35	QUE	CE	IRISH	CARPENTER	082	G		58
MOORE	EDWARD				27	ONT	CE	IRISH	F	081	J	1	26
MOORE	EDWARD		2		1	ONT	CE			081	J	1	D
MOORE	EMERY				37	QUEBEC	CE	AMERICAN	FOREMAN	084	D		1
MOORE	EMERY		1		26	O	WM	IRISH	F	084	D		6
MOORE	EMMA			1	77	MOOSE FACTORY	CE	NORWEGIAN		089	B		25
MOORE	ESIBELLE		2	1	3	ONT	CE			081	J	1	D
MOORE	GEORGE		2			O	RC			089	B		D
MOORE	HARMEN				70	US	WM	IRISH	IMPROVER OF RIVERS	082	G		58
MOORE	ISABELLA		1	1	20	ONTARIO	CE	SCOTCH		082	A		21
MOORE	JAMES				33	ONT	CE	IRISH	F	081	J	1	26
MOORE	JAMES				60	IRELAND	CP	IRISH	FARMER	082	I		34
MOORE	JOB				54	QUE	CE	SCOTCH	F	082	K	1	18
MOORE	JOHN				55	O	EM	ENGLISH	CARPENTER	081	B		3
MOORE	JOHN				29	ONT	RC	IRISH	F	081	J	1	25
MOORE	JOHN		2		5	ONT	CE			081	J	1	D
MOORE	JOHN				40	IRELAND	CS	IRISH	F	082	A		21
MOORE	JOHN		1		52	QUE	RC	ENGLISH	LUMBERMAN	082	K	1	19
MOORE	JOHN				30	US	PB	IRISH	F	082	K	2	2
MOORE	JOHN				41	BERMUDA	PS	SCOTCH	FIREMAN	086	C	1	7
MOORE	JOHN	SNR			52	QUE	RC	ENGLISH	LUMBERER	082	K	1	14
MOORE	LUCY		1	1	30	O	WM	ENGLISH		089	B		8
MOORE	MARTHA		1		30	O	PB	IRISH		082	K	2	2
MOORE	MARY	AN	1	1	45	O	CE	IRISH	SERVANT	082	L		6
MOORE	MAURICE				27	IRELAND	RC	IRISH	FARMER	081	G	2	10
MOORE	MITCHEL		1		26	ONT	RC	INDIAN	LUMBERMAN	088	B		5
MOORE	NANCY			1	31	QUE	CE	ENGLISH		082	K	1	12
MOORE	REBECCA			1	38	QUE	WM	IRISH		084	D		6
MOORE	RICHARD				55	IRELAND	CP	IRISH	F	082	G		6
MOORE	ROBERT				50	IRELAND	WM	IRISH	F	086	A	2	5
MOORE	ROBT				23	ENGLAND	BA	ENGLISH	LIGHTERMAN	082	E		23
MOORE	SARAH		1	1	6	O	CE	IRISH		082	L		7
MOORE	SARAH	ANN	2	1		O	WM			082	G		D
MOORE	STEADMAN				33	QUE	WM	IRISH	MECHANIC	082	G		54
MOORE	SUSAN		1	1	23	O	WM	IRISH	SERVANT	082	E		9
MOORE	THOMAS		1		5	O	WM	ENGLISH		089	B		8
MOORE	WILLIAM				38	QUEBEC	CE	IRISH	F	081	C		16
MOORE	WILLIAM				72	IRELAND	CP	IRISH	BLACKSMITH	082	C	2	37
MOORE	WILLIAM				42	O	WM	IRISH	F	082	C	2	37
MOORE	WILLIAM				30	IRELAND	CP	IRISH	FARMER	082	I		33
MOORE	WILLIAM				42	SCOTLAND	ME	SCOTCH	F	085	A		6
MOORE	WILLIAM				41	IRELAND	CN	IRISH	F	086	A	2	3
MOOREHEAD	DAVID		1		4	ONT	CS	SCOTCH		081	J	1	83
MOQUA	JONIAS				52	O	RC	INDIAN	HUNTER & FISHERMAN	081	F		25
MORAN	ADAM		1		21	O	RC	SCOTCH	SERVANT	081	A	2	30
MORAN	ANNY		1	1	23	O	RC	IRISH		081	C		9
MORAN	AUSTIN		1		24	O	RC	ENGLISH	TEAMSTER	082	D		10
MORAN	CELIA		1	1	20	IRELAND	RC	IRISH	SCHOOL MISTRESS	081	E		17
MORAN	CHARLES		1		22	O	RC	IRISH	LAB	081	K		14
MORAN	DANNIE				23	O	RC	ENGLISH	BRICKLAYER	082	D		6
MORAN	ELIZABETH		2	1	4	ONTARIO	RC			081	G	1	D
MORAN	JAMES				67	IRELAND	RC	IRISH	FARMER	081	F		9
MORAN	JAMES				37	QUE	WM	IRISH	F	085	B		14
MORAN	JOHN		1		17	O	RC	IRISH	PRINTER	081	B		53
MORAN	JOHN		1		27	O	RC	IRISH		081	C		9
MORAN	JOHN				28	ONTARIO	RC	IRISH	STOREKEEPER	081	G	1	17
MORAN	JOHN				60	IRELAND	RC	IRISH	FARMER	081	G	1	38
MORAN	JOHN				35	IRELAND	RC	IRISH	LUMBERER	083	B	1	1
MORAN	MARIA		1	1	19	O	RC	SCOTCH	SERVANT	081	A	2	30
MORAN	MARIA		1	1	21	O	RC	IRISH		081	C		9
MORAN	OWEN		1	1	18	O	RC	IRISH		081	C		9
MORAN	PATRICK				55	IRELAND	RC	IRISH	F	081	C		10
MORAN	ROBERT		1		12	O	RC	IRISH		081	K		73
MORAN	THOMAS				59	IRELAND	RC	IRISH	FARMER	081	G	1	21
MORARTY	THOMAS				35	IRELAND	RC	IRISH	FARMER	082	B		21
MORAW	FELIX				50	QUE	RC	FRENCH	FUR TRADER	088	C		5
MORDOCH	ROBERT				46	IRELAND	EM	IRISH	F	082	A		2
MORDY	JOSEPH				31	ONTARIO	CS	SCOTCH	F	082	A		39
MORDY	JOSEPH				65	ENGLAND	CE	ENGLISH	F	082	A		59
MORELY	JOHN				20	O	BA	ENGLISH	F	085	D		22
MOREN	THOMAS		1		18	O	RC	IRISH	BLACKSMITH	081	A	1	12
MORGAN	EDWARD		1		36	ENGLAND	CE	ENGLISH	COPPER SMELTER	089	A		46
MORGAN	JAMES		1		75	IRELAND	CE	IRISH	SHOEMAKER	081	I		22
MORGAN	JAMES				48	IRELAND	PS	IRISH	FARMER	089	A		49
MORGAN	JOHN		1		38	ENGLAND	EP	ENGLISH	CARPENTER	090	D		1
MORGAN	MARY	JANE	1	1	56	IRELAND	RC	IRISH		082	E		17
MORGAN	ROBT				35	ENGLAND	CE	ENGLISH	CABINETMAKER	082	E		34
MORGAN	WALTER				53	WALES	CE	WELSH	F	085	D		34
MORIARTNEY	SARAH			1	32	UNITED STATES	RP	IRISH		081	G	1	47
MORIARTY	DANIEL		1		88	IRELAND	RC	IRISH		081	D		15
MORIARTY	DANIEL		1		25	IRELAND	RC	IRISH	CARPENTER	081	J	2	4
MORIARTY	PATRICK				70	IRELAND	RC	IRISH	FARMER	081	D		5
MORIARTY	PATRICK		1		27	IRELAND	RC	IRISH	F	081	J	2	4
MORIGAN	HUGH				40	IRELAND	RC	IRISH	F	082	H		19
MORIN	JEAN	B T			45	O	RC	INDIAN	LABOURER	090	C		2
MORISON	DANNIAL		1		4	QUE	PS	IRISH		082	D		23
MORISON	DONALD				51	NB	PS	SCOTTISH	LABOURER	082	D		10
MORIZEAU	GAPETTE		1		26	QUEBEC	RC	FRENCH	FARMER	084	C		7
MORLEY	CHARLES				25	ENGLAND	CO	ENGLISH	F	085	L		4
MORLEY	JOHN				60	ENGLAND	CE	ENGLISH	F	085	D		18
MORLEY	WILLIAM				31	O	CE	ENGLISH	F	085	D		27
MORRAH	FRANCIS		1		38	PRUSSIA	RC	POLAND	LAB	081	H	2	18
MORRESY	LAWRENCE				58	IRELAND	RC	IRISH	FARMER	081	G	1	17
MORRIS	JAMES				53	SCOTLAND	CS	SCOTTISH	SHERIFF	082	E		6
MORRIS	JOHN	C	1		7	UNITED STATES	WM	ENGLISH		081	B		84
MORRIS	JOHN	E			24	O	CP	SCOTCH	CARPENTER	081	B		84
MORRIS	THOMAS		1		41	ENGLAND	CE	ENGLISH	CARPENTER	081	I		14
MORRISEAU	ANTOINE				33	O	RC	INDIAN	LABOURER	090	C		2
MORRISEAU	JOSEPH				61	ONT	RC	INDIAN	FISHERMAN	090	B		11
MORRISEAU	JOSEPH				53	O	RC	FRENCH	LABOURER	090	C		2
MORRISON	HUGH				35	SCOTLAND	PS	SCOTCH	F	085	D		10
MORRISON	JOHN				55	SCOTLAND	CS	SCOTCH	HOTEL KEEPER	089	B		7
MORRISON	MALCOM				40	IRELAND	CS	SCOTCH	F	082	A		4
MORRISON	MICHAEL				43	IRELAND	RC	IRISH	F	086	A	1	22
MORRISON	MURDO		1		29	SCOTLAND	PS	SCOTCH	SERVANT	090	C		1

SURNAME	NAME1	NAME2	STRAY	SEX	AGE	BIRTHPL	RELIGION	ORIGIN	OCCUP	DIST	SUB_DIST	DIV	PAGE
MORRISON	MURDOCH				38	QUE	CP	SCOTCH	SHOEMAKER	082	C	2	10
MORRISON	MURDOCK				45	SCOTLAND	PS	SCOTCH	F	085	D		10
MORRISON	PATRICK				34	IRELAND	CE	IRISH	F	086	A	1	22
MORRISON	WILLIAM				55	SCOTLAND	CP	SCOTCH	F	085	A		4
MORRISON	WILLIAM				55	SCOTLAND	CP	SCOTCH	F	085	B		2
MORROW	BROONO				45	QUEBEC	RC	FRENCH	F	082	A		14
MORROW	JOHN				34	IRELAND	RC	IRISH	STOREKEEPER	081	D		8
MORROW	RICHARD				46	IRELAND	WM	IRISH	F	085	H		1
MORROW	WILLIAM				70	IRELAND	ME	IRISH	FARMER	082	B		66
MORTON	ANGELINE		1	1	19	O	WM	IRISH	TAILORESS	082	E		30
MORTON	CATHERINE		1	1	14	O	RC	IRISH		082	E		69
MORTON	JANE			1	63	IRELAND	PS	IRISH		085	H		1
MORTON	JOSHUE				29	ENGLAND	FW	ENGLISH	WOOL SPINNER	081	J	1	74
MORWAY	BENJAMIN		1		24	ONTARIO	RC	FRENCH	HUNTER	084	A		4
MOSELY	ROBERT				48	O	CE	ENGLISH	MINISTER	086	A	1	24
MOSES	JOHN				35	O	RC	INDIAN	HUNTER	086	C	2	1
MOSEY	WILLIAM				39	ENGLAND	CE	ENGLISH	F	085	H		15
MOULTON	GEORGE				26	ONTARIO	PR	IRISH	MERCHANT	081	G	2	13
MOULTON	JANE		2	1	22	QUEBEC	RC			081	G	2	D
MOUSEAW	EXEFRIN				22	QUE	RC	IRISH	LAB	082	K	1	4
MOVELL	CHARLES		1		20	QUEBEC	RC	FRENCH	SHANTY MAN	081	G	1	40
MOWBRAY	THOMAS				43	ENGLAND	CE	ENGLISH	SAW MILL P OWNER	085	J		23
MOXAM	JAMES				29	QUE	EM	ENGLISH		082	C	1	39
MOXAM	SUSAN			1	36	IRELAND	CE	IRISH		082	A		7
MOYER	AMOS				34	O	WM	PRUSSIAN	F	086	A	1	4
MOYER	W	ANDREW			27	O	WM	GERMAN	F	086	A	1	4
MOYNIHAN	TIMOTHY				47	IRELAND	RC	IRISH	BLACKSMITH	081	A	1	2
MUCWABIS	PAUL				40	O	PA	INDIAN	HUNTER & TRAPPER	090	B		3
MUDGE	GEORGE				52	ENGLAND	WM	ENGLISH	MINE LABOURER	089	A		10
MUDGE	HENRY				19	ENGLAND	WM	ENGLISH	MINER	089	A		11
MUDGE	JAMES				15	ENGLAND	WM	ENGLISH		089	A		11
MUIKAVAGESICK	WM				40	O	RC	INDIAN	HUNTER	086	A	3	8
MUIR	THOMAS				38	SCOTLAND	CS	SCOTCH	TAILOR	081	I		5
MULAND	PETER		1		19	QUE	RC	FRENCH	LAB	081	B		62
MULCACHEY	MICHAEL				55	IRELAND	RC	IRISH	LAB	081	A	2	14
MULDOON	PATRICK		1		40	LEINSTER	RC	IRISH	F	087	A		1
MULENHORE	WILLIAM				50	GERMANY	WM	GERMAN	F	082	G		13
MULLEN	JAMES				50	IRELAND	RC	IRISH	F	082	L		7
MULLEN	MICHAEL				27	IRELAND	RC	IRISH	FARMER	082	B		15
MULLER	WILLIAM		1		34	ENGLAND	EP	ENGLISH	LAB	090	D		7
MULLIGAN	BRIDGET		1	1	18	O	RC	IRISH	SERVANT	082	E		1
MULLIGAN	DANIAL				50	IRELAND	RC	IRISH	FARMER	082	D		23
MULLIGAN	JOHN				38	ONTARIO	RC	IRISH	FARMER	082	B		3
MULLIGAN	JOHN				46	ONTARIO	RC	IRISH	FARMER	082	B		36
MULLIGAN	MICHAEL				71	IRELAND	RC	IRISH	FARMER	082	B		3
MULLIGAN	ROSE	A	1	1	18	O	RC	IRISH	SERVANT	082	E		55
MULLIGEN	DAVID				44	IRELAND	RC	IRISH	PILOT	082	D		10
MULLINS	CATHERINE		1	1	30	IRELAND	CE	IRISH		081	K		70
MULLINS	JOHN				60	IRELAND	CP	IRISH	F	081	H	2	42
MULLINS	JOHN	JR			23	O	WM	IRISH		081	H	2	35
MULLINS	PAT		1		26	O	RC	IRISH	FARM SERVANT	082	E		28
MULLINS	PATRICK				22	O	RC	IRISH	F	082	H		5
MULLINS	STEPHEN				35	ENGLAND	CE	ENGLISH	HARNESSMAKER	081	K		70
MULOY	JOHN				40	IRELAND	RC	IRISH		082	C	1	33
MULRANG	NEIL				52	IRELAND	RC	IRISH	F	081	K		41
MULROY	BRIDGET		2	1		O	RC			081	F		D
MULROY	MICHAEL				59	IRELAND	RC	IRISH	FARMER	081	F		7
MULVIHILL	DANIEL				90	IRELAND	RC	IRISH	FARMER	081	D		17
MULVIHILL	ELLEN			1	60	IRELAND	RC	IRISH		081	D		17
MULVIHILL	MARTIN				40	IRELAND	RC	IRISH	FARMER	081	D		17
MULVIHILL	MARTIN				50	IRELAND	RC	IRISH	F	081	J	1	28
MULVIHILL	MARTIN				60	IRELAND	RC	IRISH	F	081	J	1	89
MULVIHILL	MICHAEL				50	IRELAND	RC	IRISH	FARMER	081	D		25
MULVIHILL	MICHAEL				54	IRELAND	RC	IRISH	F	081	J	1	56
MULVIHILL	PATRICK		1		8	ONT	RC	IRISH	ADOPTED	081	J	1	59
MULVIHILL	THOMAS				60	IRELAND	RC	IRISH	FARMER	081	D		16
MULVOHIL	CATHARINE		1	1	28	O	RC	IRISH		081	B		7
MULVYHILL	MICHAEL				40	IRELAND	RC	IRISH	F	081	A	2	4
MUNCASTER	JOHN				31	ENGLAND	EP	ENGLISH	F	087	B	3	9
MUNDAY	WILL'M				26	ENGLAND	CE	ENGLISH	FISHERMAN	087	B	2	4
MUNDLE	JOHN				76	SCOTLAND	CS	SCOTCH	TAILOR	085	I		4
MUNRO	GEORGE				27	O	CP	SCOTCH	MILLER	082	C	2	38
MUNRO	GEORGE				48	SCOTLAND	PS	SCOTCH	F	086	B		3
MUNRO	JAMES				26	O	CS	SCOTCH	WHEELWRIGHT	082	C	2	64
MUNROE	DONALD				54	O	CP	SCOTCH	SHOEMAKER			1	80
MUNROE	ELIZA		1	1	14	O	CP	IRISH		081	B		55
MUNROE	JESSIE	A	1	1	11	O	CP	IRISH		081	B		55
MUNROE	JOHN				63	SCOTLAND	CP	SCOTCH	FOREMAN	081	B		76
MUNROE	WILLIAM		1		55	QUE	PS	SCOTCH	F	086	A	2	2
MUNROE	WILLIAM	J	1		9	O	CP	IRISH		081	B		55
MUNSON	GEORGE								SEE MONSON	081	F		11
MUQUO	MARY		1	1	60	MOOSE FACTORY	PA	INDIAN		090	F		18
MURDE	REBECCA		1	1	19	O	CE	ENGLISH		082	F		32
MURDOCH	JAMES				47	IRELAND	EM	IRISH	F	082	A		3
MURDOCK	ELIZABETH		1	1	40	SCOTLAND	PS	SCOTCH	F	086	A	1	23
MUREY	JOHN		1		34	FRANCE	RC	FRENCH	PRIEST	084	I	2	1
MURPHEY	JAMES				26	IRELAND	RC	IRISH	LAB	081	A	2	16
MURPHEY	RICHARD				33	IRELAND	RC	IRISH	LAB	081	A	2	12
MURPHEY	WM	HENRY			31	QUE	WM	IRISH	BOOKKEEPER	081	A	2	15
MURPHY	CHRISTOPHER				67	IRELAND	RC	IRISH	F	081	E		7
MURPHY	HERCULES				56	IRELAND	CS	IRISH	F	081	A	1	63
MURPHY	JAMES		1		24	IRELAND	RC	IRISH	LAB	081	B		54
MURPHY	JAMES				45	IRELAND	RC	IRISH	F	081	E		8
MURPHY	JAMES				50	IRELAND	RC	IRISH	F	081	J	1	8
MURPHY	JAMES				35	QUE	RC	IRISH	FISHERMAN	089	A		64
MURPHY	JAMES	SNR			50	IRELAND	RC	IRISH	F	082	J		6
MURPHY	JOHN				35	QUE	CP	IRISH	CARPENTER			1	76
MURPHY	JOHN				35	IRELAND	RC	IRISH	F	081	E		9
MURPHY	JOHN				39	ONTARIO	CE	IRISH	FARMER	081	G	1	31
MURPHY	JOHN				53	IRELAND	RC	IRISH	F	081	J	1	6
MURPHY	JOHN				60	IRELAND	RC	IRISH	F	081	J	1	34
MURPHY	JOHN				53	IRELAND	RC	IRISH	FARMER	082	B		39
MURPHY	JOHN		1		20	O	WM	IRISH	FARMER	082	D		30
MURPHY	JOSHUE				38	O	WM	IRISH	HARNESSMAKER	081	I		5
MURPHY	MARGARET		1	1	19	O	RC	IRISH	SERVANT	081	D		7
MURPHY	MARGARET		1	1	9	O	RC	IRISH		082	L		2

SURNAME	NAME1	NAME2	STRAY	SEX	AGE	BIRTHPL	RELIGION	ORIGIN	OCCUP	DIST	SUB_DIST	DIV	PAGE
MURPHY	MARY		2	1	40	SCOTLAND	CE			081	G	1	D
MURPHY	MATTHEW				45	IRELAND	RC	IRISH	LAB	081	A	2	10
MURPHY	PATRICK				55	IRELAND	RC	IRISH	FARMER	081	D		6
MURPHY	PETER				25	IRELAND	RC	IRISH	FARM LAB	082	C	1	28
MURPHY	ROSEANE			1	47	0	RC	SCOTTISH		082	E		69
MURPHY	THOMAS				76	IRELAND	RC	IRISH	F	081	C		2
MURPHY	THOMAS				40	IRELAND	RC	IRISH	F	085	J		10
MURPHY	TIMOTHY				50	IRELAND	RC	IRISH	F	081	K		57
MURPHY	WILLIAM				48	IRELAND	CE	IRISH	FARMER	081	G	1	39
MURPHY	WILLIAM		1		24	0	RC	IRISH	BLACKSMITH	082	C	1	13
MURPHY	WILLIAM	EDWARD	1		32	QUE	RC	IRISH	BOOKKEEPER	082	E		48
MURPHY	WILLIAM	EDWARD	2		4	0	WM			082	D		D
MURRAY	CHARLOTTE		1	1	25	ONTARIO	CE	IRISH		084	C		5
MURRAY	FRANCIS		1		40	IRELAND	RC	IRISH	LAB	081	K		45
MURRAY	JAMES				27	IRELAND	RC	IRISH	FARMER	083	A	1	15
MURRAY	JAMES		1		40	IRELAND	RC	IRISH	BLACKSMITH	083	A	2	3
MURRAY	JANE		1	1	89	IRELAND	RC	IRISH		082	E		48
MURRAY	MICHAEL				61	IRELAND	RC	IRISH	FARMER	081	G	1	1
MURRAY	PETER				36	SCOTLAND	CE	SCOTCH	MILL OWNER	088	C		6
MURRAY	SAM'L				31	IRELAND	CE	IRISH	F	087	B	2	8
MURRAY	THOMAS				34	0	RC	IRISH	MERCHANT	082	E		47
MURRAY	WILLIAM				31	0	RC	IRISH	MERCHANT	082	E		47
MURTON	EDWARD				40	ENGLAND	CE	ENGLISH	CARPENTER	089	B		18
MURY	ELIZABETH		1	1	8	0	RC	IRISH		081	I		25
MUSCOLO	CARL				48	GERMANY	LU	GERMAN	FARMER	081	F		32
MUSCOLO	JOHN				51	GERMANY	BA	GERMAN	FARMER	081	F		32
MUSGROVE	HENERY				35	US	CE	ENGLISH	FOREMAN	086	B		2
MUTTLEBURY	JOHN		1		45	ENGLAND	CE	ENGLISH		089	B		15
MYER	HENRY				32	ENGLAND	CE	ENGLISH	BOAT BUILDER	082	E		64
MYERS	FRIEND				35	US	WM	GERMAN	CARPENTER	085	B		9
MYERS	THOMAS				36	ENGLAND	WM	ENGLISH	MILLER & GENT MERCHA	085	I		4
MYERS	WILLIAM		2			0	WM			085	I		D
MYLES	DAVID		1		21	0	PS	SCOTTISH	SHOEMAKER	082	E		47
MYTIZ	FREDERICK		1		63	GERMANY	LU	GERMAN		082	I		55
MYTIZ	GUSTAV				28	GERMANY	LU	GERMAN	FARMER	082	I		55
MYTZ	HENRY				30	GERMANY	LU	GERMAN	F	085	A		7
MYTZ	VALENTINE				56	GERMANY	LU	GERMAN	F	085	A		8
MYTZ	VALENTINE				24	GERMANY	LU	GERMAN	F	085	A		8
NABANEGIJY	LOUIS				64	US	RC	INDIAN	F	087	A		30
NACOUCHE	MARY		1	1	50	0	RC	INDIAN		090	F		10
NADOE	ALMERE		1	1	6	0	RC	FRENCH		081	E		17
NADON	JOHN		1		28	ONTARIO	RC	FRENCH	FARMER	084	C		6
NADON	XAVIER				22	QUEBEC	RC	FRENCH	TAVERN KEEPER & FARM	084	B		3
NAHGONEGONAI	JOSEPH				45	US	RC	INDIAN	F & FISHERMAN	087	B	1	21
NAHONAY	KEJICK					0	PA	INDIAN	HUNTER & TRAPPER	090	C		18
NAHWAKIGHEH	JOHN		1		14	0	CE	INDIAN		089	B		36
NAHWAY	KEJICK					0	PA	INDIAN	HUNTER & TRAPPER	090	C		17
NAHWEGEZHIK	JAMES				38	US	CE	INDIAN	BLACKSMITH	088	B		4
NAISMITH	JAMES				32	SCOTLAND	WM	SCOTCH	F	081	J	1	31
NAISMITH	JAMES				62	SCOTLAND	PS	SCOTCH	F	081	J	1	42
NAISMITH	LAURENCE				27	SCOTLAND	CP	SCOTCH	F	081	J	1	35
NAITAHWOSH	JOHN				25	0	RC	INDIAN	F & FISHERMAN	087	B	1	20
NAIWOBAIKERHIK	JOS				37	0	RC	INDIAN	F & FISHERMAN	087	B	1	1
NAMABIN	BAPTIST				25	0	RC	INDIAN	HUNTER	090	F		8
NANSEW	ELIZABETH			1	49	QUE	RC	FRENCH	F	081	E		12
NAPIER	GEORGE				45	ENGLAND	CE	ENGLISH	F	085	I		19
NARELOW	ANNIE			1	18	PRUSSIA	RC	PRUSSIAN	HOTEL KEEPER	083	A	1	4
NASBEGICKEGUN	CHARLOTTE			1	65	0	RC	INDIAN		088	B		27
NASH-QUE-SASC	ANTOINE				70	QUE	RC	INDIAN	HUNTER	084	E		5
NASH-QUE-SASC	FRANCIS		2			0	RC	INDIAN		084	E		D
NASMITH	ELLEN			1	30	0	PS	SCOTTISH		082	E		61
NASMITH	LAURANCE		2		34	0	CP		CARPENTER	082	E		D
NATOWE	(WIDOW)			1		ONTARIO	PA	INDIAN	HUNTER & TRAPPER	090	E		6
NAUGHTON	CATHERINE			1	50	IRELAND	RC	IRISH	F	081	C		35
NAUGHTON	CHARLES				24	ONT	RC	IRISH	F	081	C		35
NAUGHTON	MARY		1	1	13	ONTARIO	RC	IRISH		081	G	1	20
NAUPIGH	SIMON				19	0	PA	INDIAN	HUNTER	088	B		24
NAVEN	JOHANNA		1	1	24	0	RC	IRISH		081	F		25
NAVEN	JULIA		1	1	26	IRELAND	RC	IRISH		081	F		24
NAWAKKABOSS	JOSETTE		1	1	13	0	RC	INDIAN	STUDENT	087	A		1
NAWASHKESK	ALEX				35	US	RC	INDIAN	F & FISHERMAN	087	A		11
NAWOAKWEGIJY	MICHAEL				51	US	RC	INDIAN	F & FISHERMAN	087	A		15
NEDO	ALEXANDER				21	QUE	RC	FRENCH	SECTION FOREMAN	081	B		33
NEFF	BENJIMAN				51	0	MN	GERMAN	F	085	I		32
NEGONEKEZHIK	PETER				40	US	RC	INDIAN	F & BOAT BUILDER	087	C		6
NEGONEWAINAH	J	BTE			57	0	RC	INDIAN	F & FISHERMAN	087	C		2
NEGONEWAINAH	LOUIS				32	0	RC	INDIAN	F & FISHERMAN	087	C		2
NEGONEWAINAH	WILLIAM				30	0	RC	INDIAN	F & FISHERMAN	087	C		2
NEGONONOQUET	MICHEL				32	0	RC	INDIAN	F & LABOURER	087	B	1	7
NEIAWANGEANG'S	(DAUGHTER)		2	1		ONTARIO	PA			090	E		D
NEIL	EDWIN				24	ENGLAND	CE	ENGLISH	F	086	A	1	3
NEIL	JAMES				36	0	EM	IRISH	COOPER	081	B		46
NEILL	FRANCIS				50	IRELAND	CE	IRISH	F	082	A		42
NEILSON	ALEXR				25	QUE	ME	SCOTTISH	BAKER	082	E		72
NEILSON	E	GEORGE			37	IRELAND	CP	IRISH	BOOK STATIONER	081	B		7
NEILSON	SAML		1		20	0	WM	IRISH	BUTCHER	082	E		57
NEITS	FREDERICK				33	GERMANY	CE	GERMAN	LAB	081	B		66
NELAN	ISEBELLA			1	36	IRELAND	RC	IRISH		081	F		16
NELAN	MARGARET			1	55	IRELAND	RC	IRISH		081	F		5
NELDEN	JOHN				58	ENGLAND	WM	ENGLISH	F	087	B	3	5
NELSON	ADAM				44	SCOTLAND	PS	SCOTCH	CARPENTER	089	A		39
NELSON	BERNARD				35	ONTARIO	PR	ENGLISH	FARMER	081	G	2	13
NELSON	DAVID				49	0	PS	IRISH	FARMER	086	B		6
NELSON	JACOB		1		13	0	NG	ENGLISH		081	K		13
NELSON	JAMES				56	IRELAND	WM	IRISH	F	082	C	1	17
NELSON	JAMES				26	QUE	WM	IRISH	SCHOOL TEACHER	082	C	1	18
NELSON	JOEL				24	0	WM	IRISH		082	C	1	17
NELSON	JOSEPH				38	CANADA	CE	IRISH	F	085	A		23
NELSON	MICHAEL				22	0	RC	IRISH	F	082	H		5
NELSON	MICHAEL				65	IRELAND	RC	IRISH	F	082	H		7
NELSON	ROBERT				28	QUE	WM	IRISH	BLACKSMITH	082	C	1	58
NELSON	ROBERT				45	SCOTLAND	PS	SCOTCH	MINER	089	A		38
NEMBICK	MICHAEL		2		34	PRUSSIA	RC		FARMER	081	G	2	D
NEPPEL	JOHN				30	IRELAND	WM	IRISH	W METHODIST MINISTER	089	A		13
NEROY	AMBERT		1		24	NOVA SCOTIA	NG	ENGLISH	CARPENTER	085	E		16
NESBIT	HENRIETA		1	1	19	0	WM	IRISH	SERVANT	086	A	1	25

SURNAME	NAME1	NAME2	STRAY	SEX	AGE	BIRTHPL	RELIGION	ORIGIN	OCCUP	DIST	SUB_DIST	DIV	PAGE
NESIKEGABOSSI	AUGUSTIN				62	US	RC	INDIAN	F & FISHERMAN	087	A		31
NESIKEGABOSSI	PIERRE				32	US	RC	INDIAN	F & FISHERMAN	087	A		31
NESIKEGUBOSSE	CATHERINE		2	1	36	US	RC	INDIAN		087	A		D
NETHERLY	HENRY		1		35	IRELAND	CE	IRISH	LUMBERMAN	086	B		3
NETTLETON	ALGINE		1	1	6	O	CE	IRISH		082	H		15
NETTLETON	ANNIE		1	1	17	O	WM	ENG	SERVANT	081	B		50
NETTLETON	JAMES				34	O	EM	ENGLISH	LAB	081	B		24
NETTLETON	MARY		1	1	22	O	CE	IRISH	WEAVER	082	H		14
NETTLETON	SAMUEL				29	O	EM	ENGLISH	SAWYER	081	B		39
NETTLETON	SAMUEL	S			62	O	EM	ENGLISH	LAB	081	B		40
NEURAUVAYIRET	PETER				75	O	RC	INDIAN	HUNTER	086	A	3	6
NEVIENS	JOHN				19	O	PS	SCOTCH	F	085	C		5
NEVIL	JAMES				35	QUEBEC	RC	IRISH	FARMER	081	G	1	44
NEVIL	JOHN				29	QUEBEC	RC	IRISH	FARMER	081	G	1	41
NEVIL	MICHAEL				44	IRELAND	RC	IRISH	BLACKSMITH	082	B		63
NEVIL	THOMAS				40	IRELAND	RC	IRISH	FARM LABOURER	082	B		65
NEVILL	MICHAEL				27	ONTARIO	RC	IRISH	F	082	A		79
NEVILL	THOMAS				60	IRELAND	RC	IRISH	F	082	A		79
NEVIN	JOHN				31	O	CE	IRISH	TAVERN KEEPER	089	B		39
NEVIN	MICHAEL				56	IRELAND	RC	IRISH	FARMER	081	G	1	38
NEW	JAMES				40	ENGLAND	EM	ENGLISH	F	081	H	2	13
NEW	JOSEPH				54	ENGLAND	CE	ENGLISH	F	081	H	2	13
NEW	THOMAS				50	ENGLAND	WM	ENGLISH	F	081	H	1	17
NEW	WILLIAM				38	ENGLAND	EM	ENGLISH	F	081	H	2	28
NEW	YOUNG				47	ENGLAND	EM	ENGLISH	F	081	H	2	15
NEWBURRY	PETER				34	ENGLAND	CE	ENGLISH	F	081	J	1	15
NEWCOMB	FRANK				50	NEW BRUNSWICK	NG	ENGLISH	LUMBERMAN	089	B		24
NEWCOMB	OCTAVINE		1		23	ENGLAND	WM	ENGLISH	ACCOUNTANT	082	C	1	5
NEWELL	EDWIN		1		25	ENGLAND	CP	ENGLISH	CARPENTER	090	F		25
NEWELL	JOHN				51	IRELAND	RP	IRISH	F	082	H		12
NEWLOVE	CHARLES				23	O	CE	ENGLISH	F	085	K	2	9
NEWMAN	JOHN				31	ENGLAND	CE	ENGLISH	CARPENTER	081	I		21
NEWSOME	HENRY				56	ENGLAND	BA	ENGLISH	F	085	H		22
NEWSOME	HENRY	F			26	ENGLAND	CE	ENGLISH	F	085	H		22
NEWTON	ANNIE		1	1	12	O	CP	SCOTTISH		082	E		1
NEWTON	ELIAS	I			27	O	RC	FRENCH	HARNESSMAKER	082	E		41
NEWTON	SARAH	A	2	1	22	ONT	RC			082	E		D
NEWTON	WILLIAM				42	ENGLAND	CE	ENGLISH		085	E		14
NEY	JOHN				22	IRELAND	RP	IRISH	F	085	L		11
NEY	ROBERT				26	IRELAND	RP	IRISH	F	085	L		11
NEY	THOMAS	I	1		20	O	RP	IRISH	F	085	L		11
NIBLET	ED	JOHN			50	ENGLAND	CE	ENGLISH	LAB	081	B		35
NIBLET	ROBERT		1		16	O	CE	ENGLISH		081	B		30
NICHOEL	CHRISTOPHER				36	ENGLAND	CE	ENGLISH	LAB	081	B		34
NICHOL	DAVID				50	SCOTLAND	CS	SCOTCH	F	081	C		45
NICHOL	JOHN				75	GERMANY	LU	GERMAN	F	085	J		18
NICHOL	THOMAS				43	SCOTLAND	CP	SCOTCH	F	086	A	2	11
NICHOLAS	JOHN				56	ENGLAND	CE	ENGLISH	MINER	089	A		25
NICHOLES	RICHARD				26	ENGLAND	WM	ENGLISH	MINER	089	A		8
NICHOLLS	JOHN				48	ENGLAND	CE	ENGLISH	MINE LABOURER	089	A		25
NICHOLLS	JOHN	HENRY			24	ENGLAND	CE	ENGLISH	CARPENTER	085	I		9
NICHOLS	ROBERT				44	IRELAND	CE	IRISH	F	085	C		22
NICHOLSON	EDWARD				29	ENGLAND	CE	ENGLISH	F	085	I		19
NICHOLSON	JOHN				25	O	CE	ENGLISH	LAB	081	A	2	16
NICHOLSON	JOHN				40	O	RC	IRISH	F	081	J	2	2
NICHOLSON	PETER				36	SCOTLAND	PS	SCOTCH	STORE KEEPER	089	A		45
NICHOLSON	RALPH				55	ENGLAND	CE	ENGLISH	GARDENER	085	I		17
NICHOLSON	WILLIAM				30	O	RC	IRISH	F	081	J	2	7
NICKELSON	JOHN				37	NORWAY	LU	NORWEGIAN	F	090	F		17
NICKOLAS	SUSAN		1	1	82	ENGLAND	WM	ENGLISH		089	A		18
NIGANIKWAAM	GEORGE				37	US	RC	INDIAN	F & FISHERMAN	087	A		16
NIGHT	CAMERON				39	ENGLAND	CE	ENGLISH	ENGINEER	085	D		7
NIGONIGIJY	FRANCOIS				30	O	RC	INDIAN	F & FISHERMAN	087	A		29
NILKEY	JULIOUS		1		28	GERMANY	PS	GERMAN	LABOURER	082	D		4
NIMAN	CHARLES				32	GERMANY	CE	GERMAN	LAB	081	A	2	5
NIMAN	FREDERICK				36	GERMANY	CE	GERMAN	LAB	081	A	2	5
NIMAN	FREDERICK				33	GERMANY	LU	GERMAN	F	082	H		15
NIMAN	LUDWICK				65	GERMANY	NG	GERMAN		081	A	2	10
NIMAN	RICHARD				55	GERMANY	NG	GERMAN	LAB	081	A	2	9
NIORDAN	DANIEL		1		48	IRELAND	RC	IRISH	SCHOOL MASTER	090	F		10
NIS	HARMON				25	O	CE	DUTCH	ENGINEER	085	I		13
NISCOB	FELIX		1		23	O	RC	INDIAN	LAB	090	F		26
NITZEL	WILLIAM				31	GERMANY	LU	GERMAN	F	081	K		56
NIVAL	MARGRET		1	1	19	QUEBEC	RC	IRISH		082	D		13
NIVAL	WILLIAM				21	IRELAND	RC	IRISH	FARMER	082	D		13
NIVEAN	MICHEL				45	O	RC	FRENCH	TRADER	090	A		6
NIXON	JOHN				22	O	WM	IRISH	F	085	E		19
NIXON	WILLIAM				26	IRELAND	WM	IRISH	F	086	A	2	11
NOAD	JOHN		1		18	O	RC	IRISH	SERVANT	081	A	2	47
NOAK	CHRISTE				26	GERMAN	LU	GERMAN	LABOURER	082	F		24
NOAK	MARTEN				42	GERMAN	LU	GERMAN	F	082	F		24
NOARK	MATTK				35	GERMANY	WM	GERMAN	F	081	K		56
NOBAY	JOHN				35	O	RC	INDIAN	HUNTER	090	F		11
NOBLE	EDWARD				44	IRELAND	CE	IRISH	FARMER	086	B		8
NOEL	WILLIAM		1		18	QUE	RC	FRENCH	LAB	090	F		25
NOGRA	CHRISTIAN				48	GERMANY	EV	GERMAN	F	082	G		91
NOICE	CHARLES				51	ENGLAND	CE	ENGLISH	FARMER	081	G	1	34
NOJEKAM	J	BTE			42	US	RC	INDIAN	F & COOPER	087	A		27
NOLAN	GEORGE				26	IRELAND	CE	IRISH	F	085	B		12
NOLAN	MRS			1	52	IRELAND	PS	IRISH	FARMER	081	J	1	2
NOLAN	WILLIAM				30	IRELAND	CE	IRISH	F	085	B		10
NOLTEN	HENRY		1		38	ENGLAND	WM	ENGLISH	CARPENTER	085	E		3
NORMAN	WILLIAM				26	ENGLAND	CE	ENGLISH	F	085	D		14
NORRIS	WILLIAM					SCOTLAND	NG	SCOTCH	F	085	E		21
NORTON	ALFRED		1		19	ENGLAND	CE	ENGLISH	LUMBERMAN	086	C	1	7
NORTON	ANNIE		1	1	21	O	RC	IRISH	SERVANT	081	B		69
NORTON	FRANCIS		1		21	ENGLAND	CE	ENGLISH	MASON	086	C	1	7
NORTON	GEORGE				37	ENGLAND	CE	ENGLISH	F	085	L		3
NORTON	JOSEPH		1		20	O	CP	IRISH	F LAB	085	E		24
NORTON	NATHAN				42	ENGLAND	CE	ENGLISH	F	085	L		4
NOVUK	AUGUSTUS				40	GERMANY	RC	GERMAN	F	082	C	2	39
NOWINEGAHBOU	ALEX		2		2	O	CE	INDIAN		087	B	1	D
NOWWAHGWONABE	PETER				25	O	CE	INDIAN	LABOURER	087	B	1	17
NOWWEGAHBOW	JOHN				40	O	CE	INDIAN	F	087	B	1	18
NOWWEKEZHIK	FRANCIS				56	US	RC	INDIAN	F	087	A		44
NOWWEKEZHIK	JOHN				38	US	CE	INDIAN	F&TINSMITH&BLACKSMIT	087	B	1	19

SURNAME	NAME1	NAME2	STRAY	SEX	AGE	BIRTHPL	RELIGION	ORIGIN	OCCUP	DIST	SUB_DIST	DIV	PAGE
NUIHEKA	SAMUEL				65	0	WM	INDIAN	HUNTER	086	A	3	7
NUJSELL	LEONARD				65	ENGLAND	WM	ENGLISH	F	085	J		1
NUNUNANCE	PIERRE		1		30	0	RC	INDIAN	SERVANT	087	C		7
NYCHMAN	AUGUST				35	GERMANY	WM	GERMAN	F	082	G		91
O BRION	THOMAS				35	0	WM	IRISH	F	082	C	1	29
O'BOYLE	JAMES				45	IRELAND	RC	IRISH	LUMBERMAN	083	A	1	6
O'BOYLE	MARIA		1	1	24	QUE	RC	IRISH	HOUSEMAID	081	D		26
O'BRIAN	CHARLES				23	0	WM	IRISH	F	082	C	1	14
O'BRIAN	HENRY				28	0	WM	IRISH	F	082	C	1	14
O'BRIAN	HENRY		2		21	IRELAND	RC			082	I		D
O'BRIAN	JENNETT		1	1	62	SCOTLAND	WM	SCOTCH		082	C	1	14
O'BRIE	ISIDORE		1		30	QUE	RC	FRENCH		081	K		32
O'BRIE	JULIE		1	1	19	QUE	RC	FRENCH		081	K		32
O'BRIEN	ALICE		1	1	12	0	RC	IRISH	SERVANT	082	E		15
O'BRIEN	CHARLES				67	IRELAND	RC	IRISH	F	081	K		19
O'BRIEN	DAN		1		26	IRELAND	RC	IRISH	LABOURER	082	E		18
O'BRIEN	ELESEBATH			1	35	ENGLAND	RC	ENGLISH		082	J		13
O'BRIEN	JOHN				50	IRELAND	RC	IRISH	LAB	081	B		82
O'BRIEN	JOHN				40	IRELAND	RC	IRISH	F	081	K		22
O'BRIEN	JOHN				58	IRELAND	RC	IRISH	F	082	A		51
O'BRIEN	JOHN		1		24	0	RC	IRISH	TEAMSTER	088	B		3
O'BRIEN	JOHN	SR			63	IRELAND	RC	IRISH	F	082	H		2
O'BRIEN	MAREY			1	40	IRELAND	RC	IRISH	F	082	K	1	12
O'BRIEN	MICHAEL				36	IRELAND	RC	IRISH	MERCHANT	081	K		69
O'BRIEN	MICHAEL				55	IRELAND	RC	IRISH	F	082	G		69
O'BRIEN	PATRICK				35	IRELAND	RC	IRISH	FARMER	081	G	1	45
O'BRIEN	PATRICK		1		25	0	RC	IRISH	BLACKSMITH	081	K		1
O'BRIEN	PATRICK				50	IRELAND	RC	IRISH	F	081	K		30
O'BRIEN	PATRICK						NG		SEE ABRINE	082	F		26
O'BRIEN	PATRICK				52	IRELAND	RC	IRISH	GARDENER	086	A	1	23
O'BRIEN	RICHARD				36	IRELAND	RC	IRISH	F	081	K		19
O'BRINE	JOHN				40	IRELAND	RC	IRISH	FARMER	081	G	1	26
O'BRINE	MARGRET			1	70	IRELAND	RC	IRISH		081	G	1	6
O'BRINE	MICHAEL				33	ONTARIO	RC	IRISH	FARMER	081	G	1	39
O'BRINE	MORRIS				32	ONTARIO	RC	IRISH	FARMER	081	G	1	44
O'BRINE	PATRICK				62	IRELAND	RC	IRISH	FARMER	081	G	1	43
O'CONNER	JAMES				40	0	RC	IRISH	F	081	A	2	40
O'CONNER	JOHN				40	IRELAND	RC	IRISH	FARMER	081	G	1	14
O'CONNER	WILLIAM				51	IRELAND	RC	IRISH	F	081	A	1	64
O'CONNER	WILLIAM				44	IRELAND	RC	IRISH	FARMER	081	G	1	14
O'CONNOR	DENNIS				28	IRELAND	RC	IRISH	F	081	J	1	45
O'CONNOR	JAMES				69	IRELAND	RC	IRISH	F	081	J	1	45
O'CONNOR	JAMES				60	IRELAND	RC	IRISH	LABOURER	081	J	1	67
O'CONNOR	MARTIN				60	IRELAND	RC	IRISH	FARMER	081	F		3
O'CONNOR	MARY		2	1		ONTARIO	RC			081	G	1	D
O'DAY	JOHN				58	IRELAND	RC	IRISH	F	081	J	1	66
O'DAY	JOHN				27	IRELAND	RC	IRISH	F	081	J	1	66
O'DONNELL	RICHARD				61	IRELAND	RC	IRISH	FARMER	089	B		17
O'DONNELL	WILLIAM				38	QUE	RC	IRISH	TRADER	081	K		1
O'DRISCOL	MICHAEL				36	IRELAND	RC	IRISH	F	082	G		46
O'DRISCOL	PAT				53	IRELAND	RC	IRISH	F	082	G		63
O'DRISCOLL	JAMES				24	0	RC	IRISH	F	082	G		51
O'DRISCOLL	MICHAEL				33	IRELAND	RC	IRISH	BARRISTER	082	E		11
O'FLANNAGAN	JAMES				33	0	RC	IRISH	F	082	K	1	8
O'FLANNAGAN	JOHN				42	QUE	RC	IRISH	F	082	J		2
O'GORMAN	JAMES				58	IRELAND	RC	IRISH	SCHOOLMASTER	081	J	2	5
O'GRADY	CORNELIUS				25	IRELAND	RC	IRISH	F	083	C		8
O'GRADY	HENRY		2		28	ONTARIO	RC		F	083	C		D
O'GRADY	JOHN				30	ONTARIO	RC	IRISH	F	083	C		8
O'GRADY	MARGARET			1	52	IRELAND	RC	IRISH	F	083	C		8
O'GRADY	WINNIFRED			1	22	IRELAND	RC	IRISH	F	083	C		9
O'HAIR	MARYANN			1	40	IRELAND	RC	IRISH		081	G	1	23
O'HARE	HUGH				74	IRELAND	RC	IRISH	F	081	J	1	61
O'HARE	MARY		1	1	20	0	RC	IRISH	SERVANT	081	B		41
O'HARE	MARY	ANNE	2	1	3	0	RC			081	E		D
O'HEAR	EDWARD				50	IRELAND	RC	IRISH	F	081	E		9
O'KANE	MICHAEL				50	IRELAND	RC	IRISH	F	082	G		64
O'MEARA	EDWD				38	IRELAND	RC	IRISH	TAILOR	082	E		17
O'MEARA	JAMES		1		35	IRELAND	RC	IRISH	SERVANT	082	E		20
O'NEIL	JERMIAH				38	0	RC	IRISH	F	082	G		66
O'NEIL	JOHN				31	ONTARIO	RC	IRISH	FARMER	082	B		71
O'NEIL	WILLIAM				28	0	RC	IRISH	F	082	G		67
O'SHAUGHNESSY	PATRICK				42	IRELAND	RC	IRISH	FARMER	081	F		13
O'TOOL	MARTIN				44	IRELAND	RC	IRISH	FARMER	082	B		64
OAKDEN	JOHN		1		35	ENGLAND	RB	ENGLISH	LIVERYMAN	081	B		30
OAKDEN	WILLIAM				48	ENGLAND	CP	ENGLISH	BUTCHER	081	B		2
OASLTER	JAMES				31	SCOTLAND	PS	SCOTCH	CARPENTER	086	A	1	30
OASTLER	ANDREW				28	SCOTLAND	PS	SCOTCH	F	086	A	1	9
OATS	RICHARD				38	IRELAND	CE	IRISH	F	082	A		38
OBASQUAT	JOSEPH				7	0	RC	INDIAN		090	A		7
OBBETOSOWAY	GEORGE		2		45	US	CE	INDIAN	F & LABOURER	087	B	1	D
OBBETOSSWAY	GEORGE	MRS		1	47	IRELAND	CE	IRISH		087	B	1	12
OBBETOSSWAY	KITTY		1	1	28	US	CE	INDIAN		087	B	1	12
OBBETOSSWAY	PIERRE				27	0	RC	INDIAN	HUNTER & F & FISHERM	087	B	1	9
OBRIAN	DAVID				55	IRELAND	RC	IRISH	FARMER	082	B		16
OBRIAN	HENRY				66	IRELAND	RC	IRISH	FARMER	082	I		26
OBRIE	ALFRED		2			0	RC			081	K		D
OBRIEN	HONOURA			1	43	IRELAND	RC	IRISH	WASHWOMAN	082	E		36
OBRIEN	JOHN				41	QUE	WM	IRISH		082	C	1	24
OBRIEN	PATRICK				35	IRELAND	RC	IRISH	F	081	K		49
OBRIEN	PATRICK		2		68	IRELAND	WM		F	082	C	1	D
OBRIEN	WILLIAM		1		23	IRELAND	RC	IRISH	LAB	090	D		7
OBRINE	JOHN		1		9	0	RC	IRISH		082	D		16
OBRINE	PATRICK				48	IRELAND	RC	IRISH	F	082	F		26
OBRINE	THOMAS				40	IRELAND	RC	IRISH	F	082	C	2	50
OBRINE	THOMAS				30	IRELAND	RC	IRISH	LABOURER	082	D		20
OBRION	JAMES				47	IRELAND	RC	IRISH	LAB	081	A	2	3
OBRION	JOHN		2		17	0	RC		LAB	081	A	2	D
OBRY	EARNEST				31	GERMANY	CE	GERMAN	LAB	081	A	2	12
OCHICK	MDM			1		0	PA	INDIAN		090	C		16
OCONNERS	ROBERT				34	IRELAND	CP	IRISH	FARM LAB	082	C	1	52
OCONNOR	CHARLES				30	IRELAND	RC	IRISH	BOOT & SHOE MANUFACT	081	B		6
OCONNOR	JAMES				68	IRELAND	RE	IRISH	F	081	A	2	17
OCONNOR	MARYANNE		1	1	20	ONTARIO	RC	IRISH	SERVANT	084	C		2
OCONNOR	PATRICK				39	0	RC	IRISH	SHANTYMAN AGENT	082	E		49
OCONNOR	STEPHEN				58	IRELAND	RC	IRISH	F	081	A	2	50

SURNAME	NAME1	NAME2	STRAY	SEX	AGE	BIRTHPL	RELIGION	ORIGIN	OCCUP	DIST	SUB_DIST	DIV	PAGE
OCONNOR	WILLIAM		1		21	0	CE	IRISH	CARPENTER	081	A	2	17
ODBER	HENRY				42	0	RC	IRISH	F	081	A	2	50
ODOSKWEOB	JEAN	BTE			38	0	RC	INDIAN	F & FISHERMAN	087	A		11
OFARRELL	PETER				39	IRELAND	RC	IRISH	MERCHANT	081	K		69
OFFRAGE	FERDINAND				38	QUEBEC	RC	FRENCH	FARMER	083	A	1	14
OGILVIE	JOHN		1		32	SCOTLAND	CP	SCOTCH	LAB	090	F		25
OGLVIE	THOMAS				30	IRELAND	PS	IRISH	F	086	A	2	2
OGORMAN	PETER		2			0	RC			081	I		D
OGORMAN	SINAN				42	IRELAND	RC	IRISH	COOPER	081	I		27
OGOUSQUAQUAH	MARIE		1	1	90	US	CE	INDIAN		089	B		34
OGRADEY	MARY	A	1	1	22	0	RC	IRISH		081	B		73
OHARA	GEORGE				30	0	CE	IRISH	F	085	J		8
OHARA	JOHN				36	0	WM	IRISH	WAGGONMAKER	081	I		7
OKANE	FRANCIS		1		21	ST J QUE	RC	IRISH	CLERK	082	E		48
OKELLY	EDW D		1		27	IRELAND	RC	IRISH	STEAMBOAT AGENT	082	E		48
OKELLY	ELIZABETH		1	1	19	0	RC	IRISH		082	E		48
OKER	MATTHEW				40	GERMANY	LU	GERMAN	F	082	G		3
OLDENBERG	FREDRICK				52	GERMANY	EV	GERMAN	FARMER	082	I		59
OLDENBOUGH	AUGUST				42	GERMANY	NC	GERMAN	FARMER	082	I		16
OLDFIELD	SAMUEL				26	ENGLAND	CE	ENGLISH	F	086	A	1	28
OLDHAM	JOHN	L			43	ENGLAND	PM	ENGLISH	F	085	D		16
OLEARY	JAMES				30	IRELAND	RC	IRISH	FARMER	082	I		26
OLEARY	JOHN				47	IRELAND	RC	IRISH	FARMER	081	J	1	2
OLEARY	MARY	ANN	1	1	24	ONT	CP	IRISH		082	I		29
OLEARY	MICHAEL				63	IRELAND	RC	IRISH	FARMER	082	I		25
OLIMER	WM				34	0	WM	ENGLISH	F	085	J		14
OLIVER	JOSEPH				45	ENGLAND	CE	ENGLISH	F	085	J		13
OLIVER	RICHARD				23	0	WM	IRISH	F	087	B	3	5
OLIVER	WILLIAM		1		53	IRELAND	RC	IRISH	F	087	B	3	5
OLMSEAD	ALBERT				37	ONTARIO	CE	GERMAN	F	082	A		63
OLMSTEAD	CHESTER				21	0	CE	DUTCH	TINSMITH	086	A	1	30
OLMSTEAD	VOGMAN				36	0	EM	IRISH	LAB	082	C	1	40
OLMSTED	COLONEL		2		22	ONTARIO	EM			082	A		D
OLMSTED	NATHANIEL				46	ONTARIO	EM	GERMAN	F	082	A		69
OMEARA	MARGARET		1	1	40	QUE	RC	IRISH		082	E		42
OMEARA	MICHL				50	IRELAND	RC	IRISH	MERCHANT	082	E		28
OMEARA	PATRICK				38	IRELAND	RC	IRISH	FARMER	082	I		32
OMEARA	WILLIAM				42	IRELAND	RC	IRISH	MERCHANT	082	E		56
OMERRA	JOHN		1		15	ONTARIO	RC	IRISH		083	C		8
OMOMOIE	GEORGE		2		21	0	ME		HUNTER & TRAPPER	090	C		D
ONAIL	CATHERIN			1	68	IRELAND	CS	IRISH		081	I		20
ONANGISSE	JOSEPH				42	US	RC	INDIAN	F & COOPER	087	A		41
ONEAL	JOHN		1		32	IRELAND	WM	IRISH		086	B		1
ONEIL	ANN		1	1	15	IRELAND	RC	IRISH		090	D		5
ONEIL	E		1		40	IRELAND	RC	IRISH	LAB	090	D		6
ONEIL	JAMES				70	IRELAND	RC	IRISH		081	K		66
ONNES	SIMON		1		35	0	CE	ENGLISH	LAB	081	B		85
ONQUETTO	MICHEL				71	US	RC	INDIAN	F	087	B	1	7
ONWAHTIU	ISAAC				36	0	RC	INDIAN		087	B	1	5
ONWAHTIU	JACOB				30	0	RC	INDIAN	F	087	B	1	5
ONWATIU	OLD	JOSEPH	1		74	0	RC	INDIAN		087	B	1	5
OQUASBUN	ELIZABETH			1	81	0	RC	INDIAN		088	B		28
OQUONAI	JOSEPH				30	0	RC	INDIAN	F & FISHERMAN	087	B	1	5
ORAM	ANNA		1	1	19	0	PS	ENGLISH		081	H	2	24
ORAM	GEORGE				32	0	CP	ENGLISH	F	081	A	2	18
ORAM	JAMES				77	NS	CE	ENGLISH	SHIP CARPENTER	081	A	2	19
ORBETSKY	ADAM				45	POLAND	RC	POLISH	F	083	C		19
ORILEY	PETER				27	0	RC	IRISH	LAB	081	I		33
ORMOND	DANL		1		27	0	PR	GERMAN	CLERK	082	E		29
ORMSBY	JAMES				48	IRELAND	WM	IRISH	F	082	C	2	48
ORORK	JAMES		1		40	IRELAND	CE	IRISH	LABOURER	082	D		19
ORR	GEORGE				30	0	WM	IRISH	F	081	A	2	59
ORR	IDA			1	19	0	WM	IRISH	TEACHER	081	A	2	59
ORR	JOHN				27	IRELAND	CE	IRISH	F	085	I		43
ORR	ROBERT				50	IRELAND	CE	IRISH	F	085	I		43
OSAWAGA	JOHN				65	0	WM	INDIAN	HUNTER	086	C	2	4
OSAWAINIS	JOSEPH				50	US	RC	INDIAN	COOPER & F	087	A		33
OSAWAMIK	J	B			40	US	RC	INDIAN	COOPER & F	087	A		41
OSAWASNGA	JOHN				30	0	WM	INDIAN	HUNTER	086	C	2	2
OSAWIBIURSE	AUGUSTIN				53	US	RC	INDIAN	F & FISHERMAN	087	A		40
OSBORNE	JAMES		1		29	0	NG	IRISH	LAB	081	K		63
OSBORNE	THOMAS				34	ENGLAND	WM	ENGLISH	F	085	J		9
OSGOOD	B	S	1		40	US	CE	ENGLISH	MILLWRIGHT	088	A		7
OSHAUGHNESSAY	MICHAEL				30	IRELAND	RC	IRISH	FARMER	082	B		42
OSHAUGHNESSAY	MICHAEL					IRELAND	RC	IRISH	FARMER	082	B		42
OSHAUGHNESSEY	JOHN				28	IRELAND	RC	IRISH	FARMER	082	B		67
OSHAUGHNESSEY	MICHAEL				32	IRELAND	RC	IRISH	FARMER	082	B		67
OSHAWASEGA	JOSEPH				25	0	WM	INDIAN	HUNTER	086	C	2	3
OSHKABEWISSENS	ANTOINE				35	US	RC	INDIAN	F & FISHERMAN	087	A		21
OSHKABEWISSENS	FRANCOIS				61	US	RC	INDIAN	F	087	A		21
OSHKABEWISSENS	MICHEL				29	0	RC	INDIAN	F	087	A		22
OSHOUGNESSY	KATE		1	1	28	0	RC	IRISH	SERVANT	082	E		48
OSORRHEGAHBOSS	SHEBOCE				42	0	RC	INDIAN	F & FISHERMAN	087	B	1	2
OSOWWAHQUOGWAN	JOHN		2		30	0	CE	INDIAN	F & FISHERMAN	087	B	1	D
OTAIANG	ANGELIQUE			1	57	0	RC	INDIAN	F & FISHERMAN	087	A		31
OTAQUELAGARDE	PAUL					ONTARIO	RC	INDIAN	HUNTER & TRAPPER	090	E		10
OTOOL	ANN	J	1	1	17	ONTARIO	RC	IRISH		082	B		53
OTTAWAAMAHIWENSI'S	(WIFE)		2	1		ONTARIO	PA			090	E		D
OTTERSON	JAMES				31	IRELAND	RC	IRISH	F	081	A	2	32
OTTERSON	JOSEPH				21	0	RC	IRISH	F	081	A	2	56
OTTERSON	MARY		1	1	19	0	RC	IRISH		081	B		77
OTTERSON	SARAH		1	1	70	IRELAND	RC	IRISH		081		1	77
OUDERKIRK	ALLEN				28	0	WM	GERMAN	F	085	J		1
OUDERKIRK	JACOB	A			65	0	WM	ENGLISH	F	085	J		2
OUGHNEY	PATRICK				50	IRELAND	RC	IRISH	FARMER	082	B		14
OULSON	RASMUS				45	NORWAY	LU	NORWEGIAN	F	085	D		11
OWEN	WILLIAM		1		27	IRELAND	RC	IRISH	SHOEMAKER	082	E		43
OWENES	ANN		1	1	62	IRELAND	RC	IRISH	SERVANT	082	J		18
OWENS	EDWARD		1		19	0	CE	IRISH		081	K		5
OWENS	EDWARD		1		10	0	CE	IRISH		081	K		12
OWENS	ELIZABETH		1	1	3	0	CE	IRISH		081	K		3
OWENS	HENRY		1		10	0	CE	IRISH		081	K		6
OWENS	JAMES				35	IRELAND	RC	IRISH	LAB	082	A		54
OWENS	JOHN				36	ENGLAND	CE	ENGLISH	F	081	A	2	47
OWENS	JOSEPH				42	IRELAND	CE	IRISH	F	081	K		4
OWENS	THOMAS	MITCHEL	1		13	0	CE	IRISH		081	K		5

SURNAME	NAME1	NAME2	STRAY	SEX	AGE	BIRTHPL	RELIGION	ORIGIN	OCCUP	DIST	SUB_DIST	DIV	PAGE
OWENS	WILLIAM		1		15	0	CE	IRISH		081	K		5
OWENS	WILLIAM	JAMES	1		10	0	CE	IRISH		081	K		3
OWNES	BERNARD				30	IRELAND	RC	IRISH	FARMER	082	B		11
OWNES	CATHERINE		2	1	4	0	RC			082	B		D
OWNES	JAMES				60	IRELAND	CE	IRISH	FARMER	082	B		35
OWNES	ROBERT				38	IRELAND	RC	IRISH	FARMER	082	B		7
OWNIES	YANTEE				34	GERMANY	CP	GERMAN	LAB	081	A	2	13
OZAWANIMIKI	J	BTE			54	US	RC	INDIAN	COOPER & F	087	A		24
PABAMAWEDONG	PETER				50	0	RC	INDIAN	TRAPPER	086	A	3	1
PACEY	WILLIAM		1		38	ENGLAND	CE	ENGLISH	TANNER	081	A	2	2
PADDLE	GEORGE		1		50	ENGLAND	CE	ENGLISH	LAB	087	B	2	8
PADDY	ANDREW		1		16	RED RIVER	RC	IRISH		090	F		11
PADEN	JOHN				26	ONTARIO	CS	SCOTCH	LUMBERMAN	083	A	1	12
PADWAWAH	MOSES		1		19	0	RC	INDIAN	LABOURER	089	B		34
PADWAWAH	THERESE		1	1	15	0	RC	INDIAN		089	B		34
PAGHOUG-BY	WILLIAM				28	0	PA	INDIAN	TRAPPER	086	A	3	3
PAGMAJAOME	PETER				51	0	RC	INDIAN	HUNTER	086	A	3	5
PAGOHMEGOHBOW					70	0	PA	INDIAN	TRAPPER	086	A	3	1
PAGOHMEGOHBOW	JAMES				26		PA	INDIAN		086	A	3	2
PAGOHMEGOHBOW	JOHN				30	0	WM	INDIAN	TRAPPER	086	A	3	1
PAHNAHNEY	AUGUSTINE				30	ONTARIO	ME	INDIAN	HUNTER & TRAPPER	090	B		2
PAHQUADGENINE	HENRY				56	US	CE	INDIAN	CHIEF	089	B		35
PAISON	GEORGE				25	ENGLAND	CE	ENGLISH	F	085	L		12
PAISTOGONABE	PIERRI				33	0	RC	INDIAN	HUNTER	088	B		24
PAKIKANOKWE	PHILOMEN				59	US	RC	INDIAN	F	087	A		40
PAKSTON	THOMAS		1		48	QUE	ME	ENGLISH	FARMER	082	D		8
PALATZKY	JOHN				31	GERMANY	WM	GERMAN	FARMER	082	I		44
PALL	GEORGE		1		30	0	CS	SCOTCH	LUMBERMAN	088	C		10
PALLIS	WILLIAM		1		23	0	RC	IRISH	LAB	085	F		5
PALMER	ALBERT				28	ONT	PS	ENGLISH	F	081	J	1	44
PALMER	ANDRESS				56	0	EM	ENGLISH	F	081	H	2	28
PALMER	BENJAMIN				29	ENGLAND	CE	IRISH	FARMER	086	B		7
PALMER	C	A	1		38	UNITED STATES	EP	ENGLISH	CLERK	090	D		1
PALMER	FREDERICK				26	ENGLAND	CE	ENGLISH	CLERK	084	B		3
PALMER	JOHN				31	ENGLAND	CE	ENGLISH	F	085	C		8
PALMER	ROELOPHEUS				28	0	OM	ENGLISH	F	081	H	1	13
PALMER	THOMAS				33	ENGLAND	CE	ENGLISH	F	086	A	1	32
PAMOWA	BOSANA				70	0	WM	INDIAN	HUNTER	086	C	2	2
PAMRIGE	WILLIAM				35	0	WM	INDIAN	HUNTER	086	A	3	7
PANGOWISH	IGNACE				31	0	RC	INDIAN	F	087	A		20
PANGOWISH	PIERRE				63	US	RC	INDIAN	CRIPPLE	087	A		20
PAPA	ABEL		1		76	QUE	RC	FRENCH	F	082	C	2	56
PAPA	JOSEPH				43	0	RC	FRENCH	F	082	C	2	62
PAPA	PETER				35	0	RC	FRENCH	F	082	C	2	55
PAPA	ROSE		1	1	66	QUE	RC	FRENCH		082	C	2	56
PAPKEY	JOHN				40	GERMANY	LU	GERMAN	L	082	G		5
PAPKEY	MICHAEL				72	GERMANY	LU	GERMAN		082	G		4
PAPKEY	WILLIAM				32	GERMANY	LU	GERMAN	F	082	G		4
PAPKINA	JEAN	BAPIST			49	0	RC	INDIAN	HUNTER	088	B		23
PAPPASANCE	MARY			1	23	0	RC	INDIAN		090	A		6
PAQUATTE	NARCISE				29	QUE	RC	FRENCH	MERCHANT	082	E		40
PAQUCHEWAY	SUSAN			1	60	0	RC	INDIAN		090	F		11
PAQUETH	JOHN				27	0	RC	FRENCH	F	082	J		13
PAQUETTE	BAPTISTE		1		20	QUE	RC	FRENCH		082	D		19
PAQUETTE	JOHN				19	QUEBEC	RC	FRENCH	LUMBERER	083	C		5
PAQUETTE	LOUACE				39	QUE	RC	FRENCH	FARMER	082	I		72
PAQUETTE	OLEVER				32	QUE	RC	FRENCH	F	082	J		11
PARAUT	PAUL		1		20	QUE	RC	FRENCH	LAB	082	K	1	15
PARIS	JOHN				63	SCOTLAND	CP	SCOTCH	F	081	A	1	1
PARIS	WILLIAM				29	0	CP	SCOTCH	SAWYER	081	A	1	19
PARK	JAMES				33	SCOTLAND	PR	SCOTCH	F	085	A		26
PARK	JOHN				57	ENGLAND	CE	ENGLISH	CLERK	082	C	2	66
PARK	W	N			38	US	CE	ENGLISH	HOTEL KEEPER	085	E		6
PARKER	ANDREW				38	IRELAND	CP	IRISH	SHOEMAKER	081	B		72
PARKER	BETSAY		1	1	94	UNITED STATES	CP	SCOTCH		081	B		5
PARKER	IRE				52	UNITED STATES	WM	IRISH	FARMER	081	G	1	44
PARKER	JOHN				29	IRELAND	CE	IRISH	F	081	K		23
PARKER	JOSEPH				19	ENGLAND	CE	ENGLISH	CARPENTER	085	B		8
PARKER	ROBERT				45	IRELAND	CE	IRISH	BOILERMAKER	085	B		17
PARKER	WILLIAM				40	IRELAND	RC	IRISH	FARMER	082	I		8
PARKET	JOHN		1		20	QUEBEC	RC	FRENCH	FARM LABOURER	081	J	1	81
PARKIN	THOMAS				54	ENGLAND	CE	ENGLISH	LUMBERER	083	C		5
PARLETT	GEORGE				30	ENGLAND	CE	ENGLISH	F	085	F		1
PARLEY	JOSEPH		1		20	0	RC	IRISH	LAB	085	F		5
PARR	DAVID				32	ENGLAND	WM	ENGLISH	FARMER	089	B		4
PARR	GEORGE				32	ENGLAND	CE	ENGLISH	LABOURER	089	B		11
PARR	THOMAS				40	ENGLAND	CE	ENGLISH	BUTCHER	089	B		3
PARRETT	HENRY	W			29	QUE	WM	ENGLISH	TEACHER	082	C	2	31
PARRETT	ROBERT				27	0	WM	ENGLISH	F	082	C	2	18
PARRETT	THOMAS				63	ENGLAND	WM	ENGLISH	F	082	C	2	18
PARSON	CHARLES				25	ENGLAND	WM	ENGLISH	F	085	L		8
PARSONS	EDWARD				29	UNITED STATES	EM	ENGLISH	SAWYER	081	B		33
PARSONS	ELIAS	S			52	UNITED STATES	NR	ENGLISH	SAWYER	081	B		79
PARSONS	W	J			27	US	WM	ENGLISH	SAWYER	081	A	2	28
PARSONS	WILLIAM				41	ENGLAND	WM	ENGLISH	MINER	089	A		41
PARTON	WILLIAM				39	ENGLAND	CE	ENGLISH	F	086	A	2	10
PATERSON	AGNESS		1	1	35	0	CP	SCOTCH	SERVANT	081	A	2	19
PATERSON	HUGH				60	SCOTLAND	CS	SCOTCH	F	082	A		1
PATERSON	JAMES				54	SCOTLAND	WM	SCOTCH	ENGINEER	088	B		21
PATERSON	MATHEW				45	QUE	CE	IRISH	F	085	H		7
PATERSON	TIMOTHY				41	IRELAND	PS	IRISH	F	085	H		3
PATREN	PIERE				40	QUEBEC	RC	FRENCH	LUMBERMAN	083	A	1	12
PATTEN	EDWARD		1		81	SCOTLAND	PS	SCOTCH	F	085	E		8
PATTERSON	ARCHIBALD				43	ONT	CP	SCOTCH	F	081	J	1	61
PATTERSON	CATHARINE		1	1	33	0	CE	IRISH	HOUSEKEEPER			1	81
PATTERSON	CHARLES				44	IRELAND	WM	IRISH	F	082	C	2	46
PATTERSON	DAVID				26	IRELAND	WM	IRISH	F	086	A	2	6
PATTERSON	ISABELLA		1	1	73	SCOTLAND	CP	SCOTTISH		082	I		66
PATTERSON	JAMES				39	IRELAND	CE	IRISH	F	085	J		5
PATTERSON	JOHN				45	IRELAND	RC	IRISH	FARMER	082	B		10
PATTERSON	JOHN		1		80	IRELAND	RC	IRISH	FARMER	082	B		11
PATTERSON	JOHN				59	IRELAND	PS	IRISH	FARMER	082	B		61
PATTERSON	JOHN				77	IRELAND	WM	IRISH	F	082	C	2	47
PATTERSON	JOHN				48	0	WM	SCOTCH	F	085	J		2
PATTERSON	KATE		1	1	24	0	CP	SCOTTISH	SERVANT	082	E		25
PATTERSON	MARY		1	1	18	0	CS	SCOTCH	SERVANT	081	A	1	41

SURNAME	NAME1	NAME2	STRAY	SEX	AGE	BIRTHPL	RELIGION	ORIGIN	OCCUP	DIST	SUB_DIST	DIV	PAGE
PATTERSON	MARY			1	60	IRELAND	RC	IRISH	SPINNER	081	A	1	73
PATTERSON	MICHAEL				61	IRELAND	RC	IRISH	FARMER	082	B		9
PATTERSON	ROBERT		1		75	IRELAND	RC	IRISH	FARMER	082	B		11
PATTERSON	SAMUEL				50	IRELAND	CP	IRISH	HOTELKEEPER	082	G		61
PATTERSON	WILLIAM				27	IRELAND	PS	IRISH	FARMER	082	B		61
PATTERSON	WILLIAM				56	ENGLAND	CE	ENGLISH		082	L		5
PATTESON	JAMES				63	IRELAND	RC	IRISH	F	081	A	2	48
PATTISON	CATHERINE			1	48	SCOTLAND	RC	SCOTCH		081	A	2	60
PATTON	CHARLES				61	IRELAND	RC	IRISH	MASON	087	B	3	7
PATYWIELD	AUGUST				47	GERMANY	LU	GERMAN	F	082	G		83
PAUL	ALEXIS		1		50	QUE	RC	FRENCH	LABOURER	084	E		4
PAUL	ELIZABETH		1	1	70	O	RC	INDIAN		081	D		20
PAUL	JAMES				51	IRELAND	BA	IRISH	F	082	G		1
PAUL	JOSEPH				36	QUE	RC	FRENCH	FARMER	084	E		3
PAUL	ROBERT				26	O	CP	IRISH	F	082	G		1
PAUL	SAMUEL		1		23	ENGLAND	WM	ENGLISH	MINER	089	A		37
PAWANSKUS	JONES				50	O	WM	INDIAN	HUNTER	086	C	2	3
PAWER	JAMES				52	IRELAND	RC	IRISH	F	081	J	1	7
PAWIS	GILBERT				34	O	WM	INDIAN	HUNTER	086	C	2	4
PAWIS	JAMES				32	O	WM	INDIAN	HUNTER	086	C	2	5
PAWIS	MARY		1	1	60	O	WM	INDIAN		086	C	2	2
PAWIS	PETER				30	O	WM	INDIAN	HUNTER	086	C	2	3
PAYETTE	ANIAS				59	QUE	RC	FRENCH	FISHERMAN	089	A		62
PAYETTE	DESIRE				48	QUEBEC	RC	FRENCH	FARMER	081	G	1	3
PAYETTE	GIBERT				34	QUE	RC	FRENCH	CARPENTER	081	I		22
PAYMENT	FELICITE			1	55	QUE	RC	FRENCH	HOUSE KEEPER	089	B		32
PAYMENT	FRANCIS				25	O	RC	FRENCH	FISHERMAN	089	A		65
PAYNE	FRIDRICK				25	ENGLAND	CE	ENGLISH	FARMER	085	E		28
PAYNE	JOHN				40	IRELAND	CE	IRISH	F	081	H	2	40
PAYNE	JOHN		1		27	O	BA	SCOTCH	LABOURER	088	A		8
PAYNE	JOSEPH				29	O	WM	IRISH	F	081	H	2	39
PAYNE	RICHARD		1		24	IRELAND	CE	IRISH	FARMER	083	A	2	3
PAYNE	WILLIAM				64	IRELAND	WM	IRISH	F	081	H	2	39
PAYNE	WILLIAM				47	IRELAND	CE	IRISH	F	085	C		13
PAYNTER	JOSEPH				78	ENGLAND	WM	ENGLISH	COOPER	089	A		46
PAYNTER	THOMAS				33	ENGLAND	WM	ENGLISH	STORE KEEPER & COOPE	089	A		46
PEACHEY	WILLIAM				26	O	CP	ENGLISH	BARBER	081	B		77
PEACOCK	CHRISTOPHER				31	ENGLAND	WM	ENGLISH	F	085	L		2
PEAKE	SAMUEL				57	ENGLAND	RC	ENGLISH	F	086	A	1	18
PEAN	JOHN		1		38	FRANCE	RC	FRENCH	PRIEST	084	I	2	1
PEAR	MARAY			1	13	O	RC	INDIAN		084	I	1	6
PEARSON	GEORGE		1			O	CP	SCOTCH		081	A	1	49
PEARSON	GEORGE				19	SCOTLAND	CP	SCOTCH	CLERK	081	B		70
PEARSON	JANE		1	1	18	O	CP			081	A	1	49
PEBELS	WILLIAM		1		21	O	CP	SCOTCH		081	B		27
PEEVER	DAVID				32	IRELAND	CE	IRISH	F	082	A		66
PEEVER	DAVID				26	ONTARIO	EM	IRISH	F	082	A		83
PEEVER	JAMES				42	IRELAND	EM	IRISH	F	082	A		65
PEEVER	WILLIAM				59	IRELAND	WM	IRISH	F	081	H	1	9
PEEVER	WILLIAM				45	IRELAND	EM	IRISH	F	082	A		75
PEGOHMYOHBOV	ABRAM				35	O	PA	INDIAN	TRAPPER	086	A	3	2
PEGONEIASANG	J	BTE			61	US	RC	INDIAN	F & FISHERMAN	087	A		35
PEGONEIASANG	MOISE				29	O	RC	INDIAN	F & COOPER	087	A		36
PEGONEIASANG	PIERRE				26	O	RC	INDIAN	F & COOPER	087	A		36
PEGONEIASANG	STEPHEN				23	O	RC	INDIAN	F & COOPER	087	A		36
PEHAWANAKWED	PAUL				42	US	RC	INDIAN	F & FISHERMAN	087	A		13
PEIREEY	JOSEPH				61	ENGLAND	CE	ENGLISH	F	085	B		21
PELKIE	MARGARET		1	1	30	QUE	RC	FRENCH	SERVANT	082	E		43
PELL	ALFRED				37	ENGLAND	CE	ENGLISH	MILLER	081	G	1	29
PELL	SAMUEL				39	ENGLAND	CE	ENGLISH	FARMER	081	G	1	37
PELLETIER	JOHN				64	O	RC	FRENCH	F	082	F		15
PELLETIER	JOHN				38	O	RC	INDIAN	F & FISHERMAN	087	A		11
PELLETIER	JOSEPH				67	US	RC	INDIAN	F & FISHERMAN	087	A		10
PELOU	JOSEPH		1		20	QUE	RC	FRENCH	LABOURER	082	E		29
PELREN	CHARLES				29	QUE	RC	FRENCH	F	082	K	1	15
PENASANABIC	SUSAN		1	1	62	RED RIVER	RC	INDIAN		090	F		12
PENASSIE	JOHN				38	O	RC	INDIAN	LAB	090	F		13
PENDER	WILLIAM				26	ONT	WM	IRISH	F	081	J	1	32
PENDER	WILLIAM				50	ONT	FK	IRISH	F	081	J	1	35
PENDERGAST	WM				25	O	CE	IRISH	F	082	G		72
PENESSEWAHBAI	ANTOINE				45	US	RC	INDIAN	F & FISHERMAN	087	C		2
PENESSEWONQUET	ANTOINE		1		34	US	RC	INDIAN	LAB	087	C		5
PENMAN	DAVID		1		22	ONTARIO	CS	SCOTCH	LAB	082	A		27
PENNO	HENRY				34	ENGLAND	WM	ENGLISH	LABOURER	089	A		17
PENNOCK	FREDRICK				37	O	WM	ENGLISH	F	082	C	2	31
PENOCK	CLARENCE				18	O	CE	ENGLISH	F	085	K	2	8
PENSON	RICHARD				42	ENGLAND	CE	ENGLISH	FARMER	085	E		32
PEPEJIGONGAJIN	(WIDOW)		1			ONTARIO	PA	INDIAN	HUNTER & TRAPPER	090	E		19
PEPIGNIS	GEORGE				80	O	RC	INDIAN	HUNTER	088	B		23
PERA	FELIX				48	QUE	RC	FRENCH	TINSMITH	082	E		51
PERANT	LUKE				53	QUE	RC	FRENCH	LABOURER	082	E		45
PERAULT	EUGENE		1	1	11	QUE	RC	FRENCH		082	E		52
PERAULT	EZRA		1		3	O	RC	FRENCH		082	E		52
PERAULT	FABINA		1	1	1	O	RC	FRENCH		082	E		52
PERAULT	VICTORIA		1	1	9	QUE	RC	FRENCH		082	E		52
PERCHA	NICHOLAS				50	PRUSSIA	RC	PRUSSIAN	F	081	J	1	6
PERCIVAL	HENRY				65	ENGLAND	CE	ENGLISH	DIE INKER AND ENGRAV	085	C		13
PERCIVIL	LIZZIE		1	1	15	O	CP	SCOTCH	SERVANT	081	A	2	2
PERFECT	SARAH		1	1	50	ENGLAND	CE	ENGLISH		082	C	2	65
PERGEAU	BISENEAV		1		16	QUE	RC	FRENCH		082	I		72
PERGEAU	DELEMOUS		1	1	3	ONT	RC	FRENCH		082	I		73
PERGEAU	JOSEPH		1		6	ONT	RC	FRENCH		082	I		73
PERGEAU	LEASAN		1	1	10	QUE	RC	FRENCH		082	I		73
PERGEAU	LOUACE		1		39	QUE	RC	FRENCH	FARMER	082	I		72
PERGEAU	LOUACE		1		14	QUE	RC	FRENCH		082	I		73
PERGEAU	MARY		1	1	35	QUE	RC	FRENCH		082	I		72
PERGEAU	OGEOS		1		4	ONT	RC	FRENCH		082	I		73
PERIGO	MARIA		1	1	18	O	RC	FRENCH	SERVANT	082	H		21
PERKINS	VICTORIA		1	1	18	O	CP	ENGLISH		081	B		80
PERO	FRANCOIS				69	QUE	RC	FRENCH	F	081	C		12
PERRAULT	ADOLPHE				23	QUE	RC	FRENCH	FARMER	090	F		16
PERRAULT	ANTOINE				58	FRANCE	RC	FRENCH	FARMER	090	F		16
PERRAULT	FRANCOIS				34	O	RC	FRENCH	FARMER	089	B		27
PERRAULT	JOSEPH				24	QUE	RC	FRENCH	COOK	090	F		15
PERRAULT	MARY		2	1	41	QUE	RC	FRENCH		090	F		D
PERRAW	HENRY				34	QUE	RC	FRENCH	LAB	081	B		57

SURNAME	NAME1	NAME2	STRAY	SEX	AGE	BIRTHPL	RELIGION	ORIGIN	OCCUP	DIST	SUB_DIST	DIV	PAGE
PERRE	NANCY		2	1	28	O	RC	FRENCH	LAB	090	F		D
PERREY	JOHN				44	QUE	RC	FRENCH	LAB	081	B		34
PERRIE	JOHN		1		17	QUE	RC	FRENCH		081	B		86
PERRIGO	JOHN				28	O	RC	FRENCH	F	082	G		63
PERRIGO	REBECCA		1	1	25	IRELAND	RC	FRENCH	SERVANT	081	K		1
PERRISHER	CHARLES				24	UNITED STATES	RC	FRENCH	LUMBERMAN	088	B		1
PERRO	JAMES		1		49	ENGLAND	CE	ENGLISH	MINER	089	A		46
PERRY	PATRICK				48	IRELAND	RC	IRISH	F	081	J	1	34
PERRY	ROBERT	D			27	US	CE	ENGLISH	MANAGER	088	B		3
PERRY	ROBERT	E			45	O	CE	ENGLISH	POST MASTER	085	I		4
PERSIAN	ANTHONY				52	ONTARIO	RC	FRENCH	FARMER	083	A	1	10
PERSICK	JOHN				24	PRUSSIA	RC	PRUSSIAN	FARMER	083	A	1	16
PERSICK	VALENTE				67	PRUSSIA	RC	PRUSSIAN	FARMER	083	A	1	16
PERSON	S	H			60	US	NR	ENGLISH	F	081	A	2	48
PERSONS	CAROLINE		1	1	25	UNITED STATES	EM	ENGLISH		081	B		13
PERVEY	ROBERT				41	GERMANY	LU	GERMAN	F	082	G		28
PERVIS	GEORGE				28	ENGLAND	CE	ENGLISH	LUMBERMAN	081	A	2	6
PESHKONSIWAB'S	(SISTER)			1		ONTARIO	PA	INDIAN	HUNTER & TRAPPER	090	E		19
PESNIWATCH	ANGULINE		1	1	70	O	RC	INDIAN		082	H		28
PESNIWATCH	DAVID				1	O	RC			082	H		D
PESNIWATCH	JOSEPH				28	O	RC	INDIAN	HUNTER AND FISHERMAN	082	H		28
PESNIWATCH	LOUIS				36	QUE	RC	INDIAN	HUNTER AND FISHERMAN	082	H		28
PESNIWATCH	MICHAEL		1		77	QUE	RC	INDIAN		082	H		28
PETAWNI	PETER				45	O	RC	INDIAN	LAB	090	F		24
PETEGREW	GEORGE				34	IRELAND	EM	IRISH	F	082	A		9
PETEGREW	JAMES				32	IRELAND	CE	IRISH	F	082	A		40
PETEGREW	MATHEW				26	IRELAND	CE	IRISH	F	082	A		40
PETER	ALEXANDER				40	O	RC	INDIAN	HUNTER	084	I	1	6
PETER	HARRY		1	1	37	O	RC	IRISH	PILOT	086	C	1	9
PETER	JOHN				60	O	RC	INDIAN	HUNTER	086	C	2	4
PETER	MOSES				30	O	RC	INDIAN	HUNTER	084	E		2
PETERKIN	ELIZABETH			1	54	SCOTLAND	CP	SCOTCH		085	H		15
PETERS	FORBES				25	IRELAND	CE	IRISH	F	086	A	2	6
PETO	ANWELL				65	QUE	RC	FRENCH	F	081	A	2	51
PETRIDGE	ANTWIN				60	O	RC	INDIAN	HUNTER	081	I		41
PEVER	JAMES				68	IRELAND	CE	IRISH	F	081	J	1	43
PEVER	JAMES				35	IRELAND	CE	IRISH	FARMER	082	B		43
PEVER	JOHN				33	IRELAND	CE	IRISH	FARMER	082	B		44
PEVER	ROBERT				34	IRELAND	CE	IRISH	F	081	J	1	48
PHAILEN	JOHN				26	IRELAND	RC	IRISH	FARMER	082	I		33
PHELEN	MARGRET		1	1	33	QUE	RC	IRISH	SCHOOL TEACHER	082	D		19
PHILIPS	ALEXANDER				29	O	CE	ENGLISH	F	085	E		15
PHILIPS	FLETCHER				29	O	WM	IRISH	F	085	H		17
PHILIPS	HEDWARD		1		34	ENGLAND	CE	ENGLISH	SCHOOL TEACHER	082	F		6
PHILIPS	JOHN				60	SCOTLAND	CP	SCOTTISH	CARPENTER	082	B		57
PHILLIPS	BERNARD		1		25	ENGLAND	CE	ENGLISH	F	085	L		4
PHILLIPS	DAVID				50	SCOTLAND	CP	SCOTCH	F	081	A	1	70
PHILLIPS	GEORGE				47	ONT	CE	ENGLISH	F	081	J	1	52
PHILLIPS	HYROM				20	O	WM	DUTCH	F	086	A	1	20
PHILLIPS	ISAAC				23	O	CE	ENGLISH	RAILWAYMAN	081	A	2	28
PHILLIPS	JAMES				36	ENGLAND	CE	ENGLISH	SHOEMAKER	081	A	2	21
PHILLIPS	JAMES				56	SCOTLAND	PS	SCOTCH	F	081	H	2	9
PHILLIPS	ROBERT		1		31	ENGLAND	CE	ENGLISH	F	085	L		4
PHILLIPS	WILLIAM				44	IRELAND	WM	IRISH	BARBER	081	B		51
PHILLIPS	WILLIAM				52	SCOTLAND	PS	SCOTCH	F	081	H	2	9
PHILLIPS	WILLIAM		1		25	ENGLAND	WM	ENGLISH	MINE LABOURER	089	A		37
PHILTACEA	THEO				33	QUE	RC	FRENCH	LUMBERMAN	088	C		6
PHIPPS	JAMES	C			42	WALES	CE	ENGLISH	MERCHANT	089	B		11
PHURESMAN	JOHN		1		3	O	WM	SWEDE		081	I		21
PICHE	JOE		1		22	QUE	RC	FRENCH	SAWYER	082	E		30
PICHE	JOSEPH		1		24	QUE	RC	FRENCH	SAWYER	082	E		70
PICHERIN	NELSON				57	US	EM	ENGLISH	F	085	D		7
PICHERIN	PETER				24	O	PM	GERMAN	F	085	D		22
PICHETTE	PAUL				36	QUE	RC	FRENCH	CARPENTER	082	E		43
PICKERIN	THOS				52	ENGLAND	CE	ENGLISH	WEAVER & F	081	J	1	63
PICKERINE	JAMES		1		40	O	ME	FRENCH	SHANTYMAN	085	E		27
PICKINS	WILLIAM				47	IRELAND	WM	IRISH	F	081	H	1	12
PIDDINGTON	SAML		1		19	ENGLAND	WM	ENGLISH	BANK CLERK	082	E		54
PIECHER	ELIZABETH			1	50	U STATES	PS	FRENCH	OCCUPANT OF LAND	082	G		70
PIELOH	ABRAHAM				45	QUEBEC	RC	INDIAN	HUNTER	083	E		1
PIERCE	PHILIP				52	ENGLAND	CE	ENGLISH	F	082	G		45
PIERCE	THOMAS				22	O	CE	ENGLISH	F	082	G		44
PIERCE	WILLIAM				48	ENGLAND	CE	ENGLISH	F	082	G		45
PIERRAULT	AUGUSTA		1	1	19	QUE	CP	FRENCH	SCHOOL TEACHER	082	I		42
PIERRAULT	CATHERINE		1	1	25	QUE	RP	FRENCH	SCHOOL TEACHER	082	I		10
PIERRE	BIG				35	MILL LAC	PA	INDIAN	HUNTER	090	F		4
PIERRE	LITTLE		1		19	O	RC	INDIAN	LAB	090	F		8
PIKA	JOHN				15	ONTARIO	RC	INDIAN	HUNTER	083	D		1
PIKERSKY	MATHIAS				49	PRUSSIA	RC	PRUSSIAN	FARMER	083	A	1	1
PILATSKE	JOHN						NG		SEE PALATZKY	082	I		44
PILGIR	HERMAN		2			O	LU			085	A		D
PILGIR	JACOB				51	PRUSSIA	LU	PRUSSIAN	F	085	A		7
PILGRIM	HENRY		1		58	ENGLAND	UT	ENGLISH	CLERK DISTRICT COURT	089	B		4
PILGRIM	WILLIAM				51	GERMANY	WM	GERMAN	FARMER	081	G	1	33
PILKY	WILLIAM		1		54	O	WM	ENGLISH	CARPENTER	085	E		1
PILLON	MARGARET		2	1	1	ONT	RC			081	C		D
PILLON	MICHAEL		2		16	ONT	RC		RAFTSMAN	081	C		D
PILON	JOSEPH				66	QUE	RC	FRENCH	CARPENTER	090	D		8
PILON	PIERRE	SR			45	QUE	RC	FRENCH	LABOURER	088	A		5
PIM	MARGARET			1	38	SCOTLAND	WM	SCOTCH	POST MISTRESS	089	B		4
PINASHUGUYIE	PIERRE				22	O	RC	INDIAN		090	A		8
PINEL	HANNAH			1	43	ENGLAND	WM	ENGLISH		085	C		25
PINK	THOMAS				27	ENGLAND	ME	ENGLISH	BLACKSMITH	082	E		65
PINKERTON	JAMES		1		6	IRELAND	CE	IRISH		081	K		70
PINKERTON	JOHN		1		15	IRELAND	CE	IRISH	HARNESSMAKER	081	K		70
PINKERTON	MARY	CATHERINE	1	1	7	IRELAND	CE	IRISH		081	K		70
PINKERTON	ROBERT				60	SCOTLAND	CP	SCOTCH	F	081	A	1	71
PIONS	MADAM		1	1	36	O	WM	INDIAN		090	C		7
PIPER	CHARLES				59	IRELAND	CE	IRISH	F	085	I		32
PIRENIASH	JOHN				43	QUE	RC	INDIAN	F	082	C	2	54
PISCAUF	JOSEPH				45	PRUSSIA	RC	PRUSSIAN	F	081	J	1	13
PISCAUF	LAURINCE				38	PRUSSIA	RC	PRUSSIAN	F	081	J	1	12
PISKEY	JOSEPH				30	O	RC	INDIAN	HUNTER	090	F		8
PISKUF	PERRE				43	O	RC	INDIAN	LAB	090	F		6
PLANT	THOS				30	ONT	RC	FRENCH	F	081	J	1	46
PLAUNT	ALFORD				26	QUE	RC	FRENCH	BUTCHER	081	I		31

SURNAME	NAME1	NAME2	STRAY	SEX	AGE	BIRTHPL	RELIGION	ORIGIN	OCCUP	DIST	SUB_DIST	DIV	PAGE
PLAUNTE	XAVIER				63	QUE	RC	FRENCH	FARMER	081	F		9
PLAYTER	SARAH	B	1	1	75	ENGLAND	CP	ENGLISH		082	E		64
PLEAU	JOSEP		1		24	Q	RC	FRENCH		086	B		1
PLEETE	JOHN				32	GERMANY	CE	GERMAN	LAB	081	B		65
PLEUNT	JOSEPH				29	0	CP	SCOTCH	HOTELKEEPER	081	I		2
PLOS	JOHN				61	QUE	RC	FRENCH	F	082	H		20
PLOSS	MARY		1	1	60	POLAND	RC	POLISH		081	I		37
PLPLNSKE	JACOB				20	POLAND	RC	POLISH	LAB	081	I		38
PLUFFIE	JAMES				80	ENGLAND	CP	ENGLISH	F	081	J	1	77
PLUMBER	DORA		1	1	19	0	CE	IRISH	SERVANT	082	E		5
PLUMBER	SERAH		1	1	19	0	CE	IRISH	DOMESTIC	082	E		10
PLUMBER	WILLIAM				52	ENGLAND	CE	ENGLISH	INDIAN SUPRDT	087	B	2	10
PLUMMER	JOHN				28	ENGLAND	CE	ENGLISH	MINING ENGINEER	089	A		48
PLUMMER	RICHARD				51	IRELAND	CE	IRISH	F	082	G		33
PLUPH	GILBART		1		32	FRANCE	RC	FRENCH	LAB	084	I	2	1
PODREY	MOSES				53	QUE	RC	FRENCH	F	082	G		29
POFF	HENERY				38	IRELAND	EM	IRISH	F	082	F		38
POFF	JOHN				24	0	EM	IRISH	F	082	F		39
POFF	MARY		1	1	55	IRELAND	WM	IRISH		082	F		40
POFF	PETER				60	IRELAND	JM	IRISH	F	082	C	2	58
POFF	THOMAS				41	IRELAND	EM	IRISH		082	C	1	24
POKITT	DOLFIRE				22	QUEBEC	RC	FRENCH	FARMER	081	G	1	45
POKYFKE	JOHN				38	POLAND	RC	POLISH	LAB	081	I		37
POLICK	THOMAS				50	SCOTLAND	PS	SCOTCH	MERCHANT	085	E		4
POLLEY	RICHARD				28	ENGLAND	PM	ENGLISH	F	085	D		29
POLLEY	WILLIAM				35	ENGLAND	PM	ENGLISH	F	085	D		20
POLLOCK	ABRAM				53	IRELAND	CP	IRISH	F	082	G		26
POLLOCK	ROBERT				40	0	CP	SCOTCH	F	082	G		42
POLMAN	IDA		1	1	15	PRUSSIA	LU	GERMAN	SERVANT	082	E		28
POLTEN	ANNE			1	35	POLAND	RC	POLISH		081	I		40
POMBARE	CHARLES		1		45	QUEBEC	RC	FRENCH	RAFTSMAN	084	D		1
POMERAING	ERNEST				33	PRUSSIA	LU	GERMAN	FARMER	082	B		14
POMERAING	WILLIAM		2			0	LU	GERMAN		082	B		D
POOLE	JOHN		1		25	ENGLAND	CE	ENGLISH	F	085	K	2	8
POOLE	W	JOHN	1		12	ONT	CP	IRISH	ADOPTED	081	J	1	59
POORMAN	CHARLES	FREDRICK			76	GERMANY	LU	GERMAN	SURVEYOR	082	I		45
POORMAN	IDA		1	1	15	GERMANY	LU	GERMAN		082	I		45
POORMAN	POLENA	CHARLOTTE	1	1	50	GERMANY	LU	GERMAN		082	I		45
POORMAN	POWELL		1		19	GERMANY	LU	GERMAN	SHANTYMAN	082	I		45
POPE	ROBERT				39	IRELAND	CE	IRISH	C ENGINEER	086	B		4
POPE	THOMAS				44	ENGLAND	WM	ENGLISH	F	085	C		11
POQUETTE	OSSILLI		1	1	19	0	RC	FRENCH		081	K		26
POQUETTE	TEOPHILE		1		23	QUE	RC	FRENCH		081	K		26
POQUIN	DAVID		1		50	QUEBEC	RC	FRENCH	CARPENTER	083	A	1	12
PORTAS	THOMAS	HENRY			26	0	CE	ENGLISH	DRUGGIST	085	I		44
PORTEGUE	PETER				28	0	RC	FRENCH	BLACKSMITH	081	D		7
PORTEOUS	ARCHIBALD				28	0	PS	SCOTCH	F	082	C	2	36
PORTEOUS	CLARISA		1	1	71	USA	WM	ENGLISH		082	C	2	37
PORTEOUS	JOHN				67	SCOTLAND	CP	SCOTCH	F	082	C	2	36
PORTEOUS	MARY	JANE		1	24		WM	ENGLISH		082	C	2	37
PORTER	ALEXANDER				38	0	CP	SCOTCH		082	C	1	40
PORTER	DAVID				37	0	CP	SCOTCH	F	082	C	1	55
PORTER	DAVID		1		38	0	PS	ENGLISH		086	C	1	1
PORTER	ELMIRA		1	1	58	US	WM	SCOTCH	HOUSE KEEPER	089	B		12
PORTER	ROBERT				39	IRELAND	CP	IRISH	F	085	J		4
PORTER	SARAH	AN	1	1	24	0	CP	IRISH	DOMESTIC SERVANT	082	E		19
PORTER	THOMAS				47	0	PS	IRISH	F	082	G		90
PORTERO	LAURENT		1		19	QUE	RC	FRENCH	SERVANT	089	B		2
PORTGAVE	JOSEPH				39	QUE	RC	FRENCH	LAB	081	I		43
PORTIOUS	WILLIAM		1		52	SCOTLAND	CS	SCOTCH	FARM SERVANT	081	A	1	49
PORTISS	ROBERT				28	NB	PS	SCOTTISH	FARMER	082	D		5
PORTOUS	ROBERT				43	SCOTLAND	CS	SCOTCH	CARPENTER	081	H	1	10
PORTURSON	EDWARD				33	0	RC	FRENCH	TINSMITH	081	I		39
POSEY	DURHAM				31	QUE	RC	FRENCH	CARRIAGEMAKER	081	A	1	12
POTCTVIN	LOUIS				50	QUE	RC	FRENCH	F	081	K		15
POTTER	AUSTIN		1		26	ENGLAND	WM	ENGLISH	MINISTER	085	I		4
POTTER	CARL				33	PRUSSIA	FW	GERMAN	BLACKSMITH	081	G	1	24
POTTER	FREDERICK				42	GERMANY	LU	GERMAN	WAGON MAKER	081	F		10
POTTER	JAMES				39	0	CP	IRISH	SAWYER	082	E		70
POTTER	JAMES				38	ONT	CP	IRISH	FOREMAN	082	I		44
POTTER	JOHN				44	GERMANY	BA	GERMAN	BLACKSMITH	081	F		10
POTTER	JOHN				57	IRELAND	CS	IRISH	F	081	J	1	38
POTTER	JOHN	W			37	ENGLAND	CE	ENGLISH	STONE & MARBLE CUTTE	082	E		14
POTTER	RICHARD		1		20	ENGLAND	CE	ENGLISH	STONECUTTER	082	E		30
POTTER	THOMAS				53	IRELAND	CP	IRISH	FARMER	082	B		54
POULETTE	WILLIAM		1		21	0	ME	FRENCH	TEAMSTER	090	F		23
POULIN	JULES				40	QUE	RC	FRENCH	CARPENTER	090	F		5
POUNDER	GEORGE				35	0	WM	ENGLISH	F	082	C	2	25
POUNDER	JOHN				66	IRELAND	WM	IRISH	F	082	C	2	24
POUPLOUS	ISRIAL		1		25	QUE	RC	FRENCH	LAB	082	K	1	15
POUPLOUS	SALLAY		1	1	27	0	RC	ENGLISH		082	K	1	15
POUPLOUS	T	WILLIAM	2			0	RC			082	K	1	D
POUPORE	SARAH			1	65	IRELAND	CE	IRISH		082	C	1	8
POUQUETTE	JOHN		1		18	QUEBEC	RC	FRENCH		083	A	1	8
POWELL	SAMUEL				60	IRELAND	RC	IRISH	LAB	081	A	2	8
POWELL	WILLIAM				36	IRELAND	RC	IRISH	LAB	081	A	2	9
POWER	EDWARD				45	IRELAND	RC	IRISH	F	081	K		35
POWER	EDWARD				27	0	RC	IRISH	SHOEMAKER	081	K		63
POWER	JAMES		1		17	QUEBEC	RC	IRISH	LAB	083	C		3
POWER	JOHN				32	IRELAND	RC	IRISH	F	081	K		38
POWER	MARGARET			1	50	IRELAND	RC	IRISH		081	A	1	11
POWER	MARY ANN		1	1	40	ONTARIO	RC	IRISH		082	B		4
POWER	MORRIS				50	IRELAND	RC	IRISH	F	082	A		13
POWER	PATRICK				27	QUEBEC	RC	IRISH	LUMBERER	083	B	2	1
POWER	PETER				55	IRELAND	RC	IRISH		081	K		35
POWER	SARAH		1	1	75	IRELAND	RC	IRISH		082	B		4
POWER	THOMAS				51	IRELAND	RC	IRISH	F	081	K		35
POWER	WILLIAM				52	IRELAND	RC	IRISH	F	081	J	1	75
POWERS	JAMES		1		33	IRELAND	RC	IRISH	LAB	081	B		55
POWERS	RICHARD				24	0	RC	IRISH	F	082	C	1	43
PRANKAY	AGUSTUS				31	PRUSSIA	RC	GERMAN	F	082	J		15
PRATT	A	W			22	NEW BRUNSWICK	FW	ENGLISH	LUMBERER	083	B	1	1
PREBBEL	STEPHEN				54	ENGLAND	WM	ENGLISH	F	085	J		22
PREMO	BAPTISTE				48	QUE	RC	FRENCH	F	081	K		34
PREMO	JOACHIM		1		64	QUE	RC	FRENCH	FARM LAB	082	C	1	27
PREMO	JOSEPH				28	QUE	RC	FRENCH		082	C	1	34

SURNAME	NAME1	NAME2	STRAY	SEX	AGE	BIRTHPL	RELIGION	ORIGIN	OCCUP	DIST	SUB_DIST	DIV	PAGE
PREMO	JULE				23	QUE	RC	FRENCH	LAB	082	C	1	33
PREMO	LOUIS				32	QUE	RC	FRENCH		082	C	1	33
PREMO	LOUIS	SUG			55	QUE	RC	FRENCH		082	C	1	33
PREMO	THOMAS				23	QUE	RC	FRENCH	F	081	K		42
PRENE	JOHN		1		31	0	RC	INDIAN	LAB	090	F		6
PRENTISS	ELESABATH		1	1	23	0	RC	IRISH	SERVANT	082	K	1	19
PRESCOT	JOHN				29	0	CE	IRISH	FARMER	082	F		3
PRESCOT	THOMAS		2		1	0	CE			082	F		D
PREUI	ARCHABLE				25	QUE	RC	FRENCH	WAGGONMAKER	081	I		11
PRICE	ADAM				35	0	WM	ENGLISH	F	085	J		14
PRICE	CHARLES		1		07	ONTARIO	RC	IRISH		082	B		2
PRICE	DAVID				37	IRELAND	CE	IRISH	F	081	H	2	41
PRICE	DAVID				28	QUE	JM	IRELAND	F	082	C	2	61
PRICE	DAVID	SEN			50	IRELAND	WM	IRISH	F	081	H	2	35
PRICE	ENOCH				35	IRELAND	CE	IRISH	F	082	C	2	29
PRICE	JAMES		1		7	0	RC	IRISH		081	H	2	40
PRICE	JAMES				32	IRELAND	EM	IRISH	F	082	G		48
PRICE	MARGARET	A	1	1	13	IRELAND	WM	IRISH		081	H	2	39
PRICE	MARY		1	1	17	0	RC	IRISH		081	H	2	40
PRICE	MARY		1		67	IRELAND	EM	IRISH		082	G		49
PRICE	THOMAS		1		15	0	RC	IRISH		081	B		12
PRICHARD	ALFRED				36	ENGLAND	CE	ENGLISH	BOOKKEEPER	082	D		11
PRICHARD	THOMAS				20	ENGLAND	CE	ENGLISH	F	085	E		20
PRIEBE	FREDRICK				44	GERMANY	LU	GERMAN	FARMER	082	I		19
PRIEST	JOHN				30	0	RC	ENGLISH	F	082	F		23
PRIMO	BAPTISTE				27	QUEBEC	RC	FRENCH	LUMBERER	083	B	2	1
PRINCE	ADAM				35	PRUSSIA	RC	GERMAN	FARMER	081	G	1	15
PRINCE	ADAM				74	PRUSSIA	RC	PRUSSIAN	FARMER	081	G	2	5
PRINCE	FRANCIS				35	PRUSSIA	RC	PRUSSIAN	FARMER	083	A	1	3
PRINCE	JOHN		2		75	ENGLAND	CE	ENGLISH	JUDGE	089	B		D
PRINCE	JOSEPH				40	PRUSSIA	RC	PRUSSIAN	FARMER	083	A	1	20
PRINCE	JOSEPH				59	POLAND	RC	POLISH	F	083	C		19
PRINCE	MICHAEL				32	PRUSSIA	RC	PRUSSIAN	FARMER	083	A	1	20
PRINCE	MICHAEL				47	POLAND	RC	POLISH	F	083	C		19
PRITCHARD	MARY	JANE	2	1	7	0	BA			090	F		D
PRITCHARD	WARREN				40	US	BA	SCOTCH	EXPLORER	090	F		15
PROBYEN	LOUISE			1	32	SCOTLAND	CE	SCOTTISH		082	E		5
PROCTOR	RICHARD				32	IRELAND	CE	IRISH	F	081	J	1	37
PROCULE	LAFRANCE		1		18	QUE	RC	FRENCH	BLACKSMITH	082	D		7
PROCULE	LEDUC		1		22	QUE	RC	FRENCH	CLERK	082	E		26
PROPHET	JOHN				38	ENGLAND	WM	ENGLISH	MINER	089	A		3
PROUDFOOT	ALEXANDER				54	SCOTLAND	UP	SCOTCH	F	085	J		20
PROULX	ALEXANDRE				23	0	RC	FRENCH	FISHERMAN	088	A		2
PROULX	ANDREW				32	QUE	RC	FRENCH	LUMBERMAN	088	B		6
PROULX	J	BTE			30	0	RC	FRENCH	COOPER	088	A		1
PROULX	PHILEMIN				54	QUE	RC	FRENCH CAN	LIGHTS KEEPER	088	A		6
PROUT	FRANK				30	ENGLAND	CE	ENGLISH	MINER	089	A		12
PROUT	MARGRET			1	60	IRELAND	RC	IRISH	HOTELKEEPER	081	B		59
PROVO	ANTOINE		1		25	QUE	RC	FRENCH	LAB	081	B		82
PROVOS	MICHEAL	SR			60	QUE	RC	FRENCH	F	082	J		7
PROVOST	PHREM		1		33	QUE	RC	FRENCH	LUMBERMAN	088	B		17
PRUDAIN	NED		1		18	QUE	RC	FRENCH	SADDLER	081	B		73
PRUNTY	PATRICK				54	IRELAND	RC	IRISH	F	085	B		3
PRUSS	CHARLES				47	GERMANY	LU	GERMAN	FARMER	082	I		21
PUDAH	BUSILE				66	QUE	RC	FRENCH	FARMER	081	F		20
PUGH	WILLIAM				52	ENGLAND	CE	ENGLISH	CARPENTER	089	A		34
PULLARD	SUSAN		1	1	78	ENGLAND	WM	ENGLISH		085	I		40
PULOT	ALEXANDER				24	QUE	RC	FRENCH	LAB	081	B		15
PULSE	LEVI				50	PRUSSIA	LU	GERMAN	F	081	C		31
PUNARD	MORICE		1		24	QUEBEC	RC	FRENCH	BLACKSMITH	083	E		2
PURCEL	ELLEN		1	1	80	IRELAND	RC	IRISH		081	K		58
PURCELL	JAMES		1		26	ENGLAND	CE	ENGLISH	PLASTERER	085	I		10
PURCELL	WILLIAM				35	IRELAND	RC	IRISH	MINER	090	D		3
PURCIL	HENRY				50	IRELAND	RC	IRISH		081	A	2	5
PURCY	MICHAEL				21	0	RC	IRISH	F	082	G		69
PURDY	GEORGE				33	ONTARIO	CE	IRISH	FOREMAN	081	G	1	43
PURIL	JOSEPH				18	ONTARIO	RC	INDIAN	HUNTER	083	D		1
PUTCHAT	LOUIS				45	0	RC	INDIAN	HUNTER	090	F		14
PUTNAM	PHILANDER				48	0	PM	ENGLISH	F	085	D		22
PZPHER	PHERMAN				56	QUE	RC	FRENCH	F	082	H		21
QUADE	AUGUST				22	GERMANY	LU	GERMAN	F	082	H		24
QUADE	AUGUST				51	GERMANY	LU	GERMAN	F	082	H		24
QUAHAN	ANASTANIA		1	1	17	GERMANY	LU	GERMAN		081	F		30
QUAHAN	YOIN		1		15	GERMANY	LU	GERMAN	FARMER	081	F		30
QUAIT	WILLIAM				40	ENGLAND	CE	ENGLISH	TAILOR	081	B		42
QUALY	TIMOTHY		1		20	IRELAND	RC	IRISH	BLACKSMITH	081	I		41
QUAST	GOTLIP				43	GERMANY	WM	GERMAN	F	082	H		11
QUAST	WILLIAM		1		87	GERMANY	WM	GERMAN		082	H		10
QUEENLIVEN	BRIDGET		1	1	23	IRELAND	RC	IRISH	SERVANT	082	E		56
QUEGLY	JOHN				48	IRELAND	RC	IRISH	MERCHANT	081	K		1
QUICFE	SAMUEL	S			48	ENGLAND	WM	ENGLISH	F	085	L		8
QUIGLEY	MICHAEL				29	IRELAND	RC	IRISH	F	081	K		51
QUIGLY	CATHERINE		1	1	32	IRELAND	RC	IRISH		081	F		25
QUIGLY	JOHN		1		1	0	RC	IRISH		081	F		25
QUIGLY	MICHAEL		1		29	IRELAND	RC	IRISH	FARMER	081	F		25
QUIGLY	PATRICK		1			0	RC	IRISH	F	081	F		25
QUILTY	THOMAS				60	IRELAND	RC	IRISH	F	081	C		34
QUIM	LAWRENCE		1		24	IRELAND	RC	IRISH	SHOEMAKER	081	I		7
QUIN	JAMES				60	IRELAND	RC	IRISH	FARMER	082	B		22
QUIN	JOHN				30	IRELAND	RC	IRISH	FARMER	082	B		26
QUINLAN	JOHN				27	IRELAND	RC	IRISH	MINE LABOURER	089	A		7
QUINN	DANIEL		1		27	0	RC	IRISH	FARM LABOURER	081	K		64
QUINN	JAMES				35	IRELAND	RC	IRISH	F	081	K		60
QUINN	JOHN				7	ONTARIO	RC	IRISH		082	B		9
QUINN	MARTIN				52	IRELAND	RC	IRISH	FARMER	081	F		28
QUINN	MICHAEL		1		11	0	RC	IRISH		081	K		64
QUINN	PATRICK		1		30	IRELAND	RC	IRISH	F	081	H	2	31
QUINTON	THOMAS				43	ENGLAND	CE	ENGLISH	F	085	I		40
QUITTY	NICHOLAS				26	IRELAND	RC	IRISH	F	081	J	1	8
QUNESMO	JOHN				26	0	CE	INDIAN	LUMBERMAN	088	B		18
RABADOUR	PHILIMIENE		1	1	24	QUE	RC	FRENCH		082	I		48
RADDITZ	HENRY				54	GERMANY	CE	GERMAN	FARMER	081	F		8
RADINGTON	THOMAS				38	QUE	RC	IRISH	LAB	081	B		46
RADKAY	FREDRICK				38	GERMANY	WM	GERMAN	FARMER	082	I		58
RAE	SAMUEL				56	IRELAND	WM	IRISH	F	081	A	2	51
RAEUME	EUGUEME		1		2	0	RC	IRISH		082	D		2

SURNAME	NAME1	NAME2	STRAY	SEX	AGE	BIRTHPL	RELIGION	ORIGIN	OCCUP	DIST	SUB_DIST	DIV	PAGE
RAEUME	MARGRET		1	1	25	O	RC	UNKNOWN		082	D		2
RAFFERTY	HUGH				26	IRELAND	CE	IRISH	F	086	A	1	31
RAFFERTY	JOSEPH				30	IRELAND	CE	IRISH	F	086	A	1	31
RAGAN	RICHARD		1		20	O	RC	IRISH	LAB	085	F		5
RAGLON	CHAS				23	GERMANY	LU	GERMAN	F	082	G		83
RAGLON	CHAS				29	GERMANY	LU	GERMAN	F	082	G		84
RAIMUS	JULIOUS				33	GERMANY	LU	GERMAN	FARMER	082	I		45
RAINS	ALLAN				28	O	RC	ENGLISH	FARMER	089	A		55
RAINS	ARTHUR				30	O	RC	ENGLISH	FARMER	089	A		56
RAINS	EVAN				33	O	RC	ENGLISH	FARMER	089	A		56
RAINS	OWEN				40	O	RC	ENGLISH	FARMER	089	A		57
RAINS	WILLIAM				82	ENGLAND	CE	ENGLISH	FARMER	089	A		56
RAJOTTE	LOUIS		1		26	QUE	RC	FRENCH	STORE CLERK	082	E		48
RALPH	JAMES				55	IRELAND	RC	IRISH	FARMER	082	I		2
RAMO	JOSEPH				48	QUE	RC	FRENCH	F	082	C	1	8
RAMSAY	DANIEL				43	IRELAND	CE	IRISH	CARPENTER	081	B		51
RAMSBOTTOM	J				27	O	CE	ENGLISH	LABOURER	088	A		7
RANGER	XAVIER		1		24	QUE	RC	FRENCH	LUMBERMAN	088	B		2
RANKIN	MATHEW				37	IRELAND	CE	IRISH	F	086	A	1	14
RANKIN	SAMUEL				37	IRELAND	CE	IRISH	F	082	A		76
RANKIN	THOMAS				39	ENGLAND	PS	INDIAN	STONE CUTTER	085	A		24
RANSON	ROBERT				48	ENGLAND	RC	ENGLISH	HOTELKEEPER	084	B		1
RAPPRISH	CARL				40	GERMANY	CE	GERMAN	CARPENTER	081	G	1	34
RAPSON	MARY		1	1	13	ENGLAND	EP	ENGLISH		090	D		5
RASTOOL	JOSEPH		1		42	ONTARIO	RC	FRENCH	HUNTER	084	D		1
RATH	CHARLES				30	IRELAND	CE	IRISH	F	082	F		2
RATHWELL	ANDREW		1		18	O	RC	IRISH	F	082	B		15
RATHWELL	CATHERINE		1	1	38	IRELAND	RC	IRISH		082	B		15
RATHWELL	JOHN				40	IRELAND	RC	IRISH	FARMER	082	B		63
RATHWELL	JOHN		1		12	O	RC	IRISH		082	B		15
RATHWELL	RICHARD				31	IRELAND	EM	IRISH	PUMPMAKER	081	B		8
RATHWELL	STEPHEN		1		15	O	RC	IRISH		082	B		15
RAVELE	JOHN		1		40	QUE	RC	FRENCH	LAB	081	B		42
RAVIEL	ISAAC		1		19	QUE	RC	FRENCH	LAB	081	B		55
RAWLAND	D	WILSON			55	ENGLAND	CE	SCOTCH	F	081	J	1	78
RAWSON	ROBERT				23	ENGLAND	CE	ENGLISH	F	085	J		9
RAWSON	THOMAS				25	ENGLAND	CE	ENGLISH	F	085	D		1
RAWSON	WILLIAM				51	ENGLAND	CE	ENGLISH	F	085	D		1
RAYMOND	AGUST		1	1	21	GERMANY	LU	GERMAN	SERVANT	082	E		50
RAYMUS	FREDRICK				67	GERMANY	LU	GERMAN	FARMER	082	I		46
RAYMUS	WILLIAM				30	GERMANY	LU	GERMAN	FARMER	082	I		46
RAYN	JAMES				50	IRELAND	RC	IRISH	FARMER	081	G	1	41
READ	JAMES				28	QUEBEC	CE	IRISH	FARMER	083	A	1	10
READ	JAMES		1		30	ENGLAND	CE	ENGLISH	LABOURER	089	A		46
READ	JOHN				41	IRELAND	CE	IRISH	MINE LABOURER	089	A		48
READY	JAMES				40	IRELAND	RC	IRISH	F	081	C		7
READY	JOHN				44	IRELAND	RC	IRISH	F	081	C		5
READY	JOHN				30	IRELAND	RC	IRISH	F	081	C		8
READY	JOHN		2			ONT	RC			081	C		D
READY	PATRICK				65	IRELAND	RC	IRISH		081	C		8
REAHEOBINA	THOMAS		2		8	O	WM	INDIAN		086	A	3	D
REAR	JOSEPH				25	O	WM	ENGLISH	F	085	H		20
RECO	MARY			1	50	POLAND	RC	POLISH		081	I		37
RECOLET	FRANCOIS				54	O	RC	FRENCH	FARMER	089	B		34
RECOLLET	JEAN	BTE			24	O	RC	INDIAN	F & FISHERMAN	087	A		9
RECOLLET	JOSEPH				47	O	RC	INDIAN	F & FISHERMAN	087	A		9
RECOSKY	STANASLUS				35	PRUSSIA	RC	PRUSSIAN	FARMER	083	A	1	3
RECROFT	CHARLES				58	IRELAND	CE	IRISH	F	081	K		24
RECULLIE	ANTHONY				58	QUE	RC	FRENCH	FISHERMAN	089	A		60
REDDAN	DANIEL				57	IRELAND	RC	IRISH	F	081	K		21
REDMAN	EDWARD				39	IRELAND	WM	IRISH	FARMER	082	I		77
REDMAN	FREDERICK				64	GERMANY	BA	GERMAN	MINISTER	081	F		21
REDMOND	FREDERICK				32	GERMANY	BA	GERMAN	LAB	081	A	2	43
REED	ADAM				35	SCOTLAND	CP	SCOTCH	F	082	F		23
REED	JOHN		1		29	ENGLAND	CE	ENGLISH	GENT	085	J		24
REED	ROBERT				33	ONTARIO	CE	IRISH	FARMER	083	A	1	7
REEKIE	GEORGE				72	SCOTLAND	PS	SCOTCH	F	086	A	1	3
REEMAN	JAMES		1		60	IRELAND	RC	IRISH	LAB	083	C		2
REESE	MARTIN				39	GERMANY	LU	GERMAN	F	082	G		28
REEVES	ALEXANDER				32	QUE	CE	ENGLISH	MERCHANT	082	G		55
REEVES	JAMES				37	QUE	CE	ENGLISH	MERCHANT	082	G		58
REEVES	ROBERTSON				22	QUE	CE	ENGLISH	TURNER & CARPENTER	082	G		58
REGAN	CATHARINE		1	1	20	IRELAND	RC	IRISH	SERVANT MAID	081	J	1	63
REGAN	DANIEL				30	ONTARIO	RC	IRISH	FARMER	081	G	1	7
REGAN	DANIEL				60	IRELAND	RC	IRISH	FARMER	081	G	1	11
REGAN	JAMES				35	ONTARIO	RC	IRISH	FARMER	081	G	1	7
REGAN	MRS		1	1	50	IRELAND	RC	IRISH	HOUSEKEEPER	081	J	1	63
REGAN	PATRICK				26	ONTARIO	RC	IRISH	FARMER	081	G	1	11
REGAN	PATRICK				40	IRELAND	RC	IRISH	FARMER	081	K		74
REHNEW	JOHN				42	QUE	RC	FRENCH	LUMBERMAN	086	C	1	3
REID	ANN		1	1	26	UNITED STATES	CE	IRISH		085	C		13
REID	CHARLES				44	IRELAND	CS	IRISH	F	081	K		59
REID	EPHRIAM				51	SCOTLAND	CP	SCOTCH	FARMER WOOLEN FACTOR	081	J	1	74
REID	HENERY				56	ENGLAND	PR	IRISH	FARMER	081	G	2	12
REID	JAMES		1		21	SCOTLAND	CP	SCOTCH	CLERK	081	I		10
REID	JOHN		1		27	QUE	PS	SCOTTISH	CARPENTER	082	E		30
REID	ROBERT				34	SCOTLAND	CP	SCOTCH	WEAVER F	081	J	1	63
REID	ROBERT				37	SCOTLAND	CP	SCOTTISH	CARPENTER	082	E		71
REID	THOMAS	BL	1		23	O	WM	IRISH	SCHOOL TEACHER	087	B	3	3
REID	WILLIAM		1		24	O	CP	SCOTCH	SHOEMAKER	081	B		6
REID	WILLIAM				48	SCOTLAND	CP	SCOTCH	LUMBERER	083	F	2	1
REILLY	DANIEL				45	IRELAND	RC	IRISH	FARMER	082	B		8
REILLY	JOHN				44	ONTARIO	RC	IRISH	FARMER	082	B		17
REILLY	MARLOW		1		42	IRELAND	WM	IRISH	SCHOOL TEACHER	082	C	1	4
REILLY	MICHAEL				30	ONTARIO	RC	IRISH	FARMER	082	B		9
REILLY	ROBERT				48	IRELAND	CE	IRISH	F	082	A		20
REILLY	THOMAS		2		16	ONTARIO	CE			082	A		D
REILY	GEORGE				60	IRELAND	WM	IRISH	F	082	G		9
REILY	PATRICK				28	IRELAND	RC	IRISH	STOREKEEPER	081	G	1	40
REISTOW	CHARLES				53	GERMANY	CE	GERMAN	F	083	C		16
REMFRY	JOHN				37	ENGLAND	WM	ENGLISH	MINER	089	A		20
REMMINGTON	FREDERICK				38	ENGLAND	CE	ENGLISH	MILLER	081	F		29
REMO	EDWARD				45	QUEBEC	RC	FRENCH	LAB	082	A		18
REMUS	TULIOUS						NG		SEE RAIMUS	082	I		46
RENFREW	DAVID				40	SCOTLAND	CP	SCOTCH	CLERK	081	B		82
RENNIE	WILLIAM				40	SCOTLAND	PS	SCOTCH	F	085	C		14

SURNAME	NAME1	NAME2	STRAY	SEX	AGE	BIRTHPL	RELIGION	ORIGIN	OCCUP	DIST	SUB_DIST	DIV	PAGE
RENY	WILLIAM				35	AMERICA	WM	ENGLISH	CLERGYMAN	081	I		28
REO	VICTOR		1		26	FRANCE	RC	FRENCH	FARM SERVANT	082	A		6
REOPEL	EUSEBE				52	QUE	RC	FRENCH		081	K		37
RESTUL	MARGARET		2	1	19	O	RC	INDIAN		084	I	1	D
RETTIG	BARTHOLIMEW				45	O	RC	GERMAN	F	082	C	1	7
RETTY	JOHN				55	IRELAND	CE	IRISH	F	082	C	1	16
RETZA	PETER				50	PRUSSIA	RC	PRUSSIAN	FARMER	083	A	1	6
REVET	FRANCIS				27	QUE	RC	FRENCH	F	082	C	1	33
REVITT	JOOHANNA		1	1	18	O	EM	ENGLISH		081	B		11
REVITTS	WILLIAM				49	ENGLAND	EM	ENGLISH	LAB	081	B		34
REYNALDS	JAMES				39	ENGLAND	CE	ENGLISH	PAINTER	081	I		15
REYNOLDS	BERNARD				34	IRELAND	RC	IRISH	FARMER	081	G	1	9
REYNOLDS	EDWARD				37	IRELAND	RC	IRISH	FARMER	082	B		8
REYNOLDS	JOHN				49	IRELAND	RC	IRISH	BLACKSMITH	081	G	1	18
REYNOLDS	JOHN				48	IRELAND	EM	IRISH	F	082	A		20
REYNOLDS	MICHAEL				39	IRELAND	RC	IRISH	FARMER	082	B		33
REYNOLDS	WILLIAM				31	ENGLAND	WM	ENGLISH	LIVERY KEEPER	081	I		7
RHODE	NICHOLAS				24	GERMANY	LU	GERMAN	F	085	H		4
RIARDAN	TIMOTHY				42	O	RC	IRISH	F	082	G		67
RIAZENE				1	37	QUE	RC	FRENCH	NUN	084	I	2	1
RICE	JAMES				73	IRELAND	RC	IRISH	FARMER	082	B		64
RICE	JOHN		1		26	ONTARIO	RC	IRISH	CLERK	082	B		56
RICE	JOSEPH				27	ONTARIO	RC	IRISH	FARMER	082	B		65
RICHARD	ISEDORE				48	QUE	RC	FRENCH	F	082	K	1	4
RICHARD	LYON		1		19	O	CP	ENGLISH	CARPENTER	081	B		85
RICHARDS	DAVID				24	QUEBEC	RC	IRISH	FARMER & TAVERN KEEP	084	B		2
RICHARDS	DAVID				45	WALES	BA	WELSH	F	087	B	3	9
RICHARDS	EDWARD		1		24	ENGLAND	WM	ENGLISH	MINER	089	A		37
RICHARDS	ELIZA		2	1	2	ONTARIO	CE			082	A		D
RICHARDS	HERBERT	A			26	ENGLAND	CE	ENGLISH	CARPENTER	085	I		16
RICHARDS	ISAIAH		1		22	ENGLAND	WM	ENGLISH	MINER	089	A		37
RICHARDS	JAMES				28	ONTARIO	CP	SCOTTISH	FARMER	082	B		25
RICHARDS	JOHN				33	ENGLAND	WM	ENGLISH	MINER	089	A		27
RICHARDS	JOHN				40	WALES	PS	WELSH	MERCHANT	089	B		9
RICHARDS	JOHN	JOSEPH	2			QUEBEC	RC			084	B		D
RICHARDS	RICHARD				35	IRELAND	CE	IRISH	F	082	A		55
RICHARDS	SAMPSON				33	ENGLAND	WM	ENGLISH	MINER	089	A		11
RICHARDS	THOMAS				48	ENGLAND	WM	ENGLISH	F	085	I		12
RICHARDS	WILLIAM				54	SCOTLAND	CE	SCOTCH	F	081	H	1	15
RICHARDS	WILLIAM				29	O	CE	ENGLISH	LUMBERMAN	081	K		14
RICHARDS	WILLIAM				39	WALES	EP	WELSH	F	087	B	3	2
RICHARDS	WILLIAM				34	ENGLAND	WM	ENGLISH	MINER	089	A		33
RICHARDSON	ANNE		1	1	60	IRELAND	CE	IRISH	SERVANT	082	E		70
RICHARDSON	FREDERICK				41	ENGLAND	CE	ENGLISH	SHOEMAKER	085	D		6
RICHARDSON	JAMES		1		25	O	CE	IRISH	LAB	081	H	2	20
RICHARDSON	JOHN				58	IRELAND	WM	IRISH	F	081	H	2	33
RICHARDSON	MARGARET		1	1	11	O	CE	IRISH		081	H	2	39
RICHARDSON	MARTHA	A	1	1	9	O	CE	IRISH		081	H	2	39
RICHARDSON	MARY			1	42	O	CE	SCOTCH		086	C	1	6
RICHARDSON	MARY	J	1	1	14	O	CE	IRISH		081	H	2	21
RICHARDSON	MOSES				78	IRELAND	CE	IRISH	F	085	H		15
RICHARDSON	NANCY		1		17	ONTARIO	CE	IRISH		082	A		42
RICHARDSON	RICHARD				23	QUE	WM	IRISH	F	082	C	2	15
RICHARDSON	SAMUEL				23	ENGLAND	CO	ENGLISH	CARPENTER	085	I		20
RICHARDSON	SARAH		1	1	1	O	CE	IRISH		081	H	2	39
RICHARDSON	WILLIAM				47	SCOTLAND	CS	SCOTCH	F	082	C	1	42
RICHIE	HUGH				38	IRELAND	CS	IRISH	F	082	A		8
RICHIE	JAMES				60	IRELAND	CS	IRISH	F	082	A		24
RICHIE	ROBERT				54	IRELAND	EM	IRISH	F	082	A		22
RICHMOND	STEPHEN				40	O	WM	ENGLISH	CARPENTER	086	A	1	19
RIDDEL	LILLIAS			1	34	O	PS	SCOTCH		081	K		7
RIDGE	EARNEST	WILLIAM	1		22	ENGLAND	CE	ENGLISH		084	A		4
RIEL	BENJAMIN				22	O	RC	FRENCH	FISHERMAN	090	A		1
RIELLY	ANDREW				27	QUE	RC	FRENCH	LUMBERMAN	088	C		11
RIELLY	LAWRANCE				60	IRELAND	RC	IRISH	F	081	H	1	9
RIELLY	PATRICK				22	O	RC	IRISH	F	082	L		5
RIELY	JOHN				25	QUE	RC	IRISH	F	081	K		38
RIELY	THOMAS				57	IRELAND	RC	IRISH	FARMER	081	G	2	5
RIJIGOWININI'S	(SON)		2			ONTARIO	PA			090	E		D
RINEHEART	SAFIELD		1		26	GERMANY	LU	GERMAN	FARM SERVANT	082	I		42
RING	DAVID				34	ONTARIO	RC	IRISH	FARMER	081	G	1	6
RING	EDMOND				62	IRELAND	RC	IRISH	FARMER	081	G	1	8
RING	EDWARD				35	ONTARIO	RC	IRISH	FARMER	081	G	1	20
RING	JAMES		2		1	ONTARIO	RC			081	G	1	D
RING	ROBERT		1		20	O	RC	IRISH	LAB	085	F		5
RINGLE	CHARLES				46	GERMANY	LU	GERMAN	FARMER	082	I		60
RINGLE	JULIOUS				34	GERMANY	LU	GERMAN	FARMER	082	I		64
RIPPINGTON	JOHN		1		23	ENGLAND	CE	ENGLISH	LAB	090	F		25
RISCOU	MARY			1	37	QUE	RC	FRENCH		082	C	1	20
RISKY	WILLIAM				37	GERMANY	LU	GERMAN	FARMER	081	F		30
RITCHEY	FRANCIS		1		55	QUE	RC	FRENCH	LAB	082	C	1	12
RITCHIE	GEORGE		1		24	O	CS	SCOTCH	LUMBERMAN	088	C		10
RITT	JOHN				35	O	RC	IRISH	SADDLER	081	I		11
RIVET	GUSTAVUS		1		23	O	PS	ENGLISH	F	087	B	3	11
RIVIERE	JOSEPH				29	ONTARIO	RC	FRENCH	HUNTER	084	C		7
ROACH	ALEX		1		25	ONTARIO	RC	IRISH	F	081	C		55
ROACH	JAMES				26	ONTARIO	RC	IRISH	LAB	082	A		47
ROACH	JANE		1	1	19	ENGLAND	PM	ENGLISH	SERVANT	089	A		8
ROACH	JOHN		1		22	ONT	RC	IRISH	RAFTSMAN	081	C		55
ROACH	JOHN				34	ONTARIO	RC	IRISH	F	082	A		67
ROACH	MARY	ANN	1	1	18	ONT	RC	IRISH		081	C		55
ROACH	MICHAEL		1		22	IRELAND	RC	IRISH	F	082	A		66
ROACH	MICHAEL				60	IRELAND	RC	IRISH	F	083	C		2
ROACH	NICHOLAS				35	IRELAND	RC	IRISH	F	081	A	1	74
ROACH	SAMUAL		1		14	O	WM	ENGLISH		089	A		2
ROACH	SARAH			1	58	ONTARIO	RC	IRISH		082	A		66
ROACH	TIMOTHY		1		20	ONT	RC	IRISH	RAFTSMAN	081	C		55
ROACH	WILLIAM				27	ONTARIO	RC	IRISH		082	A		67
ROACH	WILLIAM				24	ENGLAND	WM	ENGLISH	MINER	089	A		3
ROAN	ANN		1	1	18	O	RC	IRISH		081	B		12
ROAN	CATHERINE		1	1	23	O	RC	IRISH		081	B		12
ROAN	JOHN				70	IRELAND	RC	IRISH	F	083	C		13
ROBB	HUGH		1		19	O	CP	SCOTCH	SHANTY MAN	085	E		27
ROBBINS	BENJAMIN				40	O	WM	IRISH	FARMER	085	B		19
ROBBINS	PHILIP				20	O	EM	UNKNOWN	F	085	K	2	9
ROBBOTTAM	WILLIAM				47	ENGLAND	CE	ENGLISH	SHOEMAKER	081	I		12

SURNAME	NAME1	NAME2	STRAY	SEX	AGE	BIRTHPL	RELIGION	ORIGIN	OCCUP	DIST	SUB_DIST	DIV	PAGE
ROBCHOULD	JOSEPH		1		35	0	RC	FRENCH	LAB	082	K	1	5
ROBEAR	CHARLES				40	QUE	RC	FRENCH	LUMBERMAN	089	A		52
ROBECHOU	ADELINE		1	1	25	0	RC	FRENCH	SERVANT	082	K	1	15
ROBERSON	WILLIAM		1		62	SCOTLAND	CE	SCOTCH	FARMER	081	G	1	34
ROBERT	H	RODGERS	1		19	ENGLISH	CE	ENGLISH	TELEGRAPH OPERATOR	083	A	1	12
ROBERTS	EDWARD		1		27	ENGLAND	CE	ENGLISH	CLERK	081	H	2	26
ROBERTS	ELIZABETH		1	1	33	QUEBEC	CS	IRISH	SERVANT MAID	081	J	1	83
ROBERTS	ELIZEBETH		1	1	17	ONT	OM	IRISH	SERVANT	081	H	1	17
ROBERTS	REBBINA		1	1	19	ONTARIO	OM	IRISH	SERVANT	081	H	1	17
ROBERTS	THOMAS				43	ENGLAND	PM	ENGLISH	MINER	089	A		23
ROBERTS	WILLIAM				46	QUE	CE	IRISH	LAB	081	I		31
ROBERTSON	ALEXANDER				33	0	CP	SCOTCH	CARPENTER	081	A	1	12
ROBERTSON	ALEXANDER				32	0	RC	SCOTCH	LABORER	090	A		3
ROBERTSON	BETSY			1	47	SCOTLAND	CP	SCOTCH		081	A	1	1
ROBERTSON	DONALD				46	SCOTLAND	CP	SCOTCH	F	081	A	1	71
ROBERTSON	ISABELLA			1	26	0	CP	SCOTCH	DRESSMAKER	081	A	1	19
ROBERTSON	JAMES				64	SCOTLAND	CP	SCOTCH	F	081	A	1	27
ROBERTSON	JAMES				35	0	CP	SCOTCH	F	081	A	1	50
ROBERTSON	JAMES				62	SCOTLAND	BA	SCOTCH	SHOEMAKER	081	I		9
ROBERTSON	JAMES				34	0	WM	IRISH	F	086	A	2	8
ROBERTSON	JOHN				58	SCOTLAND	CP	SCOTCH	F	081	A	1	50
ROBERTSON	JOHN				35	SCOTLAND	CS	SCOTCH	LABOURER	082	F		31
ROBERTSON	JOHN				55	IRELAND	CE	IRISH	F	086	A	2	1
ROBERTSON	MARY		1	1	22	0	RC	IRISH		081	B		29
ROBERTSON	MATHEW				37	SCOTLAND	CS	SCOTCH	F	081	H	1	3
ROBERTSON	NEIL				70	SCOTLAND	CS	SCOTCH	F	081	A	1	58
ROBERTSON	NEIL				50	SCOTLAND	CP	SCOTCH	LUMBER MERCHANT	081	A	2	2
ROBERTSON	PATRICK				33	SCOTLAND	CE	SCOTCH	BANKER	081	B		72
ROBERTSON	PETER		2		26	0	CP		F			1	D
ROBERTSON	ROBERT				39	0	RC	SCOTCH	WORKMAN	089	B		2
ROBERTSON	WILLIAM				60	0	RC	SCOTCH	CARPENTER	090	A		2
ROBICHOU	HENRIET		1	1	8	0	RC	FRENCH		082	K	1	13
ROBICHOU	LOUIS				50	QUE	RC	FRENCH	LAB	082	K	1	12
ROBICHOU	MENNIE		1	1	1	0	RC	FRENCH		082	K	1	13
ROBICHOU	THEOPHILE		1		10	0	RC	FRENCH		082	K	1	13
ROBILLARD	PRISGNE				45	QUEBEC	RC	FRENCH	LUMBERMAN	083	A	2	1
ROBINSON	CHARLES		1		62	0	CE	IRISH	FARM SERVANT	085	A		24
ROBINSON	CHARLES				47	SCOTLAND	PS	SCOTCH	F	085	E		7
ROBINSON	G	C	1		34	ENGLAND	CE	ENGLISH	CLERK	082	C	1	5
ROBINSON	HENRY				33	ENGLAND	CE	ENGLISH	BRICKLAYER	082	E		52
ROBINSON	JAMES				53	IRELAND	CE	IRISH	F	082	C	2	32
ROBINSON	JAMES				33	SCOTLAND	PS	SCOTTISH	MILLER	082	E		44
ROBINSON	JAMES				33	0	ME	IRISH	F	085	A		29
ROBINSON	JAMES				35	0	PS	IRISH	F	086	A	1	10
ROBINSON	JAMES				49	ENGLAND	CE	ENGLISH	FARMER	089	A		49
ROBINSON	JANE			1	29	HUDSON BAY	CE	ENGLISH	WASHERWOMAN	090	F		23
ROBINSON	JOHN				30	0	WM	IRISH		082	C	1	38
ROBINSON	JOHN				58	SCOTLAND	CS	SCOTCH	F	082	C	1	53
ROBINSON	JOHN				58	IRELAND	CP	IRISH	F	082	C	2	35
ROBINSON	JOHN		1		33	IRELAND	EP	IRISH	FARMER	090	D		2
ROBINSON	JOSEPH		1		25	0	PS	IRISH	FARMER	082	E		28
ROBINSON	MRS			1	80	SCOTLAND	CP	SCOTCH		081	A	2	15
ROBINSON	SAMUEL				23	0	WM	IRISH	F	082	C	2	30
ROBINSON	THOMAS				38	0	ME	IRISH	F	085	A		24
ROBINSON	THOMAS				35	ENGLAND	IN	ENGLISH	TAILOR	085	B		16
ROBINSON	THOMAS		1		26	IRELAND	NG	IRISH	LUMBERMAN	088	B		5
ROBINSON	WILLIAM				37	0	CS	IRISH	F	084	E		1
ROBINSON	WILLIAM				30	0	CE	IRISH	F	086	A	1	10
ROBINSON	WM				24	IRELAND	CE	IRISH	F	085	L		7
ROBISON	CATHERINE		1	1	36	0	CP	SCOTCH		081	B		6
ROBISON	DUNCAN				43	0	CP	SCOTCH	F	081	A	2	47
ROBISON	ELIZABETH		1	1	18	0	CP	SCOTCH		081	B		70
ROBISON	HENRY				21	ENGLAND	CE	ENGLISH	WAGGONMAKER	081	A	2	27
ROBISON	JAMES				24	0	CP	SCOTCH	F	081	A	2	18
ROBISON	MARGARET		1	1	23	0	CP	SCOTCH	SERVANT	081	A	2	19
ROBSON	CHARLES				29	ENGLAND	CE	ENGLISH	F	085	H		19
ROCHE	MARTIN	JR			27	0	RC	IRISH	F	082	H		1
ROCHE	MARTIN	SR			61	0	RC	IRISH	F	082	H		1
ROCHESTER	GEORGE				50	QUE	WM	ENGLISH	LUMBERER	081	A	1	34
ROCHFORD	PATRICK				48	ONTARIO	RC	IRISH	F	082	A		28
ROCHON	MARTIN				37	QUE	RC	FRENCH	RAFTSMAN	082	E		14
ROCKWAY	FRANCES				30	0	RC	INDIAN	HUNTER	084	I	1	4
ROCQUE	FERDINAND				46	QUE	RC	FRENCH	MAIL CONTRACTOR	088	A		1
RODA	EVAL		1		7	GERMANY	LU	GERMAN		081	F		22
RODA	MINA		1	1	8	GERMANY	LU	GERMAN		081	F		22
RODDAN	EDWARD				60	IRELAND	RC	IRISH	FARMER	081	F		26
RODDEN	BARNABAS	EDWARD			24	0	RC	IRISH	MERCHANT	081	K		62
RODDEN	CHARLES		1		50	IRELAND	RC	IRISH	LAB	081	K		50
RODDEY	MICHAEL				38	0	RC	IRISH	F	081	A	2	58
RODDIN	ROBT				37	SCOTLAND	PS	SCOTTISH	MILLER	082	D		22
RODGERS	ANNE		1	1	13	ONT	RC	IRISH	ADOPTED	081	J	1	59
RODGERS	JAMES		1		11	0	RC	IRISH		081	K		74
RODGERS	ROBERT	H							SEE ROBERT	083	A	1	12
RODOLPH	COTTY				34	PRUSSIA	LU	PRUSSIAN	STONEMASON	085	C		6
ROE	GEORGE				38	ENGLAND	WM	ENGLISH	F & HAT MANUFACTURER	085	K	2	2
ROE	JOHN				59	IRELAND	CE	IRISH	FARMER	082	I		40
ROFS	SAMUEL				62	IRELAND	CE	IRISH	F	082	G		73
ROGERS	JOHN				39	QUE	CE	ENGLISH	FOREMAN	084	D		8
ROGERS	JOHN		1		25	ENGLAND	CE	ENGLISH	YEOMAN	085	B		14
ROGERS	JOSEPH		1		18	0	CE	ENGLISH	COOPER	089	A		29
ROGERSON	JOSEPH				41	IRELAND	CE	IRISH	F	086	A	1	30
ROHLOFF	MICHAEL						NG		SEE ROLSLOFF	082	I		36
ROI	EUSEBE		1		43	QUE	RC	FRENCH	LABOURER	084	E		5
ROLANDS	WILLIAM				31	0	CE	IRISH	F	082	C	2	57
ROLF	RICHARD		1		9	QUE	CE	IRISH		081	B		58
ROLLANS	EDWARD				70	IRELAND	CE	IRISH	F	081	H	1	21
ROLLANS	THOMAS				27	0	CE	IRISH	F	081	H	1	18
ROLLINS	FRANCIS				28	ONTARIO	CE	IRISH	FARMER	082	B		25
ROLLOF	JOSEPH				38	GERMANY	EV	GERMAN	F	082	I		64
ROLLONS	JOHN				40	0	CE	IRISH	F	081	H	1	19
ROLSLOFF	MICHAEL				46	GERMANY	LU	GERMAN	FARMER	082	I		36
ROMAN	JAMES				63	IRELAND	WM	IRISH	F	082	F		19
ROMANE	VIANGORE				52	QUE	RC	FRENCH	CARPENTER	082	C	1	57
RONALD	JOHN				50	SCOTLAND	CP	SCOTCH		081	A	1	51
RONDEAU	CALBOIR				34	QUE	RC	FRENCH	F	082	K	1	10
RONEY	HENERY				49	IRELAND	CE	IRISH	FARMER	082	F		2

SURNAME	NAME1	NAME2	STRAY	SEX	AGE	BIRTHPL	RELIGION	ORIGIN	OCCUP	DIST	SUB_DIST	DIV	PAGE
RONSON									SEE RORISON	081	B		5
ROOK	JOHN				34	ENGLAND	WM	ENGLISH	F	085	J		8
ROOS	CATHERINE		1	1	18	0	CS	SCOTCH		081	H	1	1
ROOTS	AUGUST				47	GERMANY	LU	GERMAN	F	082	G		85
RORISON	JAMES				49	SCOTLAND	CP	SCOTCH	GROCER	081	B		5
ROSE	GEORGE				55	MOOSE FACTORY	CP	INDIAN	LAB	090	F		20
ROSE	GUSTA		1	1	16	GERMANY	CE	DUTCH		081	B		30
ROSE	J	W			63	0	ME	SCOTCH	STIPENDIARY MAGISTRA	086	A	1	31
ROSE	JOSEPH		1			0	RC	IRISH		081	K		48
ROSE	MARTIN				40	HUNGARY	RC	FRENCH	F	086	A	1	17
ROSE	WILLIAM				53	ONTARIO	CE	ENGLISH	F	082	A		68
ROSEBORO	JAMES				23	0	BA	ENGLISH	F	085	L		11
ROSEBOROUGH	JAMES		1		24	0	WM	IRISH	LAB	085	I		16
ROSEHM	JOSEPH		1		38	QUEBEC	RC	FRENCH	RAFTSMAN	084	D		1
ROSS	AGNES		1	1	19	0	CP	IRISH	SCHOOL MISTRESS	082	C	1	52
ROSS	ALEXANDER				65	0	PS	ENGLISH	F	085	D		34
ROSS	BENI				27	0	BA	ENGLISH	F	085	I		32
ROSS	BENJAMIN	W			33	0	CE	SCOTCH	HOTEL KEEPER	085	I		6
ROSS	CHARLES				24	PROSSIA	RC	PRUSSIAN	ENGINEER	081	A	2	23
ROSS	COLIN				36	SCOTLAND	CS	SCOTTISH	FARMER	082	B		34
ROSS	DAVID				44	SCOTLAND	CS	SCOTCH	F	082	A		41
ROSS	DAVID				36	QUE	BA	SCOTTISH	CARPENTER	082	E		63
ROSS	EDMOND				38	ONTARIO	WM	IRISH	F	082	A		10
ROSS	GASSAWAY				56	US	WM	AFRICAN	FARMER	089	B		10
ROSS	GEORGE		1		18	ONTARIO	CE	ENGLISH		082	A		42
ROSS	GEORGE		1		23	0	CE	SCOTCH	LUMBERMAN	086	B		2
ROSS	HARRIET		1	1	9	ONTARIO	WM	IRISH		082	A		11
ROSS	HELEN			1	57	SCOTLAND	CP	SCOTCH		081	I		11
ROSS	HUGH				60	SCOTLAND	CP	SCOTCH	F	082	C	2	17
ROSS	JAMES				72	SCOTLAND	CS	SCOTCH	F	082	A		56
ROSS	JAMES				32	ONTARIO	EM	IRISH	FARMER	082	B		70
ROSS	JAMES		1		45	SCOTLAND	CS	SCOTCH	CLERK	088	A		6
ROSS	JESSIE			1	40	SCOTLAND	CE	SCOTCH	DRESSMAKER	081	I		4
ROSS	JOHN				36	ONTARIO	CS	SCOTCH	SHOEMAKER	082	A		50
ROSS	JOHN				59	SCOTLAND	CS	SCOTCH	F	082	A		56
ROSS	JOHN	M			66	IRELAND	CE	IRISH	FARMER	082	B		69
ROSS	ROBERT				36	ONTARIO	EM	IRISH	FARMER	082	B		70
ROSS	SAMUEL				26	ONTARIO	CS	IRISH	F	082	A		10
ROSS	SAMUEL	J			31	IRELAND	CE	IRISH	F	082	G		51
ROSS	WILLIAM				44	ONTARIO	WM	IRISH	F	082	A		11
ROSS	WILLIAM				38	ONTARIO	EM	IRISH	FARMER	082	B		68
ROSS	WILLIAM				50	SCOTLAND	CP	SCOTCH	SCHOOL TEACHER	085	C		6
ROSSA	JULIAS				33	GERMANY	LU	GERMAN	F	082	H		12
ROTHWELL	ANDREW				35	IRELAND	RC	IRISH	FARMER	082	B		36
ROTKEY	FREDRICK				39	GERMANY	EV	GERMAN	F	082	G		30
ROUGIER	PAUL				34	FRANCE	RC	FRENCH	PRIEST	081	I		20
ROUKS	CHARLES				36	GERMANY	EV	GERMAN	FARMER	082	I		20
ROUN	FERDINAND		1		84	GERMANY	LU	GERMAN		082	I		39
ROUN	HERMAN		1		21	GERMANY	LU	GERMAN	RAFTSMAN	082	I		39
ROURKE	EDWARD				59	IRELAND	RC	IRISH	FARMER	082	B		23
ROUSHOM	HENRY				51	QUE	PR	IRISH	F	085	A		18
ROUSHOM	MARJORY		2	1	90	MONTREAL	ME			085	A		D
ROUSKE	CARL		1		60	GERMANY	LU	GERMAN		081	K		57
ROUSKE	VILAMENA		1	1	60	GERMANY	LU	GERMAN		081	K		57
ROUSSEAU	DOMINIQUE				6	0	RC	FRENCH		088	A		3
ROUSSEAU	EDWARD				36	0	RC	FRENCH	MINE LABOURER	089	A		7
ROUSSEAU	WILLIAM				35	0	RC	FRENCH	FISHERMAN	089	A		58
ROUSSIN	CHARLES				50	0	RC	FRENCH	FISHERMAN	090	A		6
ROUX	EARNEST		1		9	GERMANY	LU	GERMAN		082	I		21
ROUX	JOHN		1		51	GERMANY	LU	GERMAN	FARMER	082	I		21
ROWAN	JOHN				36	ONT	WM	IRISH	FARMER	082	I		10
ROWAN	JOHN				36	0	WM	IRISH	LUMBER MERCHANT	082	J		3
ROWAN	JOHN				34	IRELAND	RC	IRISH	LABOURER	083	A	1	14
ROWAN	JOSEPH				25	0	CP	IRISH	LUMBERER	082	E		24
ROWAN	THOMAS				21	0	RC	IRISH	MERCHANT	081	K		15
ROWAN	THOS				45	IRELAND	RC	IRISH	F	081	J	1	24
ROWAN	WILLIAM				24	0	WM	IRISH	LAB	082	J		3
ROWAT	WILLIAM				23	0	CP	SCOTCH	SADDLER	081	B		53
ROWE	GEORGE				38	ENGLAND	WM	ENGLISH	MINER	089	A		1
ROWE	JOHN				37	0	CE	ENGLISH		086	C	1	1
ROWE	RICHARD				52	ENGLAND	CE	ENGLISH	MINER	089	A		4
ROWE	SAMUEL				43	ENGLAND	CE	ENGLISH	MINER	089	A		1
ROWE	THOMAS				46	ENGLAND	CE	ENGLISH	MASON	081	B		23
ROWE	WILLIAM				39	ENGLAND	WM	ENGLISH	F	087	B	3	2
ROWLEY	GEORGE				28	0	WM	ENGLISH	F	085	I		30
ROWLEY	NATHANIEL				49	0	PM	ENGLISH	F	085	I		23
ROWLEY	THOMAS				46	0	WM	ENGLISH	F	085	I		30
ROXCAGE	LOUIS				28	ONTARIO	RC	INDIAN	HUNTER	084	D		2
ROY	JEAN				32	QUE	RC	FRENCH	F	081	E		3
ROY	JOHN		1		52	QUE	RC	FRENCH	CARPENTER	090	F		10
ROY	LOUISON				38	0	RC	INDIAN	F & FISHERMAN	087	A		10
ROY	PETER		2		79	QUE	RC		LABOURER	089	B		D
ROYCE	WILLIAM		1		18	0	CP	SCOTCH	SHOEMAKER	081	A	1	18
RUDDY	PATRICK				67	IRELAND	RC	IRISH	FARMER	082	B		2
RUDDY	PATRICK				27	ONTARIO	RC	IRISH	FARMER	082	B		3
RUDDY	WILLIAM				30	0	RC	IRISH	F	083	C		1
RUFFIE	JAMES								SEE PLUFFIE	081	J	1	77
RUNTZ	CARILINA		1	1	14	GERMANY	BA	GERMAN		081	F		23
RUNTZ	WILLIAM				48	GERMANY	BA	GERMAN	FARMER	081	F		22
RUSH	WILLIAM				38	0	NG	ENGLISH	FARMER	089	B		39
RUSK	CHARLES				57	GERMANY	LU	GERMAN	F	082	G		18
RUSK	JAMES				28	IRELAND	WM	IRISH	F	085	B		5
RUSKEY	FREDRICK				45	PRUSSIA	CE	GERMAN	F	085	C		6
RUSOLER	JOHN		1		32	GERMANY	LU	GERMAN	F	082	H		24
RUSSEL	HUGH				40	IRELAND	CE	IRISH	F	082	C	2	42
RUSSEL	ROBERT		1		19	SCOTLAND	CP	SCOTTISH	CLERK	082	E		26
RUSSELL			2	1		0	EM			081	H	2	D
RUSSELL	CALVIN				20	0	WM	SCOTCH	F	081	H	2	17
RUSSELL	CALVIN		2			0	CS			081	H	2	D
RUSSELL	CALVIN	F	2		69	U S	EM		F	081	H	2	D
RUSSELL	GEORGE				42	SCOTLAND	CP	SCOTCH	GARDNER	081	A	2	30
RUSSELL	ISABELLA			1	39	0	CP	SCOTCH		081	B		85
RUSSELL	ISABELLA		2	1	65	SCOTLAND	EM			081	H	2	D
RUSSELL	JAMES				39	UNITED STATES	WM	SCOTCH	F	081	H	2	18
RUSSELL	JOHN		2			0	EM			081	H	2	D
RUSSELL	MARTIN	L			40	0	CE	SCOTCH	F	081	H	2	12

SURNAME	NAME1	NAME2	STRAY	SEX	AGE	BIRTHPL	RELIGION	ORIGIN	OCCUP	DIST	SUB_DIST	DIV	PAGE
RUSSELL	REUBEN				35	0	CS	SCOTCH	F	081	H	2	12
RUSSELL	WILLIAM				45	SCOTLAND	CP	SCOTCH	MERCHANT	081	B		80
RUSSELL	WILLIAM		1		6	0	PS	IRISH		081	H	2	21
RUSSELL	WILLIAM				31	QUEBEC	RC	FRENCH	FARMER CARPENTER	081	J	1	19
RUSSELL	WILLIAM				71	US	CS	ENGLISH	SHOEMAKER	082	C	2	66
RUSSELL	WILLIAM				46	SCOTLAND	PS	SCOTTISH	BUSH RANGER	082	E		72
RUSSELL	WILLIAM				27	0	CP	IRISH	F	085	D		29
RUSSELSOM	JOHN		1		50	US	WM	ENGLISH	FARM SERVANT	082	E		28
RUSSET	PEIRRE				45	QUE	CP	FRENCH	F			1	78
RUSTOOL	FRANSES				44	0	RC	FRENCH	HUNTER	084	I	1	1
RUTARO	JOHN		1		28	ONTARIO	WM	IRISH	MINISTER	081	G	1	13
RUTLEDGE	JOHN				24	IRELAND	CE	IRISH	F	082	G		63
RUTLEDGE	JOHN				50	CANADA	CE	IRISH	F	087	B	2	8
RUTLEDGE	WILLIAM				33	IRELAND	CE	IRISH	F	082	G		75
RYAN	ANDREW				60	IRELAND	RC	IRISH	F	081	C		6
RYAN	EDMOND				72	IRELAND	RC	IRISH	F	081	C		3
RYAN	EDWARD				38	IRELAND	RC	IRISH	FARMER	081	D		26
RYAN	EDWARD				48	IRELAND	RC	IRISH	F	082	A		4
RYAN	HANORA		1	1	12	0	RC	IRISH		082	H		20
RYAN	JEREMIAH				31	IRELAND	RC	IRISH	F	085	D		9
RYAN	JOHN				50	IRELAND	RC	IRISH	FARMER	081	F		19
RYAN	JOHN				36	ONTARIO	RC	IRISH	FARMER	081	G	2	10
RYAN	JOHN				40	IRELAND	RC	IRISH	F	082	C	1	62
RYAN	JOHN				40	IRELAND	RC	IRISH	LABOURER	082	E		53
RYAN	JOHN				44	ONT	CE	IRISH	FARMER	082	I		24
RYAN	MAREY		1	1	21	QUE	RC	IRISH	SERVANT	082	K	1	11
RYAN	MARGIRIT		1	1	13	0	RC	IRISH	SERVANT	082	J		4
RYAN	MARGT		1	1	19	QUE	RC	IRISH	SERVANT	082	E		56
RYAN	MARY	ANN	1	1	14	0	CP	IRISH		085	H		25
RYAN	MATHIAS				26	ONTARIO	RC	IRISH	LABOURER	083	A	1	12
RYAN	MICHAEL				70	IRELAND	RC	IRISH	FARMER	081	J	1	1
RYAN	MICHAEL				60	IRELAND	RC	IRISH	FARMER	082	B		23
RYAN	MICHAEL				47	IRELAND	RC	IRISH	F	083	C		10
RYAN	PATRICK				22	0	RC	IRISH	F	081	A	1	45
RYAN	PATRICK				28	IRELAND	RC	IRISH	MERCHANT	081	C		38
RYAN	PATRICK				40	ONTARIO	RC	IRISH	FARMER	081	G	2	10
RYAN	PATRICK				41	0	RC	IRISH	HOTELKEEPER	081	I		2
RYAN	PATRICK				72	IRELAND	CE	IRISH	F	086	A	2	7
RYAN	SOPHIA		1	1	12	0	RC	IRISH		082	K	1	11
RYAN	STEPHEN				50	IRELAND	RC	IRISH	F	082	H		5
RYAN	TIMOTHY				34	IRELAND	RC	IRISH	F	081	A	2	47
RYAN	WILLIAM		1		17	UNITED STATES	RC	IRISH	TINSMITH	081	B		54
RYAN	WILLIAM				56	ONT	RC	IRISH	F	081	C		36
RYAN	WILLIAM				27	0	RC	IRISH	F	082	C	2	29
RYAN	WILLIAM				60	IRELAND	RC	IRISH	F	082	H		30
RYDER	THOMAS		1		40	IRELAND	RC	IRISH	SAILOR	083	A	2	3
RYKER	FREDRICK				35	GERMANY	LU	GERMAN	F	082	G		82
RYSIN	MARY		1	1	41	IRELAND	RC	IRISH	SERVANT	081	I		20
SAAR	ARAN				27	GERMANY	LU	GERMAN	F	082	F		25
SAAR	CHARLES						NG		SEE SEARR	082	I		54
SABASTIN	JOHN				39	QUE	RC	FRENCH	LAB	081	B		54
SABDER	ARTOM		1	1	10	0	RC	FRENCH		082	F		15
SABINAY	ARCHIE				30	QUE	RC	FRENCH	LAB	081	I		32
SABOURIN	MDM			1	45	0	RC	INDIAN		090	C		5
SACHE	JAMES		1	1	36	0	CE	ENGLISH		081	B		77
SACK	AUGUST				28	GERMANY	LU	GERMAN	F	082	G		20
SACK	MARTAN				40	GERMANY	LU	GERMAN	LABORER	082	F		35
SACK	WILLIAM				36	GERMANY	LU	GERMAN	F	082	G		20
SACRIBUSKY	POWL				40	PRUSSIA	RC	PRUSSIAN	FARMER	083	A	1	4
SACY	DANIEL				42	IRELAND	RC	IRISH	MERCHANT	081	K		64
SADDLER	JOHN				36	0	CE	IRISH	F	082	G		75
SADDLER	JONATHON				45	IRELAND	CE	IRISH	F	082	G		36
SADDLER	ROBERT				55	IRELAND	CE	IRISH	F	082	G		74
SADLEY	WM				24	0	CE	IRISH	CARRIAGE WAGONMAKER	082	C	1	3
SAFFRON	JOHN				40	IRELAND	RC	IRISH	F	081	A	2	48
SAGAR	LOUACE				51	GERMANY	LU	GERMAN	FARMER	082	I		62
SAHGAHNUCKKE	THOS				42	US	RC	INDIAN	F & FISHERMAN	087	A		43
SAHQUAIBUNESS	SAUL		2		17	0	CE	INDIAN		087	B	1	D
SALFER	ALBERT				23	POLAND	RC	POLISH	LAB	081	I		37
SALMAN	JAMES				48	IRELAND	RC	IRISH	F	081	J	1	89
SALMON	JAMES		1		17	ONTARIO	RC	IRISH	FARMER	082	B		4
SALMON	MARY		1	1	24	IRELAND	RC	IRISH	DOMESTIC	082	E		7
SALMON	MARY ANN		1	1	14	ONTARIO	RC	IRISH		082	B		4
SALMON	THOMAS		1		20	ENGLAND	CE	ENGLISH	F	085	K	2	7
SALOR	PATRICK				28	IRELAND	RC	IRISH	F	081	J	1	7
SALTER	PETER				29	ONT	CE	IRISH	BLACKSMITH	082	G		34
SAMAKIVE	(WIDOW)			1		ONTARIO	PA	INDIAN	HUNTER & TRAPPER	090	E		13
SAMMON	ANDREW				60	IRELAND	RC	IRISH	FARMER	082	B		26
SAMMON	ANNIE		1	1	10	IRELAND	RC	IRISH		082	B		20
SAMMON	BRIDGET		1	1	12	IRELAND	RC	IRISH		082	B		20
SAMMON	DANIEL		1		14	IRELAND	RC	IRISH		082	B		20
SAMMON	JAMES		1		11	IRELAND	RC	IRISH		082	B		20
SAMMON	JOHN				27	ONTARIO	RC	IRISH	FARMER	082	B		19
SAMMON	MICHAEL				35	IRELAND	RC	IRISH	FARMER	082	B		26
SAMMON	MICHAEL		1		5	IRELAND	RC	IRISH		082	B		20
SAMMON	THOMAS		1		7	IRELAND	RC	IRISH		082	B		20
SAMONDE	ELLEN		2	1	25	0	RC			086	C	1	D
SAMPLE	JOHN		1		23	0	CP	IRISH		081	B		12
SAMPLE	JOHN				62	IRELAND	CP	IRISH	LAB	081	B		83
SAMPLE	JOHN				36	IRELAND	PS	IRISH	F	085	A		19
SAMPLE	WILLIAM				35	IRELAND	WM	IRISH	F	085	A		19
SAMSON	ROSAN			1	65	IRELAND	RC	IRISH		081	K		16
SAMUEL	JAMES		1		20	0	CE	IRISH	F	085	C		15
SANBURN	JAMES				88	US	PS	ENGLISH	FARMER	081	F		14
SANDERS	CHARLOTT		1	1	9	ONTARIO	CE	ENGLISH		082	A		42
SANDERS	EMANUEL				40	ENGLAND	CE	ENGLISH	LAB	082	A		28
SANDERS	FRANCIS	M			36	0	WM	ENGLISH	FARMER	089	B		14
SANDERSON	EDWARD				36	0	JM	IRISH	MINISTER	082	C	2	8
SANDERSON	WILLIAM				44	IRELAND	WM	IRISH	MINISTER	082	I		75
SANDERSON	WM				22	ONTARIO	ME	ENGLISH	F	085	A		19
SARGENT	SAMUEL				40	0	CE	ENGLISH	F	081	A	2	42
SARGISON	JOSEPH		1		69	ENGLAND	WM	ENGLISH	BLACKSMITH	085	I		14
SARSAW	DEMYEA		1		19	QUE	RC	FRENCH		084	E		1
SARSFIELD	ELIZABETH		1	1	80	IRELAND	RC	IRISH		082	I		35
SARVIR	JOSEPH		1		15	SCOTLAND	RC	FRENCH	FARMER	082	B		34
SARVIR	JULIA		1	1	13	ONTARIO	RC	IRISH		082	B		

SURNAME	NAME1	NAME2	STRAY	SEX	AGE	BIRTHPL	RELIGION	ORIGIN	OCCUP	DIST	SUB_DIST	DIV	PAGE
SARVIR	MARGARET		1	1	17	0	RC	FRENCH		082	B		34
SARVIR	MARY A		1	1	10	0	RC	FRENCH		082	B		34
SATER	ALEXANDER				27	QUE	CE	IRISH	F	085	H		9
SATOUR	JOSSELLE		2	1	112	NS	RC			089	B		D
SAUGHNAU	JAMES								SEE FAUGHNAU	082	B		28
SAULIE	FRANCIS				42	QUE	RC	LABOURER	LAB	082	E		35
SAULSBERY	WILLIAM				23	0	BC	GERMAN	LAB	085	H		24
SAUNDERS	EDWARD				40	ENGLAND	CE	ENGLISH	STAVE MAKER	088	B		3
SAUNDERS	EDWIN				45	ENGLAND	CE	ENGLISH	STAVE MAKER	088	B		21
SAUNDERS	JOHN				38	ENGLAND	NG	ENGLISH	FARMER	089	B		39
SAUNDERS	MARIE		1	1	20	QUE	WM	IRISH		089	B		4
SAUNDERS	SAMUEL		1		19	ENGLAND	WM	ENGLISH	MINER	089	A		11
SAUNDERS	THOMAS		1		17	0	RC	FRENCH	LAB	090	F		26
SAUVA	GREAL		1		17	0	RC	FRENCH	CLERK	082	E		26
SAVAGE	FREDERICK				29	ENGLAND	CE	ENGLISH		089	B		9
SAVAGE	JAMES		1		60	IRELAND	RC	IRISH	STONEMASON	082	E		17
SAVAGE	JOHN	M			73	ENGLAND	CE	IRISH	REGISTRA	089	B		12
SAVAGEAU	JOSEPH				26	QUE	RC	FRENCH	LAB	090	D		2
SAWER	HENERY				33	ENGLISH	CE	ENGLISH	FARMER	082	F		3
SAXON	PETER				37	QUEBEC	RC	FRENCH	SHOEMAKER	081	C		22
SAYAH	FRANCES				30	0	RC	FRENCH	LABOURER	081	B		31
SAYER	EDWARD				57	RED RIVER	RC	GERMAN	FUR TRADER	088	C		9
SAYER	EDWARD				38	0	RC	INDIAN	BOATMAN	089	B		29
SAYER	GEORGE				40	0	RC	SCOTCH	CARPENTER	088	B		2
SAYER	JAMES				22	0	RC	IRISH	BOATMAN	089	B		28
SAYER	JOSEPH				63	0	RC	INDIAN	CHIEF	089	B		28
SAYER	JOSEPH				30	0	RC	INDIAN	BOATMAN	089	B		29
SAYER	JULIE		1	1	76	0	RC	FRENCH		089	B		30
SAYER	ROBERT				32	0	RC	FRENCH	LUMBERMAN	088	B		2
SAYER	THOMAS				24	0	RC	INDIAN		089	B		29
SAYER	TOUISSAINT	M			51	RED RIVER	RC		BOATMAN	089	B		11
SAYERS	GEORGE				24	US	WM	ENGLISH	BAKER	082	E		34
SCANLAN	JOHANN		1		27	IRELAND	RC	IRISH	SERVANT	081	I		9
SCARLETT	JOHN	S			26	IRELAND	CE	IRISH	STORE KEEPER	085	J		7
SCHALA	JOSEPH				60	PRUSSIA	RC	PRUSSIAN	FARMER	083	A	1	2
SCHAWLA	POWL				29	PRUSSIA	RC	PRUSSIAN	FARMER	083	A	1	5
SCHAYART	GODTLIB				54	GERMANY	EV	GERMAN	FARMER	082	I		68
SCHELLIN	WILLIAM	A			72	QUEBEC	RC	FRENCH	TINSMITH	090	B		1
SCHELLIN	WILLIAM	B			38	ONTARIO	RC	FRENCH	CARPENTER	090	B		2
SCHELP	PATRICK				43	0	CE	FRENCH	TAVERN KEEPER	085	A		23
SCHIMMUNG	GODTLIP				36	GERMANY	LU	GERMAN	FARMER	082	I		38
SCHNEIDER	CHARLES				51	GERMANY	CE	GERMAN	MINE LABOURER	089	A		2
SCHNEIDER	FREDERICK				25	0	CE	GERMAN	MINER	089	A		2
SCHOFIELD	MARY	ANN		1	48	ENGLAND	CE	ENGLISH	STOREKEEPER	081	B		25
SCHOFIELD	WILLIAM				26	ENGLAND	CE	ENGLISH	CARPENTER	081	B		38
SCHOLARD	JAMES				48	IRELAND	RC	IRISH	F	081	C		15
SCHOLEY	GEORGE				51	ENGLAND	CE	ENGLISH	F	085	C		19
SCHOLEY	HARIAT		2	1	44	ENGLAND	CE			085	C		D
SCHOLVAIN	FREDERICK				40	GERMANY	LU	GERMAN	FARMER	081	F		28
SCHOOF	FREDRICK				36	GERMANY	NC	GERMAN	FARMER	082	I		4
SCHOONER	SILAS		1		25	CANADA	WM	ENGLISH	FISHERMAN	087	B	2	4
SCHOTTS	FREDRICK				52	GERMANY	LU	GERMAN	FARMER	082	I		46
SCHULENBERGH	A	R			27	US	CE	GERMAN	SAW MILL OWNER	088	A		7
SCHULTZ	AUGUST				31	GERMANY	LU	GERMAN	FARMER	081	F		14
SCHULTZ	ERNEST				34	PRUSSIA	LU	PRUSSIAN	F	085	A		8
SCHUMENTZ	CHRISTIAN				35	P GERMANY	LU	GERMAN	F	082	G		2
SCHURANDT	WILLIAM		1		36	GERMANY	EV	GERMAN	MINISTER	082	I		59
SCHUSICK	JOSEPH				35	PRUSSIA	RC	PRUSSIAN	FARMER	083	A	1	1
SCHUTT	CHARLES				23	GERMANY	LU	GERMAN	F	082	G		61
SCHUTT	FREDRICK				28	GERMANY	LU	GERMAN	F	082	G		18
SCHUTT	WILLIAM				21	GERMANY	LU	GERMAN	F	082	G		19
SCHUTTES	CARREL				44	GERMANY	CE	GERMAN	LAB	081	B		64
SCHWAPP	JOSEPH				22	AUSTRIA	RC	AUSTRIAN	F	082	L		4
SCOBIE	JAMES				26	0	CS	SCOTCH	F	081	H	2	35
SCOLLICK	JOHN		1		32	ENGLAND	CE	ENGLISH	CLERK	083	A	1	14
SCOTLY	ROBERT		1		31	0	CE	ENGLISH	SCHOOL TEACHER	081	I		10
SCOTT	AARON				29	0	PM	SCOTCH	F	085	H		15
SCOTT	ALEXANDER				32	SCOTLAND	PS	SCOTCH	FARMER	089	A		59
SCOTT	DAVID				41	US	PM	ENGLISH	F	085	B		7
SCOTT	EMMA		1	1	5	0	WM	GERMAN		085	K	2	3
SCOTT	FRANCIS				65	0	WM	SCOTCH	F	082	C	2	46
SCOTT	FRANCIS		1		41	0	CS	SCOTTISH	LAWYER	082	E		33
SCOTT	FRANK				30	RED RIVER	RC	SCOTCH	MINER	090	F		17
SCOTT	FRANK		2		4	0	RC			090	F		D
SCOTT	HENRY				36	US	CP	SCOTCH	MILLOWNER	081	A	2	27
SCOTT	HENRY				30	ENGLAND	WM	ENGLISH	CARPENTER	085	E		3
SCOTT	HIRAM				32	0	WM	SCOTCH	F	082	C	2	46
SCOTT	JAMES				56	IRELAND	CE	IRISH	F	086	A	1	19
SCOTT	JOHN				29	SCOTLAND	CS	SCOTCH	BUTCHER	081	I		18
SCOTT	JOHN				37	ENGLAND	CE	ENGLISH	F	085	A		25
SCOTT	THOMAS				43	0	CE	IRISH	F	082	C	1	46
SCOTT	THOMAS				40	IRELAND	CP	IRISH	F	082	C	2	24
SCOTT	THOMAS				31	0	CE	ENGLISH	F	085	E		11
SCOTT	WILLIAM				32	SCOTLAND	PS	SCOTCH	F	081	J	1	37
SCOTT	WILLIAM				28	0	CP	SCOTTISH	BLACKSMITH	082	E		13
SCOTT	WILLIAM				26	0	WM	IRISH	F	086	A	1	18
SCOTT	WINF		1		21	US	PS	SCOTCH	LABOURER	090	B		1
SCRIM	DAVID								SEE SCRIVER	081	B		1
SCRIVER	DAVID				50	SCOTLAND	CP	SCOTCH	GARDENER	081	B		1
SCUDDER	MARY		1	1	64	GERMANY	LU	GERMAN		082	G		28
SCUDDER	MATT		1		71	GERMANY	LU	GERMAN		082	G		28
SCULLY	DANIEL				41	IRELAND	RC	IRISH	FARMER	081	D		10
SCULLY	DANIEL				60	IRELAND	RC	IRISH	FARMER	081	D		18
SCULLY	GERALD				50	IRELAND	RC	IRISH	F	081	C		1
SCULLY	JAMES				48	IRELAND	RC	IRISH	F	081	C		1
SCULLY	JOHN				58	IRELAND	RC	IRISH	FARMER	081	D		24
SCULLY	MICHAEL				60	IRELAND	RC	IRISH	FARMER	081	D		23
SCULLY	MICHAEL		2			0	RC			081	D		D
SCULY	MAURICE				50	IRELAND	RC	IRISH	FARMER	081	G	2	9
SEABELL	AUGUST				35	GERMANY	EV	GERMAN	FARMER	082	I		63
SEAKE	GEORGE				49	IRELAND	BA	IRISH	CARPENTER	082	G		1
SEALES	EDWIN	P			33	ENGLAND	CE	ENGLISH	LABOURER	082	E		67
SEALS	JOSEPH				55	IRELAND	CE	IRISH	F	081	H	2	34
SEALS	MARTHA		1	1	50	IRELAND	CE	IRISH		081	H	2	39
SEALS	MARY		1	1	18	0	CE	IRISH		081	H	2	39
SEALS	SARAH		1	1	25	0	CE	IRISH	SERVANT	081	H	2	21

SURNAME	NAME1	NAME2	STRAY	SEX	AGE	BIRTHPL	RELIGION	ORIGIN	OCCUP	DIST	SUB_DIST	DIV	PAGE
SEAMER	LOUACE				46	GERMANY	EV	GERMAN	LABOURER	082	I		63
SEANEY	WILLIAM				47	IRELAND	CE	IRISH	F	082	J		5
SEARR	CHARLES				54	GERMANY	LU	GERMAN	FARMER	082	I		54
SEARSON	MARY	ELLEN	1	1	5	O	CE	IRISH		082	G		8
SEARSON	WM	JOHN	1		8	O	CE	IRISH		082	G		8
SEBAT	AUGUST				46	GERMANY	RC	GERMAN	LAB	081	A	1	20
SECANL	JOSEPH		1		7	QUE	RC	FRENCH		082	E		27
SEELEY	JUSTICE				31	O	CE	IRISH	LAB	081	B		10
SEELEY	OBIDARE				60	NB	CE	ENGLISH	F	085	K	2	7
SEELEY	WILLIAM	JOHN	2		2	O	CE			081	B		D
SEELY	GEORGE		1		38	O	CP	ENGLISH	RAFTSMAN	081	A	1	56
SEELY	HARRIET		2	1	8	O	CE					1	D
SEELY	JOSEPH				47	O	CE	ENGLISH	F	081	A	1	45
SEEPER	WILLIAM				26	O	CP	IRISH	COOPER	089	B		6
SEGAN	JACOB				50	ONTARIO	CP	GERMAN	FARMER	083	A	1	8
SEIDLER	AUGUST				51	GERMANY	LU	GERMAN	FARMER	081	F		14
SELKIRK	WILLIAM	SR			56	SCOTLAND	CP	SCOTCH	F	082	J		3
SELLAR	CARL				46	GERMANY	CE	GERMAN	FARMER	081	F		11
SELVEST	JOSEPH				35	QUE	RC	FRENCH	F	082	J		10
SEMMENS	JOHN				54	ENGLAND	WM	ENGLISH	MINE LABOURER	089	A		25
SENISTRUM	ELLEN		1	1	19	O	RC	IRISH		081	A	2	27
SERGEANT	JULE				25	QUEBEC	RC	FRENCH		084	A		1
SERGENT	MATHEW				44	O	CE	IRISH	SAWYER	081	B		39
SERRETTE	ANTOINE				31	O	RC	FRENCH	CARTER	089	B		29
SERSON	WILLIAM				28	IRELAND	RC	IRISH	F	081	K		28
SERSON	WILLIAM				69	IRELAND	RC	IRISH	F	081	K		30
SESSON	JOHN		2		66	IRELAND	RC		F	082	B		D
SESSON	MARY	JANE	2	1	1	O	CE			082	B		D
SESSON	THOMAS				36	ONTARIO	CE	IRISH	FARMER	082	B		66
SETTLE	CHARLES		1		32	O	CE	IRISH	CLERK	086	C	1	11
SEVORE	ABRAHAM				39	QUE	RC	FRENCH	F	081	A	2	46
SEYMOR	JOSEPH				50	QUE	RC	FRENCH	SHOEMAKER	081	I		17
SHABBOTT	FRANCES				65	QUE	RC	FRENCH	LAB	081	B		76
SHABENEWESE	LOUIS				35	O	RC	INDIAN	LAB	090	F		6
SHAE	JAMES				59	O	EM	IRISH	F	085	D		27
SHAE	JANE			1	70	IRELAND	RC	IRISH		081	A	2	52
SHAE	WILLIAM				24	O	CP	IRISH	F	085	D		22
SHAE	WILLIAM				23	O	EM	IRISH	F	085	D		28
SHAFER	FRIDRICK				37	O	ME	GERMAN	FARMER	085	E		30
SHAFER	TUSO				32	O	RC	FRENCH	LAB	082	F		19
SHAFRA	ISIDORE				46	O	RC	FRENCH	F	082	F		17
SHAJANASH	JAMES				20	O	RC	INDIAN	LAB	090	F		8
SHAMER	BEN				25	QUEBEC	RC	FRENCH	LAB	082	A		18
SHANAHAN	EDMOND				53	IRELAND	RC	IRISH	FARMER	081	J	1	2
SHANAHAN	JAMES				62	IRELAND	RC	IRISH	F	081	C		33
SHANE	MICHAEL				61	GERMANY	RC	GERMAN	F	081	A	1	20
SHANNON	ALEXANDER	B				ENGLAND	PS	ENGLISH	STORE KEEPER FARMER	085	D		26
SHANNON	EDWAN				62	ONTARIO	RC	IRISH	F	082	A		82
SHANNON	ISABELLA		1	1	60	IRELAND	RC	IRISH		081	D		7
SHANNON	JOHN		1			O	RC	IRISH		082	C	1	20
SHANNON	RICHARD				58	IRELAND	RC	IRISH		082	C	1	36
SHAPLEY	MARY		1	1	18	QUE	CE	ENGLISH		081	B		29
SHARBINO	ZOA			1	48	QUE	RC	FRENCH		081	B		16
SHARP	ANNIE		1	1	19	ENGLAND	CE	ENGLISH	SERVANT	082	E		2
SHARP	JAMES		1		25	O	CE	IRISH	F	081	K		6
SHARP	JAMES				26	ENGLAND	CE	ENGLISH	F	085	L		7
SHARP	JANNETT		1	1	72	SCOTLAND	CP	SCOTCH		085	H		26
SHARP	JOHN		1		47	ENGLAND	CE	ENGLISH	MACHINIST	082	E		33
SHARP	JOHN				62	ENGLAND	WM	ENGLISH	FARMER	089	B		22
SHARP	JONATHON		1		11	ONT	CE	ENGLISH		081	J	1	85
SHARP	MARY	JANE	1	1	21	O	WM	SCOTCH		081	K		6
SHARP	ROBERT				50	IRELAND	RC	IRISH	F	081	K		3
SHARP	ROBERT				32	IRELAND	CE	IRISH	FARMER	081	K		6
SHARP	THOMAS				29	O	CE	IRISH	F	081	K		3
SHARP	WALTER				38	US	CP	SCOTCH	F	085	H		24
SHARP	WILLIAM		1		15	ENGLAND	CE	ENGLISH	LABOURER	081	J	1	85
SHARPE	JAMES				49	SCOTLAND	CP	SCOTCH	F	085	B		7
SHARPE	JAMES		2		74	SCOTLAND	PS		FARMER	085	H		D
SHAS	MARY			1	5	ONTARIO	RC	INDIAN		083	C		6
SHAUGHNESS	SIMON				50	IRELAND	RC	IRISH	F	082	G		68
SHAUGHNESSY	MARY		1	1	60	IRELAND	RC	IRISH		081	G	1	24
SHAUGHNESY	MARTIN				35	O	RC	IRISH	JACK OF ALL TRADES	082	G		79
SHAUNESY	ROBERT		2		2	O	RC			082	G		D
SHAUNESY	THOS		2		10	O	RC			082	G		D
SHAVER	MICHAEL				58	PRUSSIA	RC	GERMAN	F	085	I		41
SHAW	DANIEL				46	US	WM	ENGLISH	F	082	C	2	62
SHAW	HENRY				30	O	CE	IRISH	INNKEEPER	081	H	2	25
SHAW	JOHN				65	IRELAND	PS	IRISH	F	081	H	2	8
SHAW	JOHN				54	SCOTLAND	CP	SCOTCH	MILLER	082	G		53
SHAW	WILLIAM				40	O	WM	IRISH	F	086	A	1	1
SHAY	ALLEN				30	USA	WM	ENGLISH	F	085	L		1
SHAY	FRED				36	USA	WM	ENGLISH	F	085	L		10
SHAY	PHILIP				64	USA	WM	IRISH	F	085	K	2	3
SHEA	JEREMIAH				60	IRELAND	RC	IRISH	F	082	K	2	1
SHEA	MICHAEL				26	ONTARIO	RC	IRISH		084	B		2
SHEAHAN	MRS			1	60	IRELAND	RC	IRISH	F	081	J	1	22
SHEAHAN	PATRICK				32	ONT	RC	IRISH	F	081	J	1	22
SHEAHAN	PATRICK		2		70	IRELAND	RC		F	081	J	1	D
SHEALS	THOMAS				35	ONTARIO	RC	IRISH	FARMER	081	G	1	25
SHEARER	MARGRET		1	1	74	SCOTLAND	CP	SCOTCH		081	A	1	63
SHEBAGIZI	JOHN				70	RED RIVER	CE	INDIAN	LABOURER	089	B		34
SHEBAGIZI	WILLIAM				38	US	CE	INDIAN	BOATMAN	089	B		34
SHEBRICK	WILLIAM				43	GERMANY	CE	GERMAN	F	081	A	2	43
SHEEDY	JOHN				47	IRELAND	RC	IRISH	F	081	K		18
SHEEDY	MARTIN				45	IRELAND	RC	IRISH	FARMER	081	D		2
SHEEHAN	PATRICK				60	IRELAND	RC	IRISH	F	082	A		78
SHEFFIELD	GEORGE				20	O	CE	ENGLISH	LAB	081	A	2	23
SHEFFIELD	JOSEPH				27	QUE	PS	IRISH	SHANTYMAN	082	E		72
SHEILD	ELESEBATH			1	66	QUE	CE	IRISH		082	K	1	6
SHEILDS	DANL				52	IRELAND	RC	IRISH	HOTELKEEPER	082	E		25
SHEILDS	FREDERICK				25	GERMANY	CE	GERMAN	LAB	081	B		63
SHEILDS	MARY			1	62	IRELAND	RC	IRISH		082	B		33
SHEILDS	MICHAEL				50	IRELAND	RC	IRISH	FARMER	082	B		44
SHENNON	JOHN				47	SCOTLAND	PS	SCOTCH	MILLER	085	D		25
SHEPHERD	WILLIAM				53	ENGLAND	CE	ENGLISH	LIGHT KEEPER	089	A		53
SHERBINO	EUSTACHE				38	QUE	RC	FRENCH	FILER	081	B		41

SURNAME	NAME1	NAME2	STRAY	SEX	AGE	BIRTHPL	RELIGION	ORIGIN	OCCUP	DIST	SUB_DIST	DIV	PAGE
SHERBINO	GEORGE				28	O	RC	FRENCH	LAB	081	B		33
SHERBINO	JNO		2		8	O	RC			081	B		D
SHERBINO	THOMAS				51	QUE	RC	FRENCH	CARPENTER	081	B		42
SHERICK	PARMELIE				12	O	CE	ENGLISH		085	J		5
SHERIDAN	ELLEN	JANE	1	1	15	IRELAND	RC	IRISH		085	D		12
SHERIDAN	PATRICK				62	IRELAND	RC	IRISH		082	G		50
SHERIDAN	THOMAS				36	IRELAND	RC	IRISH	FARMER	081	G	1	23
SHERIDAN	THOS				52	IRELAND	RC	IRISH	F	082	G		50
SHERLOCK	ANN		1	1	15	O	RC	IRISH		081	A	1	5
SHERLOCK	BRIDGET	ELLEN	1	1	13	O	RC	IRISH		081	A	1	5
SHERLOCK	JAMES				68	IRELAND	RC	IRISH	BUTCHER	081	B		46
SHERLOCK	MARY		1	1	11	O	RC	IRISH		081	A	1	5
SHERMAN	DANIEL				33	O	RC	IRISH	FISHERMAN	090	A		5
SHERMAN	GEORGE		2		1	O	RC			090	A		D
SHERMAN	HENRY				50	US	CP	IRISH	CARPENTER	082	C	2	5
SHERMAN	SYLVESTER				44	US	BA	ENGLISH	MANAGER	086	C	1	1
SHERNBINO	JOSEPH				62	QUE	RC	FRENCH	CARPENTER	081	I		6
SHERWIN	J	B	1		23	ENGLAND	CE	ENGLISH	ENGINEER	088	A		8
SHESTS	WILLIAM				30	GERMANY	CP	GERMAN	LAB	081	B		67
SHEWETAHGIN	JOSEPH				60	O	CE	INDIAN	F	087	B	1	11
SHIDDY	DENNIS				40	IRELAND	RC	IRISH	FARMER	082	B		24
SHIDDY	MARTIN				37	IRELAND	RC	IRISH	FARMER	082	B		22
SHIDDY	MATHEW				22	ONTARIO	RC	IRISH	FARMER	082	B		26
SHIDDY	MICHAEL				45	IRELAND	RC	IRISH	FARMER	082	B		20
SHIDDY	PATRICK				66	IRELAND	RC	IRISH	FARMER	082	B		26
SHIDDY	TIMOTHY				53	IRELAND	RC	IRISH	FARMER	082	B		26
SHIDDY	TIMOTHY	J			44	IRELAND	RC	IRISH	FARMER	082	B		27
SHIELDS	ANDREW				40	QUEBEC	CS	IRISH	MASON & FARMER	084	C		2
SHIELDS	BENJAMIN				25	QUEBEC	CE	IRISH	FARMER	084	C		3
SHIELDS	FREDERICK				53	GERMANY	BA	GERMAN	F	081	A	2	43
SHIELDS	HENRY				40	O	RC	IRISH	INNKEEPER	081	H	2	36
SHIELDS	HUGH				25	IRELAND	CE	IRISH	F	086	A	1	1
SHIELDS	JOHN				50	IRELAND	RC	IRISH	FARMER	082	B		33
SHIELDS	JOHN				53	IRELAND	RC	IRISH	F	082	H		7
SHIELDS	THOMAS				28	QUEBEC	RC	IRISH	LUMBERMAN	083	D		1
SHIELDS	WILLIAM				29	GERMANY	CE	GERMAN	FARMER	081	F		32
SHILK	CHARLES				40	GERMANY	WM	GERMAN	F	082	G		30
SHINEAUMAN	FRED				37	GERMANY	LU	GERMAN	F	082	G		83
SHINWAWK	AUGUSTINE				67	O	CE	INDIAN	CHIEF	089	B		41
SHINWAWK	JIRVAIS				30	O	RC	INDIAN	LABOURER	089	B		42
SHINWAWK	LOUISAINE				35	O	CE	INDIAN	LABOURER	089	B		42
SHIRE	MARTIN		1		28	O	CE	IRISH	LUMBERMAN	088	B		5
SHIRLEY	JOSEPH				50	IRELAND	RC	IRISH	F	082	H		6
SHITE	LOUIS				28	QUE	RC	FRENCH	SHANTYMAN	082	E		73
SHOLDICE	DAVID		1		21	QUE	CE	IRISH	LAB	081	A	2	17
SHOLDICE	JOHN	F			28	O	CE	IRISH	FOREMAN	081	A	2	15
SHOMPHONG	GEO				32	O	WM	INDIAN	HUNTER & TRAPPER	090	C		7
SHONDASS	JOHN					O	WM	INDIAN	HUNTER & TRAPPER	090	C		7
SHONDASS	LONG				57	O	WM	INDIAN	HUNTER & TRAPPER	090	C		7
SHONSHONG	(1ST SON)		2		7	O	WM			090	C		D
SHONSHONG	(2ND CHILD)		2	1	5	O	WM			090	C		D
SHONSHONG	JOHN		2		22	O	ME		HUNTER & TRAPPER	090	C		D
SHOROW	MAXIM				38	QUE	RC	FRENCH	LAB	081	B		14
SHORTHUR	CHAS		1		30	QUE	RC	FRENCH	STABLEMAN	082	G		61
SHORTREED	THOMAS				52	SCOTLAND	PS	SCOTCH	FISHERMAN	087	B	2	2
SHOULDICE	CHRISTFER				65	IRELAND	CE	IRISH	F	085	E		21
SHOULDICE	GEORGE				28	O	CE	IRISH	F	085	E		21
SHOULIST	THOMAS				52	PRUSSIA	RC	PRUSSIAN	FARMER	083	A	1	1
SHOULTZE	CHARLES				45	GERMANY	LU	GERMAN	FARMER	082	I		79
SHOULTZE	CHARLES				35	GERMANY	LU	GERMAN	FARMER	082	I		79
SHOULTZE	JOHN				37	GERMANY	LU	GERMAN	FARMER	082	I		79
SHOWRO	EMERAL		1		30	QUEBEC	RC	FRENCH	LUMBERMAN	083	E		3
SHOWWAINOSHE	JACOB				37	O	RC	INDIAN	F & FISHERMAN	087	C		6
SHOWWAINOSHE	JOSEPH				70	US	RC	INDIAN	F	087	C		5
SHRUDER	AUGUST				40	GERMANY	LU	GERMAN	F	082	H		24
SHRUDER	WILLIAM				51	GERMANY	WM	GERMAN	F	082	H		10
SHULTS	WILLIAM				25	GERMANY	LU	GERMAN	F	082	F		21
SHUSCOSKEY	FRED				48	GERMANY	EV	GERMAN	F	082	G		86
SHUTLY	JOHN		1		48	GERMANY	RC	GERMAN		082	G		21
SHUTLY	MARY		1	1	46	GERMANY	RC	GERMAN		082	G		21
SHUTTE	GEORGE		1		21	ENGLAND	CE	ENGLISH	LAB	082	C	2	6
SHUTTLEWORTH	ROBT				37	O	ME	ENGLISH	CARPENTER	085	E		4
SIBERAT	CHARLES				33	QUE	RC	FRENCH	LAB	082	C	1	65
SIBERRY	THOMAS				63	ENGLAND	CE	ENGLISH		081	K		65
SIBIWENS	JOSEPH				41	O	RC	INDIAN	F & FISHERMAN	087	A		6
SICORE	MATILDA		1	1	11	QUE	RC	FRENCH		082	D		12
SIEBEL	AUGUST						NG		SEE SEABELL	082	I		63
SILAS	FREDERICK				48	GERMANY	WM	GERMAN	F	082	H		15
SILLIB	HENRY				44	GERMANY	PR	FRENCH	F	085	A		27
SILUS	CARALINE		1	1	21	GERMANY	CE	GERMAN	SERVANT	081	G	1	30
SILVERWOOD	JOHN				51	ENGLAND	WM	ENGLISH	F	085	L		5
SILVERWOOD	SAMUEL		1		19	ENGLAND	WM	ENGLISH	SERVANT	085	I		11
SIM	ROBERT				31	O	CP	SCOTCH	PHOTOGRAPHER	081	I		17
SIMARD	ANDREW		1		15	O	RC	FRENCH	LAB	081	B		86
SIMINGTON	JAMES				33	IRELAND	CE	IRISH	CARPENTER	085	I		6
SIMINGTON	JOHN				37	O	CE	IRISH	F	085	A		22
SIMMENS	JOHN				28	IRELAND	RC	ENGLISH	MINER	090	D		4
SIMMENS	MARGARET		2	1	2	UNITED STATES	RC			090	D		D
SIMMINGTON	WILLIAM				65	IRELAND	CE	IRISH	F	085	A		22
SIMMONS	JOSEPH				41	QUE	RC	IRISH	FARMER	082	D		3
SIMON	JOSEPH				60	US	RC	INDIAN	LABOURER	089	B		40
SIMPSON	AGNES		2	1		O	CE			089	B		D
SIMPSON	HUGH				50	IRELAND	CP	IRISH	FARMER	082	I		36
SIMPSON	JAMES		1		26	O	WM	IRISH	PREACHER	082	C	1	11
SIMPSON	JOHN				47	IRELAND	PS	IRISH	F	081	J	1	50
SIMPSON	JOHN		1		35	ENGLAND	WM	ENGLISH	TAILOR	089	A		24
SIMPSON	JOHN	H			49	IRELAND	CE	IRISH	CLERGYMAN	082	C	2	64
SIMPSON	MARY		2	1	14	ONT	CP			082	I		D
SIMPSON	SAMUEL				63	IRELAND	CS	IRISH		081	A	1	67
SIMPSON	SAMUEL				29	O	CE	ENGLISH	LUMBERMAN	084	E		1
SIMPSON	THOMAS		1		20	O	RC	IRISH		086	B		1
SIMPSON	THOMAS				38	CANADA	CE	SCOTCH	SURGEON MD	087	B	2	9
SIMPSON	W	I			37	QUE	CP	ENGLISH	SAILOR	090	D		8
SIMS	FREDK	LLOYD			50	ENGLAND	UP	ENGLISH	F	085	D		11
SIMS	MARY	ANN		1	37	ENGLAND	EP	ENGLISH	F	087	B	3	9
SIMSPON	WEMYSS				46	ENGLAND	CE	ENGLISH		089	B		1

SURNAME	NAME1	NAME2	STRAY	SEX	AGE	BIRTHPL	RELIGION	ORIGIN	OCCUP	DIST	SUB_DIST	DIV	PAGE
SINCLAIR	BRUCE	IRWIN	1		21	QUEBEC	CS	SCOTCH	FARMER	084	D		2
SINCLAIR	CATHERINE			1	32	0	RC	SCOTCH		081	F		9
SINCLEAR	DUGAL				19		NG		F	085	E		29
SINGER	FRED		1		24	GERMANY	LU	GERMAN	BAKER	082	E		39
SINGLETON	ROBERT				51	ENGLAND	EP	ENGLISH	MINER	090	D		8
SINN	FREDERICK				29	GERMANY	CE	GERMAN	CLERK	081	B		69
SINTON	HENRY		1		51	QUE	CE	IRISH	BOOKKEEPER	082	C	1	1
SIR	JOHN				37	0	ME	IRISH	F	086	A	1	7
SIVEAR	JAMES				26	ENGLAND	CE	ENGLISH	F	085	I		40
SKEBO	FRANK				60	PRUSSIA	RC	PRUSSIAN	LAB	081	A	2	23
SKEETAH	ALEXANDER				62	MILL LAC	PA	INDIAN	HUNTER	090	F		5
SKEGLO	JACOB				30	POLAND	RC	POLISH	LAB	081	I		37
SKELLY	JAMES				35	IRELAND	RC	IRISH	F	082	H		22
SKIPPEN	JOHN		1		57	ENGLAND	BA	ENGLISH	F	087	B	3	8
SKIPPEN	WILLIAM				23	0	BA	ENGLISH	F	087	B	3	8
SKUCE	JOHN				29	ONTARIO	CE	IRISH	FARMER	083	A	1	10
SKUCE	RICHARD				56	IRELAND	CE	IRISH	FARMER	083	A	1	11
SLACK	H	L			27	QUE	CE	ENGLISH	TEACHER	081	B		66
SLACK	JAMES	W			49	ENGLAND	CE	ENGLISH	TAILOR	082	E		60
SLADE	GEORGE				29	ENGLAND	BA	ENGLISH	F	086	A	1	24
SLATER	HENRY				39	ENGLAND	WM	ENGLISH	TAILOR	085	I		2
SLATER	J	C			47	ENGLAND	WM	ENGLISH	WESLEYAN MINISTER	082	E		1
SLATERY	PATK		1		29	IRELAND	RC	IRISH	STORE CLERK	082	E		18
SLEATER	GEORGE				35	IRELAND	CE	IRISH	F	085	D		30
SLEITH	THOMAS		1		40	IRELAND	RP	IRISH	WEAVER	081	K		10
SLONE	JOHN				40	IRELAND	RC	IRISH	F	081	B		65
SLOOPER	THOMAS				32	ENGLAND	CE	ENGLISH	PLASTERER	085	I		33
SLOUGH	GEORGE	H			39	0	EM	ENGLISH	F	085	J		21
SLY	RILEY				53	0	WM	SCOTCH	F	086	A	1	23
SMALL	GEORGE				45	IRELAND	RP	IRISH	FARMER	082	I		2
SMALL	MATTHEW				48	IRELAND	RP	IRISH	FARMER	082	I		2
SMALLBONE	WILLIAM				64	ENGLAND	CE	ENGLISH	F	085	D		25
SMALLPEICE	HANNAH			1	46	ENGLAND	CE	ENGLISH		081	G	1	46
SMALLPEICE	THOMAS		2		51	ENGLAND	CE	ENGLISH	FARMER	081	G	1	D
SMILING	FREDERICK				37	GERMANY	LU	GERMAN	F	082	H		34
SMITH	ADONIRUM				35	ONTARIO	EM	ENGLISH	F	082	A		70
SMITH	ALBERT				53	ONTARIO	WM	IRISH	FARMER	081	G	1	13
SMITH	ALBERT				25	ENGLAND	PM	ENGLISH	F	085	D		14
SMITH	ALEX				60	ONT	CS	SCOTCH	F	081	C		56
SMITH	ALEXANDER	LECKIE			16	0	CS	SCOTCH	F	081	A	1	41
SMITH	ALFERD				30	ENGLAND	PM	ENGLISH	F	085	F		1
SMITH	ALFRED				49	ONTARIO	EM	ENGLISH	F	082	A		70
SMITH	ANDREW				59	SCOTLAND	PS	SCOTCH	F	085	J		16
SMITH	ANDREW	ORR			33	ONTARIO	CS	SCOTCH	FARMER & HUNTER	084	D		2
SMITH	ANNIE		1	1	8	0	CP	SCOTCH		081	A	2	26
SMITH	ARCHIBALD				29	0	CS	SCOTCH	FOREMAN	081	A	1	42
SMITH	BAKER				40	0	OM	SCOTCH	F	081	H	1	15
SMITH	BENGEMAN		1		18	IRELAND	CE	IRISH	F	082	F		40
SMITH	BERNARD		1		19	QUE	RC	IRISH	TAILOR	081	B		86
SMITH	CARL				27	US	WM	GERMAN	F	085	H		12
SMITH	CHENCEY				34	0	OM	ENGLISH	F	081	H	1	12
SMITH	DANIEL				29	ONT	CE	SCOTTISH	FARMER	082	I		69
SMITH	DONALD		1		26	0	CS	SCOTCH	LABOURER	088	A		7
SMITH	EDWARD				43	NB	CE	ENGLISH	BLACKSMITH	082	D		17
SMITH	ELIZA		1	1	25	ENGLAND	WM	ENGLISH	F	082	C	1	10
SMITH	ELIZABETH		1	1	63	SCOTLAND	CS	SCOTCH	F	085	L		11
SMITH	FRANCIS		1		24	ONTARIO	EM	ENGLISH	LAB	082	A		19
SMITH	FRANCIS				40	0	CE	IRISH	LUMBERMAN	086	C	1	11
SMITH	FRED				30	ENGLAND	RC	ENGLISH	BOARDING HOUSE	090	F		19
SMITH	FREDRICK		1		19	ENGLAND	WM	ENGLISH	BLACKSMITH	082	C	1	10
SMITH	GEORGE				28	IRELAND	CE	IRISH	F	082	G		41
SMITH	GEORGE				27	0	WM	ENGLISH	F	085	D		18
SMITH	GEORGE				44	GERMANY	PS	GERMAN	F	085	H		18
SMITH	HANNA		1	1	20	GERMANY	PS	GERMAN	SERVANT GIRL	082	D		3
SMITH	HARRY		1		14	ENGLAND	WM	ENGLISH	LAB	082	C	1	10
SMITH	HENRY				30	GERMANY	EV	GERMAN	F	082	H		26
SMITH	HENRY				40	GERMANY	WM	GERMAN	F	086	A	1	22
SMITH	HUGH				75	IRELAND	CE	IRISH	F	081	J	1	20
SMITH	HUGH				48	SCOTLAND	CS	SCOTCH	F	085	J		15
SMITH	INFANTS		1			ONT	CP	SCOTTISH		082	I		24
SMITH	ISAAC				40	IRELAND	CE	IRISH	FARMER	084	C		2
SMITH	ISAIAH				26	0	BA	GERMAN	F	085	I		26
SMITH	JAMES		1		19	0	CP	SCOTCH	LAB	081	A	2	19
SMITH	JAMES				43	UNITED STATES	OM	IRISH	F	081	H	1	17
SMITH	JAMES				73	IRELAND	CE	IRISH	F	082	C	2	32
SMITH	JAMES				35	SCOTLAND	PS	SCOTTISH	SCHOOL TEACHER	082	D		4
SMITH	JAMES		1		24	ONTARIO	CP	SCOTCH	LAB	083	C		3
SMITH	JAMES				54	SCOTLAND	PS	SCOTCH	F	085	C		3
SMITH	JAMES				34	ONTARIO	CP	IRISH	F	085	H		7
SMITH	JAMES	B			27	0	FW	SCOTCH	F	081	A	1	7
SMITH	JANE		1	1	22	ONT	CP	IRISH		082	I		29
SMITH	JOHN		2		63	SCOTLAND	CS		F			1	D
SMITH	JOHN				49	IRELAND	CE	IRISH	LAB	081	B		35
SMITH	JOHN				45	0	BA	ENGLISH	FARMER	081	I		12
SMITH	JOHN				52	IRELAND	CP	IRISH	HOTELKEEPER	081	I		26
SMITH	JOHN				68	IRELAND	RC	IRISH	F	081	K		17
SMITH	JOHN				37	IRELAND	CE	IRISH	F	082	C	2	33
SMITH	JOHN		1		20	0	CE	IRISH	SADDLER	082	E		59
SMITH	JOHN				40	IRELAND	EM	IRISH	F	082	G		41
SMITH	JOHN				23	SCOTLAND	CP	SCOTCH	LUMBERER	083	G		1
SMITH	JOHN		1		26	ENGLAND	CE	ENGLISH	F	085	H		10
SMITH	JOHN				63	ENGLAND	CE	ENGLISH	F	085	I		25
SMITH	JOHN	R			38	QUE	CP	SCOTCH	F	082	G		44
SMITH	JONAS				40	0	EM	IRISH	F	081	H	2	36
SMITH	JOSEPH		1		35	IRELAND	RC	IRISH	SHOEMAKER	081	G	1	47
SMITH	JOSEPH		1		60	ENGLAND	CE	ENGLISH		081	H	2	41
SMITH	JOSEPH		1		32	IRELAND	RC	IRISH	SHOEMAKER	081	K		65
SMITH	MALCOLM		2		34	SCOTLAND	CS	SCOTCH	FUR TRADER	088	B		D
SMITH	MARGRET		1	1	27	0	CP	SCOTCH	SERVANT	081	A	1	43
SMITH	NANCY			1	50	RUPERTS LAND	CE	SCOTCH		088	B		14
SMITH	PHILANDER				37	0	OM	IRISH	F	081	H	1	11
SMITH	RICHARD		1		14	QUE	WM	SCOTCH	LAB	082	K	1	17
SMITH	RICHARD	OPHOR	1		1	ONT	CP	SCOTTISH		082	I		24
SMITH	ROBERT				26	0	RP	SCOTCH	F	081	E		4
SMITH	SARAH	ANN	2	1	29	0	CE			085	I		D
SMITH	SARAH	SEN	2	1	42	0	CE			081	I		D

SURNAME	NAME1	NAME2	STRAY	SEX	AGE	BIRTHPL	RELIGION	ORIGIN	OCCUP	DIST	SUB_DIST	DIV	PAGE
SMITH	SIMION				41	IRELAND	CE	IRISH	F	086	B		4
SMITH	SOLOMAN				50	SCOTLAND	PS	SCOTCH	F	085	I		19
SMITH	THOMAS				39	0	RC	IRISH	FARMER	081	F		25
SMITH	THOMAS				54	IRELAND	CE	IRISH	F	082	A		15
SMITH	THOMAS				50	IRELAND	CE	IRISH	BOOT SHOEMAKER	082	B		56
SMITH	THOMAS				30	IRELAND	CP	IRISH	LUMBERMAN	082	C	1	27
SMITH	THOMAS				29	ENGLAND	CE	ENGLISH		085	J		26
SMITH	THOMAS	G			48	ENGLAND	WM	ENGLISH	F	085	H		16
SMITH	THOMAS	JOHN	1		28	ENGLAND	CE	ENGLISH	LAB	081	B		36
SMITH	WALKER		1		50	0	RC	INDIAN	F	085	G		1
SMITH	WILLIAM		1		10	0	CP	SCOTCH		081	A	2	26
SMITH	WILLIAM		1		24	ENGLAND	CE	ENGLISH	B LAB	081	B		11
SMITH	WILLIAM				32	0	RC	IRISH	HOTELKEEPER	081	K		70
SMITH	WILLIAM				25	ONTARIO	CE	IRISH	LAB	082	A		46
SMITH	WILLIAM				38	IRELAND	CE	IRISH	F	082	C	1	48
SMITH	WILLIAM				50	IRELAND	CE	IRISH	F	082	C	2	53
SMITH	WILLIAM				48	ENGLAND	CE	ENGLISH	F	085	D		1
SMITH	WM		1		14	0	CS	SCOTCH	LABOURER	088	A		7
SMITH	WM	H			36	ENGLAND	WM	ENGLISH	TANNER	082	C	1	4
SMITTERS	LAWRENCE				31	SCOTLAND	PS	SCOTCH	F	085	D		35
SMYTH	ALEXANDER				40	IRELAND	CE	IRISH	F	081	H	2	18
SMYTH	SAMUEL				29	IRELAND	WM	IRISH	F	081	H	2	18
SMYTH	WILLIAM				45	IRELAND	CE	IRISH	F	081	H	2	19
SNELL	WM				40	ENGLAND	CE	ENGLISH	F	085	J		18
SNIDELY	FREDRICK		1		34	IRELAND	WM	ENGLISH	LUMBERMAN	086	B		2
SNIDER	CHARLES				36	GERMANY	LU	GERMAN	FARMER	082	I		5
SNIDER	DAVID				44	GERMANY	LU	GERMAN	F	085	H		2
SNIDER	RANDOLPH		1		38	GERMANY	WM	GERMAN	SERVANT	082	G		22
SNODDEN	STEWART				71	IRELAND	CE	IRISH	SHOEMAKER	082	C	1	14
SNODDON	ROBERT				42	QUE	CE	IRISH	F	082	C	1	28
SODUSKEY	MATHIAS				45	PRUSSIA	RC	PRUSSIAN	FARMER	083	A	1	6
SOLOMAN	ELIZA			1	20	0	RC	INDIAN		090	F		15
SOLOMAN	JESSE		1		16	US	ME	ENGLISH		090	F		18
SOLOMAN	MARIE			1	45	0	RC	FRENCH	FISHERMAN	088	A		1
SOLOMAN	PHILLISTE		1	1	16	0	RC	FRENCH		086	C	1	8
SOLOMON	AGATHE		1	1	21	0	RC	CANADIAN	STUDENT	087	A		1
SOLOMON	HENRY				50	0	RC	FRENCH CAN	TRADER	088	A		4
SOLOMON	HENRY				22	0	CE	INDIAN	LABOURER	089	B		39
SOLOMON	JAMES				53	US	RC	FRENCH	FISHERMAN	088	B		7
SOLOMON	JOSEPH				35	USA	RC	FRENCH	LIGHT HOUSE KEEPER	086	C	1	6
SOLOMON	JOSEPH				70	QUE	RC	FRENCH	F	086	C	1	6
SOLOMON	LOUIS		1		10	0	RC .	FRENCH		088	A		5
SOLOMON	WILLIAM				25	0	CE	FRENCH		086	C	1	6
SOLOMON	WILLIAM				45	0	RC	FRENCH	HUNTER	088	B		20
SOLOMON	WM	JUNR			25	0	RC	FRENCH	LABOURER	088	A		3
SOLOMON	XAVIER				48	0	RC	FRENCH	FISHERMAN	088	A		2
SONCISE	ABRAM				58	QUE	CE	FRENCH	F	082	G		66
SONVIN	DELEVO		1		37	QUEBEC	RC	FRENCH	LUMBERMAN	083	E		2
SORANSTIN	ROBERT		1		24	MOOSE FACTORY	CE	ENGLISH	LAB	090	F		25
SORELL	VENOIS		1		25	QUE	RC	FRENCH	PAINTER	082	E		43
SORIPHA	LAMEL		1		5	0	RC	FRENCH		082	H		28
SORIPHA	MARY		1	1		0	RC	FRENCH		082	H		28
SORIPHA	SUSAN		1	1	25	0	RC	INDIAN		082	H		28
SORIPHA	THOMAS		1		4	0	RC	FRENCH		082	H		28
SORITT	EBENIZER				55	ENGLAND	WM	ENGLISH	F	085	E		2
SOUCO	ALBERT				33	GERMANY	EV	GERMAN	FARMER	082	I		67
SOUCO	WILLIAM				61	GERMANY	EV	GERMAN	FARMER	082	I		67
SOULIER	ANTOINE				40	0	RC	INDIAN	LABOURER	090	C		1
SOULIER	JEAN	BAPTIST			50	0	RC	FRENCH	LABOURER	089	B		30
SOULINE	J	B	1		20	ONTARIO	RC	FRENCH	LABOURER	090	B		1
SOURAY	IZACK				20	QUE	RC	FRENCH	LUMBERMAN	086	C	1	4
SOVER	ROBDAT				51	GERMANY	RC	GERMAN	FARMER	081	F		30
SPARK	WILLIAM		1		13	GERMANY	LU	GERMAN		082	F		33
SPARKS	ABRAHAM				45	IRELAND	WM	IRISH	FARMER & LUMBERER	084	C		3
SPARLING	GEORGE				42	IRELAND	WM	IRISH	F	082	F		36
SPARLING	JOHN		1		17	0	WM	IRISH	CLERK	082	E		29
SPARLING	JOHN				42	IRELAND	WM	IRISH	FARMER	082	I		75
SPARLING	JOSEPH				37	IRELAND	EM	IRISH	F	082	F		34
SPARLING	WM				37	IRELAND	CP	IRISH	CARPENTER	082	E		2
SPEEDIL	JOHN				32	SCOTLAND	UP	SCOTCH	F	085	C		23
SPEER	JOHN	H			35	0	WM	IRISH	PAINTER & CABINETMAK	085	I		3
SPEID	JOHN		1		23	SCOTLAND	PS	SCOTTISH	CLERK	082	E		30
SPEIDLER	AUGUST		1		23	GERMANY	RC	GERMAN	LAB	090	D		7
SPENCE	FINLEY				35	IRELAND	CP	IRISH	STONECUTTER	081	B		63
SPENCE	GEORGE				26	IRELAND	WM	IRISH	F	085	H		8
SPENCE	GILBERT				32	SCOTLAND	PS	SCOTCH	POST MASTER H B CO	090	B		1
SPENCE	JACOB				57	IRELAND	WM	IRISH	F	085	H		5
SPENCE	JOHN				33	SCOTLAND	CS	SCOTCH	F	081	A	1	74
SPENCE	MOSES				69	IRELAND	CE	IRISH	BLACKSMITH	082	C	2	59
SPENCE	SANDY				21	ONTARIO	CP	SCOTT	FARMER	082	B		62
SPENCE	VIOLET			1	44	IRELAND	CE	IRISH		082	G		49
SPENCE	WILLIAM				66	IRELAND	CP	IRISH	MASON	081	B		62
SPENCER	ABEL				39	ENGLAND	CE	ENGLISH	F	085	I		28
SPENCER	CHARLES				25	0	WM	ENGLISH	F	086	A	1	3
SPENCER	WILLIAM				37	IRELAND	CE	IRISH	SCHOOL TEACHER	085	C		26
SPERBERG	FREDRICK				33	GERMANY	LU	GERMAN	FARMER	082	I		57
SPERBERG	WILLIAM				55	GERMANY	EV	GERMAN	FARMER	082	I		57
SPICER	CHARLES		1		61	0	WM	ENGLISH	LAB	082	C	1	10
SPIKE	GEORGE		1		23	0	WM	SCOTCH	LABOURER	088	A		8
SPIKE	R		1		35	0	CO	SCOTCH	LABOURER	088	A		8
SPILLANE	RICHARD		1		15	IRELAND	RC	IRISH		082	E		16
SPINK	CAROLINE		1	1	24	0	CE	ENGLISH	SERVANT	081	A	1	17
SPINKS	ELIZABETH	ANN	1	1	19	0	EM	SCOTCH		081	A	1	55
SPLAIN	ROBERT				39	0	CE	IRISH	SECTION MASTER	081	A	2	30
SPLAN	THOMAS		1		16	0	RC	IRISH	RAILWAYMAN	081	A	2	29
SPOTSWOOD	JAMES				31	0	CS	SCOTCH	FARMER	082	C	1	5
SPOTSWOOD	JANE			1	56	SCOTLAND	CS	SCOTCH		082	C	1	5
SPOTSWOOD	WILLIAM		2		60	SCOTLAND	CS	SCOTCH	F	082	C	1	D
SPRAGE	EDWARD				33	US	CP	ENGLISH	SAWYER	081	A	2	28
SPREADBOROUGH	GEORGE				36	ENGLAND	CE	ENGLISH	BLACKSMITH	086	A	1	31
SPREADBOROUGH	WILLIAM				42	ENGLAND	CE	ENGLISH	F	085	H		23
SPRING	ALBERT				50	0	CP	SCOTCH	F	085	H		10
SPRINGBELT	ANN		2	1	32	ENGLAND	CE	ENGLISH		089	B		D
SPRINGBETT	ANNIE		1	1		0	RC	ENGLISH		089	B		20
SPRINGBETT	MARY		1	1	4	0	CE	ENGLISH		089	B		3
SPRINGBITT	JOHN	EDWARD			27	ENGLAND	CE	ENGLISH	FARMER	089	B		22

SURNAME	NAME1	NAME2	STRAY	SEX	AGE	BIRTHPL	RELIGION	ORIGIN	OCCUP	DIST	SUB_DIST	DIV	PAGE
SPRINGBITT	WILLIAM		1		2	O	CE	ENGLISH		089	B		22
SPRINGER	JOHN				47	PRUSSIA	LU	GERMAN	F	082	G		11
SPROAT	MARY	I	2	1	35	O	CE			087	B	2	D
SPROAT	WM				38	IRELAND	CE	IRISH	F	087	B	2	8
SQUAGISIDE	CLARK				50	O	RC	INDIAN	HUNTER	086	A	3	8
SQUIRES	CLOEY		1	1	42	ONTARIO	EM	IRISH		082	A		69
SQUIRES	EDWAN				45	ONT	EM	ENGLISH	F	082	A		71
SQUIRES	ROBERT				40	ONTARIO	IM	ENGLISH	FARMER	082	B		60
ST AMOND	AMBROSE				23	QUE	RC	FRENCH	SHOEMAKER	082	E		51
ST AMOND	FRANCIS		2		1	QUE	RC			082	E		D
ST AMOND	PAUL				32	QUE	RC	FRENCH	SHANTYMAN	082	E		50
ST AMOND	PEIR				31	QUE	RC	FRENCH	BOARDING HOUSE KPR	082	E		46
ST AMOND	PERE				70	QUE	RC	FRENCH	LABOURER	082	E		46
ST AMOUR	ANTOINE				52	O	RC	FRENCH	F	082	J		5
ST ANTWIN			1	1	37	QUE	RC	FRENCH	NUN	084	I	2	1
ST AUGE	ABRAHAM				42	O	RC	FRENCH	FISHERMAN	089	A		62
ST AUGE	ANTHONY				52	O	RC	FRENCH	LABOURER	089	A		53
ST DENI	JOSEPH				55	QUE	RC	FRENCH	LAB	082	C	1	32
ST DENIS	JOSEPH				41	QUE	RC	FRENCH	LABOURER	082	E		52
ST GEORGE	LEWIS		1		33	O	NG	FRENCH	TEAMSTER	085	B		7
ST GODORE	PETER				27	QUE	RC	FRENCH	LAB	082	J		4
ST JACK	JOSEPH				28	QUE	RC	FRENCH	LABOURER	082	D		14
ST JOCK	MICHL		1		13	QUE	RC	FRENCH	SERVANT	082	E		65
ST JOHN	NAPOLEON				30	QUE	RC	FRENCH	SHOEMAKER	082	E		51
ST LOUIS	EUSTACE				50	QUE	RC	FRENCH	F	081	K		33
ST LOUIS	GUSANT				67	QUE	RC	FRENCH	F	081	K		26
ST LOUIS	HYACINTH				59	QUE	RC	FRENCH	LAB	082	C	1	9
ST LOUIS	MOSES				65	QUE	RC	FRENCH	F	081	K		32
ST LOUIS	SAMUEL				42	QUE	RC	FRENCH	F	081	K		39
ST LOUIS	TUSANT				21	O	RC	FRENCH	F	081	K		39
ST MARTIN	JOSEPH		1		26	QUE	RC	FRENCH	LUMBERMAN	088	B		2
ST ONGE	LOUACE				34	QUE	RC	FRENCH	FARMER	082	I		49
ST PEIR	JOSEPHINE		1	1	9	O	RC	FRENCH		082	K	1	10
ST PEIRE	JOSEPH				27	QUE	RC	FRENCH	SHANTYMAN	082	E		73
ST PIERRE	JOSEPH		1		13	O	RC	FRENCH		089	B		16
ST PIERRE	MARJERITE		1	1	18	O	RC	FRENCH	WORK WOMAN	089	B		16
ST PIERRE	PIERRE		1		18	QUE	RP	FRENCH	SERVANT	082	I		6
ST REVSIN	SUSAN			1	29	ONTARIO	RC	INDIAN		083	C		6
STACK	ELLEN		1	1	20	O	RC	IRISH		081	B		81
STACK	JOHN				60	IRELAND	RC	IRISH	F	081	J	2	6
STACK	JOHN				43	IRELAND	RC	IRISH	F	081	K		70
STACK	MICHAEL		1		23	O	RC	IRISH	LABOURER	081	D		24
STACK	MICHAEL				30	IRELAND	RC	IRISH	F	083	C		14
STACK	PATRICK				40	IRELAND	RC	IRISH	F	083	C		10
STACKPOOL	JOHN	MASSY	1		41	IRELAND	CE	IRISH	SHANTYMAN	081	F		25
STAFFORD	BENJAM				31	O	CE	ENGLISH	CARPENTER	081	B		67
STAGGA	CHARLES				35	GERMANY	LU	GERMAN	FARMER	082	I		18
STANE	JOSEPH				29		ME		COOPER	086	C	1	10
STANGER	JAMES		1		16	O	RC	SCOTCH	HUNTER	084	H		1
STANLEY	JOHN				28	O	CE	ENGLISH	WAGONMAKER	082	E		5
STANTON	JOHN				27	O	RC	IRISH	F	081	A	1	7
STARKEY	ARTHUR				23	INDIA	CE	ENGLISH	F	086	A	1	22
STARKWETHER	JAMES				30	O	RC	AFRICAN	LABOURER	088	A		9
STARKWETHER	NOT GIVEN		2	1		O	NR			088	A		D
STARNS	LOUIS		1		35	U STATES	CP	IRISH	CARDER	081	J	1	74
STARRITT	HANNAH			1	53	IRELAND	CP	IRISH		085	I		27
STATH	MARY		1	1	12	QUE	RC	IRISH		082	C	1	28
STAY	DILISH		1	1	30	QUE	RC	FRENCH	SERVANT	082	I		66
STEAPLETON	JOHN				39	IRELAND	RC	IRISH	FARMER	082	I		27
STEEL	AGNUS			1	58	SCOTLAND	RP	SCOTCH		081	K		8
STEEL	JAMES				38	SCOTLAND	RP	SCOTCH	F	081	K		10
STEEL	JANE		2	1	1	O	CP			082	B		D
STEEL	ROBERT		2			O	PS			081	K		D
STEEL	THOMAS				34	ONTARIO	CP	SCOTTISH	FARMER	082	B		50
STEEP	MICHAEL				28	ONTARIO	RC	IRISH	FARMER	081	G	1	24
STEEP	MICHAEL				51	IRELAND	RC	IRISH	FARMER	081	G	1	30
STEERS	MARGETT		1	1	17	ONTARIO	CE	IRISH		081	G	1	38
STEIN	WM				51	ENGLAND	CE	ENGLISH	F	085	J		25
STEINBRICK	REINHOLD				33	GERMANY	RC	GERMAN	FARMER	081	F		29
STEPHEN	JAMES				37	SCOTLAND	CP	SCOTCH	F	085	E		23
STEPHEN	JAMES		1		26	SCOTLAND	EP	SCOTCH	COOPER	090	D		2
STEPHENS	ALEX				28	O	PS	SCOTCH	PHYSICIAN	086	A	1	27
STEPHENS	ANNIE		1	1	22	O	CE	ENGLISH		089	B		24
STEPHENS	CHARLES				38	ENGLAND	WM	ENGLISH	F	085	I		17
STEPHENS	RICHARD				50	IRELAND	WM	IRISH	F	085	B		6
STEPHESON	ALEXANDER				70	SCOTLAND	CP	SCOTCH		081	A	2	55
STEPHESON	CATHERINE		1	1	20	O	CP	SCOTCH	SERVANT	081	A	2	19
STEPHESON	DONALD				40	SCOTLAND	CP	SCOTCH		081	A	2	52
STEPHESON	HUGH				32	O	CP	SCOTCH	F	081	A	2	54
STEPHESON	JAMES				60	SCOTLAND	CP	SCOTCH	F	081	A	2	54
STEPHESON	WILLIAM		1		23	O	CP	SCOTCH	RAILWAYMAN	081	A	2	28
STERLING	WILLIAM				21	O	CP	SCOTCH		081	A	2	25
STERRICK	LOUISA		1	1	19	Q	CE	SCOTCH	GOVERNESS	082	C	1	5
STEVENS	JOSEPH				29	NS	CE	IRISH	F	085	D		24
STEVENS	WM				40	O	EM	ENGLISH	F	085	J		4
STEVENSON	ANN		1	1	6	O	CE	IRISH		081	K		51
STEVENSON	GEORGE				30	O	CS	SCOTCH	F	081	A	1	72
STEVENSON	JAMES				51	SCOTLAND	CS	SCOTCH	F	082	C	1	54
STEVENSON	MATHEW				53	SCOTLAND	CS	SCOTCH	F	082	C	1	54
STEVENSON	MATTHEW				22	O	CS	SCOTCH	BLACKSMITH	082	C	2	64
STEVENSON	WILLIAM				60	ENGLAND	CE	ENGLISH	CABINET MAKER	081	I		15
STEWARD	JOHN				41	SCOTLAND	CS	SCOTCH	F	081	H	1	4
STEWARD	PETER				30	ONTARIO	CS	SCOTCH	F	082	A		38
STEWARD	ROBERT				26	ONTARIO	PS	SCOTTISH	FARMER	082	B		69
STEWART	AGNES		1	1	63	SCOTLAND	CS	SCOTCH		081	A	1	70
STEWART	ALEXANDER				50	O	CP	SCOTCH		081	A	1	10
STEWART	ALEXANDER				45	SCOTLAND	CP	SCOTCH	F	081	A	1	25
STEWART	ALEXANDER				48	SCOTLAND	CS	SCOTCH	F	081	A	1	62
STEWART	ALEXANDER		2			O	EM			081	B		D
STEWART	ALLAN				66	SCOTLAND	CP	SCOTCH	F			1	81
STEWART	ALXAND		2			O	CP			081	I		D
STEWART	ALXANDER				43	SCOTLAND	CS	SCOTCH	F	081	H	1	19
STEWART	ANDREW				50	SCOTLAND	CS	SCOTCH	F	081	A	1	44
STEWART	CHARLES				42	O	CP	SCOTCH	F	081	A	2	62
STEWART	CHARLES		1		32	O	CP	SCOTCH	LAB	081	B		82
STEWART	CHARLES				48	O	RP	SCOTCH	F	082	H		31

SURNAME	NAME1	NAME2	STRAY	SEX	AGE	BIRTHPL	RELIGION	ORIGIN	OCCUP	DIST	SUB_DIST	DIV	PAGE
STEWART	CHRISTINA			1	66	SCOTLAND	CS	SCOTCH		081	A	1	40
STEWART	DANIAL				67	SCOTLAND	CP	SCOTCH	F	081	H	1	18
STEWART	DANIAL				29	SCOTLAND	CP	SCOTCH	BUTCHER	081	I		43
STEWART	DANIEL		1		37	SCOTLAND	CP	SCOTCH	SAWYER	081	A	1	20
STEWART	DAVID				51	QUE	CP	SCOTCH	F	081	A	2	61
STEWART	DAVID		1		73	SCOTLAND	CS	SCOTCH	F	081	J	1	85
STEWART	DONALD				41	O	CP	SCOTCH	STOREKEEPER	081	A	1	2
STEWART	DONALD				46	SCOTLAND	CS	SCOTCH	F	081	A	1	51
STEWART	DONALD				32	O	CP	SCOTCH	LABOURER	081	B		32
STEWART	DONALD				56	SCOTLAND	CP	SCOTCH	LAB	081	B		74
STEWART	DUNCAN		1		4	O	RP	SCOTCH		081	E		20
STEWART	ISABELLA		1	1	10	O	RP	SCOTCH		081	E		20
STEWART	JAMES				37	SCOTLAND	CP	SCOTCH	F	081	A	1	3
STEWART	JAMES				35	O	CP	SCOTCH		081	A	2	52
STEWART	JAMES				29	O	CP	SCOTTISH	TINSMITH	082	E		59
STEWART	JAMES				50	SCOTLAND	PS	SCOTCH	F	085	D		14
STEWART	JANE		2	1	23	O	CP					1	D
STEWART	JANETT		1	1	87	SCOTLAND	CS	SCOTCH		081	H	2	23
STEWART	JOHN				68	SCOTLAND	CS	SCOTCH	F	081	A	1	17
STEWART	JOHN				35	O	CS	SCOTCH	F	081	A	1	40
STEWART	JOHN				43	O	CP	SCOTCH	LAB	081	A	2	26
STEWART	JOHN				30	SCOTLAND	CP	SCOTCH	F	081	A	2	37
STEWART	JOHN				57	IRELAND	CE	IRISH	WEAVER	081	D		1
STEWART	JOHN				39	SCOTLAND	CP	SCOTCH	MERCHANT	081	I		7
STEWART	JOHN				30	O	CS	ENGLISH	LAB	081	I		24
STEWART	JOHN				38	SCOTLAND	PS	SCOTCH	F	081	J	1	54
STEWART	JOHN	D			36	QUE	CP	SCOTCH	LAB	081	A	2	23
STEWART	MARGARET		1	1	30	SCOTLAND	CS	SCOTCH		081	H	2	3
STEWART	NIEL				39	O	CP	SCOTCH	F	081	A	1	73
STEWART	PETE		1			SCOTLAND	CP			081	I		43
STEWART	PETER				33	O	CP	SCOTCH	F	081	A	1	73
STEWART	RICHARD				41	IRELAND	CP	IRISH	F	082	C	2	41
STEWART	RICHARD				45	ENGLAND	RC	ENGLISH	F	085	J		22
STEWART	ROBERT				45	SCOTLAND	CS	SCOTCH	F	081	A	1	21
STEWART	ROBERT				25	O	CP	SCOTCH	F	081	A	1	42
STEWART	ROBERT				33	QUE	CS	SCOTCH	F	081	A	1	52
STEWART	ROBERT				24	O	WM	ENGLISH	F	081	I		1
STEWART	ROBERT		1		22	O	CS	SCOTCH	SADDLER	081	I		42
STEWART	ROBERT				38	SCOTLAND	CS	SCOTCH	F	082	A		37
STEWART	ROBERT				34	IRELAND	CS	IRISH	F	082	C	2	59
STEWART	RODERICK				40	SCOTLAND	CP	SCOTCH	F	085	H		25
STEWART	THOMAS				31	O	CP	SCOTCH	F	081	A	2	55
STEWART	THOMAS				41	O	CP	SCOTCH	WOOLEN MANUFACTURER	081	B		75
STEWART	WILLIAM				35	QUE	CP	SCOTCH	F	081	A	2	47
STEWERT	DANIAL				28	O	CS	SCOTCH	BLACKSMITH	081	I		3
STICKLER	PETER				43	SCOTLAND	CS	SCOTCH	F	086	A	2	12
STIEP	JOHN				26	IRELAND	WM	IRISH	LUMBERMAN	086	C	1	2
STILLER	LOUIS				27	O	WM	ENGLISH	SAW MILLER	086	A	1	1
STINSON	EPHRIM		1		9	O	CP	IRISH		085	H		12
STINSON	ROBERT				29	IRELAND	WM	IRISH	F	085	I		37
STINSON	WILLIAM				42	IRELAND	EP	IRISH	SCHOOL TEACHER	087	B	3	10
STIRLING	ALEXANDER				50	O	CP	SCOTCH	SHOEMAKER	081	A	1	17
STIRLING	DAVID				35	O	CE	SCOTCH	MINE LABOURER	089	A		45
STITT	JANE		1	1	27	QUEBEC	CS	IRISH	SERVANT	082	A		46
STITT	THOMAS				36	QUEBEC	CE	IRISH	F	082	A		46
STJACK	JOSEPH				37	QUE	RC	FRENCH	LABOURER	082	D		12
STOCKS	JAMES				50	ENGLAND	CE	ENGLISH	FARMER	082	B		71
STOGUA	MARY		2	1	85	QUE	RC			082	C	2	D
STOKER	CHARLES				48	ENGLAND	PM	ENGLISH	BOAT BUILDER	085	C		2
STOKES	EDWARD				74	IRELAND	RC	IRISH	CARPENTER	085	C		12
STOKES	HENRY				21	O	WM	ENGLISH	SADDLER & HARNESS MA	082	C	2	5
STOKES	HENRY				24	ENGLAND	CE	ENGLISH	LABOURER	082	E		32
STOKOUA	LAMAPE				57	O	RC	INDIAN	HUNTER AND FISHERMAN	082	H		26
STOKOULA	DANIEL				4	O	RC			082	H		D
STONE	CHARLES				22	QUE	CE	SCOTCH	LAB	081	B		35
STONE	JOHN				49	IRELAND	CE	ENGLISH	F	082	G		41
STONEMAN	WILLIAM				33	ENGLAND	CE	ENGLISH	F	085	E		15
STOODLEY	ROBERT				54	ENGLAND	RC	ENGLISH	STONEMASON	081	D		7
STOPON	JOHN				66	PRUSSIA	RC	PRUSSIAN	FARMER	083	A	1	16
STOREY	JOSEPH				31	O	BA	SCOTCH		081	A	2	55
STORIE	CHARLES								SEE STONE	081	B		35
STORIE	ELIZABETH		1	1	85	SCOTLAND	CP	SCOTCH		081	A	1	69
STORIE	JAMES				38	SCOTLAND	CP	SCOTCH	F	081	A	1	69
STORIE	JAMES				80	SCOTLAND	BA	SCOTCH	F	081	A	2	58
STORIE	JAMES	JR			37	O	BA	SCOTCH	F	081	A	2	57
STORIE	JOHN				45	SCOTLAND	CP	SCOTCH	F	081	A	1	69
STORIE	JOHN	J			57	QUE	RC	SCOTCH	CARPENTER	081	B		19
STORIE	ROBERT				57	SCOTLAND	BA	SCOTCH	F	081	A	2	56
STORIE	ROBERT		1		40	SCOTLAND	PS	SCOTCH	F	081	H	2	10
STORIE	THOMAS				44	SCOTLAND	EM	SCOTCH	CARPENTER	081	B		25
STORIE	WILLIAM				48	SCOTLAND	FW	SCOTCH	F	081	A	1	72
STORY	CHARLES				43	O	WM	ENGLISH	CARPENTER	085	I		7
STOTEN	ALEXANDER				67	O	CP	ENG	LAB	081	B		57
STOUGHTON	ALEX D				27	O	WM	ENGLISH	LAB	081	B		77
STOUGHTON	WILLIAM				59	US	WM	AMERICAN	F	081	C		49
STRACHE	CAROL				44	GERMANY	BA	GERMAN	F	081	A	2	44
STRADO	AUGUSTA		1	1	21	PRUSIA	ZZ	PRUSIAN	SERVANT	081	B		49
STRAIN	FRANCIS				35	IRELAND	CE	IRISH	F	086	A	1	27
STRANE	EUGENE				35	IRELAND	RC	IRISH	F	081	E		9
STRANG	ELIZABETH			1	51	UNITED STATES	MO	ENGLISH		089	A		59
STRATHY	ROBERT		1		10	O	CP	SCOTCH		090	F		25
STRATON	GEORGE				26	SCOTLAND	CP	SCOTCH	LUMBERER	083	B	2	1
STRATTON	WILLIAM				55	ENGLAND	CE	ENGLISH	FARMER	089	B		1
STREET	CASPER				56	PRUSSIA	PR	PRUSSIAN	F	085	A		9
STRESMAN	FREDRICK				43	GERMANY	LU	GERMAN	FARMER	082	I		21
STRINGER	JOHN				65	ENGLAND	CS	ENGLISH	F	081	C		23
STRINGER	JOSEPH				31	ENGLAND	EP	ENGLISH	F	087	B	3	10
STRINGERS	WILLIAM				70	IRELAND	CE	IRISH	CARPENTER	082	A		55
STRONGMAN	WALTER				22	O	CE	ENGLISH	LUMBERMAN	088	B		17
STROUD	MICHAEL				58	IRELAND	CE	IRISH	FARMER	081	D		3
STRUTHERS	JANE			1	73	SCOTLAND	CP	SCOTTISH		082	B		56
STUARD	JAMES				25		CP	SCOTCH	LABORER	085	E		30
STUART	CHARLES				50	IRELAND	PR	SCOTCH	F	082	G		49
STUART	THOMAS				21	IRELAND	WM	IRISH	F	086	B		4
STUBBS	FREDRICK				23	ENGLAND	CE	ENGLISH	F	085	E		21
STUBS	DEAN				47	ONTARIO	EM	ENGLISH	LABOURER	082	A		68

SURNAME	NAME1	NAME2	STRAY	SEX	AGE	BIRTHPL	RELIGION	ORIGIN	OCCUP	DIST	SUB_DIST	DIV	PAGE
STUBS	EDWARD				65	IRELAND	PR	IRISH	FARMER	081	G	2	4
STUDDARD	WILLIAM				56	IRELAND	CE	IRISH	F	082	K	2	3
STURRACK	AGNES		1	1	10	QUE	CS	SCOTCH		081	I		41
STWERT	DUNCAN				27	0	CS	SCOTCH	MERCHANT	081	I		2
STYLES	ROBERT				34	0	PS	SCOTCH	F	085	E		7
SUCIER	CLEMMENT				34	QUE	RC	FRENCH	TRADER	082	C	1	49
SUDGER	MAYRAND				28	QUE	RC	FRENCH	LUMBERMAN	088	C		11
SUFFERN	ANTHONY				34	IRELAND	PS	IRISH	F	085	D		4
SUFFERN	JAMES				63	IRELAND	PS	IRISH	LABORER	085	D		4
SUGDEN	CHARLES		1		21	ENGLAND	CE	ENGLISH	SERVANT	085	I		16
SULAVIN	MARY		2	1	22	0	CE			082	D		D
SULAVIN	PATRICK				102	IRELAND	RC	IRISH	UNABLE TO WORK	082	D		25
SULAVIN	ROBERT				23	0	CE	IRISH	FARMER	082	D		31
SULAVIN	TIMOTHY				54	IRELAND	RC	IRISH	FARMER	082	D		24
SULIVAN	HANNAH		2	1	22	0	RC			082	C	2	D
SULIVAN	JOHN				40	0	WM	IRISH	F	082	C	2	66
SULIVAN	MICHAEL				32	IRELAND	RC	IRISH	F	082	C	2	65
SULIVAN	THOS				30	IRELAND	RC	IRISH	INN KEEPER	082	C	2	5
SULLAVAN	JEREMIAH		2		70	IRELAND	RC	F		082	K	1	D
SULLAVAN	MAREY			1	71	ENGLAND	RC	ENGLISH	F	082	K	1	10
SULLAVIN	DANIEL				34	IRELAND	RC	IRISH	FARMER	081	G	1	26
SULLIVAN	ANDREW				51	IRELAND	RC	IRISH	FARMER	081	J	1	81
SULLIVAN	BABY		1			0	CP	SCOTCH		082	C	1	46
SULLIVAN	CORNELIUS				40	IRELAND	RC	IRISH	LAB	081	A	2	7
SULLIVAN	CORNELIUS				37	IRELAND	RC	IRISH	F	081	J	2	2
SULLIVAN	DEBORAH			1	40	IRELAND	RC	IRISH		081	J	2	2
SULLIVAN	DENNIS				54	IRELAND	RC	IRISH	F	081	K		72
SULLIVAN	DINNIS				60	IRELAND	RC	IRISH	FARMER	081	G	1	26
SULLIVAN	ELLEN		1	1	21	IRELAND	RC	IRISH	SERVANT	081	G	1	43
SULLIVAN	JAMES				59	IRELAND	RC	IRISH	F	081	J	1	6
SULLIVAN	JEREMIAH		1		27	IRELAND	RC	IRISH	LAB	090	D		1
SULLIVAN	JEREMIAH		1		27	IRELAND	RC	IRISH	LAB	090	D		6
SULLIVAN	JOHN		1		32	IRELAND	RC	IRISH	SHOEMAKER	081	B		6
SULLIVAN	JOHN				40	IRELAND	RC	IRISH	FARMER	081	F		6
SULLIVAN	JOHN		1		18	ONTARIO	RC	IRISH	FARMER	081	G	1	43
SULLIVAN	JOHN		1		36	IRELAND	RC	IRISH		081	H	2	36
SULLIVAN	JOHN				55	IRELAND	RC	IRISH	F	081	J	1	67
SULLIVAN	JOHN				30	IRELAND	RC	IRISH	F	083	C		11
SULLIVAN	JOHN				32	0	RC	FRENCH	LUMBERMAN	086	C	1	5
SULLIVAN	LAWRENCE				24	IRELAND	RC	IRISH	F	083	C		7
SULLIVAN	MICHAEL		1		15	ONTARIO	RC	IRISH		081	G	1	43
SULLIVAN	MICHAEL				57	IRELAND	WM	IRISH	MINER	089	A		28
SULLIVAN	PATRICK				58	IRELAND	RC	IRISH	F	081	J	1	6
SULLIVAN	PATRICK				30	IRELAND	RC	IRISH	MINER	090	D		3
SULLIVAN	THOMAS				44	IRELAND	RC	IRISH	FARMER	081	F		5
SULLIVAN	WILLIAM		1		45	IRELAND	RC	IRISH		087	B	3	11
SUMMACH	CARL				44	GERMANY	BA	GERMAN	FARMER	081	F		23
SUMMERS	ELIZABETH		1	1	18	ONT	CP	SCOTTISH		082	I		65
SUMMERS	LOUIS				40	SCOTLAND	CS	SCOTCH	F	085	D		28
SUMMERSKILL	JOHN				49	ENGLAND	CE	ENGLISH	F	085	A		12
SUMMERVILLE	SAML				32	SCOTLAND	CS	SCOTCH	F	085	L		12
SUMMERVILLE	THOS		1		17	0	CP	SCOTCH	APPRENTICE	081	B		11
SUMMERVILLE	WM				26	SCOTLAND	CS	SCOTCH	F	085	L		12
SUNDERLAND	ANGUS				45	SCOTLAND	CP	SCOTCH	F	085	E		26
SUNDSTRUM	SAMUEL				57	QUE	RC	SWEDEN	F	082	H		22
SUNSTRUM	WILLIAM				39	QUE	CE	SWEDE	F	082	H		32
SUPPLE	JOHN				66	IRELAND	CP	IRISH	GENTLEMAN	082	E		27
SUPPLE	JOHN		2		28	QUE	CP	SCOTTISH	MILLOWNER	082	E		D
SUPPLE	MARRIANNE			1	23	0	CP	SCOTTISH		082	E		8
SUPPLE	WILLIAM				22	0	CP	IRISH	LUMBERER	082	E		28
SURMAN	FREDERICK				40	ENGLAND	CE	ENGLISH	COOPER	089	B		24
SUSKE	JACOB				45	POLAND	RC	POLISH	LAB	081	I		36
SUTCHLIFFE	LISTER				40	ENGLAND	WM	ENGLISH	FARMER	081	G	1	13
SUTHERLAND	ALEXANDER				50	SCOTLAND	JM	SCOTCH	F	082	C	2	55
SUTHERLAND	ANGUS				40	0	CP	SCOTCH	F	082	G		10
SUTHERLAND	ARCHIBALD				28	US	CP	SCOTCH	F	081	A	1	55
SUTHERLAND	DANIEL				31	0	CP	SCOTCH	F	082	F		7
SUTHERLAND	DAVID				42	SCOTLAND	CP	SCOTCH	F	082	F		5
SUTHERLAND	JAMES				31	0	CP	SCOTCH	F	082	G		6
SUTHERLAND	JAMES				38	0	CP	SCOTCH	F	082	G		40
SUTHERLAND	JAMES				51	SCOTLAND	CP	SCOTCH	F	085	B		17
SUTHERLAND	JESSY		1	1	4	0	CP	SCOTTISH		082	E		5
SUTHERLAND	JOHN				71	SCOTLAND	CP	SCOTCH	TAILOR			1	77
SUTHERLAND	JOHN				35	0	OP	SCOTCH	F	082	H		15
SUTHERLAND	WILLIAM				21	ENGLAND	WM	ENGLISH	F	085	J		26
SUTHERLAND	WM				72	SCOTLAND	CP	SCOTCH		082	G		40
SUTLIFF	EDWAN				50	IRELAND	RC	IRISH	F	082	A		83
SUTLIFF	THOMAS				60	IRELAND	RC	IRISH	F	081	H	2	38
SUTLIFF	THOS				34	IRELAND	RC	IRISH	F	082	A		35
SUTTABY	WILLIAM				25	ENGLAND	CE	ENGLISH	F	085	B		5
SUTTON	EDWARD				47	IRELAND	CE	IRISH	F	082	F		5
SUTTON	HENRY				25	ENGLAND	CE	ENGLISH	BLACKSMITH	081	A	2	14
SUTTON	JOHN	P			31	ENGLAND	CE	ENGLISH	BARBER	082	E		30
SUTTON	MARY	ANNE	1	1	20	0	CE	ENGLISH	SERVANT	082	E		29
SUTTON	RICHARD				40	IRELAND	CE	IRISH	F	082	G		22
SUTTON	SAMUEL		1		30	IRELAND	CE	IRISH	FARM LABOURER	082	G		1
SUTTON	SAMUEL				32	IRELAND	CE	IRISH	FOREMAN ON FARM	082	G		22
SUTTON	SAMUEL	I	1		18	0	CE	IRISH	CLERK	082	E		11
SWALWELL	JOANN			1	41	SCOTLAND	WM	SCOTTISH	FARMER	082	I		69
SWAN	CHARLES				54	ENGLAND	CE	ENGLISH	BUTCHER	081	B		46
SWANPIPER	CHRISTOPHER				32	Y STATE	WM	GERMAN	SHOEMAKER	085	I		25
SWANS	THOMAS		1		24	0	CE	ENGLISH	LUMBERMAN	088	B		5
SWARTZ	CHARLES				60	GERMANY	LU	GERMAN	FARMER	082	I		18
SWEELE	WILLIAM				27	0	WM	ENGLISH	MINER	089	A		35
SWEENY	ISABELLE			1	60	IRELAND	CE	IRISH		082	G		27
SWEENY	JAMES		2			0	CE			082	G		D
SWEENY	JAMES		2		36	IRELAND	CE		F	082	G		D
SWEENY	JANE			1	29	0	CE	IRISH		082	G		26
SWEENY	JOHN				33	IRELAND	CE	IRISH	F	082	G		25
SWEENY	THOS				40	IRELAND	CE	IRISH	F	082	G		23
SWEET	CHARLES		1		20	ENGLAND	WM	ENGLISH	SERVANT	085	I		11
SWEETMAN	RACHEL		1	1	44	JERSEY	CE	ENGLISH		082	E		3
SWEETMAN	WILLIAM		1		53	ENGLAND	CE	ENGLISH	TAILOR	082	E		3
SWEETMAN	WILLIAM	P	1		18	JERSEY	CE	ENGLISH	BOOKKEEPER	082	E		3
SWENY	SPENCER				36	0	CE	IRISH	F	082	C	2	16
SWESEY	SIMON				29	0	WM	SCOTCH	F	082	F		24

SURNAME	NAME1	NAME2	STRAY	SEX	AGE	BIRTHPL	RELIGION	ORIGIN	OCCUP	DIST	SUB_DIST	DIV	PAGE
SWITZER	JOSEPH				65	IRELAND	CE	IRISH	F	082	C	2	31
SWITZER	MARTIN				50	GERMANY	LU	GERMAN	F	082	G		94
SWORD	JOHN				21	SCOTLAND	CP	SCOTCH	F	086	A	2	13
SWORD	THOMAS				56	SCOTLAND	CS	SCOTCH	F	086	A	2	13
SYKES	THOMAS				84	0	CE	ENGLISH	F	082	C	2	61
SYLVESTER	EMBRES		1		21	0	CE	ENGLISH	LAB	085	F		5
SYLVOYS	MARY			1	37	0	RC	FRENCH		089	A		40
SYMINGTON	WILLIAM				43	SCOTLAND	EM	SCOTCH	F	085	D		33
TABAHQUIN	JOHN				32	0	RC	INDIAN	LAB	090	F		26
TABAHQUNIN	ALEXIE				32	0	RC	INDIAN	HUNTER	090	F		10
TABERT	MARTHA		1	1	12	GERMANY	RC	DUTCH		082	C	2	34
TABERT	MATILDA		1	1	18	GERMANY	LU	GERMAN		082	D		9
TABOR	ROBERT				35	0	CE	ENGLISH		085	I		39
TABURG	HENERY		1		20	GERMANY	LU	GERMAN	LABOURER	082	D		18
TACIA	AMBROIS				52	QUE	RC	FRENCH	F	082	C	1	22
TAGGERT	GEORGE				27	NEW BRUNSWICK	CE	SCOTCH	LUMBER MERCHANT	084	C		2
TAGGERT	GEORGE	RINALDS			4	0	CE			084	C		
TAGGERT	MARGARET		1		20	QUEBEC	ME			084	C		D
TAIBOSEGAI	FRANCIS				37	0	RC	INDIAN	F & LABOURER	087	B	1	6
TAIBOSEGAI	LOUIS				47	0	RC	INDIAN	F & MECHANIC	087	B	1	3
TAIBOSEGAI	LOUIS	SENIOR			62	0	RC	INDIAN	F	087	B	1	1
TAICUM	(1ST SON)		2		21	0	IF		HUNTER & TRAPPER	090	C		D
TAIFARE	JOSEPH	JR	1		26	QUEBEC	RC	FRENCH	RAFTSMAN	084	D		1
TAIFARE	JOSEPH	SR	1		48	QUEBEC	RC	FRENCH	RAFTSMAN	084	D		1
TAILOR	CHARLES				26	0	WM	IRISH	BLACKSMITH	082	C	1	26
TAIT	ROBERT				40	SCOTLAND	WM	SCOTCH	CARPENTER	089	B		5
TAIT	SAMUEL				49	SCOTLAND	CS	SCOTCH	F	081	J	1	71
TAIT	SERAH		2	1	16	ONT	CS			081	J	1	D
TAIT	WILLIAM				56	SCOTLAND	PS	SCOTCH	BLACKSMITH	085	C		12
TAKAMISE	ANTOINE				61	US	RC	INDIAN	F & FISHERMAN	087	A		38
TAKAMISE	LOUIS				25	0	RC	INDIAN	COOPER & F	087	A		38
TAKAMISE	PAUL				32	0	RC	INDIAN	F & FISHERMAN	087	A		38
TAKMAN	CARL				38	GERMANY	BA	GERMAN	FARMER	081	F		21
TAKWADJWON	J	BTE			43	US	RC	INDIAN	F & FISHERMAN	087	A		14
TAKWADJWON	LOUIS				39	US	RC	INDIAN	F & FISHERMAN	087	A		14
TALAHQUIN	PAUL		2		2	0	RC			090	F		D
TALLON	MARY	ANNE	2	1	44	IRELAND	RC			082	E		D
TALLON	PATRICK				37	IRELAND	RC	IRISH	LABOURER	082	E		14
TALOR	ARTHER				54	SCOTLAND	CP	SCOTCH	F	082	F		22
TALYEA	MADAM				30	QUE	RC	INDIAN		084	D		7
TANENN	DERUONE				37	QUE	RC	FRENCH	LAB	082	C	1	21
TANG	EMMAY		1	1	11	0	LU	GERMAN		082	J		10
TANG	FREDRICK		1		14	GERMANY	LU	GERMAN	SERVANT	082	E		34
TANG	LISSEE		1	1	14	GERMANY	LU	GERMAN	SERVANT	082	J		10
TANG	MAGEE		1	1	6	0	LU	GERMAN		082	J		10
TANG	ROSA		1	1	8	0	LU	GERMAN		082	J		10
TANNER	ELWIN	E	1		21	USA	BA	ENGLISH	CLERK	086	C	1	1
TANTERSON	DORIN		1		34	NORWAY	PS	NORWEGIAN	SAILOR	089	B		25
TANTERSON	JEMINA		1		28	MOOSE FACTORY	CE	SCOTCH		089	B		25
TANTERSON	SARAH		1	1	5	0	CE	NORWEGIAN		089	B		25
TATE	HENRY				32	ENGLAND	WM	ENGLISH	F	082	C	1	10
TATE	JAMES				35	ENGLAND	WM	ENGLISH	LAB	082	C	1	6
TAY	JAMES		1		17	IRELAND	RC	IRISH	SADDLER	082	E		44
TAY	JOHN		1		11	0	RC	IRISH		082	E		44
TAY	MARY		1	1	50	IRELAND	RC	IRISH		082	E		44
TAY	MARY	ANN	1	1	10	0	RC	IRISH		082	E		44
TAY	THOMAS		1		18	IRELAND	RC	IRISH	LABOURER	082	E		44
TAYLER	ABRAHAM				46	0	EM	ENGLISH	BLACKSMITH	085	B		18
TAYLER	WILLIAM				38	ENGLAND	WM	ENGLISH	F	085	B		6
TAYLOR	ALLAN	B			29	SCOTLAND	PS	SCOTCH	WAGGON MAKER	085	I		33
TAYLOR	ANDREW				33	0	CP	SCOTCH	F	081	A	1	58
TAYLOR	ARCHIBALD				36	0	CP	SCOTCH	MILLWRIGHT	085	D		26
TAYLOR	DAVID		1		13	0	CE	IRISH		081	F		13
TAYLOR	GEORGE				23	0	WM	IRISH	GROCER	081	B		55
TAYLOR	JAMES				36	IRELAND	CP	ENGLISH	F	081	A	2	35
TAYLOR	JAMES		1		52	0	CE	ENGLISH	LAB	081	H	2	26
TAYLOR	JAMES		1		25	ENGLAND	CE	ENGLISH	F	085	I		35
TAYLOR	JOHN				27	0	CP	SCOTCH	F	081	A	1	58
TAYLOR	JOHN				40	ENGLAND	CE	ENGLISH	CABINET MAKER	085	C		24
TAYLOR	JOHN				26	SCOTLAND	CS	SCOTCH	F	085	L		3
TAYLOR	JOHN				45	IRELAND	CE	IRISH	F	086	A	2	7
TAYLOR	JOHN	N	1		24	ENGLAND	CE	ENGLISH	F	085	L		6
TAYLOR	JOSEPH				63	SCOTLAND	CS	SCOTCH	F	081	C		19
TAYLOR	JOSEPH				45	ENGLAND	WM	ENGLISH	F	085	H		17
TAYLOR	MARGARET		1	1	9	0	CE	IRISH		081	F		13
TAYLOR	MARY		1	1	22	ONTARIO	CE	ENGLISH	SERVANT	082	B		42
TAYLOR	MINNA		1	1	11	0	CP	ENGLISH		082	C	1	2
TAYLOR	PRECIVAL				47	ENGLAND	WM	ENGLISH	F	085	H		17
TAYLOR	ROBT		1		21	0	PS	SCOTTISH	FARM SERVANT	082	E		28
TAYLOR	SAMUEL				34	ENGLAND	CE	ENGLISH	F	085	I		35
TAYLOR	THOMAS				43	SCOTLAND	CP	SCOTCH	TAILOR	082	C	2	2
TAYLOR	WILLIAM				31	IRELAND	CE	IRISH	SHOEMAKER	086	A	1	30
TAYLOR	WILLIAM				43	IRELAND	CE	IRISH	F	086	A	2	7
TCHINGEWAK	ANTOINE				47	US	RC	INDIAN	F & FISHERMAN	087	A		29
TEASIC	DONALD				46	0	CP	SCOTCH	MERCHANT	082	C	2	6
TEBO	BABTIST				60	0	RC	FRENCH	F	082	F		19
TEBO	FRANK				28	0	RC	FRENCH	MINE LABOURER	089	A		32
TEBO	JOSEPH				48	RED RIVER	RC	FRENCH	LABOURER	089	B		37
TEBO	MARY		2	1	9	0	RC			082	F		D
TEBO	MOSES				29	0	RC	FRENCH	F	082	F		20
TEBODAU	FRANCISE				36	QUE	RC	FRENCH	F	082	K	1	17
TEEVENS	ELLEN		1	1	17	0	RC	IRISH		082	E		56
TEGIL	AUGUST				45	GERMANY	LU	GERMAN	F	082	G		90
TEGIOSH	PETER				75	US	RC	INDIAN	FARMER	089	B		35
TEHKUMMAH	AUGUSTA		2		2	0	RC	INDIAN		087	B	1	D
TEHKUMMAH	FRANCES				42	US	RC	INDIAN	F & COOPER	087	B	1	22
TEHKUMMAH	LOUIS				56	US	RC	INDIAN	F	087	B	1	22
TEIGS	GUSTAV				28	GERMANY	LU	GERMAN	F	081	K		58
TEIGS	JOHN				58	GERMANY	LU	GERMAN	F	081	K		58
TEIRNEY	JOHN		1		42	IRELAND	RC	IRISH	LAB	081	A	1	36
TEKASTO	MARGRET			1	42	0	WM	UNKNOWN	SEAMSTRESS	082	C	2	45
TELFER	ANDREW				33	QUE	CP	SCOTCH	LAB	081	A	2	20
TELFER	DOROTHY		2	1	1	ENGLAND	CE			085	B		D
TELFER	JOSEPH	W			49	ENGLAND	CP	ENGLISH	F	085	B		20
TELLIER	JOSEPHINE		1	1	12	ONTARIO	RC	FRENCH		084	C		3
TEMPLE	CHARLES				40	ENGLAND	RP	ENGLISH	F	081	K		9

SURNAME	NAME1	NAME2	STRAY	SEX	AGE	BIRTHPL	RELIGION	ORIGIN	OCCUP	DIST	SUB_DIST	DIV	PAGE
TENANT	WILLIAM				50	0	RC	IRISH	CARPENTER	081	F		18
TENNANT	GEORGE				42	0	WM	IRISH	TANNER	082	G		96
TENNANT	MARY		1	1	20	SCOTLAND	WM	SCOTCH		089	B		5
TENNANT	RICH'D				80	IRELAND	CE	IRISH	F	082	G		94
TENNANT	RICHARD				36	0	CE	IRISH	F	082	G		91
TENNANT	ROBT				31	0	CE	IRISH	L	082	G		94
TENNANT	THOMAS				36	0	CE	IRISH	F	082	G		94
TENNENT	JOHN				38	0	WM	IRISH	MECHANIC	082	J		3
TERIA	BATIST				28	QUE	ME	FRENCH	FARMER	082	D		9
TERRY	GEORGE				30	ENGLAND	BA	ENGLISH	F	085	C		3
TESBOINNIL	JEROME		2		7	ONT	RC			090	B		D
TESCON	MARGRET		1	1	14	QUE	RC	FRENCH	SERVANT	081	A	2	42
TESSIER	AMBROISE								SEE TACIA	082	C	1	22
TEVIVDALE	JOHN				36	SCOTLAND	CS	SCOTCH	MERCHANT	085	I		13
THACKRAY	RICHARD				41	ENGLAND	CE	ENGLISH	CARPENTER	081	G	1	30
THEABO	JOSEPH		2		1	0	RC			089	A		D
THEABO	PETER				28	0	RC	FRENCH	FISHERMAN	089	A		59
THEABO	SAMUEL				56	UNITED STATES	RC	FRENCH	LABOURER	089	A		60
THEABO	WILLIAM				25	0	RC	FRENCH	FISHERMAN	089	A		62
THEBOULT	TIFFIELD				21	ONT	RC	FRENCH	SHANTY CLERK	082	I		79
THIBAULT	ALEX				27	0	RC	FRENCH	F	082	F		16
THIBAULT	THEOPHILE						NG		SEE THEBOULT	082	I		79
THIBEDEAU	NERBURE				34	QUE	RC	FRENCH	F	082	C	1	20
THIBO	S	T			65	0	RC	FRENCH	MERCHANT	088	A		5
THIEMANN	ADAM				51	GERMANY	LU	GERMAN	F	082	H		8
THIRD	WILL'M				38	SCOTLAND	PM	SCOTCH	F	087	B	2	7
THISS	THOMAS				43	SCOTLAND	ZZ	SCOTCH	LABOURER	085	B		1
THIVERGE	ANTOINE		1		51	QUEBEC	RC	FRENCH		084	C		5
THIVERGE	ANTWIN	ANTOINE	1	1	13	0	RC	FRENCH		084	I	2	1
THIVIERGE	JOSEPH		1		6	ONTARIO	RC	FRENCH		084	B		5
THOBOKESHICK	JOHN	BATIS			48	0	RC	INDIAN	HUNTER	084	I	1	3
THOBOKISIK	OSULEBEAK			1	60	0	RC	INDIAN	HUNTER	084	I	1	4
THOMA	CHRISTINA		1	1	56	GERMANY	WM	GERMAN		082	G		13
THOMA	GOTLIP		1		20	GERMANY	WM	GERMAN	SERVANT	082	G		13
THOMAS	A	H			29	ENGLAND	CE	ENGLISH	WHARFINGER	081	H	2	23
THOMAS	ALEXANDER				34	0	CE	ENGLISH	F	082	H		21
THOMAS	BRUN				57	IRELAND	RC	IRISH	FARMER	082	B		40
THOMAS	EDWARD				45	0	CE	ENGLISH	F	082	H		33
THOMAS	FRANCES		1	1	25	ONTARIO	CE	SCOTCH	SERVANT	084	C		5
THOMAS	GEORGE		2			0	CP			082	G		D
THOMAS	HENRY				55	PRINCE RUPERTS LAND	CE	ENGLISH	LAB	083	C		6
THOMAS	JOHN				35	IRELAND	CP	IRISH	F	082	G		10
THOMAS	JOHN	W			33	US	CP	UNKNOWN	HOTEL & STORE KEEPER	085	E		23
THOMAS	MARY			1	27	ENGLAND	WM	ENGLISH		089	A		47
THOMAS	PRINCE				35	GERMAN	RC	GERMAN	SERVANT	081	H	1	8
THOMAS	RICHARD				31	0	CE	ENGLISH	HOTELKEEPER	082	H		31
THOMAS	ROBERT				73	IRELAND	CP	IRISH	F	082	G		43
THOMAS	THOMAS				43	QUEBEC	CE	WELSH	FARMER	084	D		5
THOMAS	W	H			35	ENGLAND	CE	ENGLISH	F	085	J		22
THOMAS	WALLACE		1		9	ONTARIO	PM	ENGLISH		082	B		61
THOMAS	WILLIAM				49	0	CE	ENGLISH	F	082	H		34
THOMAS	WILLIAM				36	IRELAND	PB	IRISH	F	082	K	2	2
THOMPSON	ALEXANDER				70	SCOTLAND	CS	SCOTCH	F	082	A		22
THOMPSON	ANDREW				40	IRELAND	WM	IRISH	F	085	H		6
THOMPSON	ARCHD				49	SCOTLAND	PS	SCOTTISH	D CLERK OF THE CROWN	082	E		57
THOMPSON	CATHERINE		1	1	18	ONT	CP	SCOTTISH	SERVANT	082	I		66
THOMPSON	EDWARD				43	IRELAND	WM	IRISH	SHOEMAKER	082	C	1	3
THOMPSON	EDWARD				37	0	CP	ENGLISH	FARMER	085	E		28
THOMPSON	FRANK		1		20	0	PS	IRISH	SHOEMAKER	082	E		43
THOMPSON	GEORGE		2		65	SCOTLAND	CS		MINISTER	081	I		D
THOMPSON	GEORGE				28	ONTARIO	IM	ENGLISH	FARMER	082	B		47
THOMPSON	GEORGE				31	0	CP	IRISH	F	082	C	2	8
THOMPSON	GEORGE				50	IRELAND	CE	IRISH	F	082	G		66
THOMPSON	GEORGE				42	0	CE	ENGLISH	F	085	F		2
THOMPSON	HENRY		1		22	US	BA	ENGLISH	BUSHMAN	084	E		3
THOMPSON	JACOB				40	0	CE	INDIAN	HUNTER	089	B		42
THOMPSON	JAMES				23	ONT	CE	IRISH	BLACKSMITH	082	G		55
THOMPSON	JAMES				50	SCOTLAND	CP	SCOTCH	FARMER	082	I		37
THOMPSON	JAMES	C			28	0	CP	IRISH	LUMBER MERCHANT	082	G		53
THOMPSON	JANNET		1	1	23	0	PS	SCOTTISH		082	E		38
THOMPSON	JN'E				28	0	CP	SCOTCH	MERCHANT	081	B		71
THOMPSON	JOHN				42	SCOTLAND	RP	SCOTCH	F	081	E		20
THOMPSON	JOHN		1		68	SCOTLAND	CS	SCOTCH	LAB	082	A		5
THOMPSON	JOHN				27	ONTARIO	WM	IRISH	F	082	A		19
THOMPSON	JOHN				30	0	CP	IRISH	F	082	C	2	31
THOMPSON	JOHN				33	IRELAND	CE	IRISH	F	085	C		26
THOMPSON	JOHN				39	ENGLAND	PM	ENGLISH	F	085	D		2
THOMPSON	JOHN				49	SCOTLAND	PS	SCOTCH	F	085	H		3
THOMPSON	JOHN		1		19	0	CP	SCOTCH	FARM LABOURER	085	H		21
THOMPSON	JOHN		1		38	SCOTLAND	CP	SCOTCH	LAB	090	D		7
THOMPSON	LAMT	R			23	IRELAND	CE	IRISH	F	085	A		13
THOMPSON	MARK				35	ONTARIO	PM	ENGLISH	FARMER	082	B		60
THOMPSON	MARK		1		28	0	CE	IRISH	SADDLER	082	E		58
THOMPSON	MARY			1	55	IRELAND	CE	IRISH	F	082	G		75
THOMPSON	PHILIP				67	ONTARIO	CE	ENGLISH	FARMER	082	B		46
THOMPSON	ROBERT				25	SCOTLAND	CP	SCOTTISH	CARPENTER	082	B		56
THOMPSON	ROBERT				42	0	WM	IRISH		082	C	2	29
THOMPSON	SARAH		1	1	65	SCOTLAND	CS	SCOTCH		081	I		16
THOMPSON	W	H			29	0	CP	SCOTCH		081	B		71
THOMPSON	WILLIAM				32	0	OP	SCOTCH	F	081	E		19
THOMPSON	WILLIAM				27	ONT	RC	IRISH	FARMER	082	I		33
THOMPSON	WILLIAM	H			32	0	PS	IRISH	FARMER	082	D		30
THOMPSON	WILLIAM	STALLARD	1		60	ENGLAND	CE	ENGLISH	TEACHER	081	K		9
THOMPSON	WM				42	IRELAND	CP	IRISH	F	082	C	1	3
THOMSON	ALEXANDER				35	0	CP	SCOTCH	LAB	081	B		40
THOMSON	ALEXANDER				32	SCOTLAND	CS	SCOTCH	F	081	H	2	11
THOMSON	ESTHER	E	2	1		0	CS			081	H	2	D
THOMSON	GEORGE				35	SCOTLAND	CS	SCOTCH	F	081	H	2	11
THOMSON	JOHN				58	QUE	CP	SCOTCH	WHARFINGER	081	B		71
THOMSON	JOHN				37	U S	EM	ENGLISH	F	081	H	2	26
THOMSON	JOHN				40	0	CP	SCOTCH	F	086	A	2	13
THOMSON	ROBERT				25	0	CP	SCOTCH	FOREMAN FOR HOTCHKIS	085	F		5
THOMSON	WILLIAM				25	0	WM	IRISH	F	086	A	2	9
THORBORN	ELIZABETH		1	1	19	QUEBEC	PS	ENGLISH		090	B		1
THORNTON	DAVID				38	SCOTLAND	CS	SCOTCH	LUMBERMAN	083	A	2	1
THORNTON	RICHARD				35	ENGLAND	WM	ENGLISH	F	085	L		10

SURNAME	NAME1	NAME2	STRAY	SEX	AGE	BIRTHPL	RELIGION	ORIGIN	OCCUP	DIST	SUB_DIST	DIV	PAGE
THRALEY	JOHN				58	GERMANY	LU	GERMAN	F	082	G		93
THRASHER	ABRAHAM				36	O	WM	ENGLISH	F	082	C	2	44
THRASHER	GEORGE				49	O	WM	ENGLISH	F	082	C	2	44
THRASHER	HIRAM				34	O	WM	ENGLISH	F	082	C	2	42
THRASHER	MARY	JANE	2	1	9	O	WM			082	C	2	D
THRASHER	PHILAMON				48	O	WM	ENGLISH	F	082	C	2	44
THROWER	WILLIAM				26	O	CE	ENGLISH	F	085	K	2	5
THUN	MATILDA		1	1	15	QUE	RC	ENGLISH		082	K	1	4
THURE	WILLIAM				41	PRUSSIA	LU	GERMAN	F	082	G		17
THUROW	CHARLES				35	GERMANY	WM	GERMAN	FARMER	082	I		56
TIBBETT	WILLIAM				38	ENGLAND	WM	ENGLISH	PAINTER	085	D		11
TIERNEY	CHRISTOPHER				45	IRELAND	RC	IRISH	RAILWAY EMPLOYEE	081	B		9
TIERNEY	DENIS				33	ONTARIO	RC	IRISH	LABOURER	082	B		6
TIERNEY	JAMES		1		24	ONT	RC	IRISH	LUMBERER	081	C		53
TIERNEY	JAMES				39	ONTARIO	RC	IRISH	F	082	A		33
TIERNEY	JESSIE	ELIZABETH	2	1	1	O	RC			081	B		D
TIERNEY	JOHN				33	O	RC	IRISH	MERCHANT	081	B		18
TIERNEY	JOHN				34	IRELAND	RC	IRISH	LABOURER	081	B		33
TIERNEY	MARY	ANNE		1	9	QUEBEC	RC	IRISH		084	A		1
TIERNEY	W	P			21	O	WM	IRISH	CLERK	081	B		84
TILLEY	ARTHUR				39	O	CP	SCOTCH	DEALER IN FURNITURE	081	B		13
TIMMANS	ROBERT				37	ONT	CP	IRISH	F	081	J	1	59
TIMMINS	NOAH				43	QUEBEC	RC	ENGLISH	MERCHANT & HOTEL KEE	084	C		4
TIMMON	JOSEPH				59	QUE	RC	FRENCH	CASTER	081	B		42
TIMSON	ANGEL		1	1	10	QUE	RC	ENGLISH		084	I	2	1
TINDISHAGARDE	JOSEPH					ONTARIO	RC	INDIAN	LABOURER H B CO	090	E		10
TINGA	CAROLINE			1	55	GERMANY	LU	GERMAN		082	G		87
TINGEY	AUGUST		1		21	GERMANY	LU	GERMAN	LABOURER	082	D		18
TITCHNER	JOHN				62	ENGLAND	CE	ENGLISH	F	085	D		1
TOBEY	MARY		1	1	25	O	RC	IRISH	DOMESTIC	082	E		9
TOBIN	JOSEPH				55	IRELAND	RC	IRISH	FARMER	085	E		32
TOBIN	MARY		1	1	30	O	RC	IRISH	SERVANT	081	B		49
TOMBEAU	LOUIS		1		60	QUE	RC	FRENCH	LABOURER	082	E		18
TOMLIN	JOHN	HENRY			31	ENGLAND	WM	ENGLISH	STRAW HAT MANUFACTUR	085	I		1
TOMLIN	LOUISA		2	1		O	WM			085	I		D
TOMLINSON	MARY			1	60	IRELAND	CE	IRISH	F	081	K		12
TOMPKINS	MYRON				54	UNITED STATES	CO	ENGLISH	PHYSICIAN	090	D		3
TOMRAS	WILLIAM				30	GERMANY	CE	GERMAN	LAB	081	B		58
TONER	ANN		1	1	15	MONTREAL	CE	IRISH	NURSE	082	G		58
TONGUE	SAML		1		15	O	CE	ENGLISH	APPRENTICE	082	E		55
TONGYER	THOS		1		38	QUE	RC	FRENCH	TINSMITH	082	E		47
TONOR	WILLIAM				40	IRELAND	RC	IRISH	F	082	A		78
TOOHEY	ANTHONY				70	IRELAND	RC	IRISH	F	081	K		16
TOOKEY	JAMES				47	ENGLAND	CP	ENGLISH	F	085	I		26
TOOKEY	SARAH	LEVINA	2		1	O	CP			085	I		D
TOOLAN	MARGRET		1	1	17	QUE	RC	IRISH		081	B		17
TOOTCHISH	JANE		2	1		ONT	RC			090	B		D
TORRANS	WILLIAM				38	SCOTLAND	CP	SCOTCH	F	085	F		2
TOSH	JANE		1	1	18	O	CP	SCOTCH		082	C	2	14
TOSHEK	ELIZABETH			1	23	O	WM	IRISH	MILLINER	081	B		69
TOUGH	JOHN				60	SCOTLAND	CS	SCOTCH	CARPENTER			1	75
TOULOUSE	CHARLES				43	O	RC	INDIAN	F & FISHERMAN	087	A		9
TOULOUSE	JEAN	BTE			56	O	RC	INDIAN	F & FISHERMAN	087	A		4
TOULOUSE	MICHEL				47	O	RC	INDIAN	F & FISHERMAN	087	A		8
TOURANGEAU	JOSEPHIN		1	1	27	QUE	RC	FRENCH		081	B		18
TOURANGEAU	PRISCILA		1	1	33	QUE	RC	FRENCH	HOUSEKEEPER	082	D		19
TOUSANTT	JOHN				63	QUE	CE	ITALIAN	FARMER	082	I		40
TOWELL	MARY		1	1	5	IRELAND	CE	IRISH	SERVANT	081	A	2	29
TOWERS	THOMAS	A P			28	SCOTLAND	CE	SCOTCH		089	B		6
TOWNING	CHARLES				36	IRELAND	WM	IRISH	F	086	A	2	1
TOWNSEND	DAVID		1		18	SCOTLAND	WM	SCOTCH	SERVANT	081	B		60
TOWNSON	FREDRICK				39	ENGLAND	CE	ENGLISH	CARPENTER & F	082	F		13
TOY	FREDERICK				43	ENGLAND	WM	ENGLISH	F	085	H		4
TOY	THOMAS				42	O	RC	IRISH	BLACKSMITH	081	B		50
TOZA	JOSEPH		1		38	QUEBEC	RC	FRENCH	RAFTSMAN	084	D		1
TRACEY	PATRICK		1		23	O	RC	IRISH	SERVANT	082	E		48
TRACEY	ZACHARY				30	U STATES	RP	IRISH	LUMBERMAN	082	H		36
TRACY	JOHN				24	IRELAND	RC	IRISH	LUMBERMAN	083	C		1
TRACY	JOSEPH				29	ENGLAND	CE	ENGLISH	F	085	F		1
TRACY	MARGRET		1	1	18	O	RC	IRISH	SEAMSTRESS	082	E		2
TRAINER	ALEX	B			48	QUE	NG	IRISH	F	085	K	2	4
TRANCHE	MRS		1	1	68	O	RC	INDIAN		088	A		6
TRANSWA	CATHERINE			1		O	RC			088	H		D
TRANSWA	MICHAEL				22	O	RC	INDIAN	HUNTER AND FISHERMAN	082	H		28
TRASHER	MARY	ANN	1	1	30	CANADA	WM	IRISH	DOMESTIC	082	E		9
TRAVERS	ELIZABETH		1	1	22	QUE	RC	IRISH		081	C		4
TREACY	JAMES				23	IRELAND	RC	IRISH	LUMBERMAN	083	A	1	8
TREDO	HARRY		1		6	O	RC	FRENCH		089	A		62
TREDO	JOHN		1		10	O	RC	FRENCH		089	A		62
TREDO	JOSEPHINE		1	1	12	O	RC	FRENCH		089	A		62
TREDO	JULIA		1	1	13	O	RC	FRENCH		089	A		62
TREDO	MARY		1	1	10	QUE	RC	FRENCH		081	A	2	46
TREDOE	JOSEPH				50	O	RC	FRENCH	LUMBERMAN	086	C	1	5
TREDREA	WILLIAM				45	ENGLAND	WM	ENGLISH	MINER	089	A		6
TREGENZA	JOHN				27	ENGLAND	PM	ENGLISH	MINER	089	A		19
TREGENZA	THOMAS				50	ENGLAND	WM	ENGLISH	ENGINEER	089	A		15
TRELLA	MAXIAM		1		22	QUE	RC	FRENCH	LUMBERMAN	088	B		17
TRELOAR	THOMAS				66	ENGLAND	CE	ENGLISH	MINER	089	A		9
TRELOAR	THOMAS				41	ENGLAND	WM	ENGLISH	MINER	089	A		10
TREMBLAY	JEAN	B	1		27	QUE	RC	FRENCH	SHOE MAKER & CARPENT	089	B		32
TREMBRETH	THOMAS				31	ENGLAND	PM	ENGLISH	MINER	089	A		7
TREMELLING	WILLIAM				33	ENGLAND	CE	ENGLISH	MINER	089	A		32
TRENHAM	N	J			30	UNITED STATES	PS	ENGLISH	PHOTOGRAPHER & PAINT	081	B		72
TRETHEWAY	EMILY	R	2	1	14	O	PM			085	H		D
TRETHEWAY	JAMES				38	ENGLAND	PM	ENGLISH	MILLER	085	H		19
TRETHEWAY	PAUL				40	ENGLAND	WM	ENGLISH	F	085	H		20
TRETHEWAY	SAMUEL				44	ENGLAND	WM	ENGLISH	F	085	H		20
TRETHEWEY	THOMAS				30	ENGLAND	WM	ENGLISH	SEAMAN	089	A		2
TREVAIL	ANN		1	1	10	O	WM	ENGLISH		089	A		25
TREVILLIAN	JOHN				46	ENGLAND	WM	ENGLISH	MINER	089	A		13
TREVIN	HUGH				23	IRELAND	CE	IRISH	F	086	B		5
TREWBINSKEY	POWEL				58	PRUSSIA	RC	PRUSSIAN	FARMER	083	A	1	7
TRICKEY	BAPTIST				64	QUE	WM	GERMAN	F	082	K	1	7
TROTT	JOSHUA				83	ENGLAND	CE	ENGLISH		089	B		8
TROUT	W	A			35	O	CS	SCOTCH	MILLWRIGHT	088	C		10
TRUCET	ANDREW				21	ONTARIO	RC	FRENCH	HOTELKEEPER	083	F	1	1

SURNAME	NAME1	NAME2	STRAY	SEX	AGE	BIRTHPL	RELIGION	ORIGIN	OCCUP	DIST	SUB_DIST	DIV	PAGE
TRUCOTE	ISABEL			1	20	0	RC	ENGLISH		090	A		6
TRUDEAU	ANTOINE				25	0	RC	INDIAN	F & FISHERMAN	087	A		7
TRUDEAU	JOSEPH			1	50	0	RC	INDIAN	F & FISHERMAN	087	A		7
TRUDEAU	MARIE						NG		SEE TREDO MARY	081	A	2	46
TRUDEAUX	JOSEPHINE		1	1	6	0	RC	INDIAN	STUDENT	087	A		2
TRUSKO	MICHAEL				37	POLAND	RC	POLISH	FARMER	082	I		16
TUCK	JOHN				60	IRELAND	RC	IRISH	F	082	F		25
TUCK	JOHN				35	IRELAND	RC	IRISH	F	082	F		29
TUCKER	CHARLOTT			1	50	NEWFOUNDLAND	WM	ENGLISH	F	085	J		1
TUCKER	GEORGE	A			23	0	WM	GERMAN	F	082	C	1	26
TUCKER	GEORGE	R	2			0	WM			082	C	1	D
TUCKER	HUGH				40	0	RC	IRISH	F	082	H		4
TUCKER	JOSEPH				48	0	WM	IRISH	F	082	C	1	2
TUCKER	JOSEPH				36	ENGLAND	WM	ENGLISH	BLACKSMITH	089	A		18
TUCKER	RACHEL			1	56	QUE	WM	GERMAN		082	C	1	26
TUCKER	ROBERT		2		48	ENGLAND	WM		STORE KEEPER	085	J		D
TUCKER	SAMUEL				40	ENGLAND	WM	ENGLISH	MINISTER	086	A	1	25
TUCKER	SAMUEL		2		7		WM			086	A	1	D
TUCKER	WILLIAM				44	ENGLAND	CE	ENGLISH	CARPENTER FARMER	081	J	1	14
TUFFY	CATHERINE		2	1	1	0	RC			082	B		D
TUFFY	DANIEL				50	IRELAND	RC	IRISH	FARMER	082	B		19
TUFFY	JAMES		1		6	ONTARIO	CS	IRISH		082	A		50
TUFFY	PATRICK				63	ONTARIO	RC	IRISH	F	082	A		54
TULLOCK	GEORGE				55	SCOTLAND	PS	SCOTCH	MILL FOREMAN	086	C	1	3
TULLY	PHILIP				51	IRELAND	PS	IRISH	F	085	J		19
TULLY	WILLIAM				41	0	CE	IRISH	F	086	A	2	7
TUNN	JOHN				36	ENGLAND	CE	ENGLISH	FARMER	082	I		53
TURCOTT	EXAVIER	SR			54	QUE	RC	FRENCH	F	082	J		12
TURCOTTE	HECTOR				28	QUE	RC	FRENCH	LUMBERMAN	088	C		11
TURNBULL	ANDREW		1		30	SCOTLAND	CP	SCOTCH	F	085	H		14
TURNBULL	JOHN	JAMES	1		16	SCOTLAND	CP	SCOTTISH		082	I		66
TURNER	GEORGE				50	ENGLAND	CE	ENGLISH	F	085	J		7
TURNER	JOHN		1		17	0	CP	SCOTCH	SERVANT	081	A	2	36
TURNER	MATILDA			1	38	0	RC	SCOTCH		090	A		6
TURNER	NELSON		1		41	QUE	RC	ENGLISH	LAB	090	D		2
TURNER	ROBERT				49	QUE	CS	IRISH	LUMBERMAN	081	K		60
TURNER	THOMAS				37	ENGLAND	CE	ENGLISH	F	085	K	2	6
TURNER	WILLIAM				32	IRELAND	PS	IRISH	MERCHANT	089	B		9
TURPIEN	JULIEN	SR			34	QUE	RC	FRENCH	LAB	082	J		2
TURTUS	GEORGE				49	ENGLISH	CE	ENGLISH	MERCHANT	082	C	2	1
TUSHNER	JOHN		1		50	GERMANY	LU	GERMAN		082	G		92
TUSKO	JOHN				35	POLAND	RC	POLISH	FARMER	082	I		16
TWAKAKANA	ELIZABETH		2	1	2	0	RC			081	F		D
TYNE	ANNE		1	1	22	IRELAND	RC	IRISH		081	J	2	5
TYNE	NANCY		1	1	20	IRELAND	RC	IRISH		081	J	2	5
ULMAN	THOMAS				51	0	LU	DUTCH	F	086	A	1	15
UMPHRIES	JOHN				51	ONT	WM	IRISH	F	081	J	1	48
UPTON	WILLIAM				50	ENGLAND	CE	ENGLISH	F	085	A		25
URQUHART	JOHN		1		32	SCOTLAND	CP	SCOTCH	LAB	090	D		1
URRY	SAMUEL				38	ENGLAND	BA	ENGLISH	FARMER	085	E		29
URTA	GODFREY				27	QUE	RC	FRENCH	LUMBERMAN	081	K		62
VAIL	WILLAM		1		45	SCOTLAND	CS	SCOTCH	F	085	I		15
VALAQUETT	MAGHEONE		1		55	QUE	CB	FRENCH	TANNER CURRIER	082	E		46
VALDVIR	FREDRICK		1		50	QUE	RC	FRENCH	LABOURER	084	F		1
VALED	JOSEPH		1		22	QUE	RC	FRENCH	CARPENTER	081	I		39
VALINCENT	PAUL		1		20	QUEBEC	RC	FRENCH	LUMBERMAN	083	A	1	10
VALIQUET	ROBERT				57	QUE	RC	FRENCH	FARMER	081	D		11
VALIQUETTE	BAPTISTE				59	QUE	RC	FRENCH	F	081	K		19
VALLAR	JOHN		1		38	QUEBEC	RC	FRENCH	LAB	083	E		1
VALLEUR	PAUL		2		60	QUEBEC	RC		FARMER	083	A	1	D
VALLEY	ISADORE				66	QUE	RC	FRENCH	BLACKSMITH	081	B		26
VALLIEUR	PAUL				24	ONTARIO	RC	FRENCH	FARMER	083	A	2	1
VALLOIS	JOHN				42	0	RC	FRENCH	CARPENTER	082	E		42
VALUCK	JACOB				56	POLAND	RC	POLISH	LAB	081	I		42
VALYET	CASIMERE				56	QUEBEC	RC	FRENCH	F	081	J	1	15
VAN CAMP	GEORGE				46	0	WM	GERMAN	CABINET MAKER	086	A	1	2
VANCE	JOHN				46	IRELAND	CE	IRISH	F	081	H	2	34
VANDEWATER	HENREY		1		18	USA	WM	ENGLISH	PAINTER & F	085	L		9
VANDUSEN	BENJAMIN				44	0	WM	DUTCH	F	081	A	2	34
VANDUSEN	PETER				45	0	CP	DUTCH	F	081	A	2	36
VANEA	BAPTISTE				32	QUE	RC	FRENCH	LAB	081	K		73
VANKOUGHNETT	BENJ				62	0	WM	DUTCH	F	086	A	1	11
VANKOUGHNETT	GEORGE				25	0	WM	DUTCH	F	086	A	1	12
VANKOUGHNETT	JOHN				42	0	WM	DUTCH	F	086	A	1	11
VARNER	JANE		2	1	2	0	RC			090	F		D
VARNER	JOSEPH				30	0	RC	FRENCH	LAB	090	F		14
VARNEY	JOHN				60	ENGLAND	IM	ENGLISH	F	081	K		23
VARNIE	DAVID		1		11	0	RC	FRENCH		081	E		17
VARREL	WILLIAM				24	US	ME	ENGLISH	F	090	F		22
VARTY	WILLIAM		1		22	0	CE	ENGLISH	LAB	085	F		5
VASOE	LASORE				22	0	RC	FRENCH	F	081	E		21
VASSAIR	J		1		18	QUE	RC	FRENCH	LABOURER	088	A		7
VASSAIR	JOHN				31	0	RC	FRENCH	LUMBERMAN	088	B		1
VASSEUR	CHARLES				40	0	RC	FRENCH	CARPENTER	089	A		52
VASSEUR	LEZETTE			1	21	0	RC	FRENCH		089	A		63
VAUDERY	VETOL				35	0	RC	FRENCH	F	082	F		29
VAUDREVILLE	PAUL						NG		SEE VOUDREY	082	F		28
VAUDREVILLE	VITAL						NG		SEE VAUDERY	082	F		29
VAUGHAN	WILLIAM		1		28	ENGLAND	WM	ENGLISH	TAILOR	089	A		24
VENT	FREDERICK				43	GERMANY	BA	GERMAN	F	081	A	2	44
VENTLAND	LUDWAY				33	GERMANY	LU	GERMAN	F	082	G		14
VERMET	JOHN				28	QUE	RC	FRENCH	LAB	081	B		20
VICARY	GEORGE				30	ENGLAND	CE	ENGLISH	CARPENTER	089	A		30
VICARY	WALTER				34	ENGLAND	CE	ENGLISH	MINE LABOURER	089	A		30
VIEBECK	JANE			1	92	0	RC	INDIAN		089	A		52
VIGARS	JOHN				50	ENGLAND	WM	ENGLISH	HOTEL KEEPER	089	A		14
VIGARS	WILLIAM				29	ENGLAND	WM	ENGLISH	MASON	089	A		9
VILLA	PETER		1		19	0	RC	IRISH	LAB	085	F		5
VILOVILLE	LOSIRE				25	QUE	RC	FRENCH	LUMBERMAN	088	C		11
VINCENT			1	1	28	QUE	RC	FRENCH	NUN	084	I		1
VINCENT	JAMES				29	MANITOBA	EP	ENGLISH	CLERK	084	G	1	1
VINCER	WILLIAM		1		17	CANADA	PS	SCOTCH	LAB	087	B	2	3
VINEBERG	HIRAM				16	POLAND	JU	POLISH	MERCHANT	082	A		1
VIRGIN	ABIGAL			1	59	QUE	WM	ENGLISH	WEAVER	081	D		4
VIRGIN	EDWIN		2		14	ONT	WM			081	C		D
VIRGIN	WILLIAM				37	QUEBEC	WM	AMERICAN	F	081	C		47

SURNAME	NAME1	NAME2	STRAY	SEX	AGE	BIRTHPL	RELIGION	ORIGIN	OCCUP	DIST	SUB_DIST	DIV	PAGE
VIRTUE	WILLIAM				23	O	WM	IRISH	CARPENTER	082	C	2	14
VISENAN	ELIE				60	QUE	RC	FRENCH	F	082	C	1	8
VISENAU	JOHN				27	O	RC	FRENCH	F	082	C	1	10
VISSER	HERMAN		1		17	IRELAND	CE	GERMAN	SADDLER	082	E		58
VITZEL	JOHN				37	GERMANY	LU	GERMAN	F	082	G		18
VIVIAN	HENRY				51	ENGLAND	WM	ENGLISH	MINER	089	A		17
VIVIAN	JOHN				43	ENGLAND	WM	ENGLISH	ENGINEER	089	A		35
VIZENIA	JOHN				65	O	RC	FRENCH	CANOE BUILDER	090	F		9
VODEREY	MALQUARY		1		40	QUE	RC	FRENCH	CARPENTER	084	G	1	1
VOLK	PHILIP				33	GERMANY	LU	GERMAN	F	085	C		14
VONDETTE	BAPTISTE				78	QUE	RC	FRENCH	F	081	K		26
VONDETTE	BAPTISTE				45	QUE	RC	FRENCH	F	081	K		39
VORAH	JOSEPH				61	QUE	RC	FRENCH	F	081	E		12
VOSHES	ELIZA		1	1	50	IRELAND	JM	IRISH		082	C	2	16
VOUDREY	EXERES				35	O	RC	FRENCH	F	082	F		27
VOUDREY	PAUL				34	O	RC	FRENCH	F	082	F		28
VRITIER	JOHN		1		24	QUEBEC	RC	FRENCH	LAB	083	C		5
VSELGAG	VELENTIN				47	POLAND	RC	POLISH	LAB	081	I		38
WABANOSE	JEAN	BTE			30	O	RC	INDIAN	F & FISHERMAN	087	A		29
WABANOSSE	ONISIME				52	US	RC	INDIAN	F & FISHERMAN	087	A		11
WABB	ANDREW		1		22	O	CS	SCOTCH	LABOURER	088	A		8
WABICOOSE	MECHER				18	ONTARIO	RC	INDIAN	HUNTER	084	A		4
WABIKEKEKE	HENRY				67	US	RC	INDIAN	F	087	A		32
WABIKIJIG	MICHEL				57	US	RC	INDIAN	F	087	A		34
WABOOSE	BAPTISTE				60	O	WM	INDIAN	CHIEF	090	A		1
WABOOSE	EDWARD				35	O	WM	INDIAN	PAINTER	090	A		1
WADDELL	SARAH		1		36	ONT	CE	IRISH		081	C		45
WADDLE	ROBERT				50	IRELAND	PS	IRISH	F	086	A	1	1
WADINGTON	WILLIAM				22	ENGLAND	CE	ENGLISH	FOREMAN	081	G	1	33
WAFAMONKC	HANNAH		2	1	3	O	WM	INDIAN		086	C	2	D
WAGAMINAN	(WIDOW)			1		ONTARIO	PA	INDIAN	HUNTER & TRAPPER	090	E		5
WAGAMVULA	ISAAC				55	O	PA	INDIAN	HUNTER	086	C	2	3
WAGGUAMESHY	JOSESP				80	O	WM	INDIAN	TRAPPER	086	A	3	4
WAGNAR	CHARLES				35	GERMANY	LU	GERMAN	FARMER	082	I		24
WAGNER	JOHN		2		30	ENGLAND	CE		LABOURER	089	A		D
WAGNOR	WILLIAM				27	GERMANY	LU	GERMAN	FARMER	082	I		47
WAGONOSH	PETER				50	O	RC	INDIAN	HUNTER	086	C	2	1
WAGOSH	J	BTE			48	US	RC	INDIAN	F & FISHERMAN	087	A		10
WAHBAHKAZAIE	ANNE				35	O	ME	INDIAN	HUNTER & TRAPPER	090	B		4
WAHBEKEZHIK	MICHELLE				50	US	RC	INDIAN	LAB & BOAT BUILDER	087	C		4
WAHBEMIN	MDM			1		O	RC	INDIAN		090	C		11
WAHBONGGAI	JOSEPH				32	O	RC	INDIAN	F & LABOURER	087	B	1	7
WAHBONGGAI	LOUIS				47	USA	RC	INDIAN	F & FISHERMAN	087	B	1	4
WAHCOWSAI	FRANCIS				26	O	RC	INDIAN	F & FISHERMAN	087	C		7
WAHCOWSAI	PIERRE				55	US	RC	INDIAN	F	087	C		5
WAHEGIJY	FRANCOIS				37	US	RC	INDIAN	F & FISHERMAN	087	A		3
WAHSAIKEZHIK	PAUL				45	US	RC	INDIAN	F	087	B	1	10
WAHSAISHKUNG	JNO				27	O	CE	INDIAN	HUNTER	087	B	1	19
WAHTAHKAYAIE	JANE		2	1	6	ONT	RC			090	B		D
WAHTAHKAYAIE	THOMAS		2		9	ONT	RC			090	B		D
WAIT	ELIZABETH		1	1	15	O	CP	IRISH		081	B		81
WAIT	JOHN	T			36	UNITED STATES	CN	ENGLISH	DRUGGIST	081	B		13
WAJATAPP	LOUIS		1		20	O	RC	INDIAN	LAB	090	F		26
WAKEFIELD	ROSETTA				38	IRELAND	WM	IRISH		086	A	1	33
WAKEGIJY	ALEXANDER				41	US	RC	INDIAN	F	087	A		2
WAKEGIJY	LOUIS				64	US	RC	INDIAN	F	087	A		2
WALFORD	ESTER		2	1	32	ENGLAND	IN			081	I		D
WALFORD	STIREN				59	ENGLAND	IH	ENGLISH	DRUGGIST	081	I		5
WALKER	ANN			1	28	O	PS	ENGLISH	F	086	A	1	14
WALKER	GEORGE		1		34	ENGLAND	CE	ENGLISH	BAR KEEPER	085	B		7
WALKER	GEORGE				17	O	PS	ENGLISH	SERVANT	085	J		26
WALKER	JAMES				26	ONTARIO	RP	SCOTTISH	CARPENTER	082	B		5
WALKER	JOHN				26	QUE	CE	IRISH	Q BANK MANAGER	082	E		25
WALKER	JOHN				57	IRELAND	CP	IRISH	F	085	F		2
WALKER	WILLIAM				44	SCOTLAND	EP	SCOTCH	F	081	J	1	32
WALL	JAMES				31	ONTARIO	CE	IRISH	FARMER	082	B		31
WALL	JOSEPH				30	IRELAND	CE	IRISH	F	082	A		66
WALLACE	BETSAY			1	80	IRELAND	CP	IRISH		081	A	2	21
WALLACE	FRED		1		18	O	CE	ENGLISH	LAB	081	B		85
WALLACE	HENRY		1		25	O	CE	ENGLISH	LAB	081	B		85
WALLACE	JAMES				32	SCOTLAND	CP	SCOTCH	F	081	C		27
WALLACE	JAMES				48	IRELAND	CP	IRISH	FARMER	082	I		29
WALLACE	JAMES				41	SCOTLAND	CP	SCOTCH	F	086	A	2	10
WALLACE	JOHN				74	IRELAND	CS	IRISH	F	081	A	1	33
WALLACE	JOHN				59	SCOTLAND	CP	SCOTCH	F	081	C		28
WALLACE	JOHN		2		12	ONT	CP			081	C		D
WALLACE	JOHN		1		21	O	PS	SCOTTISH	PLASTERER	082	E		33
WALLACE	THOMAS				30	ONTARIO	CE	IRISH	F	082	A		76
WALLACE	WILLIAM				45	O	WM	IRISH	F	081	A	2	33
WALLACE	WILLIAM				69	IRELAND	CE	IRISH	F	082	A		76
WALLAS	THOMAS				30	IRELAND	CE	IRISH	F	082	F		10
WALLIS	JOHN		1		25	O	ME	SCOTCH	LUMBERMAN	086	C	1	11
WALLS	JOHN				60	IRELAND	CE	IRISH	F	081	H	1	14
WALSH	ANN		1	1	14	ONTARIO	RC	IRISH		082	B		4
WALSH	JAMES		1		31	IRELAND	RC	IRISH		081	K		20
WALSH	JAMES				27	ONTARIO	RC	IRISH	FARMER	082	B		16
WALSH	JAMES				32	IRELAND	RC	IRISH	FARMER	082	B		59
WALSH	JOHN				63	IRELAND	RC	IRISH	FARMER	081	F		26
WALSH	MARTIN				28	IRELAND	RC	IRISH	FARMER	082	F		25
WALSH	MICHAEL		1		25	IRELAND	RC	IRISH	LABOURER	083	A	1	12
WALSH	MICHL		1		16	O	RC	IRISH	SADDLER	082	E		41
WALSH	PATRICK				40	IRELAND	RC	IRISH	FARMER	082	B		13
WALSH	PATRICK				60	IRELAND	RC	IRISH	F	082	H		36
WALTER	CARL				39	GERMANY	LU	GERMAN	CARPENTER	081	F		29
WALTON	BRINELAY	M			36	ENGLAND	FK	ENGLISH	PHYSICIAN	082	C	1	5
WALTON	THOS	SMITH			33	ENGLAND	CE	ENGLISH	SURGEON	085	D		34
WAMITOGINES	JOHN		1		40	RED RIVER	RC	INDIAN	HUNTER	090	F		13
WAPQUNAQUA	SUSAN		1	1	14	O	RC	INDIAN		081	F		25
WARBRICK	JOHN				46	SCOTLAND	EM	SCOTCH	F	082	A		17
WARBRICK	JOHN		1		75	ONTARIO	CE	ENGLISH	F	082	A		19
WARBUCK	GEORGE		2		1	ONTARIO	EM			082	A		D
WARD	ALFRED		2			O	CP			081	A	2	D
WARD	BERNARD		1		11	SCOTLAND	RP	SCOTCH		082	K	1	3
WARD	CATHERIN		1	1	14	SCOTLAND	RP	SCOTCH		082	K	1	3
WARD	EDWARD				55	IRELAND	RC	IRISH	F	081	J	1	75
WARD	GEORGE		1		17	SCOTLAND	RP	SCOTCH	F	082	K	1	3

SURNAME	NAME1	NAME2	STRAY	SEX	AGE	BIRTHPL	RELIGION	ORIGIN	OCCUP	DIST	SUB_DIST	DIV	PAGE
WARD	JAMES				34	O	CS	SCOTCH	TINSMITH	081	I		6
WARD	JOHN				42	IRELAND	RC	IRISH	F	082	C	1	63
WARD	JOHN				59	ENGLAND	WM	ENGLISH	MINER	089	A		21
WARD	MATILDA		1	1	25	O	RC	IRISH		082	C	1	53
WARD	PETER		1		15	SCOTLAND	RP	SCOTCH		082	K	1	3
WARD	PETER		1		27	NOVA SCOTIA	RC	IRISH	LABOURER	090	B		1
WARD	SUSAN		2	1	26	IRELAND	RC			082	C	1	D
WARD	W	SHERMAN			39	US	CP	ENGLISH	PHYSICIAN	081	A	2	62
WARDELL	JOSEPH				44	ENGLAND	ME	ENGLISH	F	085	A		10
WARDELL	TIMOTHY				28	O	DI	GERMAN	F	085	I		26
WARDLE	WILLIAM				28	ENGLAND	CE	ENGLISH	FARMER	086	B		8
WARK	GEORGE				38	IRELAND	PR	IRISH	FARMER	081	G	2	5
WARK	JAMES				54	IRELAND	CE	IRISH	F	082	A		6
WARK	JOHN				60	IRELAND	CS	SCOTCH	F	082	A		3
WARK	MARY	ANN	1	1	34	IRELAND	EM	IRISH	SCHOOL TEACHER	082	A		65
WARK	MYRA			1	56	I	CP	IRISH		081	I		42
WARMDORF	ANNA		1	1		GERMANY	LU	IRISH		082	I		4
WARMDORF	FREDRICK				23	GERMANY	LU	GERMAN	FARMER	082	I		4
WARMDORF	LOUISA		1	1	23	GERMANY	LU	GERMAN		082	I		4
WARNER	EBENEZER				61	US	RC	ENGLISH	CLERK	090	F		15
WARNER	ROBERT				32	O	NG	ENGLISH	F	085	I		18
WARNOCK	ALFRED	T			50	O	CE	ENGLISH	F	082	C	1	15
WARNOCK	JAMES		1		28	QUE	CP	IRISH	ACCOUNTANT	090	F		22
WARNOCK	JOHN				45	IRELAND	RC	IRISH	INNKEEPER	081	H	2	22
WARNOCK	PATRICK				27	ONTARIO	RC	IRISH	FARMER	082	A		28
WARRELL	ESSEX				38	QUE	WM	ENGLISH	LUMBERER	082	D		28
WARREN	BISHOP	D	1		30	QUE	WM	IRISH	CLERK	082	E		9
WARREN	FLETCHER		1		25	QUE	WM	IRISH	STORECLERK	082	E		2
WARREN	FRANES		1	1	15	O	WM	ENGLISH	F	082	C	2	31
WARREN	GEORGE				25	ONT	CE	IRISH	F	081	J	1	77
WARREN	H		1		22	ENGLAND	WM	ENGLISH	LABOURER	088	A		7
WARREN	JAMES				27	O	CE	ENGLISH	F	085	H		9
WARREN	JEFSIC				66	QUE	CE	IRISH	F	081	C		31
WARREN	JOSEPH				45	O	CE	IRISH	FARMER & SCHOOL TEAC	082	G		40
WARREN	RICHARD				30	O	CE	ENGLISH	F	085	H		10
WARREN	ROBERT		1		21	O	CE	IRISH	TINSMITH	081	B		19
WARREN	THOMAS				68	IRELAND	CE	IRISH	F	082	G		44
WARRILLS	ELIAS				30	O	CP	IRISH	LAB	081	B		85
WARROCK	FRANCIS		1		20	ENGLAND	WM	ENGLISH	LABOURER	082	E		61
WARUN	WILLIAM				26	QUE	WM	ENGLISH	HARNESSMAKER	082	C	1	3
WASAWNEGUA	MARY			1	60	O	WM	INDIAN		086	A	3	4
WASEKEGEG	JOSEPH				38	US	RC	INDIAN	F & FISHERMAN	087	A		5
WASEKEGIG	EDOUARD				62	US	RC	INDIAN	FISHERMAN	087	A		4
WASEKEGIG	LOUIS				42	US	RC	INDIAN	F & BLACKSMITH	087	A		4
WASHINTON	GEORGE		1		20	O	NG	INDIAN		085	E		19
WASMONT	CHRISTIAN		1		68	GERMANY	LU	GERMAN		082	G		19
WASMONT	MARY		1	1	50	GERMANY	LU	GERMAN		082	G		19
WASMUND	THEYODORE				33	GERMANY	WM	GERMAN	F	082	H		9
WASSANAKIGABAN	(WIDOW)			1		ONTARIO	PA	INDIAN	HUNTER & TRAPPER	090	E		7
WASSIKINENSI	(WIDOW)			1		ONTARIO	RC	INDIAN	HUNTER & TRAPPER	090	E		9
WATAP	FRANCOIS				52	O	RC	FRENCH	LABOURER	089	B		30
WATAPP	LOUISAINE				45	O	RC	FRENCH	BOATMAN	089	B		43
WATERS	JAMES		1		22	O	RC	IRISH		086	B		1
WATKINS	HENRY				27	ENGLAND	CE	ENGLISH	F	086	A	2	6
WATKINSON	EBENESER				36	ENGLAND	BA	ENGLISH	FARMER	086	B		9
WATSON	BEATRICE	L	1	1	2	ENGLAND	CE	ENGLISH	ADOPTED	085	I		39
WATSON	DAVID				32	O	CP	IRISH	F	081	A	2	37
WATSON	GEORGE				45	SCOTLAND	CP	SCOTCH	F	081	K		12
WATSON	JAMES				61	SCOTLAND	CS	SCOTCH	WEAVER	081	C		21
WATSON	JAMES				27	SCOTLAND	CP	SCOTCH	MOULDER	085	I		21
WATSON	JOHN				45	INDIA	CE	ENGLISH	GENTLEMAN	081	G	1	28
WATSON	JOHN				19	US	WM	ENGLISH	SHANTYMAN	084	B		2
WATSON	JOHN				43	ENGLAND	CE	ENGLISH	ENGINEER	089	A		19
WATSON	MARTIN				22	ENGLAND	CE	ENGLISH	F	085	H		10
WATSON	PETER				40	ONT	WM	ENGLISH	FARMER	082	I		73
WATSON	RICHARD				30	IRELAND	CE	ENGLISH	F	082	F		38
WATSON	SANDERS				35	O	CE	ENGLISH	HOTELKEEPER	081	B		70
WATSON	SARAH			1	36	O	CP	IRISH	TAILORESS	081	B		58
WATT	FRED				37	US	PR	GERMAN	MILLWRIGHT	082	E		70
WATT	GEORGE				42	SCOTLAND	CS	SCOTCH	CLERK	090	F		19
WATT	ISABELLA		1	1	23	O	CE	SCOTCH	SEAMSTRESS	090	F		6
WATT	JAMES				35	O	BA	IRISH	CHAIRMAKER	081	I		5
WATT	JAMES				32	ONTARIO	CP	SCOTTISH	FARMER	082	B		62
WATT	JOHN				30	HUDSON'S BAY	CE	SCOTCH	LABORER	090	E		1
WATT	MALCOLM				24	ONT	CP	SCOTCH	LABOURER	081	J	1	38
WATT	MARY ANN			1	38	ONTARIO	RC	FRENCH		090	E		22
WATT	ROBERT				23	IRELAND	CP		LABOURER	090	A		3
WATT	ZACARIAH				34	US	ME	AFRICAN	F	086	A	1	16
WATTAKAIJIA	JOHN				35	O	RC	INDIAN	HUNTER	090	F		13
WATTAKAJIA	JOSEPH				25	RED RIVER	RC	INDIAN	LAB	090	F		13
WATTO	JOHN				60	GERMANY	LU	GERMAN	F	082	G		88
WATTS	THOMAS				39	O	PM	ENGLISH	F	085	J		4
WAUBINOZIH	ALEXANDER				25	O	CE	INDIAN		089	B		38
WAUGH	GEORGE				35	SCOTLAND	CP	SCOTCH	F	086	A	2	12
WAVER	MATILDA		1	1		O	CE	IRISH	SERVANT	082	G		75
WAYAGUAKESHIG	JAMES		2		2	O	WM	INDIAN		086	A	3	D
WEAVER	ISRAEL				42	ENGLAND	CE	ENGLISH	F	085	H		21
WEBBER	EDWARD				45	GERMANY	LU	GERMAN	F	081	K		55
WEBBER	JOHN				48	GERMANY	BA	GERMAN	FARMER	081	F		23
WEBBER	MATILDA		1		14	GERMANY	LU	GERMAN		081	K		59
WEBBER	WILLIAM		1		22	ENGLAND	CE	ENGLISH	FARMER	086	B		7
WEBER	CAROLIN		1	1	65	GERMANY	CE	GERMAN		081	G	1	34
WEBIKAMIGUD	JOSEPH				46	US	RC	INDIAN	F & COOPER	087	A		32
WEBSTER	JOHN				46	O	WM	IRISH	MINISTER	085	I		7
WEBSTER	THOS		1		24	O	CE	ENGLISH	STORECLERK	082	E		2
WEDGE	JOHN	OLIVER			29	O	WM	ENGLISH	F	085	I		19
WEEB	BENGAMIN	O			32	ENGLAND	CE	ENGLISH	LABOURER	081	D		14
WEEKWARK	JOHN				28	GERMANY	RC	GERMAN	F	082	G		21
WEINHOLDT	JOSEPH				30	GERMANY	LU	GERMAN	FARMER	082	I		52
WEIR	ANTHONY				65	SCOTLAND	FK	SCOTCH	F	081	J	1	35
WEIR	JANETT		1	1	37	SCOTLAND	CS	SCOTCH		081	H	2	13
WEIR	THOMAS				38	ENGLAND	CP	ENGLISH	F	085	K	2	9
WEIR	THOMAS		1		22	IRELAND	WM	IRISH	LUMBERMAN	086	B		2
WEISENBERGH	ELIZA		1		61	GERMANY	LU	GERMAN		082	I		63
WEISENBERGH	GOTTLLILP		1		71	GERMANY	LU	GERMAN	FARMER	082	I		63
WELDON	JOSEPH				51	QUE	WM	ENGLISH	F	082	C	2	15

SURNAME	NAME1	NAME2	STRAY	SEX	AGE	BIRTHPL	RELIGION	ORIGIN	OCCUP	DIST	SUB_DIST	DIV	PAGE
WELLETTE	JOSEPH				55	QUE	RC	FRENCH	FARM LAB	082	C	1	59
WELLS	JOHN				55	ENGLAND	CE	ENGLISH	F	085	I		21
WELSH	JAMES				34	IRELAND	CE	IRISH	F	082	F		6
WELSH	MICHAEL				35	IRELAND	RC	IRISH	FARMER	081	G	1	3
WELSH	ROBERT		1		38	IRELAND	RC	IRISH	LAB	090	D		6
WELSH	WILLIAM		1		48	IRELAND	RC	IRISH	LABOURER	082	D		20
WELTON	CHARLES				35	ENGLAND	CE	ENGLISH	BAKER	085	B		18
WEST	CHARLES				19	SCOTLAND	WM	SCOTCH	F	085	E		26
WEST	GEORGE				28	0	WM	ENGLISH	F	085	K	2	3
WEST	JOSEPH				56	ENGLAND	CE	ENGLISH	LABOURER	082	D		5
WEST	THOMAS				51	SCOTLAND	WM	SCOTCH	F	085	E		25
WESTCOTT	JOHN		1		16	ENGLAND	CE	ENGLISH	SERVANT	082	E		29
WESTCOTT	JOHN				44	ENGLAND	BA	ENGLISH	PAINTER	082	E		74
WESTCOTT	MARY	ANNE	2	1	2	ENGLAND	BA			082	E		D
WESTMILLER	HENRY				25	0	PS	GERMAN	F	085	H		11
WESTMILLER	HERMEN				56	GERMANY	ZZ	GERMAN	F	085	H		11
WESTOTT	EMA		1	1	14	ENGLAND	CE	ENGLISH	SERVANT	082	E		16
WETHOFFER	NICHOLAS				26	GERMANY	PS	GERMAN	F	085	H		12
WEVER	ANTHONY				63	PRUSSIA	PS	PRUSSIAN	F	081	J	1	15
WHALAN	MARGARET		1	1	35	IRELAND	RC	IRISH	SISTERS OF CHARITY	087	A		1
WHALEN	ANNIE		1	1	11	ONTARIO	RC	IRISH		082	B		21
WHALEN	JAMES				47	ONTARIO	RC	IRISH	INNKEEPER	081	G	1	4
WHALEN	JOHN				58	IRELAND	RC	IRISH	FARMER	082	B		22
WHALEN	JOHN				55	IRELAND	RC	IRISH	FARMER	082	B		29
WHALEN	JOHN				57	US	RC	IRISH	LABOURER	089	B		40
WHALEN	MARY		2	1	38	ONTARIO	RC			081	G	1	D
WHALEN	THOMAS				50	IRELAND	RC	IRISH	F	082	F		25
WHALEY	ISAAC				34	0	CE	IRISH	HARNESSMAKER	082	G		57
WHEALAN	STEPHEN				35	IRELAND	RC	IRISH	F	081	J	1	29
WHEELER	FRANK				43	ENGLAND	WM	ENGLISH	TAILOR	081	B		84
WHEELER	H	FRANCIS			40	ENGLISH	WM	ENGLISH	TAILOR	081	B		25
WHELAN	C	B			36	QUE	WM	IRISH	WATCHMAKER	082	E		34
WHELAN	DANIAL				45	IRELAND	RC	IRISH	FARMER	082	D		25
WHELAN	ELLEN		1	1	24	0	RC	IRISH	SERVANT	082	E		1
WHELAN	ELLEN		1	1	21	QUE	RC	IRISH	SERVANT	082	E		2
WHELAN	JAMES				30	IRELAND	RC	IRISH	F	081	J	1	12
WHELAN	JOHN				34	ONTARIO	RC	IRISH	FARMER	081	G	1	9
WHELAN	JOS	E			28	QUE	RC	FRENCH	FURRIER	082	E		40
WHELAN	MRS				28	ONT	RC	IRISH	F	081	J	1	16
WHELAN	PATRICK				45	IRELAND	RC	IRISH	F	081	J	1	64
WHELAN	PATRICK				42	IRELAND	RC	IRISH	F	082	A		85
WHELAN	THOMAS		1		20	IRELAND	RC	IRISH	F	082	A		80
WHELAN	THOS				73	IRELAND	RC	IRISH	F	081	J	1	12
WHELAN	THOS				45	IRELAND	RC	IRISH	F	081	J	1	13
WHILACHIN	MICHAEL				37	IRELAND	RC	IRISH	LABOURER	082	D		15
WHINGLE	NICHOLAS				45	IRELAND	RC	IRISH	FARMER	081	G	1	24
WHITE	ANDREW	T			33	0	CP	SCOTTISH	LUMBER MERCHANT	082	E		1
WHITE	ELIZA		1	1	21	STATE N YORK	RC	IRISH	TEACHER	082	D		21
WHITE	JACOB				51	QUE	RP	FRENCH	FARMER	082	I		1
WHITE	JAMES				33	0	RC	IRISH	GROCER	081	B		7
WHITE	JAMES				71	ENGLAND	CE	ENGLISH	F	082	C	2	23
WHITE	JAMES				66	IRELAND	CE	IRISH	F	085	B		3
WHITE	JAMES	B	1		24	CANADA	PS	SCOTCH	LUMBERER	087	B	2	3
WHITE	JOHN				40	ENGLAND	CE	ENGLISH	BAKER	081	B		54
WHITE	JOHNATHAN				26	0	BA	DUTCH	SHOEMAKER	086	A	1	15
WHITE	MARY	ANN	1	1	16	U STATES	RC	IRISH		082	G		68
WHITE	MORRIS		1		13	U STATES	RC	IRISH		082	G		68
WHITE	PETER	SENR			76	SCOTLAND	WM	SCOTTISH	GENTLEMAN	082	E		1
WHITE	RICHD				38	QUE	RC	IRISH	MERCHANT	082	E		25
WHITE	ROBERT	H			26	IRELAND	KB	IRISH	CARPENTER	085	I		2
WHITE	STEPHEN				23	0	RC	INDIAN	LAB	090	D		7
WHITE	THOMAS				38	0	CE	ENGLISH	F	082	C	2	30
WHITE	WILLIAM				59	SCOTLAND	RP	SCOTCH	FARMER	082	I		13
WHITE	WILLIAM				31	SCOTLAND	RP	SCOTCH	FARMER	082	I		13
WHITE	WM	R			28	0	CE	SCOTTISH	SOLICITOR	082	E		2
WHITE PARTRIDGE	THOMAS				37	0	RC	INDIAN	HUNTER	090	F		9
WHITEDUCK	EXAMIR				30	ONTARIO	RC	INDIAN	FARMER	081	G	2	7
WHITEDUCK	JOSEPH				25	0	RC	INDIAN	HUNTER AND FISHERMAN	082	H		28
WHITEDUCK	PETER				41	0	RC	INDIAN	HUNTER	081	A	2	59
WHITEHEAD	HARRY				33	0	CE	ENGLISH	F	085	B		15
WHITEMORE	HENERY				26	0	WM	IRISH	F	082	F		25
WHITESIDE	JOHN				50	IRELAND	WM	IRISH	F	085	A		14
WHITESIDE	RICHARD				26	IRELAND	PR	IRISH	F	085	A		15
WHITFIELD	WILLIAM				35	UNITED STATES	WM	ENGLISH	F	085	C		20
WHITLA	R	J	1		23	IRELAND	WM	IRISH	MERCHANT	081	B		13
WHITLEY	GEORGE		1		27	0	CE	ENGLISH		085	C		15
WHITLEY	MARGARET	E	2	1		0	CE			085	C		D
WHITNELL	CHARLES				48	ENGLAND	CE	ENGLISH	FARMER	089	A		47
WHYTE	ALEXANDER				30	SCOTLAND	CP	SCOTCH	F	081	C		24
WHYTE	ARCHIBALD				60	SCOTLAND	CP	SCOTCH	F	081	C		24
WHYTE	JAMES				44	0	CP	SCOTCH	WAGGONMAKER	081	B		81
WHYTE	JOHN				42	SCOTLAND	CP	SCOTTISH	MILLER	082	E		64
WHYTE	NEIL		1		30	SCOTLAND	CS	SCOTCH	CLERK	090	F		22
WHYTE	PARK		1	1	6	0	WM	ENGLISH		085	A		26
WHYTE	THOMAS				54	SCOTLAND	RP	SCOTCH	F	085	A		21
WIANKO	ADOLPHUS				33	PRUSSIA	LU	PRUSSIAN	F	085	A		19
WIANKO	W		1		22	PRUSSIA	LU	PRUSSIAN	F	085	A		17
WICKETT	JOHN				45	ENGLAND	WM	ENGLISH	MINER	089	A		12
WIDGE	PINAISIE				51	ONT	RC	INDIAN	HUNTER & TRAPPER	090	B		11
WIESSEBERG	FREDRICK				46	GERMANY	LU	GERMAN	FARMER	082	I		20
WIETTE	WALTER		1		72	US	PR	ENGLISH	SERVANT	082	G		44
WIGGAND	THOMAS				69	HUDSON BAY	CE	ENGLISH	F	090	F		23
WIGIMAH	JACOB				45	US	CE	INDIAN	LABOURER	089	B		42
WIGLSWORTH	HENRY				26	ENGLAND	CE	ENGLISH	F	082	C	2	65
WIGLSWORTH	JOHN		2		75	ENGLAND	CE		GENTLEMAN	082	C	2	D
WIGNEY	JOSEPH				56	ENGLAND	OB	ENGLISH	F	081	C		6
WILCOCKS	AMELIA		1	1	24	US	EM	ENGLISH		082	A		23
WILCOCKS	THOMAS				33	ENGLAND	CE	ENGLISH	F	085	C		16
WILCOX	GEORGE				50	IRELAND	CE	IRISH	F	082	G		10
WILCOX	GILBERT				67	UNITED STATES	WM	ENGLISH	F	082	C	2	4
WILCOX	MARY	ANN	1	1	90	IRELAND	CE	IRISH		082	G		66
WILCOX	WILLIAM				45	ENGLAND	CE	ENGLISH	F	086	A	1	12
WILDER	JOHN		1		20	0	WM	SCOTCH	HIRED MAN	086	A	1	15
WILEY	MARIA		1	1	16	0	CE	IRISH		089	A		
WILEY	MARIA		2	1	38	IRELAND	CP			090	F		D
WILEY	THOMAS				48	IRELAND	CP	IRISH	MARINER	090	F		25

SURNAME	NAME1	NAME2	STRAY	SEX	AGE	BIRTHPL	RELIGION	ORIGIN	OCCUP	DIST	SUB_DIST	DIV	PAGE
WILKEY	JAMES				37	SCOTLAND	CP	SCOTCH	F	082	C	1	51
WILKINSON	GEORGE				24	ENGLAND	CE	ENGLISH	F	086	A	1	32
WILKISON	T	GEORGE	1		21	ENGLISH	WM	ENGLISH	LABOURER	082	D		17
WILLET	ANDREW				25	QUE	CE	FRENCH	MILLWRIGHT	088	B		4
WILLET	PETER	ANDREW			74	QUE	WM	FRENCH	COOPER	088	B		1
WILLETT	ALFORD				26	QUE	RC	FRENCH	LABOURER	082	D		12
WILLIAM	JOHN		1		25	O	OP	SCOTCH	LAB	081	E		18
WILLIAMS	ALBERT				28	ENGLAND	CE	ENGLISH	F	085	E		5
WILLIAMS	EDWARD				70	IRELAND	CE	IRISH	F	082	A		40
WILLIAMS	EDWARD				40	WALES	UT	WELSH	FARMER	083	A	1	6
WILLIAMS	FREDERICK				37	ENGLAND	CE	ENGLISH	MINING ENGINEER	089	A		11
WILLIAMS	GEORGE				36	O	WM	ENGLISH	HOUSE CARPENTER	082	C	1	1
WILLIAMS	JAMES				45	ENGLAND	CE	ENGLISH	MINER	089	A		9
WILLIAMS	JANE		2	1	1	ONT	NG			081	C		D
WILLIAMS	JOHANA		1	1	24	ONTARIO	PR	ENGLISH	SCHOOLMISTRESS	081	G	2	7
WILLIAMS	JOHN				70	US	PS	AMERICAN	F	081	C		55
WILLIAMS	JOHN				26	O	CP	SCOTCH	F	082	C	2	19
WILLIAMS	JOSEPH				35	ENGLAND	CE	ENGLISH	LAB	081	B		45
WILLIAMS	SAMUEL				56	IRELAND	CS	WELCH	F	081	A	1	71
WILLIAMS	THOMAS				33	ENGLAND	WM	ENGLISH	F	085	D		16
WILLIAMSON	WILLIAM				25	US	WM	ENGLISH	BLACKSMITH	085	I		17
WILLICX	J	C			57	O	CP	IRISH	BUTCHER	081	B		55
WILLIS	NORRIS				30	O	PB	IRISH	F	085	D		30
WILLIS	SAMUEL				46	IRELAND	CE	IRISH	F	085	I		34
WILLSON	GILMAN				51	O	EM	IRISH	MILL OWNER	085	I		16
WILMAN	CHRISTOPHER	V			39	QUE	CE	GERMAN	TRADER & FISHERMAN	087	C		7
WILMAN	VALENTINE				74	CANADA	CE	FRENCH	FISHERMAN	087	B	2	4
WILMOT	FREDERICK				21	ENGLAND	CE	ENGLISH	F	085	D		34
WILSON	ALEXANDER				75	SCOTLAND	CS	SCOTCH	F	081	A	1	61
WILSON	ALEXANDER		1		14	QUEBEC	RC	IRISH		084	B		3
WILSON	ANDREW				40	US	CS	SCOTCH	F	081	C		19
WILSON	ANDREW				44	IRELAND	FK	IRISH	FARMER	082	I		26
WILSON	BENJAMIN				44	QUE	WM	SCOTCH	F	082	C	1	31
WILSON	DAVID				52	IRELAND	CE	IRISH	F	082	C	2	50
WILSON	GEORGE				35	O	CP	IRISH	MERCHANT	081	B		18
WILSON	GEORGE				31	ONTARIO	CS	IRISH	F	082	A		13
WILSON	GEORGE		1		35	ENGLAND	CE	ENGLISH	BAR KEEPER	085	B		8
WILSON	JAMES				30	SCOTLAND	CS	SCOTCH	F	082	C	2	59
WILSON	JAMES				50	SCOTLAND	RP	SCOTCH	F	082	K	1	2
WILSON	JAMES				29	SCOTLAND	PS	SCOTCH	F	085	D		34
WILSON	JAMES				57	IRELAND	CE	IRISH	TAILOR	086	A	1	27
WILSON	JAMES				30	O	PS	IRISH	ENGINEER	089	A		14
WILSON	JAMES		1		19	SCOTLAND	PS	SCOTCH	MINE LABOURER	089	A		38
WILSON	JANE		1	1	80	IRELAND	RC	IRISH		081	H	2	26
WILSON	JOHN				27	O	CP	IRISH	F	081	B		11
WILSON	JOHN				30	IRELAND	RC		LUMBERER	081	C		3
WILSON	JOHN				48	ENGLAND	CE	ENGLISH	F	081	C		52
WILSON	JOHN				37	O	CP	SCOTCH	F	081	E		16
WILSON	JOHN				48	IRELAND	RC	IRISH	BLACKSMITH	081	H	2	25
WILSON	JOHN				45	IRELAND	CE	IRISH	F	082	A		25
WILSON	JOHN				37	IRELAND	CE	IRISH	F	082	A		26
WILSON	JOHN				32	IRELAND	PS	IRISH	F	085	E		8
WILSON	JOHN				35	O	WM	ENGLISH	F	086	B		5
WILSON	JOSEPH		1		8	O	WM	SCOTCH		089	B		1
WILSON	JOSEPH				53	SCOTLAND	CS	SCOTCH	COLLECTOR OF CUSTOMS	089	B		9
WILSON	MARGRET		1	1	20	O	EM	GERMAN		081	B		24
WILSON	MATHEW				70	IRELAND	CE	IRISH	F	081	J	1	37
WILSON	MATTHEW				24	SCOTLAND	PS	SCOTCH	F	085	E		16
WILSON	MOSES				34	O	CE	IRISH	F	082	C	1	39
WILSON	PETER				51	SCOTLAND	CS	SCOTCH	F	082	C	2	61
WILSON	RICHARD				40	IRELAND	CP	IRISH	F	081	J	1	38
WILSON	RICHARD				35	O	CE	IRISH	F	086	A	1	29
WILSON	ROBERT				51	SCOTLAND	CS	SCOTCH	TEACHER	081	A	1	35
WILSON	ROBERT				26	ONTARIO	EM	IRISH	F	082	A		13
WILSON	ROBERT		1		1	ONTARIO	CS	IRISH		082	A		50
WILSON	ROBERT				27	IRELAND	PS	IRISH	MINE LABOURER	089	A		35
WILSON	THOMAS		1		22	CANADA	PR	CANADIAN	MERCHANT	085	A		11
WILSON	THOMAS		2		64	ENGLAND	CE	ENGLISH	SHOEMAKER	085	D		D
WILSON	THOS				32	IRELAND	CE	IRISH	F	081	J	1	40
WILSON	WILLIAM				38	IRELAND	WM	IRISH	SHOEMAKER	081	B		15
WILSON	WILLIAM				38	ONTARIO	CE	SCOTCH	F	082	A		24
WILSON	WILLIAM				46	SCOTLAND	PS	SCOTCH	MINE LABOURER	089	A		41
WILSON	WILLIAM		1		41	UNITED STATES	CP	IRISH	LAB	090	D		7
WILSON	WILLIAM		1		20	ONTARIO	RC	SCOTCH	LABOURER H B CO	090	E		22
WIMES	SARAH	ANN	1	1	20	USA	RC	ENGLISH		086	C	1	10
WINAGOOSH	PAUL				30	O	PA	INDIAN	HUNTER	090	F		3
WINDIGO	(WIDOW)			1		ONTARIO	RC	INDIAN	HUNTER & TRAPPER	090	E		5
WINDLE	JAMES				65	IRELAND	RC	IRISH	F	081	C		11
WINDLE	JOHN				60	IRELAND	RC	IRISH	F	081	C		13
WINDLE	PATRICK				45	IRELAND	RC	IRISH	F	081	C		13
WINFIELD	WILLIAM				37	O	CE	ENGLISH	F	085	D		18
WINGFIELD	JOHN	M			32	SCOTLAND	PS	SCOTCH	STONE CUTTER FARMER	085	J		6
WINGLE	PATRICK				60	IRELAND	RC	IRISH	FARMER	081	D		25
WINGLE	THOMAS				40	IRELAND	RC	IRISH	FARMER	081	G	1	27
WINGROVE	DANIEL				34	O	WM	GERMAN	CARPENTER	085	B		13
WINKIE	JOHN	C			56	GERMANY	EV	GERMAN	FARMER	082	I		67
WINKIE	WILLIAM				36	GERMANY	LU	GERMAN	FARMER	082	I		23
WINTER	CHARLES				25	ENGLAND	WM	ENGLISH	F	085	J		26
WINTER	MOSES				61	O	WM	ENGLISH	F	085	D		16
WINTERS	JOHN				60	IRELAND	RC	IRISH	FARMER	081	G	1	8
WISE	HENREY				25	ENGLAND	PM	ENGLISH	F	085	J		3
WISENBOURG	FLOURENTENA		1	1	6	ONT	LU	GERMAN		082	I		19
WISGAU	MARTIN		1		37	GERMANY	LU	GERMAN	TAILOR	082	G		89
WITT	FRANCES				36	GERMANY	LU	GERMAN	FARMER	082	I		61
WITT	FREDRICK				48	GERMANY	LU	GERMAN	FARMER	082	I		61
WITTS	CHRISTINA		1	1	68	GERMANY	LU	GERMAN		082	I		17
WITTS	DANIEL		1		76	GERMANY	LU	GERMAN		082	I		22
WITTS	HERMAN				30	GERMANY	LU	GERMAN	FARMER	082	I		18
WITTS	MICHAEL		1		73	GERMANY	LU	GERMAN		082	I		17
WITTS	WILLIAM				42	GERMANY	LU	GERMAN	FARMER	082	I		20
WOLFE	JONATHAN				37	O	CE	IRISH	MERCHANT	081	B		4
WOLFGRAM	FREDRIC				59	GERMANY	LU	GERMAN	F	082	G		19
WOLFGRAM	WILLIAM				45	GERMANY	LU	GERMAN	F	082	G		15
WOLFGRAM	WM				26	GERMANY	LU	GERMAN	F	082	G		19
WOLFORD	WILLIAM				29	ENGLAND	WM	ENGLISH	SCHOOL TEACHER	082	I		75
WOLLINP	FREDERICK		1		19	ENGLAND	BA	ENGLISH	LUMBERMAN	088	B		5

SURNAME	NAME1	NAME2	STRAY	SEX	AGE	BIRTHPL	RELIGION	ORIGIN	OCCUP	DIST	SUB_DIST	DIV	PAGE
WOOD	ANDREW				58	SCOTLAND	WM	SCOTCH	FARMER	089	B		18
WOOD	CHARLES	JAMES			28	ENGLAND	WM	ENGLISH	F	085	I		29
WOOD	ELISHA		1		23	O	EM	ENGLISH	F	085	J		14
WOOD	HENRY				35	ENGLAND	CE	ENGLISH	CLERK	089	B		3
WOODALL	JOHN				24	O	CE	SCOTCH	CAPTAIN	086	C	1	11
WOODCOCK	WILLIAM				46	ENGLAND	CE	ENGLISH	BRITANIA METALSMITH	085	C		10
WOODHOUSE	JOHN		1		30	ENGLAND	CE	ENGLISH	F	085	E		24
WOODHOUSE	RALPH				52	ENGLAND	CE	ENGLISH	FARMER	081	G	1	12
WOODLICK	ANTHONY		1		5	ONT	RC	PRUSSIAN		081	J	1	12
WOODLICK	JOSEPH		1			ONT	RC	PRUSSIAN		081	J	1	12
WOODLICK	PETER		1		2	ONT	RC	PRUSSIAN		081	J	1	12
WOODROW	D	H	1		28		NG		CLERK	085	E		27
WOODS	CHARLOTTE			1	46	ENGLAND	CE	ENGLISH		085	I		28
WOODS	ELIZA		1	1	24	IRELAND	CE	IRISH	SERVANT	081	B		80
WOODS	JONAS				76	O	PB	GERMAN	F	085	D		9
WOODS	MARY	ANN	1	1	14	ONT	RC	IRISH		082	I		35
WOODS	WILLIAM		1		41	ENGLAND	CE	ENGLISH	TAILOR	085	B		8
WOOLEY	GEORGE				31	ENGLAND	WM	ENGLISH	BAKER	085	C		2
WOOLFIELD	CHARLES		1		24	ENGLAND	CE	ENGLISH	CLERK	081	E		3
WOOLSEY	ALISI		2	1	3	O	CE			082	D		D
WOOLSEY	THOMAS				27	O	CE	ENGLISH	PUMPMAKER	082	D		21
WRAY	GEORGE				29	AUSTRALIA	CE	IRISH	F	085	C		22
WREN	THOMAS				40	IRELAND	RC	IRISH	F	081	K		29
WRENSHALL	FRED	C			31	ENGLAND	WM	ENGLISH	F	085	E		30
WRIGHT	BENJAMIN	F	1		14	O	CP	ENGLISH		082	C	1	48
WRIGHT	ELIZABETH	JANE	1	1	5	O	CP	SCOTCH		082	C	1	22
WRIGHT	EMME	JANE	1	1	11	O	CP	ENGLISH		082	C	1	48
WRIGHT	FANNY		1	1	60	O	BA	SCOTCH		081	I		16
WRIGHT	HORIS		1		25	QUE	CE	IRISH	FOREMAN	081	A	2	17
WRIGHT	JAMES				47	ENGLAND	CE	ENGLISH	F	082	A		43
WRIGHT	JAMES		1		11	O	CP	SCOTCH		082	C	1	22
WRIGHT	JAMES				46	O	CE	ENGLISH	SHOEMAKER	082	E		39
WRIGHT	JESEA		1	1	3	O	CP	SCOTCH		082	C	1	22
WRIGHT	JOHN		1		25	O	CP	ENGLISH	AGENT	081	A	2	29
WRIGHT	JOHN				55	QUE	WM	ENGLISH	F	082	C	1	19
WRIGHT	JOHN	E			43	IRELAND	RC	IRISH	AUCTIONEER	082	E		42
WRIGHT	JOHN	HILL	1		10	O	CP	SCOTCH		081	A	1	27
WRIGHT	JOHN	M	1			O	CP	SCOTCH		082	C	1	22
WRIGHT	JOSEPH				32	O	CE	ENGLISH	F	082	F		1
WRIGHT	MARGARET		1	1	30	SCOTLAND	CP	SCOTCH		082	C	1	22
WRIGHT	MARSHAL		1		17	O	EM	ENGLISH	CLERK	081	B		12
WRIGHT	MARTIN				53	IRELAND	PS	IRISH	F	081	K		51
WRIGHT	MARY			1	47	ENGLAND	CE	ENGLISH	HOTELKEEPER	081	I		29
WRIGHT	MARY		1	1	1	O	CP	SCOTCH		082	C	1	22
WRIGHT	NATHANEL				57	QUE	WM	ENGLISH	F	082	C	1	18
WRIGHT	ROBERT	WM	1		6	O	CP	SCOTCH		082	C	1	22
WRIGHT	SAMUEL				39	O	CP	IRISH	F	082	C	2	7
WRIGHT	THOMAS		1		44	SCOTLAND	CP	SCOTCH	STONEMASON	082	C	1	22
WRIGHT	THOMAS				35	US	PM	IRISH	F	085	D		20
WRIGHT	THOMAS	A	1		8	O	CP	SCOTCH		082	C	1	22
WRIGHT	WALTER				47	SCOTLAND	CO	SCOTCH	MINISTER	085	B		1
WRIGHT	WILLIAM				36	O	CP	IRISH	F	082	C	1	15
WRIGHT	WILLIAM				56	ENGLAND	CE	ENGLISH	F	082	F		1
WRIGHT	WILLIAM	A	1		10	O	CP	SCOTCH		082	C	1	22
WYLLE	WILLIAM		1		28	SCOTLAND	CP	SCOTCH	MINER	090	D		7
XEVIER	MERRIAN				63	QUE	RC	FRENCH	LAB	082	C	1	61
YADFO	BAPTISTE				38	QUEBEC	RC	FRENCH	FARMER	083	A	2	3
YANDA	THOMAS				27	ONTARIO	WM	FRENCH	FARMER	081	G	2	3
YANDT	FREDRICK		1		24	GERMANY	RP	GERMAN	BLACKSMITH	082	K	1	11
YATES	THOMAS				32	QUE	EM	IRISH	F	085	D		13
YATES	THOMAS		1		21	ENGLAND	CE	ENGLISH	CARPENTER	086	A	1	31
YEARLEY	ELIZA	MA		1	44	ENGLAND	CE	ENGLISH		085	I		36
YEASINDE	DENIS				29	O	RC	INDIAN	F	084	D		7
YEW	WILLIAM				30	ENGLAND	CE	ENGLISH	F	086	A	1	6
YOKILD	MARTIN		1		25	GERMANY	LU	GERMAN	L	082	G		85
YOKISCH	WILLIAM				38	GERMANY	EV	GERMAN	FARMER	082	I		59
YONKAY	FREDRICK				36	GERMANY	LU	GERMAN	FARMER	082	I		54
YONTOE	ANDREW				25	PRUSSIA	RC	PRUSSIAN	LABOURER	083	A	1	6
YONTOE	AUGUST				40	PRUSSIA	RC	PRUSSIAN	FARMER	083	A	1	5
YONTOE	JOSEPH				35	PRUSSIA	RC	PRUSSIAN	FARMER	083	A	1	5
YOUNG	ADAM				47	IRELAND	CP	IRISH	BOOKKEEPER	081	A	2	15
YOUNG	ALFRED	JAMES	1		4	O	CP	SCOTCH				1	80
YOUNG	ANDREW				53	IRELAND	WM	IRISH	F	082	F		40
YOUNG	ANN		2	1	80	IRELAND	CE			082	F		D
YOUNG	ANNE		1	1	8	QUEBEC	FK	SCOTCH		081	J	1	35
YOUNG	ARCHIBALD				58	SCOTLAND	CE	SCOTCH	MERCHANT	081	H	2	24
YOUNG	CHARLES				74	IRELAND	CE	IRISH	F	082	K	2	2
YOUNG	GEORGE				44	IRELAND	WM	IRISH	F	082	A		48
YOUNG	JAMES				21	QUE	CP	SCOTCH	HOTELKEEPER	081	A	2	19
YOUNG	JAMES				55	SCOTLAND	CP	SCOTCH	F	081	A	2	26
YOUNG	JANE		1	1	8	O	RP	SCOTCH		081	E		20
YOUNG	JANE			1	40	IRELAND	CE	IRISH		082	F		36
YOUNG	JOHN				56	SCOTLAND	CS	SCOTCH	F			1	80
YOUNG	JOHN				40	SCOTLAND	CP	SCOTCH	F	081	A	2	37
YOUNG	JOHN				34	ONTARIO	RC	IRISH	SHANTYMAN	082	B		59
YOUNG	JOHN		1		28	O	CE	IRISH	LAB	082	K	1	20
YOUNG	JOHN				63	SCOTLAND	PS	SCOTCH	F	085	A		1
YOUNG	JOHN				41	SCOTLAND	PS	SCOTCH	F	085	D		3
YOUNG	JOHN	SR			45	IRELAND	CE	IRISH	F	082	K	1	19
YOUNG	MARGERET		1	1	19	O	CE	SCOTCH		082	K	1	20
YOUNG	MARY	ANN	1	1	72	IRELAND	WM	IRISH		082	A		48
YOUNG	MATHEW				42	IRELAND	RC	IRISH	F	085	A		20
YOUNG	RICHARD				56	IRELAND	CE	IRISH	F	082	F		12
YOUNG	ROBERT				51	QUE	CP	SCOTCH	MERCHANT	081	B		6
YOUNG	SAMUEL				27	O	WM	IRISH	F	082	F		35
YOUNG	SAMUEL		1		22	O	RC	IRISH	LAB	085	F		5
YOUNG	WILLIAM				30	O	WM	IRISH	F	082	F		39
YUALL	WILLIAM				37	ONTARIO	PR	SCOTCH	FARMER	081	G	2	10
YUILL	CATHERINE			1	47	SCOTLAND	CP	SCOTCH		081	A	2	26
YUILL	JOHN		1		18	O	CP	SCOTCH	BARTENDER	081	A	2	19
YUILL	JOHN				57	SCOTLAND	CP	SCOTCH	F	081	A	2	39
YUILL	THOMAS				29	O	CP	SCOTCH		081	B		13
YUILL	WALTER				41	ONT	CS	SCOTCH	F	081	C		54
YULE	ALLAN		1		16	O	CP	SCOTCH	FARM LAB	081	A	1	17
YULE	ARCHIBALD				21	O	CP	SCOTCH	F	081	A	1	17
YULE	CATHARINE		1	1		O	CS	SCOTCH		081	A	1	16

SURNAME	NAME1	NAME2	STRAY	SEX	AGE	BIRTHPL	RELIGION	ORIGIN	OCCUP	DIST	SUB_DIST	DIV	PAGE
YULE	CHRISTINA		1	1	24	0	CS	SCOTCH		081	A	1	16
YULE	SARAH			1	37	0	CP	SCOTCH	TAILORESS	081	A	1	19
ZADZEK	CHARLES		1		16	GERMANY	BA	GERMAN	FARMER	081	F		10
ZEBELL	GUSTAVE				46	GERMANY	WM	GERMAN	F	082	G		93
ZEBELL	WILLIAM				53	GERMANY	LU	GERMAN	F	082	G		84
ZELL	FREDRICK				43	GERMANY	WM	GERMAN	F	082	G		13
ZEMMERMAN	JOSEPH				41	0	WM	GERMAN	F	085	I		25
ZERSKY	JOSEPH				43	PRUSSIA	RC	PRUSSIAN	FARMER	081	G	2	3
ZIBERT	ANTHONY				54	PRUSSIA	RC	PRUSSIAN	FARMER	081	G	2	3
ZIMMERMAN	GOODLY		1		70	PRUSSIA	LU	PRUSSIAN		081	J	1	80
ZIMMERMAN	SOPHIE		1	1	68	PRUSIA	LU	PRUSIAN		081	J	1	80
ZOCK	MARTIN						NG		SEE SACK	082	F		30
ZONBLESKY	JOSEPH				53	PRUSSIA	RC	PRUSSIAN	FARMER	083	A	1	17